Management
Training
CASES AND PRINCIPLES

Management Training

CASES AND PRINCIPLES

WILLIAM J. McLARNEY
Late Associate Professor of Engineering
San Jose State College, and
Supervisory Training Consultant

WILLIAM M. BERLINER
Professor of Management and
Chairman of the Department of
Management and Industrial Relations
School of Commerce, New York University, and
Management Consultant

1970

Fifth Edition
RICHARD D. IRWIN, INC., Homewood, Illinois
Irwin-Dorsey Limited, Georgetown, Ontario

FIFTH EDITION

First Printing, August, 1970

Library of Congress Catalog Card No. 74–124166

Printed in the United States of America

To

> *the late*
> WILLIAM J. McLARNEY
> *who furnished the creativity*
>
> *his wife*
> HELEN McLARNEY
> *who helped in the transition*
>
> and *my wife*
> BERTHA H. BERLINER
> *who gave me the inspiration*

Preface

Revising someone else's work presents some difficulty. Every attempt was made to build on William McLarney's contributions as expressed in earlier editions of this book. Hopefully, the blend of his industrial engineering background and this author's education, experience, and knowledge of administration, organizational behavior, and management development has produced a revision which makes a contribution to the training of managers.

The text offers a college-level course in the important areas of managerial practice necessary for first-level and middle-manager positions. It offers to the college student and the management trainee a preview of, and a preparation for, a managerial job in any complex organization. The experienced manager seeking advancement will find much information which can help him understand more fully the role and functions of the manager.

The practice of management requires just that—practice and experience. No text can create a manager. It can, however, offer the opportunity to gain understanding of the responsibilities of management and help develop the awareness necessary for effective assumption of the managerial role in either a line or staff department. This is precisely what this book tries to accomplish. Because problem solving is central to the manager's job, this text emphasizes it. Actual job problems, collected by the authors over many years of conducting supervisory conferences and management development programs as well as from their practical experience as managers, are included in significant numbers.

In fact, the main thrust of the book is a practical one. Theory is included to establish a frame of reference for the aspiring or practicing manager. The book is concerned with what a manager has to do on his job. The areas of knowledge that relate to carrying out managerial responsibility on the first and middle levels of management are explored. For this reason the subjects covered encompass those involved in management principles and practices, supervision, personnel administration, and, to a limited extent, industrial engineering. In this sense the book covers the totality of the manager's job and what he should be concerned with in effectively carrying out that job.

Each chapter is revised to some extent and several chapters have been almost completely rewritten. There are two less chapters in this edition. What had been two chapters on evaluating and developing personnel and on transferring and promoting were combined with relevant material added, into one new chapter on organization development and manpower planning. Similarly, the two previous chapters on rules and discipline and on gripes and grievances were combined and enlarged into one chapter on managing employee problems and change.

The recent emphasis on the behavioral sciences in management literature is recognized and much new material from this area of knowledge is introduced throughout. Particular emphasis is given to human relations theory, individuals and organizations, conflict, change, motivation, morale, organization development, career planning, employee mobility, and manpower planning. Some quantitative concepts that are playing an increasingly important role in managerial practice are discussed. The analysis of an organization as a total system is described along with its possible impact on organization structure and organization planning.

Several new examples of management techniques such as break-even analysis, sensitivity training, management by objectives, managerial grid, and total planning are developed, and there is a rather complete example of the introduction of a work measurement program in a large organization employing white-collar workers. This example is given in detail because of the growing importance of cost control in office operations. Leading companies supplied charts, procedures, job descriptions, and other forms to illustrate practical applications of the text material.

The bibliography at the end of each of the five parts of the book has been enlarged and updated to include recent books and articles which could supplement material in this book if the reader wants to further pursue a particular subject which interests him.

There are 55 new cases among a total of 296, which provides 15 or more cases for each chapter. The purpose of having so many cases is to afford a wide choice of problems on various levels of difficulty and to give students some indication of the variety of managerial problems they may meet in a management position. A number of the new cases deal with current problems relating to minority groups, upper management, and employee behavior. All of the cases have been derived from actual experience, and most of them have been used in management training programs conducted by the authors over a combined total of 40 years.

The author wishes to acknowledge his indebtedness to the many managers who contributed cases and problems to be used. The teachers and authors who shaped this author's thinking must also share considerable thanks. Many practicing managers, both capable and incapable, have also added to the body of the author's experience and have enabled him to more fully understand the importance of sound management. The subordinates who have allowed him to try the management theories with varying degrees of success also share his admiration. Particular thanks is due to the Manufacturers Hanover Trust Company, Frederick W. Oswald, Senior Vice President, and Robert W. Keith, Vice President, both personnel administrators, who have furnished a cooperative climate for many of the author's ideas. Nathan W. Picker, Chairman of the Board of OTI Services, Inc., is also due special thanks for sharing the management problems of a medium-size company with the author over a period of many years. From these practicing managers and others too numerous to mention, the author has gained some valuable insights into the application of management theory. It is hoped that some of these insights have contributed to this revision.

Acknowledgment and thanks are due the following companies for their kindness in supplying information about and illustrations of their management practices and techniques: Bell and Howell Company, Ford Motor Company, General Motors Corporation, Jones and Laughlin Steel Corporation, Lockheed Aircraft Corporation, Manufacturers Hanover Trust Company, Owens-Corning Fiberglas Corporation, Prudential Insurance Company of America, Sylvania Electric Products, Inc., Standard Oil Company of California, and United States Steel Company.

Appreciation is expressed also for permission to quote from publications of American Institute of Industrial Engineers; American Management Association; American Society of Mechanical Engineers; Appleton-Century-Crofts; Brookings Institution; Bureau of National Affairs; *Business Week; Factory Management; Fortune; Harvard Business Review;* Harper & Row, Publishers; Harvard University Press; Harcourt, Brace, & World Co.; Richard D. Irwin, Inc.; The Macmillan Co.; McGraw-Hill Book Co.; National Industrial Conference Board; Thomas Nelson and Sons; Prentice-Hall, Inc.; Pitman Publishing Corp.; Rand, McNally & Co.; National Association of Manufacturers; University of California Press; University of Michigan, Bureau of Industrial Relations; University of Chicago Press; and World Publishing Co.

Gratitude is expressed to Dean Abraham L. Gitlow whose managerial style has encouraged creativity; to Professor Richard D. Freedman who assisted in early research on each chapter; and to my secretary, Mrs. Florence F. Ditmar, who assisted in the typing.

Greenwich, Connecticut   WILLIAM M. BERLINER
July, 1970

Foreword and the utilization of the case approach

To the teacher and the training director

This text offers a college course in management theory and applications as a preparation for effective performance of a management position. It can be used in a college classroom for students interested in managerial careers or in company training programs for first-level and middle-manager development. The text materials and actual case problems present a combination of management fundamentals and practical operating experience—a linking of theory to relevant job problems.

There is more than enough material for a one-semester course meeting three hours a week or a two-semester course if all of the case material is utilized. For supervisory or management training programs, the text could be assigned for reading at home while the cases could be used to develop discussion using the conference method. The book is unique in the sense that it combines personnel administration and industrial management to reflect the performance characteristics of the supervisor's job. The selected materials are integrated and presented from the point of view of the manager rather than from the separate, and often conflicting, points of view of the various specialists such as the personnel manager or the production manager.

The text deals primarily with management on the first and middle-management levels—the activities that the college graduate will be undertaking in the management of a section, unit, or department. For the student preparing for a career in management or for the potential manager in business, this is the area in which he must prove his worth early in a managerial career.

From management training a student should get a method and a habit of applying management principles to the solution of job problems. The text provides the method in the seven-step problem-solving technique, and provides the job problems in the form of case studies. Thus it sets up the means and the materials for practicing a systematic approach to analyzing problems, working out solutions, and making decisions.

Working as a group member on case problems helps a student to see interpretations and solutions other than his own. The cases give him a fund of job information covering an area more diversified than would be within the personal experience of a teacher. Cases show the environment in which principles have to operate, show how things are done in a number of companies, and what will be expected of him. Many of the cases present situations that he will be in soon after starting a job—problems of trainees, of new supervisors, and of conflicts between line and staff. New cases in this edition reflect changes and trends in the industrial environment, particularly the trend toward a more highly educated work force.

This book supplies cases and principles to be used in a conference program of management training. It is fitted to the first-level supervisor and his boss and the area of management up to and including the middle-management level. It is designed to improve the performance of men on these jobs and to prepare men to advance to these jobs.

The conference case-study method of training is used because it requires and gets active participation of the men being trained in group discussion of cases and the principles involved, a management man profits by the exchange of ideas with other supervisors having like problems. He evaluates solutions not only in terms of his own job but in terms of their jobs and the organization as a whole. He develops skill in analyzing problems and applying principles and techniques within the framework of the policies of his own organization. He gets practice in achieving realistic, workable, and effective solutions. He carries back to his job an understanding of principles and techniques of good management and a method and habit of applying them to his problems.

By coordinating cases and principles and keying them to supervisors and middle management, the book saves the time of many people. It relieves the conference leader of having to spend his time gathering materials beforehand and then having to spend the time of conferees while he develops cases and principles during the conference. When the conferees have the textbook before them, then the whole time of the conferences can be devoted to the solution of cases and the application of principles.

The arrangement of 17 chapters into five parts permits a rational development of the subject matter. Starting with "Management's Job" and going through "Job Management," "Developing the Work Team," "Maintaining the Work Group," and ending with "The Management of Professional Personnel," the book covers the range of the manager's efforts and concerns. Completion of a course using text and cases should give the participant a good understanding of managerial responsibility in complex organizations.

Normally a chapter can be handled in two conferences—one for lecture and discussion of principles, techniques, and practices, and the other for discussing, analyzing, and solving cases. The plan of the text permits picking and choosing the chapters to be used. The integration of human and technical factors in each chapter enables the teacher or training director to select chapters most relevant to the training needs of the group and to get a complete and integrated treatment of the topics chosen. These particular chapters can be combined into a training course to fit the time available for handling the most urgent needs of the group. Subsequent programs and refresher courses can cover other chapters that are next in the order of need.

The text is flexible also in the levels of training it offers. The case studies cover a wide range of subject matter, depth, and difficulty—permitting the discussion to be pitched at the level appropriate to the group. The 296 cases came from a wide range of authority levels in a wide variety of enterprises in which the authors conducted training programs. Over a period of 20 years these cases were collected from and used in aircraft companies; shipyards; manufacturers of electronic equipment, of machine tools, hand tools, and furniture; railroads, public utilities, banks, insurance companies, other service organizations; college courses; and government installations.

Most of the cases have been stripped of the nonessentials of their backgrounds and are presented in a form that makes them applicable to businesses other than the ones from which they came. The wording is such that details can be added and assumptions made to fit the conditions existing in a specific company. A bare case can be slipped into the background of a big company or a small one, and this is important because problems will be solved one way in a large company and another way in a small; one way in a company that has a union contract and another way in a company that hasn't; one way in a company that is owner managed, and another way in a company that has hired management.

The cases are workable ones on which conferees can show how principles should be applied or modified to fit the situation and how company policies need to be interpreted or modified in terms of basic princples. Most of the cases involve more than one principle. Their inclusion in one chapter rather than another is not for the purpose of limiting discussion; they should not be warped to fit some particular principle. In looking for cases to fit the training needs of a group, it is advisable to consult the index. Each case is indexed under as many topics as it applies to. There is a close tieup between cases and text, with a case applying to almost every topic listed in the Table of Contents.

The principles of good management presented in the text are not new or revolutionary; they are in accord with the best in the literature of management. The presentation of them is interlarded with techniques and practices based upon them—techniques and practices that have been used and tested by supervisors in a variety of enterprises.

The contents of the text represent a selection of topics on which there is the greatest need of supervisory training and which for the time required yield the greatest results. They were chosen from successful training programs conducted by the authors, and they are selected and arranged to meet the needs of conference training programs for first-level supervisors and managerial people up to and including the middle-management level. Topics are presented to be discussed and interpreted in the framework of company policies and conditions and to be applied in the solution of problems and thus made a part of a man's thinking.

To the supervisor and the student

The cases are for group discussion. A man solving a problem by himself sees it only from his own angle and decides on a solution that is based on his own knowledge and experience. But one man's solution is seldom as comprehensive as a solution that is the product of group thinking and group experience. When a group is trying to arrive at the most practical solution—the one that will work in this instance—each man contributes his experiences of what has succeeded or failed for him, the techniques he used, and the cautions he found necessary to observe. It is from the pooling of this knowledge and experience that a solution is arrived at and agreed upon; and it is this fund of knowledge and experience that a group member should draw upon for his own use.

Preparing for case discussion. A person approaching case discussion naturally asks: What good will it do me? What can I expect to learn from it?

Active participation in group solving of case-study problems makes a person more expert in handling problems on his job. A member of a case-study group is not trying to accumulate a bagful of ready-made solutions to apply to whatever problems come along on his job. He is getting practice in methods of analyzing and clarifying problems, in looking for causes, and working out a number of possible solutions. He is getting practice in making good decisions, in choosing the solution that is best suited to the time, place, and conditions—the solution that is in line with good management principles and practices, that is practicable, acceptable, and most likely to accomplish the results desired.

A working member in a conference problem-solving group can clarify, interpret, and evaluate his own study and research on the problem. He can integrate his knowledge of separate specialties by applying it to the solution of problems. Futhermore, he can acquire a stock of ideas and techniques suggested by other conferees and evaluated by the group. In solving case problems, people contribute suggestions and pool their ideas. They evaluate other people's suggestions, improve upon them, consider alternatives, integrate various points of view, and take the best of the thinking and combine it into solutions. The decisions made should embody the thinking and experience of all the members.

Conferees should not be looking for one "right" answer to a case problem. They should be looking for all possible solutions from which to select the one—or ones—most likely to succeed under existing conditions. A solution that will work in one time and place may not work in another; a solution that will take care of this problem may create other problems. It is well to develop several solutions to be evaluated. Becoming wedded early to a single solution (or a single reason for everything) limits thinking and stands in the way of using the ideas of others.

The questions following a case are not intended to direct the discussion. They are there to help the conferee analyze the case in advance and prepare himself for the discussion of it. In the first few sessions of case study, people are inclined to jump to conclusions without digging deeply enough beneath the surface, without weighing the circumstances, or thinking through the results of proposed actions. The problem-solving technique described in the text should deter people from prescribing the cure before they've diagnosed the ailment. It should keep them from wasting time redesigning the mousetrap when they should be looking for better ways to eliminate mice.

The management principles involved in a case are not limited to the chapter in which the case appears. Job problems—and the cases describing them—are seldom limited to a single issue. The cases came from a wide variety of businesses. They are problems on which someone had to make a decision. "Facts" of a case include opinions and inferences; they must be lined up and evaluated in a thorough and orderly manner. If the group wants more data in the framework of a case, the thing to do is to make assumptions and evaluate their reasonableness.

A side value of case study is that the supervisor-student often recognizes some personalities very like the people he deals with daily, or very like himself, and he begins to see problems, motives, and relationships from the other fellow's point of view. Some of the case problems are difficult to solve—some have been going on for a long time and still have no ideal solution. But it should be encouraging to remember that a group of people working together on a problem bring to it a combination of many years of experience and individual interpretations of management theory which can lead to some remarkably effective conclusions.

Contents

operation. Procedure for making an operation study. Human engineering. Methods improvement by employees—JMT. Cost reduction. Summary. Case studies, 286.

PART IV.   MAINTAINING THE WORK TEAM

Part I

Management's job

1 The job of managing

The job of internal management. The manager's resources. Knowledge, skills, and attitudes the supervisor needs. The tools of management. Planning. Organizing. Directing. Coordinating. Controlling. Decision making. Problem-solving techniques. The seven-step problem-solving technique. Summary.

The newly appointed president of a major corporation recently stated that it was his responsibility to provide leadership, communications, and direction to employees to maximize their contributions to the policies and objectives of the company. "Management must create the right type of framework so people feel they are contributing, and this must come from the top," he went on to say.[1] It is almost axiomatic that the leadership climate created by the top management of an organization has a direct relationship to the effectiveness of that organization. While the creation of the "right type" of framework mentioned above is rather complex, there is no doubt that the quality and type of leadership on each level of management in an organization has a definite impact on employee performance.

No supervisor operates in a vacuum regardless of the amount of autonomy he may have. He reports to a superior, who in turn must also report to a higher level of authority in the organization. Naturally, there are relationships with peers and subordinates to be considered also. It is these interrelationships among levels of management in a company and the way they are carried out that creates the managerial climate for that particular company.

This text is written to show the supervisor his management position in its many and varied dimensions, to point out what it demands of him in knowledge, skills, and attitudes, and to help him meet these demands. The supervisor's job has been complicated by a multitude of scientific discoveries and technical developments that have brought about new systems, new processes, and new methods—all of which are

---

[1] "Monsanto Picks a New Catalyst," *Business Week*, August 10, 1968.

3

changing the nature of jobs and the skills needed to perform them and to supervise them. Technological advances and the rapid growth of industry combine to create a demand for supervisors who have the high level of skill and knowledge to handle technical problems. Additionally, they must have the managerial knowledge, skills, and attitudes which will allow them to work successfully with people on all levels of the organization. The complexities developing in our society make the human relations aspects of the supervisor's job particularly difficult and challenging. Perhaps the most essential contribution the supervisor can make is determined by his ability to perceive and present ideas in a way that will enlist the cooperation of others.

The job of internal management

All types of organized activity require management. While there is some difference of opinion regarding a definition of the process of management there is little doubt that the process exists in every type of organization our society has produced. Churches, hospitals, labor unions, universities, schools, foundations, government, along with the business firm are just some of the areas of our society where the function of management is carried out. It can be readily assumed that there is considerable universality to the practice of management. This does not imply, however, that it is practiced in a similar fashion in all organizations. In fact it is practiced differently on the various managerial levels of one organization. Even individual managers contribute differences in practice by their perceptions of the manager's role and their development of a particular management style. The process of management is practiced when the manager engages in the many activities such as decison making, planning, coordination, control, and general leadership, which are parts of the process.

While the manager's efforts must be applied on all levels of the organization from the chairman of the board to the first-level supervisor, there are differences in perception, emphasis, responsibility, and focus on each level. The complexity of the organization determines the number of managerial levels but for explanatory purposes most books on the subject usually describe three; top management, middle management, and first-line or supervisory management. Top management usually concerns itself with the establishment of objectives, overall planning of the long- and medium-range variety, external relationships, and the achievement of the goals established for the major components of the enterprise. The principal emphasis of this text is on the middle manager and the first-line supervisor. Their contributions to the welfare of the organization and how they go about managing will be explored rather thoroughly.

Trying to define the role of a manager has proved to be somewhat elusive as the many studies of this role seem to indicate. Perhaps one of the more well known is the philosophical one mentioned by Peter Drucker:

Who is a manager can be defined only by a man's function and the contribution he is expected to make. And the function which distinguishes the manager above all others is his *educational* one. The one contribution he is uniquely expected to make is to give others vision and ability to perform. It is vision and moral responsibility that, in the last analysis, define the manager.[2]

The concern for establishing an understandable definition of the manager's role is a valid one. Both students and practitioners would benefit from such an understanding along with the multitude of people in our society whose work is nonmanagerial but who are supervised by managers. The simple statement found in many books that managing is getting work done through other people does not seem to be reflected in practice. All of us know managers on various levels of organization who perform clerical, technical, and other tasks that could be considered nonmanagerial by any test. In fact a great many of these people are quite proud of their abilities to perform these tasks better than the people they supervise.

One can understand the desire of the first-level supervisor who was promoted because of his productivity, to continue nonsupervisory tasks. After all he knows he can do the work and managing is something new and perhaps frustrating. But when higher level managers type their own letters and take home mountains of clerical work and refuse to or do not want to delegate the more routine tasks to subordinates, the student of management begins to wonder if the management texts are at all correct. This is particularly true if the manager performing these nonmanagerial tasks has achieved some of the accepted success status factors such as title, salary, private office, and secretary.

Perhaps we must accept the evidence that managers continue to do a variety of work in addition to their managerial responsibilities even though it may be desirable for them to give up nonmanagerial work. Job pressures, satisfaction of accomplishment, lack of trained help, poor planning, misplaced emphasis, inadequate knowledge of management among others may contribute to the manager's desire to remain partly a worker. In any event this text will try to define the role of the manager in all of its chapters. To a certain extent it is desirable to recognize the role of the manager as it is practiced generally with all of the limitations imposed on or possessed by individual managers. This may lead

---

[2] Peter Drucker, *The Practice of Management* (New York: Harper & Row, Publishers, 1954), p. 350.

to a better understanding of management as it should be and the blending of theory and practice will become a reality for the reader.

The manager's resources

Probably the principal effort of all managers is devoted to effective allocation of the resources available to the tasks at hand. The resources that managers have to work with are people, money, machines, materials, time, and methods. People are the most valuable of the resources and the most difficult to utilize to maximum effectiveness.

The performance of any group of men depends upon the effectiveness of its boss, and it is to a man-boss combination that this book is directed—the first-level supervisor and his boss[3] and the area of manage-

FIGURE 1-1
Levels of Management

The supervisory hierarchy has at the top that part of management concerned with overall company policies and external relationships. Between the company officers at the top and the rank-and-file employees at the bottom is the part of management primarily concerned with the internal running of the business: middle management and the supervisors—the management group treated in this text. It includes department chiefs, section heads, and the first-level or unit supervisors.

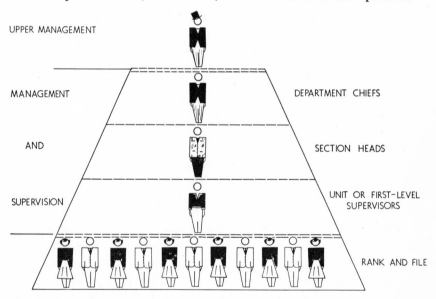

UPPER MANAGEMENT

MANAGEMENT   DEPARTMENT CHIEFS

AND   SECTION HEADS

SUPERVISION   UNIT OR FIRST-LEVEL
                             SUPERVISORS

                             RANK AND FILE

---

[3] In discussing the supervisor and his boss, the text uses the title "supervisor" to refer to both jobs in those cases where no distinction need be made between them.

Jobs vary in title and content from one type of business to another. In many companies there are levels of supervision between first-level and middle management. Figure 1–1 shows such an organization structure.

ment up to and including middle management. The picture of the first-level supervisor's job would be incomplete without his boss in it, because the boss is the one who sets the pattern for the behavior that is expected and rewarded. His attitudes and ways of operating have a profound influence upon his subordinates in shaping their jobs, molding their attitudes, and determining the way they will operate and how successful they will be.

Responsibilities of the first-level supervisor. The first-level supervisor is the management man who directs the work of operative (nonmanagement) employees.[4] He supervises work and worker. He is the management representative at the bottom of the management pyramid—the management man who is in direct contact with the rank and file. He may be called foreman, supervisor, section manager, unit manager, chief clerk, department head, group chief, head nurse, team leader, or some other similar title.

A group of first-level supervisors and middle-management men in a management training conference[5] worked out the following list of what a supervisor's boss expects of him:

1. Get out the product or the service within the requirements of time, quality, quantity, and cost.
2. Develop and maintain an effective work force.
3. Keep up-to-date on technical job knowledge.
4. Make good decisions; don't wait for the boss to make them.
5. Plan, organize, direct, coordinate, and control the work.
6. Know and apply company policies and procedures.
7. Know the union contract and live within it.
8. Handle grievances properly but try to prevent them.
9. Improve methods and get worker acceptance of the changes.
10. Maintain discipline—don't let people get by with poor performance or unsafe acts or improper behavior.
11. Build cooperation and morale.
12. Be loyal.
13. Communicate upward effectively and honestly.
14. Don't be afraid of criticism.
15. Don't make promises that leave no room for alternatives.
16. Be ready for crises but don't create them.

---

[4] Below the first-level supervisor there are a number of positions which have some supervisory duties along with operative duties. For example, there are assistants who instruct or assist fellow employees or who examine and coordinate their work. Titles of some of these jobs are assistant supervisor, assistant foreman, production assistant, working foreman, leadman, group chief, setup man, layout man, and so forth.

[5] Much of the material in this text is based upon analysis of such conferences conducted by the authors.

The first-line supervisor has in most cases advanced from a job in which he was an individual producer to a job that now requires him to get production through others. He may now have the authority to make decisions and manage or he may be an overseer who carries out orders and sees to it that rank-and-file workers carry out orders. If his job falls in this second category, the reason may lie in the design of his job, the nature of the work being done, in the managerial philosophy of his company, or in the attitude and ability of his boss. Or the fault may lie with the supervisor himself; he may not know how to handle a managerial job and he may not even consider himself a member of management. The supervisor who pictures himself as somebody squeezed but unloved between the line of workers below him and the line of managers above him needs help in developing himself to assume a managerial role. All too frequently he is promoted on short notice and little or nothing is done to orient him and help him understand his new responsibilities. He is expected to learn on the job and this is very costly and frequently disasterous.

In many organizations the supervisor's job is really not thoroughly analyzed. His expectations and interpretation of the job as contrasted with those of higher management may differ markedly yet the two viewpoints are not communicated and each party goes on its way adding confusion. Most supervisory training programs and many books on supervision place a good deal of emphasis on the desirability of good human relations skills for the first-level supervisor. He is told to keep morale high, labor turnover low and to develop a work force free from conflict and disagreement. Yet, he is promoted if productivity is high, the work gets out on time and deadlines are met. He is expected to be management's representative to the worker, yet management does not really welcome him and he frequently is the last to know things that affect his area of responsibility. In many instances he cannot hire, fire, transfer, or promote and he may have very little to do with salary changes for his employees. He may be expected to turn out a significant amount of work leaving him little time for supervision and the training and development of subordinates. In short, while he may be called a manager, many of the things managers do have been taken away from him.

The supervisor's job has been undergoing considerable change in recent years for a variety of reasons. There is no doubt that in many organizations the first-level supervisor has very limited authority. This is particularly true where a union contract carefully spells out the rights of the bargaining unit thus limiting supervisory discretion and judgment. Likewise, supervisors in many public and semipublic agencies are limited by a myriad of written rules and procedures. The same limiting characteristics hold true in those organizations where tradition and the lethargy of higher management do not allow the supervisor to function as a manager. Even though descriptions of his job include lists of virtues, qualities, and abilities possessed only by saints, the supervisor in reality rarely has the attributes he is supposed to have to be "management's representative to the worker."

Probably the outstanding change that has taken place is the increasing shortage of people to fill supervisory jobs. Two factors contribute to this shortage. Business firms as well as other organizations have increased in size quite rapidly thus creating the need for more first-line supervisors. Secondly, young people now enter the work force with more education and higher levels of aspiration. These two factors coupled with increased complexity of organized activity have caused organizations to seek managerial personnel from sources other than the apprentice route. It is not unusual for a college graduate to become a first-line supervisor after a relatively short training period and a minimum of experience in the type of work he supervises. Manufacturing, service, and other types of industries have all started to choose some supervisors in this manner.

In those organizations that have been choosing supervisors who do not have seniority but who are well educated and ambitious, the supervisor's job has become a more responsible one. The very factor of size and long lines of communication has necessitated the greater flexibility in the position. While there is still a need for technical knowledge in many supervisory jobs, there are several companies particularly in service industries such as banking, insurance, and retailing that have promoted people to supervisory positions because they demonstrated managerial attitudes and capability rather than excellent technical competence. As this trend continues the supervisor will of necessity become more of a manager rather than a lead worker. Shortages will also increase the span of control of the individual supervisor and the rising educational level of our society with its emphasis on the desirability of managerial positions will force even the organizations with strong traditions of limited authority for supervisors to carefully evaluate their view of the supervisor's role.

Responsibilities of the middle manager. The distinction between the responsibilities of the middle manager and the first-level supervisor as they apply to the two jobs is a matter of degree and emphasis. Both jobs are concerned with the direct operations of the firm, but the middle-management responsibilities are heavier and the results harder to measure. The middle manager supervises supervisors, while the first-level supervisor supervises work and workers, telling his workers what to do and training and instructing them so that they can do it. A middle manager tells his subordinate supervisors what he *wants to accomplish,* and he tells them in fairly specific terms; then he counsels them to the extent necessary for them to accomplish the objectives. Higher management sets up the overall objectives which the middle manager translates into specific projects for his subordinates. He develops plans, and directs and reviews progress toward them, but he does not supervise the details of their accomplishment.

While the first-level supervisor spends a larger proportion of his time in directing and controlling, the middle manager does more planning (medium range rather than long range), more organizing, more integrating and coordinating of the work performed by his subordinate supervisors within the department. He also coordinates the department's special function with the functions of the other departments. The middle manager designs departmental procedures, formulates departmental policies, draws up budgets, and analyzes costs. He has the responsibility of gathering information, sifting it, and transmitting it to upper management in the form of progress reports and explanations of unusual circumstances.

The same factors in our society that have produced changes in the first-line supervisor's job have naturally affected the middle manager. There is pressure from below for competence from those supervisors who know their jobs and expect their bosses to have similar ability. Pressure from higher management for more effective decisions, increased productivity and expense control truly make the word "middle" stand out in the middle manager's job.

Knowledge, skills, and attitudes the supervisor needs

Effectively utilizing human resources, getting the product or the service completed on time, keeping costs down, and maintaining established quality standards are the supervisor's primary responsibilities. Accomplishing these results calls for knowledge and skills in dealing with people, in managing, and in the particular processes and methods of the work being done. The managerial, technical, and human elements are inseparable on the job, and they are combined in the discussion presented in each chapter.

The basic managerial skills to be mastered are those of planning, organizing, directing, coordinating and controlling, solving problems, and making effective decisions. The groundwork for studying the supervisor's managerial job is presented in the first four chapters:

1. *The job of managing.* An overall look at the supervisor's job and a charting of the course designed to improve performance on it.
2. *Organizations and organization structure.* The shape and size and authority relationships which affect the supervisor's way of operating.
3. *Policies and procedures.* Policies as guides to decision making, and procedures as ways to move work through the department.

4. *Organization dynamics.* The man–boss relationships; principles and techniques of delegating responsibility and authority.

In handling the technical side of his job, the supervisor may have the help of technical staff specialists such as methods men, standards men, procedure analysts, and job analysts, or he may apply the techniques himself. In either case he needs technical knowledge of, and skill in, the work that is being performed. If he lacks skill in it, he should have the analytical ability and competence necessary to direct it, make good decisions concerning it, to compare and improve methods, instruct workers, and evaluate their work. Moreover he must keep up-to-date on technical developments, because skills and techniques become obsolete as technological advances make possible new ways of doing things.

Innovations in product or service, in process, equipment, and method are essential to the continued profitability of a business. Therefore a supervisor's attitude toward change and his skill in introducing it are matters of concern to the whole organization. Efficiency of operation calls for knowledge and skill in the application of the principles and techniques for improving methods, designing jobs, developing standards of work performance, designing procedures, and controlling costs. The supervisor's multiple problems and lack of time call for a look at the design of his own job and a careful study of the way he uses his time.

It is the purpose of the text to present understandable and usable information about staff techniques for improving efficiency. There are examples and reports of how things are being done in a variety of companies. There are samples of forms that are used and examples of ways to use them. There are reports of problem solutions that other managers have found to be effective. And there are case studies to bring out the point of what is being discussed and to provide an opportunity to apply it.

Knowledge, skill, and attitudes in dealing with people. Human relations practices are aimed at motivating people to work for management objectives. The supervisor's effectiveness in dealing with people depends upon his understanding of their abilities, wants, and behavior, upon his skill in communicating with them, and upon his attitude toward them. Attitudes are of prime importance in the job of supervising. Most misunderstandings and mishandlings of job problems occur because people's attitudes prevent them from understanding why others are behaving as they do. Figure 1–2 presents this idea graphically.

An employee may seem to be stupid, stubborn, or lazy, but his behavior may be the result of some managerial action which to his way of thinking has taken the dignity, skill, or responsibility out of his job, has reduced him to a position of less importance, has damaged his estimation of his own

FIGURE 1–2
Factors Affecting a Person's Interpretation of a Situation

Each person's perception of a situation is distorted by his values: his expectations loyalties, prejudices, likes, dislikes, ideals, and objectives. These factors may prevent him from seeing the real situation and understanding why others are behaving as they are.

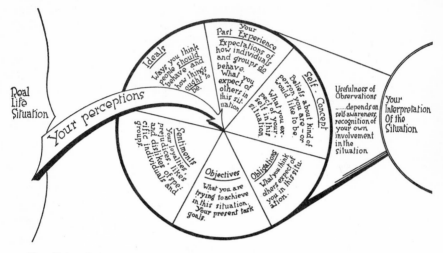

From Robert L. Katz, "Human Relations Skills Can Be Sharpened," *Harvard Business Review,* July–August, 1956.

worth, or has shut off his hopes of advancement. As he sees the situation, the job isn't worth putting in the effort.

Cases studies give the supervisor a laboratory in which to analyze attitudes of people in the case and the people who are discussing the case (himself included). Case studies help to develop the kind of attitudes that a boss should have toward his subordinates. If surveys of what people want from their jobs are translated into attitudes they want their bosses to have toward them, the list includes:

Respect for their personal dignity and worth.
Concern for their success on the job, their safety, and health.
Acceptance of their limitations and appreciation of their abilities.
Understanding of their needs for security, fair play, approval, belonging, importance, and recognition.
Willingness to listen to them, to try to understand them, to spare them from unnecessary unpleasantness and worry.

Knowledge, skill, and attitudes, and the environment. While the basic managerial skills and attitudes are similar for all managerial jobs, there are differences in approach and emphasis depending on the nature of the organization and the level of management. Generally speaking, it is more difficult for a first-level supervisor to develop a management attitude. In a sense his organizational environment is different than that of the middle manager. With the constant pressure placed on him by higher authority to get the work out, he may find it easier to sympathize and identify with his subordinates rather than with his superior. This is particularly true if he is a so-called working supervisor with a quota of work to produce along with his supervisory activities.

The middle manager is usually more concerned with coordination and control, planning and development of people. As a result he will more likely develop a managerial attitude. It is very important to his own growth that he allow his subordinates to function as managers. By doing so he then develops their supervisory abilities and their identification with management in the organization. The middle manager can make a considerable contribution to the health of the organization by developing his subordinates' managerial skills and attitudes.

Supervisory attitudes vary in relation to the nature of the work as well. Where the work pattern is relatively stable and there is no undue pressure, the supervisor may be more relaxed and less autocratic. He may also feel that he can communicate more effectively with his superior when time pressure is not as strong as it would be in a high-production, dynamic work environment. In organizations where change is rapidly taking place due to technology, methods, and procedures as well as equipment, the supervisor frequently meets resistance from subordinates. To be an effective change agent may require human relations skills that are extraordinary as well as the time necessary to properly train employees. Since this combination of time and outstanding human relations skills is not too common, the supervisor has more difficulty in the dynamic environment. This type of environment requires a high order of cooperation between the middle manager and the first-level supervisor. If both apply their collective skills and knowledge to the needed change then there is greater chance for smoother transition.

The tools of management

The five tools or main activities[6] of management mentioned earlier are supervisory skills to be learned and practiced. The discussion of

---

[6] This division into five activities comes from Henri Fayol, *General and Industrial Management*, trans. Constance Storrs (New York: Pitman Publishing Corp., 1949).

Other authors divide the activities differently—for instance, into planning, organizing, analyzing, and commanding; or into planning, organizing, and controlling. In this latter division, "controlling" would be defined to include both commanding and checking up. The difference between authors is not in essential material covered but in the way the activities are defined.

them in this chapter is a preliminary one; they are taken up again in later chapters. These five activities are:

1. *Planning.* The deciding of what is to be done to accomplish the purpose, the objective, or the mission of the department, section, or unit.
2. *Organizing.* The formal arranging and balancing of activities, the determination of who is to do what, the assigning of authority and responsibility so that that which is being planned will be accomplished.
3. *Directing.* Assigning tasks, ordering, instructing, telling subordinates what to do in order to accomplish the objective.
4. *Coordinating.* The integrating (routing) and timing (scheduling) of activities so that the plans will be carried out.
5. *Controlling.* Checking the progress of work against plans or standards to determine if activities are being carried out; making corrections and adjustments or even new plans in the light of new developments or unforeseen circumstances.

Planning

A business is dependent for its very existence on the abilities of its top planners. Failure to forecast the demand for a product and to plan how to meet a rising or shrinking demand spells the difference between success and failure of an enterprise. Top-level plans may be projected 20 years or more into the future. A paper manufacturer, for instance, forecasts the sales of its products and then plans a reforestation program to supply the wood pulp it will need.

Since top-level plans are implemented and carried out at lower levels of the organization, the first requisite in the supervisor's planning is that he know the objectives to be attained, the policies to be followed, the organizational and procedural structures to be used, the people who will be involved, and the environmental factors that have to be taken into account. In order to operate effectively toward the objectives, the supervisor must have a long-range plan, a plan for each day's work, and a plan for the apportioning of his own time. Since time is so scarce, so essential, and so easily lost, he needs to allocate it wisely. The supervisor who uses time to good advantage reserves a sizable portion of it to be spent in planning. All the work that comes into his department must be planned; it must fit into the plans of his department and into the plans of other departments. Planning requires that the supervisor answer the following questions:

What is to be done? He needs a clear idea of the work from beginning to end.

Why should it be done? Perhaps parts of the work need not be done. The most efficient way of improving those parts is to eliminate them.

When is it to be done? He must know how long the work will take, in order to fit it into his schedule and meet deadlines.

How is the work to be done? He must investigate methods.

Who is to do the work? He must fit men and jobs.

Where should it be done? He must fit jobs and machines. This is routing.

Planning is studied in more detail and in its application to the supervisor's job and his own personal planning in the chapter on, "Planning and Controlling the Department's Work."

Organizing

Organizing is defined as the formal arranging and balancing of activities, the determination of who is to do what, the assigning of authority and responsibility in order that the plan can be accomplished. Organizing an enterprise is the process of setting up the formal framework of activity groupings and authority relationships that make up the organization structure. The various kinds of structures, the authority responsibility relationships of the people within the structure and the accommodations that must be made to enable people and departments to work together effectively within the confines of the structure are analyzed and discussed in later chapters. The purpose of the present discussion of organizing is to show it in the overall picture of the job of managing.

There are certain criteria that must be observed in organizing any group effort performance, and they refer to unity of command, span of control, homogeneous assignments, and delegation of responsibility with the requisite authority.

Unity of command. The principle of unity of command is simply that a man should have only one boss and that no one but that boss should be giving him any direct orders. A superior who has delegated authority to a subordinate must operate through that subordinate and should no longer give orders directly to those who are under that subordinate. The superior sets up a channel when he delegates authority, and he should operate through that channel and not around it.

Span of control. Span of control is interpreted here as span of supervision. The span is a measure of the number of subordinates reporting directly to him that one boss can manage effectively. There is a theory (frequently disputed) that a top-level administrator's span is within the range of from three to eight. A first-level supervisor's is much larger. Reasons for the difference lie in the nature, complexity, and variety of the work, the amount of coordinating that must be done, and the amount of damage that could result from decisions made on each of the levels. Other organizational factors affecting the span of supervision are the amount of assistance available to the supervisor, the amount of responsibility he can delegate to subordinates, and the effectiveness of procedures and controls.

Personal factors that limit the number of employees a person can supervise are the extent of the energy and knowledge of the supervisor, his personality, the distance over which his subordinates are spread, and the number of hours there are in a workday.

Homogeneous assignments.   The reason for organizing in the first place is to divide the work and assign the authority and responsibility for accomplishing it. Whether this dividing is being done by the top executive or by the supervisor, the principle governing it is the same: the work must be divided into homogeneous assignments. To put it another way—an area of work must be outlined to cover related jobs, and a man's assignments must fall within that area. A man needs a specific job made up of related tasks that make sense to him—a whole job, not a half a job or a job and a half. Jobs should be designed to utilize the skills of people and to meet their psychological needs as well as to meet the company's technical, organizational, and economic needs.

Each job should be carefully defined in terms of what is to be accomplished, the skills necessary, and the amount of authority and responsibility that go with it. This information should be expressed in a formal job description which summarizes what the person does, how he does it, and what qualifications he must have. The design of a job and the way a man fits the job are important factors in motivation.

Delegation of responsibility and authority.   No matter how capable a management man is, his responsibilities are always greater than his capacity to carry them out. No one expects the company president personally to produce and package his product; he formed an organization so that these responsibilities could be delegated down the line. When any management man becomes overburdened to the point that he can't handle all his responsibilities and still do the important ones well, he needs to hand over some of his tasks to subordinates and free himself for the more important parts of his job.

Successful delegation calls for complete understanding between superior and subordinate about the tasks that are being handed over and the amount of authority the subordinate is being given to make decisions concerning them.

Directing

Directing includes assigning tasks, ordering, telling, and instructing subordinates what to do and perhaps how to do it. Since the supervisor's job is to get things done through people, his effectiveness is closely tied to getting his ideas across to them clearly and in a way that will get the action he desires. It is essential that the subordinate understand the orders or he won't be able to carry them out. In directing people it is important to know how much information and what kind of information to give them. Orders should be fitted to the receiver: the new man needs to be instructed in detail but the experienced man may need only the objectives and he can choose the means to attain them.

When supervisors get together in management training conferences and discuss order giving and receiving, many of them complain that the orders they receive contain too much emphasis on how to do it and too little on why it needs to be done. People by nature are curious; when they are doing a job they want to know what it is all about. One of the things that a man asks of his job is that it have meaning to him—that he know what he's doing. He also likes to be helpful and to contribute his own ideas to the project.

Good communication between a man and his boss is essential for intelligent performance of a job. A man has no way of knowing the significance of what he is doing unless his boss tells him. A person can't make good decisions if he lacks essential information. The man carrying out an order always has to do some planning of details because an order can never be absolutely complete or cover all possibilities. Often unanticipated conditions arise that call for interpretation of the instructions. The person understanding *why* the order was given is in a better position to adapt his actions and interpretation to the overall purpose than the person who is given only the detailed *how*.

The desirability of explaining why an order is issued will depend on a number of things:

1. The extent to which the subordinate must exercise his own judgment and initiative in carrying out the directions.
2. The capacity of the subordinate to comprehend the overall situation.
3. The importance of training the subordinate.
4. The time available for discussion when the order is issued.
5. The extent to which the subordinate already knows and understands the reasons.
6. The need of the *why* as a motivator, especially when an order might otherwise meet resistance.

Coordinating

Coordinating refers to that element of precision which makes sure the right thing will be at the right place at the right time. Anyone who has visited an automobile assembly plant and watched the right subassemblies arrive at the main assembly line at just the right time has seen a job of coordinating. Getting out the payroll is another good example of coordinating. Lack of coordination can bring about some chaotic conditions, as, for example, when a sales promotion plan breaks down because the advertising isn't ready or the samples aren't there, or the mailings haven't gone out, or there has been no provision for taking care of the extra load of office work or production work.

Middle-management people do a great deal of coordinating in fitting together the work of their subordinate managers and integrating it into the work of other departments. The basis of this fitting together is good planning. When a supervisor subdivides a department job and hands out the parts for various people to do, he must fit together the activities of those people so that the whole job is done in the proper manner and on time. In order to meet deadlines, he must know how long it takes to do the jobs and when they must be started. It is a sure sign that coordination is breaking down if a piece of work is held up because some part is not finished on schedule. Coordination becomes even worse if the needed part is cannibalized from another job.

Certain parts of jobs have to be completed before other parts can be begun. Therefore, the supervisor must coordinate the activities of his department with those of other departments. To do this, he must know where his department fits into the whole picture and how it affects the operation of other departments. This knowledge of how the various parts of a job fit together enables a supervisor to plan the work so that there is no duplication of effort and no parts are left undone—no gaps.

Vertical coordination is the means by which a supervisor integrates the activities of his own department into the plans of his superior. He must do the job that his superior wants done, do it in the way his superior wants it done, and get it done on time. Coordination involves all levels of management from the receiving clerk and receiving inspector checking in a newly purchased piece of equipment on up to the treasurer of the company raising the cash to pay for it.

The need for coordination increases as specialization increases, because the more an activity is subdivided, the more it needs to be integrated with other activities in matters of sequence and timing. The need to coordinate is one of the factors that limit specialization, because as organization becomes more complex, coordination becomes more necessary and difficult. Management has at its disposal certain aids to coordination, such as organization charts, budgets, procedures, job descriptions, routing, scheduling, and follow-up techniques.

Additional coordination can be achieved by the creation of more elaborate systems of procedures, with the expensive paper work they involve. On the other hand, coordination can sometimes be better achieved by developing cooperation or teamwork, keeping the organization structure simple, delegating authority and responsibility, avoiding overspecialization, and having more effective communicating.

Controlling

Controlling involves the checking of performance against standards or goals to find out what people are doing and comparing it to what they should be doing. It is a type of inspection activity. A superior must know how well his subordinates are performing. He must find out whether the job is being done in the desired manner, whether men are putting out work of a satisfactory quality and in a satisfactory quantity.

In order for a supervisor to perform this inspection aspect of his job, he must have standards by which to measure. How much work can a qualified employee put out in a unit of time? What should be the accuracy or quality requirements of the job?

These standards of quantity and quality should be determined as accurately as possible. Until they are determined and established, a job is going to be judged by three standards—the worker has his ideas of a fair day's work and also what he thinks might be expected of him; the supervisor has his ideas of what he would like to have done and what he thinks can be done; and top management has its criteria and expectations. Whether or not quantity and quality standards are recognized, they exist, and each level in the organization—the workers, the supervisor, and the big boss—may be judging jobs by different standards. Until uniformity is achieved, there will be misunderstandings. Good standards set up and recognized let the department head know what he can expect and let the first-level supervisor and each worker know just what is expected of him and how much.

Measuring supervisory performance. Cost and performing records give a supervisor a measure of his own performance against a common standard. A standard against which the middle-management man can measure his own performance is the budget: Are actual expenses of the department staying within the amount that was budgeted? If cost figures are higher than the amount budgeted, then he must investigate the causes *while the work is still in process.* The governing philosophy of this type of control—as with all controls—should be to prevent poor performance rather than just assess the blame after the job is done.

The ideal form of control is management by objectives and self-control. A supervisor is able to operate that way when (1) he has reached an understanding with his boss about objectives of the company and what contributions his department is expected to make toward attaining those objectives; (2) he knows not only what kind of performance is expected of him but by what kind of statistics or records it is measured; (3) he is kept supplied with information in a form that enables him to check up on his own performance and he gets this information soon enough to enable him to take corrective action. Management by objectives and self-control motivates managers to set high goals for themselves because their performance is measured by the actual contribution they make to the company rather than by the showing they make on certain reports.

Decision making

Managers are paid to make good decisions. The very existence of a business can depend upon decisions made by its top-level administrators. The importance of management's decision-making function is indicated by the growing number of training programs and training devices designed to improve it.

The supervisor's area of decision making is in managing work and worker. His boss makes decisions about managing the department, supervising the supervisors, and coordinating their work. Making good decisions about the work to be done calls for knowledge and skill in the technical side of the job and an understanding of the managerial techniques of planning, directing, and controlling the work of others. And since decisions must be made in terms of the whole organization, a supervisor must know the organization's policies and procedures, the union contract, the extent of his own authority, the way the boss wants things done, and the way the decision will affect areas other than his own.

Decisions in order to be workable must not only be technically sound but must take into account the attitudes of the people who will be affected by them. How will this decision be interpreted by subordinates? Is there anything in it that will upset them unnecessarily and have a bad effect on their will to work? No decision is going to be very successful if it arouses fears or hostility in the people who are expected to give their best efforts to carrying it out.

Almost every decision the supervisor makes involves people in some way, and the problems arising from decisions stem from the fact that the situation doesn't look the same to the other person as it does to the decision maker. Figure 1–2 shows how a person's perception of a situation and his interpretation of it are conditioned by his own involvement in it and by his own background. Of all the people viewing a situation, no two see it in the same way. Each person sees things through a lens shaped and colored by his own experiences, beliefs, and sentiments; his perception is distorted by his values, his expectations, loyalties, prejudices, likes, dislikes, ideals, and objectives.

If a supervisor is aware of his own attitudes and how they affect his judgment, he is better able to evaluate the information on which he makes his decisions. Case study conferences give a supervisor a laboratory in which to observe the processes by which people bring their widely differing backgrounds of knowledge, attitudes, interests, and ambitions into the analysis of case problems.

Problem-solving techniques

Most of the supervisor's daily problems are fairly routine in nature and can be handled by the commonsense method—a quick evaluation of the situation against experience and logic. Some problems require deeper and wider consideration, however, particularly problems relating to planning, improving methods, disciplining, and handling grievances. There are various methods of handling difficult problems: the more complicated the problem, the more elaborate the technique. Six problem-solving techniques are presented here. Each has merit and is particularly adaptable to certain types of problems.

Technique A. What is the problem? Why did it arise? What can be done about it? Who should do it? When should it be done? How should it be done?

Technique B. What is wrong? Evidences? Causes? What can be done?

Technique C. The problem. Effects of the present method or policy. Suggestions for improvement. Evaluation of suggested methods. Conclusions as to method to be adopted.

Technique D. The problem. Facts. Analysis. Evaluation. Conclusions.

Technique E. The JMT formula. This formula (Job Methods Training) has been used with success in getting workers to study their own jobs and discover better ways to perform them. JMT can be found in Chapter 8 in the discussion of methods improvement.

Technique F. The seven-step problem-solving technique which will be described below and illustrated in subsequent chapters. It was chosen for presentation in detail here because it contains all the essentials of the other five techniques and has the advantage of being more precise.

The seven-step problem-solving technique

Students of management and people in management who want to increase their scores for sound decision making should try the seven-step problem-solving technique on their more difficult problems. Even though they have to spend a fair amount of time going through the seven steps, they will gain speed and proficiency with practice. As a result of the practice they will make better decisions and will form the habit of using the seven steps—even applying them rapidly to their less-impor-tant problems and getting better results on them also. The technique can be practiced by applying it to the more difficult cases in the text, using the seven steps instead of the specific questions that are attached to each case.

Here are the seven steps of the technique:

Step 1.   Clearly define the problem or problems.
Step 2.   Gather the information.
Step 3.   Interpret the information.
Step 4.   Develop solutions.
Step 5.   Select the best practical solution.
Step 6.   Put the solution into operation.
Step 7.   Evaluate the effectiveness of the solution.

Step 1.   Clearly define the problem or problems.   A supervisor's awareness of a problem may be a feeling of concern over a number of undesirable conditions that he hasn't the time to do anything about—poor performance by subordinates, schedules not met, and work piling up. His first statement of the problem may be that he needs more people or more overtime. If he examines this idea critically, he discovers that he is drawing conclusions too soon and that he isn't considering the situation in terms of his objectives of high production at low cost.

If the problem has arisen because of poor management, he may need one solution to take care of the immediate problem and then some long-range improvement to avoid future problems. In other words, he needs a cure for now and then a plan of prevention which might include methods improvements, training, delegating, motivating, and other good supervisory practices. (Chapter 7 prescribes a course of action for the supervisor who goes from one crisis to another and never has the time to take action necessary to prevent the problems from arising.)

In defining a problem, the supervisor should determine the area it covers and ask: Do I have the authority to do anything about this myself? Do I have the knowledge? The time? Could I get somebody else to do it? Suppose I don't do anything, what then? If the total problem is too big for me, what are the parts that are most urgent? How broad should the investigation be? How deep? What benefits can be expected from solving the problem? A list of the expected benefits serves as the criterion by which to evaluate and compare alternative solutions. Also, the list puts a price tag and perhaps a priority number on the investigation. How important are these benefits? How much are they worth? What expense should be gone to to attain them?

Step 2.   Gather the information.   Although information gathering is listed as the second step in the process, it is actually an activity that continues all through it. Information has to be gathered in order to define the problem, in order to work out and evaluate solutions, and in order to check up on the effects of the chosen solution. The information gathered will probably be a combination of facts and feelings, because in any problem that involves people there will be attitudes, prejudices, opinions, inferences, and maybe illusions that must be considered.

Experience is a good source of information—the supervisor's own experience, the experience of other men in management, and the experience of the people involved in the problem. Everybody involved has ideas of what should be done about it, and many of these ideas turn up good information and suggestions. But whether these ideas are fruitful or not, *asking for them* is important because the person who is consulted in the analysis and solution of a problem will have a better attitude toward that solution and any changes it entails than would a person who was not consulted. People are anxious to tell what is wrong with a situation (providing it's not their fault). If they think the company is making it hard for them to do a good job, it is important that they get a chance to air their opinions. Employees want a voice in matters that affect them, and asking their opinions is one way to help satisfy this want.

If the problem being investigated is a personnel problem, something can be learned about the people involved in it by asking their former supervisors. Good information can often be gotten from production, personnel, and office records, time and attendance reports, inspection reports, history of transfers, promotions, raises, layoffs, etc. The information gathered will never be complete; some of it will be useless, some inaccurate, some of it will open up new avenues for investigation.

Step 3. Interpret the information. Information should not be judged piece by piece as it is gathered; there is too much danger that the investigator will develop a theory (This employee is a born troublemaker or accident prone or insecure) and then ignore or discount any evidence that doesn't fit into the pattern. Conflicting accounts have to be pieced together and evaluated against additional evidence. Information might be sorted into some orderly arrangement, such as one of the following:

1. Line up the information in the order of its reliability.
2. Arrange the information in terms of major importance, minor importance, and no importance.
3. Set the information up in terms of time: What happened first? Next? What came before what? Why did it? What were the surrounding circumstances?
4. Set the information up in terms of cause and effect: What is the cause of what?

5. Classify the information into categories: Human factors such as personality, health, age, relationships between people, off-the-job problems. Technical factors such as method, skill, training, tools, machinery, workplace. Time factors such as stage of growth or development of the company, length of service, overtime, night shift, or the question, "How long has this been going on?" Policy factors such as policies, procedures, or rules applying to the problem.

Since the information is never complete, it is necessary to make assumptions, and all assumptions should be supported by evidence and logical thinking. The investigator should be aware of his own prejudices and try to be objective in his judgments. In considering circumstances he should try to get the point of view of the people who were involved in the incident. For example, was everybody violating the smoking rule? Or the chain of command? Or was only one person doing it? Did the sequence of events have something to do with it? If this sort of thing has been going on for a while, what has been the attitude toward it?

The investigator might put himself in the place of the person being investigated and ask: If I were in his place, how would I see the situation? Would I have acted the same way? Would the "normal" person have acted as he did or was there something special in the situation or in the person that made him react the way he did? Is he new on the job? What is his physical condition? His age? What difficulties does this person have or what does he think he has? Was this behavior a mask for some feeling he didn't want to show? Is he afraid he'll lose his job or that he won't be able to do the work?"

Step 4. Develop solutions. As a person interprets information, numerous ideas about possible solutions suggest themselves to him. The first one might well be: What will happen if I do nothing about it? Some problems clear up by themselves; others call for immediate action. In considering possible solutions, the supervisor must be guided by established policy and the principles and practices of good management. What principles or practices of good management are being violated, thus causing the difficulty or contributing to the undesirable situation? What principles or practices, if applied, would offer solutions to the problem? What obstacles stand in the way of a solution? Sometimes considering obstacles one by one yields ideas for solutions.

After several possible solutions have come to mind and have been put in writing, the supervisor should start developing ideas about them. He should not limit himself to a single solution, because doing so seems to limit thinking and cause too much concentration on detail. Developing several alternative solutions makes it possible to combine the best parts of them into one superior solution. Also, alternatives are valuable to have in case the boss finds something wrong with the first one—a bad flaw in it or incompatibility with the broader company plans that he has information about.

Step 5.   Select the best practical solution.   In selecting the best solution to a problem, the supervisor should consider the short-term and long-term effects of each of the possible solutions. He might compare the solutions in terms of the following questions:

1.   How far has the situation deteriorated? Must drastic steps be taken or can time aid as a cure? Is the problem just arising or has it been existing a long time?
2.   To what extent will the objectives in Step 1 be realized by each of the solutions?
3.   What will be the effect of each possible solution on the quality and quantity of production?
4.   Which solution is most readily applicable and will produce the quickest results?
5.   Have these solutions been used before and what have been their results?
6.   What will be the side effects of each of the possible solutions?
7.   What are the difficulties involved in the application of each of these solutions?
8.   What will be the cost of each solution?
9.   How does the cost of each solution compare with the results that it will give?

Step 6.   Put the solution into effect.   Some solutions have to be put into effect quickly—matters of discipline, for instance, may have to get some kind of immediate treatment. Company policy and union contract must be followed; so the supervisor should know in advance what authority he has to act in an emergency, and what the penalties are for various offenses.

If the problem is a technical one and the solution to it brings a change in the method of doing work or calls for a new arrangement of facilities or a new type of machine, it may run into resistance. People become disturbed by changes that break up their habit patterns and threaten their security or status. Rather than have a good plan fail because people resist the changes it entails, the supervisor might consider breaking his plan up into a chain of events, each to be introduced when the time is ripe.

Sometimes changes can be tried out in a limited area and the bugs uncovered and corrected before the area of application is widened. Pilot studies and dry runs permit a person to adjust plans to unforeseen circumstances and to make corrections and refinements before final application under full operating conditions. A change may be put in on a temporary basis and then modified in terms of the reactions to it. (A policy might be introduced in this manner.) A change in procedure might be put in step by step and the installing schedule worked out with the people who would be affected by it. If the change is a new program to be launched—for instance, a job evaluation program—people could be prepared for it by a great amount of advance publicity. In whatever way a change is introduced, people should be assured that they will get training and assistance for adjusting to the new situation, and they should be helped to see the new situation in a favorable light.

Step 7.   Evaluate the effectiveness of the solution.   Periodically a supervisor should review the plan he put into operation and he should compare the actual practice with the ideal of the solution. (People are prone to fall back into old habit patterns.) The benefits resulting from the plan should be measured against the objectives set up in Step 1: Are the objectives being realized? If not, why not? If the results are better than expected, what favorable factors cause this to be so?

Periodic checkups on solutions give the supervisor valuable experience to use in solving other problems. The supervisor should study the operation of his solutions somewhat as the quarterback studies the films of the football game. Where did he make mistakes? How can he avoid repeating them? What decisions were brilliant successes? What were the contributing circumstances? If the supervisor will evaluate and build on his experience and deliberately direct his efforts in practice, he can develop skill in solving problems.

Summary

This chapter was designed to give both the supervisor and the student an idea of the broad responsibilities of management. To function effectively, the manager must develop the knowledge, skills, and attitudes necessary for the practice of management. The fact that these can be developed is demonstrated by the thousands of people who each year go through management development programs of various kinds. The practice of management can be learned although each practitioner will bring to his efforts his particular individualism in much the same way an artist will interpret a scene in his own unique way on the canvas.

Of particular importance is the development of a managerial attitude and a problem-solving approach. It is desirable for the supervisor to identify with other members of management in his workplace and to try and establish personal goals which closely resemble the goals of his organization. Because the manager is largely concerned with solving a variety of problems, this subject was covered rather thoroughly. The cases which follow this chapter and all other chapters in this book present typical managerial problems and group discussion of these cases will help the manager sharpen his problem-solving ability. It will be helpful to read the Foreword of this text for a further explanation of the use of cases and their value as a development tool for the supervisor.

CASE 1

Bill Roberts had been with his company three years when he was promoted to manager of the tax department which was part of the controller's division.

He started with the company when he graduated from college and he completed the company's one-year management training program. After that he spent two years in the department as a tax accountant and a supervisor of 10 tax accountants. He served as a supervisor for eight months prior to his promotion.

The department has 45 employees including clerical and secretarial people. Several people in the department are senior personnel with more than 30 years' experience. Some of these are more technically knowledgeable in taxation than Bill. There is some resentment in this group that so young a person was made manager and three or four are particularly upset because they desired the promotion and felt they deserved it.

1. What can Bill Roberts do about the resentful senior employees?
2. Can higher managenent do anything to help Mr. Roberts make the transition to his greater responsibility?
3. Will his lack of technical know-how hinder Bill's managerial effectiveness?
4. Should Bill's superior have discussed his pending promotion with the senior members of the department before announcing it?
5. Should Bill have turned down the promotion to gain more technical experience?
6. Can a person turn down a promotion to a significant managerial position without hindering his career in a company?

CASE 2

Leo Harris, one of your assistants in a fire insurance company, is in charge of a group of clerical workers who review changed policies, endorsements, and riders, calculate commissions, and maintain records. He is very meticulous, and everything coming out of his group is perfect. He does not delegate authority and responsibility but rechecks in detail all the work turned out by his group. He keeps turning back to them careless and inaccurate work until it is perfect. As a result, he is busy from early morning until late at night doing detail work and neglecting his role as supervisor.

His workers have figured him out and are taking it easy. They do slapdash work and correct it as often as he returns it.

You are afraid that Harris is overworking and heading for a nervous breakdown. You have told him in general terms to delegate authority and responsibility and to discipline his group. He says that you just can't find people any more who have pride in their work or concern for the company, and that if he fires any of his people or they quit, the replacements would probably be worse.

1. What are some of the reasons why people do not delegate authority and responsibility?
2. What are Harris' responsibilities as a supervisor?
3. Which can he delegate?
4. How should he go about delegating them?
5. What are some of the leadership characteristics that Harris lacks?
6. How can you go about developing them in him?

CASE 3

Very recently, Jack and Harry were made first-level supervisors. They had no previous supervisory experience. Following are three of the situations they fell into last week:

Situation 1. An order came down through regular channels to Jack for him to have a certain job done. He assigned three men to it and told them to see that the job was done correctly. Three days later he was called in by his supervisor and reprimanded because the job was not done correctly. Jack claimed that he was not to blame—that he had assigned the job to three of his men and they must have fallen down on the job.

What principle of good management did Jack fail to observe?

Situation 2. An order came down through channels to Supervisors Jack and Harry to use their combined groups to do a piece of work. The work was done but not in a satisfactory manner. When Jack was called in by his supervisor, he said that he had understood that Harry would make the final check on the work. When Harry was called in, he said that his understanding was that Jack would make the final check.

What is wrong in the above situation?

Situation 3. Supervisor Harry, while walking through Supervisor Jack's section, saw two of Jack's subordinates talking and laughing at the water cooler during working hours. He reprimanded them and told them to get to work.

What principle of good management did Harry violate?

Harry and Jack come to you, a fellow supervisor, and ask you for some tips on how to supervise. List a half-dozen additional principles you would set up for them to observe in order for them to keep out of trouble.

CASE 4

You were working as a first-level supervisor in a branch plant (or make this a branch office or chain store) when your boss told you that you were being promoted to a better position (in the home plant, office, or headquarters) within two weeks and you should pick one of your rank-and-file employees to take over your job.

You chose Harry Wilson because his production was good, he was well liked by the other employees, and he had seniority. (It was not necessary, however, that the promotion be based on seniority.) You explained your choice to everyone involved and started Harry off handling the paper work to be sure he would be well acquainted with the system and the forms and reports he would be responsible for. This took up a whole week, since you couldn't devote all your time to Harry. You expected to crowd a lot into the second week but you didn't have the opportunity, because your boss told you that you were needed at once on the new job. You told him that Harry wasn't too well acquainted with his new job, but he said for you to keep in touch with Harry by phone.

Your new position occupied all of your time, and you did not phone Wilson. Since he did not call you, you assumed he was not getting into trouble. After you had been on your new job for a month your new boss called you into his office one morning and wanted to know what was the matter with Wilson—the production of his group was far below normal. He then told you to go back to the branch and stay there until you had the situation straightened out.

1. List and define the duties of a first-level supervisor.
2. What kind of supervisory skills might Wilson be lacking to cause "production far below normal"?
3. How should Wilson have been prepared for his new job? Be specific.

CASE 5

The superintendent wants to set up a management training program for first-level supervisors. He has set up a committee of first-level supervisors and middle-management people to: (1) set up ways of determining the training needs of first-level supervisors, (2) determine what training they should have in order to meet the most obvious needs, (3) devise some way for measuring the effectiveness of the program.

Decide if this is in a product industry or a service industry, and as members the committee:
1. Set up a checklist of questions that might be used for uncovering training needs of first-level supervisors.

2. List the topics or subjects that might be included in such a program.
3. List a number of methods of conducting training.
4. How can the effectiveness of training programs be measured? See "Uncovering Training Needs" in Chapter 12.

CASE 6

John Matthews, a new salesman for the company, had just returned from a trip to the company's headquarters where he had undergone a six-week training program. Before John left the regional office where he was hired he drew $500 for expenses, which was normal practice. His travel and hotel expense had been paid for by the home office. Upon his return he carefully prepared his expense account itemizing all expenditures. His total expenses for the trip came to $350 and he was prepared to return the surplus to the cashier. He turned in his expense account for the sales manager's approval which was required of all salesmen.

The sales manager called John to his office and told him he was a fool for returning the surplus. John replied that he only spent the amount stated and naturally thought the surplus must be returned. The sales manager smiled and then proceeded to show John how to pad his expense account. He remarked that John's honesty would make the other salesmen and the sales manager look bad when the expense accounts were checked by the company's internal auditing staff.

1. What should John do in view of the sales manager's objection to his honest expense account?
2. Can John refuse to comply with the sales manager's request for expense account padding and still stay with the company?
3. Should John go to the sales manager's superior with his problem?
4. What would cause the sales manager to encourage expense account padding when it increases the cost of doing business and this would tend to reflect on his managerial competence?

CASE 7

You have recently been promoted to the position of branch manager. In the six weeks since you were transferred to this branch as its manager you have been able to assess the various capabilities of your subordinates.

The operations manager who is in charge of all clerical work at the branch has been with the company for 18 years and has held most of the clerical positions in a branch. He has been at the branch for four years as its operations manager. His knowledge of operations is excellent but he is very excitable and tends to speak very loudly when under pressure.

The assistant branch manager has 25 years of service with the company, the last 14 years in this branch. He has also held most branch positions and is one of the best when it comes to technical knowledge. He was first assigned to the branch as chief clerk and he subsequently served as operations manager until he was promoted to his present post and was replaced by the present operations manager. The assistant manager has, with the consent of two former branch managers, retained most of the responsibilities he held as chief clerk and operations manager. As a result there is a weak chief clerk, a staff with a feeling of dependency on one man and an operations manager who is frustrated since he cannot do his job.

You want to realign duties and responsibilities and accomplish more delegation to strengthen the staff. You have found however, that your assistant manager resists change and he has worked himself into a position where he can make change very difficult. He is a man who is set in his ways and once he has taken a position on a subject he is almost impossible to change on a friendly basis.

1. What can you do to properly assign managerial responsibilities and utilize your staff more effectively?
2. Why does the old operations manager refuse to relinquish his past responsibilities?
3. Can such a man be utilized effectively under the circumstances?
4. Should you maintain the status quo as your predecessors have done?

CASE 8

You are interested in delegating some of your authority and responsibility in order to free yourself of detail. However, the men in your department do not show any initiative, nor do they seem interested in advancement. When any problems arise about the way to handle a job or anything unusual shows up in their work, which is all routine, they just come to you for the solution. It takes you more time to explain the solution than to do the job yourself. As a result, you are snowed under most of the time.

1. What are some of the causes of a lack of initiative?
2. How can you stimulate initiative in your men?
3. How should you go about delegating authority and responsibility?

CASE 9

Ralph Taylor was recently hired for the job of mechanical installation foreman in a communications industry. One of the duties he regularly performed was to supervise the installation of preassembled rack-mounted electronic circuit boxes. In laying out one particular job he found that the number of boxes to be mounted would not fit on the racks provided if he maintained the spacing between boxes that was called for on the specifications. So he shortened the spacing between boxes to get them all in.

When the mounting was finished, he turned the job over to the electricians who, under the direction of their foreman, provided the necessary power to the circuit boxes. This completed the installation.

When the circuits were "cut over" they functioned satisfactorily for several days, then failed because of overheating. The engineering department investigated and found that the overheating was caused by lack of proper ventilation, which in turn was caused by having the boxes too close together. Further investigation of the mistake revealed: (1) that the buyer in the purchasing department had ordered 12-foot channels rather than the 16-foot channels specified on the requisition made out by engineering, (2) that the receiving inspection department had overlooked the fact that the order received did not match the requisition, and (3) that the costs of the job and the error were as follows:

Pair of 12-foot racks (channel) ....$	12
Circuit boxes which were mounted on the channels	16,000
Mechanical and electrical installation	500
Revenue lost to the company through the failure of the circuitry	50,000
Engineering cost of investigating the failure	1,500
New electronic components to replace the ones that failed	1,000
Remounting the boxes with proper spacing on the 16-foot racks	200
Rewiring the power to fit the new spacing	300

1. To whom would you charge this error?
2. What means should be taken to prevent repetition of such costly mistakes?

CASE 10

The boss in a well-run company gives to a committee of his middle-management subordinates the names of four first-level supervisors he wants them to consider for promotion to a single position in middle management. Each committee member knows enough about the four to make a good decision. The boss wants the group to recommend one man and be able to justify the recommendation.

1. List a half-dozen or so requirements a man must meet if he is going to be a success as a middle-management supervisor.
2. Agree on the meaning of, and work out a definition for, each of the above requirements.
3. What kind of evidence does the committee need in order to compare the four candidates in relation to each requirement?

4. To what extent are the requirements similar to, and to what extent are they different from, those necessary for success in first-level supervision?

CASE 11

Assume that you are a recent college graduate working in the personnel department of a company. Your boss has just turned over to you a letter from a local health organization that performs a community service—chest X ray, polio shots, or blood bank (choose one). The health organization wants to inaugurate its services on the premises of the company. The time required is three hours either in the morning or afternoon on a day convenient to the company. Your boss tells you to take over the assignment.

The company is proud of its record of close cooperation with the community and will want the project to be successful. You want it to be an outstanding success because you know your boss is using this assignment as a means of testing your managerial ability. He says that the company nurse has been informed and will cooperate, and that you may have any necessary clerical assistance.

1. Select a type of business that you are acquainted with or interested in—such as retail sales, insurance, manufacturing (jobbing or mass production). Gather as much data as you need about the business. Make any necessary assumptions as to the number of employees. Choose a number somewhere between 100 and 1,000. Apply the planning, organizing, directing, coordinating, and controlling techniques to the project.
2. Prepare an outline for your boss, showing step by step how you will accomplish your assignment. Be prepared to defend each step.
3. Compare your outline with the outlines of other members of the group who may have chosen different types of businesses and different sized companies. Observe how the nature and size of the business affect the outlines.

CASE 12

An independent wholesaler dealing in goods handled by retail stores employs 150 order fillers and packers in the warehouse. The workers are union members and until recently were supervised by six working foremen, also union members and selected strictly on the basis of seniority.

Management believes that the warehouse employees do as little work as possible for the pay they receive and has tried the following remedies: setting work quotas, having two foremen patrol the warehouse, using overtime as an incentive to produce more, and stopping the employees from conversing on the job. These measures did not improve performance but did stir up resentment; the employees claimed they were being treated unfairly.

Management diagnosed the problem thus:

1. The foremen, selected on a seniority basis, are not qualified for the job.
2. The foremen are in sympathy with the employees rather than with management.
3. The foremen have the same grievances as the employees.

Management decided, therefore, to eliminate the job of working foreman and to incorporate the position into management's structure. The job created was not really different from the one that previously existed, but the job title changed and the prestige that went along with it increased. The men who were placed in the newly created positions were distinguished from the rank-and-file workers by a symbol—a white shirt. The result of this action was a further drop in production. The workers claim that the foreman's job belongs to a member of the rank and file.

What action should the company be taking?

CASE 13

Recently you were promoted from the job of first-level supervisor to that of middle management, and you now have under your supervision several of your former equals. You get along well with them, and there is no resentment about your advancement because they recognize that you are the best man available for the job.

You know from past associations that you will have to straighten out three of these subordinates; the rest are all right. The three are Black, Blue, and White. Black has always been against the organization, Blue has always been snowed under by work, and White has always been a weak sister.

Black, the anticompany man, always sides with his men against the organization and sympathizes with them when things go wrong. He wants conditions to be perfect and is always pointing out to his men the defects in the company and finding fault with the way the organization is run. (Conditions, while not perfect, are above average.) He does his job grudgingly and does not get along well with the other men in the organization. The morale of his men is low, and they, too, are always grumbling.

Blue, on the other hand, is snowed under by his work; he carries the whole load of the department on his shoulders. His men take no initiative, and he is continually correcting their mistakes. He sees that whatever little work comes out of his section is letter-perfect even if he has to have his men do their jobs over and over again and he has to put on the finishing touches himself. Often his men are standing around waiting for him to get around to checking their work. They know their jobs but wait for Blue to make all the decisions.

Finally, there is White, the weak sister. Instead of running his men, he is letting them run him. The men do their jobs in any manner they wish. They do not respect his authority, and they question all his decisions. They argue with him when he gives orders, and they raise so many objections that he lets them do whatever they want. Often they boast of how they tell him off.

All the other supervisors under your jurisdiction are doing a good job. You would like to take the easy way out and fire Black, Blue, and White, but they have been with the company for quite a while. Besides, you feel that, if you can lick these problems, you will receive quite a bit of recognition from upper management.

1. How would you go about straightening out Black?
2. How would you go about straightening out Blue?
3. How would you go about straightening out White?

CASE 14

The accident rate in the receiving department has been increasing rapidly; the injuries are falls, wrenched backs, banged-up fingers or toes, and the like. The head of the receiving department, Mr. Wright, reports directly to you. He has been with the company 10 years in his present capacity. He is a quiet, unassuming person, and, since the receiving department never was much of a problem, you seldom bothered about it or him.

Since this accident rate needs attending to, you call Wright into your office and ask him how he plans to clear it up. He tells you that it will work itself out. Then you suggest that he should do some reading on safety and supervision or take a course in supervisory development. This remark seems to hit a sore spot, because he tells you emphatically that he does not believe in learning a lot of catch phrases such as "Accidents are caused," or "An unsafe condition plus an unsafe act equals an accident," or "Plan your work and work your plan." He states that all anyone needs is the Golden Rule—"Do unto others as you would have them do unto you." With this statement, he leaves your office.

Following this incident, you look closer into the affairs of the receiving department and find that, in addition to the accident situation, the turnover rate is high and there are indications of pilfering. Formerly, most of Wright's personnel was made up of men he hired from a rescue mission where he preaches at night. But, since the personnel department took over all hiring, the new workers are not from the rescue mission, and there seems to be a fair amount of conflict between the new men and Wright. They refer to him as "Holy Joe."

1. What are the problems involved in this case?
2. What are the "facts"? What sources might supply you with additional information?
3. Assume that other conditions are about average. Make additional assumptions, if necessary, to fit the company. What is the cause of what? What is the effect of what? What principles or policies are involved?
4. Develop several solutions.
5. What seems to be the best possible solution?
6. How would you go about achieving this solution?
7. How would you follow up on the effectiveness of the solution?
8. Outline step by step the procedure Wright should follow in correcting the accident situation in his department.

CASE 15

You are employed in an airline company. Your boss has asked you to represent him on a committee working on the problem of reducing the turnover of stewardesses. He feels that you can supply the recent graduate point of view.

Your company, as well as other airlines, has the problem of half the stewardesses quitting each year. According to the personnel department's records and the exit interviews, they quit to get married; some of them marry people within the company, some marry passengers, but most of them marry the boy back home. The turnover rate and causes in your company are similar to those in the other airline companies.

To qualify for the job of stewardess on a plane, a girl must be between the ages of 21 and 26, single, slender, attractive, and have a pleasant disposition and voice. The company feels that the above qualifications are necessary for dealing with the traveling public. The company will be slow to modify these requirements unless there are good reasons. The stewardess's pay is on a level with a stenographer's.

Each girl, before being assigned as a stewardess, is trained for six weeks in a school maintained by the company. About 250 girls finish the course each year. It costs well over $1,000 to recruit and train a stewardess.

At the present time there are more qualified applicants than there are vacancies.

Apply the seven-step problem-solving technique to this case.

FOLLOWING UP ON THE JOB

The five M's: men, materials, money, machines, methods

1. Are your men assigned to jobs that use their best skills as much as possible?

2. Is the spoilage and waste of materials kept at a minimum in your unit?
3. How careful are you about spending the company's money?
4. Are the machines in your department kept busy doing the jobs they were designed to do?
5. Are efficient methods being used?

Planning, organizing, directing, coordinating, and controlling

1. Do you plan the work of your unit in terms of: What? Why? When? Where? Who? How?
2. Do you organize your work so that you are not overburdened by routine work? Do you delegate authority and responsibility?
3. When new work comes into your department, do you analyze it in terms of the skills required?
4. Do you give orders in a manner that ensures that they will be understood?
5. Do you coordinate the jobs in your department with one another? Do you coordinate the work of your unit with other units? With your boss's requirements?
6. Do you check up on the progress of the jobs in your department frequently enough?

Responsibilities of the supervisor

Do you and your boss agree on the definition of your responsibilities? The outline under the head "Responsibilities of the first level supervisor" early in this chapter offers a means of finding out.

2 Organizations and organization structure

Development of the structure—The traditional viewpoint. The bases upon which organizations are built. Line and staff in organization. The tall organization. The flat organization. Decentralizing authority and responsibility. Rule of the exception. Some recent developments in organization theory. Summary.

Organizations are one of the complexities of modern life but few of us realize the impact they have on our daily lives. Perhaps in a desire to simplify our daily activity we refuse to recognize the role organization has in our existence. If we pause to reflect for a moment we can think of some of the many organizations, large and small, informal and formal, that affect us. The family, church, schools, hospitals, fire and police, other governmental agencies, businesses, social clubs, charities, work groups, and informal leisure groups such as card players and gardeners are among the many and varied organizations we are affected by and of which we are members. One could say that civilization and organization have been handmaidens throughout history. Philosophers, statesmen, militarists, clergymen, and educators among others have devoted considerable time and energy to the analysis of organization and organized effort. The patriarchal family group, the tribe, the army, the church, the government, and in our society, the business organization have all been carefully studied and evaluated to try and discover effective ways of organizing effort.

Chris Argyris in a recent book presents a clear rationale for the creation of organizations.

Organizations are usually created to achieve objectives that can best be met collectively. This means that the sequences of activity necessary to achieve objectives are too much for one individual and they must be cut up into "sequential units" that are manageable by human beings. At the individual level the units are roles; at the group level the units are departments. These units are integrated or organized in a particular sequence or pattern designed to achieve the objectives, and the resulting pattern constitutes the organization structure.[1]

The discussion in this chapter is concerned with organization structure[2]—that framework of activity groupings and authority relationships within which people work together to achieve objectives. For a supervisor to understand where he fits into an organization and how he should operate within it, he needs to understand the design of the structure and how it will influence his relationships and regulate his behavior.

Development of the structure—The traditional viewpoint

The most prevalent approach to the study of organization structure is the one that looks upon the individual enterprise as a unit with a hierarchial arrangement. Few companies start out with the idea of building a particular type of structure. In most cases a new business is just put together by the founder who divides the work up among a few subordinates on the basis of their talents and abilities—or maybe on the basis of which one has the least to do at the moment and can take on a few more responsibilities. New functions are struck into this or that department or split between departments in a hit-or-miss fashion. There is little consideration given to whether the activities belong together or whether having them together promotes a logical work flow and harmonious working relationships.

Eventually lack of sound organizational relationships shows up in delays and disagreements in decision making, overlaps and gaps in responsibility, duplication and waste motion, jealousies, frictions, and buck-passing between managers. No one is sure who is responsible to do what or who has the authority to do it.

Traditional principles. The chaos that usually envolves as a new organization grows generally leads to a more orderly approach if the enterprise is to survive. In order to operate smoothly and efficiently a company needs a structure built according to sound organizational principles. The subject is a complex one, but the following guides are offered here because they apply to organizing on any level. The supervisor can use them in studying the structure of the company or in organizing his own department.

---

[1] Chris Argyris, *Integrating the Individual and the Organization* (New York: John Wiley & Sons, Inc., 1964), p. 35.

[2] Chapter 3, "Policies and Procedures," considers the organization from the standpoint of why the company is in business, what it wants to achieve, and how it wants to conduct itself. Chapter 4, "Organization Dynamics," analyzes authority and responsibility and the process of delegation through which the manager shares his work with subordinates. Chapter 6, "Teamwork in Management," takes up the human problems of working together to achieve the purpose for which the organization was formed.

1. The organization structure must be designed to provide for the activities necessary to accomplish the objectives of the business. What work has to be performed? What kinds of work belong together? What amount of emphasis should be given to each activity?
2. The structure should be as simple as possible and have the fewest possible levels of management necessary to accomplish its purpose.
3. Decisions should be made as close to the scene of action as practicable. That is, they should be made at the lowest level at which can be taken into account all the areas that will be affected by the decision.
4. No one in the organization should report to more than one line supervisor. (The principle of unity of command.)
5. The organization should be set up primarily in terms of the jobs to be done rather than around the personal characteristics of individuals.
6. Employees reporting to a manager should not be more in number than he can effectively direct and whose work he can coordinate. This is the span of control principle (also called span of supervision or span of management). The number of subordinates a manager can handle effectively depends on his knowledge, ability, energy, and personality. It depends also on his level in management, the design of his job, the type of business, the complexity and variety of the work his subordinates perform, the ability and geographical dispersion of his subordinates, the interrelationship and interdependence of the work of his subordinates.
7. Responsibility should be coupled with corresponding authority and should be published and understood.
    Authority is the power and the right necessary to make possible the performance of the assigned work.
    Responsibility is the work assigned to a position and the obligation to do it in a suitable manner or see that it is done. Responsibility = performance of work + accountability.
    Accountability is the obligation of a subordinate to report to his superior on the way the authority is being used and the work being done, to report in terms of standards and goals.

The bases upon which organizations are built

The organization structure is simply a means of achieving the purpose of the enterprise. It is successful if it is operating at the lowest overhead cost and utilizing its human and material resources at their highest capacities. There is no one perfect organizational plan. Each structure must be tailored and adjusted to meet the specific requirements of the business. The usual bases for dividing the work of a company are according to function, product, operation, customer, and region, or a combination of these.

Function as a basis of organizing. Most businesses in their beginnings are organized on the basis of their main functions. These primary functions or responsibilities in a manufacturing business would be manufacturing, sales, and finance. Organization on this basis puts people together according to their specialties—all the sales people together, all the accountants, all the engineers, etc. This type of organization is economical and flexible to start with but it tends to grow tall. A further disadvantage is the clannishness that develops and interferes with teamwork between departments. Each department thinks its work is more important than that of other departments and tends to promote its own specialty at the expense of the total enterprise. Since this cleavage runs from top to bottom of the organization, an elaborate system is required to coordinate and control the specialties.

Product as a basis of organizing—Mass production. Where several standard products are made in large quantities, an organization according to product sets up separate divisions so that each type of product is produced in its own division or department and not mixed with the other types of products. A company making office machines would have a separate line of equipment for manufacturing adding machines, another line for manufacturing typewriters, and a third line for manufacturing cash registers. (See Figure 2–1.) A company might have separate plants to manufacture its separate products.

FIGURE 2–1

**A Line Organization with Manufacturing
Departments Divided on a Product Basis**

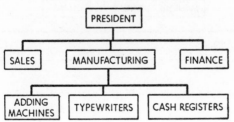

Mass production fits into organization according to product. The economies of mass production are achieved by turning out a great quantity of good quality product on special purpose machines. In a typical mass-production industry, the tasks which make up a worker's job may be so few and so simple that they fit into a time cycle of less than a half minute. Such employees are easily replaced because training time is short. Many of the jobs are machine paced. When a worker is performing a small segment of work over which he has little control he may feel no responsibility for the outcome. He may find the job monotonous and frustrating.

In some companies job enlargement has resulted in a better grouping of tasks so that the individual worker performs more operations and has responsibility for the quality and quantity of an identifiable stage of the work. Job design is discussed in Chapter 10.

From the supervisor's standpoint, each unit or department tends to be immediately dependent on other units for its work. Any changes in one department would affect other departments. Interlocking operations call for close supervision because if one machine stops, others may have to stop also. Planning is done on a high level. Control is centralized at a high level. A number of responsibilities have been removed from the line managers' jobs and are handled by staff departments. The supervisor must maintain a schedule set by the production control department. Conditions are highly standardized, and he has little opportunity to develop his own way of doing things.[3]

Operations, processes, or equipment as a basis of organizing—The jobbing shop. At the opposite extreme from mass production is the business that is organized according to the operations or processes that are performed on the products—or according to the equipment needed

FIGURE 2–2
A Line Organization with Manufacturing Departments Divided on an Operational Basis

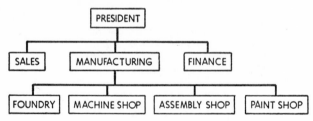

to perform these operations. Such an organization is charted in Figure 2–2. The departments shown in this chart might be further divided according to operations. The machine shop might have within it a milling machine section, a drill press section, a grinding section, etc. An order for 50 pumps to be made according to the customer's specifications

---

[3] For a study of the foreman's job on an automobile assembly line, see Charles R. Walker, Robert H. Guest, and Arthur N. Turner, *The Foreman on the Assembly Line* (Cambridge, Mass.: Harvard University Press, 1956). For worker reaction to assembly line jobs, see Charles R. Walker and Robert H. Guest, *The Man on the Assembly Line* (Cambridge, Mass.: Harvard University Press, 1952), or *Harvard Business Review*, May–June, 1952. The studies were made by the Institute of Human Relations of Yale University.

would be routed from one section to another according to the type of operations that need to be performed in the fabrication of the parts.

A jobbing shop is a type of organization set up according to operations. It may be a distinct business by itself or it may be a department within a manufacturing business. Its distinguishing characteristic is variety of work: it is set up to manufacture orders to customers' specifications. (The customers may be other divisions of the same company.)

Each order as it comes in for the first time must be analyzed to determine the types of operations required, the proper machines on which to perform them, the proper order or sequence in which to schedule them, and the operators who should perform them. Job shop machines are a general purpose type which can be adapted to a variety of operations by the attachment of auxiliary tooling and equipment and by the application of operator skills. Work is put through the shop in batches (intermittent manufacture) rather than in a continuous flow through fixed production lines (as in mass production). The flexibility of the machines and the adaptability of worker skills enables the job shop to accept one-of-a-kind orders and experimental work. The control of manufacturing operations is decentralized, and the line supervisor has greater managerial responsibilities than in mass production.

As compared to mass production, job shop workers have higher skills, a wider variety of skills, and more flexibility. Their work has in it more variety, more decision making, more responsibility for using proper methods, taking care of equipment, saving material, and turning out work of the required quality and quantity without close and continuous supervision. The jobs in a jobbing shop are more apt to belong to a family of jobs, graded according to skill, and the machine operator can see a pathway to advancement through acquiring higher skills.

Customers as a basis of organizing. A company may be divided according to the types of customers it serves; a supplier of furniture might be organized into divisions to serve wholesale, retail, and institutional customers. An advantage of this type of division is that it can adapt its products, prices, terms, and selling approach to fit the three kinds of customers.

Region as a basis of organizing. Region (territory or geographical location) is the basis for dividing many companies—oil companies, railroads, chain stores, insurance companies, manufacturing organizations, and sales organizations. A company that does business nationally might divide the country into a number of zones and operate from a headquarters in each zone. Or a company might have headquarters in one part of the country and branches or plants throughout the country. Plants and offices set up to serve various parts of the country may be run from headquarters with an elaborate system for directing and controlling activities. Or regional divisions may be almost as independent as if they were in business for themselves and simply contributing their profit to the company.

From the standpoint of the supervisor, decentralization of authority and responsibility puts fewer layers of management above him, gives him more opportunity to use his initiative, make decisions, and prepare himself for advancement into jobs that exist throughout the company.

Organization according to several bases. It is seldom that a company is organized completely on any one base. At the top it may be divided according to the product; then the product divisions split into manufacturing, sales, and finance. Then the sales department may be divided according to customer or region. The manufacturing division of a company mass-producing several standard products can be departmentalized according to product or according to operations, or a combination of the two.

New engineering companies are apt to be organized according to project. As they take on additional projects of a similar nature, several divisions may be manufacturing the same components and performing other duplications of activities. Then new departments are set up on a functional basis to take care of the overlap. Such hybrids are common in aircraft and in some electronics companies.

Organizing the service company. The years since World War II have seen a tremendous growth of various service companies such as banks, insurance companies, finance companies, real estate firms, retail stores, and advertising agencies. Most of these types of businesses follow the same evolutionary pattern of organization structure that the manufacturing company does. Usually starting with the basic functions characteristic of the particular business, the structure evolves into regional, project, and divisional structures similar to the complex manufacturing enterprise. For instance, a large commercial bank will have a metropolitan division to administer branches in the city in which it is located, an international division to manage its overseas operations and branches, a national division to supervise its correspondent banking relationships with banks all over the country, a personnel department, a treasurer's department, a controller's department, an auditing department, a security department, a data processing department, and an internal operations department. Marketing and advertising departments along with business development, personal and corporate trust, personal loans, credit cards, and others indicate that banks organize around product lines as well as functions.

Similar structures have evolved for retailing, finance companies, and other service companies in our economy. A word might be said for the multitude of nonbusiness organizations in our society. Schools, colleges, universities, hospitals, government agencies, religious and charitable organizations all evolve into complex structures as they grow. They do, however, follow the same pathways that other organizations do. Starting with functional areas, they break up into specialized divisions as the need for additional management becomes evident. All of the structure problems experienced by complex business firms are shared by the public, quasi-public, and nonprofit organization as well.

Line and staff in organization

The line organization has direct responsibility for accomplishing the objectives of the enterprise. This responsibility and the authority to perform the work are delegated by the head of the organization down the line of managers—each boss to his subordinate managers.

Most companies start out with an organization that is predominantly line; that is, a boss runs his department with a minimum of outside interference or help—doing his own hiring, firing, purchasing, maintenance, and inspection. When the number of his employees becomes too large for him to manage, he appoints some subordinate managers. Vertical expansion of this type reaches a point of diminishing returns because each management man is handling a great variety of tasks calling for a variety of talents and duplicating the tasks that the next man is handling. As these tasks increase in volume and complexity, it becomes advisable to start taking some of them away from the line managers and giving them to specialists.

Staff Service. Activities that are removed from the line managers' jobs can be handled centrally as staff functions. Maintenance can be done on a plantwide basis by skilled repairmen; purchasing can be centralized and the buyers can give full time to contacting suppliers. A production control department can be set up to coordinate and facilitate production; a credit department can check on the credit of the customers of the sales department; a time study department can set up standards; a personnel department can recruit employees and take care of some of the personnel and labor relations matters; and an engineering department can design products and processes. See Figure 2–3 for an organization chart showing line and staff departments. See Figure 2–4 for industrial engineering services that are available to the line organization.

It is well to remember that what is line in one company may be staff in another. If a company's business is manufacturing and selling, then purchasing would be a staff activity. If the business is buying and selling, then purchasing would be a line activity. Research and development is a staff activity in a manufacturing company, but a line activity in a design and development firm. Generally speaking, office functions are staff activities in a manufacturing company and line in an insurance company. Theoretically the distinctions between line and

FIGURE 2–3
A Line and Staff Organization

The staff departments (dotted lines) are Controller, Chief Engineer with Drafting and Design, Personnel, Purchasing and Inventory Control, Industrial Engineering with Methods and Standards, Production Planning and Control, Quality Control with Inspectors.

The Personnel Department might be placed higher in the structure; it might be called Employee Relations, Industrial Relations, or Labor Relations. Among the variations in the organization of Personnel Departments are: (1) Labor Relations and Personnel Administration may be combined under one head as shown here. (2) Labor Relations and Personnel Administration may be separate departments. (3) Public Relations may be included in the Personnel Department or be a department by itself.

The activities handled by the Personnel Department might be set up as sections within or, in a small company, combined as duties.

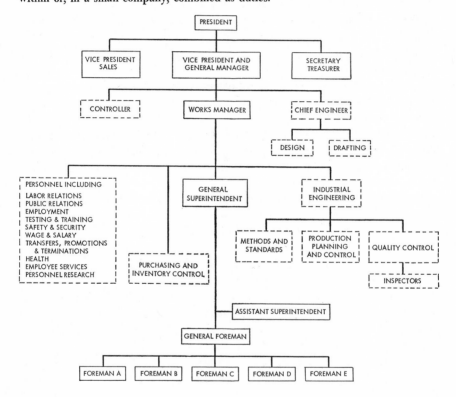

staff are easy to understand. In practice, however, the distinctions are not so clear and are likely to cause confusion between line and staff executives. In a recent book, Ernest Dale attempts to simplify the distinction between line and staff.

Line people are those who carry out the functions that contribute directly to the achievement of the organization's goal; staff people are those who contribute indirectly by helping the line to do its job—by performing services

FIGURE 2–4

A Management Directive Outlining the Services That the Industrial Engineering Department Renders to the Line Organization

MANUFACTURING BRANCH _____ **Directive**_____ NUMBER 1-101
PAGE 1 of 1

LOCKHEED AIRCRAFT CORPORATION   REPLACES   DATE THIS
MISSILE SYSTEMS DIVISION   ISSUE OF 6-10- *   EFFECTIVE 9-22-

APPROVED _____ DIRECTOR   SUBJECT   INDUSTRIAL ENGINEERING REQUESTS

REFERENCE: Management Directive 101.

Industrial Engineering, reporting to the Manager of Manufacturing Control, is a staff organization for the Director of Manufacturing. As such, it is engaged primarily in coordination and evaluation work for the Director of Manufacturing. Its services include issuance of Directives, Procedures and Form/Report Instructions defining Manufacturing policy and operating systems.

Industrial Engineering services are available to line organizations as required to aid in resolving problems which are complex, involve several organizations and/or concern basic operating systems.

Requests for new/revised Directives, Procedures, Form/Report Instructions or systems analysis shall be directed to Industrial Engineering by IDC. Requests shall be acknowledged, outlining actions to be taken and establishing Estimated Completion Dates.

*Completely rewritten

Industrial Engineering, John Truesdale

Reproduced by permission of Lockheed

for it and/or providing advice and counsel on the basis of their specialized knowledge.[4]

Staff advice. As business problems increase, line managers need information and advice as well as service. In an advisory capacity, staff specialists make investigations, and draw up plans and procedures for the approval of line management. For example, market research is expected to investigate and report on the demand for products. These reports should be accurate and complete because management decisions are based on them. To show the quality of investigations and reports expected of a staff specialist, the following quotation is taken from the Marine Corps *Management Improvement Handbook.*

Completed Staff Work is the study of a problem and presentation of a solution by a staff officer, in such form that all that remains to be done

---

[4] Ernest Dale, *Management: Theory and Practice* (New York: McGraw-Hill Book Co., 1965), p. 281.

on the part of the head of the staff section, or the commander, is to indicate his approval or disapproval of the composed, completed action. The words "Completed Action" are emphasized because the more difficult the problem is, the more the tendency is to present the problem to the commander in piecemeal fashion. It is the duty of a staff officer to work out the details, no matter how perplexing they may be. He may, and should, consult other staff officers. The product, whether it involves the pronouncement of a new policy or affects an established one, should, when presented for approval or disapproval, be worked out in finished form.[5]

Staff plans might be for such things as job evaluation, wage incentives, methods improvements, merit rating, or employee training. Line management is free to accept or reject these plans because, theoretically at least, advisory staff has no authority.[6] Staff is expected to sell its ideas and services by fitting them to the needs of the line. If the line accepts the plans, then the staff agency may be authorized to install them, watch over their operation, and report to higher line management on the way they are being carried out. In this manner, staff moves out of the area of advice and into the area of service (when it installs) and control (when it checks up and reports).

Staff control. The control function of staff is one of checking up—of measuring the performance of line people with regard to the way they are carrying out certain parts of their jobs. The accountant exercises a control over the line by keeping track of labor and material expense, comparing it to the amount budgeted, and reporting the figure to a higher level of line management. The personnel manager exercises a control when he checks on the line supervisors to see if they are abiding by personnel policies that have been accepted by top management for uniform application. Factory inspection exercises a control when it examines products made by the line departments and rejects some as unsatisfactory. The credit department exercises a control in checking customer credit and refusing to approve a sale if the credit is not up to the standard.

The assistant to. The staff activities discussed up to this point are called *specialized* staff or *technical* staff. Such services are available for plantwide application. A staff job of another type is that of assistant *to* (the *to* is the important word). A line executive may turn over part of his work to an assistant to without giving up immediate and personal control over it. The assistant to may handle either highly specialized

---

[5] *Management Improvement Handbook,* Vol. III, NAVMC 1088–2 ADM (April, 1955), p. 19.

[6] In thinking of staff as having no authority, it is well to remember that the head of a staff department has line authority in his own department over his own subordinates. For example, quality control is a staff department and the head of it has direct line authority over his subordinate, the chief inspector, who in turn has direct line authority over the subordinate inspectors.

work or general paper work and details. He does not ordinarily act in his own name but only in the name of his boss. He does not take over in the boss's absence except under unusual conditions. He has no one reporting to him; therefore he has no direct authority. He operates in a more restricted area than does a line assistant (an executive vice president, assistant chief engineer, assistant quality control manager, assistant superintendent). The line assistant has line authority delegated to him—that is, he acts in his own name. It is rather established practice for him to take over in the boss's absence.

The tall organization

The supervisor's job is shaped by the organization structure—the bases upon which the organization is set up and the type and amount of staff development. Another factor—a related and important one—is the tallness or flatness of the organization.

The "tall" organization is one that has added so many levels of supervision between top and bottom that the people at the top have lost contact with the ones at the bottom and have to depend upon elaborate procedures, reports, and other devices for keeping informed. Tallness is not limited to huge companies; some medium-sized ones have as many as 10 layers of management through which information must find its way to the top for a decision to be made.

If a salesman phones in a change on a customer's order that is already in production, and the change requires overtime to meet delivery dates, how far up the line must the foreman go for approval? How many levels must be consulted before reaching the one that can authorize the extra expense of overtime? Or suppose the customer phoned his order change to the president of the company, how long would it take for the information to trickle down to the bottom and how accurate would it be when it finally got there?

The piling of layer upon layer of management is apt to take place in the types of business in which each unit and department is immediately dependent on others for its work. Mass production is an example of the interlocking and interdependent operations which must be closely coordinated in order to keep the whole company working as a unit. Layering of management is less common in a retail store because there is little interaction between departments: the men's clothing department is not affected by inefficiencies in the housewares.

In a tall organization, decision making is done at the upper levels, and upper management has a tight system of controls to see that orders are carried out in the proper manner. These controls call for additional staff people to operate them, which in turn piles a greater burden on the system for communicating, controlling, and coordinating.

When an organization grows too tall, people are apt to lose sight of its objectives. Just keeping the system running becomes an objective in itself. When the opportunity to get ahead depends upon conforming to the system, then people up and down the line conform to the utmost; they do just what they are told, they won't take any chances, they protect themselves at all times, they take every problem to the boss (and he takes it up with his boss). The organization man feels that he must be sure that each man under him can be depended upon to behave just as he is supposed to behave.

Whenever the number of employees in an organization is increasing at a faster rate than business, then top management should suspect that some of these people are there just to keep the system going and that the system is becoming more important than the business.

The flat organization

The flat organization with its three or four levels of management escapes the disadvantage of impersonal leadership; but personal leadership can be good or bad, depending on the leader. In the flat organization the lines of communication are short. Decisions can be made quickly, mistakes can be discovered quickly, and the consequences of mistakes are not usually as serious as they are in a tall organization. Where the levels of management are few, the coordination problem is not so great, and controls can often be exercised by spot checks by department heads as they pass through their departments. There is less turning of wheels within wheels.

Just having fewer levels of management does not guarantee that authority and responsibility will be decentralized, however, because some companies have flat organizations and still have a highly centralized management.

A flat organization in a big company is an indication that managers have a fairly wide span of control (span of supervision) and therefore don't have the time to supervise their subordinates closely. Sears Roebuck Retail is an example of flat organization: president, vice president, store manager, section manager. A vice president may have a hundred stores under him, each one an autonomous unit. A store manager may have 30 section managers under him, each responsible for the marketing and profit in his own section.

Decentralizing authority and responsibility

As an enterprise grows in size and complexity, it becomes apparent that the manager cannot do everything by himself. Human factors have to be taken into consideration. Many companies have grown and geographically decentralized their operations so that they could be nearer their markets or nearer raw materials or both. In addition the growth pattern of an individual company may result in its expansion into other industries. Oil and rubber companies have moved into chemicals, companies in basic industries have moved into consumer products, and consumer products companies have moved into wholesaling and retailing. Such diversification has caused organizational structure problems. Questions arose as to the efficiency of the old structure since control with a high degree of centralization became very difficult. There were also the attendant problems of doing business in a new or different sphere. A decentralized organization structure with decision-making authority on the lowest possible managerial level was the result. Of course, managerial decentralization cannot be achieved overnight. It requires the retraining of people all the way up and down the line; it requires a change of attitude toward the job—a willingness to risk having subordinates make more managerial decisions. Bittel contrasts centralized and decentralized control indicating both problems and rewards.

One of the key decisions to be made when establishing policy is the extent to which control will be centralized or decentralized. Centralized control tends to provide greater assurance that top management goals will be achieved. Decentralized controls—especially when they apply broadly to profit responsibility—present four difficult problems. First, they are costly to administer. Second, they require a tighter, more complex information system. Third, they depend upon a more highly qualified middle-management staff. Finally, there is always the danger that the lower echelon managers will not be motivated, or act, in the best interests of the company.

Weighed against these disadvantages are the greater resilience, balance, and diversity that a decentralized system can develop and maintain.[7]

Decentralization of management involves:

1. Giving subordinates more authority to make decisions and holding them responsible for these decisions.
2. Providing guidance in the form of realistic policies.
3. Using procedures to save time and labor but not to stifle initiative and judgment.
4. Telling subordinates more of the *what* and *why* and less of the *how to*.
5. Retraining the people in management so that they can handle authority and make better decisions and do it on a greater variety of problems.
6. Instilling in the personnel a feeling that they don't always have to be 100 percent correct.

---

[7] Lester R. Bittel, *Management by Exception* (New York: McGraw-Hill Book Co., 1964), p. 106.

7. Having people feel that they will have time to gather and prepare information—that having a lot of precise data on tap at all times is not a measure of their managerial ability.
8. Simplifying the system and placing more dependence on people.
9. Enlarging jobs.
10. Making more use of staff activities.
11. Making more use of the *Rule of the Exception* at each level in order to prevent authority and responsibility from climbing upward.

Rule of the exception

The rule of the exception provides that a manager does not have to pass personally on every matter that comes within his jurisdiction, but should have only the exceptions called to his attention. Under this system a manager should delegate to his subordinates as much of routine operations as possible, leaving for himself the difficult problems and exceptions to routine. In order to delegate successfully, the manager must have policies, procedures, and standing plans to guide his subordinates; he must have trained and equipped them to handle matters; and he must have established a system of controls in order to get reports telling him how well the subordinates are carrying out the job.

In line with the rule of the exception (or exception principle, as it is also called), when a problem is outside a person's jurisdiction, he passes it up the line to the point at which there is sufficient authority to solve it. If the solution is not within the authority of the superior, he passes it up to the next level and so on until it reaches a level at which the requisite authority exists. There it is settled as a routine problem. This concept is an extension of F. W. Taylor's principle that a manager should receive only condensed and comparative reports pointing out all the exceptions—both good and bad—to the past averages and standards.[8]

Some recent developments in organization theory

The purpose of organization is to coordinate the many diverse elements of the enterprise and to optimize the goal achievement of the total structure. The traditional viewpoint with its many principles of organization has attempted to achieve this. To a certain extent, the success of American business is a tribute to the success of its managers in their application of traditional organization theory. Nevertheless the search for more effective ways of organizing goes on. As our organizations grow both in size and complexity there is an increasing recognition that traditional approaches are found wanting. As a result management theorists have been paying greater attention to both human and environ-

---

[8] F. W. Taylor, *Shop Management* (New York: Harper & Bros., 1911).

mental factors in their search for more effective ways of organizing. Traditional theory emphasizes formal structure, principles applicable to all organizations, policies, rules, and procedures, thus leading to the view that an individual organization is a closed system operating with little or no relationship to its environment. Additionally, people are viewed as being governed by the structure, principles, and rules with little or no attention given to their individual aspirations, needs, goals, and behavior patterns.

Any recognition of reality will demonstrate that traditional organization theory does not give us a broad enough framework for understanding the modern complex organization. William G. Scott develops the following viewpoint in his recent book.

The distinctive qualities of modern organization theory are its conceptual-analytical base, its reliance on empirical research data, and, above all, its synthesizing, integrating nature. These qualities are framed in a philosophy which accepts the premise that the only meaningful way to study organization is as a system.

System analysis has its own peculiar point of view. Modern organization theory accepts system analysis as a starting point. It asks a range of interrelated questions which are not seriously considered by the classical and neo-classical theories of organization. Key among these questions are:

1. What are the strategic parts of the system?
2. What is the nature of their mutual interdependency?
3. What are the main processes in the system which link the parts and facilitate their adjustment to each other?
4. What are the goals sought by the system?

Modern organization theory is in no way a homogeneous body of thought. Each writer and researcher has his special emphasis when he considers the system. Perhaps the most evident unifying strand in modern organization theory is the effort made to look at human systems in their totality.[9]

The systems viewpoint. A study of the recent literature[10] of management theory indicates a ferment as part of the evolutionary process

[9] William G. Scott, *Organization Theory: A Behavioral Analysis for Management* (Homewood, Ill.: Richard D. Irwin, Inc., 1967), pp. 122–23.

[10] For example, see Scott, *ibid.*, chap. 6; John A. Seiler, *Systems Analysis in Organizational Behavior* (Homewood, Ill., Richard D. Irwin, Inc., 1967); R. A. Johnson, F. E. Kast, and J. E. Rosenzweig, *The Theory and Management of Systems* (2d ed.; New York: McGraw-Hill Book Co., 1967); Rocco Carzo, Jr., and John N. Yanouzas, *Formal Organization, A Systems Approach* (Homewood, Ill., Richard D. Irwin, Inc., 1967); Adrian M. McDonough and Leonard J. Garrett, *Management Systems, Working Concepts and Practices* (Homewood, Ill., Richard D. Irwin, Inc., 1965); Joseph A. Litterer, *The Analysis of Organizations* (New York: John Wiley & Sons, Inc., 1965); Stanley Young, *Management: A Systems Analysis* (Glenview, Ill.: Scott, Foresman & Co., 1966); Stanford L. Optner, *Systems Analysis for Business and Industrial Problem Solving* (Englewood Cliffs, N.J.: Prentice-Hall, Inc., 1965); David L. Cleland and William R. King, *Systems Analysis and Project Management* (New York: McGraw-Hill Book Co., 1968).

to develop more effective ideas about organization. Essentially the manager is concerned with the allocation of the resources available to him and the rationale for organization is to optimize this allocation. By approaching the organization from a systems point of view the manager becomes aware that it is made up of many interdependent but individual managers working on problems and processes requiring a variety of techniques, knowledge, and capabilities. The systems approach makes an attempt to analyze and integrate the human beings, processes, technology, information needs, communication networks, and the goals of the total organization.

The basic differences in the systems approach when contrasted to the traditional approach to organization seems to be the recognition that process is more important than structure. The traditional approach with its fixed hierarchical authority and responsibility relationships is changing into the recognition of the organization as a group of interrelationships of people, materials, money, and information with behavior, time, and change as critical factors. The rapidly growing and widely accepted activity of organization planning and development, taking the total system into account, seems to be the wave of the immediate future.

Organization restrictions. In every organization, every person is delegated some degree of authority and responsibility; at the very least he is accountable for his job or assignment. In management, each man is accountable to someone for something and also for somebody (for the actions of his subordinates). He must function within the organizational constraints of his firm as well as the external and internal environmental limitations. The amount of freedom he has in doing his job depends on his boss, on the stage of growth and profitability of the company, the health of the economy in general and for the individual industry in particular, and upon the complexity and level of sophistication of the entire firm. It will also depend on the philosophy of top management as evidenced by policies, objectives, and strategic planning.

If the supervisor is aware of the ways in which the organization restricts him, he can determine what can be changed around him, and he can strive to bring about these changes. Also he can determine what changes he must make within himself—what adjustments he has to make to fit the organization. The person who knows himself and the situation is generally better adjusted to it than the person who is ignorant of or does not understand the pressures upon him and what he must do to accommodate to them.

No man fits his job perfectly; each man has his own strong and weak points, his own interests, goals, drives, and attitudes which determine somewhat the parts of his job he will do well and the parts he will not do so well. Also, his personality causes him to work better with some people than with others; its influences him in the amount of authority and responsibility he will delegate to his subordinates and the amount he wants his own boss to delegate to him.

Because a man does not fit his own job perfectly, his strong and weak points affect the jobs around him. Collectively, each activity in the firm has a similar relationship. These interdependencies and their degree of effectiveness determine the level of success of the firm. The departmental and hierarchial compartments of traditional organization structure do not fully allow for the recognition of the mutual dependency of all parts of the company. If the enterprise is to take full advantage of the emerging managerial techniques encompassing quantitative methods, the computer, information systems, and the behavioral sciences, then it seems that it must move away from the traditional approach to organization structure. As innovation continues and control and measurement of operations improves, traditional departments and lines of authority will tend to blur. By approaching the organization as a total system operating in an external environment, management will be able to more effectively allocate resources and optimize results.

Summary

Whenever the services of more than one person are necessary to carry out a project, an organization must be formed to divide up the work and delegate to others the authority to perform it. The organization structure is the framework within which people work together to carry out company objectives. There is no one best structure. The best organization is the one that operates at lowest overhead cost and makes the best use of people and material resources. The work of a company may be divided up and assigned according to function, product, operation, customer, or region, or some combination of these bases.

Increase in size and technical complexity cause a business to make a further division in its work—this time along the basis of line and staff. Line departments are those carrying out the main responsibilities for which the company was organized (buying and selling, for example). Staff performs specialized functions which provide advice, service, or control.

The shape and size and authority relationships of an organization determine the amount of freedom the supervisor will have in doing his job. A tall organization with tight controls and big staff departments to operate them will restrict his decision making. Managerial decentralization, on the other hand, gives him more freedom but makes greater demands upon him for a high level of performance.

If a supervisor understands the organization he is a part of, he is better able to make the adjustments necessary to get along in it. He is also better able to organize the work of his own department.

Recent developments in organization theory indicate that there are changes in thinking regarding the traditional structure with its lines of authority and departmentalization. To take advantage of rapidly developing managerial techniques utilizing quantitative methods, the computer, information systems, and the behavioral sciences, many firms are approaching their organization as a total system. This concept allows for the more effective utilization of the available resources and helps the firm to optimize results.

CASE 1

The general manager has hired the services of a personnel administrator but has purposely not defined the new man's role in the organization.

You, a line supervisor, have become involved in several arguments with this personnel administrator when he attempted to relieve you and other supervisors of the authority for transferring and promoting employees, changing pay rates, and other matters on which he should only be advising line management. You feel that he does not have the proper perspective for his job and that he is trying to take over more and more power in order to create a good job for himself.

You have mentioned this usurping of authority to your boss, the general manager, and have asked him to define the man's job. The boss answered that he is allowing the personnel administrator to find his own niche in the organization. You feel that the morale of the men in your department will suffer unless the personnel administrator's position is made clear.

1. Discuss the above situation from a line point of view.
2. Discuss the situation from a personnel administrator's point of view.
3. Develop a practical working relationship based on the principles of good organization.

CASE 2

Bill Corwin was employed by a large bank for several years. He started as a messenger, then was assigned to a branch. He progressed in this branch from a bookkeeping clerk to a platform assistant. In this position he had a variety of duties largely centering on administrative assistance to the officers of the branch.

The bank's many branches were divided regionally with each region having a group of officers responsible for the branches in that region. Bill was transferred from the branch in which he worked for 12 years to a branch in another region. At the time of his transfer he was told that the branch was completely "run down" as to operational procedures and systems. The branch had a normal complement of 4 officers and 35 staff members. One month prior to Bill's transfer one of the four officers retired and two weeks after this retirement, the branch manager was hospitalized with a serious illness.

When Bill arrived at his new assignment, he found a rather demoralized situation. Complete lack of interest was shown by the two remaining officers and the rest of the staff was not properly trained or disciplined. The two officers did not know Bill and they were informed by the regional office that he was being assigned to the branch as a platform replacement for only two weeks.

During his first week at the branch, Bill discovered that the senior clerks were not qualified to train other staff members, customer complaints were rampant, there was both a record of excessive absenteeism and excessive overtime, and the branch had received very poor audit reports by the bank's internal auditors with the same major exceptions reported on the previous four audits.

After two weeks, Bill was called to the regional office and offered the job of operations officer. He was told that he would receive the official title in two months. He was also told that the present operations officer, who had held the job at this branch for seven years, was to be relieved of all operational responsibilities and that he would be instructed to work with Bill until the branch was functioning effectively.

Bill returned to the branch and started on his assignment. He found the former operations officer cooperative for about one week. Bill then decided to go ahead without the help of the former operations officer. Over the next three months he worked almost every night until 8 or 9 P.M. He tried to correct the problems that had developed over several years. The training of employees involved considerable time and he found it necessary to release 12 clerks who were causing trouble in various ways. The remaining staff and replacements started to function smoothly. He received his title as promised and then the officer in charge returned to work after his prolonged illness. A week after his return he called Bill to his office and questioned his efforts in the branch. He told Bill that the former operations officer had mentioned that he was an upsetting influence in the branch, had fired several good people, did not know his job, and that he left his job early several days a week.

1. If you were Bill, how would you answer the officer in charge?
2. Did the regional office handle Bill's transfer properly?
3. What should be done by the regional office now?
4. Do you believe that Bill can function effectively in this branch?

CASE 3

Quite a few of the small companies engaged in manufacturing and experimental work have been started by small groups of hardworking, ingenious individuals with good ideas and technical know-how. As these companies expand, it becomes necessary to bring in people with managerial ability to handle the administrative work. The original founders of the company are doing the technical work and are not trained to handle the higher administrative jobs; as a result, they find that the company they own is getting out from under their control.

Or, if they don't want to risk turning over the management of the company to outsiders, they don't hire any management people but just struggle along by themselves, using poor management techniques.

1. What are some of the results of an organization's not having sufficient managerial ability?
2. What are the "dangerous ages" in the growth of a company?
3. What are some of the ways the founders of a company can direct and maintain active control over it as it grows?

CASE 4

You are a supervisor in the shop of a manufacturing company. One of your operators complains that his machine does not have an adequate safety guard. You and he make a sketch of an improved guard and submit it—as is the custom—to the safety committee. It comes back with their approval.

You make out a work order for $75 and send it with the sketch to the maintenance department for them to make and install the guard. A week goes by and you ask the maintenance supervisor how the order is progressing. He tells you that the order was canceled by your boss. You talk to your boss and he informs you that the order was canceled because the maintenance foreman told him that the amount of safety added did not justify the cost of the work order.

1. List the things wrong in this situation.
2. How much authority should a safety committee of first-level supervisors and workers have in order to be effective?
3. Work out a plan for controlling expenditures for safety improvements.

CASE 5

You have recently been assigned as supervisor over a group of workers. The lead man of the group, whose duties are to order the materials and lay out the work for each man, is conscientious and has had many years of experience. One morning he comes into your office all upset and tells you that one of the workers in the group is changing his layout and doing the work to suit himself. The lead man wants you to order the worker to do the job as originally laid out, as the lead man does not have the authority to force him to do so.

As you are leaving the office, you meet the worker, and he tells you that he had to change the method of doing the job because the material was cut incorrectly in the previous operation, that the lead man knew about this but ordered him to go ahead with the job because he wanted to put the worker on the spot. The workman says that the lead man is always trying to assume the duties of a supervisor, with the result that the morale of the group is breaking down. He suggests that you should contact other members of the group about some of the things that the lead man is doing and the amount of authority he is trying to assume.

1. Should you confront the lead man with the accusations?
2. Should you tell the worker that he should do the job as ordered?
3. Should you question the rest of the group? How?
4. If the lead man is in the right, how should you settle the problem?
5. If the worker's accusations are true, how should you settle the problem?
6. How might the situation have been avoided?
7. What kind of responsibility should lead men have? How much?
8. What kind of authority should lead men have? How much?

CASE 6

A young man who had been working in a gas station while going to school got a job as assistant manager in a drugstore. He expressed his problem this way:

I wonder why women are so hateful on the job—always pecking one another. Ask one of them to go to another department where they're shorthanded and you can scarcely pry her off her perch. Or send her to wipe up some spilled perfume or broken glass in another department and she'll tell you that's not her job. And send somebody in to work in her department, and she'll pick apart everything the woman does. Out of the dozen of them, somebody is always scrapping or crying.

I keep telling them that it's company policy they have to work the whole store—they have to move around wherever they're needed. The store is open 100 hours a week and each one of them works only 40 hours. They're supposed to keep their prices marked and the stock arranged on the shelves according to the chart so that anybody can go into that department and take over. But I really believe they put the stock out of place on purpose so that whoever tries to work in there will look stupid.

I asked the boss what made them so unwilling to work together and move around where they're needed, and he said it was the fault of the previous managers. They let the women boss the departments and make up orders and set up displays and do the kind of thing that management is supposed to be doing. I thought maybe it was because I'm so much younger than they are and they're used to bossing their families at home. But still, they aren't all that way. Some of the new ones aren't young and they cooperate with me and we get along fine.

What are some of the problems here?

CASE 7

You are in charge of a group of office workers doing stenographic, typing, filing, and clerical work. In the past you have made it a practice to hire all-around workers so that, whenever anyone was absent, almost any other worker could take her place or, whenever any type of work began to pile up, everyone would pitch in until the backlog was cleared. The morale of the group was good, although there was some complaining that a person had to jump from one job to another and that some people were not doing a full job.

Recently the work load has been increasing, and you have been hiring additional help, but the output is not increasing proportionally. The girls you were able to get are not all-around workers, and you notice an increasing amount of errors and goldbricking.

Something has to be done; so you are thinking of changing this line type of organization into something different. One of your ideas is to get together with some other sections and create a stenographic and typing pool with a woman as the head. The other section heads and your boss think it is a good idea.

You approach some of your better stenographers and typists with the plan, which you feel they will like, but they tell you that the present setup is the lesser of the two evils. Next you approach some of the workers who don't like typing and ask their opinions. To your surprise, they also object. When you try to get reasons from them, they don't seem to know why they object.

1. What might be some of the reasons for these reactions?
2. What kind of reorganization should you put into effect?
3. How would you prepare your workers for it?

CASE 8

The president of a small company that had been growing rapidly engaged a management consultant to conduct an organization survey so that proper organizational development and planning could result. After considerable analysis the consultant developed a proposed organization structure. Before preparing the necessary position descriptions and an organization manual, he discussed the proposal with the president. The recommended structure was thought to be sound by the president but he believed that all employees should be involved in the discussion so that they could see the reporting relationships and lines of authority and responsibility. The consultant advised against this idea, suggesting that only supervisors be involved. He felt it should be their responsibility to discuss it further with their subordinates. The consultant further believed that many of the employees were unsophisticated about management theory and practice and that such a discussion would be confusing.

The company president was insistent in his desire to communicate the proposed structure to all employees. A meeting was scheduled one evening after the close of the business day. Approximately 100 employees crowded into the company's reception area where a blackboard had been set up. The president opened the meeting with a brief statement of its purpose and then turned it over to the consultant. The consultant explained the desirability of organization planning and the need for sound structure to allow the company to achieve its objectives. He discussed responsibility and authority and the need for establishing accountability and effective reporting relationships. He then proceeded to draw the proposed structure on the blackboard indicating the major functional areas, their relationship to each other and the resultant lines of authority down from the chief executive. In short, he depicted a typical organization chart on the blackboard. Several questions ensued since the company had never had any chart and this was all new information to the majority of those present. After answering several questions, the consultant closed the discussion by emphasizing the fact that the chart was one aspect of sound organizational development and that it wasn't static but would be changed as the company developed and grew. The president thanked the group for coming to the meeting and concluded the program.

Several employees then came forward to talk to both the president and the consultant. Additional questions were raised and the consultant answered them. The consultant felt that the meeting was successful since all of the questions were good ones and he thought the discussion created greater understanding of the proposal among the employees. Just as he was mentally congratulating himself on the apparent success of his efforts, one of the clerks from the accounting department grabbed him by the arm and took him to the blackboard. The clerk, an old-timer with the company, then said, "Where is my box on the chart?"

1. How would you answer the clerk's question?
2. Should the president have included all employees in this discussion group?
3. What do you think prompted the clerk to raise his question?

CASE 9

A small research group of 15 people was assembled by a university to handle a specific type of research problem under a military contract with the U.S. government. The group did not function well as a unit even though each member was excellent in his own specialty. Organization and planning were lacking. The scientists were continually stymied by normal business problems, routines, decisions, and contracts.

The director of the project hired a businessman to act as an administrative assistant to the group. His job was to take over all management details so that the scientists could devote full time to research activities. The duties of the administrative assistant were to take care of business relationships, contracts, personnel work, records, etc. As an indication of the size of the project, the cost of the equipment alone came to several hundred thousand dollars.

After working with the group for a year, the administrative assistant concluded that very little progress had been made in either the research or the management of the project. He stated that the scientists could not be directed into any predictable routine and that the only thing he could do was to operate on a day-to-day basis, just handling problems as they arose.

1.   What are the areas that are common to managing a research project and a business project?
2.   What are the areas that are different?
3.   What suggestions do you have for the manager to help him in his problem?

CASE 10

The normal arrangement of a credit department would be to have the department head report to the controller. The problem in our company is that the credit manager of the division reports to the credit manager of the parent company, who in turn reports to the controller of the parent company. The division controller is thereby completely bypassed by people whose activities are directly his responsibility.

The way things are set up, the parent credit manager and the division controller are on about the same management level. The division controller has no say in credit matters although he is responsible for the amount of accounts receivable outstanding. This makes for a frustrating situation for him.

No complaints have been made to management, as the various heads do not want to suggest that management may be wrong in using this setup.

1.   In a large corporation having a number of manufacturing divisions, what might be the reason for this form of organization?
2.   What is the relation of organization structure to responsibility?
3.   What problems exist in this type of setup?

CASE 11

Ben Williams had just been promoted to the position of department head. Along with the private office, he inherited the previous department head's private secretary, Dottie Staples. Dottie was a departmental fixture, having been there for over 20 years. She was unmarried and her whole life seemed to revolve around her job. She was an excellent typist and stenographer and she enjoyed her status which was often referred to as "departmental mother."

During his eight years with the company, Ben had ample opportunity to observe Dottie in action and he was unimpressed with her gossipy approach to the job. Dottie had several favorites in the department, but Ben Williams wasn't among them. Ben's feelings about Dottie were well known and several of the employees wondered what would happen now that Ben Williams was the boss.

When Ben was told of his promotion he asked the personnel vice president about transferring Dottie. He was told that company tradition had long established the practice of leaving secretaries in their jobs when new managers were appointed. With the exception of the company's president, none of the executives dictated the choice of their secretaries. It was felt that an experienced girl helped make the new manager's transition into his job an easier one by lending continuity. Since Ben was just promoted, he felt that discretion was necessary and he did not press his request.

When Ben moved into his office, Dottie congratulated him and said, "Well, you're the fifth department head I've broken in." Ben simply thanked her for her congratulations and said nothing further. Having decided that he had no choice at present, he thought he would try to work with Dottie. Over the next few months there were several polite clashes between them, particularly when Ben tried to introduce new methods and approaches and Dottie kept reminding him that this was not the way it was done in the past. Ben then heard through the grapevine that Dottie had been talking about him to her previous boss who had been transferred to another job when Ben was promoted. The final straw among the many came when Ben discovered that Dottie had countermanded an order he had given earlier to a subordinate to prepare some data for an analytical report Ben was developing on departmental operations. He called Dottie to his office and asked her why she had done this. She replied that she was only trying to save the man from extra work which she thought was unnecessary. She said that in her opinion the report would not be welcomed by Ben's superior and she was just saving him from criticism. Ben exploded and furiously berated Dottie. She rushed out of his office in tears and Ben called the personnel vice president vowing to tell him that either Dottie be transferred or the company could look for another department head.

1. Was the company tradition a wise one?
2. Should an executive be allowed to choose his secretary? Why?
3. Should Ben have been more forceful in trying to have Dottie transferred when he took over the department head's position?

4. Should he now threaten to quit if Dottie is not removed from her job?
5. What can a company do about employees like Dottie who seem to over-step their authority because of long seniority on the job?

CASE 12

The plant superintendent responsible for manufacturing operations of the plant had on his staff a process engineer whose function was to advise as to the most economical ways of fabricating the parts of the product. The staff engineer's findings were seldom questioned by either the supervisors or the assistant plant superintendent.

The plant superintendent decided to reorganize part of his organization. He abolished the position of assistant plant superintendent (to whom all the first-level supervisors of the operating departments and the maintenance department had reported) and he created two new positions: superintendent of manufacture and superintendent of maintenance. He promoted the assistant plant superintendent to superintendent of maintenance, and he moved the process engineer from a staff position to the line position of superintendent of manufacture. Both men got raises.

The new superintendent of maintenance (that is, the former assistant superintendent) is unhappy about the change. He claims that he was, in reality, demoted. He resents the new superintendent of manufacture who has supplanted him as boss of the operating department supervisors. Most of the operating department supervisors also resent reporting to their new boss, even though they were happy working with him when he was a staff man.

1. What are some of the problems involved in shifting a man from a staff to a line position?
2. How should the above reorganization have been handled?

CASE 13

The X company was started about five years ago. It was primarily a jobbing shop, filling orders for special hand tools. Its organization was simple and predominantly of the line type. There were about 100 employees, most of them all-around machinists. The foremen were highly skilled and dealt continually with top management. The engineering department was small but efficient.

A recent rapid expansion has increased the payroll from 100 to 1,000 employees. The products have been reduced in variety and they have been upgraded in quality so that tolerances have to be held closer. Orders are for larger quantities than they used to be and the customers demand prompt delivery.

The shop is unable to meet its production schedules. The top officials seem to spend most of their time stalling off the customers, and the engineering department is not able to coordinate production between the departments. Because of scarcity of labor, the company can no longer get all-around machinists but instead must hire machine operators. The old machinists will have nothing to do with the new operators. The supervisors are complaining that they are no longer supervisors but merely clerks and instructors.

1. What procedure would you follow in analyzing this situation in order to correct it?
2. What would you need to know?
3. How would you go about finding it out?
4. Making some assumptions, what kind of basic organization structure would you set up?

CASE 14

A young engineer slated for rapid advancement in the company was rotated from staff to line jobs in his training program, then after six years with the company he was given the post of assistant *to* the president. He had scarcely started on his new duties when the president left on a business trip of two weeks. The new assistant *to* wanted to have something worthwhile to show for the two weeks, and he had a great many ideas for improvements that he had never been able to put through in his previous positions. Since several new products were being readied for production, he sent word to the heads of manufacturing, industrial engineering, and industrial relations that he would like a report on the possibilities of using the learning curve for setting up learners' incentive rates.

These three department heads had never been very receptive to his suggestions. Since they were not sure how much attention they had to pay to him in his new position, they sent him a memo that it would take a couple of weeks to assemble the information. Then, when the president returned, they asked for a clarification of the young man's authority.

What is the authority of the assistant *to?*

CASE 15

For a number of years a company manufactured a line of open-end wrenches, alligator wrenches, and ratchet wrenches, and enjoyed practically a monopoly until the patents ran out.

There were 350 shop employees. The shop consisted of a milling machine department, a broaching department, a drill press department, and a grinding department. These departments performed most of the operations on the forgings, which were purchased; a few operations were subcontracted. The various products were manufactured in batches. There was an inspection department with a foreman. He and the foremen of the departments previously mentioned reported to the general foreman, who in turn reported to the general manager. Among the other departments were a maintenance department, a toolroom, a small drafting department, a receiving and shipping department, a sales department, and a general office, all reporting to the general manager.

Maintenance of both plant and equipment was inadequate with the result that the plant was allowed to run down.

In the last few years of patent protection, some feeble attempts were made to improve production methods by putting in an incentive system, but this did not help. The company's situation became desperate when the patents ran out and other companies came into the field, producing superior wrenches at lower cost.

The sales manager by a lucky stroke found that the company could buy sole manufacturing rights for a dial indicating gauge and he sold top management on the idea of buying up these rights. The same jobbers could be used for distribution as were used for the hand wrenches, which had a good name in the trade. Money was secured and the rights were purchased.

The new product—the dial indicating gauge—looks like a stopwatch and contains stampings, springs, gears, and other parts that have to be held to closer tolerances than wrenches. The demand for the product will be steady. The dollar volume will be three times that of the wrenches.

1. Apply the seven-step problem-solving technique to the case.
2. Develop step by step a plan for reorganizing the shop. Justify each step.
3. Draw an organization chart of your proposed reorganization. Be prepared to defend your chart.

FOLLOWING UP ON THE JOB

The relationship of the department to the organization

1. Are you keeping your department in step with major changes in the structure of the whole organization?
2. Do you know the function and boundaries of your department and its relationship to other departments?
3. Do you know what staff services are available to you? Are you taking sufficient advantage of them?
4. Are you performing line or staff functions that could (or should) be performed better by some other department?

Decentralization

1. Do you delegate authority and responsibility as far down the line as possible?
2. Do you make sufficient use of the rule of the exception?
3. Do you place too much dependence on the system and not enough on people?
4. Is maintaining the system becoming more important than running the business?

Personalities and the organization

1. Is the organization in your department built around jobs and not around personalities?
2. When a vacancy occurs, do you try to fill the boots of the man who held the job or do you hire according to the job description?
3. Do you choose people for their potential competence or because they are compatible with you?
4. Do you short-circuit the organization structure and confide in those executives you like even though they are not your formal superiors?

3 Policies and procedures

Formulating and establishing policies. An example of policy implementation. Characteristics of a good policy. The supervisor interprets
and applies policies. Departmental policies. Transforming policy into
action. The purpose of procedures. Why supervisors should be interested in procedures. How procedures should be developed. Why
procedures should be kept simple. Procedures depend on people.
Application of the seven-step problem-solving technique to the
redesign of a simple procedure. Summary.

Organizations differ in their approach to the management of the several
functions making up the enterprise. Even companies in the same industry
vary in their dynamism and their emphasis on the importance of various
activities. All of us know companies that are sales oriented, research
oriented, production oriented and so on. Then there is another classification system with which we are all familiar. In any given industry there
are conservative companies, innovative companies, leader companies,
follower companies, and those that could be described as ambivalent
since they seem to shift from one pattern to another. In essence this
is the organization's style and attitude. It could also be called the firm's
philosophy of management.

To understand policy formulation there first must be understanding
of the development of a management philosophy. Haynes and Massie
describe this process:

A *philosophy of management* covers those general concepts and integrated
attitudes fundamental to the cooperation of a social group. Philosophies for
firms may differ. One might be good for firm A but not useful for firm
B. Often a firm's own members may not be conscious of a philosophy, yet
it is effective. To understand the philosophy of a given firm, the *concept
of the firm* must be understood. This will provide a picture of the "character"
of the firm—how the firm got where it is, the place that it occupies in
the industry, its strengths and weaknesses, an idea of the viewpoints of its
managers, and its relationship to social and political institutions.

Specifically, this concept can be determined from understanding:

(1) the existing personnel and their relationships,
(2) the history of the firm,
(3) the ethical framework of its managers, employees, customers, competitors, and suppliers,
(4) the industrial setting, which includes its operating processes and economic structure of the industry,
(5) the institutional setting, including the social forces and framework of government relationships.[1]

Formulating and establishing policies

An organization's philosophy evolves by day-to-day practice, conscious effort on the part of management in the establishment of goals and strategies, or some combination of both. A successful company's philosophy must be developed by taking into consideration several factors beyond the internal needs of the company. Increasing social awareness on the part of business has resulted in policies which affect the company in its relationships not only with employees, customers, and stockholders, but with the government on all levels, communities in which the company is located, suppliers and various national organizations including political parties.

Policies evolve out of the philosophy of the company as it is expressed by its management. Objectives are arrived at and a means to accomplish these objectives result in the formulation of policies. These policies should be broad enough to allow employees to exercise creative action but they should also establish parameters so that the whole company is directed toward optimum achievement of its goals. In short, a policy is a guide for action. It is also a statement of the company's intentions to achieve certain goals. As such it should be clear in language and readily understandable by those who must implement the policy. Above all, policy should not be so restrictive that it eliminates judgment by managers, for one of the most significant developers of managerial ability is decision making in an environment which allows for individual initiative and judgment. With this thought in mind, it becomes apparent that the amount of policies formulated by the top management of an organization should be kept to a minimum. Only those that contribute to the attainment of established objectives in a broad sense and those that give direction toward these goals should be considered as necessary.

Policy is recognized by most managers as a form of authority imposed on them by the top management. Because of this restrictive interpretation, it becomes necessary to evaluate each existing policy periodically

---

[1] W. Warren Haynes and Joseph L. Massie, *Management Analysis, Concepts and Cases* (Englewood Cliffs, N.J.: Prentice-Hall, Inc., 1961), pp. 142–43.

to determine its relevance to current organizational objectives. In fact, some companies build in a review procedure at the time a policy is formulated by indicating a date for its reevaluation. In other companies, this review takes place annually. Certainly some review is necessary if policy is not to become red tape which is bent and skirted by managers down the line. The obvious danger of obsolete policies is that all policies become suspect and implementation by line managers is very difficult.

Significantly, effective policy formulation takes place when the individuals charged with this responsibility are aware of the needs of the organization as well as its goals. This means that line managers should be brought into the discussions whenever possible. Feedback on the effect of policy is vital to its proper evaluation and continuance. Such feedback will only take place where the managers feel their opinions are listened to.

An example of policy implementation

When an organization increases in size and complexity and there are several levels of management, top managers cannot make every decision. Policy allows them to indicate broad guides for action down the line so that lower level managers will make decisions implementing the thinking of top management when the policy was formulated. If a policy is traced from its formulation by top management to its implementation by a first-line supervisor, this process will be easy to understand.

Personnel policy committee of the board of directors. This company intends that its rates of pay be commensurate with compensation practices in the markets in which it competes for people.

Personnel vice president. Establishes job evaluation program to determine the relative value of one job compared to all others in the company in purely objective terms without regard to the person who holds the job. Then salary ranges are established taking into account the results of the job evaluation effort and the salaries paid for comparable jobs in other companies. A performance review program is then developed and all managers in the company are made aware of the salary ranges for the jobs they supervise as well as the salaries being paid to the incumbents. Additionally they are instructed in the use of the performance review and are given the dates when this is to take place.

Middle manager. Gathers all the first-line supervisors reporting to him for a meeting to discuss the salary ranges, the performance review form and is prepared to answer any questions and make himself available for consultation. He instructs supervisors to be objective in evaluating performance, emphasizing the problems that can arise by playing favorites and makes them aware of the need for thoroughly discussing the results of the performance review with the employee. He goes on to mention that he will assist them in their recommendations of specific amounts of increase in rates of pay should the performance review warrant an increase for a particular employee.

First-level supervisor. Looks at lateness and absentee records of all employees; studies production records and error ratio; evaluates employees on the other criteria established by the personnel department, such as ability to work with others, cooperativeness, promotability, and accuracy. He rates each employee working for him and then discusses the rating with each employee in private, indicating good points and offering suggestions for the improvement of those areas where the employee is lacking. He then indicates his recommendation for salary action for each employee and passes both his salary recommendations and performance reviews to his superior making himself available for discussion. He notes that several of his employees are being paid below the minimum of the range established for the job they occupy and he firmly recommends increases which will bring their pay above the minimum.

Characteristics of a good policy

A supervisor should have some criteria for judging the quality of policies, since they have so much influence on his actions. Some policies are out of date; they haven't been examined and revised to keep up with changes inside and outside the company. Economic conditions and markets may have changed. The company may now be mass producing instead of jobbing; it may be producing a different line of products and in need of a different type of labor skills; it may have expanded into branches far from the home office. It may have changed completely to meet changing conditions yet never revised its policy manual. Some of the policies may have always been ineffective because they just grew out of a few decisions that set a precedent. Some other decisions might have been better, more timely, more in line with objectives, and more in harmony with other company policies.

There are certain characteristics to look for in evaluating policies. Good policies are *stable, flexible, compatible, understandable, sincere, realistic,* and *written.*

A policy should be as *stable* as it is possible to make it. It will be necessary to discard policies when they have outlived their usefulness, and it is necessary to modify them to keep up with the times, but these are changes that should not be made lightly. The stability of a policy can be improved by making it sufficiently *flexible* to take care of problems that vary from the normal, and flexible enough not to have to be adjusted too frequently to allow for changing conditions. If, however, a policy doesn't require reformulation from time to time to take care of inevitable changes, then that policy may be too vague to ever have much meaning or it may be so inflexible that it is actually a rule.

A good policy must be *compatible* with the "body" of policies; that is, it must not contradict or be in conflict with other policies. If it is a department policy, it should be subordinate to, and in harmony with, broader company policies. If the company has a policy of promotion from within, the department's hiring and training policies must be designed to take people in at the bottom and train them for advancement.

Policies are a way of publicizing the philosophy and ethics of a company—at least they are a commitment by management on how the company will act. Therefore they should be *sincere*. In their intent and in their wording they should express trustworthiness and build goodwill and cooperation, but they still have to be *realistic*. They can't be just high-sounding platitudes which would be followed if things were different. They must be guides to steer a business and must provide for its survival and profitability in the actual working world.

Finally, a policy must be *understandable* if it is going to have a chance to be uniformly interpreted and applied. The meaning of it must be clear not only to the supervisors who will interpret and apply it but to everyone who will be affected by it. A policy maker will make his policy more understandable, plan it more carefully, and express it more clearly if he knows that it is going to appear in writing. For these reasons, and for many other reasons, a policy should be *written* and it should be written in the policy manual. It should be reviewed periodically—preferably by a committee—and kept up-to-date and in harmony with changing conditions.

If a policy meets most of these conditions, it stands ready to serve its purpose.

The supervisor interprets and applies policies

When a supervisor is confronted with a problem requiring a decision—such as a discipline problem or whether to allow overtime or to lay off some workers—he first determines whether he has the authority to render the decision. If he does not have sufficient authority, he passes the problem up to his boss (the rule of the exception, in Chapter 2). If on the other hand the decision should be made on a level of management lower than his own, he sends the problem back down the line to his subordinate and with it he sends guidance to aid in the solution. If such guidance or policy does not already exist, he formulates it and in so doing he is formulating policy.

Once the supervisor knows that he has the authority to render a decision, he looks to policy for guidance. And policy will mean more to him if he knows why it was adopted in the first place, what changes have been made in it and why, and what trends will influence its application in the future. Being aware of trends is particularly advisable in the field of equipment replacement policies, hiring policies, and policies toward the union. When a supervisor has background information on policies, he is better equipped to interpret them and use them for their true purpose—as a guide to decision making rather than as an inflexible formula for action.

Understanding the reason for a policy and knowing its history makes the supervisor feel more in accord with the policy. His attitude toward policy is sensed by his subordinates and influences their attitude toward it and toward the decisions made in accordance with it. The supervisor must interpret policy accurately and clearly, in language that employees can understand; he must do it impartially, in the spirit in which the policy was intended; and he must give the reasoning behind it, the why and the wherefore.

The supervisor cannot assume that his subordinates know the policies just because they were explained in the induction program or in a talk a year ago. Workers come and go, they forget, and any piece of information becomes garbled in time. When a supervisor gives a decision on a controversial matter, he will do well to remind his subordinates of the policy under which he made that decision. Then his men will know that he is not being arbitrary, operating by whim, or playing favorites. If an employee wants a raise or a transfer and he isn't worth it or shouldn't have it, the supervisor should not blame policy or hide behind policy; it's better to tell the employee where he stands than to say something like, "Company policy says that the average should be close to the middle of the range."

Policies commit management to specific courses of action and specific types of decisions. If the company acts contrary to policy or if decisions down the line are made contrary to policy, the result is consternation and confusion. Policies that are strictly adhered to and well publicized help the personnel to understand, anticipate, and accept specific management decisions. For instance, if a company has a policy of a trial working period before an employee becomes permanent, and during that trial period the company can fire without cause, then people are forewarned. Or if during a recession it is known that the company will first cut out overtime and then shorten the work week before a wholesale layoff, people will be prepared to accept what is coming.

Uniformity of application is essential. Employees lose respect for a policy if they see it being violated with impunity in other departments or units—or worse still, if they see their own supervisor being inconsistent in his decisions that should be based on it.

Departmental policies

Since policies formulated by top management have to be broad enough to cover the whole organization, they are seldom detailed enough to guide the various major departments in their internal operations.

Using the broad general management policies as a guide, the major department head must develop policies to guide his own department. He must also interpret broad policies to determine their relevance to his area of responsibility. The example of a compensation policy given earlier in this chapter indicates how a major department head (the personnel vice president) would develop a policy from the broader policy formulated by higher management.

When the head of a department or section finds his subordinates coming to him for decisions rather than with decisions, he should suspect that he has been spending too much time solving their problems for them and too little time formulating policies to help them do the problem solving themselves. In formulating policies for his own department he might use the following outline:

1. Ask the questions: *Why is this problem reoccurring? Why isn't it solved automatically without coming across my desk?*
2. Find out if the principles and practices of good management are being applied to the situation that has given rise to the problem. If the company has staff specialists in policy and procedure analysis work, consult them and get their assistance.
3. Investigate or have a staff specialist investigate to find the best practices elsewhere in the company and in other companies in handling this type of problem.
4. Determine a tentative course of action for solving the immediate problem.
5. Develop a guide or policy for solving this type of problem in the future.
6. Make sure the proposed policy is not in conflict with company policy.
7. Discuss the proposed policy with the people who will have to enforce, interpret, and abide by it; get the benefit of their ideas and experience. Find out from them some of the difficulties that may arise when the proposed policy is applied to specific cases or situations.
8. Apply the policy on a temporary basis and modify it if necessary to get greater acceptance.
9. Put the policy in writing and explain it to all concerned.
10. Keep informed on the experiences of those enforcing the policy, the reaction of others to the policy, and any changes going on that are making it difficult to apply the policy.
11. Revise the policy when it no longer serves its purpose—that is, when there have been changes in the labor situation, the product, the skill requirements, or the broad company policies. A policy should be revised when there is an increasing number of exceptions

to it, when the interpretations have to be farfetched, and when people start coming for decisions and interpretations. In revising, consider what the effect will be on the commitments and procedures based on the policy.

12. If there is a policy manual, remove the old policy from it and put in the new one. Explain the change to all concerned.

Transforming policy into action

One of the essential responsibilities of all managers is problem solving. The seven-step problem-solving technique described later in this chapter can be very useful to the manager once he has decided that the problem is worth solving. Each day on the job presents several occurrences which the manager must confront and do something about. Given the guide of overall company policy, he must translate this policy into action so that the objectives established for his area of responsibility can be accomplished. To do this effectively he must identify those situations which recur frequently.

In the previous pages, policies have been defined and discussed as guides to be used in deciding *what* to do. The following discussion will consider the development of procedures that allow for the implementation of policy. Procedures can be defined as standing plans or predetermined courses of action for recurring situations telling *who* should do it, *where* it should be done, and *when* it should be done. The detailed description of *how* it should be done (machine and motions) is considered as method. Procedures form a network that extends throughout a company and ties together its various parts. This network of procedures is part of the total system which encompasses people, devices, and plans.[2]

The activities covered by procedures are the ordinary recurring ones of a business, and the routines are established to make sure that these activities are accomplished in the proper manner, at the proper time, by the proper people, in the proper place, and in the correct sequence.

In the personnel department the employment procedure is the process of putting people on the payroll—a systematic manner of handling the application forms, initial screening of applicants against openings, the interviews, tests, physical exams, checking of references, assigning payroll number, and other steps necessary to the process.

---

[2] Anyone discussing procedures should be prepared to meet differences in definitions. Procedures may be defined as orderly and logical arrangement of functions (acts). They may be considered the same thing as system and defined much as system was defined above. They may be given the importance of lifeblood in the organization structure. Or, at the other extreme, they may be likened to red tape—the forms, paper work, control reports, and oral and written instructions that prescribe and govern the steps (operations) that make up a process.

The routine for making up the payroll is a procedure of the accounting department. The routine for processing a piece part is a procedure in a manufacturing department. These are departmental procedures.

An example of a procedure that crosses departmental lines and involves several departments is Figure 3–1 showing the activities and operations necessary to ship equipment under a government contract. This procedure involves the project engineer, technical liaison people, packing, carpenter shop, purchasing, quality control, and shipping departments. Reading the steps of this procedure and analyzing them as they appear on the flow chart of Figure 3–1 serves to show how a procedure arranges for things to get done. Each step serves to tell someone to do something: to fill out information on a form and distribute it to the people who must use it, to type up a list and distribute the copies to the people who need them, to order materials, to get approvals, to fabricate parts, to have inspections made.

It can be seen from this example that procedures involve several people, oral or written instructions, a sequence of steps, information to be moved, forms to be filled out, checkings and verifications to be made. The recurring activity governed by a procedure is not just a repetitive task performed at a work station—not, for instance, typing a letter or filing one. What the typist and the file clerk are doing is termed an operation. Such an operation would be a step in a procedure. The equipment used and the motions involved in performing an operation are the *method*.

The purpose of procedures

It would be difficult to run a business if upper management had to issue a series of specific orders covering all the details for each transaction. The establishment of standing plans (organization structure, policies, procedures, and methods) makes it possible for subordinates to carry on the actions according to plan. When procedures and methods are set up and standardized, it becomes possible to delegate responsibilities to a low level in the organization. Less time is needed for explanations of what is to be done. Methods can be made more efficient; standards of performance can be established. Coordination and control become easier because consistent actions are taken on similar cases, and actions are predictable.

Procedures may follow the chain of command or they may flow horizontally across the organization. When an order comes into a business house, information about it must somehow be carried to all the departments that will work on it—sales, credit, billing, fabricating, shipping, accounting, to name a few—where the proper chain of events will be set off for doing all the things that need to be done. The work relationships for this horizontal flow are set up by procedures.

The type of procedure that flows from department to department acts as a horizontal coordinator and controller: it ties the organization together by horizontal lines that are channels for carrying information across the network of vertical lines that separate one department from another. If there were no procedures cutting across departments, theoretically it would be necessary for information between departments to go up the line to a common point and then come down again (see Chapter 4). Theoretically, if there were no procedure to cover the requisitioning of materials, each time a supervisor needed something for a job it would be necessary for his department head and the heads of all the other departments involved to meet with the plant superintendent and work out the details. When procedures exist it becomes possible for the whole transaction to flow across the organization at a low level, in most cases never going any higher than the first-level supervisor. If procedures did not exist, management men would have to develop a whole body of plans for organizing, directing, controlling and coordinating each piece of work.

A procedure by definition is a routine for processing the ordinary activities of the business; therefore, if a process has become or is going to become repetitive, a procedure should be established for it so that it can be handled automatically and without the waste of managerial time and effort.

Why supervisors should be interested in procedures

A supervisor should be interested in procedures because he can make them work for him, can use them to relieve him of a load of routine and save his time for the more important aspects of his job. Also, if he understands procedures he can do a better job of explaining their purpose and their importance to the subordinates who are expected to carry them out.

If the supervisor looks critically at some of the procedures in his department, he may see that they are not being followed—that steps are being skipped—and some of the failures he has been blaming on subordinates may be caused by weaknesses in the procedures. Procedures usually grow from the bottom of the organization and they aren't always in line with policies, which start from the top. Procedures develop from custom or habit, or they may be put in as stopgaps. They develop piecemeal; part of an old procedure doesn't work well or people make too many mistakes under it, so a new procedure is tacked on to take care of the weak place. A procedure that has not been carefully planned is probably inefficient.

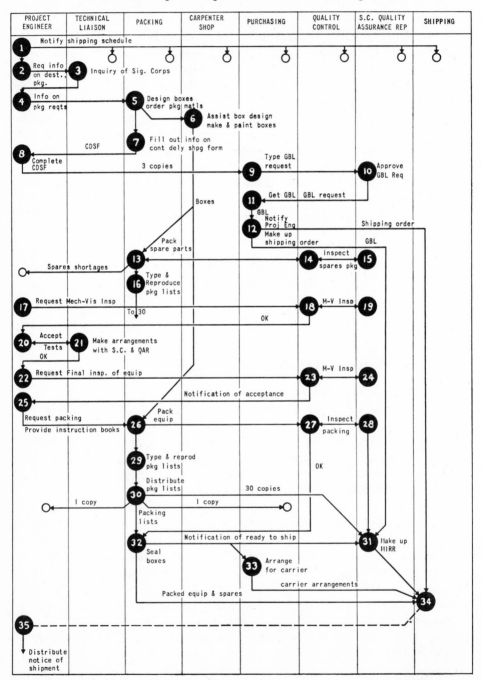

FIGURE 3–1
Flow Chart 35 Steps of the Procedure for Shipping Equipment under a
Government Contract
The first four steps of this procedure are described in Figure 3–2.

FIGURE 3–2
The First Four Steps of the Procedure for Shipping Equipment under a
Government Contract

All 35 steps of this procedure are charted on the flow chart in Figure 3–1.

SYLVANIA ELECTRIC PRODUCTS INC.
ELECTRONIC DEFENSE LABORATORY

INDEX NO. 70.01
PAGE 1 OF 6

POLICY AND STANDARD PRACTICE

SUBJECT: PROCEDURE FOR CONTRACT SHIPMENTS

(Supersedes No. 82.01 of 4/11/57)
DATE ISSUED: April 7, 1958
APPROVED BY: A. Brolly
J. Lien

I SCOPE

The activities and operations necessary to ship equipment fabricated under an EDL contract.

II POLICY

The Project Engineer will be responsible for meeting contract requirements. Shipping arrangements may be delegated by him to the Products Control group, technical matters excepted.

III PROCEDURE

The procedural steps listed below refer by number to steps on the attached flow diagram.

1. At the earliest date on which the Project Engineer can reasonably anticipate when equipment will be shipped on his project, he should notify all people concerned with the shipment of the schedule. Two weeks advance notice is desirable and preferably will be given with an internal memorandum. Schedule delay or acceleration deserves the same notifications.

   A tickler file will be maintained by Contracts Administration to provide an advance check for all projects in the Laboratory.

2. The Project Engineer will request of Technical Liaison information regarding destination of the equipment, the type of packing required (domestic or overseas) and the level of classification.

3. Technical Liaison will inquire of USASERU to obtain the desired information and will transmit it back to the Project Engineer.

4. The Project Engineer will advise the Packing group of his requirements. He will provide the following information:

   (a) Itemized list of all units to be shipped, including quantities, full description and serial numbers.

   (b) Type of packing (Will some packing boxes also be used as permanent carrying cases?)

   (c) Security Classification.

   (d) Spare parts list.

Flow chart (Fig. 3–1) and page 1 of the procedure are reproduced with the permission of Sylvania Electric Products Inc., Electronic Defense Laboratory, Mountain View, California.

Some procedures have outlived their usefulness but are still followed because people resist change. The product changes, the organization changes, people change, related procedures change, but still some of the expensive old routines are continued like bad habits. The supervisor who is called upon to cut costs will find a fruitful field in the investigation and redesign of the procedures under his control.

He may find that some of the information being collected in his department is no longer needed or that it is also being collected elsewhere. Some of the forms being filled out may be useless. Some of the records being kept in the department may be just "protection" in case someone should ask for information that could be gotten elsewhere. One of the benefits of procedural analysis is in getting rid of needless work. There is more saving in abolishing the *need* for the sorting, checking, typing, posting, distributing, or filing than there is in improving the methods of performing these operations.

How procedures should be developed

Procedures that cross department lines should be developed by staff specialists who have experience in systems analysis. These specialists are equipped to make complete investigations crossing department lines, to draw elaborate interrelations, design forms, put proposed procedures in writing, and help install them. When companies do not have these specialists, the supervisor who knows the fundamental principle of procedure design can set up efficient procedures for his own department.

A supervisor should learn the fundamentals of procedure design even though the company procedures are designed by specialists from the system design department. The line man who knows what staff specialists can and cannot do can get full value from their services. He knows what kinds of information they need in order to do a better job of designing procedures, and he knows how to relate the procedures to the abilities and status relationships of his subordinates who will be responsible for carrying them out.

Why procedures should be kept simple

A procedure is effective if it fulfills its purpose and does it at the lowest possible cost. Procedures cost money because it takes time to handle information—to gather it, record it, transport it, and check it for accuracy. The more complicated the procedure, the more costly it is. Involved procedures arise from trying to make the procedure foolproof—putting in a great number of checkpoints so that nothing can possibly go wrong. The boss who hates to assume any blame for mistakes made in his department may build extra steps into procedures just to be sure that there will be no slipups that he would be held responsible for; his signature would be required before any action could be started and then again after it was accomplished. If a mistake cannot be made under a procedure, the procedure is probably too complicated.

There are a number of things that cause procedures to become complicated. They may be designed to cover too wide an area—that is, cover the unusual as well as the routine. For example, if the processing of a special order can follow the same routine as that of a regular order, the procedure is probably too complicated. Special cases and cases that occur rarely should be treated as exceptions to the routine. Procedures have a tendency to become elaborate in manufacturing establishments because of the need to meet deadlines and coordinate various activities in preparation for assemblies. As a company gets larger there is a tendency for procedures to become more elaborate so that more control can be achieved.

Procedures depend on people

Although procedures are spoken of as being automatic and self-starting, they are not. A form cannot fill itself out and start its several copies on their way to the departments that need the information. Procedures and systems have to be designed for the people who are going to carry them out. The best a form can do is be designed so that people will use it promptly, fill in the information accurately, interpret the information correctly, and take the proper action on it. Procedures need to be designed to cut down the possibilities of human error. People forget, they have bad days, they put things off, they make mistakes in copying information, they mislay things; so procedures should be designed to catch errors and correct them before they have caused much damage. For instance, forms should have numbering systems to call attention to any that are missing from the series. Copies should be matched together at some control point to catch any that have gone astray or been improperly handled.

The various steps of procedures should be assigned to people who are fitted to perform them adequately and economically; highly paid personnel should not be assigned detailed routine work. A procedure will be carried out more effectively if people accept it as logical and necessary and if it is also an easy starter, quick and simple to handle, with all the steps designed to reduce the possibility of any being skipped or of action being stopped before reaching completion. Procedures need built-in attention callers.

Since procedures cannot and should not cover every situation, one of the dangers of management-by-procedure is that people will hesitate to use their own good judgment even when they can see that the application of a procedure is not in the best interests of the company. In some organizations, systems become an end in themselves rather than a means to an end. When getting ahead depends on how well a man follows procedure, then any deviation from procedure is frowned upon and nobody will risk using his initiative or judgment but will follow along, keeping his nose clean.

There should be more emphasis on the purpose or *why* of routines, more dependence upon people, and less upon the system. The trend in better management today is to build meaning into jobs—to design jobs in such a way as to promote individual responsibility. If a man feels that responsibility rests upon him rather than upon a system, he will exercise initiative and judgment. But if he feels that he has to buck the routine in order to protect the company's interests, he may choose to follow routine. As a result he will be of less value to the company and he will have less satisfaction in his job. Procedures can't operate without people, and the performance of people hinges upon their knowledge, ability, and attitude, the design of their jobs, and the quality of the supervision.

Application of the seven-step problem-solving technique to the redesign of a simple procedure

The supervisor (also the person preparing to enter management) should get some practice in procedure analysis and design. Even though he may work in an organization that has staff experts to design procedures for him, he needs to be able to understand procedures so that he can use them intelligently and teach his subordinates how to use them.

The problem to be presented here is the redesign of a simple procedure. Actually, a person isn't equipped to change procedures until he has learned the techniques of methods improvement and until he has an understanding of the human relations problems involved in changing a routine and tampering with job content. The classroom problem of redesigning a procedure is tackled here for the purpose of learning about procedures by taking one apart and putting it together again. The procedure chosen for this study should be a simple one such as the requisitioning of supplies from the storeroom, or the procedure for starting a new employee, or the procedure for handling an injury on the job. The college student who is preparing for a management job will find a very good subject for study in some part of the school's registration procedure.

The technique to be applied to the procedure analysis and redesign is the problem-solving technique[3] illustrated in Chapter 1. The seven steps are:

1. Clearly define the problem or problems.
2. Gather the information.
3. Interpret the information.
4. Develop solutions.
5. Select the best practical solution.
6. Put the solution into operation.
7. Evaluate the effectiveness of the solution.

Step 1. Clearly define the problem or problems. Put in writing what you think the problem is, what the manifestations of the problem are, and what benefits you expect to derive from the solution of the problem.

Manifestations of procedural problems might be bottlenecks, rush jobs, people having to wait for information, for material, or for machines, needed items out of stock, orders not filled on time, billing not up-to-date, bills not paid on time, or perhaps information getting lost or coming too late to accomplish its purpose.

Benefits to be expected from solving such problems might be in having the work go through smoothly, jobs completed on time, work better balanced, or savings in time or steps or money. Listing these desired results serves to clarify the problem and to evalute the effectiveness of the solution. Setting the problem up in terms of benefits to be expected from its solution gives a basis for judging how much expense should be gone to in the investigation: What are these benefits worth?

The investigator always has to remember that procedures are related to policies. In analyzing a procedure he needs to know what policy the procedure is based upon, he needs to judge if the procedure is doing its job of carrying out the policy, and he may need to ask whether the policy should be revised.

Step 2. Gather the information. In the information-gathering phase of the problem-solving technique, it soon becomes apparent that it is necessary to limit the scope of the investigation. Procedures become part of a system and lead from one department to another. Therefore

---

[3] Other techniques can be used; the choice would depend on the difficulty of the problem. A simple problem might not require seven steps—in fact, Steps 3 and 4 are often combined. The solution of a complicated procedure problem is beyond the scope of this text. For complicated procedure problems that cross department lines, consult Norman Barish, *Systems Analysis for Effective Administration* (New York: Funk & Wagnalls Co., 1951); or Victor Lazzaro (ed.), *Systems and Procedures* (Englewood Cliffs, N.J.: Prentice-Hall, Inc., 1959). For information on the techniques of investigating a procedure, see John M. Pfiffner, *A Manual for Administrative Analysis* (School of Public Administration, University of Southern California) (Dubuque, Ia.: William C. Brown Co., 1951).

the investigator has to limit his study to the area which he can do something about—where he can make modifications, changes, and decisions. He has to limit the width of the study and then he must limit the depth: How detailed should it be? Will the possible benefits justify the cost of the study and the innovations?

The information gathered about a procedure would be unwieldy and difficult to analyze if presented in essay form. The investigator has to know exactly what happens at each step: This piece of paper that is the subject of the investigation—was it worked on at this step? or checked for accuracy? or carried from one place to another and, if so, how far? or stored in a file and, if so, for how long? This kind of information can best be handled in chart form—the same kind of printed form that an investigator uses for following a product through a manufacturing plant. The form to be used in this procedure problem is a *Process Chart*[4]; (see chapter on methods improvement). The sample form filled out is Figure 3–3.

The investigator should now gather information on his own procedural problem and put it down step by step on a process chart. Figure 3–3 shows how to break a procedure into its separate activities and describe each activity in sequence on the chart. (For additional information on filling out the chart, consult Chapter 8 on "Improving Methods.")

The investigator should gather and study each printed (or typed or handwritten) form used in the procedure, find out its purpose, and judge how well the information on that form fills this purpose. The investigator of a procedure should talk to each person who is involved in any way in the procedure, ask him what he does in connection with it and what he would suggest for improving the procedure. This is the time to get the employee's participation in what may mean a change in his job. It is never too early to take into account the fact that people have a better attitude toward changes if they have a hand in planning them, particularly if they are given credit and recognition for their good ideas and their contributions in working out improvements.

In questioning the necessity of performing some part of a procedure, it is well to keep in mind the feelings of the person performing it. It comes as a shock to a man to learn that what he has been doing so carefully isn't worth wasting the time on and that a piece of his job is being pulled out from under him. For this reason people should be encouraged to participate in the investigating and planning stages of a procedure change. Then they are *improving* their job, not having it taken away from them.

---

[4] There are a number of other widely used methods of portraying information in chart form. There is the organizational flow chart, the activity analysis chart, the department analysis chart, the forms distribution chart, and variations of these charts. For further information on charts see Barish or Lazzaro, *ibid.*

FIGURE 3–3
Portion of a Process Chart

A study of this process chart will show that the investigation of the procedure begins at a desk where the incoming case is waiting to be handled. This waiting is called a *storage* and is represented on the chart by putting a line through the triangular symbol at line 1. Then at line 2 something is done to the case and it is done right there on the same desk. This doing something is an *operation* and is represented on the chart by drawing a line through the larger circle opposite line 2. Then at line 3 the case goes into storage again, this time in the outgoing basket where it stays for 10 minutes; so the line is drawn through the storage triangle that is on a level with line 3. At line 4 the case is carried 120 feet to the file clerk, and this *transportation* is charted by drawing the line through the small circle in the transportation column at the level of line 4. This line that is drawn from one symbol to another traces the path followed by the case as it is being processed in the office. The left-hand columns list the distance the case is moved and the time it spends in storage. A study of this chart shows how to break a routine into its steps, how to enter the steps on the chart, how to describe them and how to classify them according to whether they are operations, transportations, storages, or inspections, and how to list the distance and time involved.

Actually this chart had 46 steps on it. The *Supervisor's Guide* from which it was taken discusses some of these steps in detail.

WORK SIMPLIFICATION PROGRAM
PROCESS CHART

PROCESS CHARTED __Certification__   UNIT_____ __Certification__
                Procedure   DIVISION, BRANCH, ETC., __Field__
DATE_____ October 15, 19---

O IN FEET	TIME IN MIN.	OPERATION	TRANSPORT	STORAGE	INSPECT.	STEP NO.	DESCRIPTION OF EACH STEP (SHOW WHAT IS DONE — WHO DOES IT)
		○	○	▲	□	1	Incoming case at master register desk
		●	○	△	□	2	Case entered in master register
	10	○	○	▲	□	3	In outgoing basket
120		○	●	△	□	4	To file clerk
	20	○	○	▲	□	5	In incoming basket
		●	○	△	□	6	Case entered in file room register
		●	○	△	□	7	File searched for previous action
		●	○	△	□	8	File pulled and attached to case
		●	○	△	□	9	Charge-out slip made on file
	40	○	○	▲	□	10	In outgoing basket
180		○	●	△	□	11	To clerk A
	120	○	○	▲	□	12	In incoming basket
		○	○	△	■	13	Case checked against file for change of address
120		○	●	△	□	14	To correspondence clerk
		●	○	△	□	15	Acknowledgment dictated
10		○	●	△	□	16	To stenographer's desk
		●	○	△	□	17	Acknowledgment
60		○	●	△	□	18	To s
	130	○	○	▲	□		

Taken from *Supervisor's Guide to the Process Chart*, Work Simplification Program (Washington, D.C.: U.S. Government Printing Office).

Step 3. Interpret the information. Step 4. Develop solutions.
Steps 3 and 4 of the problem-solving technique can be combined in
handling this problem of investigating a procedure. The investigator
has in his hand a process chart on which he has charted every step
of the procedure he is going to redesign. His job now is to analyze
the information on his chart—to question every step on it. *What* does
this step accomplish? *Why* is it necessary? *Where* and *when* should
this step be done? *Who* should do it? *How* should it be done? By
attacking each step with these questions, he expects to find ways of
eliminating, combining, rearranging, and simplifying steps in a way that
will improve the procedure. The investigator can use the following
checklist to question each of the steps and each of the printed forms
involved in the procedure.

1. Each step should be necessary. If it is not, then eliminate it.
2. Each step should have a reason for being by itself. Can it be com-
    bined with others?
3. Each step should have an ideal place in the sequence. Where should
    it be?
4. Each step should be as easy as possible.
5. Each distance traveled should be as short as possible. Can distances
    traveled be reduced?
6. Each form should have a real purpose. Verify it. Is the form neces-
    sary? Can it be eliminated? Combined with another form? Replaced
    with a copy of another form?
7. If a form is finally destroyed, maybe it should never have been
    originated.
8. Information that is taken off one form and put on another suggests
    that more copies should have been made in the first place. Are all
    information takeoffs and readings necessary? Transferring informa-
    tion from one form to another is an occasion for omissions and errors.
9. What would happen if the form were lost?
10. What equipment might be used to make it easier to process the
    form?
11. Files should have a purpose. Do they? Avoid duplication. Avoid
    unnecessary files.
12. Does someone sign all copies? How can this be avoided? Signers
    are busy people.
13. Is there excessive checking?
14. Where is the best place to check? Calculate the risk of letting
    a subordinate put his OK on it instead of getting the boss's signature.
15. Does one person have too much of the procedure to follow in
    terms of unrelated skills? His job should be made up of related skills
    of about the same level.

16. Does one person have too little of the procedure to follow? Each person who handles the procedure has to spend time in reading or recognizing what is to be done. Rather than hand it along to have each person perform one operation on it, why not have one person do more, thereby cutting down on the makeready time? Giving one person more of the procedure to follow may enlarge his job by increasing the variety of tasks in it and building into it more responsibility for accuracy.
17. Are as many steps as possible given to the lowest classification of personnel? Detailed routines should not be performed by highly paid people.
18. What is the worst that could happen if any of these steps were omitted?

The investigator should evaluate the steps of the procedure and the jobs they touch upon to see how they measure up to the principles of good management: *Are authority and responsibility being delegated as far down the line as possible? Is the supervisor using his time for actual managing or is he spending too much time doing routine work? Are the jobs in the department made up of related tasks all requiring about the same level and type of skill and training, or are they a hodgepodge of unrelated tasks? Is the work load distributed evenly?[5] Is there a logical flow of work? Are desks and equipment properly placed with regard to light, heat, noise, flow of traffic, distances to be traveled?*

The investigator is now studying the possibility of eliminating steps or of taking steps away from the people performing them and giving them to someone else. He is measuring distances and wondering if it might be better to move some desks or some files; he is studying printed forms to see if they could be eliminated or improved or combined with other forms. He writes down each improvement as it comes to his mind, and by the time he has covered every step on the chart, he has uncovered quite a number of possible changes.

Step 5. Select the best practical solution. The investigator now wants to settle on what improvements he should adopt, and he wants to get his revised procedure charted on a process chart form so that people can see his new plan, can see the reduction in the number of steps, in the distances traveled, and in the time spent. He wants to get his boss's approval wants to find out how people will react to the changes he is considering, wants to double-check all along the line to make sure the new procedure is going to be an improvement, that it is going to be worth the cost of installing it, and that it isn't going to stir up any serious personnel problems.

In general it is well to develop several solutions; there may be bad

---

[5] There is a work distribution chart in Chapter 10.

holes in the one that is first choice or the boss may have reasons to reject it. It is well to have an alternative solution that is more limited in its scope. The best solution would be the one that is least costly, does an adequate job, is sure-starting, and—once set in motion—goes to completion and is completed on time. The procedure should not be complex; it does not have to cover all possible situations; its purpose is to handle routine activities adequately at the lowest possible cost.

So, once the steps that will be in the revised procedure have been chosen, the new process chart is filled out and the advantages of the proposed plan are written up.

Step 6. Put the solution into operation.   Before installing a new procedure or a revision of an old one, it is wise to be sure that it has been thought out. In the case of the procedure revision being done for practice in this chapter, it would be well to delay the installing phase of it until the investigator has covered the material in Chapter 8 on methods improvement, Chapter 9 on standards of work performance, Chapter 10 on fitting men and jobs, and Chapter 11 on human relations.

But when a procedure is going to be installed, it must be explained and justified to the people who will have to use it. They must understand the reasons for the change as it affects the processing of the work, but—more important—they must see how the change will affect them. Each man must be assured that the need for a change was not due to any failure on his part and that if some of his duties are being given to someone else or if his desk (or the files or the phone) are being moved, that he is not being stripped of authority or reduced in importance or being moved toward the exit. A change in procedure should not make a man lose face.

Sometimes a new procedure can be installed part by part and corrections made when flaws show up, or the procedure can be used in a limited area on a trial basis. Sometimes, of course, it is necessary to take out the old procedure and replace it with the new one all at one time. In any case, the procedure should be studied in advance so that, after it is set up, it will require a minimum amount of adjusting. If too much adjusting takes place after a procedure is installed, people lose confidence in it and in its installer.

Step 7. Evaluate the effectiveness of the solution.   Now that the revised procedure is in operation, what benefits have come from making the change? The investigator made a list in Step 1 of the results that he hoped to get through improving the procedure. Now he should check the operation of the revised procedure to see if these expected benefits have been realized. If some of them have not been, then he needs to find out why and make the necessary modifications. The process charts and idea sheets should be retained not only for this checkup but for use in the future whenever further improvements are being considered.

The steps of a procedure should be checked periodically to see if any steps are being skipped or any being added. If any steps are being skipped—for instance, parts of forms not being filled out—and the objective is still being reached, then such steps should have been left out in the first place. If steps are being added—particularly steps from the old procedure—it is probably because someone is overcautious and wants a double check. If these steps are not necessary, they should be removed.

Summary

Policies evolve from an organizational philosophy and effort on the part of management to establish goals and strategies. To give the organization direction toward its objectives policies must be formulated by top management. Each major department head must also develop policies for his area of responsibility that are in the context of broad company policy.

Policies are guides to action to help all levels of management in their decision making—to let them know what kind of action is expected of them and to let others know what kind of action to expect. Policies enable all levels of management to make decisions that are in line with the organization's philosophy and goals. They also give management criteria by which to judge the decision-making capability of managers on all levels. Lower level managers usually interpret policy to guide their actions although they may be involved in policy formulation if consulted by higher management.

Procedures are standing plans establishing the manner, step by step, for handling the recurring activities of the organization. They provide for coordination and control of the flow of work through an organization and cut down on the need for carrying routine matters through the chain of command for a decision.

Procedures should be designed to minimize the possibility of human error. They should be sure-starting, uncomplicated, and fitted to the people who will use them. They should not become an end in themselves or be permitted to discourage initiative and judgment. They should be examined periodically and redesigned to bring them up to date and make them more efficient.

CASE 1

Stone, Roberts and Jackson Company, a firm of stockbrokers with several branches in a large city decided to open a branch in a wealthy suburb about 35 miles from the central office. The branch manager decided to keep the office open two evenings a week so that he could more effectively serve the customers.

At this branch it is necessary for employees to drive to work since there is no public transportation available. Because of the salary ranges for lower level clerical jobs the manager has experienced difficulty in recruiting such help. Those that are employed are aware of this difficulty and they have been exhibiting considerable independence and they are difficult to discipline. The manager has been unable to convince most of them to work overtime on the two evenings a week the branch is open.

The manager sought the help of the company's personnel director. In particular he wanted to increase the salaries and the ranges for the clerical positions which were giving him trouble. The personnel director told him that this could not be done because it would mean changing the ranges for all clerical positions and, of course, it would mean increases for all clerks, not just those in the suburban branch. He went on to say that this would be too costly and that the company was not having any unusual difficulty with clerks at its metropolitan branches.

1. Should a company have a flexible salary policy to handle unusual situations such as the one depicted in this case?
2. Was the personnel director being realistic in his explanation to the branch manager?
3. What can the branch manager do to effectively operate his branch?
4. Do you feel the employees' independent behavior was attributable solely to the salaries paid?

CASE 2

You are head of the general services department made up of five sections—correspondence, stenographic, stationery, files, and reproduction. The supervisor of the filing department has just brought you this problem:

One of her file clerks, Miss Kamp, will be celebrating her 25th anniversary with the company next month—celebrating, that is, if anybody can be found who will celebrate with her. It's a medium-sized company, family-owned, and upper management pays no attention to what goes on with the people at the lower levels. The problem never came up before because the only people who ever stayed that long were a few salesmen and engineers who started with the founder (now dead) and they had their own celebration.

Miss Kamp is well known all over the office but her job and her personality haven't endeared her to anybody. In the early days of the company she was the combination mail clerk and file clerk, and she still takes full responsibility for the handling of all the important mail that comes into the house. Her job now is to get customers' folders so that new correspondence can be attached to them and turned over to the people responsible for handling their accounts. She spends her day rummaging through the work on people's desks, urging them to finish with folders right away, or to copy out what they need, or to promise them to her within the hour. She has a memory for customers' names and she knows everything that is going on in the business and who should be handling it. She is probably the most conscientious worker in the company. She is also pushy and raspy along with being speedy, efficient, and dependable.

Her supervisor has tried to stir up some enthusiasm for a filing department lunchtime party or a gift collection to give some token of appreciation for these 25 years of devotion, but the girls she approached don't want to handle it. Their reaction is, "She bugs everybody." Miss Kamp has been on the giving end of office collections for years—baby showers, bridal showers, wedding presents, housewarmings, and hardship cases. But nobody wants to pass the hat for her, and the supervisors never do any collecting.

1.　What are you going to do about the occasion?
2.　What would be the effect if you do nothing?
3.　Would this be a good time to shut off on all the collections, gift presentations, and lunchtime festivities that girls seem to spend so much time on?

CASE 3

Top management feels that there is a need for setting up in writing a practical policy covering the discharge of employees. Top management considers a discharge a serious matter and wants to avoid any unfavorable repercussions in the application of the policy. You (a personnel man) are assigned the problem of developing such a policy, also a foolproof procedure to implement it. You are to submit them to top management for its consideration. The company is nonunion.

1.　Develop and defend a policy to cover the discharge of employees.
2.　Develop a procedure to implement this policy.
3.　If this were a union shop, what might be the difference? Why?

CASE 4

Because of a tight labor market, the personnel department has been overselling jobs to prospective employees—indicating that sick leave is a right, that raises are frequent, and that they can get a day off when they need it, etc. The new men feel that they can get away with anything short of murder.

On the other hand, line management wants to get out production.

It insists that sick leave is a privilege, that raises must be earned, and that the job comes first.

After the new employees are on the job for a short time, they become resentful. They feel that they have been "taken in" if their every wish is not granted. The old employees also are demanding and availing themselves of all the privileges promised to the new ones. You and the rest of the supervisors are trying to keep everybody happy, but with little success.

1. Evaluate the actions of the personnel department.
2. Evaluate the actions of the line management.
3. Evaluate the actions of the new men.
4. Evaluate the actions of the old employees.
5. Whose problem is this?
6. How should it be worked out?
7. Set up a policy to cover the situation.

CASE 5

There is an expansion program going on within the organization. So, in accordance with the company policy of promotion from within, the company has been transferring and promoting some of the supervisors and employees from one department to another.

In the beginning this worked well, but lately it seems as if everyone in the organization is shifting from one job to another in order to benefit himself. Supervisors are pirating employees from their old departments, and employees are shopping around the various departments for better jobs. All this is resulting in confusion and is causing quite a training job. Each time someone is shifted, he has to be given some training, and his replacement has to be trained. Production is suffering.

1. What are the advantages of the promotion-from-within policy?
2. What are the disadvantages of the promotion-from-within policy?
3. How should transfers have been kept under control?
4. Set up a procedure for transferring employees.

CASE 6

The other day you walked into your unit and found two of your men fighting. Smith was beating Jones quite badly. You stopped the fight and saw that Jones needed medical attention; so you called first aid, and they sent him to the hospital. You immediately suspended Smith without pay for a week and told him that you would make a final decision after you got the facts of the case. Also you phoned Mrs. Jones and told her about her husband's being in the hospital and assured her that the company would take care of everything and that he would receive full pay while he was out. The above procedure seemed the best to follow.

When things calmed down, you started to gather the facts. According to the workers, Jones (the injured man) had been annoying Smith for several weeks and trying to pick a fight. On the day of the fight, Smith pushed Jones away from him, and Jones pulled out a knife. Then Smith really thrashed him, using self-defense as the justification.

The employees feel that Smith was in the right and Jones was in the wrong. Also that you made a mistake when you suspended Smith without pay. They feel that Jones instead should have been penalized.

You feel that you are getting beyond your depth; so you consult your boss. He goes up the line and finds that there is no policy or procedure to cover such situations.

1. What should you do?
2. What should your boss do?
3. How should fights be handled?
4. Set up a policy to show what the company's attitude should be toward fights.
5. Set up a procedure for handling fights.

CASE 7

When staff people are assigned a problem, usually the study calls for investigating, analyzing, compiling, and evaluating information, then drawing conclusions or making recommendations. When the investigation is completed, all the conclusions and supporting evidence are submitted to the assigner for his action. A report of this type is often called *completed staff work*.

Top management wants to set up a policy relating to the training of recent college graduates for managerial positions. Management wants the answers to such questions as: Should they have such a program? How specialized should the program be? What should be included in the program? How long should it take the trainee to complete the training?

Select for your project a type of business or industry you are familiar with or interested in. Write letters to representative companies in the field and try to obtain information, brochures, and outlines of their programs so that you can get enough information to enable you to make recommendations and justify them.

CASE 8

You are a second-level supervisor in the R.&D. division of a company. The company policy is that only graduate engineers or those having equivalent background may be considered for first-level supervisory jobs.

You have under your jurisdiction Sid Smith, an engineering designer. He has no college training or equivalent background, but he has such outstanding ability and leadership qualities that you promote him to the job of first-level supervisor. The other first-level supervisors in the department, as well as your boss, believe that Smith is the man for the job. The boss advised you to process the necessary papers. Smith has now been on the job for two weeks and he looks very promising. In the mail this morning you received from the personnel department a rejection of the promotion because Smith does not have the necessary background. There is a good chance that Smith will quit if he is demoted.

1.   Evaluate the company's policy. Justify your answer.
2.   What should you do now?
3.   How could the situation have been prevented from occurring?
4.   Work up a procedure to prevent similar situations from occurring.

CASE 9

The reproduction department in a large corporation handles a heavy load of security-classified documents. Lack of sufficient automatic equipment prevents the manager of the department from establishing production line techniques even with the routine blueprint operations. He has a limited budget and believes that his biggest problem is to avoid the "brush fire" type of operation associated with excessive rush requests, so he has established detailed procedures and follows them rigidly. One of these procedures is to require the signatures of section supervisors on all rush jobs.

The department manager feels that he is doing his best within his budget, although there are complaints about having to wait for service. The scheduling and engineering departments constantly complain that they can't get a "few quick copies" of their working papers and sketches. Because of the delays and the inflexible procedures, some engineers have been copying by hand their sketches and material lists. The chief engineer, wanting to put a stop to this waste of time, requested his own departmental copying machine. The request was turned down by management because all reproduction services fall within the responsibility of the reproduction department and all the machines are located in that one area.

The chief engineer believes that the inadequate reproduction service is hampering his department and decreasing output, but he hasn't sufficient records of job and time charges to prove his point.

1.   Should engineering have its own copying machine?
2.   What can be done to improve the reproduction service?

CASE 10

Because of a tight clerical labor market, the company had been making a special attempt to recruit older married women for open clerical and secretarial positions. During the last year the recruiting effort was successful and several married women were now on the payroll.

The nature of the company's business was such that employees were encouraged to take their vacations in the fall and winter rather than the usual summer vacation period. Each employee was entitled to a two-week paid vacation and over the years the company had experienced little difficulty with their informal vacation policy. The company also had a leave of absence policy to cover emergencies and other special circumstances. An employee was allowed one paid leave of absence day for each year of employment and if they were not used the employee received compensation for the unused days at the end of the calendar year.

During the month of May, three of the recently hired married women put in requests for their vacations. Each asked for two weeks during the summer as well as a third week leave of absence. They said they did not expect to be paid for the third week. When their supervisor told them that not only they couldn't have their two weeks during the summer but the requested leaves of absence were out as well, he was greeted with incredulous stares and then the spokesman for the three told him that each of them had to have their vacations to coincide with those of their husbands. All of the husbands received three weeks and the wives wanted to travel with their families. They said that if the company would not allow the requested time off they would have to resign.

All three were excellent employees and the other married women were working out very well also. The supervisor wondered what to do about the problem.

1. Should the company allow the three married women to take their vacations as requested?
2. Is the company's vacation policy outmoded?
3. If a company recruits married women should they recognize the special problems this may create?
4. Should special consideration be given to these employees?

CASE 11

A manufacturing company in a medium-sized town is being reorganized. It is a moderately profitable business that was sold because the owner wanted to retire. One of the problems facing the new management is that of having a large number of older people among the operating employees. Seven men and 18 women (5 percent of the work force) are over 60 years old. Each of these employees has been with the company more than 20 years and does not wish to be terminated. While they are doing their work to the best of their capabilities, they can't keep up with the younger employees. The company had no retirement plan.

The new owners (a large company) think that these older people should be taken care of. The new heads are anxious to work out some sort of a plan that will prepare people for retirement. They believe that too many people die within a year or two after retirement, and that this is a poor recompense for a lifetime of honest work.

1. What are some of the adjustments people have to make when they retire?
2. How can the transition be made easier in relation to each?
3. What are some of the pertinent provisions of the Social Security Act?
4. Outline a set of policies to handle the problem of the older worker.

CASE 12

One Friday morning Gloria and Joan, two friends, arrived at work together. They were going away for the weekend and each was carrying a suitcase. When they got to the time clock Gloria asked Joan to punch her in so she would not have to put the suitcase down and could continue to her desk. Neither girl noticed their supervisor, Dave Johnson, who happened to be passing the time clock just as the two girls came in. He observed Joan punching in Gloria and herself. He called to Joan and criticized her behavior mentioning the fact that the company had a strict rule which did not permit one employee to punch another employee's timecard. He went on to say that she could be fired for this infraction but that his discipline would consist of a smaller raise recommendation during the salary review period which was approaching. Joan was aghast at both the severity of Mr. Johnson's tone as well as the type of punishment. She told him that Gloria was right next to her and that she was only doing a favor for Gloria and was not attempting any subterfuge. She walked away from Dave Johnson muttering about her ruined weekend and her need to do something about what she considered unfair treatment.

1. Was Dave Johnson correct in disciplining Joan for her apparent rule infraction? Why? Why not?
2. If Joan was to be disciplined, should not Gloria receive similar disciplinary treatment?
3. Should Dave Johnson have bothered to discipline Joan at all?
4. How would you handle a similar situation?

CASE 13

You are the manager of a branch bank in a section of a large city which is now considered a ghetto area. Formerly it was a residential and retail business neighborhood. The complexion of the area has changed in a few years from middle income to a predominance of welfare recipients. There has been a marked increase in crime causing former residents to relocate. Many of the homes and stores are abandoned and boarded up.

During a normal business day it is not unusual to hear of robberies and muggings taking place, with the branch's customers the victims in several instances. As a result of these conditions, several employees are alarmed about their safety coming and going to work.

In the past month, two employees have requested transfers because they claim their families do not want them to work in this section. Both are key employees, excellent workers and have been with the bank over 10 years. You have little choice but to grant their requests for transfer, for if you don't they have threatened to resign and thus two superior employees would be lost to the bank. This leaves two vacancies that will be hard to fill. It seems that the bank's personnel department has been finding it exceedingly difficult to recruit either new or experienced employees for this branch.

Despite the conditions mentioned above, the branch is maintaining high balances in checking accounts and loans. Although many of the business accounts have moved, they continue to bank in this branch because of the years of pleasant relationships they have had with you as manager and financial adviser.

1. Should you have allowed the two key employees to transfer?
2. Could you have done anything to convince them to stay at the branch?
3. Can you help the personnel department with their recruiting efforts?
4. How will you continue to serve your customers effectively if you lose more employees and you cannot get replacements?
5. Even though business continues to be profitable, should you recommend that the bank close your branch?
6. Can a large organization such as a bank afford to stop doing business in depressed areas?

CASE 14

A group of students taking a course in management training want to get some practice in procedure analysis and design. Here is a good problem for them: Redesign part or all of the school's registration procedure. Use the information supplied in Chapter 8. Apply the seven-step problem-solving technique. Work in groups of three or four.

A representative of each group should present his group's findings, compare them with the findings of other groups, and make any necessary adjustments.

CASE 15

The president of a medium-sized company needed a new secretary since his present one was leaving to be married. After screening several applicants sent to him by the personnel department, he chose Mrs. Jane Black. She had considerable experience as a secretary and her last position was very similar to the one she was chosen for.

When she started her new job she was given the usual formal orientation program that all new employees of the company received. This program was done by the personnel department and it encompassed among other things, an explanation of all company personnel policies and how they affected the employee. These policies included such items as vacations, holidays, insurance, other fringe benefits, probationary period, and sick leave.

In relation to sick leave, the company policy clearly stated that an employee was entitled to five days' sick leave after three months of employment, which was the normal probationary period for new employees.

After being employed for 1½ months, Mrs. Black was absent for two days. When she received her next paycheck, two days' pay had been deducted. She stormed into the president's office complaining quite bitterly about the deduction and the fact that she thought it very unfair. The president waited until she was finished complaining and then told her he did not have time to discuss it with her. Two more weeks passed then Jane Black complained to her boss once again. He called the personnel manager and asked him to handle the problem. Another week passed and Mrs. Black was now complaining to anyone who would listen to her. Finally, the personnel manager called Jane Black to his office and asked her about her problem. She went into a lengthy explanation particularly emphasizing the unfairness of the salary deduction. He asked her if she had been informed of the company policy on sick leave when she was hired and she replied in the affirmative. He then asked if she fully understood that she was not entitled to any sick leave until she had been with the company for three months. She again replied in the affirmative. He then stated to her that he could not understand why she was complaining so forcefully. Jane then stated with great emphasis, "But I was really sick!"

1. Did Jane Black have a legitimate complaint? Explain.
2. Did the president handle the problem properly?
3. Did the personnel manager handle the problem satisfactorally?
4. Why do you think Jane Black complained about her salary deduction?

FOLLOWING UP ON THE JOB

Policies

1. Do you know company policy on raises? Promotions? Demotions? Transfers? Layoffs?
2. Are your departmental policies on these matters in line with company policies?
3. Do you apply policies when making decisions?
4. Do you make it a point to show your subordinates that your decisions are made in line with company policies?

Procedures

1. Are there some activities in your department that are repeated often enough to be reduced to routines and handled by procedures?
2. Do you periodically examine present procedures with the thought of eliminating steps and uncovering a better way of doing things?
3. Do you know the *why* for each step of each procedure you use?
4. Do your men know that you are following company procedures in your handling of absences, reprimands, and the like?

4 Organization dynamics

Authority and responsibility. Delegation of authority. Learning to delegate. Barriers to delegation. Span of supervision. Extending the span of supervision. Managerial attitude. Unity of command. Violations of the chain of command. The supervisor's view of the short circuit. Analyzing violations of the chain of command. Preserving the chain of command. Flexibility in the chain of command. Summary.

Even though classical organization theory is being critically analyzed in much of the current management literature, it is still a vital factor in organization life. Most large organizations adhere to its concepts of formal structure and prepare charts depicting the various levels of management and the reporting relationships of each level. The formal organization chart is still very much in use as a depictor of career tracks for budding executives and it also serves as the indicator of authority relationships and scope of responsibility for managers on all levels.

The increasing interest of behavioral scientists in organization theory has given us many useful insights in the application of traditional concepts to the day-to-day activity of the organization. Structure is recognized as one of the variables to be considered by the manager along with delegation of authority and responsibility, assignment of accountability, span of control, status, and power, among others. What is emerging is a more dynamic, cohesive, and multidimensional view of organization theory.

Given objectives, policies, procedures, and a formal structure, it becomes necessary to take these relatively static concepts and make them dynamic. It is reasonable to assume that if an organization structure evolves from the work to be accomplished then the people in the organization require direction and knowledge as to how they will get their jobs done. The dilemma that the modern manager faces in trying to get work accomplished in his area of responsibility has plagued managers through the ages. The Bible indicates that Moses had this same managerial problem several thousand years ago.

On the morrow Moses sat to judge the people, and the people stood about Moses from morning till evening. When Moses' father-in-law saw all that he was doing for the people, he said, "What is this that you are doing for the people? Why do you sit alone, and all the people stand about you from morning till evening?" And Moses said to his father-in-law, "Because the people come to me to inquire of God; when they have a dispute, they come to me and I decide between a man and his neighbors, and I make them know the statutes of God and his decisions." Moses' father-in-law said to him, "What you are doing is not good. You and the people with you will wear yourselves out, for the thing is too heavy for you; you are not able to perform it alone. Listen now to my voice; I will give you counsel, and God be with you! You shall represent the people before God, and bring their cases to God; and you shall teach them the statutes and the decision, and make them know the way in which they must walk and what they must do. Moreover choose able men from all the people, such as fear God, men who are trustworthy and who hate a bribe; and place such men over the people as rulers of thousands, of hundreds, of fifties, and of tens. And let them judge the people at all times; every great matter they shall bring to you, but any small matter they shall decide themselves; so it will be easier for you, and they will bear the burden with you. . . ."

So Moses gave heed to the voice of his father-in-law and did all that he had said. Moses chose able men out of all Israel, and made them heads over the people, rulers of thousands, of hundreds, of fifties, and of tens. And they judged the people at all times; hard cases they brought to Moses, but any small matter they decided themselves.[1]

In this short quotation from the Book of Exodus we see the problems of delegation of authority, span of control, and reporting relationships. It is also interesting to note that Moses' father-in-law was playing the role of a management consultant.

Authority and responsibility

In the traditional sense all authority and responsibility is vested in the chief executive of an organization and is delegated by him in varying amounts to his immediate subordinates, who in turn delegate to their immediate subordinates and so on through all the levels of management in the organization. This is called the authority of position and the path along which authority and responsibility go downward and accountability goes upward is known as the chain of command.

The concept of "authority of position" deserves further explanation. Chester I. Barnard in his classic work describes it as follows:

Thus men impute authority to communications from superior positions, provided they are reasonably consistent with advantages of scope and perspective that are credited to those positions. This authority is to a considerable extent independent of the personal ability of the incumbent of the position.

---

[1] The Holy Bible, Revised Standard Version, "Book of Exodus," (Thomas Nelson and Sons, New York, 1953), pp. 74–75.

It is often recognized that though the incumbent may be of limited personal ability his advice may be superior solely by reason of the advantage of position.[2]

It is quite common for subordinates to react to the authority of a superior in an organization without much regard to the person who occupies the position. Simply stated, when a vice president asks a subordinate to do something he usually gets compliance because he is a vice president. Obviously, there is no qualitative dimension to the authority of position. An individual executive who possesses considerable ability and who has a professional viewpoint along with a positive personal characteristic may have more authority over subordinates than his position may indicate in the formal structure. Conversely, the poorly performing executive may find it difficult to exercise authority even with a high position in the formal structure.

Superior-subordinate relationship. It becomes apparent that the key to understanding concepts of authority is a full awareness of the relationships of superiors with their subordinates in the formal organization structure. Positions of delegated authority in the formal organization result from the process of organizing and the subsequent development of the formal structure as depicted by the familiar hierarchial organization chart. These positions have little to do with the occupant of the position at any particular time. In other words, a company needs a sales manager and his position is shown on the formal chart. The chart also indicates his reporting relationships and the scope of his authority. An accompanying organization manual and position description will give in great detail, his duties, responsibilities, and accountabilities. Such charts and manuals have relative permanence usually going beyond the incumbency of any given individual. Changes may take place in the formal structure from time to time as the need arises for such change but the structure rarely changes when a new person is moved into the particular authority position. It is in this sense then, that we arrive at the concept of the authority of position.

While the authority vested in the position is a determinant of the exercise of authority by the superior over the subordinate, nevertheless, the ability of the superior along with his leadership style, experience, and knowledge enable him to control subordinate performance with varying degrees of success. There is no doubt that an authority relationship exists when one individual has the power to exercise control over another individual by using rewards and punishments commonly accepted in the particular organization. Given the authority of position, we find that in practice some managers are better able to exercise their

---

[2] Chester I. Barnard, *The Functions of the Executive* (Cambridge, Mass.: Harvard University Press, 1938), p. 173.

delegated authority than others. For instance, a given manager may train his subordinates more effectively, he may be better able to secure raises for them, he may have better relationships with his superiors, he may be considered fair and competent by peers, and subordinates. In short he may be a better manager and his subordinates react to this by more readily accepting his authority.

Another concept of authority that should be considered is called the acceptance theory of authority. William G. Scott describes it as follows:

Authority is proposed in this theory as emanating from those led rather than from the delegation process in hierarchial systems. This theory, as the name indicates, is based upon the acceptance by followers of the authority exercised by those in superordinate positions. The idea essentially is that authority is meaningless unless consent is secured from subordinates. Action is impossible without the willing cooperation of those who are led to act.[3]

It might be said that a subordinate allows his superior to exercise authority over him in exchange for a certain salary, a given quality of working conditions, and a certain amount of job security. If these things among others are present then the subordinate has job satisfaction and he willingly accepts the authority of his superior.

The subject of authority is a rather complex one and it will be considered further in this book. There is no doubt that the style of leadership is an important factor in the exercise of authority. But such things as a fringe benefit program, work hours, job title, and general working conditions loom large in any superior-subordinate relationship.

Delegation of authority

As an organization grows in complexity it soon becomes apparent that delegation must take place. Organization dynamics requires that authority-responsibility relationships be established so that the hierarchial structure can accomplish its objectives. The process of delegation must take place whenever a supervisor's responsibilities become too heavy for him. The only way he can do his job effectively is to delegate some of his work to others. Delegation frees him from a multitude of time-consuming tasks and permits him to give proper attention to the important parts of his job. Delegation involves authority, responsibility, and accountability.

Authority. Authority involves the right to make decisions, give orders, and expect to be obeyed in relation to work assignments. It is the right to require action of others. It is a permission to make com-

[3] William G. Scott, *Organization Theory, A Behavioral Analysis for Management* (Homewood, Ill.: Richard D. Irwin, Inc., 1967), pp. 202–3.

mitments, use resources, and take other necessary action to make possible the performance of the assigned work. Authority is described and defined in job descriptions, policies, procedures, instruction manuals, routines, and special instructions.

Responsibility and accountability. Responsibility is a double obligation: (1) the obligation to perform the assigned work in a suitable manner or to see that someone else does it in a suitable manner, and (2) accountability for its proper performance. Accountability is defined as the obligation of a subordinate to report to the delegating superior upon the exercise of authority and the performance of the assignment. The report may involve a statement of causes and grounds explaining or justifying an act, event, or circumstance. Actually, an employee is responsible for two things: performance of the work assigned, and then feedback to the boss as to the way the authority was exercised and the work performed. Accountability is being answerable for one's conduct in respect to obligations fulfilled or unfulfilled; it is a rendering of stewardship.

Generally, the activities a man has to do himself are called *duties.* The word *responsibilities* is used in this text to include his duties plus the activities he can delegate to somebody else. The process of delegation does not relieve the delegator of any responsibility, accountability, or authority. The delegator is still responsible for seeing that the work is done satisfactorily and for reporting on it to his own boss. If need be, the delegator can take back the authority and keep it, or he can give it to someone else.

Responsibility and authority must be coextensive. If a person is responsible for an activity, he must have sufficient authority to carry it out or to see that it is carried out. On the other hand, if a person has authority (permission to perform an activity or have it performed) he should be responsible for the wise use of that authority.

Delegation. Delegation is the act of transferring selected responsibilities, with commensurate authority, to one or more subordinates.

Delegation of authority should be from a superior to his immediate subordinates. Theoretically the delegation should be to the position and not to the man, but actually the kind of man determines the kind of delegation. First of all, the subordinate must be able and willing to receive the authority. To be able, he must have sufficient knowledge and experience to make good decisions and he must be able to exercise his authority so that the goals will be achieved. And he must be willing to accept responsibility.

In the second place, the amount and kind of delegation depends on the delegator; some people can't bring themselves to let go of authority. The third factor influencing delegation concerns the philosophy and attitude of the company about the level at which decisions should be made; some companies believe in holding authority close to the top.

Learning to delegate

The first problem in delegation is *what* to delegate. Each job has certain residual duties that the jobholder himself must perform. There may also be tasks too difficult, confidential, or delicate to be turned over to a subordinate. But the essential criterion is a matter of how *important* the responsibility is. The boss should delegate his less-important responsibilities in order to be able to give himself more time to devote to the more important ones.

How much authority to delegate depends upon the ability and training of the subordinate. Starting out small and increasing steadily is much better practice than throwing an unprepared subordinate in to sink or swim. Whatever the amount of authority, it must be equal to the amount of responsibility and it should be defined and published. Decisions which the subordinate is authorized to make can be divided into categories:

1. The area in which the subordinate is free to be on his own, reporting results rather than actions.
2. The area in which he can make decisions but should report them to the boss.
3. The area in which he should contact staff before making decisions.
4. The area in which he must consult the boss before taking final action.

Before a boss can delegate, he must accept the fact that his subordinates will make mistakes and that he will be responsible for them. He must be prepared to stand up and protect subordinates against criticism by others. He must not let anyone else punish them for their mistakes. He must also realize that the work isn't going to be done just the way he would do it himself. A boss who expects perfection is apt to get excuses rather than actions. If he is too meticulous, he may need to remind himself occasionally that the business would carry on without him if he should quit or die.

Teaching a subordinate to exercise authority is a matter of building up a relationship of mutual trust. The subordinate must be confident that the boss won't sacrifice him in order to escape blame. A boss must show that he's interested in results rather than details and that he's willing to help the subordinate over bad spots. A boss must be consistent in his behavior and in his decisions; otherwise the subordinate won't know what to do or what to expect.

Good management practices which a supervisor should observe when delegating authority and responsibility to a subordinate can be summarized as follows:

1. Observe the principle of the unity of command: each person should have one and only one boss and should know who that boss is.

2. Assign homogeneous tasks; that is, when making up a job, see that it consists of tasks that call for the same or similar skills.
3. Define the amount and extent of authority and responsibility involved in each job; avoid overlaps and gaps.
4. Set up standards of performance so that people know what is expected of them.
5. Set up policies and procedures—policies to guide subordinates in making decisions, and procedures to take care of routine activities.
6. Train subordinates so that they know how to manage; then rely on them.
7. Develop a control system so that work can be checked during performance.
8. Delegate authority and responsibility as far down the line as possible, so that decisions will be rendered as close as practical to the origin of the problems.
9. Be available to help the subordinates when they get into difficulty.
10. Make use of the *Rule of the Exception* so that a problem outside a person's jurisdiction is passed up the line to the point where there is sufficient authority to solve it. According to the Rule of the Exception, if the solution of a problem is not within the authority of the supervisor, he passes it up the line to the next level. If it cannot be settled at that level, because of lack of authority, it is passed up to a level at which the requisite authority exists. Here it is settled as a routine problem.

Barriers to delegation

Most managers acknowledge the need to delegate but some of them find themselves unable to let go of authority. They are responsible for the proper performance of the work and they feel that no one can do it as well as they can. Even on relatively unimportant tasks, they are unwilling to settle for a performance that is merely adequate. They insist on giving minute instructions and checking up on details. Such bosses are afraid to take a chance because they don't want to be blamed for mistakes. They lack confidence in the ability of their subordinates, but they give the subordinates no opportunity to improve by practice.

Sometimes a boss can't delegate because he simply doesn't plan his work far enough ahead to be able to line up a project and turn it over to someone else to handle. If he doesn't have it worked out in his own mind, he is unable to describe the problem to a subordinate or tell him what it is that he wants done.

Some bosses won't delegate because they enjoy the importance of being in on everything that goes on, and they feel they would lose some power or prestige if they turned over a part of the job to a subordinate. Some bosses have had unsuccessful experiences in delegating because they turned over authority without preparing the subordinate to handle it. Or they may have tried to delegate without having any standards by which to measure performance or any system of controls by which to get reports on how well the work was being done.

A boss may complain that subordinates just don't want responsibilities and won't use the authority he gives them—that all the problems come home to roost. Perhaps his subordinates find the risks are greater than the rewards. If they've been criticized unmercifully for making mistakes, they'll avoid making decisions. Or if there are ironclad procedures and rules to cover every minor matter, subordinates may be afraid to use their own good judgment.

Some subordinates complain that they just don't have enough authority to do their jobs. It's true that many bosses assign responsibilities but hold back on the authority. It's possible also that subordinates aren't using the authority they have. They may be reluctant to face up to unpleasant decisions or afraid to stick their necks out. Some people are unable to handle authority; they can't discipline themselves or they can't stand the uncertainty that goes with decision making. Sometimes the trouble is that they simply don't know what it is the boss wants.

Span of supervision

Span of supervision[4] refers to the amount of managing a person is able to do as measured by the number of subordinates reporting directly to him. The relationship of the span of supervision to delegation and to the chain of command can be seen most easily by looking at the way an organization develops from its beginnings as a shop supervised by one man.

When a company grows to the point that the president cannot personally supervise all the foremen and salesmen and accountants, he hires a production manager and delegates to him the authority and responsibility for production. He hires a sales manager and delegates to him the authority and responsibility for the sales department, and he hires a treasurer and delegates to him the authority and responsibility for finance. The president has put a link in the chain of command between himself and his workers because he could extend his span of supervision no farther.

As his business continues to expand, he turns over his work of purchasing to a purchasing manager, hires an engineer, and so on until

---

[4] Span of supervision is more commonly called span of control. The word *control* is used in this text in its meaning of establishing performance standards and then measuring performance against the standards. Control includes a checking and reporting system for information on performance.

he has 10 managers reporting to him. Then he finds that he does not have the time to plan, organize, direct, coordinate, and control the work of these 10 and at the same time take care of his own duties. This time the president appoints a vice president to help him and to take over from him the responsibility for sales, purchasing, and finance. The new vice president is an added link in the chain of command.

It can be seen then that the chain of command results from the fact that one boss can't do everything himself, nor can he keep adding indefinitely to the number of people reporting directly to him. As he directs more and more people, he exceeds his span of supervision and begins to become less effective. The span is limited by such factors as the nature of the work—its complexity, importance, and amount; the competence of the subordinates, the amount of authority that can be delegated to them, the effect of poor decisions (how much damage they could do), the availability of staff assistance, the growth rate or stability of the enterprise, the existence of policies and of objective standards for measuring performance, and a system of controls for checking and reporting information.

A first-level supervisor has a wider span of supervision than a higher level manager. In the higher levels of the organization, problems are more complex, more people are affected by decisions, and a greater variety of interests must be considered; therefore a boss in the higher levels usually has fewer people reporting directly to him than does a boss on the lower levels.

But outside of these factors that are tied to the nature of the job, there is another set of limiting factors that is tied more closely to the man. In the number of subordinates one boss can have reporting directly to him, he is limited by time, distance, attention, knowledge, energy, and personality.

Time.   There aren't enough hours in the day to do an unlimited amount of managing. For each person reporting to him, a boss has to plan assignments, give instructions, check the progress of work, and listen to problems. And in addition to supervising his subordinates, he has other managerial duties to perform—such as overall planning, working with staff departments, and attending conferences—which activities also use up his time.

Distance.   The supervisor has to keep in contact with his men even though they are spread out over large areas as in maintenance, custodian, and sales work, and in any work done outside the shop or office.

Attention.   Some people are able to attend to many activities, while other people become flustered when a number of demands are made upon their attention. Each person reporting to the boss adds to the number and variety of problems the boss has to handle and the number of decisions he has to make.

Knowledge. As problems increase in variety and complexity, a boss needs more and more specialized and technical information in order to make good decisions. People vary in their backgrounds of education and experience and in their ability to assimilate information.

Energy. Jobs vary in the amount of energy they consume and people vary in the amount of energy they can generate and expend effectively. The energy involved is both physical and mental. The mental energy or nervous energy provides the drive by which people get things done. The exhausted or half-alive supervisor can't extend himself as far as the human dynamo.

Personality. The relationship of personality to the span of control is not simply one of how effective a person is at communicating or at motivating and guiding his subordinates. There is involved also that facet of personality that enables a man to see and handle a whole project and not get mired down in the details—to keep his sights on the objective and push steadily toward it, letting others take care of the details. The boss who frets over trifles is limited in the extent of his span of supervision.

Extending the span of supervision

Each new link added to the chain of command is an additional level of supervision, putting more distance between the people at the bottom and the leaders at the top. The people at the top lose contact with the ones at the bottom and have to depend on elaborate procedures, reports, and devices for keeping informed—a tight system of controls to see that orders are carried out in the proper manner. Authority may be tightly held at the top, and a person may be better off to conform to procedure than to use his own good judgment.

In order to keep down the number of levels and maintain a short chain of command, a manager should try to increase his span of supervision; that is, he should try to do a more effective job with his present subordinates rather than create another level of management below him to handle them. Starting with the personal factors that limit him, he can get better control of *time* by planning and scheduling and seeing that recurring problems can be handled by procedures. He can reduce the drains on his *energy* by cutting down on confusion, crises, and anger. Remedies here are better planning, establishing routines, and changing his attitude toward people who give him trouble. Conflicts and hostilities become less distressing if a person makes an attempt to understand the other fellow's problems and point of view.

The demands on a manager's *attention* can be made fewer if he teaches his subordinates to use the rule of the exception—that is, to handle the normal routines themselves and bring to the boss's attention only the unusual situations outside their authority. A manager's limits of knowledge can be pushed back by study, by use of the problem-solving technique, and by use of staff help. *Personality* factors can't be changed easily but if a man becomes aware of the effect of his behavior upon others, he can do much to improve it.

Managerial attitude

There is general agreement in management literature that executive growth is enhanced when delegation is practiced. Equal emphasis is placed on the desirability of forcing the supervisor to supervise by expanding his span of supervision. As is the case with many sound managerial principles, there is considerable difference between theory and practice. In most organizations there are several variables which cause the gap between acceptance of theoretical principles and daily managerial practice.

The formal organization chart depicts a static situation in the dynamic framework of ongoing organizational activity. This does not mean that formal structure should be criticized because it doesn't inform the manager as to how he should do his job. Formal structure supports the manager in that it indicates reporting relationships, areas of responsibility, the chain of command, and who his peers are. What it does not do is indicate how he shall exercise his authority, what relationships he shall have with his peers, how he will report to his superiors, and how he will discharge his responsibilities.

To a very great extent the style of an organization is established by its leaders. If a concerted effort is made by higher management to delegate work downward and constant pressure is exercised to force supervisors on all levels to devote the major portion of their effort to the tasks of supervision by consciously expanding their span of supervision, then the climate is created for decentralized managerial activity. Effective decentralization of authority exists only where top management is convinced of its value and is willing to risk a few mistakes in order to have the flexibility that comes with having decisions made as close as possible to the scene of action.

When upper management subscribes to, and practices decentralization of authority, individual supervisors have the opportunity to exercise general supervision rather than close supervision over their subordinates. General supervision is distinguished from close supervision in the greater amount of authority delegated, in setting goals rather than giving detailed orders, in providing the training and support that enables subordinates to accept responsibility and exercise authority, in supervising by results and meeting standards, and in spending more time on long-range planning and little time doing the same work being done by the subordinates.

General supervision is not laxness; it demands results and sets up definite limits within which people are to work, but it lets the subordinate make his own decisions within those limits and doesn't hover over him clucking while he does it.

General supervision isn't a magic formula which will take care of all the supervisor's problems. Some people don't want responsibility on the job. A subordinate who has been poorly supervised and has developed attitudes antagonistic to management will not perform well under general supervision. And general supervision won't work well if there are poor relations between union and management or if there are internal conflicts. A supervisor can't very well use general supervision if upper management exercises tight controls or if his boss exercises tight controls.

A supervisor has to take all these factors into account and suit his method of supervision to the company situation, the type of work to be done, the ability and personality of the subordinates, and his own personality, ability, and experience.

Unity of command

Unity of command means that each person, from the bottom to the top of the organization, has just one boss, and no one but that boss should be giving him direct orders. In the average business this principle of unity of command—that no man can serve two masters—is violated frequently and flagrantly. Organization structure may be properly designed and policies and procedures carefully set up, and yet the principle on which the whole structure is built—and the principle with which everyone agrees—is violated left and right.

A superior has direct authority and responsibility for his subordinates; he is responsible for their actions. But if someone else is coming in and giving orders to them, that someone is assuming authority over them, taking the authority away from their boss, and leaving him with the responsibility. This is contrary to the principle that authority and responsibility must be coextensive. A person giving orders to someone else's subordinates is violating the chain of command.

Violations of the chain of command make management's job more difficult as well as less effective: the organization structure becomes distorted, authority and responsibility are no longer coextensive, people are taking orders from more than one boss, and there is no accountability for the discharge of duties and responsibilities. The supervisor finds it difficult to plan and organize the work of his department under these conditions. He can't direct his men effectively if someone else is giving them orders or if they can choose to accept one order and reject another. Coordination becomes next to impossible if other people are issuing orders, assigning work, and interfering with the planned flow of work while the supervisor is trying to set up priorities and schedules. Controlling the work of the department becomes impossible when the people who are giving the orders do not have the responsibility for seeing that the orders are carried out.

Violations of the chain of command

The chain of command is violated when one organization member communicates in an official capacity with another who is not his immediate superior, subordinate, or colleague. These violations occur in a number of ways. The big boss comes into a section and tells a worker to do a job. Or someone from a service department tells a worker that a certain job ought to be done. Or a staff specialist gets a line worker to push one of his projects. The superintendent may go directly to a trouble spot and instruct the worker to use a different method. The head of another group may come over to see how a job is progressing and start giving the worker orders about it—all this without keeping the man's immediate superior informed. Or a subordinate may go to one or all of these people and ask for directions. Thus numerous people are giving orders to the subordinates of another, and the supervisor is held responsible for work he may know nothing about and which may even be contrary to his orders.

In a well-organized business in which authority and responsibility are properly delegated, why are there so many violations of the chain of command? It is because organization merely sets up the framework for unity of command; the business of maintaining unity of command is a matter of the functioning of personnel.

Most of the violations arise from wanting to get things done in a hurry. The big boss may be in a hurry to get certain things done and be trying to save time by going directly to the worker. Again, he may want a particular job done in a certain way, and, to be sure that it will be, he thinks that he has to give the information to the worker firsthand. Or the big boss, wanting to keep close contact with everyone in the organization, likes to talk things over with the boys, and so, before he knows it, instead of just discussing jobs and working conditions, he is issuing orders on how to do things and what to do next.

Some violations can be charged to ignorance, some to failure to consider the consequences, and some to the ambition of a supervisor who is trying to take over the authority for a particular activity in order to enlarge the area of his job.

A staff specialist, concentrating on his own specialty and sometimes forgetting that it is only part of the whole picture, often oversteps his bounds and gives orders to the men under the line supervisor.

Finally, a subordinate may short-circuit his superior and seek directions from others. Some of the reasons here could be ignorance, malice, or a desire to promote his stock with someone close to the top. Or the reason could lie in the attitude of the boss. He may be unapproachable, critical, blustering, or impatient. The subordinate may be afraid to admit ignorance or to insinuate that the boss can't express himself clearly or might have made a mistake.

The supervisor's view of the short circuit

Supervisors who meet in management training conferences have a great deal to say about violations of the chain of command. They claim that short circuits lower morale in general, reduce the incentive of the person being bypassed, and cause good people to quit. They find that short cuts across the lines of authority interfere with them in their getting the work out—that a job ordered by an outsider may not get done properly and may actually result in wasted time, that outside interference unbalances the work loads, interferes with scheduling, and defeats the purpose of planning.

When supervisors gathered in training conferences discuss Case 1 of this chapter, each man seems to see the case situations existing right in his own company. Even though the case has been analyzed by a number of groups and the groups have been made up of supervisors from a variety of organizations, the answers to the questions always fall into the same pattern. To show what experienced supervisors have found to be the causes of violations of the chain of command in their own companies, their analysis of the case is reproduced here:

Situation 1: Why does employee D ask boss A instead of his supervisor U for orders and receive them?
Because:
   Supervisor U is too busy.
   Employee D formerly reported directly to boss A.
   U renders poor decisions.
   D is seeking recognition.
   A and D do not realize the importance of maintaining the chain of command.
   U avoids responsibilities.
Situation 2: Why does B, another line supervisor, give orders to employee D?
Because:
   B is in a hurry; U is not available.
   D is doing an operation in an incorrect or unsafe manner.
   Boundaries are not clear cut between the departments or sections supervised by U and B.

B wants to absorb U's section.

D is wasting materials or time.

D is violating a company rule.

Situation 3: Why does C, a service supervisor, give orders to employee D?
Because:

C sees D abusing equipment.

The distinction isn't clear between the responsibilities of the operating and service departments.

D is using inefficient methods.

U is avoiding his full responsibilities.

C wants to get a special job done in a hurry.

D is doing a job for C in payment for a special favor or job that C has previously done for D.

Situation 4: Why does E, staff specialist, give orders to employee D?
Because:

E wants to avoid the bother of explaining a project to both U and D.

U does not cooperate with E.

U is permitting staff to usurp his authority.

E forgets that he has no line authority.

E is impatient with going through channels.

E wants to make sure his project is handled promptly and properly.

Situation 5: Why does A, the supervisor's boss, give orders to employee D?
Because:

U is not available.

A likes to keep in close contact with what is going on.

A thinks he is giving advice, while D thinks he is receiving an order.

D and A are old friends.

A does not have confidence in U in relation to a special job.

A does not realize the importance of maintaining the chain of command below him.

Analyzing violations of the chain of command

When a supervisor finds that the chain of command is being violated or short-circuited, he should study each case of violation and find out the cause. Starting with himself—is he a bottleneck? Perhaps he is not issuing orders correctly or clearly. Perhaps he is not giving his subordinates enough authority and responsibility. Perhaps he has not thought through the job on which he is giving orders. Perhaps he is not explaining the why of each job. Perhaps he is too vague in giving orders or directions or possibly too precise and detailed.

Is the boss short-circuiting him in order to get a true picture of what is going on in the group? Maybe the boss is not being properly informed or is afraid that he is not. Perhaps the supervisor is filtering the information that he gives to the boss—just relaying the favorable things and suppressing or coloring the unfavorable ones. Perhaps he needs to find out exactly what the boss wants.

Why is the supervisor running into conflict with the departments that were established to provide service to him? Is there a clear demarcation between the activities of his department and those of the service departments? Perhaps he is antagonistic. Does he know how to utilize their services in order to do a better job? Do the service departments know his problems? Would an understanding with them clear things up?

As to the staff specialist—does he realize that he is stepping outside his bounds? Because the staff man is close to the top boss, is the subordinate kowtowing to him and inviting the violation?

Why are the supervisors of other departments interfering with his men? Perhaps they are impatient to get things done. Maybe they are after part of his job. It may be that the boundaries of the activities of the various departments are not clearly defined.

Why do his subordinates accept, allow, or seek directions from someone who is not their boss? Perhaps the supervisor is not giving them the recognition they want, and they are seeking it elsewhere. Maybe his orders are not clear. Maybe he is not approachable or available. Maybe he is disagreeable. Some of the workers may be out to show him up and get rid of him or get his job.

Preserving the chain of command

In order to correct and prevent violations of the chain of command, a supervisor needs to let outsiders know that he runs his department efficiently and that all work must clear through him so that he can route and schedule it. He himself must be a strong and necessary link in the chain of command and must manage his group so well that his subordinates will not be receptive to orders from outsiders.

Short circuits can often be controlled by good job descriptions and good supervision. The supervisor should examine the job descriptions to see if they:

1. State the purpose of the job and its relationship to other jobs.
2. Carefully define the duties and responsibilities of the job.
3. Define authority in relation *to what, to whom,* and *for whom.*
4. State the standards of work performance.

He can improve his supervision if he will:

1. Schedule work assignments in advance.
2. Check the progress on work assignments frequently.
3. Distribute work equally.

4. Keep subordinates fully occupied doing the work assigned to them.
5. Train subordinates to report immediately if outsiders assign work to them.
6. Be available for consultation about work assignments.

Flexibility in the chain of command

Maintaining the chain of command does not mean that all information must go all the way to the top of the organization in order to be cleared before it can be acted on. One way that the flow of information on routine matters is sent horizontally is by means of procedures, as described in Chapter 3. They follow paths laid out for them at low levels across the organization. But there are other matters, not controlled by procedures, that need to be taken care of by means of informal cross contacts that expedite the exchange of information.

People in separate chains of command need work contacts with one another. They need to get and give advice and information and coordinate their work. It would be impossible for them to take any kind of prompt action on daily problems if each matter had to be carried up the line to a common boss and then back down the other side.

Fayol's Bridge. The need for a cross channel was recognized by Fayol in his writings on management in 1916. He was particularly concerned about government agencies and the tendency to send everything

FIGURE 4–1

Fayol's Bridge for Cross-Communication

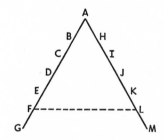

up the chain of command for decisions rather than take the responsibility for action. He illustrated his remedy as a plank, "Fayol's bridge," across the lower span of a double ladder representing two chains of command united at the top in a single boss. In the illustration, employee F and employee L are in contact, but the plank is a short cut to be used at every level in order that people may work together directly and speedily without sacrificing the unity of command.

If F and L were to stick to the channels of the chain of command, the matter of their discussion would have to be sent on a climb up the ladder of authority, stopping at the desks of managers E, D, C, and B on the way to boss A, who would send it down the other side through managers H, I, J, K, and finally to L who would work on it and send it back up the chain for the return trip. All of this might take months, the time of many people, and the need for great masses of paper work. Fayol emphasized the need for direct contacts at all levels and the necessity for the superior to grant permission for them, and to be kept informed of what went on in them.

Channels of communication. In a big organization the channels of the chain of command become overloaded and unable to give expeditious handling to the quantity of information that must be transmitted for the running of the business. To improve the situation, upper management establishes channels of communication in which staff specialists perform an active role. Permission to maintain direct contacts with people in other lines of authority is established through policies and executive decisions and through authority and responsibility assignments in the design of procedures. In this way, specialized technical knowledge can be brought to the point of application without being handed down the chain of command from boss to subordinate. And conversely, reports on the performance of the line organization at various levels are sent up the channels of communication in staff reports.

The line managers' view of these upward reports is colored by the fact that part of the success of staff lies in finding faults in line operations. Staff communications downward may become so heavy that the line supervisor complains that he is smothered by them. Staff people in direct contact with him are bringing advice, instructions, and suggestions from personnel, accounting, industrial engineering, production scheduling, quality control, and safety—to name a few.

A *policy for cross contacts.* As an example of the way an industry provides the benefits of cross contacts while still protecting the chain of command, the following section is quoted from Jones and Laughlin Steel Corporation's *Organization Planning Guides.*

Channels of Communications

Organization structure defines lines of responsibility and authority but it should not place restrictions on channels of communication. J&L permits and requires the exercise of common sense and good judgment, at all organizational levels, in determining the best channels of contact necessary for expeditious handling of work. All are urged to follow these simple rules:

1. *In making contacts*
   Be simple, direct and practicable
   Use common sense and good judgment
   Seek rather than demand information.

2. *Keep your superior informed*
   When he will be held accountable
   When differences of opinion exist
   When change in policy is involved
   When coordination with other organization units is required
   When you need his advice
   When changes in established policies may result.[5]

Summary

Classical organization theory is still a vital factor in organizational life. Behavioral science concepts have given us many useful insights in the application of traditional concepts to the day-to-day activity of the organization. Among the organization dynamics that are critical to management are delegation, span of control, and the chain of command.

An understanding of various concepts of authority enables the manager to use the formal structure to achieve organizational goals. The authority of position is not enough, for if the manager is to function effectively he must earn authority from his subordinates by virture of his performance as a manager.

There is little disagreement on the desirability of delegation as a managerial process. Nevertheless many managers are reluctant to use delegation so that they may function as managers in a better manner. Barriers to effective delegation must be overcome if a manager is to fully utilize his available resources. Increasing the span of supervision to require full-time attention to supervisory duties plus strong examples of delegation established by higher management tend to force lower level managers to practice supervision more effectively. One way to widen the span is to delegate more responsibility to subordinates and to give them the authority necessary to handle the responsibilities. Delegation does not relieve the delegator of any responsibility, authority, or accountability.

In order to delegate, a manager must plan and organize the work, train subordinates to handle it, and set up policies and procedures to guide them and controls to keep track of what is going on. He must also overcome a number of barriers that stand in the way of successful delegation. He must accept the fact that he is responsible for the subordinate's mistakes and must take the blame for them. If a boss expects perfection, is too harsh about mistakes, too interfering, changeable, or hard to get along with, the subordinate is apt to avoid using the authority.

---

[5] From the Organization Manual of Jones and Laughlin Steel Corporation (rev. ed., 1960). Used with permission.

General, rather than close, supervision is a means of developing capable subordinates and increasing their job satisfaction.

The principle of unity of command is that each person—from the bottom to the top of the organization—should have just one boss, and no one but that boss should be giving him direct orders. A person violates (short-circuits) the chain of command when he gives direct orders to someone else's subordinates.

The organization provides channels of communication in addition to those of the chain of command. It would be inefficient to send each matter up the line of authority to the top boss, down another line of authority, and then on a return trip to the point of origin. The boss, therefore, gives permission to his subordinates to maintain cross contacts with people in other chains of command—just so long as he is kept informed and approves of what they are doing.

CASE 1

How can you overcome violations of the chain of command?

1. D asks A for orders and gets them.
   What might be five or six plausible reasons?
   What should U do about each reason?
2. B gives orders to D.
   What might be five or six reasons?
   What should U do about each reason?
3. C (Service) gives orders to D.
   What might be five or six reasons?
   What should U do about each reason?

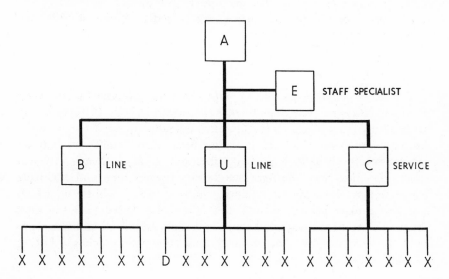

4. E (Staff) gives orders to D.
    What might be five or six reasons?
    What should U do about each reason?
5. A gives orders to D.
    What might be five or six reasons?
    What should U do about each reason?

CASE 2

You are the supervisor of the receiving department. One of the buyers in the purchasing department regularly gives instructions to your receiving clerks without keeping you informed. He phones them to tell them that they should direct certain incoming shipments through receiving inspection although your department has received no orders to that effect. He instructs them to handle paper work in new ways; recently he told them to change the procedure for handling requisitions—that they should now be attached to the receiving reports.

Each time this buyer has given your clerks instructions to do something contrary to established procedure, you have gone to him to ask why. He has three stock reasons:

1. A present procedure is too slow.
2. A procedure is being revised.
3. A modification of a procedure is being tried out.

His reasons turn out to be true, because weeks later upper management publishes new procedures that are in line with the buyer's instructions to your clerks. In the meantime you are operating in the dark.

1. How can you get control when the cause is 1? 2? 3?
2. Set up a method for installing a new procedure so that it will cause the least amount of disturbance.

CASE 3

The safety engineer has taken upon himself the authority for enforcing the safety rules in your department. He stops in about 10 times a day to check up, particularly on the lift truck operators to see if they observe the safety rules. If they are traveling more than 5 miles an hour in an area where visibility is partially obscured, he stops them and warns them. The men have become antagonistic toward him, and accidents are increasing. Recently he equipped himself with a whistle on which he blew a blast behind a truck that was going faster than the limit allowed. The operator stopped short, and the load fell off and was damaged. To make it worse, one of the cartons came within inches of hitting an employee.

The safety engineer holds you accountable for all of this. He says that the foreman is responsible for the safety of his men.

1. Is the safety man correct in his attitude?
2. Is the foreman responsible for the safety of his men? Explain.
3. Should the safety engineer take upon himself the authority for enforcing the safety rules? Explain.

CASE 4

One of your subordinates is always bypassing the chain of command and getting information from your superiors which he could have gotten from you. He is a handshaker by nature and wants to mingle with upper management as much as possible. Your superior notified you of this on one occasion. You have admonished the man several times, but it hasn't done any good.

1. What action should you take?
2. Should you advise your superior of your action?
3. Should you request your superior to handle him?
4. How can this type of behavior be corrected?

CASE 5

Quite frequently the chief enters your department and gives orders and changes the work methods of your subordinates. As a result, the men are confused and want to know who is boss. Your chief thinks that his efforts are helping production, but there is no evidence that they are.

1. What should you say to the chief?
2. What should you say to your men?
3. Even though your chief is responsible for plant production, to what extent has he the right to interfere in your department?
4. What might be some of the results of his actions?
5. How can the situation be corrected?

CASE 6

The manager of engineering purchasing supervised one buyer and five assistant buyers serving a research and development organization. Rapid growth, organizational problems, and space limitations made it necessary to separate research from development and move research to another building which happened to be several miles away. A purchasing group made up of three of the assistant buyers was sent to the new location.

The manager of purchasing decided that he should appoint one of the three to supervise the other two. His choice was between the man with the most seniority and the one with the least. The senior man had been with the company for 12 years but only 1 year on this job and he was somewhat lacking in technical knowledge. The junior man was very well qualified technically and had been doing an excellent job in his two years in the purchasing department, but he was much younger than the other two men in the group.

The manager chose the older man and gave him the title of acting buyer, but told the younger one in private to keep an eye on the new boss and make sure that things ran well.

Evaluate this type of delegation.

CASE 7

You are the manager of a large clerical department and seven supervisors report to you. One of these supervisors is causing you a problem because of his lack of appreciation of the responsibilities of supervision. The problem is complicated by the fact that he is an effective supervisor when he chooses to exercise his managerial prerogatives.

The supervisor in question is a senior employee with many years of experience who was promoted to his position as a reward for long service shortly before you came to the department as its manager. He is intent on doing nothing but the routine work and leaving all supervisory matters to wait until he finds it convenient to handle them. Naturally some of them are neglected and it is this neglect which has caused your problem.

Because this supervisor busies himself so frequently with everyday routine work he has failed to set disciplinary standards for his subordinates. As a result they are taking longer lunch hours, excessive coffee breaks, making personal telephone calls, and there is frequent tardiness. The other supervisors in your department have complained to you about these infractions since it is becoming difficult for them to control their employees effectively.

1. What can you do to motivate this senior employee to assume his supervisory role more effectively?
2. Should a senior experienced employee be promoted to a supervisory position as a reward for long service?
3. Can this man be returned to a nonsupervisory job in the department?
4. How do you handle the complaints of the other supervisors under your jurisdiction?

CASE 8

Frank Benner was the plant manager of a small electronics manufacturing company. He recently had a heated discussion with the company president about the plant porter. The porter was the lowest paid employee and it was his job to keep the floors clean in the plant and office, empty trash, keep aisles free from debris, pack shipments, and do general maintenance work. Since the plant is a small one, the porter usually completed his tasks before the workday was over and when he did, he would occupy himself reading comic books or just do nothing.

In the opinion of the plant manager, the porter performed his tasks efficiently, promptly and with a good attitude. This was the heart of the discussion Frank had with the company president. After noticing the porter's inactivity on several occasions, he told Frank Benner that the porter should always be doing something useful such as learning how to be a wireman or a solderer so that he could advance. Mr. Benner told the president that the porter had no desire or interest in learning new or additional duties since he had already tried to teach him other jobs without success. Mr. Benner could not understand the president's desire to push a man who was doing a fine job as a porter and had no ambition. The discussion ended when the president told Frank Benner to fire the porter and hire a more ambitious replacement.

1. Did the president have an unrealistic level of expectation for the porter?
2. What can a supervisor do, if anything, about an employee who is performing his job well but has no ambition?
3. Should an employee be criticized because he finishes his work assignment before the end of the workday?
4. Was the president justified in forcing the plant manager to fire the employee?

CASE 9

You are in charge of a department employing a large number of men. You have two men working on a project which, when completed, you think will help you expedite production in your department. One day while you are working on this new idea, the superintendent walks by and asks you what they are making. You explain your idea to him. He says it is very good and tells you to go ahead with it.

The next day your immediate supervisor, the general foreman, walks by. He sees the men working on your project, comes to you, and wants to know what they are making, also why they are not on some other work directly connected with production. You explain your idea to him. He tells you to discontinue the project and rebukes you for doing that kind of work without first getting his permission. You tell him that you wanted to have it in a more complete form before showing it to him and taking up his time. You also mention to him that the superintendent saw it and told you to go ahead with the job.

The general foreman has always been very obliging as well as considerate and quite friendly toward you. But apparently he is annoyed because you did not tell him of your plans, even though he knows you had good intentions and planned to tell him before anyone else. He says now that *he* is your foreman and you must do as *he* wishes. You comply with his request, and the following afternoon the superintendent pays you a visit to see how you are progressing. He sees that you have stopped the project and asks why.

1. What would you say to the superintendent?
2. If you told him the facts, would you lose your boss's friendship and confidence?
3. Is this what we call "short-circuiting"? On whose part?
4. What effect would this situation have on the two workmen?
5. Explain briefly how this situation could have been avoided.

CASE 10

Recently you were transferred from one branch office (or shop) of the company to another, to relieve Dan Davis, the second-level supervisor who is being shifted to a recently started branch. He will move within the next couple of weeks, but he is still in charge. He is supposed to be acquainting you with his job but instead is spending his time cleaning up his work. He introduced you as his successor and then left you on your own. You are becoming acquainted with your new subordinates—the first-level supervisors. From what you gather, Davis has delegated a minimum amount of authority and responsibility to these subordinates. There are no job descriptions but there are rather complete personnel records available.

Since you are from another branch of the same company, you are familiar with the overall policies. One of these policies is to delegate authority and responsibility as far down the line as possible. You believe that your predecessor's violation of this policy may be the main reason he is being shifted to the new branch; in a newly formed branch, liberal delegation is not advisable at first.

The company has been turning out a standard product (or service) for a long period. This and other conditions indicate that the decentralization of authority and responsibility is desirable. You plan to delegate as much authority and responsibility as possible to the first-level supervisors under you.

1. How would you go about finding out the what, who, where, when, and how of the work of the branch?
2. How would you go about delegating authority and responsibility?

CASE 11

You are the manager of a small pharmaceutical manufacturing subsidiary of a large corporation. The small company was purchased two years ago from its founder-owner, a chemist who continues to head the experimental work and testing of products. He supervises four bench chemists. His assistant who has been with him for 20 years is a very capable woman technician. At her request a second woman technician was added to the staff a year ago to assist her with the increased work load.

The new woman is technically qualified for the job, capable, extremely meticulous, and well liked. Both women are in their forties but the junior woman's training is quite recent.

The two women worked well together for a year. Then, while the senior woman was on her summer vacation, her assistant undertook some tidying up and rearranging which somehow snowballed into quite a project as she had some excellent suggestions for improving the layout of the lab and a few of the procedures. The changes cost very little and the chemist approved them, so they were made. While things were being moved around it seemed a good time to paint the walls, as no one had ever done much about keeping up the appearance of the place. Everyone was pleased with the improvements—everyone, that is, except the senior woman who, when she returned and saw the changes, was furious. She has been angry now for a month and everybody in the lab is extremely uncomfortable. The chemist seems unable to accomplish anything without her close collaboration. The new woman is afraid to talk to her about assignments, and the work is suffering. The new woman has taken a few days off, saying she was sick.

1. Why would the senior technician get so angry?
2. What can be done now to improve the situation?

CASE 12

Bill Boylan was a college graduate who had successfully completed the company's executive training program. At the time of his completion he was interviewed by the regional manager who was impressed with Bill's ability and who promised him the manager's job in a new branch the company was opening in a suburban city. The branch was going to be both a wholesale distribution center and a retail store for the company's many products. Bill was pleased with the offer and looked forward to the job.

A few weeks before the branch opened he again met with Joe Flint, the regional manager. At this time he was told that management had decided to give the branch manager's job to Lou Stern who had been with the company for 17 years and who at present was serving as credit manager in a large branch in the central city. The regional manager went on to say that even though Lou was not a college graduate and had not completed the executive program, it was felt that his loyal service for 17 years made him deserving of the promotion. Mr. Flint then mentioned that Bill was young and other opportunities would certainly arise. Bill was offered the assistant manager's post in the new branch and he reluctantly accepted.

It soon became apparent to Bill that Lou was not a very competent manager. He was very autocratic and petty and was constantly creating animosity among the 15 employees in the branch. Because Bill was responsible for the preparation of the weekly branch control report sent to regional headquarters, he found that the branch was running at a loss due to Lou's poor pricing of wholesale sales. He pointed this out to Lou who replied that these customers were being cultivated and had to be given a price break. Bill became quite unhappy with his job and began thinking about leaving the company for a better opportunity.

One Thursday afternoon Bill was alone in the office he shared with Lou who was out calling on customers. Joe Flint, the regional manager, came in and started questioning Bill about Lou's performance. Bill felt awkward about talking about his boss, but when Joe pressed him he merely confined his comments to material known to Mr. Flint, such as the information contained in the branch control reports. He refused to gossip about Lou, telling Flint that he was not responsible for evaluating the performance of his superior. Flint then asked him if he thought he could run the branch. Bill replied in the affirmative, mentioning that he thought he could six months earlier when Joe Flint had first offered the position to him. Flint then replied that Bill should take over effective the next day and that when Lou came back from his customer calls, Bill should fire him. Bill was flabbergasted at this request and protested vigorously, stating that it was Flint's responsibility to fire Lou. Flint replied that he didn't want to see Lou at all because he would only lose his temper.

1. What would you now do if you were Bill Boylan?
2. Why do you think the regional manager did not want to personally fire Lou?
3. Should Bill Boylan have accepted the assistant manager's job and then having done so, should he now accept the manager's job?
4. Do you feel Joe Flint has fallen down on his responsibilities in ways other than his refusal to fire Lou?
5. Can an effective superior-subordinate relationship be effected between Bill Boylan and Joe Flint?

CASE 13

Up until six months ago you were quite successful in achieving high morale and efficiency in your organization by maintaining close contact with all your employees on the several levels of supervision. Each person felt that he could drop in on you at any time and discuss his work and personal problems, and many availed themselves of the opportunity. The organization ran smoothly. You were in close contact with the work situations and could render many spot decisions which promoted efficiency.

Six months ago, because your work load and your organization were expanding rapidly, you added another assistant to your staff. You had a choice between Smith and Jones. Smith is a brilliant, aggressive, lone wolf, who often rubs people the wrong way and does not have too much respect for regulations. Jones is well liked by everyone, has average intelligence, follows directions closely, but does not have a great deal of initiative. You chose him for the job instead of the more brilliant Smith.

Since then, owing to the pressure of work, you have been too busy to keep in close touch with the lower supervisors and have been getting more and more of your information from your several assistants. As far as you know, everything is going pretty well in all departments except Jones's. The other supervisors are old-timers and their work is under control.

However, in Jones's department you are getting worried about what might develop. For two months Smith has been dropping into your office quite frequently. You have encouraged the visits because he is a good man and you want to adjust him to his new relationship with Jones. Often you give him a few hints on how to handle a job he is doing for Jones, with the result that he exerts the maximum effort and goes beyond the requirements. However, on any job handled exclusively through Jones, Smith's work is just passable. You ask him about this, and he replies that Jones either does not know how, or does not wish, to lay out a job for him in the best manner. According to Smith, Jones wants his subordinates to do just as they are told and nothing more.

Recently Jones has been complaining to you that Smith is unsatisfactory and that his work, though fundamentally superior, does not coordinate well with the work of the rest of the group, with the result that other jobs often have to be modified to fit Smith's work or Smith's work has to be modified to fit regulations. Smith knows that his work is superior and has been indicating to Jones and others that they had better follow his pattern if they want to keep up the group's efficiency.

1. What are the issues involved?
2. How should you handle Smith?
3. How should you handle Jones?
4. What are the advantages and disadvantages of the open-door policy?
5. What are the advantages and disadvantages of the chain-of-command policy?

6. How could the situation have been prevented?
7. What are the possible solutions for the problem? Which is the best?
8. Can the open-door policy and the chain-of-command policy be integrated? If so, how?
9. Formulate a policy to prevent the occurrence of similar situations.

CASE 14

You are a young dispatcher in a manufacturing plant. Your job is to release move tickets, setup requests, material requests, inspection tickets, work orders, etc. and to do it at the right time so that the schedule of work can be maintained. You have the related task of observing the progress of jobs in the shop. If they are falling behind to the extent that they should be rescheduled, then it is your responsibility to notify your boss in the production control department soon enough so that adjustments can be made in the schedule. Both your boss and the shop people wish to avoid these adjustments, which can be extensive.

Your boss tells you to watch the progress of work and to "expedite" when it begins to fall behind—that is, to tell the shop supervisor to speed up the work. You do not have that kind of authority; furthermore the shop supervisor resents any kind of pushing from outsiders. However, your boss keeps pushing you. You are in the middle.

Work out a way for handling the situation.

CASE 15

When an order is placed in the company's shop, part of the procedure is as follows:

The accounting department OKs the sales order and then makes out a work order, a copy of which goes to the engineering department, which prepares the bills of materials, specifications, and blueprints and sends them to the production control department. The production control department fills out material requisitions and sends them to the stores department where materials are apportioned. The production control department also fills out routing and scheduling sheets and sends them to the dispatcher who uses them as the basis for filling out move tickets, setup requests, inspection tickets, time tickets, etc. which he releases to the shop so that the schedule can be maintained.

Most of the time the work flows smoothly. However, emergencies occasionally arise when customers want to change their orders—either in amount or delivery date or in some details relating to design. Theoretically any such change should be the basis for initiating a change order which then should start at the beginning and go through the whole procedure, but this takes time and might jeopardize sales. The salesmen, to protect their sales, have been short-circuiting some of the procedure and going directly to the shop to tell the general foreman about the changes. (They give him a box of cigars occasionally.) He makes the changes and adjusts the affected cost sheets.

Management has been closing its eyes to the situation. You, a procedures man, see potential dangers in what is going on and want to get the situation under control by devising a procedure that will cut across department lines at as low a level as possible and still be effective.

1. What are some of the potential dangers in this short circuit?
2. Design a procedure to take care of the situation.
3. Show by example how procedures increase horizontal communication and make it unnecessary to go up and down the chain of command.

FOLLOWING UP ON THE JOB

Delegation of authority and responsibility

1. Do you plan your work well enough and far enough ahead to enable you to delegate the less-important tasks?
2. Do you know what responsibilities to delegate?
3. Do you prepare your subordinates to accept responsibility and to exercise authority?
4. Do you give your subordinates an opportunity to use their initiative and judgment?
5. Do you criticize mistakes in a way that discourages subordinates from exercising initiative or accepting responsibility?
6. Do you give your subordinates the information they need to make good judgments?
7. Do you have policies to guide subordinates in making decisions?
8. Do you have standards by which subordinates can measure their performance?
9. Do you have controls by which to keep informed of performance?
10. Have you checked your responsibilities with your boss?

Span of supervision

1. What activities take up most of your time on the job?
2. Can you share or delegate some of your activities?
3. Can you increase your span of supervision in relation to the factors of distance, time, energy, personality, attention, and knowledge?

Organization dynamics

1. Do you violate the chain of command?
2. Do your workers receive orders from people in other units?
3. Do your workers solicit orders from people in other units?
4. Does your boss short-circuit you?

5. Do your subordinates short-circuit you?
6. Do your workers keep you informed when they receive orders from outsiders?
7. Are you available when workers need directions?
8. Do your workers avoid coming to you for directions?
9. Do you always know what jobs your workers are doing?
10. Do you check the progress of work frequently enough?
11. Do you schedule work carefully?

5 Communicating more effectively

The supervisor's area of communicating. Communicating is an art. Words are tricky. Learning to listen. Distractions muddle orders. Putting across a new idea. Difficulties in discussion. Unfavorable attitudes build up listener resistance. Good attitudes facilitate understanding. How to give orders. Getting orders from the boss. Keeping the boss informed. Lack of understanding between subordinate and boss. How bosses can promote more effective communicating. The flow of management information. Communication systems. Summary.

The rationale for organization is to develop a cohesive unit which can achieve a common purpose. The initial step toward the accomplishment of this common purpose is communication. Obviously all parties involved in goal achievement must know and understand the goals before they can do anything about them. The effectiveness of the manager hinges to a great extent on his ability to communicate these goals to subordinates and to encourage feedback indicating positive response to his direction.

The field of communicating takes in all the ways in which men try to impart their ideas to others—spoken words, written words, pictures, gestures, even silence or a raised eyebrow. Communicating in business may be face-to-face, by phone, memos, letters, bulletins, reports, house organs, notices in pay envelopes, etc. The emphasis on the importance of communications in business raises the questions: What are these messages that are being sent? Why is it so important that they be understood and accepted? What are the hindrances to the giving and getting of information?

The supervisor's area of communicating

It's the supervisor's job to get things done through and with people; thus his effectiveness depends on getting ideas across so that people understand what to do and are willing to do it. His is face-to-face communicating; it is the talking and listening *about which he can do something.*[1]

In order to gain skill in communicating, he must have an understanding of those things that get in the way when a man tries to impart his ideas to another. Why is it that people don't get what is said to them and do get meanings that were never intended? Some of the trouble arises because people attach their own meanings to words. Some comes from the way the words are arranged in the sentence, and the sentences arranged in relation to one another. Some of the difficulties can be charged to the interference of distractions; some have their roots in feelings, attitudes, backgrounds, and experiences.

He told me: "Now hear this. That number has to go on every job you handle and don't ever forget it." So I copied the number down and I've put it on every job just like he said. I didn't know I was supposed to put a different number down every time. I didn't know those numbers on the sheet were contract numbers. I thought I was supposed to use my special number on everything I handled.

It's up to the supervisor to make himself understood and to find out what the other fellow has in mind. Poor communication results in stupid mistakes and costly failures. The subject, therefore, is a profitable one to investigate.

The supervisor communicates all day long. He is communicating when he is interviewing applicants and trying to find out if they can and will do the work and if their personalities, backgrounds, interests, ambitions, and goals fit them for the job. His manner of talking gives the applicants a picture of the company and of the job and of the kind of boss this supervisor would be. Can he be relied on for a square deal? Is he approachable, considerate, friendly? Does he describe the job in an understandable way?

The supervisor is communicating when he introduces new employees to the department and to the job, teaches them, trains them, finds out their job interests, encourages them to develop their talents, lets them

---

[1] The emphasis in this chapter is on talking and listening because the supervisor does so much of it. He can do something about his reading and writing skills also. A study of this chapter will alert him to the causes of misunderstandings. A study of technical writing will help him improve the structure and effectiveness of his written orders, instructions, reports, memos, disciplinary records, warnings, answers to written grievances, and so forth. For an easy start in the evaluation and improvement of business writing, see William R. Van Dersal, *The Successful Supervisor in Government and Business* (New York: Harper & Row, Publishers, 1962). His chapter on writing shows how to use the Fog Index to measure readability of a 100-word sample. Or see Rudolph Flesch, *The Art of Readable Writing* (New York: Harper & Row, Publishers, 1949).

know that he is interested in them as individuals and that he wants to help them get ahead on the job.

He is communicating when he delegates authority and responsibility to them, directs their efforts, praises their work, points out mistakes, lets them know how they are measuring up to the standards, listens to their gripes, answers their questions, counsels them in merit rating interviews, disciplines them, settles grievances, asks for their suggestions, gets them to participate in improving job methods and in putting changes into effect.

He is communicating when he makes assignments, gives orders, explains standards of quality and quantity, checks the progress of the work, gives assistance, suggestions, or encouragement, sells management's ideas, interprets policies, explains and enforces rules, gives training in safety, assigns overtime, or asks for extra effort.

Almost everything the supervisor does involves communication. And the communicating may be done in a way that antagonizes the subordinate and causes him to be suspicious, resistant, and resentful, to do a minimum and to pass the buck. Or the communicating may be done in a way that makes the subordinate feel pride in his work, responsibility for his part in it, and willingness to do his best.

The supervisor should suspect that his communicating is at fault whenever jobs are not carried out according to his instructions, when his people are working at cross-purposes, when they work grudgingly, refuse to accept changes, duck their responsibilities; and when misunderstandings, gripes, and grievances interfere with production.

Communicating is an art

Communicating is an art by which a person finds a way to reach the mind of another and share with him an idea or create an understanding. The sender of a message may write it or speak it, or he may draw a picture of his idea. Whatever art form he uses to carry his message, he must learn the principles and techniques of the art and the rules governing structure and arrangement of its parts. In writing he must depend on words and the way he puts them together to convey the message he intends. In speaking, he can reinforce his meaning with tone of voice, motions, and facial expression; he can see how the message is being received and make adjustments to fit the receiver.

For a supervisor, communicating is an art to be studied and practiced. When he communicates a message it is for the purpose of getting a response from the receiver—getting him to do something or to know something or to accept something. Whether the communication will be successful depends in great measure on the meaning which the receiver attaches to it. Dictionary meanings of words don't tell what meanings the receiver has in mind. The words themselves are merely symbols to which each person attaches meanings of his own.[2]

Study of communication includes a study of the characteristics of human behavior and the factors that influence a person's reaction to the messages he receives. Figure 1–2 in Chapter 1 illustrates why one person will never perceive anything exactly as someone else would or exactly as he himself would perceive it at some other time or place, in some other state of mind, or under other circumstances.

Predicting the reaction of a person to a message is the basis of persuasion. The TV commercial is pitched to a particular type of customer and designed with the expectation of getting a favorable response. The supervisor has an advantage when it comes to predicting the responses of his subordinates to a message: he is close to them and to the group that influences them. If he was once a member of that group, he knows its system of values—the things that are important to it. He can choose words, examples, and approaches that fit their experience; he can shape his communication in terms of their attitudes.

Words are tricky

When a speaker uses a word, he is inclined to assume that his listeners would use that word just the way that he is using it. Few people take into account that the 500 most used words in the English language have more than 14,000 meanings listed in the dictionary. There is a real risk that a word used one way by the speaker will be interpreted another way by the listener.

The word "job" for instance is a simple one. What trouble could there be with it? The job analyst considers a job as a group of tasks or duties which are performed by a person. The employment interviewer normally takes the word "job" to mean a vacant position that some applicant will be hired to fill. To the supervisor of a production department a job may mean order no. 402 for 500 pieces to be fabricated by Wednesday.

A worker says, "I'll be glad to get off this job; it's driving me nuts." What does he mean? What is the supervisor going to think he means? What happens if the supervisor is thinking of job no. 402 (which has really been a tough one) and he replies, "Tomorrow's your last day

---

[2] For a discussion of communication theory, see David K. Berlo, *The Process of Communication* (New York: Holt, Rinehart & Winston, Inc., 1960). His treatment of communication as a process emphasizes its similarity to the learning process in its use of stimulus, response, and reward as builders of habit patterns in responding to messages.

on it and I hope it's a long time before you get another one like it."
But the worker wasn't thinking of no. 402; he was just talking about
knocking off work at 4:30 and getting a chance to relax after a hard
day. So here's the supervisor trying to fire him and blacklist him.

How can the supervisor prevent things like this from happening?
Once a misunderstanding has occurred, how is he going to spot the
trouble, get it out into the open, and clear it up before its gets any
worse?

He can't go around all day defining terms and asking his employees
to define theirs, but he can detect misunderstandings by improving his
listening and keeping in mind the questions: *Do I really know what
he is talking about? Does he know what I am talking about?*

Learning to listen

The supervisor is lucky that his communicating is the face-to-face
kind, because he has the opportunity to detect and correct misunderstandings before they become serious. Communicating in writing enjoys
no such advantage; the words stand there to be read over and over,
to be interpreted one way or another according to the background,
experience, or mood of the reader. It is no accident that delicate negotiations are carried on in face-to-face contacts so that each participant
can sound out and observe the reactions of the other, make adjustments,
ask questions, and tailor the presentation to fit the person receiving
it.

The supervisor who misunderstood the worker's statement, "I'll be
glad to get off this job," needs only to be an observant listener in order
to catch the mistake. The worker's face may register surprise, anger,
consternation, or some other emotion that seems unwarranted. Whatever
he will say or do at this time just won't make good sense in the situation
as the supervisor sees it. Here is where the supervisor has to assume
that there has been a misunderstanding, and he can ease some of the
tension by taking the blame for it. The other fellow is probably upset
and it won't help any to insinuate that he's stupid and can't understand
plain English. "Did I say something that didn't sound right? I didn't
intend to," will spread oil on the waters while the rescue boat is operating. It is much easier to straighten out a mistake in an atmosphere
of friendliness than in one of bitterness.

The supervisor has to ask questions in a manner that inspires trust
and draws out information. He has to resist the inclination to think
that if he just repeats what it was he said before (and what caused
all the confusion) and does it in a louder voice, everything will be all
straightened out.

Distractions muddle orders

In management training conferences, role playing serves as an excellent means of awakening supervisors to the realization of how their words and meanings are misinterpreted. In a role-playing interview as part of a training conference, two supervisors discuss and try to solve a problem when each knows only his own side of it. (The audience of supervisors knows both sides.) When tape recordings are made of interviews, the supervisors are always surprised by the playbacks. ("Did I say that?") Before the playback, the whole group discusses the way the two supervisors handled the interview: How did they define the problem? What solution did they work out? What course of action did they agree on? The listeners are never in complete agreement. ("He said. . . ." "That wasn't what I thought he said." "You promised him a raise." "No, I only said that. . . ." "You were threatening him." "I only told him. . . .") The two who did the talking are positive that they didn't say the things being attributed to them. Each wonders how everybody missed the point. When the tape is played back they want to borrow it in order to find out for sure what happened to the things they intended to say and how they could have missed the import of the other fellow's words. They are surprised to learn that a part of the time they were just talking *past* one another rather than *to* one another.

If it were possible for a supervisor to make a tape recording of the orders he gives, he would discover on the playback that there are gaps in the information: things he thought he said just aren't there; ideas he had all worked out in his mind and ready to pass along got lost somewhere. Some of the gaps could be charged to having his attention distracted by phone calls or something interesting going on across the room. Some thoughts are lost because words were drowned out by noises or weren't spoken clearly and sounded like something else.

As the supervisor studied the recorded instructions, he could see where he failed to pass along some important pieces of information and he could understand why his subordinates would run into trouble on these points. But how about instructions that are complete? Why are they misunderstood?

Putting across a new idea

A man who teaches school for a living knows the amount of effort it takes to put across a new idea. He must first set the stage for it, tell what is the need for it, distinguish it from things that it resembles and might be confused with, then express it one way, give examples, ask questions, express it another way for those who might be confused by word meanings, hit the high points again, and then summarize the whole business.

An idea that the supervisor has been working on for weeks becomes so familiar to him that he may assume that the listener should be able to keep right up with him. Actually the poor fellow may not even be able to figure out what this new idea relates to. Veteran public speakers have a three-step formula for putting across a message.

1. *Tell them what you're going to tell them.*
2. *Tell them.*
3. *Tell them what you told them.*

People are not able to grasp many ideas at a time; a motorist getting travel directions has trouble remembering more than three turns in the road. If information is given in big doses, some of it spills over and is lost. The order giver needs to observe the listener's reactions to see if he is getting the order. If the subordinate has lost the thread of the story, the speaker can summarize, tell the relationship of the new idea to familiar ideas, give examples, and repeat the key points in different words than he used before.

The listener's mind may be occupied with problems he is going to have in carrying out the order. The order giver needs to observe the attitude of the listener to see whether he is accepting the idea or building up objections to it. If the worries or objections can be brought out into the open, the explanation can be presented in a way that will take them into account.

Here is where it is important for the boss to be a good listener, to be approachable and friendly so that his men will ask questions about what is puzzling them. The boss can't fill in gaps in the information until he learns where the gaps are; he needs to ask questions himself and to be alert to the meaning and feeling of the answers and then in terms of these answers to modify what he says and how he says it. This is *feedback*—the principle by which a machine checks on its own performance and corrects it; this is the way the thermostat on the wall regulates the amount of heat from the furnace according to the information (the temperature of the air) fed to it. Accuracy and speed of comprehension increase with the amount of feedback in conversation. Experiments indicate that certain types of information cannot be communicated accurately without feedback—that is, without permitting the receiver to ask questions and get answers to them.[3]

---

[3] Dr. Alex Bavelas's experiments at MIT referred to in George Strauss and Leonard P. Sayles, *Personnel: The Human Problems of Management* (2d ed.; Englewood Cliffs, N.J.: Prentice-Hall, Inc., 1967), p. 233.

When people like and trust each other and know some of the diffi-culties involved in communicating ideas, they can question and listen in a way that will result in understanding.

Difficulties in discussion

The supervisor has to deal with many complaints, requests, and ex-cuses that sound unreasonable to everyone but the person making them. When the supervisor is listening to a complaint that sounds foolish or unfounded, he asks himself, "What's wrong with this person or situation to make him say such a thing?" Maybe there isn't much wrong with the person except the way he is expressing himself. It could be that his statement is true from the angle that he is looking at it. Each person sees a situation with himself at the center; so his point of view is going to be different from that of the next person.

If a girl employee complains, "This is an unfriendly company," the supervisor might wonder what quirk in her personality keeps her from making friends among so many congenial people. Rather than contradict her and point out all the instances of friendliness he is thinking of, he should ask himself, "Is she making a sweeping statement to express a couple of instances of unfriendliness?" He might ask her, "Are we talking about everybody in the company or just a few people who give us a lot of trouble?" Expressing the question that *we* (not *you*) are having trouble will make it unnecessary for the girl to build up her story; she will probably feel free to admit that it's the two girls next to her who are making her life miserable. The essence of this type of questioning is to avoid any display of superiority, criticism, amuse-ment, or disbelief. The purpose is to get information and avoid any contest in which the employee feels obliged to defend his stand.

Most supervisors can recall occasions on which people have argued over sweeping statements, contradicting one another, stirring up ill-feel-ing, and wasting a lot of time. In many of these cases, a simple question asked in a helpful way would have exposed the fact that the sweeping statement was intended simply to express a particular instance, and the speaker hadn't considered the matter any further than that. A ques-tion instead of a contradiction will often bring to light that there is no real difference of opinion—the seeming difference is simply a matter of stating the problem.[4]

---

[4] For an excellent discussion of sweeping statements and talking past one another, see Irving J. Lee, *How to Talk with People: A Program for Preventing Troubles That Come When People Talk Together* (New York: Harper & Row, Publishers, 1952).

For gaining an insight into the emotional impact of words, read S. I. Hayakawa, *Language in Thought and Action* (New York: Harcourt, Brace & World, Inc., 1949).

Facts or conclusions? It makes a man angry to have someone dispute a fact—something that can be verified, weighed, measured, or attested to by records or by unimpeachable witnesses. Some of the ill-feeling that enters into discussions arises because a man thinks his facts are being contradicted. Actually, many of the statements that people offer as facts are really opinions, inferences, conclusions, or judgments.

If a supervisor says to his boss, "I need more men to get job no. 402 out on time," he regards this statement as a fact. If the boss replies, "I don't think you do," it sounds like a contradiction of a fact. If they will move the discussion over to facts, they might set it up this way: Job no. 402 is half finished. Production records show that it took 100 man-hours to do that half. Continuing at this rate, it would be only three fourths completed by the deadline.

It may still turn out that the only way to finish on time is to use more men, but if the problem can be handled by considering facts rather than arguing about conclusions, at least the door hasn't been shut on other possibilities and there will be less emotion involved in the exchange of ideas. When a man's conclusions or opinions are attacked, he is inclined to feel that he is being attacked personally, and he concentrates his attention on defending himself and his position.

Unfavorable attitudes build up listener resistance

The discussion thus far has dealt with the communication of ideas which were fairly logical to start with but became distorted either at the sending or at the receiving end. The supervisor in his communicating will encounter thinking on the part of subordinates that isn't logical—thinking in which feelings, attitudes, and prejudices strongly influence the selection and weighing of facts as well as the inferences and judgments that are made from them.

Employees may feel that the supervisor is discriminating against them, that he is the cause of all their troubles on the job. They may build up hostility and resentment about changes made in their jobs. They become so stirred up emotionally that they simply do not hear explanations or arguments that run counter to their beliefs. People hear what they expect to hear, because their emotions and attitudes filter out evidence that contradicts their stand. Figure 5–1 illustrates the barriers between the sender and receiver of a message.

A subordinate who dislikes and distrusts his boss will build up a resistance to understanding him. Such an employee will be so intent on getting the most unfavorable interpretation of every communication that he won't hear what the boss is actually saying. A person's problem may be based more on feelings than on facts, but those feelings look like facts to him, and he'll go to some lengths, often unconsciously,

FIGURE 5–1
Communicating

Barriers to understanding and how to penetrate them. The supervisor needs to recognize these barriers in himself as well as in others and to cultivate the attitudes and techniques that will enable him to understand and be understood.

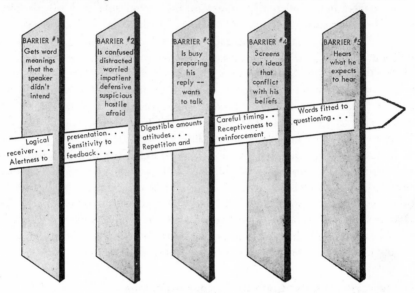

to make them look like facts to others. The subordinate doesn't feel that he is being unreasonable; he feels that the boss is being unreasonable. It takes wise and sympathetic listening and questioning on the part of the supervisor to find out what is actually on the person's mind, to overcome the resistance, clear the channels of communication, and arrive at a better understanding of each other's point of view.

Good attitudes facilitate understanding

The supervisor can't spend his day playing psychiatrist; he has work to get out. Luckily many of the day's work assignments are routine and require only a few words to get them rolling. His subordinates are so accustomed to the assignments and the words that go with them that they are listening only to find out his mood and assure themselves that everything is going along all right. The supervisor's manner when he is handing out assignments communicates some kind of emotion to his workers, and it will have an effect—good or bad—on their will to do the work.

If he is grumpy, surly, threatening, or sarcastic, his subordinates will feel imposed upon, angry, resentful, uncertain, afraid to ask questions, and unwilling to use their initiative, stick their necks out, or do anything to please him. If, on the other hand, he knows his people as individuals with their good points and their shortcomings and their needs for reassurance, friendliness, human warmth, and importance, he can at least let them know he's not mad at them. In the few seconds that it takes to make an ordinary assignment, he may be able to convey the feeling that he knows they can do the work well and he expects that they will want to do it well. And most people tend to do what they feel is expected of them.

Subordinates who feel secure in their relationships with the boss— who respect and trust him—are not out to misunderstand his words and misinterpret his intentions. They will overlook occasional slips on his part—things he wouldn't have said (or said that way) had he taken time to think them over. They know he's under pressure and that everybody has to let off steam once in a while.

If they have good attitudes toward him, they will work with him to achieve understanding. The supervisor builds up this attitude of receptiveness in his subordinates by demonstrating to them in his words and actions that he is interested in their welfare, understands their problems, and appreciates them as people. The better his relationships with his subordinates, the more they will help him in his job of communicating with them.

How to give orders

Ask some supervisors how they give orders and they say they don't— or at least seldom—find it necessary to order anyone to do anything. They have the work set up so that people know what they're expected to do and take the responsibility for getting it done. When work has to be assigned piece by piece, these supervisors say they issue their orders in the form of requests. But the directing of subordinates is an essential part of supervising, and authority is the right to give orders and have them obeyed; so the word "orders" is used here to include all the ways of assigning work and instructing subordinates how to do it.

Whether the supervisor will say, "I'd like you to take care of this when you have time," or "I want this finished by four o'clock" depends on the circumstances and the kind of person receiving the order. Fitting the order to the receiver means knowing the extent of his competence, remembering his strong and weak points in previous situations, knowing his attitudes and how he is motivated. Fitting an order to the receiver requires that words be used in the sense that he uses them. ("Hit it hard" means one thing to the dentist and something quite different to the stakedriver.) Examples and explanations used to put across the meaning of words must refer to something within the experience of the listener. The amount of instruction and attention to detail must be suited to the receiver and the situation.

In a candy factory the workers took turns working a late shift to clean the sticky residue out of the machines. The foreman assigned a new man to take a turn, and left him with the same three words of instruction that he'd been using very successfully on the others: "It's all yours." The candy hardened in the machines overnight into an expensive mess.

An order giver must organize his presentation of ideas into a logical pattern based on his knowledge of *what* is to be done and *why* it is to be done, and how much leeway the subordinate has in choosing his method and making decisions. In delivering this information, the supervisor may have to divide it into digestible portions, making them clear one at a time by asking and answering questions. If a supervisor will invite questions as he goes along, he can modify his presentation in terms of the difficulties revealed in the answers. Repetition helps to clear up misunderstandings, particularly if different words and examples are used; but it is well to let the listener know that what he is learning *is* a repetition—a reinforcement of what was said before and not a presentation of an additional new idea.

The supervisor has to reconcile himself to the fact that, no matter how careful the presentation, a certain amount of the information won't get through and another portion of it will be forgotten. He should spot check while the order is being carried out. Then if the job is going wrong because of a misunderstanding, he can find and repair the weak spot in the communicating. An order will be carried out more intelligently and willingly if the subordinate knows why he was chosen to do it, how important it is, and what it will be used for. People want to know that what they are doing is important. Man has a basic need to feel that what he is doing is worthwhile; it is one of the factors that motivates him to do a good job. He also wants to know the why of quality requirements: What does the part have to fit to? What are these figures going to be used for? How legible does this reproduction have to be?

If safety instructions go along with the job, the supervisor can give them in a manner that shows he's interested in the well-being of the subordinate.

Getting orders from the boss

When supervisors taking a management training course discuss the topic of communicating, the discussion is always brought around to what they find wrong with the oral orders they get from their bosses.

The faults they find with their bosses' order giving will cover a range like this: too vague, not thought out clearly, too hurried, too detailed, not complete enough, too much how and not enough why, too much in one package, not practical, mixed up, indistinct, interrupted by phone calls. Some supervisor will say, "I go out of his office not knowing what he wants and just hoping I can make a lucky guess." But supervisors who can't find out what the boss wants undoubtedly have under them workers mumbling, "Why didn't he say what he meant? How was I to know? I'm no mind reader."

Each man is inclined to think what he is saying is crystal clear, just like taking a detailed picture out of his own mind and setting it up on an easel in the listener's mind. It's natural for a supervisor to say of his boss, "I can't find out what he wants; he doesn't make himself clear," and then of his own workers: "They're either stupid or inattentive or stubborn, or they couldn't make the mistakes they do after I've told them exactly what I have in mind."

Keeping the boss informed

The supervisor should supply his boss with complete and accurate information for the boss to use in making decisions, issuing orders, and reporting in turn up the line to his own boss. A subordinate has an obligation to his boss (accountability) to report on the way he is carrying out his responsibilities and using his authority. One of the difficulties in carrying out this obligation is the unexpected demands that a boss may make for information that he wants right away because upper management has called upon him to account for some item or condition brought to light in a control report.

A man has to protect his boss from being caught unaware of, and uninformed about, things he holds the responsibility for. But the supervisor should not be called upon to produce instantaneous information 100 percent correct on matters that do not in themselves require such record keeping. If the boss should need to ask for such figures, the supervisor should be able to tell him that he doesn't have them and that it will take a certain length of time to gather them and prepare the information. Keeping the boss informed should not obligate the supervisor to have on tap all kinds of assorted information just as a precaution in case the boss should suddenly ask for it. Collecting and compiling information unnecessarily is a waste that can be avoided if the boss will give the supervisor time to prepare special reports.

But there is a great deal of regular day-to-day information that the supervisor is expected to supply to his boss. The boss needs to know, for instance, how work is progressing, what difficulties are being encountered, what improvements are needed, how orders are being carried out, if any actions of management are getting unfavorable reactions at the work level, and if there is any trouble brewing.

It can be seen from this communication between a man and his boss that the channels of the chain of command exist not only to send orders down from the top to the bottom of an organization, but also to pipe information back up the same line—each man to his boss.

Coloring the information. If upward communications are to fulfill their purpose, everyone in the chain of command must recognize those human traits that tend to distort information. There is a natural tendency to keep the boss happy by overemphasizing the good aspects and playing down the unfavorable aspects of a situation. It is human nature to distort information so as to escape blame—to color up reports so that the boss will think you're on the ball, to filter out anything that might make you look careless, stupid, or unfit for the job.

The amount of censoring, filtering, and coloring of information hinges upon the kind of relationship a man has with his boss. If the relationship is one of mutual helpfulness, a man can admit that he made a mistake, that things aren't going too well at the moment, that it looks like trouble ahead and something needs to be done about it. If a supervisor doesn't have to phrase his reports in terms of protecting himself, he can send up the channel the kind of information that upper management needs to make its decisions and to formulate its communications in terms of the people who will receive them.

Lack of understanding between subordinate and boss

Research reports indicate that there is a sad lack of understanding between man and boss. One survey[5] of high middle-management men and their bosses revealed that man and boss had not reached a good understanding of the duties of the subordinate's job and that they had even less agreement about the qualifications required to fill the subordinate's job, the future changes that would affect his job, and the difficulties that he was encountering in doing the job.

Without such an understanding, a manager doesn't really know what his boss expects of him, doesn't know how his performance is going to be measured, and doesn't have any way of knowing how well he is doing or what he should be doing differently.

Another survey[6]—this one of foremen and their bosses—revealed that

---

[5] Norman R. F. Maier, L. Richard Hoffman, John J. Hooven, and William H. Read, *Superior-Subordinate Communication in Management* (American Management Association Research Study No. 52) (New York: The Association, 1961).

[6] Chester E. Evans, *Supervisory Responsibility and Authority* (American Management Association Research Report No. 30) (New York: The Association, 1957). Based on this report is an article by Lee E. Stern, "The Foreman's Job. What Are the Boundaries?" *Supervisory Management,* Vol. 3, No. 7 (July, 1958).

they didn't agree on the extent of the foreman's authority. The foreman in most cases thought that his authority was more limited than the boss said it was. On some matters the foreman thought that he had more authority than the boss said he had.

A survey[7] of what foremen and general foremen *think* their subordinates want from the job showed little agreement with what the subordinates themselves said they wanted. The bosses overestimated the importance subordinates attach to economic factors and underestimated the importance they attach to human factors: such things as getting along well with boss and fellow workers and having a chance to do interesting and good quality work. If a boss is misinformed about what his subordinates consider important on the job, he doesn't know what motivates them to high performance.

Barriers to understanding.   In addition to the ordinary hindrances in the way of getting information, there are a number of other barriers that make it difficult for a man to achieve understanding with his boss. Supervisors worry about the existence of these barriers and they bring them up for discussion in management training conferences. It is from such conferences that the material for this discussion was derived.

Fear seems to be a very important barrier to the free flow of information. The relationship of a man to his boss is not a free and easy one. A man is dependent on his boss for security, status, recognition, and success on the job. He wonders if he's pleasing the boss and he worries about what the boss thinks of him.

Supervisors admit that they are afraid to ask questions of the boss— afraid of appearing dumb or insubordinate. They are afraid to doubt the infallibility of information coming down the line through the boss and afraid to raise objections to the boss's ideas even though the objections would be valid. Many of these fears seem to come from lack of security.

Supervisors tend to feel that the boss looks with favor on the bearer of good news and with disfavor on the bearer of bad news; and nobody wants to look bad in the eyes of the boss. Nobody wants to tell the boss about failures or mistakes. A man looks like a blunderer if he tells his own mistakes, and he's an informer if he tells someone else's.

Some supervisors say their bosses' attitudes tend to shut off communicating. The bosses either have a "just-do-as-you're-told" attitude or they act bored or they seem to be too busy to listen ("Can't spend all day sifting through a lot of chaff and chatter just to get a few grains of useful information").

---

[7] Robert L. Kahn, "Human Relations on the Shop Floor," in E. M. Hugh-Jones (ed.), *Human Relations and Modern Management* (Amsterdam: North-Holland Publishing Co., 1958). This survey is summarized in Rensis Likert, *New Patterns of Management* (New York: McGraw-Hill Book Co., 1961), pp. 49–51.

Or the bosses insinuate that the subordinates can't see the whole picture or aren't intelligent enough to understand it. Some bosses think they don't need to be told because they already know what subordinates think. Some bosses are not receptive to information because they lack open-mindedness. Some resent having their decisions questioned by subordinates. Some bosses like to avoid reality—no news is good news; what they don't know won't hurt them, and they don't want to get involved in the personal problems of their subordinates.

On the other hand, some supervisors are not interested in communicating; others do not see the importance of passing along information either up or down the line. Some supervisors stop communicating up the line because no action was taken on previous communications they sent up. Some supervisors won't communicate because they are suspicious of upper management.

How bosses can promote more effective communicating

In order to promote more effective communicating, management men must realize the value of the free flow of information and establish a climate in which truthfulness and openness can prosper. A relationship of helpfulness and trust between man and boss is needed all the way up and down the chain of command if people are going to overcome those human failings that cause them to doctor up information as they pass it along.

Bosses must realize that their own attitudes determine to a great extent the kind of information they will get from their subordinates. It takes courage for a subordinate to tell his boss the whole truth and nothing but the truth; if the boss has a bad reaction to it or shows displeasure toward the bearer of the news, then the diet of information is apt to be cut down and flavored to suit the boss's taste. Information can be selected that will please him, doubtful situations can be colored up with optimism, and bad news can be withheld until he finds it out for himself.

A good way for a boss to build up a relationship of openness and trust with his subordinates is to reduce to a minimum his social distance from them. He must have them work closely with him so that they can know how he operates and will feel free to confide in him. He should let them know that an occasional error won't be held against them. A boss can set up the framework for an easier exchange of information by showing interest in his subordinates' ideas, seeking their suggestions, and providing opportunities for them to take part with him in the discussion and solution of departmental problems. This type of participation in problem solving is discussed in Chapter 6.

The flow of management information

One of the maxims of traditional organization theory is that information in the form of orders flows down the chain of command and acceptance of these orders in the form of accountability flows upward. Because most complex organizations have managements which are essentially autocratic in nature, this concept has some validity. There is, however, a filtering process on each level of the organization as managers interpret and explain what they believe has to be accomplished based on their understanding of the orders and direction of higher management.

Classical theory further assumes that upward communication takes place in much the same way with each level of management passing on information upward so that higher levels of management can know what is happening in the entire organization. While this view is basically correct, incisive study of any organization and its communications flow will indicate that management information systems are more complex.

Since communication involves transactions between people it is vital to the understanding of organizations. By studying and identifying all of the channels of communication in an organization, the organization becomes recognizable as a network of information centers. Coordination becomes possible with a flow of this information and the persons who receive and send information tend to gain status and power in the organization. Communication can be the stimulus to perform and this performance can be measured, hence communication is also vital to any control system.

The manager can transmit information as an order or a command. This is a "chain of command" communication and as such it has an effect on those subordinates reporting to the particular executive. They will tend to react to such an order quite differently than they would to an order coming from someone else in the organization. For instance, an employee may receive an order from a staff executive, such as the personnel manager, and even though he may follow it, he is not under the same responsibility to comply as he is with an order from his immediate line superior. An informal group leader may also give orders but no one in the group need follow these orders since the informal leader does not have a chain of command position. Nevertheless, even the communications of the informal leader contribute to the network of organizational information and in this sense have a bearing on group behavior. The staff executive may be trying to usurp line authority and by giving orders he may confuse the work group, but here, too, there is an information flow which contributes to the total network. Each organization is made up of several senders and receivers of communications on all levels. Some senders have the authority of position while others are just senders in the informal sense.

Rumors and the grapevine. Perhaps the best example of informal sending and receiving is the grapevine. It is the unofficial carrier of information in an organization. In most instances the grapevine is speedy and it serves to spread the news of management's plans whether or not management intends them for publication. Some employees are more active news passers than others, possibly because of their personalities, possibly because they have more opportunities and more contacts with people. Almost anyone becomes more active on the grapevine when he is confused and apprehensive about what is going on. When people feel helpless and threatened, spreading rumors is one way of expressing and alleviating anxiety. Rumors tend to become most rampant in those departments where the manager deliberately withholds information because he believes this allows him to exercise power and control his subordinates.

While some managers believe that the grapevine is a useful device because it is considered by them to be the normal passing along of news about what is going on in the company, most other managers call it a necessary evil. In fact, it is usually an unreliable communications technique, very often harmful in its effect on the work force. A rumor about an impending change could distress employees who may believe that the change is going to cause firings or increase the work load. When the official news finally comes through, the proposed change may not be at all bad but the employees have been conditioned against it and their response is hostile. There also seems to be a relationship between the grapevine and the level of management in an organization. The tendency among employees to tell the boss what they think he wants to hear may effectively insulate him from the rumors that are being spread among employees. J. W. Keener, president of The B. F. Goodrich Company comments on the grapevine:

> Every company has an executive suite or its equivalent. Once you get up there people will not talk to you the way they used to, and certainly you get off the grapevine. The higher up in the organizational structure I went, the further off the grapevine I got. I don't think that is unusual. There are people still on the grapevine who are supposed to keep me informed of what I can't find out for myself. I am sure that I don't get the full flavor, but I get enough of it to be able to see that any problems that develop receive the attention or support they deserve.[8]

It is apparent that the grapevine is not efficient as either a sending or receiving communications device. Perhaps management's best efforts

---

[8] "The President Looks at His Job," *Management Record*, National Industrial Conference Board, May, 1962, pp. 2–11.

should be applied to an analysis of the frequency, number, and type of rumors circulating on the grapevine. This would indicate where the formal communications networks are not functioning and would show areas of employee interest, poor morale, misinformation, and other communications difficulties. Then, it would seem that if the employees were given accurate, timely, and optimal information in areas of their major interest, the effect of the grapevine would be minimized.

Communication systems

There is little doubt that the success of any organization is directly related to the efficiency of its communication system. All of the management functions such as goal definition, policy formulation, planning, direction, control, coordination, and staffing require an accurate and consistent flow of communications. Since human organizations are imperfect, it becomes necessary for management to develop a system of internal communication which minimizes these imperfections.

Data or information must be acquired, processed, analyzed, distributed, and displayed to and from all levels of the organization. Feedback is as essential as the distribution of information. To effectively control as well as to develop an awareness, management must know what is going on. Feedback and peer communication should be an integral part of the communication system.[9]

Above all, communication must be timely. People who should know have to receive the information before the grapevine distorts it. Nothing is as frustrating or disappointing to the supervisor than to hear about a promotion, raise, or transfer of one of his employees or himself through the grapevine before he gets an official notification of the event. Everything management can do to encourage a free and open flow of the information necessary for the effective functioning of the organization will more than contribute to the efficient functioning of that organization.

Summary

There is hardly any part of management's job that does not involve communication. All of the managerial functions require effective communication if they are to be carried out successfully. Poor communication can develop fear, anxiety, distrust, and dislike among the people in an organization. Serious mistakes can be made because orders are misunderstood and casual kidding can cause unnecessary anger. Offhand

---

[9] For a thorough analysis and discussion of the entire subject of communication, see Lee Thayer, *Communication and Communication Systems* (Homewood, Ill.: Richard D. Irwin, Inc., 1968).

remarks by senior management can lead to rumors which cause considerable unrest among employees.

Since the supervisor's job is to get things done through and with others, his effectiveness depends on his ability to reach an understanding with them. The supervisor's attitude toward his subordinates is the basis on which understanding is built.

Misunderstandings between the supervisor and his boss have their roots in attitudes. Fear of the boss deters the supervisor from questioning him and causes the supervisor to color and filter information.

Misunderstandings between fellow supervisors and between line and staff arise when each is protecting his own area from the other and there is no shared purpose.

Misunderstandings arise about management's intentions in making changes and about the effects these changes will have on jobs. Employees oppose changes for a number of reasons: fear of losing the job or the "advantage" of the job; feeling that the change criticizes or belittles them; resentment about not being consulted; pressure from the group to oppose it. Fear and resentment stand in the way of becoming proficient on the changed job. If status relationships are reversed and people have to take orders from their inferiors, they may be unable to work together. Job security, changes that take care of human needs, and good two-way communication will prevent some of the disturbance caused by change. If employees participate in planning the change, they are less apt to resist it.

The grapevine, while a necessary evil, is not an effective transmitter of internal communications in an organization. It is best countered by a free and open flow of accurate and timely communications on a "need to know" basis. The flow of information in an organization evolves into a series of networks which enable a greater understanding of the organization. Because human organizations are imperfect, it is necessary for management to develop internal communications systems which minimize these imperfections.

CASE 1

The president of the company discovered that confidential management plans were being discussed throughout the organization within hours after middle-management conferences, so at the next conference he emphasized the need for protecting the company by not betraying its confidences. The leak continued, and the president questioned the 10 middle managers about the amount of information they were giving out.

Since there had been no problems of this type in previous years, the president wondered if perhaps the newest man, Ames, might be the culprit. To test a hunch he called Ames in and talked to him about being prepared in a general way for possible expansion of his department that could come about if some company plans worked out well, told him that it was all uncertain and cautioned him against discussing the matter with anyone. Within three days the organization was buzzing with a rumor that a big expansion was on the way.

Ames admitted that he had divulged the information but his defense was "I tell my subordinates what I feel they are entitled to know." A check with Ames's previous boss revealed no trouble of this type but indicated that he was well liked, cooperative, and a high producer. He had been hired as a first-level supervisor for the company four years ago and after three successful years on that job was promoted to his present position. The president didn't want to lose the man, so talked to him at length about the seriousness of the breach and told him his job depended upon respecting confidences. Two months later Ames leaked an important piece of information to his subordinates.

1. What are a management man's obligations for protecting company secrets?
2. Why would a middle-management man give out confidential information to his subordinate supervisors?
3. Was there a better way to handle this problem?
4. What should be done with Ames now?

CASE 2

As supervisor in charge of a designing and drafting section, you have to choose the man to fill the vacancy of the job of chief draftsman. Al Adams, the man you wish to place in the job, is outstanding in every qualification except one—communicating. He has a speech impediment—he stutters. He says the stuttering began while he was in the military service. He is making a wholehearted effort to overcome the affliction and has shown improvement during the two years he has been with the company, but he still has a long way to go before he can achieve complete control.

Since you need a man who can bridge the gap between your section and the departments it services in the company, the job will involve a great deal of face-to-face discussion. Because of this you hesitate to promote Adams to the job even though he is next in line for it. If you pass him over, you might destroy all the progress he has made in speech improvement; also he might leave the company.

1. To what extent is stuttering a handicap in communicating?
2. What should you do in the case of Adams? Justify your answer.

CASE 3

Your chief often rushes into your department and gives you vague and general orders. When you question him, he tells you to work out the details yourself. You use your judgment, and the results are often quite different from those he anticipated. He then tells you that you are not carrying out his orders.

1. Should you ask him for orders in writing?
2. How would you go about getting more specific and detailed orders from him?
3. How should the situation be handled?
4. What are some of the causes of misunderstandings relating to orders?

CASE 4

Lillian Martin, one of Art Henderson's best employees, was known to be an habitual gossip. By the end of each day, Art was filled in on everything that went on in the department. Usually she stopped him as he went by her desk during the course of the workday to give him the latest details of events. At times she would come to his office on a pretext so that a particularly interesting item could be communicated immediately.

Art Henderson had been giving considerable thought to the situation. At lunch one day he discussed Lillian and her gossip with one of his friends who had been a department head in the company for many years. The "old-timer" advised him to continue the relationship. He stated that every department had such a person who seemed to enjoy telling the boss everything that went on. He went on to say that Art might as well be realistic and make use of the gossip even though most of it wouldn't amount to anything, there would be some that he could use to his advantage in running his department.

As a result of his conversation with his fellow department head, Art allowed Lillian Martin to continue feeding him information. Some of it proved useful to him in his job and from time to time he checked the validity of her stories and found them to be true. Lillian apparently was an accurate reporter of departmental happenings.

1. Should Art have continued to use Lillian as a communications vehicle?
2. Are there any disadvantages to such a relationship?
3. What effect could it have on departmental morale?
4. Could the employees be using Lillian to communicate with their boss?
5. What can a supervisor do to discourage an employee like Lillian Martin?

CASE 5

Your boss is a believer in the open-door policy, with the result that a number of your subordinates go to see him and make complaints. He listens to their side of the story and half-promises them favorable action. However, when he hears your side of the story, he changes his stand and agrees with you. He tells you to take appropriate action, but he does not indicate his change of position to the men. When your action on the matter is unfavorable to the men, they become angry with you and slow down production.

1. What are the advantages and disadvantages of the open-door policy?
2. Is the boss ever justified in using you as a buffer between himself and the workers?
3. Should you send the men in to see the boss after he has reversed his decision?
4. To what extent should you back up the boss?

CASE 6

You believe that each man down through the organization should be a "booster in the line"—that he should be a supplier of extra ideas relating to his assignments and thus strengthen rather than weaken the chain of command.

John Doe is your weakest assistant. He has a pleasant personality and can handle regular assignments but is limited in initiative, technical knowledge, and ideas.

Lately the work of the organization has become more complicated and follows less and less of a regular pattern. As the nature of the work changes, you see that Doe is becoming more and more of a yes man. As you outline a project to him, he keeps yessing you along. Occasionally you test his understanding by asking pertinent questions, to which he is unable to give quick answers. However, you pass over the points, giving him time to work out the details at his desk and muddle through. You do not know how much he grasps and how much he misses. You feel that, if you could have a meeting of minds with him, you could save his time and yours by explaining more in detail the points he may be missing, but he never asks questions or brings up objections— simply yesses every statement you make.

Doe has developed the philosophy of agreeing with you and keeping you happy to the point where he is overemphasizing the favorable aspects of his department and suppressing the unfavorable ones. For example: Recently two of his best men quit to take jobs at the same pay in California. They gave as an excuse the climate. Doe knew that they planned to quit, but he did not inform you. When you question him about it, he says that he expected them to change their minds, and anyway he did not want to trouble you with the internal problems of his department.

1. What are some of the things wrong with Doe?
2. Why does he act as a yes man?
3. How can you help him get over it?

4. What steps can you take to make your subordinates "boosters in the line"?
5. What gives rise to the philosophy of keeping the boss happy?
6. What are the advantages and disadvantages of keeping the boss happy?

CASE 7

The president of a medium-sized company had long been dissatisfied with the performance of the controller. He decided to have the entire matter of corporate financial management discussed at a board of directors' meeting. After much discussion the board authorized the hiring of a treasurer who would be the chief financial officer of the firm. The question of the controller was not completely settled, since it was decided to allow the new treasurer to make a judgment as to his competence after a period of time, and it was felt that the controller would be helpful in assisting the treasurer until he became familiar with the financial aspects of the company.

The company's public accounting firm was enlisted to help in the search for the new treasurer. The accounting firm was one of the largest in the country and had numerous contacts. They offered executive search as a service for their clients. All interviewing was to be done on the premises of the public accounting firm and the effort was to be carried out by the board chairman, the president, and two board members. The company's personnel department was bypassed since the board chairman wanted the selection of a new treasurer to remain secret so that there would be no upsetting influence on the present controller and the accounting department.

One afternoon about two weeks after the secret recruiting effort had begun and several applicants had been interviewed at the public accounting firm's offices, the manager of the data processing section sought out the personnel manager. He said he was bursting with curiosity and had to speak to someone. A friend of his had been interviewed for the treasurer's position and had called him to find out more about the company. The data processing manager now confronted the personnel manager with this information and demanded to know what the story was.

The personnel manager, not being privy to the secret recruiting program could only claim ignorance and, of course, the data processing manager did not believe him. Even though the data processing manager asked the personnel man to keep the information in confidence because he did not want to jeopardize his position or the chances of his friend, the personnel manager told the story to the board chairman. He was then informed by the chairman about the recruiting effort and the apparent need for secrecy.

1. Should the personnel manager have been made aware of the recruiting effort before it was undertaken?
2. Why would a company attempt secret recruiting for a managerial position?
3. Is it desirable and a sound practice?
4. How should the data processing manager be handled?

CASE 8

You are the supervisor in an office. Your boss has just phoned you that he wants the weekly report today instead of tomorrow because he is going out of town.

Annie, the girl who usually works up the report, is absent; so you call Joan over and start to explain the job to her. She interrupts, protesting that it is Annie's job. You counter by telling her that you can't wait until Annie gets back tomorrow. You give Joan all the figures and a copy of the last weekly report and tell her to follow it exactly. You say, "You understand, don't you?" She yesses you and does the job instead of her regular work. Three hours later she puts the report on your desk. It is all wrong. All the figures are a column out of place. There was a holiday in the week of the report you gave her. When you show her mistake to her, she says that she did exactly what she was told.

There is still enough time to have Joan do the report over again.

1. What principles of good communication were violated?
2. How would you go about having Joan redo the report and get it out on time?

CASE 9

You have a boss who is brilliant technically but deficient in organizational procedures. He often drops into your office and gives you orders that are vague and general and tells you that he wants you to work out the details. When the project turns out well, he takes the credit; when it does not, you get the blame.

In addition, he engages your subordinates in long technical discussions, opening up different avenues of procedure to them. Some of your subordinates take this as a go-ahead signal; others come to you for verification. If the ideas work out, your boss claims the credit. If they do not, he blames you.

1. What might be some of the causes for orders that seem to be vague and general?
2. How should you go about closing this gap in communications between you and your boss?
3. Where does a technical discussion end and an order begin?

4. What are some of the results of the short-circuiting by your boss?
5. How are you going to control this short-circuiting?
6. Set up a half-dozen rules that a person should observe when giving orders to a subordinate.

CASE 10

You and the other supervisors attend periodic coordinating meetings at which you report to the boss the conditions within your respective departments. Your associates are inclined to overemphasize the favorable and discount the unfavorable conditions. You try to give as factual a picture as possible, often to your disadvantage. You know that the boss bases his reports to top management on the information he gets at these meetings. You believe that he discounts all the reports—thereby making your department look bad to top management.

1. How important is it that such information be accurate?
2. What difficulties result when information given to the boss is inaccurate?
3. Should you tell your boss that your information is accurate, while that from the other supervisors is not?
4. How can the reliability of such information be improved?

CASE 11

Mr. Smith is the plant superintendent. It is his custom to take frequent tours of the plant. During these tours he stops and engages the workers in conversation. It is his theory that this boosts the morale of the rank and file. He asks them questions about the equipment, production, materials, etc. Often the information he receives from the workers is incomplete or inaccurate; sometimes it is absolutely false.

At his weekly conference meetings with his section chiefs, he demands explanations of pieces of information he received during his tours. His subordinates would have to spend hours making investigations and collecting data to account for and explain away the erroneous impressions he picks up on these tours.

His subordinates have asked him if they might accompany him on his tours and thus be able to answer his questions on the spot. He states that when he is talking to the rank and file he is getting the truth; when he is talking to his assistants all he gets is a bunch of statistics. He also states that the workers will not talk when their immediate superiors are around.

1. What might be some of the reasons for the superintendent's actions?
2. To what extent might his subordinates have contributed to this condition? Explain.
3. Develop a plan that the section chiefs could work out which would provide a good channel of communications up and down.

CASE 12

A professional man was hired to work in a new and rapidly expanding government agency under a boss whose policy it was to hire aggressive, ambitious, well-qualified professional men and let them alone to carve out their jobs and stake out claims in their areas of knowledge before other divisions of the agency expanded into them. His subordinates saw very little of him except when they overstepped the few boundaries he had established; then he let them know they could either abide by his policies or get out. An administrative assistant handled the routine contacts.

Here is the way the new man's coming was announced to the two men he would be associated with: An article appeared in the newspaper about his hiring. It extolled his education (Ph.D.) and his experience (teaching) and indicated (but didn't come right out and say) that he would be top man in the field that was now occupied by the two associates. The article did not mention the associates.

When the new man arrived on the job, the boss did not take him around to introduce him but instead sent him with another employee (the friend who had been influential in getting him the job). This friend was unpopular—too tactless and too ambitious. He introduced the new man to the two men he would be working with and said, "He's here to take over, and the boss said for you two to show him the ropes and get him started."

The two associates who had previously been dividing the work on a power grab basis promptly united to protect their area from being taken over by the newcomer. They carved a work load for him out of projects they had already explored and discarded as either unfruitful or already claimed by others and not worth fighting for. The projects they gave the new man led him nowhere except into conflicts and frustrations. They provided him with space remote from the mainstream and froze him out of any opportunity to show what he could do.

At the end of his contract year the new man quit for reasons of health. When he was able to work again, he took a job with the YMCA.

What can a man do when he gets into a spot such as this?

CASE 13

You are a supervisor and have under you several assistants and a number of workers. It is your policy to pass down the line as quickly as possible any information that might affect your men. The information is passed by written memoranda, orientation interviews with new em-

ployees, informal group meetings and individual contacts with your subordinates. Your men know that you keep them informed.

In the past, top management has always kept you and the other
supervisors informed.

Recently there has been a rumor that the plant is going to be moved
to another town. The employees are becoming increasingly disturbed.
They are worrying about the possibility of having to move, sell their
houses, or lose their jobs. Morale and production are falling off.

You and other supervisors have on several occasions informed top
management about the rumor. Top management refuses to deny or con-
firm it.

1. Is top management ever justified in holding back information that will
    affect its workers? If so, justify your answer and give examples.
2. If the company is planning to move to another town, what would be
    the advantages and disadvantages of informing its employees several
    months in advance? Several weeks in advance? The very last minute?
3. What steps can you take to bolster up the production and morale of
    your group if top management continues refusing to confirm or deny
    the move?
4. How should top management handle the problem?
5. Suppose you were to find out from a friend of yours in another city that
    the plant is going to move there, should you pass on this information?
    If so, to whom?

CASE 14

Top management wants to encourage upward communicating and
to do so has just introduced a new policy stating that each supervisor
will be expected to inform his superior promptly of the reactions and
attitudes of his subordinates to policies and procedures—and that includes this new policy.

You and several other supervisors will be discussing the new policy
during the coffee break and you have in mind some questions about
the interpretation of the policy. You want to get the ideas of your associates on the following questions:

1. What is the dividing line between passing information up the line and
    "informing" or tattling?
2. Does top management really want to hear criticism of its pet ideas and
    projects?
3. What will top management think of the supervisor who reports a lot
    of unfavorable comment?
4. How can people be protected against retaliation?
5. How can communications upward be made more fruitful for everyone
    concerned?

CASE 15

A personnel service company had been undergoing several cost control programs along with a moratorium on the hiring of new employees as replacements for unfilled jobs. These economies had caused considerable unrest among the employees. A rumor began to circulate that the company was in poor financial condition and had to borrow money to meet its payroll. In fact, it had just negotiated new banking arrangements which allowed borrowing at a more favorable rate than from its previous bank. The normal practice of borrowing by a business had probably given rise to the rumor about the company's financial condition.

To stop the rumor the chairman of the board held a meeting with all executives and informed them of the new banking arrangement and assured them that the company was solvent. He instructed them to pass this information along to their subordinates so that the entire staff could be made aware of the incorrect impression the rumor was creating among the staff.

Quite independently of the above circumstances, the company had a disagreement with the landlord in the building in which it was located. The disagreement was based on the amount of service to be rendered by the landlord. One evening after the building had closed, the landlord in a fit of resentment removed all of the company's listings from the building directory in the lobby. The next morning one of the employees noticed the missing listings when he came in to work. He started the going out of business rumor all over again, citing the removed listings as evidence.

1. Did the board chairman handle the rumor effectively?
2. What should be his course of action in view of the rekindled rumor?
3. Should the employee who started the rumor again be disciplined?
4. How can a company offset the occurrence of rumors such as those in the case?

FOLLOWING UP ON THE JOB

Listening

1. Are you waiting impatiently for the other fellow to shut up so that you can talk?
2. Are you in such a hurry to offer a solution that you don't wait to hear the problem?
3. Are you listening only for what you like to hear?
4. Do emotional blocks get in the way of your listening?
5. Do your prejudices interfere with your listening?
6. Do your thoughts take side excursions while the other fellow is talking?

7. Are you memorizing mere details instead of getting the main points?
8. Do you quit listening when the subject matter gets difficult?
9. Do you have a negative attitude while listening?
10. Do you just pretend to listen?
11. Do you put yourself in the speaker's place to understand what makes him say that?
12. Do you take into account that you and the speaker may not be discussing the same question?
13. Are you alert for misunderstandings that could arise because the words don't mean the same to you as they do to the speaker?
14. Do you try to find out what the argument is about—a real difference of opinion or just a matter of stating the problem?

Speaking

1. Are you careful to watch for signs of misunderstanding in your listeners?
2. Do you choose words that fit the listener's intelligence and background?
3. Do you think out directions before giving them?
4. Do you break down orders into small enough packages?
5. If a subordinate doesn't ask questions about a new idea you are presenting, do you assume that he understands it?
6. Do you speak distinctly? Control distractions as far as possible?
7. Do you "bale" your thoughts before speaking so that you won't ramble?
8. Do you put the listener at ease? Encourage questions?
9. Do you assume that you know what the other fellow has in his mind, or do you ask questions to find out?
10. Do you distinguish between facts and opinions?
11. Do you stiffen up the opposition by contradicting his statements?
12. Do you influence your subordinates to be yes men?
13. Do you use a technical jargon unfamiliar to your listeners?
14. Is what you say clear, complete, concise, correct, and courteous?

6 Teamwork in management

Individuals and organizations. Sources of organizational conflict. Improving cooperation between line and staff. Expansion of staff. The service activity of staff. The advising activity of staff. The control activity of staff. Working with the industrial engineer. The first-level supervisor as a member of management. Superior—subordinate cooperation. Cooperating with fellow supervisors. Teamwork, conformity, and conflict. Summary.

Each man in management has the task of giving and getting the help that enables men to operate jointly. If managers are ·to give and get help, they must have a common cause: they must see that they will benefit if the cause is successful and that they will lose if the cause should fail. In a business enterprise the "cause" is the attainment of the objectives for which the business exists. In order for the personal aims and ambitions of people to be directed toward achieving the aims of the organization, people must see that they have a stake in its success. Since the objectives of a business can be attained only through group effort, top leadership must organize the team and set up the conditions and rewards for teamwork.

When an organization loses its sense of mission and its ability to direct personal ambitions toward a common goal, the organization is torn apart by strife and contention. The production head who deliberately slows down production on a large order to get even with the sales manager whom he dislikes, the secretary who breaks her typewriter hoping to get a new one, and the military commander ordering his troops to take a useless hill so that he can amass a greater combat record are some examples of individual and organizational goal conflict. A person has only to look at the spontaneous cooperation of people performing wonders in volunteer organizations to realize the amount of waste in business enterprises when frictions and hostilities set people to working against one another. Recognition and analysis of some of the issues involved in teamwork and the nature of cooperation in organizations should be helpful to the manager concerned with achieving

161

group goals, reconciling individual differences and developing his own career.

Individuals and organizations

It has been said that the person whose personal goals most closely coincide with those of the organization he works for has the greatest chance for achieving success. Formal organizations encourage the individual to accept and perform a job according to methods and desired results chosen by the organization. Ideal employees are those who accept the job description and produce results accordingly.

During the last several years, a number of writers have developed a thesis which places the individual and the organization in conflict. One of these, Chris Argyris wrote in 1957: "An analysis of the basic properties of relatively mature human beings and formal organization leads to the conclusion that there is an inherent incongruency between the self-actualization of the two. This basic incongruency creates a situation of conflict, frustration, and failure for the participants."[1] Obviously the organization of any group involves common restraints on its members. The very purpose of organization is to achieve goals collectively which the group members believe they cannot achieve individually.

To achieve these goals they accept constraints which they might not if they were acting as individuals. Individuality and conformity are opposing forces, and all persons find that certain organizational demands are disagreeable from time to time. Returning from a vacation, getting to work on time after a late party, and disagreeing with a superior's opinion can all cause an individual to come in conflict with the organization. It is natural for man to seek some independence and freedom, but the very fact that we live in a society implies restraint on some of our actions. By working with others in an organization the individual may have to modify or change some of his goals as he seeks the security and greater effectiveness of group achievement.

In some of the literature there is an implication that large organizations are more restrictive of individual initiative than are small enterprises. The "big frog in a small pond" notion is believed to indicate that in smaller organizations the individual would have more power. In other words, bigness is the problem. Research, however, seems to indicate that managers believe that large companies provide them more challenge, satisfaction, and reward than small firms. Apparently large organizations provide much psychological support to go along with the economic support they provide.

---

[1] Chris Argyris, *Personality and Organization: The Conflict between the System and the Individual* (New York: Harper & Row, Publishers, 1957), p. 175.

In every organization there are malcontents who never seem to be satisfied with their lot. This does not mean that an individual can only succeed if he is a conforming "organization man" who exercises great caution and has traded his birthright for the security of the large enterprise. Robert Dubin, a sociologist, has developed an interesting thesis about man and society. He characterizes man's attachments to the institutions of his society as follows:

Most men have certain central life interests at any given time focused in one, or at most, several institutional settings. They have to participate in other institutions, but do so in terms of the behaviors required in them, and without reference to the voluntary choices that may be available in them. Thus the areas of voluntary social action are precisely the institutions that are central to a man's life interests and that are therefore at the focus of his attention. . . . Self-realization may, however, be a matter of indifference to people for whom work is not a central life interest. Their self-realization comes in other institutional settings outside the productive institution.

What about those people in industry and commerce for whom work is a central life interest? These are the people who find the fulfillment of their life goals in work itself. They make the work institution central to their lives. The interesting fact is that for such people the work environment is challenging and rewarding. . . . The consequence is that he becomes a real striver in the institutional setting, securing many rewards and often encountering deprivations and frustrations. But this is no different from the man who experiences his family life as the institutional center of his interests. The point is that there is nothing about the organization of productive work, or the supervision of people doing it, that is so antithetical to human personality needs as to result only in frustration and disappointment.[2]

It becomes apparent that it is difficult to generalize about any particular individual and his relationship with an organization. While there are many similarities among a work group, each person perceives his work differently and it meets needs shaped very much by his personal value system.

What is significant is the idea that not all people desire autonomy, nor do they want to participate in the activities of management. Many individuals desire direction and prefer to know what is expected of them. The development of an autonomous or participative work climate may stir considerable anxiety and fear in such individuals and destroy the security for which they voluntarily joined the organization.

This is not to say that participative managerial techniques are not desirable under certain conditions such as highly creative work in a research laboratory or an advertising agency. It does mean that many individuals can adapt themselves to the needs of the organization, per-

---

[2] Robert Dubin, *Human Relations in Administration* (3d ed.; Englewood Cliffs, N.J.: Prentice-Hall, Inc., 1968), pp. 90–91.

ceive its goals and work productively toward them. In fact the gregarious nature of human beings causes them to voluntarily associate in a variety of groups to achieve group-desired results.

Herbert Simon adds another dimension to the holistic nature of organizational behavior with what he calls the process of composite decision:

> The central theme around which the analysis has been developed is that organization behavior is a complex network of decisional processes, all pointed toward their influence upon the behaviors of the operatives—those who do the actual "physical" work of the organization. The anatomy of the organization is to be found in the distribution and allocation of decision-making functions. The physiology of the organization is to be found in the processes whereby the organization influences the decisions of each of its members— supplying these decisions with their premises.
>
> It should be perfectly apparent that almost no decision made in an organization is the task of a single individual. Even though the final responsibility for taking a particular action rests with some definite person, we shall always find, in studying the manner in which this decision was reached, that its various components can be traced through the formal and informal channels of communication to many individuals who have participated in forming its premises. When all of these components have been identified, it may appear that the contribution of the individual who made the formal decision was a minor one, indeed.[3]

It can be seen that behavior in an organization is a series of interactions, all accomplishing with various degrees of success, the purposes of the organization. There are superior-subordinate, peer, line-staff, and many other relationships that make up the daily activity in the organization. That all of these do not always go smoothly is surely an understatement.

Sources of organizational conflict

The very nature of large organizations is apt to discourage spontaneous cooperation. A particularly significant factor is the conflict between teamwork and individualism. One of the primary desires in the business organization is for a smooth-functioning team. A great deal of emphasis is placed on the competitive nature of business and the need for cooperation and loyal teamwork so that the company can succeed in the marketplace. The organization is divided into departments, each concentrating on only one phase of the total operation. This specialization of managerial labor was designed to bring about efficiency but it also brings about frictions and conflicts between departments. Each

---

[3] Herbert Simon, *Administrative Behavior* (2d ed.; New York: The Macmillan Co., 1957), pp. 220–21.

department may push its own special interests and resist demands made upon it by other departments. Each feels that its own work is most important, that it knows more about it than anyone else, and that it should protect itself at all costs against encroachments on its territory.

Adding to this conflict is the well-publicized ideal that every employee should be personally ambitious to achieve a good record. Each manager is eager to do a good job as far as his own specialty is concerned because that is where his performance is measured. Each may be sincere in thinking that what is good for his specialty must be good for the enterprise as a whole. Organizations set up formal devices for coordinating the activities within them, but managerial plans require the efforts of people to carry them out successfully, and people can use their ingenuity either to make the plans successful or to find ways to beat the system.

In a sense each manager is encouraged to outperform his fellows. In fact, he may even be encouraged to outperform his superior. If he can demonstrate that a person, department, or group is not doing a good job, and he can further point out that he can do a better job himself, he is usually rewarded by higher management. It becomes apparent that competition and cooperation, individualism and group loyalty, and personal goals and company goals are not necessarily compatible concepts. Conflict within the individual exists also. Very few of our actions and reactions are black and white. All of us have experienced ambivalence quite frequently in our lives. How can a person be honest and not hurt others? When the boss asks for an opinion should you tell him the truth as you perceive it or what you think he wants to hear? Can you satisfy a boss who asks you to speed up production, eliminate errors, cut overtime and keep the workers happy, all in the same breath? Should you tell him what you really think or does your personal survival override your desire to be truthful?

In effect, we reach compromise solutions to most of the ambivalent situations we face and in this manner we resolve personal conflict. The individuals who do not do this generally seek other work where there may be greater compatibility between personal goals and group goals.

Organizations must be concerned with the resolution of conflict in much the same way that individuals are. To keep the parts of an organization working toward company objectives, the structure, policies, procedures, and controls must be designed to make cooperation rewarding. Each manager from top to bottom must be able to see that his personal objectives are closely related to the objectives of the firm. He must understand what is expected of him and his unit toward achieving these objectives. He should also know what help he is expected to give to other units and what help he can expect to receive.

When upper management establishes the conditions for teamwork and rewards people for playing their parts on the team, then each man knows that he must learn how to give and get the help that it takes to operate as a member of the team.

Improving cooperation between line and staff

Line (or operating) departments are defined as the ones directly responsible for accomplishing the main purpose of the organization—the creation of some product or the performance of some service for which the customer will pay. Staff departments are those which perform specialized functions to aid other activities. The use of the word "department" in referring to staff functions is not too accurate. Staff functions are not necessarily performed by departments. Some staff functions can be handled by one man as his full-time or part-time assignment: he provides advice or some specialized service to another.

In distinguishing between staff functions and staff departments, it should be pointed out that staff functions may be performed also by line departments. For example, production (a line department) may give advice (a staff function) to the sales department. An understanding of the proper duties and functions of each other is essential to improving cooperation between line and staff. The line supervisor needs to know about the nature and role of staff departments and how their work relates to his own.

Expansion of staff

Staff departments tend to grow in size and authority. In times of general expansion, when problems increase in size and complexity, staff tends to take more and more activities from the line. For example, the personnel department might start out primarily as a record-keeping and recruiting agency for the line organization. Then in a period of rapid expansion complicated by human relations problems, personnel might be authorized to handle all the company's hiring, firing, transfers, raises, and discipline.

Theoretically, staff has no authority over line. Actually, authority relationships develop in a number of ways. Line managers are required to conform to policies and procedures (purchasing procedures, for example) set up and administered by staff agencies. Or line managers may surrender authority to staff by handing over unpleasant duties (discipline, for instance), or by making a habit of accepting staff advice rather than taking the responsibility for decisions contrary to it. On the other hand, a staff specialist may be authorized to issue orders in the name of his line superior. Or he may just assume authority and start giving directions to line people. Or management might, wittingly or unwittingly, shift an activity over from line to staff simply by saying, "That's a good idea. Go out in the plant and put it into effect."

Some shifting of the balance between line and staff is necessary to make adjustments to meet changing conditions. An organization should be flexible enough to distribute power in a way that meets the demands of the moment. But shifting must be controlled so that the organization continues to serve the purpose for which it was intended.

Line men in a training conference set up the following criteria by which to judge whether there is too much or too little staff in an organization:

Indications of Too Little Staff	*Indications of Too Much Staff*
Line men doing a great variety of tasks	Too much paper work
Faulty or nonstandard procedures	Too many conferences
No innovations	Too many coordinators
Lack of planning	Too many changes
Lack of progress; stagnation	Too many opinions
Poor coordination	Too many people involved in decisions
Upper management always asking for reports	Too many people being hired and no corresponding increase in output
Going outside the firm for information and assistance	

The service activity of staff

As explained in Chapter 2, activities such as purchasing, maintenance, engineering, and personnel are turned over to staff specialists to get the benefit of their particular skills, the economy of centralized handling, or the uniformity needed in plantwide application. Staff people render services, but conflicts sometimes develop between them and the line people receiving the services. Staff and line people have trouble working together because they have different backgrounds, different bosses, and different outlooks. Each sees the situation from his own angle and may not understand the problems of the other. One such trouble area concerns relations between the production and the maintenance departments. A machine operator on an incentive wage may abuse the equipment, but he expects the maintenance department to give him immediate and top quality repair service; his earnings depend upon it. The line supervisor has to get the work out on time. If a machine breaks down, he demands rush repairs. But the maintenance department has to spread its service throughout the plant. Its efficient operation depends on regular scheduling to eliminate or reduce emergency calls. In most cases it can't do a perfect job for each one. Within the limitations of time and budget it has to compromise and give an average service. The shop foreman complains, "If your maintenance men kept the machines in good repair, they wouldn't break down so often." The maintenance foreman answers, "If your men oiled their machines and kept them clean, they wouldn't break down so often." What hasn't been settled is: *Who* should clean and oil the machines?

Cooperation between line and service departments depends to some extent on the ability of the designers of the organization structure to fit the service functions accurately to the needs of line organization. The objectives of each department and the areas of its service should be defined. A clear understanding of responsibilities and authority will remove the cause of many frictions. Focusing the objectives of the departments on the objectives of the business helps to keep service departments from building empires and line departments from demanding extravagant services.

Conflicts of opinion in an organization are normal and desirable in that they bring trouble spots out into the open and keep people and departments from getting too far out of line. But there must be a plan and a pattern by which people can work out their differences in terms of the good of the organization. Otherwise conflicting interests build up into personal hostilities and set people and departments to opposing one another as a matter of habit.

The advising activity of staff

Technical staff specialists may serve line management in a number of ways. The service function of staff was discussed above. The advice-giving and controlling functions of staff also need line-staff teamwork to make them effective. Since a staff department—personnel, engineering, or quality control, for instance—may operate in all three capacities at one time or another and provide service, advice, and control, misunderstandings arise over the authority the staff man is exercising. Is he performing a service for which the responsibility and authority were delegated to him by upper line management? Or is he exercising a control over some action of line management? That is, has he been given the authority (again by upper management) to check up on, regulate, or ensure compliance with some particular policy or procedure or method? Or is he giving information or advice to the line? If he is giving advice, then the line is free to accept or reject it, because in the advisory capacity staff has no authority over the line but must "sell" its proposals for improvements.

Technical staff specialists are brought into an organization because line management does not have the specialized knowledge or the time or objectivity to carry on extensive investigations into the possibilities or merits of new ideas. Staff men are essentially idea men who concentrate specialized attention on specific areas. They provide line management with information and advice in the form of plans, policies, procedures, techniques, methods, and systems designed to improve the line manager's performance without taking over his job or relieving him of the responsibility for getting results. Staff improves methods, establishes standards, and works out plans for reducing costs.

The authority that staff has is delegated to it by the line manager to whom the head of a staff specialty reports. Staff's closeness to higher management carries a certain implied authority that makes lower line managers cautious about refusing staff advice. Even if the staff man has no direct authority to force the line supervisor to take his advice, he does have a type of informal authority that is accorded to him because he is an expert and because he is a persuasive salesman. He is close to upper management and might give a bad report on an uncooperative supervisor. He can always appeal up the line to the supervisor's boss or higher to get the advice accepted up there and handed down as an order. Or he might ask that an order be sent down to the line supervisor telling him to heed the advice that the staff man is going to give him directly. Staff authority was discussed in Chapter 2.

First-line supervisors sometimes complain that they are swamped by staff—that each staff department is promoting its specialty and pushing to get its ideas adopted. Supervisors in training conferences claim that even if they had the time they couldn't possibly adopt all the ideas from staff because some contradict or are incompatible with others, that the several staff departments don't get together to integrate their various proposals and fit them to the line operations.

One explanation for the situation is that the staff man's performance is measured by the *number* of improvements that he is able to install for the line. If a staff department must justify its existence (and it is overhead expense), the way to do it is, unfortunately, by exposing problems and difficulties occurring in the line and needing staff's attention. Staff's need to "look good" on reports is a stumbling block to line–staff cooperation.

Line supervisors in some companies complain that the personnel department is making decisions that should be made by the line.[4] And personnel people say that line supervisors shirk their responsibilities

[4] See Dalton E. McFarland, *Cooperation and Conflict in Personnel Administration* (New York: American Management Association, 1962). This study based on interviews with personnel executives and chief executives, reports on the scope of employee relations functions, the wide variations in the amount of authority exercised by the personnel director, and the processes by which line and staff accommodate to one another.

See also Maynard N. Toussaint, "Line-Staff Conflict: Its Cause and Cure," *Personnel*, May/June, 1962, and his "Problems of Maintaining Uniform Personnel Practices," *Personnel*, September/October, 1962. Both articles are based on a study of the authority exercised by various industrial relations departments.

For an excellent chapter on personnel as a staff function, see George Strauss and Leonard R. Sayles, *Personnel: The Human Problems of Management* (2d ed.; Englewood Cliffs, N.J.: Prentice-Hall, Inc., 1967), pp. 424–47.

and turn over to them the undesirable parts of their jobs. A line supervisor is avoiding his responsibilities if he turns over to personnel his unpleasant disciplinary duties or if he says to a subordinate, "I'd like to get you a raise, but all that is now handled by the wage and salary administration people." But a study of both sides of the problem can be expected to bring about a better understanding of the job that each is to do and the accommodations each must make in working together. The staff man in order to do his job, needs to maintain a good working relationship with the line. He has to understand line problems in order to give the kind of help the supervisor needs. "Helpfulness" is defined by the receiver rather than by the giver. A line man must *see* that he has been helped before he will turn to staff as a source of help. There will be conflicts of interest as staff brings in new ideas and challenges the old. There will be conflicts of viewpoint. Conflicts of ideas are necessary and desirable if present ways of doing things are to be improved and if proposed ways of doing things are to be evaluated. Conflicts should be recognized, analyzed, discussed, and resolved in a way that enables people to work together for the good of the organization.

The control activity of staff

The control activity of staff often produces conflicts because people don't like to be restrained or checked up on or reported up the line. For example, in inspection, the inspector is the fellow who is passing on the quality of the operator's work. He is sitting in judgment and his decisions may influence the operator's pay. As far as the operating group goes, the inspector is not one of the boys, and the situation may deteriorate to the point where inspector and operator are pitted against each other—the inspector trying to prevent work from getting through, and the operator trying to slip it by. Under these circumstances, line operators do not feel responsible for maintaining the quality of the product; they will let somebody else worry about the mistakes.

As another example, when the responsibility for safety is taken over by a staff department, then line managers quit worrying about accident prevention and the accident rate goes up. Experience in the administration of safety bears out the theory that people have to share the responsibility for, and participate in, an activity before they will give it their wholehearted support. Nobody ever has an accident while he is serving on the safety committee.

In its control capacity, the industrial relations staff may have the responsibility for obtaining compliance with companywide policies and procedures for dealing with labor matters, but if it issues direct commands to the line supervisor or threatens to discipline him for failure to conform, the result is hostility. This shouldn't be necessary if the line organization agrees with labor policies and procedures. The staff man should work *through* the line rather than *on* it in getting individual compliance. He doesn't get into the situation of giving orders to a line supervisor if the line supervisor's boss will do it. Teamwork between line managers and the labor relations staff is improved when supervisors are consulted about provisions in the labor contract, when they get the training and information they need to understand labor policies and to handle their jobs of administering the provisions of the contract.

Working with the industrial engineer

An example of line-staff problems is in the relationship between the foreman's department and the industrial engineer. The nature of this relationship breeds tension and hostility. It is the engineer's job to analyze and improve methods and to reduce costs and develop standards. When he comes into the shop it is to study people's work, find how it could be improved, and make changes in it. Workers become suspicious and sometimes alarmed about what will come out of this snooping. The man who is being time-studied is sure that it won't do him any good and is apt to either cut his earnings or make it necessary for him to work harder. He doesn't like being watched and having every move noted. He doesn't like being told what motions to make or to be timed while he does his job. In order to protect himself and his friends against any unfavorable rate changes, he is going to cover up any short cuts he has been using to make the job easier.

The line supervisor shares some of these attitudes toward the engineer and his investigations and changes. Change means a drop in production that will look bad on the reports; it means extra work of teaching and training and maybe some behavior problems if people get too upset over it. It also implies that perhaps the supervisor hasn't been doing such a good job and that the engineer is going to be carrying tales to upper management.

Since the health of an enterprise depends upon the smooth and successful adoption of innovations, improvements, and cost reductions, it is wasteful for the supervisor and the engineer to be bucking one another on the job for which they are both responsible—the efficient utilization of men, materials, machines, and methods. The first step in resolving the conflict is to recognize the reasons for the hostility and to accept the fact that the problem has two sides that must be considered. On the line man's side is the need to handle his own job well and then to get better acquainted with the technical work of the engineer. The supervisor should learn enough about the engineer's work to feel able to discuss it and evaluate it from a practical operating standpoint. The supervisor wants some influence in the way changes are made and introduced into his work group. Also he needs to understand the techniques used to measure work, set time standards, and calculate wage rates.

The engineer, for his part, needs to understand the problems that the line man meets in introducing and living with the idea of staff. The engineer as seen by the supervisor may (1) be long on theory and short on experience, (2) have the unfair advantage of being closer to upper management, (3) be giving the impression that if the supervisor doesn't cooperate, upper management will hear about it, (4) be overplaying the role of expert and being too positive about his theories, (5) may be refusing to evaluate his projects in terms of human relations and practical operating considerations, (6) have no respect for the supervisor's knowledge, (7) be antagonizing the line people with technical language. People outside a profession are inclined to consider its technical jargon as an attempt to shut them out by making the specialty mysterious, exclusive, and incomprehensible.

But the supervisor must recognize that the engineer has a job to do and like anyone else wants recognition for what he does. He wants the satisfaction of seeing his ideas put into successful operation. The recognition problem is one for upper management to handle: the staff man's performance should be judged by the way his projects are accepted and put into successful operation rather than by the number originated or the reports he makes on line inadequacies. The staff man can make his most effective contribution in a role somewhat like that of a teacher or conference leader: he finds problems that need solving and then provides the amount of information, stimulation, and guidance it takes to get people to solve their own problems.

Some companies improve the relationship between the supervisor and the new engineer by teaming them up to work on committees that call for a combination of staff theory and line practicality. Safety, job evaluation, and methods improvement make good starting places. The important thing is to get both men to see problems as mutual ones to which each has something to contribute, and to get each to seek and use the suggestions of the other. The engineer, in learning more about the supervisor's problems, gains a respect for the line man's practical knowledge of production matters. The engineer can learn from the supervisor about people's social arrangements for getting work done in the department. Many staff improvements have been wrecked by the outrage of workers whose status systems were violated. If engineer and supervisor can work as a team in designing improvements and installing changes, then the changes can be tailored to fit the value system of the group. While changes are being made, the design of jobs can be improved to fit employees' abilities and ambitions and to raise the level of satisfaction and motivation.

The first-level supervisor as a member of management

The first-level supervisor's place on the management team is some-times a disputed one. In some companies supervisors are not treated as members of management but are regarded—and regard themselves— as just an in-between group. In this situation they are very apt to feel that (1) they have no stake in management and no responsibility to support its programs for increasing output, reducing costs, or improving methods; (2) they have no chance of advancing in management; (3) they are powerless to get action in matters affecting their work group; (4) they had better look out for themselves. The work group may even reject the supervisor if they feel he is powerless to do anything for them. When supervisors are in this "in-between" position, they will look first to their own protection and later—if at all—to the good of the organization.

The supervisor who identifies with his employees rather than with management may try to win favor with his employees by relaxing disci-pline or going easy on production goals. Then when his superior pres-sures him for production, the employees will most likely resent his change of behavior as he passes along the pressure to them. He loses their confidence as he already has lost the confidence of upper manage-ment. He has to try to cultivate a dual loyalty, learning how to reconcile the conflicting interests and needs of those above him with those he supervises.

The management-mindedness asked of the first-level supervisor is that he look to the good of the organization—that his objectives be in line with those of the organization. His objectives must be those of his boss, but his techniques for achieving them will necessarily be different. The boss's techniques are designed for managing managers; the first-level supervisor is managing nonmanagement people. His sub-ordinates don't have management attitudes or management objectives. He belongs to two organizational families: he is the leader of a work group and he is a member of the management group. His job of getting subordinates to work for management objectives makes conflicting de-mands on his loyalty—demands that higher-level managers don't have to face. He must be close enough to his subordinates to see their point of view and be accepted as their leader. He must be loyal to them in order to win their loyalty. He is dependent upon their willingness to cooperate with him. They in turn depend upon him to help them get what they want from the job. He must champion his group and still keep a balance between their personal objectives and the company's objectives.

Middle management must foster those things that build the supervisor's management stature. If he is to feel and act like a member of management he must be treated as one. His financial success must be tied to management objectives. He must be given the backing he needs to reinforce his position as leader of his work group. He should be kept informed about management plans and the reasons for them. He should have opportunities to participate in management decisions. He should be included in training conferences that bring supervisors and their bosses together. There is little point in training a supervisor to do things that are against the beliefs or orders of his boss. Reducing the social distance between the supervisor and his boss helps to build relationships of mutual trust that are essential to teamwork. The supervisor needs "influence" with his boss in order to look after the interests of the work group and get action on the legitimate requests of his men.

Superior–subordinate cooperation

A supervisor has no way of knowing what his boss expects from him unless he hears it from the boss himself, but in many cases the boss fails to get the information across. Surveys indicate that there is a serious lack of agreement between superior and subordinate as to the subordinate's job: the extent of his authority,[5] his duties and their relative importance, the qualifications he needs to perform them satisfactorily, the obstacles that he has to contend with, and the changes that he can expect to affect the job (and therefore the planning) in the next few years.[6]

Some conclusions to be drawn from these surveys are: (1) that superiors have been mistaken in assuming that their subordinate supervisors see eye to eye with them, (2) that superiors are making decisions without having sufficient information about what's going on at the work level, (3) that there should be some provisions for discussing job problems, exchanging information, and arriving at a better understanding of what the boss expects of his subordinates, how well he thinks they are measuring up, and how he can give them the help they need.

---

[5] Lee E. Stern, "The Foreman's Job. What Are the Boundaries?" *Supervisory Management*, Vol. 3, No. 7 (July, 1958), pp. 15–23. The article is based on a survey of 187 first-line foremen and their bosses, reported by Chester E. Evans in *Supervisory Responsibility and Authority* (American Management Association Research Report No. 30, 1957). Most of the foremen interviewed considered their authority more limited than their bosses reported it to be.

[6] Norman R. F. Maier, L. Richard Hoffman, John J. Hooven, and William H. Read, *Superior-Subordinate Communication: A Statistical Research Project* (American Management Association Research Study No. 52, 1961). The researchers interviewed 58 superiors in high middle management and a subordinate of each, and found only a little more than 50 percent agreement on the subordinate's job duties, and much less agreement than that on job requirements, obstacles to performance, and future changes to be expected.

When supervisors in training conferences are asked what kind of help they want from the boss, their lists reveal a need to put the relationship on a personal basis. They want the boss to:

1. Back up the subordinates' decisions.
2. Tell subordinates what he expects of them and how they are doing.
3. Give recognition for work well done.
4. Be interested in subordinates as people—make them feel they belong.
5. Provide good leadership and be competent for the job.
6. Give constructive criticism.
7. Tell the why of jobs.
8. Follow the chain of command.
9. Pass along information—both up and down the line.
10. Get raises for subordinates and for the workers they recommend.
11. Have confidence in the ability of subordinates.
12. Recognize the difficulties in getting jobs done.
13. Take the responsibility rather than pass the buck.
14. Make good decisions.
15. Be loyal to the subordinates and to the company.
16. Train subordinates—teach them the tricks of the game.
17. Delegate authority equal to responsibility and make clear the extent of it.
18. Welcome ideas and opinions; let subordinates have a voice in decisions.
19. Don't play favorites; be fair.
20. Help subordinates in problems beyond their depth.
21. Carry up the line problems of subordinates that require higher level solutions.
22. Understand the problems of the subordinates' work groups.

But when these supervisors who want so much from their bosses are asked what they want from their own subordinates, the list is short and it boils down to three main items: performance, loyalty, and information. Since the man-boss relationship is the one through which the organization's work gets done, it is important that there be a way to find out what each wants, needs, and expects from the other.

The supervisor's boss can provide for this exchange of information and get vastly improved relationships with his subordinates if he will include them in problem solving and decision making. The boss who is able to lead a problem-solving conference will find that the techniques of case study learned in a training program can be applied to the solution of departmental problems. Ingenious decisions are worked out in discussions in which supervisors feel free to contribute information and opinions, to thrash out differences, to suggest and evaluate solutions, and to select the most practical solution based upon their knowledge of operating problems. There are several important by-products from such get-togethers. The discussion that is a part of problem solving provides an opportunity to exchange information about job duties and impending changes; it serves to remove misunderstandings and fears and hostilities that come from lack of information; it motivates a subordinate to carry out the decision as his own rather than one that was thrust upon him.

Decisions handed down by top management (cost cutting, rules, policies, etc.) become more palatable if the boss gives his subordinate supervisors an opportunity to discuss and decide upon the best way to carry them out. Not every problem can or should be hashed out with subordinates. There just isn't time, and some problems are so tied in with unpublished plans that they can't be put out for free discussion. The boss can still make use of coordination meetings to announce decisions, fix responsibilities, set deadlines, and let each man know what is expected of him.

Cooperating with fellow supervisors

Fellow supervisors are annoyed with one another a great deal of the time. The very nature of their contacts can easily lead to conflict. When one supervisor contacts another, it is to complain about some failure of the other or to demand something that is going to cause extra work for the other. A supervisor's success depends upon the departments that precede his in the order of operations and on the departments that render service to his; naturally, he demands that those departments deliver the goods to him on time and in satisfactory condition. And when those departments see him coming or hear him on the phone, they start working up a good offense as the best defense.

Much of the communication between supervisors is by telephone, memo, or a hurried stop in at the other fellow's department, interrupting him when he is busy. There is seldom enough personal contact—enough opportunity to find out that the other fellow is not so bad and might even be likable if met somewhere else.

One of the great benefits of having management-training conferences is that it brings supervisors together for something other than complaints and making demands on one another. Conferences give them a chance to get acquainted with each other and to study each other's problems in an atmosphere of comparative calm. A good-natured discussion of a trouble zone between departments may reveal that what looks like a power grab in one case and like a "refer to Jones" in another is actually a matter of overlap and void in the assignment of duties—one duty has been assigned to both of them and the other duty to no one. Perhaps there has never been a clear boundary between the two jobs, and the lack of definition of their duties and authorities has brought about an overlapping and inefficiency that has been a source of continual irritation or conflict.

At the start of a series of conferences for supervisors, there is some sparring, some feeling-out of the other fellows, and some caustic remarks are made to get a load off the chest. Then, as problems are discussed, the supervisors see that the other fellow has troubles, too. They begin to have ideas of how to help him, and gradually they begin to work cooperatively on those problems that have been causing conflicts. The relationship built up in problem-solving sessions carries over into other areas. For instance, supervisors can get together to study an accident or injury that happened in one department and by applying their findings to other departments can prevent such accidents from happening there.

Supervisors say that getting together in foremen's clubs, safety committees, and company social events promotes cooperation. Where supervisors get to know one another better, they are willing to go more than halfway to reduce the conflicts on the job. Then they are more apt to be in a frame of mind to understand one another's problems, to help work out solutions for them, and to regulate their own work so that they will be helping their fellow supervisors instead of putting obstacles in their paths.

Supervisors say they would like to have cooperative relationships with their fellow supervisors in which all of them would be willing to:

1. Exchange ideas and information.
2. Have work completed on time for the next fellow.
3. Give and take constructive criticism.
4. Keep one another informed about new procedures, policies, and rules.
5. Respect one another's authority.
6. Achieve uniformity in the interpretation of policies and enforcement of rules.
7. Try to understand one another's problems.
8. Render necessary assistance to one another.
9. Straighten out differences in private and among themselves rather than carry them to the boss.
10. Refrain from putting one another on the spot.
11. Practice teamwork and refrain from passing the buck.
12. Show loyalty to the company and respect for its policies.

Teamwork, conformity, and conflict

There are some who confuse genuine teamwork with conformity. Likewise, any emphasis on teamwork could be interpreted as a condemnation of conflict. Neither case is true. Every organization tends to develop some conformity among its members through the development of objectives, policies and procedures. These are necessary if there is to be a reasonably unified approach toward organizational goals. Similarly, conflict is detrimental to the organization only when it subverts these goals. If it absorbs resources and efforts without any productive result, it obviously has to be eliminated. On the other hand, conflict can be useful in an organization. In fact it can encourage teamwork of the best kind. Assuming that teamwork is a series of interactions among people in the organization, then some conflict is bound to result. A close scrutiny of the list of cooperative relationships that supervisors desired, mentioned earlier in this chapter, will surely indicate areas that could give rise to conflict. Successful resolution of this conflict, however, can result in effective and desirable organizational change. Such is the raw material of progress. Rensis Likert points out that effective organizations have extraordinary capacity to handle conflict. He mentions that their success is due to three very important characteristics:

1. They possess the machinery to deal constructively with conflict. They have an organizational structure which facilitates constructive interaction between individuals and between work groups.

2. The personnel of the organization is skilled in the processes of effective interaction and mutual influence. (Skills in group leadership and membership roles and in group building and maintenance functions.)

3. There is high confidence and trust among the members of the organization in each other, high loyalty to the work group and to the organization, and high motivation to achieve the organization's objectives. Confidence, loyalty, and cooperative motivation produce earnest, sincere, and determined efforts to find solutions to conflict. There is greater motivation to find a constructive solution than to maintain an irreconcilable conflict. The solutions reached are often highly creative and represent a far better solution than any initially proposed by the conflict interests.[7]

Lastly, teamwork requires an environment which will support it. This means that all of the managerial actions must make it desirable for the individual to be a team player. If the individual does not fully understand this he will most surely revert to individual survival goals.

A large multiproduct rubber manufacturer expected each of its wholesale salesmen to meet his territorial quota every month. The company also had regional quotas encompassing the territorial quotas of several salesmen. Many regional managers complained that regional quotas for individual products were not met on a monthly basis because of the company's policy of not making the salesman aware of the regional

---

[7] Rensis Likert, *New Patterns of Management* (New York: McGraw-Hill Book Co., 1961), p. 117.

quota and the contribution of his sales efforts to that quota. By natural inclination and established practice a salesman would delay reporting a sale of batteries, for instance, if he had already reached the battery quota in his territory for that month. This would allow him to start off the next month with a cushion in that product category. Because of this widespread behavior among the sales force, monthly regional quotas in product categories might not be reached and the regional manager was required to file an explanatory report with headquarters. The managers found this distasteful since they knew the real reason but could do little about it. Despite a regional manager's efforts to encourage teamwork, the company policy in a sense, forced the salesmen to be concerned only with their own performance.

Middle management is often cast in the role of "man-in-between" in the implementation of a poorly formulated policy. He finds it difficult to develop a cohesive work force yet he must satisfy the wishes of his superiors by adhering to policy. Teamwork, in this instance, would require a free and open exchange of information with evidence given to higher management that company policy is minimizing the development of team spirit.

Summary

The aims of an organization can be achieved only through the cooperative efforts of people. In a big organization, people are separated from one another by the particular interests and aims of their specialties, by their levels in the managerial hierarchy, and by divisions into managerial units. If their efforts are not joined together in a common purpose in which each has a stake, they may be working against one another—at the expense of one another and the company.

Even though there are situations where individuals and organizations conflict, this is not necessarily detrimental to either party. Progressive change can result from such conflict if it is handled effectively. While some writers believe the restraints imposed by organizations on individuals are negative, there are many people who prefer and accept the requirements of the organization in exchange for more orderly existence it affords them.

There are several ideas which are widely accepted in organizational life but which are sources of conflict. Among these are competition and cooperation, teamwork and individual ambition, staff advice and line responsibility, and group goals and individual goals.

Top management must set up the kind of structure, system, policies, and rewards that make it possible and mutually beneficial for people to work together cooperatively. People must see that they can attain their own objectives more fully through working for the objectives of the company, and that they need each other's help to do it. In order that people will help one another, they must be formed into teams, and the teams must be joined in a common effort toward company objectives in which they can see a benefit to themselves.

If people realize that each can gain from helping the other, they will establish better ways of working together. Then differences in background, training, interest, and point of view can be made to contribute to the success of the organization rather than be a source of discord. Each person has his position to play on the team, and his success depends upon the help of others. Line managers must learn how to get the kind of staff help they need. Staff people must learn about the line manager's needs and problems in order to be a source of help to him. Each boss must find out the needs, problems, and expectations of his subordinates and give the help they need in order to get the help he needs. Fellow supervisors must find out how to help one another in order that they can all profit from team accomplishment.

To be successful, teamwork requires a supportive environment and careful nurturing by all levels of management. There must be a free exchange of ideas and opinions since teamwork is really a series of interactions. Because individuals are usually rewarded for their own performance, they must be fully informed on how their performance relates to group goals.

CASE 1

Several of your fellow supervisors are very closely associated with one another both on and off the job. They belong to the same fraternal organization, and their families visit back and forth a great deal. In fact, they might be considered a clique. They favor one another on the job, in relation to maintenance, supplies, and priorities of work. This results in their having better production records than yours.

1. Are they justified in their action? Explain.
2. Should you try to get into the clique? Explain.
3. Should you complain to your boss? What arguments could you give him?
4. How could such a situation have been avoided?
5. Who should correct it? How?

CASE 2

You were hired from the outside as supervisor of a large department. This antagonized the supervisor of a smaller department, who, because of his seniority, had expected to get the job himself. He is attempting to create resentment against you among the other supervisors, saying that he should have gotten the job; that you as an outsider are not familiar with the policies of the company or with the work; and that, if the company is going to make a practice of recruiting rather than promoting, the other supervisors may some day have the same situation to contend with.

1. How can you overcome his resentment?
2. Should you have a talk with the other supervisors and explain to them what the rival supervisor is trying to do?
3. Should you go to the superintendent and tell him what is going on?
4. How should the outsider go about working his way into an organization?

CASE 3

The company plans to set up standards of work performance and has created an industrial engineering department to do the job. The. department consists of an industrial engineer and experienced time-study men—all from industries with long histories of piece rates. Management does not plan to set up piece rates as yet; all it wants to do at present is set up standards of work performance.

Management has asked the line organization to cooperate with the new industrial engineering department but this cooperation does not seem to be forthcoming. For example, the other day one of the time-study men entered a line department for the first time. He was going to study a job but the operator he wanted to study stopped working and refused to resume. The time-study man reported the incident to the man's superior, who replied, "That's your problem, not mine. It looks like you haven't been able to sell your services to the operator." After making this remark, the line supervisor walked away from the time-study man.

Develop a list of suggestions that will increase cooperation between the operating personnel and the time-study personnel.

CASE 4

A young engineer acquired his degree, a 19-year-old bride, and a new job in June and moved to the town where the company is located. His job calls for him to test company equipment in use in nearby installations. The company is young and still small, and the people in it were hospitable to the young couple, including them in all the social affairs. The young man and his bride don't drink and are uncomfortable around people who are drinking; so they decide not to attend any more of the parties and not to become obligated to invite people to their house for drinks. The wife enrolled for some college courses so she could claim heavy assignments as an excuse for refusing invitations.

The young man's boss keeps urging him to bring his wife to the parties and become one of the group. The young man isn't sure if this is an invitation or an order so he decided that if he put in an appearance himself at the parties and left early he would be taking care of his obligation.

1. How should the young couple handle the problem?
2. How much does advancement in such an engineering job depend on party-going and party-giving?

CASE 5

You are the superintendent of a medium-sized plant that is running on two shifts. The night shift supervisors are officially assistants to the day shift supervisors. A while back you started a little friendly competition between the shifts. It built up production but it greatly increased conflict between them. Every day you get complaints. The day supervisors complain that the night men go all out for production and neglect to keep the equipment in good shape. The night supervisors accuse the day people of taking the easy jobs and leaving the difficult ones. They accuse the day supervisors of moving the faster workers to the day shift.

1. List a half-dozen complaints that shifts usually have against one another.
2. How should each be handled?
3. What are some of the ways of building cooperation and still maintaining competition between shifts?
4. How would you correct the situation outlined in this case?

CASE 6

While you were a member of the rank and file, you were a union steward for one year. That was two years ago. During that period you did a good day's work each day, represented your constituents well, and were respected by both the management and the employees.

Recently you were promoted to a salaried position in the inspection department. It was a merited promotion and not a move to get you out of the union. However, you are finding that you are not being accepted by some of your fellow supervisors as a member of the management team. Also, some of the rank and file are rejecting you with the claim that in the capacity of inspector you are being too harsh on your old friends. You are trying to be fair to both parties.

1. What are some of the advantages and disadvantages to a supervisor of having been a union steward?
2. What are some of the obstacles he has to overcome in relation to management? In relation to the rank and file?
3. How can he overcome each?
4. What kind of training and induction should a supervisor who has been a union steward receive?

CASE 7

Jean Gordon has been with the company for about six months. She is a keypunch operator and she has developed considerable speed and accuracy. As her supervisor, you have noticed that she generally finishes her work earlier than the other employees. After observing her for several days, you find that after she completes her work, she reads a magazine, writes personal letters, or makes telephone calls.

You call her to your office to compliment her on her efficient performance and to ask her to help some of the slower operators complete their work on time. She accepts the compliment as a matter of fact and proceeds to tell you how unfair your request is. "I finish my work because I don't fool around and gossip, so I'll be darned if I'll help the slowpokes," Jean says emphatically. You go on to tell her that you know she is a very good worker, but you emphasize the need for a team spirit and a cooperative attitude. Jean still protests saying, "I work as hard as anyone in the department and I don't get paid for extra work." You tell her that you are not taking advantage of her and that you would appreciate her help in getting the department's work out. You go on to say that you do not expect her to consistently do extra work. Jean leaves your office seemingly accepting your request, but evidencing very little enthusiasm. You thought of promising Jean a raise and a promotion, but you were reluctant to do so because of her negative attitude.

During the next two weeks you notice that Jean finishes her work at quitting time each day. She has no spare time and while she is no longer using the telephone or reading, she is not available for any extra work. Her past performance definitely indicates she has slowed down her work pace, but she still is efficient and accurate.

1. What can you do now about Jean Gordon?
2. Should an efficient employee be given extra work?
3. What can you do to motivate and challenge an employee like Jean?
4. Is she justified in her refusal to do extra dork?

CASE 8

A department store branch in a suburban shopping center found that it was taking in more money in the four hours that it was open at night than it did in the previous eight hours of the day. So management decided to keep the store open five nights a week and to run the store on a two-shift basis. The second shift would work 24 hours a week—four nights plus an eight-hour day on Saturday—and would get full employee benefits of hospitalization, life insurance, discounts, paid vacations, and paid holidays.

The night and Saturday shift was to be made up of the people who had been working two nights a week and on Saturdays. They were mostly college students and public school teachers. The managers of the night crew were to be those members of the night shift who had been authorized to OK checks and fill in as acting managers after the day managers had delivered their briefings and departed for the night. Management decided, however, that the new night managers should not be left in their old departments but should be shifted to manage other departments so they would be separated from the people with whom they had been working side by side.

The day managers were going to have to give up their authority over the night crew and were to retain responsibility only for merchandising at night.

The changeover was made, the store was opened five nights a week, and problems arose immediately: The night managers in their new departments didn't know the merchandise, and the day managers stayed on into the evening to supervise them or else left long lists of instructions to be followed. These new pairs of managers hadn't worked together before and didn't get along well together. The night managers complained that the day managers were overbearing. And the day managers complained that the night managers were not following procedures or carrying out instructions. Some night managers requested that the day managers be barred from coming in at night to run things.

The night managers had no way of knowing what stock had come in or what had been ordered, and the day people had no way of knowing what the night people had done.

The night people were a lively and adaptable crew, and the revenue from the night hours was so good that top management wanted to build the best possible relations between day and night shifts.

1. Set up a plan for making a smooth transition to a two-shift management.
2. Design some system for handling communications between day and night shifts.

CASE 9

Long burdened with a growing amount of detail, Charlie Klinger decided to ask the personnel department for one of the college graduates now completing the company's executive training program. He wanted to make this employee a staff assistant who would assume responsibility for some of the detail and work on various projects which Charlie had been postponing because of lack of help. Charlie's department performed an internal sales function largely concerned with business development and the necessary research to support it.

The personnel director agreed to Charlie's request and assigned Al

Davis to the position. Al was a business school graduate who had majored in market research and he was very interested in the challenges his new assignment presented. In a few months Charlie became convinced that Al Davis was all that he had hoped for. Each assignment given to Al was completed on time and with great effectiveness. Charlie was able to increase the complexity of the assignments and also give Al greater responsibility. Al welcomed all of these assignments and continually told Charlie how grateful he was for the many opportunities he had been given. By turning over many routine chores as well as several projects to Al, Charlie was able to spend more time on planning and the supervision of the department which he had neglected before Al came to the department.

One morning Charlie was having some coffee at his desk and silently congratulating himself on his success with Al Davis, who was functioning so effectively as his staff assistant. His thoughts were interrupted by Bill Franklin, a longtime member of the department and an old friend of Charlie's. Bill asked if he could join Charlie for a cup of coffee because he had something to tell him. Charlie, of course, agreed and Bill proceeded to tell him that Al Davis had been undermining him with other members in the department. Charlie couldn't believe it and mentioned Al's gratitude and cooperativeness as well as his efficiency. Bill agreed but went on to say that while Al was convincing Charlie of his usefulness he had been telling other employees that he was doing Charlie's job and frequently commenting on how lazy Charlie was. Bill frankly stated that he thought Al was trying to get Charlie's job and that it would only be a matter of time before he would start his campaign with people in higher management and the personnel department.

Charlie thanked Bill for the information but he still couldn't believe it. He wondered about what to do next and decided to talk to a few other employees in the department. Even though they were not as frank as Bill was, by using careful questions and allowing them to talk, Charlie was able to substantiate everything Bill had told him. It was apparent that he had created the proverbial monster. He then called Al to his office and confronted him with the information he had learned. Al first denied any wrongdoing but when Charlie mentioned dates and circumstances, he admitted his criticisms of Charlie's performance. He further went on to say that he felt he was doing the lion's share of Charlie's work and that he was in fact after Charlie's job.

1. What should Charlie do about Al and his frankly stated ambition?
2. Was Bill Franklin correct in telling Charlie about Al's efforts to undermine him?
3. Could Charlie have prevented such a problem from arising?
4. If you were Charlie's boss, what would you tell him to do?
5. Can an employee like Al be retained by the company?

CASE 10

Miss Jane Clark, an employee of over 17 years' tenure, was recently promoted to head a work group of 20 female clerks and typists. The promotion was based on her demonstrated initiative, technical knowledge, ability to organize work loads, and her management attitude..

Because of her management attitude and excellent work performance, Miss Clark had developed a reputation for being a "company woman" and she was unpopular with some of the girls she now supervised. In addition, there were several personality clashes with her associates over the years, largely caused by Jane's desire to please her superiors.

Perhaps because of her vulnerability now that she is a supervisor, several of her subordinates have complained to higher authority. These complaints are very general in nature, mentioning that it is extremely difficult to work under Miss Clark's supervision.

Her superior reports that he has had several interviews with her and they reveal that she understands her situation completely and is making an honest effort to be fair and reasonable in the treatment of her work group. She is not using herself as a standard of performance for the group and she is pleasant as possible in her employee relations. Her superior feels that the criticism leveled at her is undeserved and a direct result of past grudges on the part of some of her co-workers.

Recently an employee working for Jane Clark went to the personnel department to request a transfer to another department. She was qualified in the type of work done in that department and desired to perform in that area. In the course of conversation with the personnel man, she mentioned that Miss Clark was difficult to work for, but she had no specific complaints.

1. Was it ill-advised to promote Miss Clark to a supervisory position?
2. Should popularity be an important factor in determining promotability?
3. Can a superior who has recommended promotion objectively evaluate employee criticism of a supervisor?
4. Assuming the superior is correct in his evaluation of the situation, what can he do to help Jane Clark with her supervisory problems?
5. Can he assume that the employee animosity existing now will die a natural death in time?
6. Should Jane Clark be transferred to another department as a supervisor? As a regular employee?

CASE 11

You are the supervisor of a large production department. Your newest assistant is a young man named Bill Smith. Smith is considerably younger than the other assistants and lacks their experience; however, his rapid rise to the position of assistant supervisor was based on outstanding ability. Smith learns quickly, has shown great initiative, and maintains excellent relations with the employees under his supervision.

The older supervisors under your jurisdiction resent this Johnny-come-lately intruder into their ranks. While not openly hostile, their opposition is reflected in lack of cooperation, a certain reluctance to coordinate fully, and the failure to include Smith as an insider in their group. The acts are not so open as to permit you to make a clear case; yet you are acutely aware of the situation and apprehensive that it might result in a serious lowering of your department's morale and efficiency.

Smith, meanwhile, is making the best of a bad situation. He has managed to keep his subdepartment operating in an acceptable manner and has been wise enough not to force himself upon the other assistants or to reveal his discomfort and resentment. As yet, he has not complained.

1. What might be some of the reasons for the attitude of the older assistant supervisors?
2. Is Smith approaching the problem correctly? What suggestions do you have for Smith?
3. What is your responsibility in such a situation?
4. How should you go about increasing cooperation among your assistants?
5. How should you go about creating a spirit of management-mindedness among your assistants?
6. How are you going to get your assistants to put the company interests before their own interests?

CASE 12

Blake is a Negro with a degree in industrial engineering. He was born, raised, and educated in the South. His first job after graduation from college was as a technician with a large company in its Midwest division where there was a high percentage of Negro employees. The company gave him additional technical training and after two years gave him management training and promoted him to first-level supervisor. The promotion was based on superior technical ability combined with natural leadership and drive. He performed well as a supervisor for two years and then the Midwest division was shut down and Blake was transferred to the Northwest division of the company where there were few Negro employees.

Within a year he had been relieved of three supervisory assignments, each time with a general unsatisfactory performance rating. The fourth assignment was made with the understanding all around that if he did not work out in this one, he would be terminated.

During the first month on this new assignment Blake complained regularly to the manager that he had been discriminated against in the three previous assignments and had not been given a fair opportunity. He claimed that he was being railroaded out of the company. He also objected to certain duties of this new assignment as being degrading to his position as a supervisor and thought he should have more responsibility and authority. He complained that some of the other supervisors did not cooperate with him and that some of the employees did not accept his supervision. Actually none of the other supervisors had complained about him. A few employees had made rather general complaints and asked to be transferred to a different supervisor.

Blake was bright, well groomed, and businesslike. He handled himself well in contacts with individuals and groups. He handled authority well, accepted responsibility, analyzed problems quickly, and made good decisions.

What is the problem here?

CASE 13

You are in charge of a section doing heavy production work. The safety engineer has been trying out various types of safety equipment on your men—changes of goggles, gloves, etc. In evaluating the equipment, he keeps a close watch on how your men operate and at times tells them to do jobs in a certain way.

Your men object to all this. They complain to him and to you that they are not guinea pigs and that their work is being interfered with. The safety engineer complains to you that your men are not cooperating. You figure that this is his problem and not yours; so you do nothing about it.

This morning your boss called you in and told you that the safety engineer had complained to top management about the lack of cooperation. Your boss then tells you to see that your men cooperate with the safety engineer and follow his instructions.

1.   Evaluate the attitude of the safety engineer.
2.   Evaluate the attitude of your workers.
3.   Evaluate the attitude of your boss.
4.   Evaluate your own attitude.
5.   To what extent is each justified? Not justified?
6.   What are the difficulties you are going to run into in developing cooperation among all the parties concerned?
7.   How are you going to overcome them?

CASE 14

J. Smith is a young assistant supervisor, has been in the position for two years, is doing a good job, and is well liked by everyone. When things are going smoothly he and his boss, R. Jones, get along well. However, wherever Jones gets pushed around by upper management, he descends on Smith like a ton of bricks and blames him for everything. In most cases it develops (and everybody knows it) that the boss, Jones, himself was to blame, but he never admits he was wrong—just lets the issue die.

It is pretty well recognized by the other supervisors, the rank and file, and Smith himself that Smith is the scapegoat. Smith accepts the situation, takes the blasts, and then waits for things to blow over.

1. What are some of the reasons why bosses have scapegoats?
2. Evaluate J. Smith's attitude toward being the scapegoat.
3. What are some of the undesirable consequences that might result from his continuing to be the scapegoat?
4. How might Smith go about getting himself out of this situation?

CASE 15

The policy of the company is to start young college men in the organization by assigning them to work in staff departments. While engaged in such activities as time study, methods improvement, and job analysis, they can acquire quickly an overall picture of the operating departments.

This practice, however, hinders the staff departments as a whole in their endeavor to render specialized advice and assistance to the line departments. The line people look upon the staff men as intruders. The line people complain that the eager young men from the staff departments have their noses in everything, wanting to know the ins and outs of every operation and searching hard to uncover defects. All in all these young men take up a lot of valuable time asking questions and getting explanations. Occasionally one of them comes up with a good idea but most of their suggestions have been tried out previously and found to be impractical.

1. What are the functions of staff departments?
2. What are the functions of line departments?
3. Evaluate the objections of the line people in this case.
4. What are some of the ways of improving cooperation between line and staff?
5. How should young college graduates be started in a company? Justify your answer.

FOLLOWING UP ON THE JOB

Cooperating with fellow team members

1. Do you get the kind of help you need from staff people?
2. Do you let staff know your problems?

3. Do you avail yourself fully of the services offered by other departments?
4. Do you know the needs and problems of your fellow supervisors?
5. Do you help one another or pass the buck?

Cooperating with the boss

1. Do you try to find out what your boss wants?
2. Do you supply him with both favorable and unfavorable information?
3. Do you short-circuit him?
4. Are you loyal to him?

Cooperating with subordinate supervisors

1. Do your subordinates know what you expect of them?
2. Do they know your opinion of how they are doing in each of their responsibilities?
3. Do you know what help they expect and need from you?
4. Do you provide meetings at which they can discuss job problems and clear up misunderstandings?
5. Do you give them the kind of information they want and need?
6. Do you attempt to reduce their fears and uncertainties?
7. Do you know what kind of relationship your subordinates want with you?
8. Do you consider yourself the captain or the coach of your team?

Suggested readings

BOOKS

For
Chapter:

2, 6   ARGYRIS, CHRIS. *Human Behavior in Organization.* New York: Harper & Row, Publishers, 1957.

2, 4, 6   ————. *Integrating the Individual and the Organization.* New York: John Wiley & Sons, Inc., 1964.

2, 6   ————. *Personality and Organization: The Conflict between the System and the Individual.* New York: Harper & Row, Publishers, 1957.

1, 4   BARNARD, CHESTER I. *The Functions of the Executive.* Cambridge, Mass.: Harvard University Press, 1951.

5   BERLO, DAVID K. *The Process of Communication.* New York: Holt, Rinehart & Winston, Inc., 1960.

1, 2, 4, 6   BITTEL, LESTER R. *Management by Exception.* New York: McGraw-Hill Book Co., 1964.

1   ————. *What Every Supervisor Should Know.* 2d ed. New York: McGraw-Hill Book Co., 1968.

1   BLACK, JAMES M., and FORD, GUY B. *Front-Line Management: A Guide to Effective Supervisory Action.* New York: McGraw-Hill Book Co., 1963.

2, 4, 6   BLAU, PETER M., and SCOTT, W. RICHARD. *Formal Organizations.* San Francisco: Chandler Publishing Co., 1962.

2, 4, 6   CARZO, JR., ROCCO, and YANOUZAS, JOHN N. *Formal Organization: A Systems Approach.* Homewood, Ill.: Richard D. Irwin, Inc., 1967.

2   CLELAND, DAVID L., and KING, WILLIAM R. *Systems Analysis and Project Management.* New York: McGraw-Hill Book Co., 1968.

1, 2, 4, 6   CUMMINGS, LARRY L., and SCOTT, WILLIAM E. (eds.). *Readings in Organizational Behavior and Human Performance.* Homewood, Ill.: Richard D. Irwin, Inc., 1969.

1, 2, 3, 4, 6   DALE, ERNEST. *Management: Theory and Practice.* 2d ed. New York: McGraw-Hill Book Co., 1969.

2   ————. *Planning and Developing the Company Organization Structure.* New York: American Management Association, Inc., 1952.

2, 5 DAVIS, KEITH. *Human Relations at Work.* 3d ed. New York: McGraw-Hill Book Co., 1967.

1, 2, 4, 6 DRUCKER, PETER F. *The Effective Executive.* New York: Harper & Row, Publishers, 1966.

1, 2, 6 ——. *The Practice of Management.* New York: Harper & Row, Publishers, 1954.

6 DUBIN, ROBERT. *Human Relations in Administration.* 3d ed. Englewood Cliffs, N.J.: Prentice-Hall, Inc., 1968.

1, 2, 4, 6 ETZIONI, AMITAI. *Complex Organizations.* New York: The Free Press, 1961.

1, 2, 4 FAYOL, HENRI. *General and Industrial Management.* Trans. CONSTANCE STORRS. New York: Pitman Publishing Corp., 1949.

1 FORTUNE, EDITORS OF. *The Executive Life.* Garden City, N.Y.: Doubleday and Co., 1956.

4, 5, 6 GARDNER, BURLEIGH B., and MOORE, DAVID G. *Human Relations in Industry.* 4th ed. Homewood, Ill.: Richard D. Irwin, Inc., 1964.

1, 2, 4, 6 GROSS, BERTRAM M. *The Managing of Organizations.* New York: The Macmillan Co., 1964.

2 HAIRE, MASON (ed.). *Modern Organization Theory.* New York: John Wiley & Sons, Inc., 1959.

5 HANEY, WILLIAM V. *Communication and Organizational Behavior.* Rev. ed. Homewood, Ill.: Richard D. Irwin, Inc., 1967.

5 HAYAKAWA, S. I. *Language in Thought and Action.* New York: Harcourt, Brace & World, Inc., 1949.

2, 3, 4, 6 HAYNES, W. WARREN, and MASSIE, JOSEPH L. *Management Analysis, Concepts and Cases.* 2d ed. Englewood Cliffs, N.J.: Prentice-Hall, Inc., 1969.

3 HIGGINSON, M. V. *Management Policies I,* Res. Study No. 76, New York: American Management Association, Inc., 1966.

3 ——. *Management Policies II,* Res. Study No. 78, New York: American Management Association, Inc., 1966.

3 IRESON, WILLIAM G., and GRANT, EUGENE L. (eds.). *Handbook of Industrial Engineering and Management.* Englewood Cliffs, N.J.: Prentice-Hall, Inc., 1955.

2, 3, 4, 6 JOHNSON, R. A., KAST, F. E., and ROSENZWEIG, J. E. *The Theory and Management of Systems.* 2d ed. New York: McGraw-Hill Book Co., 1967.

1, 2 JONES, MANLEY H. *Executive Decision Making.* Rev. ed. Homewood, Ill.: Richard D. Irwin, Inc., 1962.

2, 3 JUCIUS, MICHAEL I., and SCHLENDER, WILLIAM E. *Elements of Managerial Action.* Rev. ed. Homewood, Ill.: Richard D. Irwin, Inc., 1965.

1, 4   KOONTZ, HAROLD. *Toward a Unified Theory of Management.* New York: McGraw-Hill Book Co., 1964.

1, 2, 3, 4, 6   ——, and O'DONNELL, CYRIL. *Principles of Management.* 4th ed. New York: McGraw-Hill Book Co., 1968.

4   LAIRD, DONALD A., and LAIRD, ELEANOR C. *The Techniques of Delegating.* New York: McGraw-Hill Book Co., 1957.

3   LAZZARO, VICTOR (ed.). *Handbook of Systems and Procedures.* 2d ed. Englewood Cliffs, N.J.: Prentice-Hall, Inc., 1969.

1, 2, 3, 4   LEARNED, EDMUND P., and SPROAT, AUDREY T. *Organization Theory and Policy.* Homewood, Ill.: Richard D. Irwin, Inc., 1966.

2, 4, 5, 6   LIKERT, RENSIS. *New Patterns of Management.* New York: McGraw-Hill Book Co., 1961.

1, 2, 3, 4, 6   LITTERER, JOSEPH A. *The Analysis of Organizations.* New York: John Wiley & Sons, Inc., 1965.

2, 4, 6   McDONOUGH, ADRIAN M., and GARRETT, LEONARD J. *Management Systems, Working Concepts and Practices.* Homewood, Ill.: Richard D. Irwin, Inc., 1965.

2, 6   McGREGOR, DOUGLAS. *The Human Side of Enterprise.* New York: McGraw-Hill Book Co., 1960.

2, 4, 6   MARCH, JAMES G. (ed.). *Handbook of Organizations.* Chicago: Rand McNally & Co., 1965.

1   ——, and SIMON, HERBERT A. *Organizations.* New York: John Wiley & Sons, Inc., 1958.

5   MARTING, ELIZABETH, FINLEY, ROBERT E., and WARD, ANN. *Effective Communication on the Job.* Rev. ed. New York: American Management Association, 1963.

2   MOORE, FRANKLIN G. *Manufacturing Management.* 5th ed. Homewood, Ill.: Richard D. Irwin, Inc., 1969.

4, 5   NATIONAL INDUSTRIAL CONFERENCE BOARD. *Improving Staff and Line Relationships.* Studies in Personnel Policy No. 153. New York, 1956. *Organization of Staff Functions.* Studies in Personnel Policy No. 165. New York, 1958. *Managing at the Foreman's Level.* Studies in Personnel Policy No. 205. New York, 1967. *Employee Communication: Policy and Tools.* Studies in Personnel Policy No. 200. New York, 1956.

1, 2, 3, 4   NEWMAN, WILLIAM H. *Administrative Action.* 2d ed. Englewood Cliffs, N.J.: Prentice-Hall, Inc., 1963.

1, 2, 3, 4, 6   ——, SUMMER, C. E., and WARREN, E. K. *The Process of Management.* 2d ed. Englewood Cliffs, N.J.: Prentice-Hall, Inc., 1967.

1   NILES, HENRY E., NILES, MARY CUSHING, and STEPHENS, JAMES C. *The Office Supervisor: His Relations to Persons and to Work.* New York: John Wiley & Sons, Inc., 1959.

2 PFIFFNER, JOHN M., and SHERWOOD, FRANK P. *Administrative Organization.* Englewood Cliffs, N.J.: Prentice-Hall, Inc., 1960.

4, 6 ROY, ROBERT H. *The Administrative Process.* Baltimore: The Johns Hopkins Press, 1958.

1, 4, 6 SAYLES, LEONARD R. *Managerial Behavior.* New York: McGraw-Hill Book Co., 1964.

1, 2, 4, 6 SCOTT, WILLIAM G. *Organization Theory. A Behavioral Analysis for Management.* Homewood, Ill.: Richard D. Irwin, Inc., 1967.

2, 4, 6 SEILER, JOHN A. *Systems Analysis in Organizational Behavior.* Homewood, Ill.: Richard D. Irwin, Inc., 1967.

1, 4, 6 SIMON, HERBERT A. *Administrative Behavior.* 2d ed. New York: The Macmillan Co., 1957.

4, 5, 6 STRAUSS, GEORGE, and SAYLES, LEONARD R. *Personnel: The Human Problems of Management.* 2d ed. Englewood Cliffs, N.J.: Prentice-Hall, Inc., 1967.

2, 4, 6 SUTERMEISTER, ROBERT A. *People and Productivity.* New York: McGraw-Hill Book Co., 1963.

2 TAYLOR, FREDERICK W. *Scientific Management.* New York: Harper & Row, Publishers, 1947.

5 THAYER, LEE. *Communication and Communication Systems.* Homewood, Ill.: Richard D. Irwin, Inc., 1968.

5 VAN DERSAL, WILLIAM R. *The Successful Supervisor in Government and Business.* New York: Harper & Row, Publishers, 1962.

2 WALKER, CHARLES R., GUEST, ROBERT H., and TURNER, ARTHUR N. *The Foreman on the Assembly Line.* Cambridge, Mass.: Harvard University Press, 1956.

1 WHYTE, WILLIAM J. *The Organization Man.* Garden City, N.Y.: Doubleday & Company, Inc., 1957.

2, 4, 6 YOUNG, STANLEY. *Management: A Systems Analysis.* Glenview, Ill.: Scott, Foresman & Company, 1966.

ARTICLES

For Chapter:

5 ANDERSON, JOHN. What's Blocking Upward Communications?" *Personnel Administration,* January–February, 1968.

1, 4, 6 ANDREWS, KENNETH R. "Toward Professionalism in Business Management," *Harvard Business Review,* March–April, 1969.

2, 6 FISCH, GERALD G. "Line-Staff Is Obsolete," *Harvard Business Review* September–October, 1961.

5 KUSHNER, ALBERT. "People and Computers," *Personnel,* January–February, 1963.

1, 4, 6 LEARNED, EDMUND P. "Problems of a New Executive," *Harvard Business Review*, July–August, 1966.

1, 4, 6 LEVINSON, HARRY. "On Being a Middle-Aged Manager," *Harvard Business Review*, July–August, 1969.

1, 6 MYERS, M. SCOTT. "Every Employee a Manager," *California Management Review*, Vol. XI, No. 3 (Spring, 1968).

6 SCHOONMAKER, ALAN N. "Individualism in Management," *California Management Review*, Vol. XI, No. 2 (Winter, 1968).

2, 6 TOUSSAINT, MAYNARD. "Line-Staff Conflict: Its Cause and Cure," *Personnel*, May–June, 1962.

1, 6 ———. "Problems of Maintaining Uniform Personnel Practices," *Personnel*, September–October, 1962.

Part II

Job management

7 Planning and controlling the department's work

Top management's role in planning. The supervisor's responsibility in planning. Lack of time and what one company did about it. The design of the supervisor's job. Personal planning. Time utilization. Delegating to subordinates. The need for total planning. Evidence of poor planning. Why planning seems difficult. The planning formula. Types of plans. The obstacles to planning. The control function. Quantitative techniques for control. Summary.

Planning is a responsibility that no man in management can escape, whether he is the president of the company having to plan the future course of the whole concern or the first-level supervisor having to plan the work of his unit. Planning is essential to the efficient and orderly running of a business.

The utility company must do its long-term planning in terms of forecasts of population growth and industrial demands. It must consider the length of time required to put up a power plant and the availability of suitable land. In considering land acquisition, it might take into account the possibility of generating electric power by means of an atomic reactor. All plans are based on assumptions of what will happen in the future. The difference between forecasting and planning is this: forecasting is predicting the most probable course of events within a range of probabilities. Planning involves deciding what to do about them. It is necessary for top management to forecast the demand for its product and to plan all its resources in terms of these forecasts. If management does not plan or if it plans poorly, the company will suffer from great fluctuations in productivity—waves of hiring and firing, expanding and retrenching—with the result that it loses money and nobody has a secure job.

It is impossible for a manager to keep his head above water if he runs his business (or his department) by decisions made in a crisis day after day. The objective of this chapter is to show the supervisor the need for planning, how to plan his own time, and how to plan and control the work of his department.

Planning improves with practice; the more a man plans, the better he can plan. The more extensively planning is practiced in an organization, the easier it becomes for everyone to plan because there is greater certainty of how others will operate.

Top management's role in planning

As is the case with all other managerial activities, top management establishes the example for the rest of the organization in planning as well. A chief executive committed to a comprehensive planning program will go a long way toward developing an awareness of the need for and the desirability of planning among managers on all levels. Well thought out overall organization plans establish the frame of reference for operational plans throughout the company. Consistency of planning effort along with reasonable adherence to formulated plans is required to convince lower level managers that planning should be a necessary part of their activity. Including their thoughts and ideas in higher level organizational planning is also a necessary requisite to an effective planning program.

The increasingly complex environment in which business organizations operate has caused them to place greater emphasis on formal planning programs. There is also a tendency to prepare more detailed long-range plans and look further into the future. Corporate commitments are being developed for activities which may take place in the next century. Part of this is caused by a rapidly changing technology but it is also a product of the more sophisticated processing of data and the development of decision-making techniques based on quantitative methods such as operations research and linear programming.

The days of the "seat of the pants" executive operating by intuition and hunch are rapidly drawing to a close. This is true for all levels of management and it would be well for middle- and first-level managers to develop themselves in the knowledge areas necessary for understanding more sophisticated planning. As large organizations develop more comprehensive plans they will have an effect on the operation of all aspects of the company's activity. The lower level manager who prefers the luxury of not committing himself to particular deadlines or who may feel that he is too busy with daily activity to take the time necessary for the consideration of basic problems in his area of responsibility will find himself left at the starting gate.[1]

---

[1] For an excellent and comprehensive analysis of the entire area of business planning, see George A. Steiner, *Top Management Planning* (New York: The Macmillan Co., 1969).

The supervisor's responsibility in planning

Each supervisor has the responsibility and the authority for the efficient operation of his unit. His unit has a definite purpose—a mission, a definite job to do—and it is up to him to see that the job is done. In order to do this job, he has at his disposal men, materials, machines, money, and methods, and he must use these factors to the greatest advantage. To do so requires planning and controlling the flow of work through the department. Planning is deciding the *what, why, when, where, who,* and *how* of the work to be done. Controlling is the checking of the progress of work against plans to be done. Controlling is the checking of the progress of work against plans or standards and then taking corrective action when necessary.

As aids in planning and controlling, the supervisor may have the services of a production control department, a standards department, or other staff agencies. However the final responsibility for getting things accomplished lies with the supervisor. If his department is not operating efficiently, he is the one who gets the blame.

Of the five resources the supervisor has to work with (the five M's—men, materials, money, machines, and methods) the most important factor is the men because they are the ones who will use the other four factors in a way that will either save or waste them. The actions of men, therefore, are the key point in planning, but the supervisor cannot push the responsibility for planning onto his men. Most men will not, of their own initiative, conserve materials to the utmost, use machines in the best manner, use the best methods, or put their time to the most productive use. However, if the supervisor takes the lead by planning the work and checking its progress, then his subordinates know that he knows what is going on, and they act accordingly.

Lack of time and what one company did about it

The design of a foreman's job may put such excessive demands on his time and energy that he is prevented from doing the things he should be doing. The following research study provides a specific report of how a foreman had to spend his time and how his job was redesigned to permit him to use his time more effectively. The study was made in the automobile industry in a gear department where efficiency was 69.6 percent in spite of managerial efforts to improve it by training and by replacing personnel. The department had a superintendent, 2 assistant superintendents, 3 general foremen, 15 foremen and about 450 hourly production employees. The foreman selected for the study was one who was rated high by management. An observer followed him around and recorded every incident that occurred in a full working day. Here is what took the foreman's time:

> *Nearly 900 tasks.* In 480 minutes the foreman performed 876 separate incidents of behavior. In other words he did something different every half minute.
>
> *Time tickets.* He spent nearly 45 minutes getting information for time tickets, making them out, and distributing them.
>
> *Checking job lots.* He devoted another 50 minutes to checking job lots and finding out when they would be completed so he could plan subsequent operations.
>
> *Moving material.* He spent still another 25 minutes of his day either moving material or arranging to have it moved from one operation to another.
>
> *Checking tools, jigs, fixtures.* This took 55 minutes of his time. His general foreman spent two hours filling in for the foreman on one jig problem.
>
> *Quality.* During the day he spent only three minutes actively looking at quality problems—yet his scrap and rework were high.

. . . It was clear . . . that organizational shortcomings were thrusting excessive demands upon the foreman's time and energy. Management undertook four steps immediately to correct these "blocks," not only for this foreman but for all 15 foremen in the department. Here are the four steps:

> A *production planner and a clerk* were assigned to each general foreman to free him from checking completion of job lots and filling out job tickets.
>
> A system of *"move tickets"* was inaugurated, with the expediter taking a more direct responsibility for such routine movements. This system facilitated material movement.
>
> *The tool-trouble staff* servicing the department was transferred from the master mechanic's department. It was directed to report henceforth to the department superintendent.
>
> Several measures were introduced to assist the foreman on quality. One of them—a stop-gap measure—was assignment of a special "quality" operator to each foreman.

. . . Management came to look at production problems from a different angle. And they came to realize the shortcomings as these shortcomings impinged on the foreman's job. They came to see that factors beyond the foreman's control, not his personal qualifications, were the true sources of trouble and that until these were cleared up no amount of classroom training would do much good.[2]

The design of the supervisor's job

The foreman's job described in the above study was so badly designed that he had to take care of 876 separate tasks in one day, which is equivalent to jumping from one task to another each half minute. Although he had a quality problem of excess scrap and rework, he was able to give it only three minutes' attention in the day. In this study an outsider was analyzing the foreman's job. His report called attention not only to the poor design of it but to the shortcomings of the organization as they affected the job. As a result of the study, the heads of line and staff departments began to take action on things that were hindering the foreman but were outside his control. The foremen in the department were then provided with people and systems to relieve them of some of the time-consuming routine clerical work, mechanical work, and general errand running. The foremen in turn made improvements in those things that were within their control. Over a three-year period of continuing improvements, the efficiency of the department rose from 69.6 percent to over 100 percent. Schedules were met for the first time, and scrap and rework were reduced.

Many supervisory jobs suffer from poor design. It isn't that the supervisor has too many people to supervise; it's that he has too many *things* to look after personally. The answer does not lie in stripping him of his responsibilities but rather in examining his responsibilities to see which are the most important in meeting the objectives of the department, which he should perform personally, which he should delegate to subordinates, and which should be handled by other departments.

Since most companies don't think of job design as the cause of, or treatment for, problems, this chapter suggests to the supervisor that he should take the initiative in improving the design of his job and that the way to start is through planning. He is aiming for an apportioning of his time so that he will be giving a minimum to routine work, a maximum to creative work, and a comfortable cushion to emergency work.

The creative work takes in both short- and long-range planning. It takes in planning to get out the daily or weekly work load, planning for solving immediate problems and for preventing future problems from arising. It takes in planning for cost improvement in specific areas—

---

[2] Frank J. Jasinski and Robert H. Guest, "Redesigning the Supervisor's Job" (Technology Project, Yale University). Reprinted by special permission of *Factory Management and Maintenance*, December, 1957. Copyright by McGraw-Hill Publishing Co., Inc.

waste, labor efficiency, and equipment maintenance. It takes in planning for training or retraining subordinates so that they will be able and willing to take over new duties and adjust smoothly to new systems, new equipment, and new processes.

The supervisor's first step in planning is to analyze the way he spends his own time.

Personal planning

While conceding that planning, controlling, and other practices of good management are worthwhile, many supervisors say they just don't have the time for them. They claim that they are so busy just keeping up with the job that they can't get any time ahead to devote to improving their departments or themselves. The purpose of the discussion on personal planning is to show the supervisor how to investigate the manner in which he spends his time, and to point out how he may be able to redistribute his time in order to allocate more of it to the more important aspects of his job. In brief, the purpose is to show "how to take time to save time."

What are some indications that a supervisor needs to make a study of the way he is using his time? If he is just keeping up with his work— that is, taking care of one emergency after another—or if he is just getting or not quite getting his essential job done, if he needs to be in three places at the same time, if he has to put in excessive overtime, if he has not time for self-improvement, if he has to do everything himself, or, finally, if he dare not take a day off when he is ill: then it behooves him to make an evaluation of how he is spending his time.

When the supervisor evaluates and redistributes his time, he no longer operates in a panic but is master of the situation. He can achieve a certain self-confidence and peace of mind by recognizing that he can do just so much and if he is doing it, he is doing his job. Usually by time redistribution he can reduce overtime, strain, and excessive fatigue. His job becomes easier because he finds he can delegate or eliminate some of the work that has been snowing him under.

An important by-product of getting better control over the job is that the supervisor becomes better prepared for promotion; a man practicing crisis management is not ready for advancement. Advancement comes to the man who has the opportunity to plan and organize, to improve methods, cut costs, and to take time to build up the morale of his group. In other words, the higher management jobs go to the man who shows he can perform these more important managerial activities.

The supervisor's personal log sheet. Figure 7–1 is a sample of a log sheet on which a supervisor can keep a record of how he is spending

FIGURE 7-1
The Supervisor's Personal Log Sheet

For the supervisor to find out how he is distributing his time, he should list in the appropriate space just what he was doing during the previous two hours. At the end of each day he should analyze each activity on his list and label it as a 1, 2, 3, 4, or 5.

1. Duties that only he can do.
2. Responsibilities that he can delegate in part.
3. Responsibilities that he can delegate entirely.
4. Activities that might be eliminated as unnecessary.
5. Activities that might be handled by some other department.

	Monday	Tuesday	Wednesday	Thursday	Friday
A.M. 1st half					
2nd half					
P.M. 1st half					
2nd half					

his time. It is recommended that he fill out the sheet at least every two hours—at the coffee breaks, at lunchtime, and before going home in the evening. In the appropriate space he should list what he was doing during the previous two hours. He should be perfectly honest in making out this log since it is for his own personal use and need not be shown to anyone. At the end of the day the supervisor should analyze the activities he listed and classify them as to whether they are:

1. Duties that only he can do.
2. Responsibilities that he can delegate in part.
3. Responsibilities that he can delegate entirely.
4. Tasks that are unnecessary to the department and could possibly be eliminated or done by some other department.
5. Activities (necessary to the department) that could be handled by some other department.

The logging should be carried on for two, three, or four weeks to give a good picture of the way the supervisor distributes his time. Any of his duties that did not occur during that period should be taken into account. These duties might be the preparation of monthly reports, quarterly reviews, budget estimates, personnel evaluations and such items that occur infrequently but consume time.

After the supervisor has made enough log sheets to give a representative sample of what he does and how much time he spends doing it, he should evaluate the activities that are taking up his time. Investigations of how supervisors spend their time have revealed that some time is consumed by work that should be done by the other departments. In some cases the supervisor assumes these tasks; in other cases they have been dumped upon him. For example, keeping of materials available, seeing that work is moved from one place to another, seeing that machines are set up on time—all these are activities that can be handled by the production control department. Machine breakdowns and minor repairs should be handled by the maintenance department. Some types of training can just as well be done in the training department.

When supervisors study their log sheets they find tasks that could be delegated to subordinates. The following checklist divides a supervisor's responsibilities into those which he must do himself (duties), those which he can delegate parts of to subordinates, and those which he can normally delegate in full.

Duties the supervisor himself must do

1. Planning and controlling the work within his section.
2. Setting standards.
3. Estimating the budget.

4. Making accident investigations.
5. Cooperating and coordinating with other supervisors.
6. Keeping the boss informed.
7. Improving himself.
8. Maintaining an adequate work force.
9. Getting the right man on the right job.
10. Getting to know his men and taking an interest in them.
11. Promoting teamwork and cooperation.
12. Evaluating subordinates.
13. Determining areas in which subordinates need training.
14. Developing and training subordinates.
15. Transferring subordinates.
16. Keeping subordinates informed; eliminating rumors.
17. Building morale and creating better attitudes.
18. Motivating subordinates.
19. Helping subordinates with their personal problems.
20. Disciplining subordinates.
21. Handling gripes and grievances.
22. Settling disputes among workers.

Responsibilities he might delegate parts of to subordinates

1. Maintaining quality and quantity of production.
2. Improving methods and procedures.
3. Keeping costs down (conservation of time, materials, space, and tools).
4. Care of equipment.
5. Training workers.
6. Explaining jobs.
7. Inducting new workers.
8. Accident prevention.
9. Attendance control (absence and tardiness).
10. Requisitioning tools, equipment, and materials.
11. Handling details or paper work relating to routing, scheduling, and dispatching.
12. Maintaining records.
13. Preparing vacation schedules.
14. Attending meetings.

Responsibilities he can normally delegate to subordinates

1. Setting up machines.
2. Sharpening and resetting tools.
3. Keeping records and making reports.
4. Checking and inspecting raw materials.

5. Maintaining good housekeeping on the job.
6. Care of tools.
7. Running errands (getting blueprints, supplies, etc.).
8. Answering the phone.

   Middle manager's job description.   The job description in Figure 7–2, is that of an upper middle manager of the Manufacturers Hanover Trust Company, New York, N.Y., a large commercial bank. This manager has other middle managers reporting to him. They in turn have several first-level supervisors reporting to them.

   Redistributing time.   The supervisor should study the present distribution of his time so that he can redistribute it to make more time available for his more important duties. He should ask himself: What is the purpose of my department? If my department ceased to exist, what work of the organization would remain undone? He should consult his job description if there is one and see how it lists his duties and responsibilities.

   With his job purpose and job description in mind, the supervisor should study his time log to see if he has been spending time on activities that are not necessary to the running of his department. If he has, he should consult the organization manual, the procedures manual, and his boss to determine if such operations could be eliminated, or if they are necessary to someone else, could perhaps be done by some other department.

   While the supervisor is finding out if certain activities could be done by other departments, he should examine the boundaries between his activities and the various service activities to see if he can free himself of tasks that are duplicated or overlapped by or belong properly to the service departments.

   Of the activities that are to be done by his department, he should sort out those that he can delegate and those that he alone must do. In apportioning time to his own duties he should ask himself what he can spend less time on and what he should spend more time on, in order to accomplish the most effective job of managing. Figure 7–3 is an example of how an aircraft company, Martin-Baltimore, expects its supervisors to apportion their time. Mr. Kullas, chief engineer of Martin-Baltimore, has this to say of what the company expects of its line supervisors:

   Figure 7–3 describes, in the same manner, what we expect of the line supervisor. These line supervisors are essentially the fellows who get the job done on the line and have day-to-day contact with the people in the technical departments. These are the men who really set the first, and perhaps most effective, example to the new graduate just out of school and, later on, when he is developing.

FIGURE 7-2
Position Description of an Upper Middle Management Supervisor

3030—12-62				
	MANUFACTURERS HANOVER TRUST		OFFICIAL STAFF POSITION DESCRIPTION	

NAME	LAST	FIRST	MIDDLE	TITLE
	Brown	William	Michael·	Vice President

DIVISION	BRANCH OR DEPARTMENT	SUPERVISING OFFICER	TITLE
Operations	Central Operations	Robert W. Black	Senior Vice President

SCOPE OF POSITION
AND
NATURE OF WORK PERFORMED

The incumbent is the officer in charge of Central Operations, and as such, is responsible for the overall supervision of, and coordination of operational activities in, the following departments:

Archives	Demand Deposits
Central Delivery	Lock Box
Central Index	Machine Repair
Central Note Teller	Mail
Central Operations	Money Transfer and Wire
Check Clearance	National Control Unit
Check Reconcilement	Transcribing
Coupon & Securities Collection	Vault

In addition, on a staff basis, under direction from his superiors, he is charged with the responsibility of maintaining a close working relationship with other major operating centers such as the Securities Department, the International Division and the Corporate Trust Department. He consults with the officers in charge of these segments on systems, equipment, and manpower requirements for special jobs.

One Assistant Vice President and an Assistant Secretary are responsible to the incumbent for the direct staff relationship with the Securities Department, International Division and the Vault. One Assistant Vice President and an Assistant Secretary are responsible to the incumbent for the same coverage of the National Control Unit, Central Index, Money Transfer and Wire, Central Operations, Central Note Teller, Coupon and Securities Collection, Brokers and Customer Loan and Machine Repair.

One Assistant Secretary and an Assistant Manager are responsible to the incumbent for the supervison of the Achives Department, the maintenance of a records retention schedule, and the Mail Department.

The line officers of the Check Clearance, Check Reconcilement and Lock Box Departments work directly with the incumbent. He also deals directly with the operating officers of the Corporate Trust Department on overall operating problems as they affect the operations of the bank. In all of the above responsibilities, the incumbent is directed by and reports to the Senior Vice President-Operations and/or the Executive Vice President-Operations. He confers with his superiors and keeps them informed on important operational matters and obtains approval and makes recommendations he deems necessary for major changes in operating policies and major equipment purchases.

The function of Central Operations is to assure smooth operation of the various activities, to provide overall control of the considerable operating, manpower and equipment expenses involved and to provide liaison and coordination for the interrelationships involved within this area, as well as with other departments of the bank. The

FIGURE 7–2 (*Continued*)

incumbent keeps himself informed about all matters of operations, personnel, and costs in his area by means of reports and frequent conversations with his staff and department heads, on such subjects as volume, personnel complements, overtime, amount of temporary help used, differences, departmental income and expense, work quality and problems, etc. He reviews and analyzes such data, watching for undesirable trends or other indications and he initiates action when necessary based on his investigation and judgment. This might include the initiation of studies of systems and procedures, office equipment, forms and related items. He is continually guiding his officers and staff members in the handling of unusual matters, claims, complaints, etc., working with the Legal Department and the bank's investigation unit as required.

Due to the many services performed by the departments under his jurisdiction, the incumbent is involved in a number of situations individually and consults with and is consulted by senior officers of the bank on various matters. National Division officers confer with him regarding complaints received from major customers and he initiates investigations of the matters to determine causes and institutes controls and changes in systems where required to prevent recurrence. Due to his wide experience in operations, his judgment and advice is frequently sought by officers in many other areas of the bank. He answers their questions about proper handling of transactions and assists in the solution of complicated problems. He has ultimate responsibility for vault controls in his area and he approves changes and authorizations for personnel to act.

The incumbent is concerned with certain aspects of personnel administration in the departments under his supervision. He reviews their salary increase recommendations with his staff and the department heads to assure conformity with established salary policy. He confers with his superiors and makes appropriate recommendations for officers' salary adjustments, as well as appointments to official status or promotions in rank. He approves or disapproves recommendations for changes in departmental personnel complements. Through guidance counsel and job assignment, he trains his own officers and follows through to assure that they do likewise with their subordinates in order to attain maximum utilization of specific talents and to develop latent qualities for broader assignments.

The background specifications for this position are a broad knowledge of bank operating procedures and practices as well as intimate knowledge of all technical and operating aspects of the various departments under his supervision, acquired through experience, and the administrative ability to deal effectively with operational and personnel problems to promote efficient performance and harmonious relationships with all areas involved. Pertinent knowledge of the Uniform Commercial Code, rules of the Federal Reserve Bank and the Clearing House is necessary, as well as a general acquaintance with State Banking Laws and certain Federal regulations.

Through attendance at departmental meetings, he assures the dissemination of pertinent information, both upwards and downwards, and supplies systems, machine and bank operations knowledge necessary to solve particular problems or to work out ways to perform operations more efficiently or economically. He attends the meetings of the Corporate Trust and International Operating Committees and serves as a member of the bank's Emergency Preparedness Committee which deals with the protection of records and personnel in case of attack or other disasters.

PREPARED BY	REVIEWED BY	APPROVED BY	DATE
HT	JR	FWO	8/19/65

FIGURE 7–3

**A Chart Showing How the Line Supervisor Is Expected to
Apportion His Time at Martin-Baltimore**

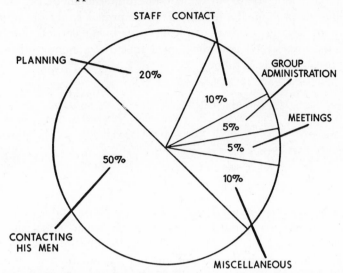

"Line and Staff Responsibilities in Engineering" by A. J. Kullas, Chief Engineer of Martin-
Baltimore (Baltimore, Maryland). In *Line-Staff Relationships in Production* (American Management
Association Special Report No. 18, 1957), pp. 62–63.

We ask the line supervisor to spend 50 percent of his time in *contact
with his men,* communicating job objectives to them, monitoring their work,
giving them guidance and counsel, and trying, in effect, to insure a reliable
product that reflects our experience while, at the same time, lending support
to the growth of every individual as fast as the individual can develop.

We expect the line supervisor to use 20 percent of his time for *planning.*
This includes two distinct kinds of activity: (1) technical planning, which
is an approach to the solution of a specific problem; and (2) calendar-time
planning, which sets the project pace and determines when we will get the
answers that we need.

Another 10 percent of the line supervisor's time should be devoted to
staff contact, because whatever success we have had in the past is generally
a reflection of the judgment and experience of our staff men, who have
many years of experience behind them. We feel that association between
the line supervisor and staff men is time well spent. New problems and
doubtful solutions are clarified in the light of the staff man's experience.
The result is a better job by the line supervisor and, of course, an improved
product.

Five percent of the line supervisor's time is allocated to *meetings,* another
5 percent to *group administration,* and 10 percent to miscellaneous activities.[3]

---

[3] A. J. Kullas, "Line-Staff Relationships in Engineering," *Line-Staff Relationships
in Production* (American Management Association Special Report No. 18, 1957),
pp. 53–64.

It is of interest to note that the time apportionment of line supervisors expected at Martin-Baltimore and discussed by Mr. Kullas in 1957 bears considerable similarity to an actual time apportionment discovered by the author in preliminary results of an empirical study of supervisory practices of a large clerical employer now being carried out by him. Supervisors were asked how they spent their time, among other things, and the breakdown is as follows:

	Percent
Contacting his men	50
Planning	20
Staff contact	10
Group administration	5
Meetings	10
Miscellaneous	5

Actually the type of work being done has considerable influence on the way supervisors apportion their time. In some situations it may be necessary for a supervisor to spend considerable time making various informal contacts with people outside his immediate work group. Although the formal structure and his job description may make no provision for such contacts, both the work flow and the supervisor's perception of the job may convince him that they are necessary. In fact there are a number of supervisors who believe that such contacts help them to be more effective supervisors. They feel that it is part of their responsibility to be well known throughout the organization so that their area of responsibility can gain support and cooperation. Further, they believe that to handle work problems properly it is desirable to establish relationships horizontally with fellow supervisors and diagonally with managers on various levels who are neither subordinates nor their direct superiors. It may be particularly fruitful for an ambitious supervisor to develop upward relationships in the organization. This is desirable if he has promotables and he is ready himself for greater responsibilities. Naturally if this is the way a supervisor perceives his job then he must plan his time apportionment accordingly.

Time utilization

Another way of looking at time may be useful for the supervisor. In most instances time is evaluated only in its quantitative dimension. It should be recognized that there are qualitative differences in time use and minutes, hours, or days are not the only way to evaluate time utilization.

An interesting comparison can be drawn between two important things many of us value—time and money. For instance, certain funds are necessary for immediate needs while others are invested for future purposes. Some we set aside for specific obligations, such as charity and education, but even the wisest individuals waste some of their money.

All that must be done is to substitute the word "time" for the word "money" in the above sentences and the comparison becomes more clear. In a supervisor's daily work all kinds of demands are placed on available time. To overcome the time problem he may frequently resort to expedient measures such as handling only pressing matters, taking short-cuts, completing only part of the task, taking work home, and turning out work that may be lower in quality than he desires it to be.

Time spent for immediate results. A certain amount of the work one does yields immediate results. These are the tasks which affect daily work. For instance, the supervisor makes work assignments to his subordinates and he expects them to meet the deadlines he has given; he helps an employee with a knotty problem; he dictates letters and prepares reports; he answers the telephone; and he coordinates the efforts of his department. All of these time uses have an immediate result. The supervisor expects a payoff in direct relation to the time invested.

Time invested for future results. This type of time expenditure is carried out with the future in mind. Weeks or months may go by before the supervisor gets a return on his investment and there is an element of risk present. He may not always get the results he expects. Nevertheless, he must invest the time if he expects future reward and improvement. The time he spends training and developing subordinates may come back to him in the form of greater efficiency for his department. Working on the development of new methods, on improving relations, or undertaking a program of self-development are investments of time in his future and the future of his employees. Planning for the next six months or year enables him to assess his needs and anticipate problems. This investment returns to him in the form of a more smoothly functioning work group with a minimum of crises.

Time for the company as a whole. While most of the effort of any supervisor is directed toward the improvement and effective functioning of his own area of responsibility, he must be concerned with the relationship of his department with others in the company and the company as a whole. After all, any organization is no more effective than the sum total of effectiveness generated by all of the units which make up that organization. Thus when he is concerned about a policy interpretation and he discusses this concern with his superior, this may return to him as greater understanding and clearer communication. Keeping staff specialists informed of the effect of installing a new procedure or program, such as work measurement, brings returns to the supervisor in the form of better cooperation with staff departments and it gives them a better understanding of line operations. Discussing matters of mutual importance with other supervisors, preparing reports for higher management, attending meetings—all of these can result in more overall efficiency, greater understanding, and better interdepartmental coordination. Following established policies and procedures, so that he does not have to continually explain his actions to his superiors, gives him time for the improvement of his own department.

Wasted time.   No matter how hard a supervisor may try not to, he will waste some time. Many individuals have been involved in conversations that are unnecessary, in misdirected telephone calls, and in searches for information that nobody really needed. Then there are the informal conferences on World Series games, pretty girls in mini-skirts, politics, and other "important" topics that steal time away from busy days.

There are some supervisors who pad their efforts to make their jobs seem more important. Others take too long on coffee breaks, telephone calls, or memorandum writing. They do work that could be delegated to subordinates or they argue needlessly with a superior and end up doing what he wants anyway.

Not all time that is spent on matters not directly connected with a supervisor's work is wasted, however. All supervisors should spend some time just thinking. This thinking could include an evaluation of his performance in the discharge of his responsibilities and plans for self-development. Conversations with superiors, peers, and subordinates can create bridges for better understanding. Reading periodicals and books that are job-related can prepare him for future responsibility.

Delegating to subordinates

Before the supervisor can relieve himself, by delegation, of any of his tasks, he must pick out subordinates who are able and willing to receive the added responsibilities—subordinates who are promotable. The supervisor should determine what additional training they need to handle the tasks and how the tasks will influence the present makeup of their jobs. He should show the subordinates that the delegation is in line with two good business practices—decentralization of authority and job enlargement. Their increased authority and responsibility will make them of more value to the company and should make their jobs more interesting, challenging, and satisfying.

When a subordinate gets new responsibilities, he needs to get, along with them, a clear picture of what he is to do and how much authority he has been given, how important the job is, and why he in particular was chosen to handle it. The people he will be dealing with must also be told about the new arrangement. In delegating a responsibility, the supervisor is not reducing his own responsibility; he is still answerable to his boss for the way the work is done. He must therefore set up a way to maintain control—that is, to keep posted on how the subordinate is doing.

The need for total planning

In Chapter 2 the systems approach to organization structure was discussed. This same concept is useful in planning. Proper coordination of all organizational activities is necessary if goals are to be met effectively. By recognizing the organization as a total system made up of several interdependent substructures, planning can and should consider the relationships of all parts of the structure. Consideration should also be given to the effect of one activity on other activities and whether or not the accomplishment of a subgoal distorts or makes difficult the attainment of other organizational goals.

Such a dilemma apparently exists in the airline industry. Airplanes have been designed to be comfortable and the jet engine has revolutionized air travel. Passenger volume has increased greatly and indications are that it will grow still further. New planes are being developed to go faster and carry more passengers than present models. In fact many airlines are using an airplane which can carry almost 400 passengers. So the goal of serving passengers in relative comfort and speeding them to their destinations seems to have been met—or has it? One of the bottlenecks that the airlines apparently did not adequately plan for is baggage handling. Baggage claim areas are crowded and confusing and they promise to be even more so when larger planes are in use delivering many more planes to destinations at one time. Baggage gets lost, stolen, mislaid, or placed on wrong flights and does not reach the same destination as the passenger who owns it. At times it catches up with the passenger on a later flight, but this may mean considerable waiting and undue inconvenience. Crowded airways, landing delays, terminal facilities that are overcrowded, poor parking for automobiles, ticket errors, among others are all factors negating goal achievement. So the objective of service to the customer-passenger has not been fully realized.

Apparently the aviation industry is the victim of poor planning and has not recognized the total dimensions involved in effective passenger service. Getting a passenger to his destination is just one part of the total system which includes such obvious things as ticket purchase, baggage handling, parking space, terminal facilities, scheduling, pricing, advertising, personnel recruitment, customer relations, airports, airways, and many others.

Obviously there are many other industries and organizations in our society that could furnish examples of the lack of total planning. Any organization should consider its planning effort as contributing to the total system. All aspects of that system should be considered if goals are to be achieved satisfactorily. Naturally this requires an uncommonly effective management team with an appreciation for the systems approach.

Evidence of poor planning

A supervisor should suspect poor planning if he is run ragged trying to get his work done; if his department is unable to meet deadlines; if it is a place of conflict and confusion; if work is held up for lack of materials, tools, or trained workers; or if his men are rushed to the point where quality suffers, housekeeping is sloppy, and accidents are high.

Some of the indications of poor planning are:

Delivery dates not met.
Machines idle.
Materials wasted.
Some machines doing jobs that should be on smaller machines.
Some men overworked; other men underworked.
Some workers stalling in order not to run out of work.
Skilled workers doing unskilled work.
Men fumbling on jobs for which they have not been trained.
Quarreling, bickering, buck-passing, and confusion.

When there is good planning in a department, section, or unit, the work flows through in a swift, shallow stream. Men are busy but not rushed. There is good housekeeping, cooperation among the workers, and respect for the leadership of the supervisor.

Some of the benefits of good planning are:

Jobs turned out on time.
Good relationships with other departments.
People using their highest skills.
Workers knowing how their jobs fit into the total pattern.
Machines doing their proper jobs.
Equipment in good shape.
Materials available.
Waste kept to a minimum.

The difference between good planning and poor planning is the difference between order and confusion, between things being done on time and not being done on time, between cooperation and conflict, and between pleasant working relationships and a workday full of discord.

Why planning seems difficult

Planning involves setting up in advance what things are to be done, when they are to be done, how they are to be done, who is to do them, and where they are to be done. Planning cannot be achieved without effort. It requires thinking, and most people like to avoid thinking. It is easier mentally to muddle through than to think one's way through. It is easier to engage in trial and error than to weigh advantages and disadvantages. It is easier to do jobs just as they occur, moving from one job to the other, keeping busy, than it is to sit down and figure out a way of getting more done and being less busy. Planning requires knowledge, foresight, judgment, and experience.

The planner—that is, the supervisor—must have *knowledge*. He must know the skills and capacities of his employees, their strong and weak points, the jobs they can do well, and the jobs that they do poorly. He must know his equipment, the type of work it can do, and the accuracy of the work it can do. He must know that one machine can do the same job as another machine but do it better. He must also know materials and their relative cost, how to handle them, and how to keep down scrap. He must know how to break big jobs down into smaller operations.

He must have *foresight*. He must know how to anticipate difficulties and thus avoid them. He must know the length of time that jobs take and what margin of safety to allow in order to meet due dates.

He must have *judgment*. He has to weigh the various factors and make decisions. He must be able to make the correct choices. He must be able to balance the short- and long-range benefits, and he must have a good sense of priorities—putting first things first. He must have the technique of coordinating work orders so that they all fit together into a neat pattern.

He must have *experience*, and he must have profited by that experience so that he will not make the same mistake twice. There is a difference between 20 year's experience and 1 year's experience repeated 20 times. The more obstacles he has overcome, the more he will be able to anticipate. The more he plans, the better he will be able to plan.

Planning, then, requires work with the head instead of with the back. It requires that things be figured out before they are tried out.

The planning formula

Most jobs that are to be planned can be analyzed by applying the questions: *What? Why? When? Who? Where?* and *How?* The answers to these questions can be set up in terms of routing, scheduling, and dispatching.

In the analysis of a job, the first question to be answered is *What?* *What* are the operations to be performed on this job? *What* is the function of this department with regard to this job? *What* are the quantity and quality requirements of this job?

The next question is *Why?* Why is it necessary to perform all the operations? *Why* is it necessary to follow a certain sequence in the performance? *Why* is it necessary to do this job at all? In answering the question *Why?* the supervisor may be able to detect unnecessary operations and perhaps eliminate them.

The next question to ask is *When* is this job to be started in order to meet deadlines? Before the supervisor can answer the question *When?* it is necessary for him to know how long the operations will take. He will need to have accurately determined standards of performance or at least good estimates based on comparable jobs. When he knows how long the operations will take, he will know when they have to be started in order to meet deadlines. He can then fit the job into a time schedule that will permit the maximum utilization of men, materials, equipment, time, and space.

Next, the supervisor asks: *Where?* He is interested in where the various operations should be performed in his unit. He wants to know what machines can perform the operations best and what machines are available to perform the various operations.

After this, he asks: *Who* will do it? He wants to know which members of his group have the skills necessary to perform the various operations, and he wants to have these men using their highest skills as much as possible.

Then, finally, comes the question *How?* There may be several methods from which he can choose for performing various operations, and there may be better methods which he can devise.

The questions need not always be asked in the above sequence, nor can one question be answered without considering the other questions; the answer to each question will influence the answers to all the other questions. As he answers the questions, the supervisor is laying out a plan for the job along the following logical steps:

1. Analyzing the job (work order) or product to be produced.
2. Determining the total number of units to be produced in a unit of time.
3. Breaking down the separate operations or tasks.
4. Arranging the operations or tasks in the sequence in which they are to be performed.

5. Determining what is needed for each operation—materials, supplies, equipment, space, blueprints, sketches—and arranging for ordering them.
6. Estimating the number of man-hours needed for each operation.
7. Estimating the total number of each kind of worker needed.
8. Working out a time schedule for each operation—when each should begin and end.
9. Providing for any training that will be necessary to prepare men for the work.
10. Showing at what points, and to whom, instructions and directions should be given.
11. Making provisions for checking the progress of the work and for making adjustments in the schedule if necessary.

These 11 steps incorporate the activities of routing, scheduling, dispatching, and controlling.

Types of plans

It is obvious that all levels of management should be involved in planning but there is no doubt that higher management probably spends more time in this activity. They, however, are concerned with overall planning for the organization, while middle- and first-level managers develop specific plans for relatively narrower areas of responsibility. They can and do use the plans established at higher levels as the frame of reference for their planning.

Supervisors are largely concerned with two types of plans. These are:

1. *Standing plans.* These are used over and over to handle situations which occur with a great amount of regularity. Included are such things as hiring of personnel to fill openings and preventive maintenance.
2. *Single-use plans.* These are designed to achieve a specific result over a short period of time, usually one year or less. Included in this category are budgets covering items such as production, sales, raw materials and other expense items.

Another type of plan that should concern managers is frequently called the contingency or standby plan. Plans of this type are developed to cover situations which may or may not occur. If they do occur, however, a sound plan will enable a company to cope with the situation more effectively. Included here are plans for courses of action in the event of a transportation strike in the area where the company is located, disasters such as fires, floods, strikes in supplier companies, early employee release on excessively warm workdays, power blackouts, national emergencies, and other unusual situations.

The obstacles to planning

The supervisor cannot plan 100 percent the work of his department. Things go wrong; employees are absent; instructions are misunderstood; machines break down; material does not arrive on time or is difficult to work; other orders have to be pushed through.

Rush jobs—wasteful as they are—have to be handled. The best that the supervisor can do about them is to get rid of them by means of overtime, by asking his men for extra effort, or by delaying some other jobs. Then, as soon as he can, he should get onto a regular schedule again so that he won't be creating more emergencies. It often pays to keep emergency jobs off the main production line and treat them separately.

If emergencies are caused by conditions which are beyond the supervisor's control and which he can't get corrected, he should tell his boss about them and their cost. Because obstacles interfere with the scheduled progress of the work, the supervisor must allow a factor of safety or some cushion to take care of delays. When delays do occur, he must revise the schedule and thus take advantage of the cushion. Then he will be on an up-to-date basis when he schedules additional jobs.

The control function

Control is essentially concerned with trying to make events conform to plans. This implies measurement of achievement and correction of deviations to assure effective goal attainment. Control is continuous and can best be described as a circular process involving:

1. An activity being performed.
2. Standards against which the performance of the activity can be measured.
3. Measurement techniques designed to indicate to managers any deviation of actual performance from expected or standard performance.
4. Corrective action which should be taken to bring performance into line with desired results.

When managers plan they must have an objective in mind. They must also decide how they are going to reach that objective. Thus a manager most likely carries on all three activities at the same time. When he formulates a goal, he plans and determines the controls simultaneously. Controlling is keeping posted on progress. It is measuring certain elements such as time, quantity, quality, or cost against a yard-stick of standards which have been set up for the purpose. Chapter 9 deals with setting up and using standards of work performance—the *how much* and the *how well*. It deals also with budgets and standard costs as they are used as measures of performance. The controlling formula as applied to the work of the department is a matter of checking and correcting work while it is in process.

Checking is a process of measuring performance against schedules or plans to determine how the work is coming along. Not every operation has to be checked, but spot checks are necessary. Care must be taken not to overcontrol or undercontrol. The supervisor must avoid breathing down the necks of his employees; he hasn't the time to do it and it has a bad effect on them. On the other hand, he can't just let things go and then be caught unaware when deadlines cannot be met.

Correcting is the making of adjustments when things are not going as planned. Some of the developments and circumstances that cause work to get behind schedule are absences, machine breakdowns, mate-rials not arriving on time or in proper kind, and jobs being done incor-rectly. When work is piling up, it becomes necessary to reschedule parts of the jobs or put some of them on a rush basis and devote overtime or extra effort or manpower to them in order to catch up.

To understand a control system it must be recognized that compliance is its most vital component. This means adherence to the established goals, policies, procedures, and rules. In a sense these and such other things as work measurement, methods improvement, budgets, and per-formance appraisal are the tools of scientific management. In using these tools, the manager must try to carefully balance the organizational neces-sity for adherence with individual creativity. No control system should be developed which puts a straightjacket on supervisors, requiring from them unquestioning compliance. This will only tend to stifle initiative and turn the supervisor into someone who does everything "by the book."

Quantitative techniques for control

If one traced the history of scientific management starting with Fred-erick W. Taylor up to the present, he could see an ever increasing use of quantitative methods on the various factors which relate to mana-gerial decision making. Taylor's time studies reduced the worker's efforts to bits of time which could be measured and could be used as the basis for determining productivity and the rate of compensation. Pres-ent-day use of mathematics is far more sophisticated. This is partly caused by increased knowledge of the applications of quantitative analy-sis to management problems and also related to the increased complexity of these problems and the nature of the decisions required to solve them. Another vital contributing factor is the development of high-speed electronic data processing which gives the manager access to far greater amounts of information than he has ever had. To use this information effectively and to apply it to problem solving and the control of operations, quantitative methods must be employed.

Operations research. Operations research was developed during World War II when the military called upon scientists for aid in solving strategic and tactical problems. Teams of various kinds of scientists, engineers, and other scientifically trained individuals use the scientific method, mathematical techniques, and other logical means to develop possible solutions to problems which confront managers. Accurately defining operations research seems to be somewhat difficult. There are several definitions in the literature which has grown in amount since the end of World War II. There is, however, common usage of the terms, "scientific method," "mathematical model," "quantitative analysis," "optimization," and "decision making." Miller and Starr describe operations research as applied decision theory.[4] Churchman, Ackoff, and Arnoff have this to say:

Each practitioner's version of O.R.'s method (if recorded) would differ in some respects. But there would also be a good deal in common. For example, most would agree that the following are the major phases of an O.R. project:

1. Formulating the problem.
2. Constructing a mathematical model to represent the system under study.
3. Deriving a solution from the model.
4. Testing the model and the solution derived from it.
5. Establishing controls over the solution.
6. Putting the solution to work: implementation.[5]

Operations research offers a systems approach to problems because it considers the way a problem (inventory size for instance) affects problems in other areas (economic lot sizes, production costs, production planning, finance, marketing, customer service, model changes, warehousing, stability of employment, motivation, etc.). It investigates these related problems in terms of the objectives of each part of the organization and seeks a solution that is best for the organization as a whole. O.R. is a problem-solving research into the economics of operations. It uses mathematical models that are part of the technique and constructs new models, using analogies from other disciplines. There are O.R.

---

[4] David W. Miller and Martin K. Starr, *Executive Decisions and Operations Research* (Englewood Cliffs, N.J.: Prentice-Hall, Inc., 1960), p. 104.

[5] C. W. Churchman, R. L. Ackoff, and E. L. Arnoff, *Introduction to Operations Research* (New York: John Wiley & Sons, Inc., 1957), pp. 12–13.

models for such problems as production lot sizes, inventory control, allocation of resources, waiting line (queuing), replacement, and maintenance.

Although the mathematical tools and techniques could be utilized by a researcher working alone, one of the particular advantages of operations research is gained through team effort. Most business problems have many sides to them—physical, biological, psychological, sociological, economic, and engineering aspects. To see them all and grasp their interrelationships requires a team approach. The professionals on an O.R. team might be a physical scientist, an engineer, and a psychologist or social scientist. The team should also contain one or more persons thoroughly familiar with the overall operations of the company—for instance, from accounting, marketing, purchasing, or administration.

When people from a variety of disciplines are confronted with a problem, each brings to it a viewpoint and a method of attack that is drawn from the theories in his own field. This diversity of background is an advantage in recognizing, identifying, and analyzing the various aspects of problems and in adapting mathematical, statistical, and other scientific techniques to their solution. An essential arrangement in O.R. is that the team consult with managers whose operations would be affected by changes, and that the team have free access to top-level management in order to get needed information and action.

If the decision maker accepts the recommendations resulting from the O.R. study, then the researchers have the responsibility for making the recommendations usable and acceptable to the people affected by them. The specialized techniques and equations employed in solving an inventory problem, for instance, would scarcely be usable on a daily basis by people without advanced mathematical training. One of the requirements of O.R. is that solutions to problems be translated into easy formulas, decision rules, and procedures for applying them.

CPM and PERT. The planning, scheduling, and controlling of huge projects can be handled by techniques such as CPM (Critical Path Method) and PERT (Program Evaluation and Review Technique).[6] These techniques are part of the growing assortment of mathematical tools for decision making. They evolved from a combination of mathematical theory and various scheduling and charting techniques.

PERT was devised between 1956 and 1958 for the Navy Department, to keep track of the thousands of details involved in the development of the Polaris submarine missile. It is a network flow chart with built-in uncertainty; there are three estimates of the time needed to complete each task—an optimistic estimate, a normal one, and a pessimistic one.

---

[6] For a detailed discussion, see Richard I. Levin and Charles A. Kirkpatrick, *Planning and Control with PERT/CPM* (New York: McGraw-Hill Book Co., 1966).

CPM was designed in 1957 by Remington Rand for Du Pont for use in scheduling the construction of a chemical plant. CPM uses a single estimate of the time each task will take. Both techniques diagram the events on a network. Figure 7–4 is an illustration of such a network and the use of CPM in selecting the most economical schedule for a tiny hypothetical project.

The key concepts of both techniques is the *critical path* as it determines which jobs should be rushed in order to get early completion of the whole project; and, conversely, which jobs if slowed down will delay the completion of the project. Of all the activities involved in a project, only a small percentage of them control the schedule for the entire project. For instance, in building a house some of the tasks can be done at almost any time but the foundation must be poured before the frame can go up and the roof go on; the heating must go in before the plaster. These essential activities are the ones that must be done in proper sequence: something must be completed before something else can be started. These events are the ones on the critical path: *the time needed for their completion determines the total time for the project.* Most jobs don't lie along the critical path; if they take a little longer than expected, they won't delay anything. They provide a certain amount of slack and even in emergencies seldom have to be put on a rush basis. Their start can be delayed, or people can be taken off of them and transferred to the more critical activities.

The first step in constructing a network is to analyze all the work that must be done, break it into tasks in their technological order, estimate the time required to complete each task, and specify the immediate prerequisite task. (Foremen may be called upon at this stage to supply time estimates and the proper order in which operations must be performed.) Each task is drawn on the graph and marked with its identifying symbol and time. In Figure 7–4 the tasks are diagramed as arrows and their completion dates as circles. (More commonly the circle represents the task and the arrow points to the next task in the sequence.)

If the scheduler wants to hasten the completion date, he estimates the costs and results of speeding up tasks on the critical path. On a small project these calculations can be made manually. On big projects a computer is needed to take into account all the variables and keep track of the interrelated projects.

The control feature of the technique is exercised by asking the questions: Did something happen that was supposed to happen on this day or did it not? If it did not, how will it affect the total performance and how much time must be regained? The next question is: How shall the time be regained? Which tasks along the critical path can be speeded (crashed) most economically?

PERT and CPM are not intended for use in repetitive operations

FIGURE 7–4
How a Computer Decides the Cheapest Schedule for a Project
CPM is illustrated on a tiny hypothetical project. Charts by *Fortune*.

How a Computer Decides the Cheapest Schedule for a Project

Job	Normal days	Normal cost	Crash days	Crash cost	Cost of crashing dollars per day
A	3	$140	2	$210	$70
B	6	215	5	275	60
C	2	160	1	240	80
D	4	130	3	180	50
E	2	170	1	250	80
F	7	165	4	285	40
G	4	210	3	290	80
H	3	110	2	160	50
Total		$1300		$1890	

Major industrial projects, such as the building of a ship or a factory or the development of a missile, involve so many activities that no human mind can keep close track of all that is going on, much less schedule every detail in the most efficient way. New mathematical techniques, however, are giving project managers a clearer view of their work and a better opportunity to use their judgment effectively. The essential steps in one of these new techniques, Critical Path Method, are demonstrated on this page by the analysis of a tiny hypothetical project. The manager begins the scheduling by listing all the jobs that must be done (see chart at left) together with estimates of normal time and cost for each. Next he estimates how much it would cost to rush each job to completion by a crash program. All this information is fed into a computer. As the totals show, the manager could get each job done as fast as possible by spending an extra $590. But he may be able to shorten the time of completing the whole project without "crashing" every job. This is what the computer will investigate.

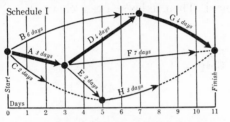

Schedule I

The manager diagrams the order in which the jobs must be done. This shows, for example, that C can be done in parallel with A but that D cannot be started until A is finished. The computer calculates the "critical path" (**ADG**) from this information. The jobs on this path determine the time (eleven days) needed to complete the whole project; the rest can be delayed somewhat (broken lines) without affecting the over-all schedule.

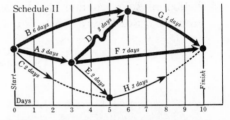

Schedule II

Next the computer calculates ways to shorten the over-all schedule by crashing some of the jobs. There may be several ways, but the computer selects the cheapest. The diagram above shows that if D is accelerated to three days instead of four, the over-all schedule can be reduced to ten days. Two more jobs, B and F, become part of a critical path, but there is still some leeway in C, E, and H. The cost of crashing D is an extra $50.

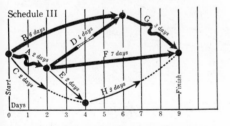

Schedule III

Again rescheduling the project so that it can be finished in nine days, the computer finds that it is best to crash both A and G by one day. Surprisingly, the extra effort put on these jobs makes it possible to relax a bit on D and allot the normal four days for its completion. Crashing A and G will cost a total of $150, but the relaxation of D saves $50, so the acceleration of the whole project from ten to nine days costs only $100 more.

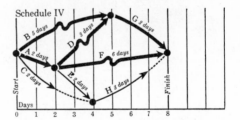

Schedule IV

If the manager wants to lop another day from the schedule, he can do so most economically by crashing three jobs: B, D, and F. Although the chart shows that F could be shortened by as much as three days, the extra hurry would have no effect on the over-all schedule, so F is shortened by only one day. The manager has now spent $300 on the crash program, compared with the $590 he might have spent to crash all the jobs.

Schedule	I	II	III	IV
Duration (*days*)	11	10	9	8
Direct cost	$1300	$1350	$1450	$1600
Indirect cost	$1210	$1100	$990	$880
Total cost	$2510	$2450	$2440	$2480

To decide which schedule is actually best from all viewpoints, the manager can instruct the computer to take other factors into account. There may be a penalty for failing to complete the project on schedule. Sometimes in actual practice contractors have found that they can make more profit by proceeding slowly and paying a penalty rather than paying heavy overtime. The chart on the left shows how the computer might include in its calculations indirect costs—e.g., overhead or penalties. In this example the indirect costs amount to a flat $110 per day, and the chart tells the manager that the cheapest schedule is the one that takes nine days.

Source: James E. Kelley, Jr., Mauchly Associates, Inc. From George A. W. Boehm, "Helping the Executive to Make up His Mind," *Fortune*, April, 1962, pp. 128 ff.

or as production control tools; they are too expensive to use when other techniques will do as well. They are used for planning and scheduling the research and development of new products, getting new products into production, constructing buildings and highways, moving plants to new locations, handling big maintenance jobs to reduce downtime, and for monitoring missiles contracts. The need for optimum control of time, cost, and manpower is spurring further developments in the basic critical path techniques, so that a wider variety of problems can be handled.[7]

Break-even analysis. Another technique used in planning is called break-even analysis. Sales volume is assumed to be the key factor in planning, and by the use of various forecasting techniques such as market research, economic forecasting, and extrapolation, a reasonable prediction of sales volume can be achieved. Then a break-even chart is prepared. (See Figure 7–5.)

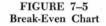

FIGURE 7–5
Break-Even Chart

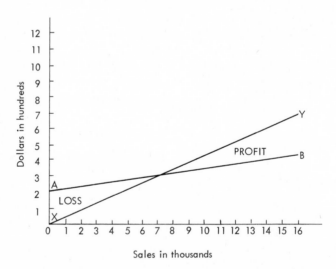

Sales in thousands

Every company has certain fixed expenses. They go on whether the company sells a thousand units or 10,000. They will not rise with increased sales. Other expenses such as those used in actually producing the product, (labor cost and material cost) rise in direct relation to sales. The cost line *AB* starts at $200 and rises with sales to $450. The

---

[7] Some of these techniques are: PERT/COST, PERT II, PERT III, PEPCO, and Super PERT. Another technique, SPAR (Scheduling Program for Allocating Resources), is an extension of the work load smoothing algorithm and is used in scheduling projects having limited resources. A technique similar to it is RAMPS (Resource Allocation and Multi-Project Scheduling).

point where line *XY*, representing sales in thousands crosses the cost line *AB* is known as the break-even point. This is the point at which the company's sales volume meets its costs exactly, but makes no profit. It can be seen that after that the profit tends to grow faster with increases in sales volume. Fixed expenses are then spread over a large number of units manufactured and are a lesser percentage of unit cost.

The break-even point in Figure 7–5 comes when the company sells 7,000 units at $300 each.

Naturally this is a simplified example. Generally a company's break-even point does not remain constant. Fixed costs can rise and if they do the break-even point will rise. It will then take more unit sales to make the same profit. A rise in price will lower the break-even point, increasing profits if costs remain constant. If variable costs such as labor and material go up then the break-even point rises and profits lower unless a price rise per unit can be passed on to the buyer.

Companies use break-even analysis by comparing projected charts with actual charts for each product manufactured.

There are many more quantitative approaches to decision making and control.[8] These have been developed in recent years to handle many of the recurring problems which managers face. The electronic computer and its capacity for handling and processing data coupled with mathematical techniques have made this possible. Routine control systems and decisions are now being processed on computers in many organizations.

Summary

Forecasting is predicting the most probable course of events of a given range of probabilities. Planning is deciding what to do about them. Planning is setting up in advance the things that are to be done, when they are to be done, how they are to be done, who is to do them, and where they are to be done. As is the case with all other managerial activities, top management sets the example for the rest of the organization in planning. Because of the increasing complexity of our society, many organizations have now established formal planning programs to assure that suitable plans will be accomplished for all organizational activities.

Each manager has a responsibility for planning. He must plan the work of his own unit and make certain that his plan coincides with the overall plans of the organization. The supervisor who fails to plan

---

[8] For a more thorough discussion, see R. E. Schellenberger, *Managerial Analysis* (Homewood, Ill.: Richard D. Irwin, Inc., 1969); and R. I. Levin and C. A. Kirkpatrick, *Quantitative Approaches to Management* (New York: McGraw-Hill Book Co., 1965).

goes from one crisis to another and never has the time to take action necessary to prevent problems from arising. His first step in improving his planning is to analyze the way he spends his own time. If his job is poorly designed it probably has too many things which demand his personal attention. Some of them are probably unnecessary, some could be done better by others in the company, some could be delegated to subordinates, and some could be eliminated. When he plans a better distribution of his own time, he is taking action to improve the design of his job. He should try to allocate a minimum amount of time to routine work, a maximum amount to creative work (solving problems), and an adequate amount to take care of emergencies.

Proper coordination of all organizational activities is necessary if goals are to be met effectively. Every activity has an effect on other activities and this effect must be considered when planning takes place. There is a need for total planning on all levels and in all activities of the organization.

The control function is concerned with trying to make events conform with plans. This implies measurement of achievement and correction of deviations to assure effective goal attainment. In recent years there has been an increase in the use of quantitative techniques in the development of control systems. Operations research is one of these and is used in a great number of organizations to aid in the solving of such recurring problems as inventory control, production control, and preventive maintenance. The planning, scheduling, and controlling of huge projects calls for techniques such as PERT and CPM. They have been and are being used by many government agencies and large organizations. Break-even analysis is another quantitative technique used by managers to aid in the determination of profitability of products manufactured and sold by a company. There are many other quantitative techniques now being utilized by managers in all types of organizations. The use of mathematics has been made possible by the advent of electronic computers with their capability to handle large amounts of data very rapidly.

CASE 1

Lou Kane is the department head of a clerical operation in the accounting division of a large firm. There are 50 people in the department, including 5 statistical typists and 8 stenographers.

During the first three months of each year, the department has to prepare a great deal of year-end work such as statements, tax forms, balance sheets, and other accounting data. The volume of work generated during this period requires considerable overtime for all of the employees. It averages 10 to 12 hours a week including Saturdays.

The labor market in which Lou's company operates is characterized by extreme shortages of competent clerical employees and high labor turnover.

Lou has been short one statistical typist and one stenographer for several months and one statistical typist has been hospitalized for several weeks and it is not known when she will return. These shortages of help have placed increased pressure on the other girls, none of whom are enthusiastic about all of the overtime work. Lou has been somewhat successful in recruiting typists from other areas of the company to work overtime during this period.

Recently one of Lou's best statistical typists who had been with the company five-and-a-half years got married. After losing her for a two week honeymoon, she indicated on her return that her husband would not allow her to work overtime.

Lou is concerned about losing her overtime contribution, but he is more worried about the effect of her refusal to work overtime on the other girls who already feel negative about overtime work.

1. What can Lou do to convince the other girls to continue overtime work?
2. Should he transfer the girl to another area of the company?
3. Is the girl justified in refusing to work overtime?
4. What other courses of action are open to Lou to alleviate his problems?

CASE 2

The men in your department are very slow starting work at the beginning of a shift. They like to stand around and chat for awhile and then slowly go after their materials and equipment, stalling as much as possible. If there is the least obstacle in the way of getting started, they will not take the initiative and clear it up, but will wait for you to come around and find out why they are not working. It would be very difficult to put the work on a piece rate.

1. What are some of the causes of not starting work promptly?
2. How should you go about getting the workers started promptly?
3. What is meant by "departmental planning"?
4. Outline the steps to be taken in setting up departmental planning.

CASE 3

The X manufacturing company has 2,000 employees, and a great deal of its work consists of special orders (jobbing shop work). Most of the employees are taking the "rest" too literally in relation to the restrooms. About 20 percent of the workers make it a practice to waste from 15 minutes to a half hour in the restrooms at the beginning of each day. However, once they get started working, they do not waste much time. Midmorning and midafternoon rest periods are provided.

The big boss has passed the word down the line that too much time is being lost, that he expects everyone to start working at the beginning of the day, and that better planning by the supervisors would help to correct the problem.

1. How can the supervisor use planning to get his men started?
2. What are some of the difficulties involved in getting prompt starting? How can they be overcome?
3. What are some of the schemes supervisors can use for cutting down the abuse of restroom privileges?

CASE 4

You are a small contractor and you are consistently underbid and outperformed by another small contractor named Early. It isn't a matter of equipment because he has much less than you have. It isn't a matter of employees because you both use many of the same construction workers; they move around as jobs are ready. A friend of yours has worked for all the contractors around, and you asked him how Early got more work out of everybody. Your friend said the work pace wasn't bad—not too much pushing, just steady, everything planned, no emergencies.

He said that Early must have influence with suppliers—that everything needed for a job was always there at the right time, of the right type and size, and in the right amount. It seemed to him that Early never ran out of anything, never had to wait for anything, never had to do work in the wrong sequence because somebody or something was missing. While other contractors had men and trucks out on the road all the time picking up materials and emergency supplies, Early never sent his men on errands. In fact, he had only one little truck which he used himself to drive to the job.

1. What savings can be made through planning and scheduling?
2. What are some of the things that must be taken into account in planning and scheduling?
3. Does planning have a snowball effect—that is, does good planning by the boss beget good planning in those who work for and with him?
4. Does poor planning by the boss cause people to relax in their efforts to carry out their commitments?

CASE 5

You are superintendent of a small production plant making a line of tables—coffee tables, lamp tables, dining tables, and end tables. It has been reported to you that some of the finishing work has been poorly done and that there are complaints from the customers.

You take up the problem with Smith, the head of the finishing department. He says that he knows of the poor work, that it is due to the speed his workers have to maintain, first, to meet delivery dates and, second, to take care of the irregular flow of work of the fabricating department. He says that sometimes he receives the work in dribbles and at other times he is swamped. He insists that if his men had enough time they could do a good finishing job.

Next you take the problem up with Jones, the head of the fabricating department. He claims that the fault is not his; that he is doing his duty by fabricating all raw materials as fast as they are sent to him, slowing down only for machine breakdowns or material shortages, which are quite frequent. As soon as these are cleared up, he goes full speed ahead.

1. Evaluate Smith's arguments.
2. Evaluate Jones's arguments.
3. Where else do difficulties lie?
4. Devise an overall planning program.
5. Who should run it?

CASE 6

Often your chief comes to you and tells you that a certain piece of work is to be rushed and he would appreciate it if you would get it out in a hurry. You give the crew a pep talk, and they step up their pace and get it out before schedule. In about half such cases, the finished work remains on the floor one or two days before it is moved to the next department. This delay makes the men angry, and they feel that they have been imposed upon.

1. Are the workers justified in this feeling?
2. What might be some of the reasons for rush jobs?
3. What might be some of the causes of this delay?
4. What excuses should you give the men?
5. What should you say to your chief?
6. How should rush work be handled?

CASE 7

In order to get extra business the sales department promises early delivery dates on special orders. The promised delivery dates are seldom met. The special orders are not very profitable. They disrupt production and they cause conflicts between the sales, the purchasing, the production control, and the manufacturing departments.

1. Describe some of the difficulties caused by special orders that have to be rushed through the plant.
2. Who should determine delivery dates? Justify your answer.
3. Set up a policy and a procedure for handling special orders so that they will cause a minimum amount of difficulty.

CASE 8

One of your assistants, a supervisor named Joe, comes to you and asks you to help him get control of his unit. He states that while you were running the unit everything went smoothly, but now he cannot keep ahead of the job. The work load has not changed to any extent, and most of the overall planning is handled by you and the production control department.

Joe tells you that he spends all his time keeping his workers busy so that due dates can be met and that he has no time left in which to develop a team spirit, take care of the problems of his men, improve the efficiency of his unit, or any of the other activities a good supervisor should engage in. All his time is spent in such routine tasks as checking the work of his men, explaining jobs, giving the machines a final checkup after they have been set up, getting supplies, and the like. Since these and similar tasks consume his whole working day, he gets out his reports after hours so that he can be free of interruptions. He states further that at times he runs some of the machines when the boys get behind because he believes that it builds morale and sets a pace for the operators.

1. How are you going to help him solve his problem?
2. What are the supervisor's major responsibilities?
3. What responsibilities can he delegate?
4. How can he retain control over those responsibilities he delegates?
5. How is he going to get his workers to assume added responsibilities?

CASE 9

You supervise a group of 15 people of various specialties who were drawn from other groups in the company and brought together six months ago to work on a project. The work requires constant interaction between the various specialists in the group. They were cooperating well until two weeks ago when on March 1 you brought up the subject of scheduling their summer vacations.

You told them to decide among themselves when each one should take his vacation, since they knew which people would be absent at the same time without disrupting the work. You gave them sheets listing the amount of vacation each was entitled to because of length of service. The periods are one week, two weeks, three weeks, and four weeks. You reminded them that company policy forbids split vacations, off-season vacations, and vacation scheduling that disrupts production.

Although seniority governs vacation scheduling for hourly workers in the shop, it has never been established as a policy in salaried groups such as yours. The company has always stated that the requirements of the work should govern the scheduling.

Since you turned over the vacation scheduling to your group, the opportunists are buzzing around making deals that will fix themselves up with the choice schedules. People are aligning first with one faction and then with another, whichever will give them the best deal. A few are refusing to deal on the grounds that their seniority or status should entitle them to first choice. All this political maneuvering is taking up time and interfering with the cooperation that is essential to the progress of the work.

1. What should you do now?
2. How should a supervisor go about setting up policies in a newly formed group?
3. What cautions should a supervisor observe in bringing subordinates into decision making?
4. How much time should be allowed between bringing up a problem like this and forcing it to a solution?
5. How can the supervisor ward off problems of conflict between status and seniority?

CASE 10

You are the superintendent of a shop doing jobbing work. The job of planning is handled by the several foremen. At present, the shop is swamped with orders, and delivery dates are not being met, so top management plans to install a production control department. The purpose of this department will be to obtain a smooth flow of work through the shop and to set up delivery dates that can be met.

As planned, this production control department will be made up of three sections—routing, scheduling, and dispatching. The routing section is to route the parts from *specific* machine to *specific* machine throughout the shop. The scheduling section is to determine how long each batch of work should take and to set up due dates. The dispatching section is to take care of all the paper work, such as move tickets, job tickets, tool tickets, material tickets, inspection tickets, etc., and follow the progress of work through the shop and report back to the routing and scheduling sections any adjustments that might be necessary.

1. Analyze this plan with the idea of making it operate successfully.
2. Should there be any modifications? Justify your answer.
3. What qualifications should the head of each of the three sections have?
4. What are some of the difficulties you might run into in the installation tion control department?
5. To what extent can the shop foremen make or break this plan?
6. How is this plan going to interfere with the jobs of the shop foremen?
7. How are you going to sell the foremen and keep them sold on the produc- and running of this production control department?

CASE 11

Engineering changes inaugurated by the main office are continually forcing modifications of the projects being built in your department. As a result, the workers often have to rework, abandon, or reconstruct jobs on which they have put many hours of labor. They are losing interest and saying that there is no need to hurry because the job will be changed several times before it is completed. Whenever you have asked your superior to give you the reason for the changes, he has answered that the home office makes them or that they are due to changes in market requirements and technology.

1. Should you contact the home office?
2. Should you stall production in the hope that the changes can be incorporated in initial constructions?
3. How can the morale of your department be raised?
4. What are some of the reasons for engineering changes?
5. Discuss ways of controlling such changes.

CASE 12

A medium-sized manufacturing job shop with excellent metalworking capabilities had been enjoying a satisfactory business manufacturing parts for aircraft firms. But its business began to fall off as the aircraft firms curtailed operations. Management, concerned over the lack of long-range planning of products, hired a highly educated engineer to develop manufacturing processes and investigate product lines that would carry the company profitably through the next five years. The new engineer was made a staff assistant to the manager.

The organization consisted primarily of line personnel in the manufacturing functions. The line supervisors agreed that long-range planning was desirable and each had his own views on what the planning should be. Their opinion of the staff assistant was (1) that he was paid too much and was of no real value to the company; (2) that he didn't know much about shop practices and techniques because the questions he asked on his infrequent visits to the shop area exposed his ignorance of how things get done in the shop. The general attitude toward the new man was to let him find out for himself; no one volunteered any information or suggestions.

The manager recognized that there was a controversy but took no action about it. The engineer resigned after eight months of making no progress.

1. What could the manager have done to make the engineer's work productive?
2. Should the manager use his line supervisors for help in long-range planning?

CASE 13

As manager of the test components laboratory, your main responsibility is to have adequately trained personnel and test equipment available to meet the needs of the other departments which use your lab for research and development testing. These departments bring hardware to your area and specify the type of test and limits they require; then it is your responsibility to figure how and if the test can be performed and to have the personnel available to run the test. Equally important to you as a manager is that your department should stay within its established budget. You have recently received the following complaints:

1. From the departments that you service: The hardware has not been moving fast enough through your laboratory.
2. From your own management: The costs of your operation are running too high.
3. From your employees: The technicians feel insecure because they are changed so often from one job to another that they are always in a learning phase—never staying long enough with one type of work to master it.

Your problem is complicated because of the difficulty of determining just what the project will need in the future. If you staff up to current requirements, you may find these reduced in a month, and you will have extra people, which is just what management is looking at today.

Also it is impossible for you to assign technicians to just one certain area because personnel have to be available to perform where the job requirements are. This means you practically have to train your technicians so that each can handle most of the test equipment within your lab.

As a manager, what would be your approach to this problem?

CASE 14

You are working in a shop (or an office) while going to school and you are kept so busy with the job and the schoolwork that you are doing justice to neither. The time has come for you to evaluate the situation—determine how much time you should devote to each and then reapportion your time so that you spend it more effectively.

1. For at least two or three weeks (or until you can get a representative sample) fill out a log sheet accounting for your waking time; do it every two hours. Include leisure time as well as school and job time.
2. Study the present distribution of your time. Find out how you distribute your time now on the job, how you distribute your time in relation to different kinds of schoolwork, and how you distribute the rest of your time.
3. Evaluate the present distribution of your time in terms of your goals.
4. Reapportion your time so that it will be used more effectively in terms of your goals.

CASE 15

Top management has decided that a standards laboratory (or a similar type of department with which you might be more familiar) should be set up in the organization. The function of the standards laboratory will be to calibrate periodically all the inspecting and testing equipment and gauges used in the plant. At present this service is rendered by a supplier of raw materials to your plant, because the supplier has the necessary personnel and equipment doing similar work in his plant. Your company wants to do its own calibration work because:

1. The supplier—having no competition—charges too much for his service.
2. Some of the departments within your company are dissatisfied with the quality of the work being done by the outsider.
3. The future expansion plans of your company indicate that the potential need for the service will be greater than the supplier has the capital, equipment, or competent technical personnel to take care of.

You have been given the task of organizing the standards laboratory. At least three months will be required to obtain sufficient equipment and personnel to put it on an operating basis. Ever since the supplier learned that the company plans this move, he has been uncooperative. In fact, the quality of his service is now so bad that your company's production has been adversely affected, and the government inspectors of goods on military orders have said that unless the quality of your product is improved promptly, contracts may be terminated.

1. How would you go about building such a standards laboratory?
2. Where should it be in the organization? Why?

FOLLOWING UP ON THE JOB

Work planning

1. Are you meeting all your deadlines?
2. Do you figure out jobs in advance in terms of What? Why? When? Where? Who? and How?
3. Are some of your men overworked while others are underworked?
4. Are some of your workers stalling in order not to run out of work?
5. Do you know the capacities of all your men and equipment?
6. Are skilled workers doing unskilled work?
7. Are your machines running at the correct speeds and feeds for the jobs on which they are working?
8. Are men and machines being held up on account of a lack of materials?
9. Do you know how long each operation should take?
10. Do you have a system for taking care of rush jobs?

Personal planning

1. Are you being run ragged trying to get your job done?
2. Do you make up a personal timetable periodically, and then analyze it?
3. Do you plan the distribution of your time?
4. Are you spending most of your time doing supervisory work?
5. Do you delegate enough responsibility and authority to your subordinates?
6. Does it take all your time to correct mistakes that wouldn't have occurred if time had been taken to train the subordinates in the first place?

Controlling

1. Do you make use of the data available to you to determine the effectiveness of performance in your area of responsibility?
2. Do you take corrective action promptly so that errors do not get out of hand?
3. Do your subordinates know what is expected of them?
4. Do you report performance data of your unit promptly so that higher levels of management are kept aware on a timely basis?

8 Improving methods

Methods improvement defined. Improving methods is part of the supervisor's job. Opposition to methods improvement. A systematic approach to methods improvement. The seven-step technique applied to a methods improvement problem. Step 1. Select a process or procedure to be improved. Step 2. Describe the present method. Step 3. Analyze the present method. Step 4. Develop several improved methods. Step 5. Select the most practical improved method. Step 6. Try out and install the new method. Step 7. Follow up the improved method. Illustration of applying the seven-step technique to a methods improvement problem. Illustration of an operation study. Technique for studying an operation. Procedure for making an operation study. Human engineering. Methods improvement by employees—JMT. Cost reduction. Summary.

Methods improvement is a systematic technique of studying and improving a work situation so that people are able to do better work with less effort, to do it in less time without hurrying, with greater safety and at less cost.

In methods improvement work, several assumptions are made:

1. That when there are several ways of doing a job, one of these ways is usually more effective than the others.
2. That effective ways of doing work can be created by combining the "best" ways of doing the several operations that make up the work.
3. That systematic thinking is more productive for improving methods than is undisciplined ingenuity.

Methods improvement defined

Methods improvement might be defined as the technique of uncovering better ways of doing work and putting them into effect. These better ways are in terms of cost, ease of operation, safety, and speed. All four of these factors have to be taken into consideration when evaluating one method against another.

"Methods improvement" is a broad term taking in everything from the quickie JMT, described later in this chapter, to the advanced techniques of the industrial engineer. The level at which the subject will be handled in this text is just below that employed by industrial engineers and consists of the fundamentals of methods improvement covered in the standard textbooks of motion and time study. The fundamentals presented here include: *a systematic approach (the seven-step problem-solving technique); description of process analysis and operation study; and principles and checklists for improving methods.*

Improving methods is part of the supervisor's job

The supervisor needs technical knowledge and skill in analyzing and improving the methods of performing the work of his department. He has the responsibility for the efficient operation of his department and for getting smooth and successful adoption of the innovations, improvements, and cost reductions that are essential to the profitability of the business.

He needs to understand the principles and techniques of methods improvement in order to recognize and correct inefficiencies in his own department and to prevent poor methods from coming into existence when new work is being set up. He must understand methods work in order to carry out his function of directing and controlling. In directing, he needs to be able to show the operator the best way to do the job and tell him why it is the best way. In controlling, he must improve methods before he can establish standards of performance.

The position of methods improvement work in the organization structure varies from one company to another. In some it takes the form of work simplification programs and is mostly a line activity; in others it is handled by the methods department; in still others it is a joint effort carried on through the cooperation of line supervisors and the staff specialists from the industrial engineering department or work measurement department. Such cooperation becomes more important as systems and equipment become more complex and departments become more interdependent.

The industrial engineering department or work measurement department is set up primarily to devise better ways of doing things. It can make methods improvement investigations on a companywide scale, starting with the raw material and ending with the finished product. Not confined by department lines, it can develop, make, or recommend major changes involving the work of many departments. When the line management man is familiar with the techniques used by these staff specialists, he can get more from the services they have to offer in solving problems involving plant layout, process layout, motion study, time study, methods improvement, and systems analysis.

The man in middle management must know enough of methods work to evaluate the programs developed by staff specialists and either approve or reject them.

Opposition to methods improvement

A group of supervisors in a management training conference compiled this list of answers when asked how their rank-and-file people felt about methods improvement.

> They don't like changes. They don't want to change their habits. They are not prepared for change. They don't see any reason to change the present method.
> They don't understand.
> They feel they will be expected to do more work for the same money.
> They fear their earnings might be reduced.
> They think they might have to learn a new job.
> They devised the present method and don't like other people changing it.
> They think that the proposed method was already tried and found to be unsuccessful.
> They fear that they will be replaced by machines.
> They feel that they are being criticized.
> They feel that maybe they should have thought of the change themselves.
> They object to having outsiders tell them how to do their jobs.
> They feel secure in the old method.
> They object to not being consulted in advance.
> They worry about how the new method will affect them and how they will learn to do the new jobs.
> They fear they may lose a portion of their jobs.
> They feel that their trade secrets are being impinged upon and their skills diluted; that they could thus be replaced more easily.
> They fear that if the new method gets more work done with fewer people, they will be out of a job, or their friends will be out of a job.

The supervisors didn't mention that employees fear a loss of status and dignity, a downgrading in importance, or loss of their hopes of getting ahead. When employees feel that a change in their jobs is depriving them of something they value, the change may be met by a prolonged drop in production, by hostility, grievances, absences, and quits. Resistance to change and ways to decrease it in introducing methods improvements is discussed in Chapter 15. Techniques for introducing change must be combined with techniques for improving methods and applied with skill with respect to human relations.

A systematic approach to methods improvement

In handling methods improvement problems, a systematic approach has been found to be more productive than undisciplined ingenuity. The systematic approach used in this text is the seven-step problem-solving technique developed in Chapter 1 and applied to the redesign of a procedure in Chapter 3. It is similar to the techniques developed by Barnes, Nadler, Mundel, and other writers in the field of motion and time study. The steps in these several techniques vary from five to nine. The seven-step technique is a rather detailed one; Steps 3 and 4 are often combined, but they are treated separately here so that they can be explained more easily.

People handling a methods improvement problem may say that they are making a process analysis or an operation analysis. Actually they are doing more than analyzing; they are applying a systematic problem-solving technique. Analysis is just the step of interpreting the information about an existing problem. A person who is improving a method must not only analyze the problem; he must also solve it. Process analysis is Step 3 of the seven-step method, and it is the step that uses the checklists and suggestion lists to analyze the information that is charted in Step 2. So that the reader will not get lost in the pages of checklists, suggestion lists, and charts that are used in Step 3, he can get his bearings from the following outline.

The seven-step technique applied to a methods improvement problem

Step 1.	*Select the process or procedure to be improved.*
Clearly define the problem or problems.	A. Pick a bottleneck, a new job, a man-hours' consumer, an unsafe or unpleasant job, an inefficient procedure, a cause of error or scrap. B. Limit the extent of the study. C. List the benefits expected.
Step 2.	*Describe the present method.*
Gather the information.	A. Make a flow process chart. B. Make a flow diagram.
Step 3.	*Analyze the present method.*
Interpret the information.	A. Decide on the depth of the study. B. Ask What? Why? Where? When? Who? How? C. Apply principles and checklists.

Step 4.   ***Develop several improved methods.***

Develop   A. Eliminate, simplify, combine, rearrange.
solutions.   B. Consult others: superiors, subordinates, associates,
                    staff specialists.

Step 5.   ***Select the best practical solution.***

Select the   A. Evaluate the solutions in terms of the human, safety,
best   cost, and time factors.
practical   B. Get necessary approvals.
solution.   C. Chart the proposed method or procedure.

Step 6.   ***Try out and install the new method.***

Put the   A. Make a limited trial application.
solution into B. Explain to, prepare, and train those affected.
operation.

Step 7.   ***Follow up the improved method.***

Evaluate the   A. Periodically compare actual performance with the
effectiveness   new standard.
of the   B. Investigate variations from the new method.
solution.

Step 1.   Select a process or procedure to be improved

In the usual treatment of the subject of methods improvement, the emphasis is placed upon originating new ways of doing things. But many supervisors claim that they have no talent for designing new ideas, that this is out of their line—something for the experts.

The supervisor who shies away from devising new ways should look upon methods improvement as a means of removing obstacles to the flow of work through his department or section. This is something that he can get his teeth into—a place to begin, a project that he has been needing. There is always some type of work (maybe a part no. 72 or a form no. 15) that he hates to see coming because of the difficulties and headaches that are attached to the processing of it in his department. A systematic study of the processing of this offender will uncover ways of removing the bottlenecks, decreasing the errors and rejections, and clearing up the troubles that beset it. The principles and techniques of methods improvement are the same whether a person applies them to open up a bottleneck or to design a whole new process.

The supervisor who is looking for methods improvement projects in his department might use the following checklist to uncover some.

1. Is this work a bottleneck?
2. Is this "new" work?
3. Is this work slowed down by chasing around for materials, supplies, tools, equipment, etc.?
4. Is this work a chronic headache?
5. Do people usually avoid or put off doing this work?
6. Does this work cause a high turnover or absentee rate?
7. Are omissions, errors, or excessive scrap associated with this work?
8. Does this work cause overtime?
9. Are there unsafe practices or conditions associated with this work?
10. Is this work usually behind schedule?
11. Is quality a problem in relation to this work?
12. Is this work fatiguing?
13. Is there excessive waste of materials? energy? time?
14. Is the work unpleasant because of dust? fumes? noise? temperature?
15. Does this work involve "Hurry up and wait"?
16. Is this work frequently a rush or a special job?
17. Does this work involve the greatest portion of time, men, materials, money, or equipment of the department, section, or unit?

Identify the area of possible improvements. Investigation of work problems may go into a number of areas which can be classified along the following lines. Investigation of:

1. The job: operations performed; hand and body motions for operation analysis.
2. The equipment on a job: tools, machines, work station, arrangement of work area.
3. The process or procedure: flow of the product; steps between receiving and shipping.
4. The product design: form, weight, finish, tolerances, packaging.
5. The raw material: size, shape, quantity, type, color, finish, or other specifications.

These five areas are closely interrelated in any work situation and must be considered from the standpoint of the way a change in one of them would affect the others. A change in raw materials or in the design of the product, for instance, might call for a change in process or equipment so that that the job being studied for improvement would be eliminated instead. In studying the list of the five possible areas of change, it can be seen that changes made in area 5 (the raw material) would have a much wider effect on the total work situation than would changes made in area 1 (the job). This numbering system (1 to 5) can be used in labeling ideas for improvements, making them easier to classify and consider. Class 5 and Class 4 changes for instance, might call for top-level decision.

Limit the problem. When investigating a problem and developing methods for solving it, the supervisor should restrict himself to those areas in which he can install changes. Many changes that will suggest themselves to him will lie outside the area of his authority and responsibility; he can suggest them to the supervisors of the departments involved or to the industrial engineers, but he should limit his *investigation* to his own section or department, where he can make the changes either under his own authority or by getting approval from his boss.

When developing methods, the supervisor has to restrict himself to improvements that do not affect other departments, and he must be particularly careful that the solutions to his own problems do not create more work for someone else.

Determine the benefits expected by the solution. When the supervisor is choosing a problem to study, he should list the benefits that he expects to get from solving it. Listing these desired results serves to clarify the problem. Also it enables the supervisor to judge whether the problem is worth studying: How much are these results going to be worth? How much expense should be gone to in such an investigation? Having the expected results listed in advance of the investigation gives the supervisor a yardstick by which to measure the effectiveness of the solution that he arrives at.

Expected benefits might be matters of reduction of steps or of effort or of distance traveled or of costs or hazards or time—things that can be measured in evaluating a proposed method against the present method.

Measuring a proposed method against a present method brings up the question of what to do if there is no present method. If this is a new job—one that is still in the planning stage—how is an investigator going to describe and chart a present method for it? The answer is to use the planning technique outlined in Chapter 7 and set up a tentative method to use as the basis upon which to develop a better method.

Step 2.   Describe the present method

The supervisor has selected a process or procedure to be improved. The subject that he is studying may be a piece part, an assembly, a letter, a form, a report, the paper work of a procedure, or the activities of a man whose job requires him to go from location to location to perform a service. The subject is something that moves from station to station, from machine to machine, or from desk to desk along a definite path. The supervisor is going to follow that subject like a shadow, observe everything that happens to it, write down each detail in the sequence in which it happens, and then chart it on a process chart. The chart provided for this purpose in Figure 8–11 is a flow process chart.[1]

The process chart. The supervisor must be careful not to change the subject of the study during the construction of the chart. If he is not careful he may start out following a gear blank through drilling and reaming operations, moves, milling operations, to an inspection, and continue following the inspector to the door of the women's washroom. Which incident should serve to remind him that:

1. He must *actually follow* the work; very often the path of work is different from what it is supposed to be—often for good reason.
2. He should include all the elements pertaining to the subject—and no other elements.
3. He should select a specific starting point and a specific ending point for his investigation.

The supervisor should be acquainted with the chart (Figure 8–11) on which he is going to describe what happens to his subject from the chosen starting point to the ending point. The chart has on each line a place for the numbering and description of each step, and a row of symbols from which to pick and mark the one that properly identifies that step.

Normally a step will include all the activities on one machine or at one workplace or at one desk, unless greater detailing would be more fruitful. Anything that happens to the subject is either an operation, transportation, inspection, delay, or storage. Figure 8–1 defines and gives examples of each of these steps and shows the symbol by which each is represented on the chart. This form of cataloging is used so that the process can be analyzed more easily.

A methods improvement problem from United States Steel Company is presented in Figures 8–2, 8–3, and 8–4. A study of these charts will not only show how to portray a methods problem in chart form but will also illustrate the kind of savings to be gained from a systematic study of a methods problem. Using the chart in Figure 8–2 as a model, the supervisor should fill in his own process chart,

---

[1] *Man Process Chart* is used for analyzing the method by which a man goes about doing a job that requires him to go from place to place.

Form Process Chart is similar to the flow process chart except that it deals with paper work: a printed form is being studied rather than a part.

Multiman Chart is used for analyzing the activities of a crew or gang as they go about doing a job.

Man and Machine Chart is used to analyze and synchronize the operations of a man and a machine.

Detailed information on how to construct the various charts will be found in the textbooks on motion and time study; they are listed in the suggested readings at the end of Part II of this text.

FIGURE 8–1
Process Chart Symbols

In charting a process, each thing that happens to the subject is either an operation, transportation, inspection, delay, or storage. The symbols below are used to portray these various steps as they are recorded on a flow process chart.

An *operation* is some form of work performed by a man or machine at a specific location. When a man is performing a job at a fixed work station or desk, any or all of his movements within approximately a 5-foot radius may be considered as one operation.

A *transportation* is a movement between specific locations. A distance traveled over 5 feet may be considered as a transportation.

An *inspection* occurs when something is checked, verified for quality or accuracy, or counted.

A *delay* is a stoppage of the work-in-process while it is waiting for an operation, inspection, or transportation.

A *storage* occurs when something is held in protective custody and requires authorization for its release.

SYMBOL (ASME)	NAME	REPRESENTS	EXAMPLES
○	OPERATION	Performance at a specific location, workplace, desk, that advances the work toward completion. Something is added, subtracted, changed, or created. An operation occurs when information is given or received or when planning or calculation takes place.	Drill, burr, mill, weld, spray, assemble, clean, pack, type, read, sign, repair
⇨	TRANSPORTATION	Movement of work-in-process, or person, or form, or letter, from one location to another.	To Dept. X by hand truck. To next machine by conveyor. To assembly by lift truck. To next desk by messenger. To accounting by pneumatic tube.
□	INSPECTION	Examining or checking an object in relation to quality or quantity requirements.	Check, count, weigh, gauge, check for damage. Verify address or amounts, proofread, read gauge.
D	DELAY	Condition that prevents the next step in the process (such as operation, transportation, or inspection) from being started.	Await truck, on skid, await elevator, in tote box, machine breakdown, waiting in line, out of information, supplies, or materials, in incoming or outgoing basket, waiting for signature
▽	STORAGE	Locating an object in a place where it is protected against unauthorized removal.	In storeroom, in storage, in safe, in file cabinet

FIGURE 8–2
Example—Flow Process Chart (Material)
Stocking Lumber Used for Car Blocking at Point of Use. Present Method.

Appendix 2 Page 3						FLOW PROCESS CHART	No. Y-4 Page 1 of 2

FLOW PROCESS CHART — No. Y-4 — Page 1 of 2

SUMMARY	PRESENT		PROPOSED		DIFFERENCE		CHART SUBJECT	Blocking Lumber - 4" x 4" x 8'	☐ MAN ☒ MATERIAL
	NO.	TIME	NO.	TIME	NO.	TIME			
OPERATIONS ○	1800							This lumber is piled in an outside storage yard by the vendor. When needed it is loaded on a truck manually, moved to the 23" Mill and unloaded manually. Move from 23" Mill pile to R.R. car as needed.	
TRANSPORTATIONS ⇨	901								
INSPECTIONS ☐									
DELAYS D									
STORAGES △	1						COMPANY ABC PLANT "X"		
TOTAL ELEMENTS	2702						DEPARTMENT Rolling Mills UNIT 23" Mill		
DISTANCE TRAVELLED	33,300Ft.	Ft.			Ft.		INVESTIGATED BY John Doe DATE 5/1 REVIEWED BY Richard Roe DATE 6/1		

DETAILS OF PRESENT METHOD	OPERATION / TRANSPORT / INSPECTION / DELAY / STORAGE	DISTANCE IN FEET	QUANTITY	TIME	ACTION (ELIMINATE / COMBINE / CHGE. SEQ. / SIMPLIFY)	NOTES
1 Pick up 1 piece 4" x 4" x 8'	○⇨☐D△		1			} 300 pieces comprise
2 Carry to truck	○⇨☐D△	16	1			} a truck load
3 Pile on truck	○⇨☐D△		1			}
4 Move to 23" mill by truck	○⇨☐D△	1800	300		x	Change location of storage pile
5 Pick up 1 piece 4" x 4" x 8'	○⇨☐D△		1			300 pieces
6 Move to storage pile by hand	○⇨☐D△	16	1			300 pieces
7 Place on pile	○⇨☐D△		1			
8 Hold for usage	○⇨☐D△		1			
9 Pick up 1 piece 4" x 4" x 8'	○⇨☐D△		1			
10 Carry to car	○⇨☐D△	75	1			300 pieces
11 Place in car	○⇨☐D△					
12	○⇨☐D△					
13	○⇨☐D△					
14	○⇨☐D△					Conclusions:
15	○⇨☐D△					Original storage of
16	○⇨☐D△					blocking should be at
17	○⇨☐D△					the mill storage area.
18	○⇨☐D△					
19	○⇨☐D△					
20	○⇨☐D△					
21	○⇨☐D△					
22	○⇨☐D△					

20

From United States Steel Company's *Methods Engineering Manual*, 1951. Explanation of the chart is on the following page.

FIGURE 8–3
Example—Flow Process Chart (Material)
Stocking Lumber Used for Car Blocking at Point of Use. Proposed Method.

As charted in Figure 8–2, blocking lumber used by one plant for loading slabs and billets in railroad cars was delivered by outside vendor trucks to a central storage building in the mill. Here, the truck drivers unloaded the lumber by hand and piled it according to size. Whenever the mill needed more lumber for blocking, they would call the service department and order a truck and several laborers to load the blocking lumber and take it to a storage point adjacent to the shipping area, unload it, and pile it by size. As the loaders blocked the car, they would carry the lumber from the pile to the car. This method of handling the lumber was an old and established one and, as a result, was accepted as standard practice. An awareness of an existing problem was brought about by the fact that labor force schedules were frequently disrupted by urgent demands for blocking lumber at the mill.

After the material flow chart was completed . . . three main points stood out: (1) excessive handling of blocking lumber, (2) two storage areas were required although neither was generally full, (3) the frequency of occurrence was very regular and the operation never varied.

Questions were raised as follows: What can be done to eliminate excessive handling? Why not unload the material directly into the pile adjacent to the railroad tracks? This would resolve the first two factors by eliminating the labor and truck for handling and freeing the main storage area for necessary material. Final ideas were recorded on chart.

As charted in Figure 8–3, the new handling operation is obviously simplified. The vendor's truck will unload the blocking and pile it by size at the storage area adjacent to the car tracks. The service department is no longer involved and the loaders work from a conveniently located supply of lumber.

Figure 8–4. is a flow diagram showing the layout conditions of this problem, the locations of the lumber storage areas in the old method and in the proposed method. The diagram is actually a picture of where the loading and unloading is performed. The diagram is keyed to the process chart by symbol and step numbers.

FLOW PROCESS CHART — Appendix 2, Page 4, No. Y-4, Page 2 of 2

SUMMARY							CHART SUBJECT: Blocking Lumber — 4" x 4" x 8'		☐ MAN ☒ MATERIAL
	PRESENT		PROPOSED		DIFFERENCE				
	NO.	TIME	NO.	TIME	NO.	TIME	DETAILS OF CHART SUBJECT		
OPERATIONS ○	1800		600		1200		Lumber is now piled in 23" Mill by vendor. Move to R.R. car as needed. Compare movement of 300 pieces with present method.		
TRANSPORTATIONS ⇨	901		300		601				
INSPECTIONS ☐									
DELAYS D									
STORAGES △	1		0		1		COMPANY ABC PLANT "X"		
TOTAL ELEMENTS	2702		900		1802		DEPARTMENT Rolling mills UNIT 23" mill		
							INVESTIGATED BY John Doe DATE 5/15/		
DISTANCE TRAVELLED	33,300ft.		22,500ft.		10,800 ft.		REVIEWED BY Richard Roe DATE 6/1/		

DETAILS OF ~~PRESENT~~ PROPOSED METHOD	OPERATION	TRANSPORT	INSPECTION	DELAY	STORAGE	DISTANCE IN FEET	QUANTITY	TIME	ACTION ELIMINATE COMBINE CHANGE SEQ. SIMPLIFY	NOTES
1 Pick up 1 piece 4" x 4" x 8'	○	⇨	☐	D	△		1			
2 Carry to car	○	⇨	☐	D	△	75	1			300 pieces
3 Place in car	○	⇨	☐	D	△		1			
4	○	⇨	☐	D	△					
5	○	⇨	☐	D	△					

describing each step clearly and concisely, numbering it, marking the proper symbol for it, and connecting the marked symbol to the marked symbol on the line above. Opposite each step he should enter the time, distance, or quantity that is pertinent. When he has entered all the information, he should add the steps of each kind and write in the totals.

The investigator should make sure he has charted all the information he will need for analyzing the method: Just what was done in the operation? What was the means of the transportation, the terminal point, and the approximate distance? What kind of an inspection? What were the reasons for the delay? He should also keep notes of any conditions that adversely affect the work—matters of safety, lighting, noise, ventilation, crowding, etc. In these matters he should try to picture the job from the point of view of the person who is performing it.

The flow diagram. An excellent accompaniment to the flow process chart is the flow diagram (Figure 8–4)—a drawing that shows the path of the work as it flows through the department. A flow diagram shows the layout conditions of the problem—the distances and relationships between units of equipment, work stations, desks, or storage areas. It shows up backtracking that might not be revealed by a process chart. The diagram is actually a picture of where the various activities are performed. It is keyed to the process chart by symbol and step numbers. The present method is portrayed in dotted or broken lines; the improved method in solid lines; work stations in light outline.

A study of the problem portrayed in the flow diagram of Figure 8–4 and on the flow process charts of Figure 8–2 and 8–3 will indicate the value of the flow diagram in suggesting solutions to certain types of problems, as well as its use in demonstrating the advantages of a new method. See "Suggestions for Analyzing the Layout Shown on the Flow Process Diagram," later in this chapter.

Step 3. Analyze the present method

Step 3 in methods improvement is analyzing the process that is described on the process chart—in other words, making a *process analysis.* The text presents two ways to do it: (1) The *work simplification technique,* which is a quick and easy handling for simple problems, and (2) some techniques of the industrial engineer for the deeper and more detailed probing warranted by more difficult problems.

Work simplification technique. The work simplification technique is a methods improvement technique which charts the present method and then develops an improved method by questioning each step so as to eliminate, combine, rearrange, and simplify the steps. The following questions are asked about each detail of the present method as it appears on the process chart:

FIGURE 8-4
Flow Diagram of the Problem That Is Charted and Explained in Figures 8-2 and 8-3

The present method is portrayed in broken lines, the proposed method (steps 1, 2, and 3 at lower right) in solid lines; work stations are in light outline. The symbol numbers in the diagram are keyed to the step numbers in the process charts.

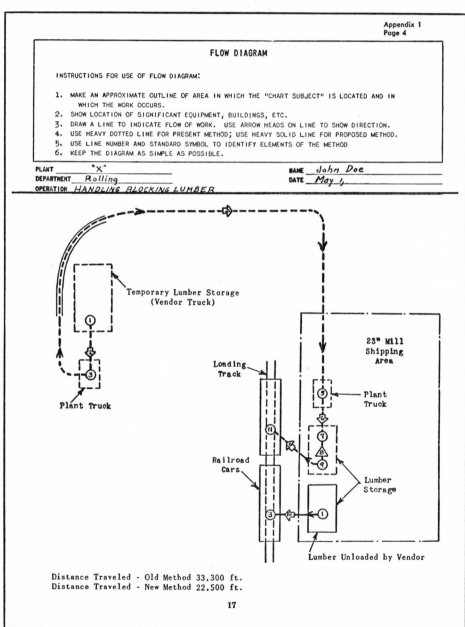

Appendix 1
Page 4

FLOW DIAGRAM

INSTRUCTIONS FOR USE OF FLOW DIAGRAM:

1. MAKE AN APPROXIMATE OUTLINE OF AREA IN WHICH THE "CHART SUBJECT" IS LOCATED AND IN WHICH THE WORK OCCURS.
2. SHOW LOCATION OF SIGNIFICANT EQUIPMENT, BUILDINGS, ETC.
3. DRAW A LINE TO INDICATE FLOW OF WORK. USE ARROW HEADS ON LINE TO SHOW DIRECTION.
4. USE HEAVY DOTTED LINE FOR PRESENT METHOD; USE HEAVY SOLID LINE FOR PROPOSED METHOD.
5. USE LINE NUMBER AND STANDARD SYMBOL TO IDENTIFY ELEMENTS OF THE METHOD
6. KEEP THE DIAGRAM AS SIMPLE AS POSSIBLE.

PLANT ___"X"___   NAME _John Doe_
DEPARTMENT _Rolling_   DATE _May 1,_
OPERATION _HANDLING BLOCKING LUMBER_

Temporary Lumber Storage
(Vendor Truck)

23" Mill
Shipping
Area

Loading
Track

Plant
Truck

Plant Truck

Railroad
Cars

Lumber
Storage

Lumber Unloaded by Vendor

Distance Traveled - Old Method 33,300 ft.
Distance Traveled - New Method 22,500 ft.

17

From United States Steel Company's *Methods Engineering Manual,* 1951.

WHAT is done? What are the steps? Do I have them all? What does each step do? What are the surrounding facts?

WHY is this step necessary? Can as good a result be obtained without it? It is an absolute must? Don't be misled by an excuse when you are looking for a reason.

WHERE should this step be done? Can it be done easier—with less time and transportation—by changing the location of employees or equipment?

WHEN should this step be done? Is it done in the right sequence? Can I combine or simplify by moving this step ahead or back?

WHO should do the job? Is the right person handling it? Or is it more logical to give it to someone else?

How is the job being done? Can it be done better with different equipment or different layout? Can I make the job easier for everyone concerned?[2]

Asking these questions at each step will suggest ways in which steps can be eliminated, combined, rearranged, and simplified into an improved method.

Answers to WHY and WHAT help to *eliminate*.

Answers to WHERE, WHEN, and WHO help to *combine* and *change sequence*.

Answers to How help to *simplify*.

In the work simplification technique the above questions are asked about each item on the chart. Asking questions produces answers, and it is from these answers that the supervisor gets the suggestions for making improvements. The improved method that is developed from this questioning is then charted on a second process chart, compared to the present method, reviewed, discussed with everyone concerned, tested, refined, and put into effect. This handling of the improved method is practically the same as Steps 5, 6, and 7 of the seven-step method. What the work simplification technique does is to substitute a short cut for Steps 3 and 4 of the seven-step method.

The basis of the work simplification technique is to get the supervisor to question everything in the present method (*Why is this done? Why is it done this way? In what other way could it be done?*) and then use his own knowledge to answer the questions.

The problem-solving technique for analyzing a process chart. The problem-solving technique uses the questions What, Why, Where, When, Who, How in analyzing a process chart but it offers also a body of

[2] *Supervisor's Guide to the Process Chart—Work Simplification Program* (Washington, D.C.: U.S. Government Printing Office).

specialized technical information and a checklist of *specific questions pertinent to each activity being analyzed.*

The supervisor can combine the work simplification technique with the problem-solving technique. Or he can shorten the problem-solving technique by combining some of its seven steps. The amount of time and analysis he should give to the problem depends upon the amount of benefit he hopes to get from solving it. Problems involving safety hazards, worker dissatisfaction, fatigue, and turnover deserve deep and careful probing. A solution that will result in a great saving of space or time deserves the expenditure of time and effort on the part of the investigator. A problem in which there is a potential saving of $100,000 deserves more care than if the savings were only $100. The $100,000 problem would in most companies be handled by staff specialists, but the supervisor needs to know how it is being done so that he can co-operate in the investigation and in the installation of the new method. He needs to know the reasoning that makes methods engineers select one method rather than another, so that he can explain to the workers the reason for change and show them the benefits that will come from it.

Furthermore, the supervisor should become familiar with these techniques of the methods men because he can put the knowledge into daily practice in the handling of his job. He can utilize it in improving methods whether he goes through all seven steps of a technique or uses a short cut.

The technique presented here contains the fundamentals of the techniques used by the industrial engineers but it represents only a selection from their total. The methods men's techniques are numerous, involved, and specialized. The principles and checklists presented here were chosen because they have a fairly general application. For additional principles and checklists, consult one of the engineering handbooks.[3]

What to do with the principles and checklists of the technique. Immediately following this section principles and checklists are presented. The checklists are in the form of questions, and their purpose is to stir up ideas for improvements—to unlock ideas that are stored in the brain waiting for a question or suggestion to trigger them off. Alongside the checklists there should be paper and pencil. An idea is a fleeting thing; if it isn't jotted down at once it may disappear and be forgotten. A person shouldn't be too critical at first of ideas that may seem outlandish. They may be valuable in themselves or they may contain the

---

[3] W. G. Ireson and E. L. Grant (eds.), *Handbook of Industrial Engineering and Management* (Englewood Cliffs, N.J.: Prentice-Hall, Inc., 1955).

H. B. Maynard (ed.), *Industrial Engineering Handbook* (2d ed.; New York: McGraw-Hill Book Co., 1963).

germs of usable ideas. The judging can come later. Good methods work combines creative thinking with a systematic procedure for stimulating, evaluating, and using ideas.

So when the industrial engineer says, "Apply principles and check-lists," he means: study, analyze, and consider an activity in terms of a body of pertinent information assembled by experts in that particular activity. This information contains essential principles, rules, guides, practices, and know-how that pertain specifically to the activity. The information is set up in the form of a list of statements (principles) supplemented by a checklist of questions. What the investigator is to do with the questions is to ask them of himself—to take up each separate step or activity and look for answers to each checklist question that relates to it.

Since Step 3 of the problem-solving technique is to analyze the process chart by applying principles and checklists, the supervisor starts with the first item on his chart. Is it an operation? Then he will study the text materials relating to operations. In the light of this information he will analyze the operation he has charted and ask himself the questions in the "Checklist for Process Analysis."

As the supervisor goes down his chart, analyzing each item with the aid of the proper set of principles and checklists, he will find many things in the present method that need to be changed, and in Step 4 he will find techniques for putting together new methods derived from the analysis of the present one. For purposes of explanation, Steps 3 and 4 need to be presented separately, but actually they overlap and use the same lists of questions. While the investigator is examining an activity and analyzing it, he is thinking in terms of eliminating it or combining it with another or rearranging or simplifying it—all of which is the subject matter of Step 4.

The materials from this page on to the beginning of Step 4 are to be used in analyzing the process that is charted on the flow process chart. They are:

> Principles and checklists for each of these activities: Operations, Transportations, Inspections, Storages, Delays; suggestions for ana-lyzing layout as it is shown on a flow process diagram; checklist for locating equipment in the shop; checklist for office layout; and suggestions for improving working conditions.

A sample Flow Process Chart to be used for charting the present method and the proposed method of a process study is presented in Figure 8–11. Figure 8–12, is an example of an Operation Chart for charting the present and the proposed method of an operation study.

Also at the end of the chapter are the following materials for use in making an operation study:

Operation analysis checklists for making detailed studies of right- and left-hand motions.

Some principles of motion economy.

Charts of physical dimensions of workers and their work-space arrangement (Figure 8–9).

An experimental model of a work station layout (Figure 8–10).

CHECKLIST FOR PROCESS ANALYSIS

◯   Operations: Some Principles and a Checklist

Each operation consists of three parts—*prepare, do,* and *put away.* Only the *do* part advances the work to completion. Elimination of this *do* part of an operation removes the need to study the *prepare* and *put away;* throw them out. If the *do* part can't be eliminated, the *prepare* and *put away* should be studied; for example, jigs and fixtures should be studied with the idea of reducing loading and unloading time.

Each machine operation should be done on the type of machine best fitted to perform it and should be set up in the most efficient manner on this machine. The machine should be of the correct capacity, and the work should be performed at the correct speed and feed.

In relation to each machine operation, investigate the materials, the design of the part, the sequence of machine operations, and the tooling to determine if substitutions or changes can be made to permit the part to be fabricated more easily.

With reference to paper work, transcribing should be kept to a minimum since transcribing information from one piece of paper to another is a source of errors and omissions. Forms (requisitions, invoices, etc.) should be set up to fit the users. Make only as many copies as needed, because time is lost in making and handling extra copies.

Avoid having high-priced personnel do low-priced work.

What is done in this operation?
Why is it done at all?
In what other way could this result be accomplished?
Where is this operation done? Why there?
Where else could it be done?
When is this operation done? Why?
At what other time could it be done?
Who does it? Why this person? Who else could?
How is it done? Why this way?
In what other way could it be done?

1. Is the operation made necessary because of an improper performance of a previous operation?
2. Can the operation be made safer?
3. What are the causes of omissions, errors, scrap?
4. Would changes in materials, design, finishes, tolerances, make this operation easier, cheaper, while still fulfilling its purpose?
5. Is the machine or equipment of the correct capacity, type, and precision for the type of work being performed on it?
6. Are the machine operations being carried on in the most efficient manner?
7. Are the correct speeds and feeds being used?
8. Could the tools, jigs, and fixtures be improved?
9. Can the principles of motion economy be applied?
10. Would an operation analysis of this operation be justified? Why? Why not?
11. Should this classification of worker be doing work of this skill level?

12. Can this transcribing (copying) be avoided?
13. Can this form be redesigned to fit better those putting information on it? Those taking information off it? Those checking the information on it?
14. Can the printed information on the form be made less subject to misinterpretations?
15. Could reports, memoranda, or letters be shortened to reduce dictating, typing, or reading time? Can a form letter be substituted?

(*See also the materials for making an operation analysis, preceding the cases at the end of this chapter.*)

⇨ Transportations: Some Principles and a Checklist

Plan the first operation as near as possible to the point of receiving the raw material. If possible, immediately upon receipt and inspection of materials, move them directly to the first operation. Provide space to set down unit loads of work in process, so prepositioned as to minimize the need for rehandling.

Wherever practical, the transportation activity should be combined with the other activities; that is, while a part is being transported, operations, temporary storages, and inspections could be performed on it.

Use the correct type of material handling equipment. (Valuable information about materials handling problems is contained in Bulletins 1, 2, 3, and 4 of The Materials Handling Institute, Pittsburgh, Pa.) Reduce the idle or terminal time of handling equipment to a minimum; don't have trucks standing around idle.

Transport as rapidly as is consistent with safety. Avoid backtracking. Shorten distances traveled. Minimize setdowns.

Use gravity as an inexpensive way of moving materials.

What is being done in this transportation?
Why is it done at all?
In what other way could this result be accomplished?
Where is this transportation going? Why?
When is this transportation done? Why?
At what other time could it be done?
Who does it? Why this person? Who else could?
How is it done? Why this way?
In what other way could it be done?

1. Is the work being delivered close to the point of use in the next operation? Is rehandling kept to a minimum?
2. Can an operation be performed during a transportation?
3. Is the most effective type of material handling equipment being used for transporting this type of work?
4. Is the material handling equipment being kept busy? Is there enough material handling equipment? Is it the right type?
5. Should this transport be planned and scheduled in advance?
6. Can the rearrangement of the sequence of operations (or of work stations, or of desks) reduce the backtracking and the amount of travel?
7. Is the batch that is being transported the most economical size?
8. Can gravity be used?
9. If a helper is needed to handle heavy parts at a work station, can a mechanical means of handling be substituted?

☐ Inspections: Some Principles and a Checklist

The closer the tolerances, the higher the costs.

Inspection of initial pieces of each operation tends to prevent the formation of scrap. Inspect materials before expensive operations. Inspect to prevent defective pieceparts from being buried in assemblies.

Statistical quality control can often reduce inspection costs.

Weighing can often be substituted for counting.

Checking and control activities should be balanced against the risk of a few errors or defects; a calculated risk may be cheaper in the long run.

What is done in this inspection?
Why is it done at all?
In what other way could this result be accomplished?
Where is this inspection done? Why there?
Where else could it be done?
When is this inspection done? Why?
At what other time could it be done?
Who does it? Why this person? Who else could?
How is it done? Why this way?
In what other way could it be done?

1. Can weighing or bulk measurement or the use of compartmental racks be substituted for counting?
2. Can a later operation or assembling act as an inspection?
3. Are tolerances closer than necessary? Are the quality requirements higher than justified by the uses of the finished product?
4. Is this inspection equipment the best for this kind of inspection?
5. Can statistical quality control be used to reduce the cost of inspecting?
6. Does this inspection prevent errors? Is it set up to uncover and report defective work so that corrective action can be taken promptly?
7. Are the check and control points in the procedure justified or would taking a calculated risk be cheaper in the long run?
8. Are there too many controls? Would delegating authority and responsibility further down the line decrease the need for some of the controls?
9. What are the inspection requirements of the operation? of the previous operation? of the following operation?
10. Would changing the inspection requirements of the operation make the operation easier to perform?
11. Are the inspection points in the process located in the most effective places?
12. Has agreement been reached by all parties as to what constitutes acceptable quality?

△   Storages: Some Principles and a Checklist

Store bulky items and items of low value close to the point of use in order to avoid rehandling.

Use adequate but not overelaborate inventory control.

Balance the cost of maintaining complete control over certain materials and supplies against the cost of loss by theft or deterioration, and against the cost of having the supply run out. Determine economic lot sizes.

Observe safety codes when storing hazardous materials such as paints, gasoline, etc.

Decentralized storage conserves workers' time in getting supplies. So does prompt and efficient service.

What is being done in this storage?
Why is it done?
In what other way could this result be accomplished?
Where is this storage? Why there?
In what other place could it be?
When does this storage occur? Why then?
At what other time could it be?
How is this storage handled? Why this way?

1. Is the amount of storage too much? Too little?
2. Is the storage of the material justified in terms of storage costs (including paper work) as against the possibility of loss or pilfering?
3. Should storage be centralized or decentralized?
4. Can the material be stored outdoors?
5. Could the space being used for storage be put to better use?
6. Are obsolete parts and files consuming valuable storage space?
7. Are parts in storage protected against damage?
8. Are inventory control records too elaborate? Are they inadequate?
9. Is the storeroom set up so that parts can be easily located and quickly obtained?
10. Are all file copies essential? Need these copies be filed? For how long?

D   Delays: Some Principles and a Checklist

Delays increase the unit cost of the product because fewer items are produced to absorb factory overhead expenses.

Idle men, idle machines, idle materials are visible signs of delays.

Delays slow down corrective action. Delayed cost control reports or inspection reports postpone the correcting of the production of defective parts.

Reduce the distances employees have to go and the amount of time they have to stand in line waiting to get parts or supplies or to get a drink of water or coffee or to punch their time.

Work should be processed in economic lot sizes. These lots should be big enough so that the operators and machines will not run out of work, and small enough to minimize other costs.

Strive for a swift, shallow flow of work through the department or unit.

What is being delayed?
What type of delay is this?
What is the cause of this delay?
How could it be avoided?
What is the waiting for?
What could be done to avoid or reduce it?
Where does this delay occur? Why there?
Who is involved in this delay?
What is affected by this delay?

1. Are there idle men, machines, materials?
2. Is work piled up? Is it causing bottlenecks?
3. Are people waiting in line at any time for any reason?
4. Do skilled or highly paid employees have to go after tools, supplies, equipment, reports, etc. that could be obtained by helpers or messengers?
5. Should deadlines or schedules be set up to expedite paper work?
6. Why is the work-in-process (or paper work) not being worked on now?
7. Is there sufficient material-handling equipment of the right kind at the right time?
8. Can the flow of work be regulated to eliminate peak periods?
9. Are delays preventing controls from being used soon enough to be most effective? Do inspection reports sit on desks while parts go through defective?
10. Are long, unnecessary conversations delaying the work?

Suggestions for Analyzing the Layout Shown on the Flow Process Diagram

Physical layout is a compromise between a number of factors, and it is frequently complicated because several different processes must be performed in the same work area and with the same facilities. The ideal layout cannot always be achieved because of the type and amount of space and equipment required.

While the ideal layout may be impossible to achieve, it is possible to improve the layout through systematic analysis and, whenever possible, through the application of the following principles:

1. The principal work flow should follow straight lines without undue backtracking and cross travel.
2. Individuals having the most frequent contact should be located near each other.
3. Files, cabinets, and other records and materials should be located for the convenience and ready access of those who use them.
4. Surplus facilities, such as furniture, tools, etc., should be released to provide space for other purposes.
5. The allocation of space should be in keeping with the requirements of the work—that is, the best lighted and ventilated space should be used for work requiring closest attention and concentration.
6. The arrangement of facilities should be such that supervision is facilitated.
7. The layout should be adapted to the maintenance of proper security precautions.
8. Individuals using the same equipment should be grouped together.
9. Individuals receiving visitors or required to maintain outside contacts should be located near entrances.
10. The capacities and characteristics of buildings should be studied to make certain that they can accommodate heavy or bulky equipment, such as safes, lifts, etc.

Checklist for Locating Equipment in the Shop

1. Is there sufficient space for the operators to perform their tasks at the machines?
2. Is there sufficient space around the machines for easy maintenance?
3. Are the machines blocked in by other machines so that they can't be moved without first moving the other machines?
4. Is there sufficient space for worked and unworked material?
5. Are the machines accessible so that the worker can get to and from them without danger of injury?
6. Are the machines too close to aisles or conveyor for the safety of the operators or others?
7. Are the work places or machines located in the best place for natural and artificial lighting?
8. Is the location safe from flying particles, explosions, fire, moving trucks, cranes, and other hazards?
9. Are the machines located properly in relation to the sequence of operations?
10. Are the machines located so as to reduce to a minimum the amount of backtracking?
11. Is there sufficient space between machines to permit the passage of material handling equipment?
12. Is there protection against excessive heat, noise, and vibration?

Checklist for Office Layout

1. Are desks and work tables arranged so that both natural and artificial light will fall on the desk from the same general angle?
2. Do workers have their backs or sides to windows, as they should have, instead of facing the windows?
3. Are files located in the less desirable space but still convenient to users?
4. Are any desks facing the wall? They shouldn't be.
5. Are sufficient aisles provided to prevent work interruptions by persons entering or leaving the area?
6. Is there aisle access to each desk?

7. Are the functions that require frequent visitors located near the entrance of each office?
8. Are the functions that require a great deal of mental concentration located away from noise and conversation?

Suggestions for Improving Working Conditions

Noise. Noise produces unnecessary fatigue, increases errors, and makes concentration difficult. Some suggestions for reducing the noise level:

1. Avoid placing typewriters or other mechanical equipment on metal desks or tables because metal magnifies normal operating sounds. If possible, use wood tables. Wood as compared to metal tends to absorb sounds. Also avoid putting equipment in front of metal partitions; they magnify noise.
2. Many equipment noises can be reduced by placing mats under the machines.
3. Acoustical materials on the ceiling will reduce noise.
4. Place reception room and all departments dealing with the public in areas where conversations do not disturb employees.
5. Isolate noisy machines as much as possible from areas where work requires concentration.

Lighting. Lighting should be of the proper intensity and quality. There should be enough light so that the worker does not have difficulty seeing, and it should have the right mixture of colors in it. There should be no glare. Light should be placed so that nobody is looking directly at it.

Temperature. The best working temperature is around 68 degrees. If the temperature has to be higher, there should be circulation of air but not drafts. There should be sufficient air changes because stale air—particularly when coupled with higher temperatures—slows down the worker and increases his errors.

Cleanliness or Housekeeping. Sufficient janitorial service should be provided to keep the workplace clean, whether it is in the shop or the office. There should be a place for everything—adequate provisions to put things in order. The general housekeeping should be as good as the conditions will permit.

Safety. Since each company has its own safety problems and its own staff to take care of safety, all proposed changes should be checked with the proper safety officials.

Step 4. Develop several improved methods

The supervisor has gotten this far in using the problem-solving technique for improving a method: In Step 1 he selected a particular problem because of the benefits he expected to get from its solution. In Step 2 he investigated the problem, broke it up into its separate activities and charted it on a flow process chart. In Step 3 he studied this process that he had charted. He analyzed the present method, studied principles that apply to each particular activity and asked a checklist of questions about each activity in order to find out the *Why* of everything.

Now in Step 4 he is still questioning the activities. He wants to eliminate as many of them as possible and rearrange the remaining ones into a new and improved method. This is the synthesis or construction part of the problem-solving technique—something like fitting together the pieces of a jigsaw puzzle. However, instead of working toward a single solution, the supervisor should develop several solutions; then if one of them turns out to have a big hole in it or is rejected by the boss for some reason, there are others to offer. When the supervisor develops several solutions, very often he can combine the better elements of each and come out with one superior solution. If the supervisor has several solutions, he can sometimes let the employees choose which of the several methods should be adopted and thus avoid some of the emotional problems that would otherwise develop at the introduction of a change.

Eliminating. When the supervisor asks *What* and *Why* of a present process, he sometimes finds that the whole process is unnecessary and can be eliminated. Or else he finds that some of the activities in the process are unnecessary and can be eliminated. He shouldn't study a step for the purpose of improving it when it should be eliminated instead. There is a saying that the best way to improve any step is to eliminate it. Ralph Barnes says: "It has been estimated that 25 to 50 percent of the manual work done in our shops, offices, factories, and homes is unnecessary—that the work might be done in a much better way, producing the same output with less expenditure of energy on the part of the workers."[4]

There are many causes of unnecessary steps. For instance, in procedures, unauthorized steps may be added for protecting individuals or for making double checks. The factor of change gives rise to unnecessary steps, and change goes on continually. When the design of a product is changed, hundreds of operations may be involved and some of them or activities related to them may be overlooked. Sometimes new operations will be added but the old ones they replace will not be removed.

In studying an operation it must be remembered that each operation is made up of three parts—*get ready, do,* and *put away.* Eliminating the *do* part, automatically eliminates the need for the *get ready* and *put away* activities, but sometimes they remain. The supervisor must be on the alert to discover and eliminate unnecessary steps. Before making any operation study—that is, an elaborate left- and right-hand analysis of an operator—the supervisor must first make a process study to find out if the operation can be eliminated. Otherwise he is apt to go ahead, make a time-consuming study of an operation, develop a new method, and even start training a worker, only to have somebody point out to him that the operation is not necessary and should have been eliminated in the first place.

A good question to ask in relation to eliminating operations is this one: "What would be the worst thing that would happen if this step were not performed at all?"

---

[4] Ralph M. Barnes, *Motion and Time Study* (4th ed.; New York: John Wiley & Sons, Inc., 1958) p. 207.

Combining. The supervisor has found out through his questioning that a number of the activities on his process chart are unnecessary and can be eliminated. He now considers the possibilities of combining some of the steps that remain. The answers to the questions *Where? When?* and *Who?* lead directly to the combining of steps. If two operations can be combined, then the transportation, inspection, and delays that previously existed between them can be eliminated; so can a *get ready* and a *put away.* Another angle on combining is that of combining the best elements of several activities and building a new activity out of this combination. For example, if a supervisor will observe a number of people doing similar work, he will find that one person does one part of the job a little better than another person; that the second person may do another part of his job better than the first person, and so on. If the supervisor will combine the "best" parts of the jobs observed, he can come up with a method that is better than any one of those observed.

Rearranging. As the supervisor studies the possibilities of eliminating some steps and combining others, he sees that steps should be rearranged. The answers to the questions *Where? When?* and *Who?* lead to sound reasons for changing the sequence of steps, thereby opening up possibilities for still further eliminating and combining.

When the supervisor is considering the rearrangement of steps, he will find that making a flow diagram will enable him to see the paths traveled and any backtracking. In the fabrication of products, the routine travels of servicemen, and the flow of paper work, very often not much attention is paid to the sequencing of steps in the original method; they just grow out of trial and error.

Several cautions must be observed in changing a sequence of steps. Sometimes there are good reasons why a certain sequence has been followed, but the reasons are not obvious; therefore it is important that the supervisor ask *Why* the steps are in their present sequence. The sequencing of operations in a certain manner might make it easier to assemble a product but harder to service or repair it.

If the supervisor is considering the possibilities of rearranging equipment, machines, desks, and such, he must consider whether they are used for other activities than the one under study. Rearranging equipment to favor the method under study might interfere with the other activities.

Simplifying. Simplifying should be handled only after the eliminating, combining, and rearranging have been done. The answer to the question *How?* leads to simplification.

Simplification reduces the variety of tasks, the number of tasks, the level of skill necessary to perform them, and the amount of energy that needs to be expended on them. Setting up tasks according to the principles of motion economy permits them to be performed with less effort and makes more effective use of the effort that is expended. Many of the gains of simplification can be gotten by making an operation study at a specific work station.

Simplification is not limited to operations. It can be used also to reduce the variety of types of material, sizes of parts, and kinds of equipment. Used in this way it can be a prelude to standardization.

Simplifying tasks reduces the amount of skill necessary to perform those tasks and the time necessary to train people for those tasks; by the same token it releases some people to do more highly skilled or productive work. For example, engineers and other technically trained personnel can be relieved of their low-skill activities and thus freed to spend more time using their special abilities. Their low-skill activities can be taken over by properly qualified clerks and technical assistants. However, when the jobs are simplified, the higher skilled people should be reassigned immediately.

People should be occupied most of the time by tasks that use their highest skills. The tasks that are below their level of skill should be moved down to people to whom these tasks will be a challenge and who are trained and have the capacity for them. The residue of meaningless work might be divided into two parts—part to be given over to machines, and the rest of it to be distributed as well as possible.

Oversimplification. While oversimplification could reduce the immediate cost of an operation, other costs—such as those connected with accidents, absenteeism, and labor turnover—might go up because the work has no meaning to the individual. Work can be deskilled to a point where it becomes meaningless as well as monotonous and actually creates inefficiency and restrictions of output. When employees can no longer see the relationship between their efforts and the end products, they lose the feeling that there is a need for careful workmanship. By recombining tasks, meaning can be rebuilt into them, and cost in its broader aspects can be reduced, because when work is more satisfying there are fewer human problems. This rebuilding of meaning into jobs is known as *job enlargement;* studies indicate that it can increase both output and morale.

Oversimplification of jobs can come about either by injudicious use of work simplification or by a change in the volume of manufacturing. What can happen is that highly specialized work, justified at one time because of a large volume demand, may no longer be necessary after the demand and the volume of production fall off. For example, during wartime there is a great demand for optical lenses and a scarcity of lens grinders. To meet this situation, the operation of grinding lenses is then greatly specialized into degrees of rough and finished grinding, so that several people are doing parts of a task that one person did formerly. After the excessive demand has stopped, such fine specialization is no longer economically justified. According to the economist, the market limits the division of labor.

The increased transfer of skill from worker to machine and the greater use of automated equipment also contributes to the loss of meaning of work in the employee's mind. Machines performing complex operations formerly done by humans make the individual feel somewhat insignificant. Automation may reduce labor costs and increase productivity but it presents problems in human resource utilization such as the retraining of those individuals displaced by the new technology.

It must be remembered that simplification is not an end in itself; simplifying may create problems as well as benefits. Simplification should be used judiciously, always with the human element in mind. The trend in management is to design jobs in a way that will promote individual responsibility.

Discuss proposed changes with others. The supervisor should consult with all those who may be affected by a proposed change. They may have some very good ideas to contribute. Also, they will have a better attitude toward the new method if they are consulted while it is being worked out. The supervisor must keep his boss informed of what he is doing; he may need the boss's authorization to put the proposed method into effect. Also he should be availing himself of valuable suggestions which the boss (having a better acquaintance with the overall picture) is in a position to contribute.

Proposed changes should be discussed with staff specialists. The safety department should be consulted with reference to hazards. The personnel department should be consulted in relation to possible changes in job classifications and job descriptions, as well as the availability of skills. The design engineer should be consulted regarding changes in tolerances and changes in design that would make fabrication easier. The production engineer should be consulted regarding changes in machining and sequences of operations. The industrial engineer should be consulted in relation to specialized methods improvement techniques and any proposed changes that would cross department lines.

When—as in the case of the smaller company—there are no staff specialists, then the line man who is willing to study and practice the principles involved in methods improvement greatly increases his value to the organization.

The supervisor should keep in mind the reasons why he should discuss proposed changes with others:

1. To find out if the suggested changes will actually accomplish the improvements anticipated.
2. To prevent the changes from causing unforeseen difficulties.

3. To be sure that everyone concerned understands why the changes should be made.
4. To make sure of having the authority to make the changes, particularly if they involve new costs and affect other work areas.
5. To find out if there are other plans afoot: the company might be planning big changes; the staff departments might be working out improvements that would make this one unnecessary.
6. To get the ideas fully accepted by the employees who will use them and by the superior who will evaluate the results.

The supervisor should discuss the proposed changes with the workers who will be affected by them. Their suggestions may be valuable. But even if they aren't, the actual consultation and the feeling of participation that it fosters is necessary to the success of the new method. Change of any kind arouses apprehension, fear, feelings of insecurity, and threats to a man's standing in the group. Changing a man's methods carries in it a suggestion that he wasn't doing his job well and that he should have improved his own methods. This criticism hurts a man's pride, makes him resentful, and causes him to oppose the improvement. This resistance to criticism shows up in supervisors, too, and in their bosses and in staff people; no one is immune. Unfortunately some methods engineers have the attitude that a change can't be any good if they didn't think of it. A change that is pushed through without regard for the people affected by it can stir up so much trouble as to cancel its technical advantages.

In order to handle the human side of a methods change, the supervisor has to put himself in the place of his employees—has to realize how he would feel if told that the work he had been doing had been eliminated as unnecessary or had been given to someone else who could do it as a minor part of a related task, or that he would be moved to another area away from his associates, or that he would have to start all over again like a beginner learning how to do a job. Once the supervisor realizes the feelings and fears that make up resistance to change, he can do a lot to ease them. He will pave the way for change by getting people to ask for it, getting them involved in the planning, giving them a choice wherever possible between a couple of possibilities in the new method, explaining the reasons for the change, and introducing it in a way that builds up the worker's confidence in himself.

Step 5.   Select the most practical improved method

In order to select the most practical improved method, the supervisor should line up the several methods he has developed and compare them in terms of the benefits he hoped to get from solving the problem.

(This is the list of expected benefits he made in Step 1.) Then he should compare the advantages of the alternative methods in terms of human factors, safety, and cost.

A less safe method should never be substituted for a safer method, no matter what the gain.

The human factors to be considered are both physical and psychological. The choice of method must take into account the amount of effort that is required of the worker and the effectiveness of that effort. It must also take into account the psychological relationships of people to their work and their social relationships in the work group.

The fact that work is broken down into its smallest elements to be studied and improved does not mean that it should be assigned that way—that jobs should be made up of just a few motions and no thinking. Elements of work should be combined into tasks and tasks should be combined into jobs in such a way that the output of the job is something meaningful to the performer. It should be an identifiable product for which he has the responsibility—something to which he could sign his name and guarantee the quality.

Costs of a method take in more than the immediate costs of hours of labor per units of product. Costs that enter the picture involve the amount of inspection, supervision, coordination, and control required by one method as over against another. Other factors influencing long-range costs are employee motivation and morale, quality of work, restriction of output, grievances, absences, and quits. The costs of training must be balanced against the amount of turnover, the increased value and versatility of the employee, and his adaptability to change.

The supervisor should select the most promising of the proposed methods and put it on a flow process chart and a flow diagram. He should total up the operations, transportations, inspections, delays, and storages, and compare the totals to the old method that he charted in Step 2. Then, as a final quick check to make sure that he hasn't missed anything in making up the new method, he should analyze it, using the checklist questions of Step 3.

If necessary, the supervisor should prepare a report on the selected method and submit it to his boss in order to get his approval to install the method. To make the decision, the boss needs to know:

1. What the proposed method is (a process chart and diagram should be furnished to him).
2. Why the proposed method is necessary.
3. What it will accomplish.
4. How it will work.
5. How much it will cost. How much it will save.
6. How it will affect the employees.
7. How it will affect other parts of the organization.

Step 6.   Try out and install the new method

If possible, the supervisor should try out the new method on a small group and correct any errors, oversights, or misjudgments in it. If the bugs are removed from a method or procedure in the tryout stage, then there is no need for tinkering after the full installation.

No matter how thoughtfully the supervisor has paved the way for the new method, he has to be prepared for a certain amount of trouble at the time of installation. The best help at this time is a company's reputation for taking care of its employees—a published policy of never firing or demoting anyone because of methods change. Also, the supervisor needs to be patient, understanding, and cheerful. He needs to encourage the employees, see that they get the training they need in the new method, and give them time to get used to it.

Step 7.   Follow up the improved method

It is necessary to follow up the improved method periodically, first to see if the improvements are actually in effect and then to determine if the improvements are actually effective. If the new method does not work, the supervisor should be the first to know it and not the last; but people sometimes develop blind spots in viewing and judging their own creations.

It is not necessary that the method work *exactly* as developed. *The method is just a means of realizing the benefits expected and as long as these desired results are achieved, the variations should do no harm.* However, it may be well to observe the variations and find out if they may not be the basis of new improvements. The supervisor should save the work sheets and charts of the new method. He will need them to use in training employees and he will want them as a reference whenever he undertakes further improvements in this method. He should see if there are other places in his department where he might be able to use these ideas for improvements.

Illustration of applying the seven-step technique to a methods improvement problem

Here is an example of how a supervisor might apply the techniques of methods improvement to an everyday problem without deliberately going from step to step or including all the steps. This problem concerns the handling of the Coca-Cola that is to be sold during the rest periods in a plant. The Employee's Club runs a snack bar during the rest periods. Joe Smith, a member of the recreation committee, has full responsibility for the snack bar and the handling of the Coke. Each day he sells about 120 bottles (five cases) across the counter. The club members don't want a dispensing machine.

Present method. The local distributor delivers 25 cases of Coke once a week to the receiving department of the plant, where the clerk checks them in, stores them, and returns the previous week's empties. Each day Joe picks up five cases of empties from the snack bar and takes them to the receiving department. In return he gets and signs for five cases of Coca-Cola. These he transports by hand truck to the snack bar, where he places them in the cooler to remain until he dispenses them during the rest periods. This is the present method but it has to be changed because the receiving department is unwilling to continue handling the Coke and the paper work connected with it. Joe will have to find some other way to handle it.

Applying the technique. In order to work out an improved method, Joe investigates the present method. He follows the path of a bottle of Coke through the plant from the time it leaves the distributor's truck until it returns as an empty to the unloading dock. He takes a process chart and fills in on it each step the Coke takes. He describes briefly (in the "Description" column) each inspection, transportation, storage, etc. He enters the pertinent distances and quantities. He makes a summary at the bottom of the chart. His completed chart showing the present method of handling the Cokes is shown on Figure 8–5.

Next Joe systematically analyzes the present method. He asks, "What is the purpose of this Coke project?" and answers, "The purpose of the Coke project is to furnish fellow employees a refreshment at cost during rest periods with the least inconvenience to the company and without involving the receiving department." This answer gives him a yardstick for evaluating the ideas that result from his analysis of each step.

Joe is going to arrive at an improved method by eliminating, simplifying, rearranging, and combining the elements of the activities of his present method—once he gets them analyzed. And he can analyze the activities by applying the What? Why? Where? When? Who? How? formula of work simplification or by using these same six questions plus the checklists and principles of the methods specialist. In this investigation Joe uses a little of each. He realizes that the work simplification questions would be adequate for a small problem like his but he feels that the principles and the checklist questions would call his attention to things he might not think of otherwise.

Line 3 on Joe's process chart is, "Transport to stockroom by platform

FIGURE 8–5
Process Chart (Present Method)

This chart shows Joe Smith's present method of handling Coca-Cola brought into the plant to be served at the snack bar. The line traces the path of the Coke through the plant beginning at Step 1 (Inspection) where the 25 cases are checked in at the unloading dock. At Step 2 (Transport) they are moved 50 feet to the stockroom where at Step 3 (Storage) they are stored until called for. Each of the 14 steps is to be analyzed in order to develop an improved process.

PROCESS CHART

PART NAME _Coca-Cola_　　SHEET NO. _1_ OF _1_ SHEETS
PART NO. _____　DATE _____
DEPT. _Employees' Recreation Club_　CHARTED BY _J. Smith_
PROCESS _Handling of Coca-Cola_

☒ PRESENT METHOD
☐ PROPOSED METHOD

STEP NO.	TIME—MIN.	DIST.—FT.	QUANTITY	OPERATION	TRANSPORT	STORAGE	INSPECTION	DELAY	DESCRIPTION
1			25 cases	○	⇨	▽	☐	D	Check in at unloading dock
2		50	"	○	⇨	▽	☐	D	To stockroom by platform truck
3			"	○	⇨	▽	☐	D	Until called for
4			5 cases	○	⇨	▽	☐	D	Count and release on requisition
5		125	"	○	⇨	▽	☐	D	To snack bar by hand truck
6			"	○	⇨	▽	☐	D	Unload into cooler
7			"	○	⇨	▽	☐	D	Until sold
8			1 bot.	○	⇨	▽	☐	D	Dispense across counter
9			5 cases	○	⇨	▽	☐	D	Pick up empties
10		125	"	○	⇨	▽	☐	D	To stockroom
11			"	○	⇨	▽	☐	D	Count empties and get receipt
12			"	○	⇨	▽	☐	D	Await pickup
13		50	25 cases	○	⇨	▽	☐	D	To loading dock by platform truck
14			"	○	⇨	▽	☐	D	Check and get receipt
				○	⇨	▽	☐	D	
				○	⇨	▽	☐	D	
Summary				3	4	2	4	1	

truck." He looks up the principles and checklists on transportation and sees:

> If possible, move materials directly to the first operation—immediately upon receipt and inspection.
> Is rehandling kept to a minimum?
> Is the batch being transported of the most economical size?

Joe applies these thoughts to his problem and gets some ideas for eliminating steps. So he continues down the lines of his chart, examining each activity with an eye to eliminating it or combining it with another or rearranging or simplifying. He decides to investigate some of these ideas further before he evaluates them. He phones the distributor and asks the price of five cases delivered daily. It is the same rate as he is paying on weekly delivery. He investigates other ideas and evaluates them against the yardstick. Then he works out the following new method.

Joe proposes to get daily delivery of five cases at the employees' entrance near the snack bar. When the truck arrives, the guard can phone him. Joe will pick up the five cases of empties at the snack bar, take them to the truck, get and sign for the five full cases, and put them in the cooler at the snack bar. He charts this process on a process chart (Figure 8–6) and presents it to management for approval. Management approves it.

Illustration of an operation study

Joe Smith did not solve all of his problems by means of the process study. In the new process, the employees still have to wait in line for their Cokes, and they want the service speeded up. Here is a bottleneck. The operation involved is Line 6, "Dispense across counter," from Joe's process chart of the new method (Figure 8–6). Joe isn't sure that a detailed left- and right-hand study of this operation is justified but he decides to do it anyway; he might learn something he could use on his job.

Present method of dispensing across counter. Joe gets an operation chart and sets down on it his present method of dispensing Cokes across the counter. This is the method: Joe reaches into the cooler, gets a bottle of Coke, opens it with a conventional hand bottle opener, and passes the bottle to the customer. The bottles are opened by Joe to keep the liquid and bottle caps off the floor. Payment is made to the cashier. The operation chart Joe makes is Figure 8–7. In it he shows separately the activities of his right hand and of his left hand. Studying the chart, Joe analyzes the activities of each hand, using the operation analysis checklist (pages 282–84) and he applies the principles of motion

FIGURE 8–6
Process Chart (Proposed Method)

This chart shows the proposed improved method of handling the Coca-Cola. Joe developed this process as a result of his analysis and investigation of the old process charted on Figure 8–5. He has eliminated the receiving department from the process by getting daily delivery of five cases to the employees' entrance (instead of weekly delivery of 25). He has reduced the number of steps from 14 to 9, has reduced the number of inspections and the distance the Coke must travel.

PROCESS CHART

PART NAME _Coca-Cola_ _____ SHEET NO. _1_ OF _1_ SHEETS
PART NO. _____ DATE _____
DEPT. _Employees' Recreation Club_ CHARTED BY _J. Smith_
PROCESS _Handling of Coca-Cola_

☐ PRESENT METHOD
☒ PROPOSED METHOD

STEP NO.	TIME–MIN.	DIST.–FT.	QUANTITY	OPERATION	TRANSPORT	STORAGE	INSPECTION	DELAY	DESCRIPTION
1		75	5 cases	○	⇨	▽	☐	ᗪ	On call from guard, return empties by hand truck.
2			"	○	⇨	▽	☐	ᗪ	Count empties, receive, and sign for Coke
3		75	"	○	⇨	▽	☐	ᗪ	To snack bar by hand truck
4			"	○	⇨	▽	☐	ᗪ	Unload into cooler
5			"	○	⇨	▽	☐	ᗪ	Until sold
6			1 bot.	○	⇨	▽	☐	ᗪ	Dispense across counter
7			5 cases	○	⇨	▽	☐	ᗪ	Collect empties
8			"	○	⇨	▽	☐	ᗪ	Stack empties beneath snack bar
9			"	○	⇨	▽	☐	ᗪ	Until returned
				○	⇨	▽	☐	ᗪ	
				○	⇨	▽	☐	ᗪ	
				○	⇨	▽	☐	ᗪ	
				○	⇨	▽	☐	ᗪ	
				○	⇨	▽	☐	ᗪ	
				○	⇨	▽	☐	ᗪ	
				○	⇨	▽	☐	ᗪ	
Summary				4	2	0	1	2	

FIGURE 8–7
Operation Chart (Present Method)

This is the chart Joe made to analyze his method of dispensing Cokes across the counter. This operation of dispensing one bottle is Step 6 in the new process Joe worked out in Figure 8–6. Because Step 6 was a bottleneck in the process, Joe put it under a magnifying glass for analysis. An operation analysis is a very detailed analysis of the right- and left-hand activities of an operator engaged in a repetitive, short-cycled task at a definite location. Joe watched to see what his right hand was doing and what his left hand was doing as he picked up a bottle, opened it, and handed it to the customer. He cataloged the activities of each hand into Doing, Moving, Hesitating, and Delaying, and he put them on the chart.

Starting with Step 1, his left hand, empty, moves to the cooler and at Step 2 selects a bottle and then in Step 3 raises the bottle up into position so that he can open it. While his left hand is so engaged, his right hand is delaying (idling) while it holds the bottle opener. In Steps 4 and 5 the left hand is delaying while holding the bottle, as the right hand positions the bottle opener and opens the bottle. Then, continuing with the left hand, Joe moves the bottle to the counter, releases it, brings his empty hand back to the cooler, selects another bottle, raises this bottle to a working position while his right hand is delaying (idling), holding the bottle opener.

OPERATION CHART

PART NAME Coca-Cola
PART NO.
DEPT. Employees' Recreation Club
OPERATOR J. Smith
OPERATION Dispensing Coca-Cola
SHEET NO. 1 OF 1 SHEETS
DATE
CHARTED BY J. Smith
MACHINE NO.
MACHINE NAME
☒ PRESENT METHOD   ☐ PROPOSED METHOD

LEFT HAND	DOING	MOVING	HESITATING	DELAYING	STEP NO.	DOING	MOVING	HESITATING	DELAYING	RIGHT HAND
Empty hand to cooler	○	○	◇	▷	1	○	○	◇	▷	Hold bottle opener
Select bottle	○	○	◇	▷	2	○	○	◇	▷	" " "
Raise bottle to working position	○	○	◇	▷	3	○	○	◇	▷	" " "
Hold bottle	○	○	◇	▷	4	○	○	◇	▷	Position bottle opener
" "	○	○	◇	▷	5	○	○	◇	▷	Open bottle
Bottle to counter	○	○	◇	▷	6	○	○	◇	▷	Hold bottle opener
Release bottle	○	○	◇	▷	7	○	○	◇	▷	" " "
Empty hand to cooler	○	○	◇	▷	8	○	○	◇	▷	" " "
Select bottle	○	○	◇	▷	9	○	○	◇	▷	" " "
Raise bottle to working position	○	○	◇	▷	10	○	○	◇	▷	" " "
Hold bottle	○	○	◇	▷	11	○	○	◇	▷	Position bottle opener
" "	○	○	◇	▷	12	○	○	◇	▷	Open bottle
Bottle to counter	○	○	◇	▷	13	○	○	◇	▷	Hold bottle opener
Release bottle	○	○	◇	▷	14	○	○	◇	▷	" " "
Summary	2	6	2	4		2	0	2	10	

economy (pages 284–85). As a result of his investigation he develops an improved method.

Proposed method of dispensing across counter. It is proposed that instead of using a hand opener, Joe install two wall-type openers on the counter ledge above the cooler. Then he can pick up two bottles at a time—one in each hand—and open them simultaneously. He charts this proposed new method on the operation chart (Figure 8–8).

Technique for studying an operation

Studying an operation might be thought of as taking any operation out of a process study and putting it under a magnifying glass. It is a very detailed analysis of the right- and left-hand activities of an operator engaged in a repetitive task of short duration at a definite location. Each operation[5] found to be essential in a process study could be the subject of an operation study if such detailed study were worthwhile. Process study must always be made before operation study; otherwise there is a risk of wasting a lot of time making a detailed analysis of an operation that is unnecessary and should be eliminated. Making the process analysis first will expose an operation that is not necessary.

When is operation study worthwhile? Operation study consumes proportionately more time than process study in terms of the resulting improvements. The detailed analysis required in operation study is worthwhile when a number of employees are doing the same kind of task or operation, when the task under study may not change for a long period of time, when the ratio of operator time to machine time is high, or when there are bottlenecks holding up a process. When these conditions exist, the savings derived from one study can be applied to all of the people performing the task, and the sum total saving will be well worthwhile. Tasks worth operation study (if the volume is sufficient) are repetitive ones such as simple assembling, soldering piece parts, simple machine operations, central inspection of parts, assembling circulars for mailing, folding paper boxes, etc.

From a cost point of view, the supervisor would seldom be justified in making an operation study. But from the point of view of learning, he should make one. It will help him to apply the principles of motion economy as a matter of course and on an everyday basis. Learning about motions will help him in designing a work station, training a worker to perform a task, making work easier, and improving the steps of a process.

---

[5] An inspection can also be the subject of an operation study. Such a detailed study of the movements of the left and right hands might be justified in a centralized inspection department where a number of women are sitting at benches performing an inspection of small parts or simple assemblies.

FIGURE 8–8
Operation Chart (Proposed Method)

This is the chart on which Joe put down the new method he worked out for dispensing two bottles of Coke at a time. He arrived at this method through his analysis of the present method charted on Figure 8–7. In analyzing Figure 8–7 he noticed the great number of delays (activities that do not advance the work). The right hand had 10 delays in 14 steps. Joe applied the Operations Analysis Checklist on *Idling* or *Delaying*. Question 1, "Can this holding be eliminated by use of a vise, clamp, clip, hook, rack, jig, or other mechanical device?" suggested to him the possibility of using a wall-type bottle opener instead of the hand type. This simple idea precipitated all the savings shown on the chart. The proposed method has two wall-type openers installed on the counter ledge above the cooler, and Joe lifts, opens, and serves two bottles at a time. The chart shows the steps by which the right hand and the left hand perform this operation.

While the left hand is moving to the cooler in Step 1, the right hand is moving there also. In Step 2 while the left hand is selecting one bottle, the right hand is selecting another bottle. In Step 3 the left hand is carrying its bottle to an opener fastened on the ledge, and the right hand is carrying its bottle to another opener fastened on the ledge. In Step 4 the top of each bottle is placed in its opener. In Step 5 a short movment of each hand opens each bottle. In Step 6 each bottle is moved to the counter, and in Step 7 each bottle is released.

OPERATION CHART

PART NAME *Coca-Cola* SHEET NO. _1_ OF _1_ SHEETS
PART NO. DATE
DEPT. *Employees' Recreation Club* CHARTED BY *J. Smith*
OPERATOR *J. Smith* MACHINE NO.
OPERATION *Dispensing Coca-Cola* MACHINE NAME
☐PRESENT METHOD ☒PROPOSED METHOD

LEFT HAND	DOING	MOVING	HESITATING	DELAYING	STEP NO.	DOING	MOVING	HESITATING	DELAYING	RIGHT HAND
Empty hand to cooler	○	○	◇	▷	1	○	○	◇	▷	Empty hand to cooler
Select bottle	○	○	◇	▷	2	○	○	◇	▷	Select bottle
Bottle to opener on ledge	○	○	◇	▷	3	○	○	◇	▷	Bottle to opener on ledge
Position bottle	○	○	◇	▷	4	○	○	◇	▷	Position bottle
Open bottle	○	○	◇	▷	5	○	○	◇	▷	Open bottle
Bottle to counter	○	○	◇	▷	6	○	○	◇	▷	Bottle to counter
Release bottle	○	○	◇	▷	7	○	○	◇	▷	Release bottle
	○	○	◇	▷		○	○	◇	▷	
	○	○	◇	▷		○	○	◇	▷	
	○	○	◇	▷		○	○	◇	▷	
	○	○	◇	▷		○	○	◇	▷	
	○	○	◇	▷		○	○	◇	▷	
Summary	2	3	2	0		2	3	2	0	

Procedure for making an operation study

Joe's operation study of the dispensing of Cokes was a sketchy one, used to illustrate the relationship between an operation and a process, and to prepare the way for a closer look at operation study.

In an operation study the activities of right hand and the left hand of the operator are analyzed in detail, and principles of motion economy and the checklist are applied for the purpose of developing a better work pattern for the operator. The fundamental principle of operation study is to increase output without increasing the amount of energy expended by the worker. (If, as a result of operation study, output is increased through the use of a new method which requires more effort on the part of the operator, he should receive more pay for having to expend that greater amount of effort.)

Such an increase in output without increasing effort can be achieved (1) by making the effort expended more productive and (2) by making work easier. The results are accomplished by applying the principles of motion economy in designing a more effective way of doing a task. (The principles of motion economy and operation analysis checklists, questioning the activities of Doing, Moving, Hesitating, and Idling, precede the cases at the end of the chapter. Charts showing the dimensions of the worker and his work area are on Figure 8–9. An operation chart form—Figure 8–11 is provided to be used in studying an operation.)

In order to study an operation or a task, it is necessary to break down the present operation into the activities performed by the right and left hands separately and list them on an operation chart. Then apply a checklist to each of these steps for the purpose of eliminating or shortening as many as possible. The activities of the right and left hands are called "therbligs" or "basic divisions of accomplishment." For ease of handling, they will be considered here under the following four groups:

◯ DOING

THIS GROUP ADVANCES THE WORK TO COMPLETION

U. Using—operating a tool or control.
A. Assembling—putting two parts together.
D. Dissassembling—the opposite of assembling.
G. Grasping—getting an object under control, picking it up.
R. Releasing—letting go of an object.

○ MOVING

THIS GROUP AIDS THE DOING

TL. Transporting Loaded—moving a piece part or a tool from one position to another—handling.

TE.   Transporting Empty—moving the hand or other body member from one position to another—reaching.

◇   HESITATING

THIS GROUP HINDERS DOING AND MOVING

SH.   Searching—trying to find something—groping.
SL.   Selecting—choosing one item from several.
PL.   Planning—making up the mind about how to proceed—deciding.
P.   Positioning—lining something up.
I.   Inspecting—examining parts in relation to quality or quantity.

▷   IDLING or DELAYING

THIS GROUP DOES NOT ADVANCE THE WORK

H.   Holding—retaining an object in a fixed position.
AD.   Avoidable Delay—idleness, stalling.
UD.   Unavoidable Delay—idleness while other hand or a machine is doing the job.
R.   Rest to overcome fatigue—overcoming tiredness.

The *steps* for studying an operation are the same as for studying a process, but the activities being studied are different, the symbols are different, and the chart forms are different. The activities studied in the process analysis were operations, transportations, inspections, storages, and delays. The operations to be studied in the operation analysis are hand motions: doing, moving, hesitating, and idling.

When studying an operation, the supervisor should study a typical trained operator. He should observe the activities of each of the two hands separately and classify them under the divisions described above. After he has observed a number of cycles of operations, he should list the present method of doing the task on the operation analysis chart (Figure 8–11). He should start with the hand that is engaging in the greatest number of activities in the cycle and should list each step by the proper abbreviation and symbol, giving a brief description of each activity.

After completing the charting of one hand, he should chart the activities of the other hand, synchronizing them with the first hand so that the chart will show what both hands are doing at the same time. After completing the charting of the present method, he should sum up the

○ Doings, ○ Movings, ◇ Hesitations, and ▷ Idlings.

Next, each activity should be studied in terms of the checklist preceding the cases at the end of the chapter, for the purpose of constructing a chart of a proposed method (Figure 8–11) that will make the effort expended more productive and the work easier.

In an operation analysis, when the supervisor is making an investigation of the present method, he should consult the workers, tell them what it is all about, and get their ideas. Also, he should observe the other operators doing the same task, in order to make comparisons of their motion patterns with those of the operator he is studying. He should find out why some operators perform different parts of the task better than other operators, and he should consider combining these "best" parts when he is constructing his proposed improved method for doing the task.

After listing the right- and left-hand activities of an improved method, the supervisor should use the checklist on them in order to see if he has missed any possibilities for improvement. He should then add the number of Doings, Movings, Hesitations, and Idlings to show the improvement over the present method of doing the task. He should go over the new method with his superior and get his OK.

In discussing the proposed improvement with the workers, the supervisor should demonstrate the need for it and the advantages of it, and he should get their suggestions. In installing the new method, he should provide the information, reassurance, instruction, and encouragement that people need when they are going through a job change.

Following up.   It is necessary to follow up periodically the results of methods improvement studies of both processes and operations. After the novelty has worn off, parts of the old procedure or method may reappear, or unforeseen difficulties may arise, or further possibilities for improvement may be uncovered. The supervisor should review step by step his procedure and determine where in each step he might have improved his investigation, and thus learn from experience how to improve his techniques of methods improvement.

Human engineering

Studying an operation, improving a method, designing a job, or arranging a workplace are activities that can profitably use the findings and techniques in the field of human engineering. Human engineering involves the relationship of man to machine and man to his physical work environment. Research in the field has been accelerated by the growing complexity of equipment and the demands it makes upon its operators. In aviation and space exploration the government has promoted research so that machines can be designed in line with the abilities and limitations of the people who are to operate them. The findings of research done on pilots and high-speed planes and on astronauts are being transferred to work situations in industry where human engineering is concerned with matters such as:

1. Light and seeing, instrument dials and legibility, visual displays.
2. Sound and hearing, speech, tonal signaling systems.

3. Human motor activities, controls for human use (knobs, cranks, wheels, levers, push buttons, etc.), the arrangement of work at a work station, working and resting.
4. The working environment, illumination, atmospheric conditions, noise, vibration.

In investigating man–machine relationships, the purpose of human engineering is to increase the efficiency and accuracy of the man–machine system by reducing the amount of effort required of the man and reducing the possibility of errors (man-caused errors greatly exceed machine-caused errors). In the performance of a man–machine system, the operator receives information from the machine, makes decisions, and then acts upon these decisions. There are certain activities that a machine performs better than a man, and there are other activities that man does better than the machine. Machines appear to surpass men in (1) storing great quantities of information, (2) erasing information, (3) reacting to control systems, (4) applying large amounts of force, (5) performing a variety of activities simultaneously, (6) performing rapid computations, and (7) performing repetitive tasks. Men, on the other hand, appear to surpass machines in the ability to (1) improvise procedures and use flexible procedures, (2) store great varieties of information, (3) detect small amounts of sound and light, (4) make judgments, (5) reason inductively, and (6) create new methods.

Designers of man–machine systems need to consider what responsibilities should be assigned to men, what responsibilities can be assigned to machines, how information needed by the operator can be best displayed to him, how the controls should be designed to give the operator the most effective control over the machine, and finally how the man–machine system should be set up to take into account human abilities and limitations. Human engineering adapts the machine, the work station, and the work environment to the physiological and psychological makeup of people.

Human engineering,[6] using a systematic research technique, draws upon the sciences of anatomy, physiology, psychology, and the various branches of engineering. It has added to the body of knowledge available to people engaged in methods improvement work. Figure 8–9 showing the dimensions of man and his work area, Figure 8–12 showing a work station layout, and the list of principles and rules of motion economy are examples of the areas that are common to motion study and human engineering.

---

[6] For more information about the principles, findings, and techniques of human engineering, consult A. Chapanis, *Man–Machine Engineering* (Belmont, Calif.: Wadsworth Publishing Co., Inc., 1965); E. J. McCormick, *Human Factors Engineering* (New York: McGraw-Hill Book Co., 1964); and R. M. Gagne, *Psychological Principles in System Development* (New York: Holt, Rinehart & Winston, Inc., 1962).

Methods improvement by employees—JMT

Each worker is a gold mine of information about his job. He can see where time and money are being wasted, but he can't always see where he will profit by suggesting improvements. Sometimes it is because the supervisor is skeptical or hostile; sometimes it is a case of "Nobody asked me." If employees' ideas are used in improving methods, the company gains not only ideas but also support for the new methods.

Employees need encouragement and a technique for developing better ways for doing their jobs. One such technique is Job Methods Training (JMT), which is much simpler than the charts and checklists for process analysis and operation study.

Job Methods Training, a 10-hour program, was developed during World War II as part of the program of Training within Industry. It was a government-sponsored course involving 10 hours of instruction, given to foremen in plants doing war work. Through it thousands of companies and their foremen became acquainted with the principles of motion study and learned how to go about making improvements in work methods in a systematic way. Many supervisors are familiar with JMT. For those who have forgotten or have become supervisors since that time, here it is:

JOB METHODS TRAINING

STEP I—BREAK DOWN the job.
1. List *all* details of the job *exactly* as done by the *Present Method*.
2. Be sure details include all:
   Material Handling.
   Machine Work.
   Hand Work.

STEP II—QUESTION every detail.
1. Use these types of questions:
   WHY is it necessary?
   WHAT is its purpose?
   WHERE should it be done?
   WHEN should it be done?
   WHO is best qualified to do it?
   HOW is the "best way" to do it?
2. Also question the:
   Materials, Machines, Equipment, Tools, Product Design, Layout, Workplace, Safety, Housekeeping.

STEP III—DEVELOP the new method.
1. ELIMINATE *unnecessary* details.
2. COMBINE details when practical.
3. REARRANGE for better sequence.

4. SIMPLIFY all *necessary* details:
   Make the work easier and safer.
   Pre-position materials, tools, and equipment at the best places in the *proper work area.*
   Use *gravity-feed* hoppers and *drop-delivery* chutes.
   Let *both hands* do *useful* work.
   Use *jigs* and *fixtures* instead of hands for holding work.
5. *Work out* your idea *with* others.
6. Write up your proposed new method.

STEP IV—APPLY the new method.
1. *Sell* your proposal to the *boss.*
2. *Sell* the new method to the *operators.*
3. Get final approval of all concerned on *Safety, Quality, Quantity, Cost.*
4. Put the new method to work. Use it until a better way is developed.
5. Give *credit* where credit is due.

Cost reduction

The pressure for cost reduction may come from either the customer or the competitor. Customer resistance to price increase works in a cycle: After the selling price gets too high, the customer demand for the product falls off, the volume of production has to be reduced so there are fewer units produced over which to distribute the costs, and therefore the cost per unit has to go up. This causes further resistance and continues the undesirable cycle.

The pressure from the competitor comes when he is able to improve his methods, making possible a reduction in the cost of production and the price.

Some cost reduction practices. An unfortunate type of cost reduction practice is the panic type wherein top management discovers that it needs to reduce costs and passes the word down the line that costs must be reduced by 10 percent or 15 percent or some such figure. Management does not say how this reduction is to be achieved—all it wants is results—and the department heads will usually try to cut costs in the easiest way and wherever they can in order to get these results. The difficulty with this technique is that results have to be accomplished very rapidly, costs are likely to be reduced in essential work as well as in nonessential work, morale suffers, and usually when the scare is over, costs creep up again.

Another technique is to put on a cost reduction drive—like a bond drive or a Red Cross drive. Under this technique a different culprit is attacked each month. One month it might be scrap and another month it might be the utility bills—light, heat, power, and phone. Or the victim might be a specific division of the company, for instance, inspection or maintenance. The cost reduction drive is usually carried on by committees, and separate committees are set up, with or without staff specialists, and one committee is assigned to each culprit.

The drive technique is superior to the crash technique but is still doing the job in a piecemeal manner—trying to reduce isolated costs. What is wrong with this approach is that products are not produced by isolated activities but by a combining of activities. For example, there is little saving in reducing direct labor costs if machines are made idle, or in cutting down inventories to the extent that people run out of work.

The supervisor and costs. In each department there are three types of costs: direct labor, direct material, and overhead. Anything that isn't direct labor or direct material is classed as overhead. Some parts of the overhead—such as depreciation, taxes, and insurance—are not under the control of the supervisor and he cannot be held responsible for them. But most of the costs are within the area of his control—the direct labor, direct material, and much of the "burden" of indirect expenses that are allocated to his department. This burden or overhead consists of indirect labor, such as that done by janitors, helpers, assistants, inspectors, etc.—all the labor that is performed in the department but cannot be attributed directly to the product. Another part of the overhead is indirect materials and supplies and utilities.

Some false economies in cost reduction. The supervisor should beware of those measures that give the appearance of reducing costs but do not actually do so. Here are some of them:

Maintenance costs of machines can be reduced by neglecting minor repairs and upkeep. Scrap can be reduced by reducing the quality requirements—letting everything get by. Output in production can be increased by overloading both the machines and the men. Tardiness can be reduced by forcing the tardy employee to take the day off and turning it into an absence. The number of reported accidents can be reduced by discouraging people with minor injuries from asking for first aid. Idleness of men can be reduced by giving them more machines to attend, but the machines waiting idle for the men to feed them may cost more per hour than the men's services.

Sources of potential cost reduction. As emphasized throughout this text, the supervisor's main responsibility is to integrate men, materials, machines, money, and methods in an effective manner, but he isn't doing this if there is idleness and waste in his department. Therefore the supervisor's cost reduction should center around reducing the idleness of men, machines, materials, and money, and doing it by the techniques of methods improvement.

The idleness of *men*—both direct labor and indirect labor—can be reduced by planning and scheduling their work in advance. The supervisor should set the example by starting each day promptly and by seeing that the work for employees is set up in advance so that they also can start promptly. Also he needs to supervise the work by directing and checking its progress. Injuries, tardiness, and absenteeism are forms of idleness and should be kept to a minimum.

Machines are idle when they are out of work. When an insufficient supply of materials or insufficient manpower are the causes, then these are problems of planning and scheduling. Machines may be out of work because of breakdowns attributable to abuse or improper use by workers who are untrained or careless.

In *materials* a certain amount of waste in the form of scrap is inevitable; however, the percentage should be established. Workers on piece rates have a tendency to cause more scrap in their haste to produce more output. However, scrap is also caused by untrained workers. Another factor causing scrap is that workers do not realize or else do not consider the cost of materials: needing a piece of wood to rest something on, they will cut it or have it cut from a full size piece of first-grade lumber rather than look around for a piece of scrap.

Money is not usually in the form of dollars in most departments; rather it is in the form of equipment, materials, space, and time. Equipment whether it is being used or not is costing money. Materials in the form of inventories represent an investment of money and therefore should be kept to a minimum. Space whether it is owned or rented costs money. Space that is used inefficiently is still being assessed taxes or charged rent for, has to be maintained, has to be heated. The supervisor is familiar with the cost of time—so much an hour for each man and for each machine. The fewer units put out by the man and/or the machine per hour, the higher the cost per unit.

The way to reduce waste is to improve methods, and the way to improve methods is to use the techniques of methods improvement.

Summary

Methods improvement is a systematic technique of studying and improving a work situation so that people are able to do better work in less time, with less effort, at less cost, and with greater safety. The supervisor needs to learn principles and techniques for improving methods so that he can analyze and improve methods in his department, stimulate worker interest in seeking better methods, and get better results from improvements originated by others.

The seven-step problem-solving technique provides a systematic approach to methods work. The seven steps are outlined in "The Seven-Step Technique Applied to a Methods Improvement Problem" earlier in this chapter and should be reviewed at this point. Steps 3 and 4 of improving a process involve the analysis of the operations, transportations, inspections, storages, and delays of the process charted on a flow process chart. This analysis uses the principles and checklist questions pertaining to the particular activities. Studying principles and asking pertinent questions about the activities stirs up ideas for eliminating unnecessary activities, for combining and rearranging the sequence of activities that are necessary, and for simplifying them (reducing skill requirements for their performance).

In devising methods and combining tasks into jobs, the supervisor must take human factors into account. An oversimplified job may be costly in the human problems it causes. A change that upsets the status system may be unworkable. A change that arouses hostility or fear will be resisted or sabotaged. The supervisor must understand his subordinates as individuals and as group members and recognize the factors that cause them to resist changes. He should pave the way for change by soliciting the suggestions of the people concerned—the workers, the boss, and the methods people.

JMT (Job Methods Training) is a technique that can be used by workers to improve their own methods. The work simplification technique on pages 249 and 251 offers another shortcut designed to encourage worker participation in methods improvement. (The term "work simplification" has another meaning: deskilling a job by reducing the variety of tasks in it, the amount of skill necessary to perform them, and the length of time necessary to train people for them.)

An operation study (an operation is a part of a process) analyzes in detail the activities of the right hand and the left hand of an operator engaged in a repetitive short-cycle task at a definite location. The principles of motion economy and checklists of specific questions are used to study the doings, movings, hesitations, and idlings. The purpose of making such a detailed study is to eliminate unproductive effort, make work easier, and thus increase output.

Learning techniques of operation study, principles of motion economy, and some of the findings of human engineering helps the supervisor to improve processes, devise methods, set up workplaces, train workers, and make work easier and more productive.

As a cost reduction tool, methods improvement makes long-term savings whereas panic cost-cutting programs may cause inefficiencies.

CHECKLIST FOR OPERATION ANALYSIS

    Doing

USING, ASSEMBLING, DISASSEMBLING

1. Can this activity be eliminated or shortened?
2. Can a better tool be used?
3. Can better leverage be obtained?

4. Can a power tool be used?
5. Are tools in good condition?
6. Are burrs interfering?
7. Can momentum be used? Can parts be spun on by hand?

GRASPING, RELEASING

8. Can this activity be eliminated or shortened?
9. Can the part be slid instead of carried?
10. Can the supply bins be furnished with lips to provide easy grasp of small items?
11. Can parts or tools be pre-positioned to provide easy grasp?
12. Can a tweezers, rubber finger, or other instrument be provided to make grasp easier?
13. Is a careful release necessary? Can it be avoided?
14. Can a drop delivery be used?
15. Can release be made in transit?
16. When the load is released, is the hand in the most advantageous position for the next activity?

O   Moving

TRANSPORTING EMPTY, TRANSPORTING LOADED

1. Can either of these movements be eliminated or shortened?
2. Can a chute or conveyor be used?
3. Should more units be moved at a time?
4. Is movement slowed down because of careful positioning required for a later activity?
5. Are the most frequently used parts or tools located nearest to the point of use?
6. Are there barriers in the path of travel?
7. Are tools and parts arranged in an arc within easy reach of the operator?
8. Can a curved motion be used instead of a straight-line motion?
9. Can hand movements be made simultaneously, symmetrically, and in opposite directions?
10. Can the part be slid instead of carried?
11. Can tools be made self-returning by means of springs and counter-balances?

◇   Hesitating

SEARCHING, SELECTING

1. Can these activities be eliminated?
2. Are parts and tools mixed?
3. Are there specific locations for parts and tools?
4. Is the lighting satisfactory?
5. Are parts and tools located in front of the operator for easy seeing?
6. Can the number of parts or tools be reduced?
7. Can color be used to facilitate the selection of parts and tools?
8. Can parts be delivered in a manner that facilitates selection?

POSITIONING

9. Is positioning necessary?
10. Can tolerances be loosened?
11. Can holes be beveled?
12. Can pins be rounded?
13. Can tools be located in holsters or funnels at a convenient angle for grasping?

14. Can self-guiding or locating tools be used?
15. Can stops be used?
16. Can jigs be used?

PLANNING OR DECIDING

17. Can this hesitation be reduced by practice? Can eye and hand movements be better coordinated?
18. Can operation be made more routine?
19. Can a rhythm be established?

INSPECTING

20. Can this inspection be eliminated or combined with another operation?
21. Can a better method be devised? Gauges? Statistical inspection?
22. Can the lighting be improved?
23. Can subsequent operations or assembling act as inspections?
24. Can this counting be eliminated? Can compartmented racks or trays be used?

 Idling or Delaying

HOLDING

1. Can this holding be eliminated by use of a vise, clamp, clip, hook, rack, jig, or other mechanical device?
2. Can a foot-activated vise or clamp be used?
3. Can a stop be used?
4. Can the holding time be shortened?
5. If hold cannot be eliminated, can arm rests be provided?

UNAVOIDABLE DELAY

6. Can steps be rearranged to keep both hands busy?
7. Can inspections or other operations be performed during machining time?
8. Can unavoidable delay be shortened by a rearrangement of the steps?

AVOIDABLE DELAY

9. Remove it from the cycle.

REST TO OVERCOME FATIGUE

10. Can it be moved to the end of the cycle to provide more complete rest?
11. Can operations be rearranged to provide rest during machining time?
12. Can regular rest periods be installed to provide complete relaxation?

SOME PRINCIPLES AND RULES OF MOTION ECONOMY FOR MAKING EFFORT EXPENDED MORE PRODUCTIVE AND/OR MAKING WORK EASIER

1. Avoid having the hand act as a vise.
2. Where possible, have both hands working at the same time and idle at the same time.
3. Motions of the arms should be made in opposite and symmetrical directions.
4. Use continuous curved motions instead of abrupt straight-line motions.
5. Shorten unavoidable delays: they can be more fatiguing than useful activity.
6. Assign work to the body member best suited for it.
7. Where possible, use momentum instead of force.
8. Use the body to the best advantage mechanically.
9. Design the workplace to fit human dimensions.
10. Arrange the height of the workplace for alternate sitting and standing.
11. Place tools and materials near place of use, in sequence of use, and prepositioned for use.

12. Reduce visual requirements (reduce number of eye fixations).
13. Arrange work for easy rhythm.
14. Balance the work among the members of the body.
15. Remove, shorten, and improve therbligs.
16. Use gravity to advantage.
17. Body motions should be confined to the lowest practical classification.
18. Use the proper tools for this task.
19. Consider the user as well as the function when designing tools.
20. Reduce "getting ready" and "putting away" time (loading and unloading time).
21. Use correct speeds and feeds.
22. Use powered and semiautomatic tools.
23. Transfer heavy lifting to mechanical lifting devices.
24. Improve working conditions that contribute to fatigue and tensions.
25. On fatiguing jobs, allow rest periods; on monotonous jobs provide for breaks and rotation.
26. Fit the man and the job.
27. Never use high-priced labor on low-priced work.
28. Keep skill level requirements balanced.
29. Never sacrifice safety.
30. Eliminate, simplify, combine, rearrange.

FIGURE 8–9

Dimensions of Normal and Maximum Working Areas in the Horizontal and Vertical Planes as Developed and Used by the Process Development Section of the General Motors Manufacturing Staff

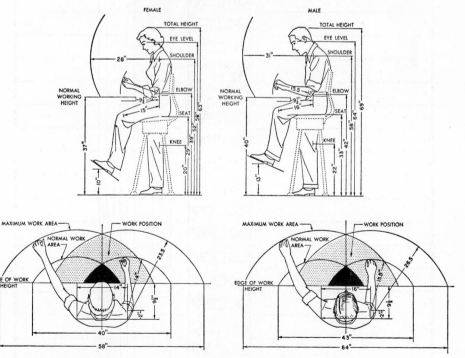

From Richard R. Farley, "Some Principles of Methods and Motion Study as Used in Development Work," *General Motors Engineering Journal*, Vol. II, No. 6 (November–December, 1955), pp. 20–25.

FIGURE 8–10

FLOW PROCESS CHART		NUMBER			

PROCESS						SUMMARY	
			ACTIONS			NO.	TIME
☐ MAN OR ☐ MATERIAL			○ OPERATIONS				
CHART BEGINS	CHART ENDS		⇨ TRANSPORTATIONS				
			☐ INSPECTIONS				
CHARTED BY		DATE	D DELAYS				
			▽ STORAGES				
DEPARTMENT			DISTANCE TRAVELLED *(Feet)*				

DETAILS OF ☐ PRESENT PROPOSED METHOD	OPERATION TRANSPORTATION INSPECTION DELAY STORAGE	DISTANCE IN FEET	QUANTITY	TIME	ANALYSIS WHY? WHAT? WHERE? WHEN? WHO? HOW?	NOTES
1	○⇨☐D▽					
2	○⇨☐D▽					
3	○⇨☐D▽					
4	○⇨☐D▽					
5	○⇨☐D▽					
6	○⇨☐D▽					
7	○⇨☐D▽					
8	○⇨☐D▽					
9	○⇨☐D▽					
10	○⇨☐D▽					
11	○⇨☐D▽					
12	○⇨☐D▽					
13	○⇨☐D▽					
14	○⇨☐D▽					
15	○⇨☐D▽					
16	○⇨☐D▽					
17	○⇨☐D▽					
18	○⇨☐D▽					
19	○⇨☐D▽					
20	○⇨☐D▽					
21	○⇨☐D▽					

FIGURE 8–11

OPERATION CHART

PART NAME_____ SHEET NO._____OF____SHEETS
PART NO._____ DATE _____
DEPT. _____ CHARTED BY_____
OPERATOR_____ MACHINE NO._____
OPERATION_____ MACHINE NAME_____

☐PRESENT METHOD   ☐ PROPOSED METHOD

LEFT HAND	DOING	MOVING	HESITATING	DELAYING	STEP NO.	DOING	MOVING	HESITATING	DELAYING	RIGHT HAND
	◯	○	◇	▷		◯	○	◇	▷	
	◯	○	◇	▷		◯	○	◇	▷	
	◯	○	◇	▷		◯	○	◇	▷	
	◯	○	◇	▷		◯	○	◇	▷	
	◯	○	◇	▷		◯	○	◇	▷	
	◯	○	◇	▷		◯	○	◇	▷	
	◯	○	◇	▷		◯	○	◇	▷	
	◯	○	◇	▷		◯	○	◇	▷	
	◯	○	◇	▷		◯	○	◇	▷	
	◯	○	◇	▷		◯	○	◇	▷	
	◯	○	◇	▷		◯	○	◇	▷	
	◯	○	◇	▷		◯	○	◇	▷	
	◯	○	◇	▷		◯	○	◇	▷	
	◯	○	◇	▷		◯	○	◇	▷	
	◯	○	◇	▷		◯	○	◇	▷	
	◯	○	◇	▷		◯	○	◇	▷	
	◯	○	◇	▷		◯	○	◇	▷	
	◯	○	◇	▷		◯	○	◇	▷	
	◯	○	◇	▷		◯	○	◇	▷	
	◯	○	◇	▷		◯	○	◇	▷	
	◯	○	◇	▷		◯	○	◇	▷	
	◯	○	◇	▷		◯	○	◇	▷	
	◯	○	◇	▷		◯	○	◇	▷	
	◯	○	◇	▷		◯	○	◇	▷	
	◯	○	◇	▷		◯	○	◇	▷	
	◯	○	◇	▷		◯	○	◇	▷	
	◯	○	◇	▷		◯	○	◇	▷	

FIGURE 8–12
Experimental Model of a Work Station Layout
for the Assembly of Valves

The model was set up to demonstrate the application of motion economy to the arrangement of a workplace. Note the fixture for holding the valve, the foot pedal for drop delivery, the grouping of the bins in an arc for easy reaching, the special open-end wrench to fit the two nut sizes.

CASE 1

A friend of yours, a supervisor in another company—one that produces a standardized product—has been telling you about methods improvement. He is quite "motion-minded" and is always figuring out ways to make jobs easier in his home and on the job. He tells you about how electric mixers and other gadgets cut down his wife's work in the kitchen. He says that his kitchen is laid out "scientifically" to save steps and strain. He then cites instances of labor savings in his company from the adoption of conveyor belts, fork trucks, "scientifically" laid out workplaces, power tools, etc. He always ends up by saying, "Who would want to throw out all these things and return to the good old days of back-breaking work?" He has half convinced you, and you are willing to give methods improvement a try.

1. List a few of the laborsaving devices that are in use in your home.
2. To what extent are the principles of methods improvement used in your home? Where might there be some further applications?
3. List a few of the laborsaving devices that are used in the plant.
4. Where in the plant are there some applications of the principles of methods improvement?
5. Where in the plant are some of the obvious places where the principles of methods improvement could be applied?

CASE 2

In order to meet the competition of plants using the techniques of efficient production, top management is faced with the problem of reducing manufacturing costs. It believes that this can be accomplished by increasing the efficiency of production instead of by cutting corners and reducing maintenance.

Each supervisor has been asked to make a conscientious effort to increase the efficiency of his section by making process analyses and operation study.

1. Where are some of the places where study of a process would show results quickly? Why?
2. Where are some of the spots where study of an operation would show results quickly? Why?
3. Why must process study precede operation study?

CASE 3

You are a supervisor, and the work load of your section has increased. Labor is quite scarce, and the personnel department is having great difficulty recruiting additional workers for you. The last few they sent you were more trouble than they were worth.

One of the ways for you to meet the increased work load is to increase the efficiency of your section. You have cleaned up the obvious inefficiencies, but now you want to do a thorough and systematic job of improving a process. You want to apply the seven-step method.

1. What process would be the most fruitful to try to improve in your section? Why?
2. What are some of the hindrances you might run into when studying the process?
3. How should you go about overcoming them?
4. Does the process analysis checklist in this chapter cover the type of work performed in your department? Should the checklist be modified? How?

CASE 4

You are the supervisor of a section in which there are a fair number of simple repetitive operations. You have studied some of the processes, and have installed improved methods that are operating successfully. Now you are thinking of studying some of the operations in detail in order further to reduce wasted effort and make work easier.

1. What types of operations are worth studying? Why?
2. What are some of the hindrances you might run into? Why?

3. How are you going to overcome them?
4. How would you go about selling new methods to your workers?
5. What are some of the ways of getting workers to substitute new habits for old habits?

CASE 5

Visualize or, if practical, visit one of the plant's departments in which there is a large group of women doing inspection or light assembly work. Pick out an operation that appears to be suitable for operation analysis. Make an operation analysis and apply the operation analysis checklist to the operation. Operation checklist and charts precede the cases at the end of this chapter.

1. Give the reasons why you chose this specific operation to analyze.
2. How would you go about explaining to the operators what you were doing?
3. What might be some of the parts of the operation on which modification would really pay off in relation to making work easier?
4. What might be some of the parts of the operation on which modifications would really pay off in making effort more productive?
5. How would you go about justifying the cost of constructing mechanical aids, special bins, tools, etc.?
6. What are some hindrances you might run into during the study?
7. How would you overcome them?
8. What are some hindrances you might run into installing a better method?
9. How would you overcome them?

CASE 6

You are the supervisor of the packing department. At a recent safety meeting with your subordinates you asked for suggestions to submit to the safety committee. Bill, a young packer, suggested that a board placed where the conveyor line turns a corner would prevent packages from falling off.

You thanked him for the idea. You investigated it and had a board placed at the turn. It did keep packages from falling off. Then you dismissed the matter from your mind. Now you hear that Bill is complaining that you are stealing his safety ideas and getting credit for them. According to the rumor, Bill is saying that the idea of the board was to prevent packages from falling off the line and either getting broken or else hitting and injuring employees.

From your point of view, the placing of the board was a commonsense act and not a safety suggestion. Since the packages were neither heavy nor fragile, there was little possibility of injury or breakage.

1. What might be some of the reasons for a lack of the meeting of the minds here?
2. How are you going to handle the rumor?

CASE 7

You are an office supervisor. As you observe your people working, you see all sorts of inefficiencies—people doing things the hard way, putting up with obstacles instead of overcoming them, taking unnecessary steps, wasting a lot of energy.

You are not interested in getting more work out of your people. You want them to work no harder than necessary to accomplish what they are doing.

1. In your spare time over a period of a week make a list of your observations of energy being expended unwisely.
2. Analyze the list, group the observations into classes, and set up ways of overcoming these wastes of energy.
3. Work out a plan for presenting your findings and suggestions to your people.

CASE 8

You want to encourage suggestions from your employees. One of your workers is continually bringing you ideas that are neither practical nor well thought out. He gives so much time to the development of new ideas that his regular work suffers.

1. How would you handle the situation?
2. How can the practicability of an idea be determined?
3. What is the distinction between a good idea and a bad idea?
4. What is meant by "thinking out" ideas?
5. Suppose that his ideas were very good but that his regular work suffered, what would you do?

CASE 9

Recently Section X was added to your jurisdiction. From observations and information you concluded that Smith, its supervisor, is not progressive. While production in his section is satisfactory, there have been no improvements in methods or equipment for years. He and his men get out production by working hard—using their backs instead of their heads. You believe that business will increase and that his department will not be able to keep up and will become a bottleneck.

1. What is meant by being progressive?
2. Give some contrasts between "new" and "old" ways of doing things in a factory or office.
3. How would you go about selling methods improvement to Smith?

CASE 10

Recently the president of a rapidly growing company hired you in the staff capacity of industrial engineer. Your primary function is to uncover better ways of doing things and to sell these improvements to the line management. Most of the men in the line organization have been with the company from its beginning. They have never had to deal with industrial engineering or similar staff activities. They look upon you with suspicion. Their attitude is (and several have gone so far as to tell you) that: (1) no outsider can know a man's department as well as the man who grew up with it from the beginning; (2) to admit that your ideas are better than theirs would be to admit that you, rather than they, should be running their departments; (3) the company has gotten along fine so far without experts.

1. Build up a convincing argument to answer each of the three objections.
2. On the positive side, build up a program whereby you can demonstrate and sell your value to the line organization.

CASE 11

You were recently appointed the supervisor of a group of experienced workers, several of whom are considerably older than you. You know that one of these older workers has the reputation of being a chronic grouch, although his work was satisfactory under the previous supervisor.

You have made several changes in method which have speeded up the work of the department without increasing the effort required. All the workers except the chronic grouch have accepted the new methods. He insists on doing the job the old way, with the result that his production is lower than that of the rest of the men.

The other workers are aware of the situation and are waiting with considerable interest to see how you are going to handle the problem. You feel that you must do something about the situation.

What should you do?

CASE 12

When trying to reduce costs, it is often worthwhile to make cost studies involving alternative actions. In simple situations it is often found that the cost of requisitioning such items as small screws, washers, and nuts exceeds their price; thus it would be cheaper to supply them without requisitions, in open bins out on the shop floor.

Similarly, the cost of sorting and reclaiming small parts from floor sweepings may exceed the price of the parts recovered. Or the cost of repairing a simple defective mechanism sent in by a customer may be more than replacing it outright. Or the cost of correspondence and other paper work about a minor item may not be justified; for example, when a customer complains of a defective article, it may be cheaper to send him a replacement and tell him to dispose of the defective one rather than return it for repair or exchange.

Look for similar situations in your office or shop. Make cost comparisons for the purpose of determining the less costly alternative.

CASE 13

Recently you hired a young industrial engineer with limited supervisory experience but a lot of good ideas. You put him in charge of a section that was poorly organized, inefficient, and badly in need of what this man had to offer. You gave him a free hand.

Through the efforts of this new supervisor, the section has rapidly become one of the most efficient and closely disciplined in your department. However, the morale is extremely poor, and many of the men—including the better ones—are seeking transfers out of his section. They claim that they cannot do their jobs the way they wish and that the supervisor is continually checking on their performance.

1. Evaluate the arguments of the men.
2. How might you have been able to avoid this situation and yet get the job done by the new supervisor?
3. What are some of the cautions that should be observed when attempting to increase the efficiency of a department?
4. What are some of the relationships between efficiency and morale?

CASE 14

Sam Leonard was recruited from outside the company to take over a department employing over 60 employees. Before Sam joined the company a work measurement and methods improvement program had been initiated for all jobs which in the opinion of the methods people could be measured. Apparently the program got off to a very bad start in this department. The employees looked upon it as a way of reducing the size of the department and they feared losing their jobs. They resented having to account for all of their actions, including telephone calls and necessary trips to other departments.

Approximately 50 percent of the department's employees are college graduates engaged in analytical and technical work and these people in particular resent the program. One of the best analysts who was thought to have considerable future potential threatened to resign, so he was excused from the program by Sam Leonard's predecessor. Resentment among the other employees increased and several resigned.

After a year of difficulty in this department all of the analytical and technical employees were removed from the work measurement program. The department head was transferred and Sam Leonard was hired to take over a rather demoralized group of employees. While the higher paid employees were no longer on work measurement, the clerical staff was. They still see no value to work measurement and Sam has found that most of the results turned in by these people are nothing better than inaccurate estimates of what they actually do. Since the company is generally satisfied with the results of its work measurement program, they are definitely going to continue it. Sam has been told by his superior that one of his first jobs as department head will be to bring order to the chaotic work measurement effort in his department.

1. Discuss the pros and cons of hiring an outsider as department head in this situation.
2. What can the new department head do to reestablish the integrity of the work measurement program in his department?
3. How can a work measurement program be sold to employees who believe it a method of job elimination?
4. Should work measurement be applied to jobs which require judgment and are technical and analytical?
5. Should the one employee have been excused from the work measurement program?

CASE 15

Upper management wants to install a companywide work simplification program—not just a one-shot affair, but a permanent activity so organized and administered that it will get the participation of all the employees, both supervisory and nonsupervisory, in a continuing campaign to increase productivity, reduce costs, and maintain good employee relations.

Draw up a complete plan for such a program. Your report will be presented to upper management for approval. Specify the size and type of company for which you are planning.

FOLLOWING UP ON THE JOB

Methods improvement

1. How long has it been since you made a major improvement in methods in your unit?
2. Are you continually looking for ways to remove obstacles? Are you motion-minded?

3. Do you do a good job of selling better methods to your superior? To your workers?
4. Are you prompt in correcting misunderstandings about methods improvement?
5. Do you encourage your employees to use the company suggestion plan?
6. Are you able to operate as a member of a team for improving methods—with subordinates, with staff, with your boss?

Application of the seven-step technique to a process

1. Do you make methods improvements by using a systematic technique instead of by trial and error?
2. Do you use and improve upon the process analysis checklist?
3. When you devise a new method, do you apply the checklist to it?
4. Do you seek the cooperation of your employees when you are making a process study?

Application of the seven-step technique to an operation

1. Do you always study the process before making a detailed study of any of the operations in it?
2. Do you carefully determine the justification for any detailed study of an operation before making the study?
3. Do you use and improve upon the operation analysis checklist?
4. Do you seek suggestions from workers when you are studying an operation? Do you explain to them what you are doing?

Cost reduction

1. During a cost reduction program, do you put more emphasis on reducing costs than on "window dressing"?
2. Do you investigate idleness of men, machines, materials, and money as a source of cost reduction?
3. Do you use methods improvements as means of reducing costs?

9 Developing standards of work performance

The fair day's work. Standards and the time study department. The work measurement program. Introducing and implementing a work measurement program. Standards and the supervisor. Laying the groundwork for standards. Gathering information for standards. Determining the quality or the "how much." Determining the quality or the "how well." Introducing standards of work performance. Checking performance against standards. Getting results from standards of work performance. Standards of managerial performance. Cost control. Cost control in a continuous process industry. Summary.

If goal achievement is a basic activity of organizations then managers must be able to determine the degree of success their units demonstrate toward such goal achievement. To the extent that standards of work performance are established—standards of quantity (*how much*) and standards of quality (*how well*)—there can be common understanding of what is required.

The common understanding of what is required is essential to any control system. The very nature of control implies measurement and if work activity is to be effectively guided toward a predetermined goal, the control system also has to indicate whether the activity is achieving desired results.

The importance of widely accepted standards of performance should be recognized by the manager. If he is to effectively supervise his employees, he must be able to indicate what he expects of them. They in turn have to know what kind of performance will bring them rewards along with the other ingredients of job satisfaction. The extent of tolerated deviations from the norm is also a requisite of the control system. Correction should promptly take place when the tolerance is breached.

In a sense an effective control system is a vital communications device indicating to all concerned what is expected of them to achieve the goals of the organization. The establishment of fair standards of work performance is of significant concern to the supervisor. Such standards give him one of the tools he needs for supervision. His success in achieving established standards allows his superior to measure the effectiveness of his performance. Cost control and budgeting also grow out of established standards so the importance of developing standards of work performance can be readily seen.

The fair day's work

One of the most troublesome questions in the employer-employee relationship is that of what constitutes a fair day's work for a fair day's pay. Problems of salaries, wages, and effort are packed with emotion, which adds to the difficulty of determining and getting an agreement on what is fair. Adding to the confusion are a number of other issues which relate to the fairness of compensation in exchange for work. A combination of increasingly complex technology in both factories and offices and a shortage of skilled labor has caused many companies to lower their expectation for what is considered acceptable performance. A tight labor market tends to increase recruitment, selection, and placement costs. Added to this is the increased cost of training what is generally a lower quality labor supply. Considerable pressure is placed on supervisors to keep labor turnover down. Under such circumstances he may tolerate poorer performance rather than discipline an employee who may quit for another easily obtainable job. Large clerical employers in particular are caught in this type of situation. In many instances, they do not have accurate job descriptions nor do they really know how much each operation really costs.

The situation is somewhat different in factories where labor unions have had a greater impact. The matter of the fair day's pay is a subject for bargaining, and so is the matter of the length of the workday. But the matter of *what rate of production constitutes a fair day's work* is a matter for measurement. The procedures and techniques for making these measurements and setting up performance standards were devised by industrial engineering and are described in this chapter. Setting and maintaining standards of work performance is a management responsibility.[1] Management's failure to establish and maintain a high level of

---

[1] Management's right to establish, determine, maintain, and enforce production standards may be subject to check through the grievance procedure. For a study and a prediction of union-management conflict over work speeds and work loads, see John G. Hutchinson, *Managing a Fair Day's Work* (Ann Arbor, Mich.: The University of Michigan Bureau of Industrial Relations, 1963), or his "Stiffer Battles Ahead over Work Standards," *Personnel*, September–October, 1963.

Hutchinson sees management's increased toughness on work standards being met by a change in union strategy. If the standards are poorly set, the union still takes a hard line on the technical imperfections. But if the standard setters seem to be competent, the union does an about-face and bases an emotional appeal on the health hazards of the faster work pace.

performance give the employees a vested interest in loose standards and leads to high costs that may render the company unable to meet the competition of a more efficiently managed firm.

Standards and the time study department

The job of setting standards of work performance is usually a function of the time study or work measurement department, but on some jobs the supervisor has to establish the standards. In order to do so, he should be acquainted with the techniques used by the industrial engineer. The supervisor should get the time study people to show him how they determine normal performance from observed performance and how they make allowances for personal needs. The following definitions will establish a basis for discussing measurements and work pace.

Definitions. A standard of work performance is defined as the quality and quantity of work that *should* be produced by a *normal* employee working at a *normal* pace under *normal* conditions. "Normal" does not mean average, because the average performance may be poor performance under poor conditions.

A *normal* employee is a trained employee with sufficient aptitude and skill plus a positive attitude and a will to work.

A *normal* pace is that pace which a conscientious person can maintain day in and day out without suffering any ill effects. It is a daywork pace and it has not been hastened by a wage incentive or any other stimulus to hurry up.

Normal conditions mean: (1) that the materials, equipment, and working environment do not hinder the employee, (2) that he is subjected to a minimum of interruptions, (3) that he is using the best available methods as determined by, or equivalent to, those developed by methods improvement techniques (see Chapter 8).

Examples of standards of work performance are shown in Figure 9–1. They are standards for office work in Standard Oil Company of California. Some other examples of standards of work performance would be:

In a shop: 3 pieces drilled per minute.
　　　　　10 percent of time devoted to safety education.
In an office: 70 to 80 invoices written per day.
In a sales department: 6 or 7 calls per day.
In a social agency: 8 to 12 cases handled per week.
In a mail-order house: 3,000 sales slips sorted per hour.

For a description of output restriction and the attitudes and social relationships that enter into it, see Orvis Collins, Melville Dalton, and Donald Roy, "Restrictions of Output and Social Cleavage in Industry," in Pigors, Myers, and Malm, *Readings in Personnel Administration* (2d ed.: New York: McGraw-Hill Book Co., 1959).

FIGURE 9–1. Work Performance Standards—Typing and Filing

PERFORMANCE STANDARDS
STENOGRAPHER-TYPIST and FILE CLERK

		Hours	Minutes	%
1.	Total Hours Paid For: (Daily)	8	480	100
.	Total Hours Allowance: (Daily)	1	60	12.5
	Total Net Productive Hours: (Daily)	7	420	87.5

LINES

2. 30 Lines Per Letter: Dictated and Transcribed
   30 Lines Per Letter: Straight Copy

LETTERS

3. Production (Net Production Time) - in Seven (7) Hours, or 420 Minutes:
   Dictated and Transcribed Letters (30 lines each) = 10-1/2 letters, or Straight Copy Work *
   (30 lines each) = 21 letters

TIME STUDY ANALYSIS

4. Fifteen (15) Minutes Average Dictation Time for 30-Line Letter
   Twenty-Five (25) Minutes Average Transcription Time for 30-Line Letter
   Twenty (20) Minutes Average Copy Time for 30-Line Letter

AVERAGE DAILY TIME

5. Net Production Time: Seven (7) Hours, or 420 Minutes:
   Minutes Per Dictated Letter (40) = 10-1/2 - 30-Line Letters in Seven (7) Hours
   Minutes Per Copied Letter (20) = 21 - 30-Line Letters in Seven (7) Hours

Note: Typing time to transcribe a full page or equivalent from voicewriting
machine cylinders or records is figured at 20 minutes per letter. The
average cylinder contains approximately 120 lines of typing. The
number of cylinders completed per day should total 7 or more.
In general, stenographers spend 65% of productive time on dictation
and transcription and 35% on typing from copy or manuscript, resulting
in a combined total production of 13 full pages per day.

FILING

6. (a) Fifty (50) Units of Mail Per Hour using a numerical file system is the average and
       includes General File upkeep.
   (b) One hundred fifty (150) Units of Mail Per Hour, filing alphabetically, is the average
       and includes General File upkeep.

These production standards are based on the results of numerous surveys of stenographic work
and represent actual production of stenographers having average ability.

CODE ARRANGEMENT:

   Have steno or typist place initials on copy.
   Use "T" for transcribing from longhand material or typed copy.
   Use "D" for dictated letters.
   Use "V" for voicewriting machine.
   Make notation on working paper describing material typed if not practical to make
       copy such as contracts, complicated statements, and legal documents.
   Show typing time on each letter or typed material.

   * From handwritten copy

From Standard Oil Company of California. Exhibit "L" part 2, page 44 of *More Profit-Less Paper*, prepared by Joseph W. Lucas with the assistance of other members of the Department on Organization of Standard Oil Company of California, 1953. Item 3 setting a standard for "Straight Copy Work" refers to typing from handwritten copy—not retyping a typed page. Used by permission.

Techniques for measuring performance. The standards set up by the time study department are used for daywork standards, wage incentives, production planning, scheduling, standard costs, and similar purposes. The three major techniques used in setting the standards are stopwatch time study, standard data, and work sampling. The stopwatch technique is the most common and it involves the following six main steps:

1. The method of doing the job is standardized by the application of methods improvement.
2. The conditions surrounding the job are standardized.
3. The job cycle is broken into parts or elements suitable for stopwatch time study.
4. Enough timings of the elements of the cycles are taken until a representative time for a cycle can be determined.
5. The pace of the operator is compared to that of the *normal* operator (the operator described above) and the observed time is adjusted.
6. Percentage time allowances to take care of interruptions and personal needs of the operator are added to the normal time. The result is the standard time or standard of work performance.

More detailed descriptions of stopwatch time study can be found in any of the motion and time study texts listed in the suggested readings at the end of Part II of this text.

The second technique of the standards people uses standard data or uses "predetermined standards." Instead of using a stopwatch reading for arriving at normal times, synthetic standards are used. The synthetic or standard data may be based on previous stopwatch studies or they may be based on fundamental manual motions. The times for these latter motions and the methods of applying them are supplied by any one of the following systems:[2]

Methods Time Measurement (MTM)
Work Factor
Motion Time Analysis
Basic Motion Time Study (BMT)

While all of the above systems have some differences in application and approach, they have common objectives. Essentially they are used to analyze work in relation to the basic motions necessary for its performance. When these motions have been identified, time values for them can be chosen from the appropriate tables of predetermined elemental time values. In this way time standards can be developed syn-

---

[2] Each of these four systems is described in detail in H. B. Maynard (ed.), *Industrial Engineering Handbook* (New York: McGraw-Hill Book Co., 1956).

thetically and can become a means of training the employee who is to perform the work.

Predetermined time systems are widely used and accepted in work measurement. When they are effectively used they do an efficient job in the setting of standards and the development of methods. Because of their consistency and relative efficiency, they have made it economically possible to measure a variety of work in both factories and offices.

The third method of determining standards of work performance is by applying a statistical sampling technique to the work for the purpose of determining the percentage of time spent doing tasks. This method is called "Working Sampling" and is described by Barnes.[3]

Ultimate and attainable standards. The standards based on the performance of the normal worker at normal pace under normal conditions are published as *attainable* or required performance. Some companies on measured daywork[4] set *ultimate* (high-task) standards which make no allowance for nonstandard conditions. Ultimate standards represent a goal to be aimed at but not necessarily to be attained. They may be kept secret so the union won't contest them. Thus if discipline is called for because an employee is putting out inadequate effort, he will be disciplined for wasting time rather than for failing to meet a standard. Ultimate standards are not required performance. Under them, methods changes and continuing improvements can be introduced without producing a contest about revising the standards upward. Ultimate standards avoid establishing a minimum acceptable amount of output which may become the maximum obtained; each employee is expected to work to the best of his ability.

The nature of the labor market may involve the work measurement department in a problem of semantics. Some practitioners believe there is a difference between *required* standards and *attainable* standards. They tend to equate the word "attainable" with "desired." Companies in tight labor markets with a shortage of skilled labor and little lead time for training accept what they call *desired* standards. One large clerical employer calls 70 percent performance of required standards, acceptable performance by its employees.

The standards discussed in this chapter are the *attainable* standards; they are the kind that must be established in order to plan and schedule work.

---

[3] Ralph M. Barnes, *Work Sampling* (2d ed.; New York: John Wiley & Sons, Inc., 1957).

[4] Measured daywork indicates pay by the hour, associated with direct or indirect control of worker efficiency through the use of production standards. For a discussion of measured daywork and incentive systems, and union-management problems over establishing and enforcing production standards, see Sumner H. Slichter, James J. Healy, and E. Robert Livernash, *The Impact of Collective Bargaining on Management* (Washington, D.C.: The Brookings Institution, 1960), chaps. 17 and 18.

The work measurement program

The importance of techniques to measure performance and ascertain results is well recognized. Work measurement is one of the "tools" of management designed to minimize the inevitable subjective judgments by which supervisors evaluate their subordinates. It is primarily concerned with improving productivity and in this sense it helps a supervisor to do a more effective job. Hopefully, a work measurement program should aid the supervisor in making work assignments, training new employees, and in the planning and scheduling of the work. Forecasting manpower requirements and determining costs are obvious additional benefits.

Since a work measurement program has a wide impact on an organization, it must have a total commitment from all levels of management. Obviously the first-level supervisor's acceptance of the program is critical to its success. After all it is at this level of supervision that the greatest involvement with the measurement and control aspects of the program take place. They should have a significant role in the development of standards and every effort should be made to make it their program. Even where a trained staff of analysts is used the supervisor should be consulted and he should approve the standards set for those jobs for which he is responsible. If the first-level supervisor accepts and supports the work measurement program enthusiastically, this will go a long way toward gaining general acceptance among all employees whose work is measured.

While middle managers are not as directly involved with work measurement as are the supervisors who report to them, they have their familiar "man-in-the-middle" role here. They are expected to support the top-management decision establishing the program and to indicate their approval to the lower level supervisors reporting to them. Middle managers are also expected to communicate to their superiors, the problems, thoughts, and opinions of their subordinates.

As the program develops and becomes well established, middle managers will find it very useful as a yardstick for the performance of first-level supervision. By holding the first-level supervisor responsible for the utilization of standards, the middle manager has a reasonably objective measurement of the effectiveness of the first-level supervisor. Such a measurement is particularly useful when recommending pay increases and promotions for first-level supervisors.

As indicated earlier the establishment of a work measurement program is usually a top-management decision. Once the decision is made there should be an indication of the wholehearted approval of senior management. It is particularly desirable that such a program have their backing for they are the individuals who establish the leadership pattern for the organization. A senior executive who reports to the chief executive should be given responsibility for the program and the chief executive should make it clear that he is interested in the success of the program.

Figure 9–2 is an example of the approach one company used to inform its employees that a work measurement program was being introduced. Not only does it clearly indicate top-management approval and support but it also gives a rather complete explanation of the reasons for the program. The letter goes on to indicate how the program will be administered and how it will operate. In anticipation of several employee questions, there is included a series of important questions which could be raised and the answers that management believes will dispel rumors and doubt about the program.

Introducing and implementing a work measurement program

To more fully understand the organizational effort required to develop a work measurement program it may be useful to explain some of the things done by the Manufacturers Hanover Trust Company in the implementation of their program. (See Figure 9–2.) With the help of an outside consulting firm they have trained their own analysts. The broad outline of this course follows:

MANUFACTURERS HANOVER TRUST COMPANY
WORK MEASUREMENT ANALYST TRAINING COURSE[5]

Analysts are trained in groups of 10 to 15 as often as necessary. The training course runs for five full weeks and is conducted in a classroom atmosphere, on the bank's premises, by members of the work measurement staff.

The course can be broken down into three separate phases:

1. The concepts and purposes of the programs.
2. MTM training and qualification.
3. Standard data and application of techniques.

1. Concepts and purposes. During the first five days of training the instructor and trainees discuss "Why a Work Measurement Program." Through role playing, the trainees are allowed to discover for themselves, the benefits and uses of work measurement control reports to all levels of management. Then through careful examination of the input and basis for the control reports, they are shown the importance of their

---

[5] Used with the permission of the Manufacturers Hanover Trust Company, New York, N.Y.

FIGURE 9–2

Letters Introducing and Explaining a Work Measurement Program Including Answers to Questions Employees Might Ask about the Program

---

MANUFACTURERS HANOVER TRUST COMPANY

350 PARK AVENUE, NEW YORK, N. Y. 10022

R. E. McNEILL, Jr.
CHAIRMAN OF THE BOARD

September 15, 1964

To the Staff of
MANUFACTURERS HANOVER TRUST COMPANY:

In the past three years, much has been accomplished to unify our Bank and to improve the quality and efficiency of its services. But, banking is a highly competitive business and we cannot rest on our laurels or relax our efforts.

To continue this progress, we are initiating a program to improve our operations through Work Measurement. This is a long range plan to help us "take stock", to evaluate what we are doing and to learn how we may do it better.

We firmly believe that the Work Measurement Program will give us the objective scientific yardsticks we need to review our work productivity and our service costs. Similar programs are being used with success by many modern businesses including a number of our competitors.

The first phase of the Program — the training of analysts selected from our own staff — will begin September 28, 1964. The study of all operations will follow in the ensuing months.

A description of the Program — its aims, purposes, and its value to you and to the Bank — is enclosed. Please read it carefully and discuss any questions you may have with your supervisor.

Our customers and stockholders properly look to us for excellence in the day-by-day performance of our duties. Efficient operations are reflected in good service, more business and, inevitably, in higher earnings, salaries and profit sharing.

I know we can count on you to give your full cooperation.

Sincerely yours,

R. E. McNEILL, JR.
Chairman of the Board.

Used with permission of the Manufacturers Hanover Trust Company, New York, N.Y.

WORK MEASUREMENT PROGRAM

THE PLAN

The Program is a long-range plan to help the bank operate as effectively and as efficiently as possible. Essentially it is an "Operations Improvement" study, a bankwide survey of our operations, work flow and habits, and the costs of producing our services. It is designed to provide the necessary facts to evaluate new services, improve operational procedures and control cost.

THE REASON FOR THIS PROGRAM

The Bank is a service organization and its success depends upon the coordinated and efficient production of its staff. By using the established analytical methods of the Program, we will determine fair standards of work output and be able to measure the quality and quantity of our production against those standards.

THE PROGRAM'S AIMS AND PURPOSE

The Program will assist in determining how many new employees should be hired. It will help supervisors make the best use of each individual's productive effort. It will aid supervisors in rating employee job performances. It will be useful in job training. It will allow better comparison of the work flow on a day-to-day and month-to-month basis so that personnel shortages can be spotted and corrected. It will call attention to methods and procedures which can be improved.

HOW EMPLOYEES BENEFIT

Probably everyone has days when his or her work effort and output are greater or less than on others. Sometimes, too, we know we have accomplished a great deal more or less than co-workers. Such variations may arise because: (1) there is an uneven flow of work, or (2) the work is unevenly distributed. Rarely is someone regularly "swamped" with work, or does he "coast" along instead of doing his share.

Each of us wants to do a "fair day's work." Each of us also wants to have his superior know how much work he is doing — and to be assured that this is recognized in salary reviews and taken into consideration for promotion.

The Program will help all of us by providing a more accurate measurement of the amount of work performed and by insuring recognition for actual accomplishment.

If the program reveals that units are understaffed, they will be brought up to par. If it shows an excess of staff, transfers will be arranged to vacancies in other departments. Most important, if upward adjustments in individual salaries are indicated, they will be made.

FIGURE 9–2 (*Continued*)

HOW THE PROGRAM WILL OPERATE

It will be installed over a period of time and will be developed in three steps. The first step involves the analysis of all operations in a specific department or branch office. The second step establishes accurately the time required for each type of work performed and relates it to normal and peak loads. The third step assembles the data in usable form to determine whether the department or branch is under, over or properly staffed.

ADMINISTRATION OF THE PROGRAM

While general administration will be the responsibility of the Operations Department, the progress of the Program will be reviewed regularly by the General Administrative Board. Analysts from our several departments and branch offices will work directly with supervisors and, where necessary, with individual members of the staff to obtain the required facts about the volume and types of work performed in each section of the Bank.

In the initiation of the Program, the Bank will have the assistance of Bruce Payne and Associates, Inc., a leading consultant firm specializing in work measurement and operational standards.

SOME ANSWERS TO IMPORTANT QUESTIONS

Q.   *How long will the Program take?*

A.   It is estimated that it will take at least two years for the bankwide analysis to be completed.

Q.   *Is the measurement of productive work the only function of the Program?*

A.   No. Improvements in methods and systems, better utilization of equipment, smoother work flow and tighter cost control; all of these will be important by-products derived from the greater knowledge of the work we do.

Q.   *Isn't this just a "speed-up" pressure program in disguise?*

A.   Most emphatically not. The Program's emphasis is on "normal" accomplishment in normal situations with proper training. The normal production of work in your specific area will be jointly determined by your supervisor and the analysts.

Q.   *Why do we need such a program when we already have evaluation interviews and reports at the time of salary reviews?*

A.   Factual and objective data will supplement personal opinions about performance. This additional information will insure a better and fairer measure of an individual's accomplishment.

FIGURE 9–2 (*Concluded*)

Q.   *Isn't this Program going to reduce our jobs to a mechanical level?*

A.   No. It is mechanical only in the measurement of production and the analysis of costs. At Manufacturers Hanover, there will always be a premium and demand for initiative, judgement, accuracy, and individual responsibility.

Q.   *Maybe the Program's all right for some jobs, but mine is different. How can you measure a job that takes a good deal of thought?*

A.   Don't stop thinking; that's what the Bank needs. Some jobs, of unusual complexity, may not be measureable; the majority do fall into established patterns and will come within the scope of the Program.

Q.   *Won't the Program emphasize quantity rather than quality?*

A.   Positively not. Quality of performance is the first requisite in our Bank and every standard will be based on the production of quality work.

Q.   *Why should personnel from other areas of the Bank survey the work of my section?*

A.   For two reasons: (1) an objective observer with a fresh viewpoint can work better with supervisors in developing fair and equitable levels of performance and, (2) it is more desirable to have our own Bank personnel analyzing our operations than outside consultants.

Q.   *In summary, what will the Program accomplish?*

A.   The Work Measurement Program will build a sounder, stronger organization by helping us to:
- Improve the quality and efficiency of our operations;
- Distribute the work load more evenly and fairly among the staff;
- Develop a more precise and objective means of measuring and setting standards for each day's output;
- Assist in scheduling operations so we can quickly adapt ourselves to changing conditions;
- Measure performance to insure proper recognition of each individual.

new job in relation to the attainment of the goals of the program and of the bank.

2. MTM training and qualification. The second phase of the training course consists of 105 hours of training in the basic measurement technique: "Methods-Time-Measurement" (MTM). This training is required by the MTM Association and is conducted by an employee of the bank who has been trained and licensed by that association. The association also provides qualification examinations and issues certificates of recognition to those successfully completing the course.

3. Standard data and consistency of application. During the last week of "formal" training, the analysts are introduced to the reference materials, forms, and techniques employed in writing work standards. They are given guidelines covering the proper approach to these assignments, the proper use of the various lines of communication, and their overall role in the area which they are measuring. They are also given the opportunity to try their newfound skills through exercises in practical application of work measurement techniques.

Orientation program. Because supervisors are vital to the success of a work measurement program, it is imperative that they understand the nature of the program and its relationship to their area of responsibility. To achieve this very necessary objective, the Manufacturers Hanover Trust Company conducts an orientation program for supervisors.

MANUFACTURERS HANOVER TRUST COMPANY
WORK MEASUREMENT ORIENTATION FOR SUPERVISORS[6]

The supervisor is the "key man" in any successful work measurement program. It is imperative that he be shown how to utilize the technician assigned to him by the work measurement department to establish fair and equitable work standards which will provide him with the information he needs in order to do his job more effectively.

 I. Why the work measurement program
    A. Tool to aid management in their basic functions
        1. Planning.
        2. Controlling.
    B. Tool to aid management in their relations with employees
        1. Motivation.
        2. Training.
 II. The work measurement program is a series of "building blocks" individually and collectively supplying information to the next level.
    A. Fundamental motions.
    B. Methods-time-measurement.

---

[6] Used with permission of the Manufacturers Hanover Trust Company, New York, N.Y.

C. Standard data.
   1. Benefits.
   2. Basic concepts.
D. Tasks.
E. Operations.
F. Work standards.
G. Performance reports.
H. Control reports.
III. What is an analyst's responsibility to the department he is analyzing and to the management of that department?
IV. What is the supervisor's role in the work measurement study?

The next link in the chain is to inform employees who will be measured by the analyst. When the program was first introduced, all employees were given an orientation program to supplement the letter of introduction. (See Figure 9–2.) This program is now carried on for all new employees who join the bank and who are assigned to departments where work measurement is in use. This orientation makes them aware of work measurement and what it means to them on their jobs.

MANUFACTURERS HANOVER TRUST COMPANY
INTRODUCTION TO WORK MEASUREMENT FOR NEW EMPLOYEES[7]

Human beings are constantly gauging their actual performance in comparison to objectives and goals which they have established. For example, in driving an automobile, we must continually compare the actual direction of the vehicle with its planned direction. If actual performance falls short of the goals, there is the danger that the vehicle will hit a pedestrian or that there will be a collision or a possibility of arriving at the wrong destination. However, a complex network of physical and mental processes helps to control the situation. These processes tell us what our direction is, enabling us to take the proper course of action.

In the same way, the bank has goals which it wishes to achieve. *Among these goals are the reduction of any excess costs and the elimination of waste and inefficiency.* To accomplish this task, we must first be able to determine the actual performance of individual employees and departments and branches as a whole. In addition, the efficiency with which time is being utilized must also be ascertained. Once these can be determined, the proper steps can be taken to improve any inadequate situations.

In order to obtain this information and therefore achieve its goals, the bank has undertaken a Work Measurement Program. In simplest terms, *work measurement is a procedure using quantitative methods to determine the amount of work that can be accomplished in a given period of time.* Every clerical job in every department and branch will have been eventually ana-

[7] Used with permission of the Manufacturers Hanover Trust Company, New York, N.Y.

lyzed under this program. The end product of work measurement is the development of work standards. These work standards show how much work can be performed in a given period of time; i.e., there are standards in branches which show the method for processing a savings deposit and how it can be accomplished in "X" number of minutes per deposit. Another standard in a department might show how much can be accomplished in "X" number of minutes with reference to the investigation of a personal loan application.

These standards have been and are in the process of being established by work measurement analysts who are employees of the bank. By analyzing the methods used for each function or job and by assigning predetermined time values, the analysts are able to establish standards.

What is the purpose of work standards as such? They serve as the basis upon which actual performance of individuals, departments, and branches can be determined. It is at this juncture that the direct involvement of each employee is required. This involvement is in the form of activity reporting; i.e., each individual will record the way in which his time is utilized. To simplify this process of reporting, tally sheets are maintained daily by each employee.

What benefits can the individual employee expect to derive from work measurement? As for the work itself, analysis and measurement aim at the establishment of the best way of performing a job. As a result, *the individual is able to work smarter rather than harder.* Work measurement provides the answers to the following questions which each employee eventually asks: "What share of the work load of my group am I supposed to carry?" and "Just what does my boss expect of me in fulfilling my assignment?"

What are the more tangible and visible benefits of this program? The most important of these can be found in the areas of *salary administration* and *promotional opportunities.* In consideration for salary increases, one's performance on his or her job can now be based on factual data. Recognition in the form of higher salary can be given as a result of work measurement. Similarly, where all other qualifications for promotion are met, his actual job performance will be judged by the tangible work measurement data. In this way the employee's productivity will be recognized objectively.

There is however, more to be gained from work measurement than increases in pay. Each individual has a desire to build and maintain a sense of personal worth and importance in relation to the job he performs. With a knowledge of his performance, *the individual will know his level of achievement and contribution on the basis of facts.* Without work measurement, one can only venture opinions as to how well a particular function is being performed. This sense of personal worth has a beneficial effect on the ego. Satisfaction is derived in part from knowing how well one is doing on his job and how well he is using his abilities.

The benefits to the bank in the form of cost reduction and waste elimination and reduction of inefficient performance have been mentioned. But, in the final analysis, when one speaks of the bank, this includes all of its employees. As the bank prospers, so does its employees. As costs are reduced, more becomes available for profit sharing. There is a long list of possible benefits to employees of an organization that is operating efficiently.

In a sense, the bank's most valuable resource is its human resource. Because it is so vital, this resource must be used effectively. Facts pertaining to the manner in which time and individual capabilities are being utilized must be obtained. When a person calls a physician to examine the existence and causes of any adverse condition, he would not expect or want him to study only outward symptoms. He would want the doctor to get all of the relevant details. Using the same logic, it can be seen that the bank cannot achieve its goals without the detailed facts on its actual performance. Work measurement provides the means by which the bank can guide itself in the critical area of employee performance and productivity.

The goal the bank hopes to achieve with its work measurement program is a better place for work performance and equitable treatment of all employees.

Standards and the supervisor

While the work measurement or time study department ordinarily sets up standards for repetitive tasks—standards that must ordinarily be expressed in definite quantitative measurements—there are many jobs that cannot and need not be measured so rigidly. These are the jobs on which the supervisor must set standards in order to plan and schedule his work, know his manpower needs, and estimate his budget needs. Another use of standards is in comparing and evaluating methods improvement suggestions one against another.

The supervisor must have standards of performance in order to evaluate the performance of subordinates and to handle disciplinary problems and grievances. If an employee is to be discharged for unacceptable performance, there must be evidence that he knew the standard and knew that his work was substantially below it over a definite period of time. When a supervisor has a set of standards of work performance, he can measure each subordinate's performance and know whether the person should be rewarded, encouraged, given extra training, transferred, or warned. If the employee knows the standard, he knows what is expected of him: he knows whether his performance is outstanding, satisfactory, or unsatisfactory and whether he is due for a reward or a warning.

Standards of performance serve both the supervisor and his boss in making possible the delegation of authority and responsibility. A delegator is still accountable for work turned over to a subordinate and must have some system of information (records and reports) to find out if the work is being done and some measure by which to judge how well it is being done. This, of course, is controlling—one of the major activities of management. A system of controls permits management by the exception principle: that is, a manager has the exceptions to the standard brought to his attention so that he can spot misuse of authority or a failure to carry out responsibility, and he can take corrective action. Standards are a help to the subordinate to whom responsibility and authority are delegated, because he knows what is expected of him.

Laying the groundwork for standards

When a supervisor is preparing to set up a standard, he analyzes a job from the standpoint of the tasks it contains and just what the worker is doing or supposed to be doing. He may find that the job is not very well set up—that the tasks are not well fitted together to make a well-designed job. Also, the workplace may be poorly arranged, or there may be delays and inefficiencies that could be corrected. He will see that it would not be a good idea to set a standard for this job now and improve the job later, because any standard he set now would have to be changed and raised when methods improvement had made possible greater output. If investigation of a job shows that a methods improvement program is needed, the job should be improved before a standard is set.

While the supervisor is still looking over the job from the standpoint of what it consists of, he should consult the job description. At this point he may wonder why he has to set up a standard at all, if the job is all written up in the job description. But if he tries to use a typical job description to evaluate performance, he will find that it describes what the man is to do, but not *how much;* it describes the skills and abilities he should possess—what he should be able to do—but provides no means of measuring *how well* he is doing it. But the job description makes a good starting spot in that it furnishes information on job content and probably lists the tasks that go to make up the job. When the job is broken down into the different tasks of which it is composed, it becomes easier to measure.

Gathering information for standards

If the supervisor performed the job while a member of the rank and file, he has a very good idea of how much should be turned out. If he has supervised the job over a period to time, he has seen it performed by a number of workers and under varying conditions. The more performances he has studied, the better will be his judgment as to what amount constitutes satisfactory performance.

By actually observing various people now working on the job, he can count output and study the spread between the various workers. By studying production records, he can get a history of output over a period of time.

By asking other supervisors what they expect for satisfactory performance on like jobs, he can evaluate his own ideas against theirs.

The time study or work measurement department can supply valuable information about the amount of work and the pace of the normal worker. The time study men are always working with this problem; they have to have an accurate idea of what constitutes the normal pace of a qualified operator in order to work out their time studies. They need to determine the difference in pace between the hourly paid employee and worker on piece rates. They also need to know the difference between the worker they are observing and the normal worker in order to set the performance requirements to fit the normal worker. With this background they can be of great assistance to the supervisor in determining what should be the pace of a normal worker.

When a supervisor is setting up standards of quantity, he must remember that it is not necessary to be as precise on hourly rated jobs and jobs of indirect labor as on piece-rate jobs. In using the standard he isn't going to be breathing down his employees' necks and counting every piece they turn out. He wishes to set up a standard by which workers can see for themselves what is expected of them and know whether they are producing at a satisfactory rate. He will spot check the output of each man at intervals. He will keep a closer check on the output of the beginner, the laggard, and the worker who seems to be slowing down. And he will have the standard to go by in investigating the *why* when the quality and quantity of a job are off.

When setting up standards it is often profitable to consult the workers as to what it is they do or should be doing. When the supervisor investigates the *what* of a job, he should keep the purpose of the job in mind so as to list the tasks in the order of their importance, and he should describe the tasks in clear, simple, specific, and definite action words. For an example of a well-written standard see Figure 9–1.

Determining the quantity or the "how much"

After lining up or writing down the tasks that make up the job, the supervisor next determines the how much—the quantity of work that will constitute satisfactory performance. Here he will have to consider both the needs of management and the capacities of competent, trained, and qualified employees. The standard he will set up should not be an ideal goal that can be attained only by an outstanding worker under conditions that are just right. The standard must be set at a mark that the normal worker—as defined under "Standards and the Time Study Department" early in this chapter—can reach and an above average employee can exceed. The preciseness with which output can be measured varies from number of pieces per hour, as determined by the time study department on repetitive jobs, to the vagueness of work that is purely creative and in which the amount is anybody's guess. The great majority of jobs in industry do not belong in the purely creative class, however, and can be measured in some manner.

Each supervisor has a good idea of the amount of work turned out by his unsatisfactory employees and by the satisfactory and outstanding ones. Pinning it down more closely, he can place the others in between and thus determine the poor, the fair, the satisfactory, the good, and the excellent or exceptional performers. By expressing these outputs in quantitative and qualitative terms, he is well on his way to establishing standards of work performance. The quantitative measure does not have to be—and in most cases cannot be—expressed in pieces per hour. Instead of a definite number of pieces, a range can be used and a longer unit of time can also be used.

Instead of setting up a standard of a specific number of units per hour, such as 15, a spread of from 13 to 17 might suffice; or the output might be expressed in terms of an eight-hour day by a spread of from 105 to 135 per day. Or it might be expressed in terms of units per week. There are advantages to expressing output in terms of a range. Work not on piece rates is usually not so closely controlled as that on piece rates; there are more interruptions, sizes may vary, and the difficulty may vary. The spread makes allowances for variations in output that are beyond the control of the worker.

The type of job under study will greatly influence the way the quantitative measure is expressed. Instead of expressing output in terms of pieces per hour or a range of pieces, it might be expressed in terms of deadlines—that is, work, such as payrolls, must be completed by a certain deadline. Or output might be expressed in terms of getting the job done so that people will not have to wait or be held up: for example, supplying materials to machines or setting up machines. Another basis might be that the job is to be completed within a certain period of time after it is received: for example, all correspondence must be answered within one or two days of receipt. The same measure might go for different types of reports.

Normally, the greater the variety involved in the tasks, the larger should be the "bundle" for measuring: for instance, if a dictaphone operator transcribes cylinders for a number of dictators, the difficulty of the letters varies, the length of the letters varies, and the number of letters per cylinder varies; so it would take a week's output to get a representative sample.

Standards of quantity must be expressed in terms that can be measured or spot-checked without too much difficulty. For example, the standard of 100 dictated words per minute for a stenographer to take in shorthand looks like a good one, but it is very difficult to measure. Measuring to that standard would require an embarrassing observation and the use of a stopwatch on the dictator. A more practical standard would be that the stenographer must seldom, if ever, have to ask the dictator to slow up, stop, or repeat because she cannot keep up.

The measurement of output must also be representative of the effort and skill expended. If an employee applies more effort and skill, his output should increase proportionately. He should not be penalized for conditions such as stoppages or lack of supplies that are beyond his control.

Standards must include allowances for interruptions and personal needs. People can't—nor should they be expected to—devote every minute of the day to work.

In measuring quantity, the supervisor must always bear in mind that he is looking for an attainable satisfactory performance on the part of his work group. He does not want to be a snooper or to measure everything; he simply wants to know what is going on, so that people are not pulling the wool over his eyes. If the supervisor makes a fetish of counting output without taking other things into consideration, he will find his men dodging difficult jobs or refusing to use their judgment if it would take time away from production. The typist whose keystrokes are being counted with a cyclometer will retype a sheet rather than take the time to make a correction on it, and, if she has been through that sort of thing before, she will not leave the discarded sheet in the wastebasket for the boss to find. She will also discover that tapping the space bar is restful and registers on the cyclometer the same as productive work.

In measuring the quantity of output, the supervisor has to set standards that encourage workers to give their best efforts to the company. A standard that emphasizes output at the sacrifice of judgment and cooperation is demoralizing.

Some examples of quantity standards are:

Punch information at the rate of 110 to 120 cards per hour.
Sort between 900 and 1,000 pieces per hour.
Validate claims at the rate of 325 to 375 per week.
Answer all outside correspondence within 12 working hours.
Finish tabulation and send to payroll department half a day before the
    payroll is to be started.
Post 750 accounts per day.

Determining the quality or the "how well"

Work may be turned out in great quantity at the expense of quality; but if it is not acceptable, it is a waste of manpower, materials, money, and equipment.

There are two ways of getting at the problem of determining satisfactory quality. The first is the positive way, in which the supervisor asks himself. "What is the purpose of this work? What is the end that it has to serve?" If the work fulfills its objective, the quality is necessarily satisfactory.

The other approach—and the easier one—is the negative approach: that is, uncovering the points wherein the work is unsatisfactory and asking why it is unsatisfactory. When a supervisor asks himself, "Why is this work being rejected?" or "Why am I rejecting this work?" he is measuring the quality aspects of the job.

It is necessary for the supervisor to relate quality and quantity in their proper balance in setting up measures of performance. Generally, the higher the quality requirements of any job, the lower the volume will be. Pieces that have to be machined to close tolerances cannot be turned but so far as those machined to loose tolerances. This theory follows through in most work. Therefore, the supervisor should not call for quality that is higher than necessary for the successful accomplishment of the job. Neither should he encourage workers to do a piece of work beyond the requirements called for. Some workers waste time doing a fine job when it is not necessary and performing operations beyond those that are called for. There is no need to put a fine finish on a piece that is going to be painted later.

In setting up standards of quality, the supervisor should be guided by the standards that are acceptable in the plant as a whole. If he is too meticulous or his standards are much higher than those of the other supervisors, he may be justly considered to be overexacting.

There are a number of bases upon which quality standards can be set up. They can be in terms of rejects by the inspection department. Or they may be set up in terms of the amount of waste—for example, an amateur painter painting a ceiling might do an excellent job but get more paint on the surrounding areas than on the ceiling. Another basis is that of reworks. This may be not only in terms of what the worker himself has to do over again, but also in terms of the amount of extra work caused for somebody else in subsequent operations: boxes piled up backward have to be turned around by someone in order to be identified. Quality may be set up in terms of errors—that is, three mistakes in a hundred. Another basis will be in terms of a worker's doing a job safely in relation to himself and others. For example: in stacking materials, a job is not satisfactory if a man does not lift properly or if the articles are piled in a manner that would allow them to fall over and injure someone or damage equipment. Quality of work should include the proper use of machines and tools.

It is necessary that the supervisor relate the quality standards to the quantity standards and give each its proper importance when setting up performance standards and when explaining them to his employees.

Some examples of quality standards are these:

Punching errors should not exceed 5 to 10 in 1,000 cards punched.

No more than 2 or 3 sorting errors in 10,000 pieces.

There should be no more than 3 or 5 claims incorrectly validated in processing 1,500 claims.

On letters, margins should be even and there should be no smudges or misspellings.

Introducing standards of work performance

The critical stage in the development of a work measurement program is gaining acceptance of the program among the employees whose performance is to be measured. As is the case with any new or different program, there is bound to be some resistance and suspicion about standards of performance. It is rather difficult for an employee to understand how standards of performance will help him before the program starts. Thus it is vital to involve and inform employees as soon as possible. Early information will help offset the inevitable rumors about a "speedup" and "cutting payroll" that accompany the introduction of any attempt at performance measurement. If at all possible, assurance should be given that the program will not result in the release of any employees. While one of the purposes of standards development is to ascertain more accurate staffing levels, recent experience has indicated that employees are not discharged because of work measurement. This is mainly due to the nature of the labor market and the fact that most companies have discovered that normal attrition is a far more effective way of reducing the size of the work force if this is necessary.

Because employees are primarily interested in their own welfare the supervisor must emphasize the relationship of performance standards to the individual employee. It is natural for employees to fear change because of the uncertainty that it implies. Obviously it is therefore necessary for the supervisor to be as specific as possible in allaying employee fears.

When the supervisor introduces standards of work performance, he should discuss them in detail with the employees involved so that they will know exactly what is expected of them. This is especially necessary in the case of the new employees, but often the old-timers are almost as ignorant of what is expected of them.

The detail which goes into writing up a standard will vary with the importance of the tasks and the number of men performing them. New standards should be tried out on a temporary basis until they are found to be satisfactory. Then they should be put on a permanent basis and not changed unless there is a substantial change in the job content or in the method of doing the job. A standard to be worthwhile must be considered a measure that will not vary.

When the work group has a good attitude toward the company, the employees themselves can participate in setting the standards; people setting their own standards usually set them high and are much better motivated to work toward attaining them. Work groups that are accustomed to taking responsibility for seeing that the total job gets done can participate in standard setting in group meetings. If a group agrees on a standard it puts pressure on individual members to conform to it and gives help to individual members to achieve it. The *process* of setting standards can result in a better understanding of the objectives of the unit and a greater willingness to accept responsibilities.

Merely discussing standards of work performance with employees can be a morale builder. If the worker knows the standards, he can measure his performance against them and can know where he stands. He will realize that the important item is work—not just pleasing the boss. When the worker knows that his output is being checked against standards, he knows that success on the job depends on himself and not on factors beyond his control. He cannot claim that his performance is being evaluated according to how the boss feels that day or what side of the bed he got out of. Nor can the worker claim that he is being overloaded or discriminated against and that other fellows are getting away with murder.

After the supervisor has explained the standards of performance, he must not let too much time elapse before he discusses with the workers how their output measures up to the standards. They must realize that the standard is a measure that is going to be used—not just hung up like a flag.

Checking performance against standards

In checking output, the supervisor has to avoid snooping or breathing down his workers' necks. He has always observed jobs to see how they were going: now he has something by which to measure them.

Some jobs, owing to their nature or importance, will require more inspection than other jobs. Some men will require closer checking than other men. New employees need to be checked often to see that they know how to turn out satisfactory work and that they understand what quality and quantity the standards call for. Employees who are on a temporary basis, before being made permanent, also need to be checked carefully. Then there is the laggard who needs frequent checking. The conscientious employee who understands the standards and tries to live up to them does not need to be checked frequently. However, it is necessary to check the work of every employee to start with and then to do it periodically, not with the idea of trying to get more work out of everybody but with the idea of determining the relative value of each man's work performance. This measuring is done by spot-checking when things are going normally. But when there are slowdowns and complaints about people being given an unequal share of the work, when certain workers appear to be goldbricking, or when production as a whole is falling off, the supervisor must keep a close measure of the output on all the jobs involved.

Getting results from standards of work performance

Standards of work performance determine in concrete terms what constitutes the satisfactory performance of a job. When actual performance is not up to the standard, the supervisor can investigate immediately to find out the cause. The material may be at fault. If material is of the wrong kind or the supply is inadequate, the supervisor can take immediate steps to try and correct the situation. Investigation may show that there is something wrong with the equipment, and he can try to have it repaired. Or the investigation may show that there is something wrong with the worker. Observing his unsatisfactory performance may disclose a specific need for further training, the fact that he is not fitted for the job and should be transferred, or that he has a gripe and needs to get it settled before he can get back to normal production.

If there is a deliberate slowdown in a section, the supervisor who has established standards of performance can put his finger on the sore spot and identify the restricters much more quickly than the supervisor who has never established such standards. A supervisor armed with published standards of performance is in a better position to combat slowdowns than the supervisor who has only his own ideas of what production ought to be and therefore must match his word against the word of the workers.

The supervisor with standards of work performance can do a much better job of planning the work of his section; he is in a position to answer more accurately the questions: *When? Where? Who?* Standards of work performance help him in estimating the number of man-hours he needs for future jobs. They permit him to balance the load better among his workers and to avoid overloading the more willing workers. The supervisor who measures work against a standard is not likely to be charged with favoritism, inconsistency, or arbitrary action.

Measuring actual performance against a standard enables the supervisor to uncover and reward outstanding performance. At the other end of the scale it enables him to prove that some performances are unsatisfactory and gives him a basis on which to take action. As far as the average qualified worker is concerned, the performance standards are a means of letting him know what is expected of him and how well he is doing it.

When a supervisor is armed with clearly stated standards of performance, he is in a better position to criticize the deficiencies of his subordinates. An employee is apt to be resentful if he thinks the boss is criticizing his personal weaknesses, but if the boss is talking about the employee's record and how it measures up to the standard, the discussion is one of facts rather than emotions, and the worker can see the need for improvement. When standards are published and the employees are able to measure their own performance, they can see for themselves when they are failing to measure up.

Quantity and quality of output are not the complete measure in evaluating an employee. A piece-rate worker may be making or surpassing the rate and still not be a desirable employee. He may quarrel constantly with his fellow workers, stir up suspicion and resentment against the supervisor or the company, engage in unsafe practices, and, in general, cause more trouble than he is worth. In an overall evaluation, such behavior would outweigh his work performance.

The same holds true of hourly paid workers; their output may be up to, or even above, the standard set by the supervisor, but their behavior may be such that they are undesirable members of the team.

Standards of managerial performance

Performance standards for managers are more difficult to develop than those for employees in most nonsupervisory positions. That managerial performance should be measured is undeniably desirable. The question is how and with what degree of objectivity. Because it is necessary for an organization's growth and survival to identify, develop, motivate, and promote managers, some method of appraising their performance should be considered. Managers resent subjective judgments about their performance as much as nonmanagerial employees do. Equally distasteful is being subjected to the whim and fancy of a superior along with the political machinations involved without any opportunity to demonstrate ability on a rational basis.

Over the years a variety of methods for appraising the performance of managers have been used. These range from checking the supervisor being rated against a list of predetermined desirable characteristics such as tactful, loyal, dependable, etc., to rather complicated forced distributions designed to arbitrarily separate good performers from poor ones.

Measurement implies a yardstick that is reliable and objective. Unfortunately such standards are not readily available for the measurement of managerial performance. Some research has indicated that managers who have an employee-centered, democratic leadership style are effective performers. Still other research demonstrates that a production-oriented, benevolently autocratic style achieves good results. The fact probably is that much depends on the nature of the work, the work group itself, the environment in which the work is performed, the individual manager, his superior, and a variety of other circumstances and variables.

The nebulous nature of managerial performance standards has given rise to a results-oriented approach to manager performance appraisal. These systems are variously called "management by results," "accountability management," and "management by objectives."[8] They all use performance standards as their basis and in many instances these standards are arrived at through superior-subordinate consultation and agreement. Obviously the standards reached are goal-oriented and these goals are related to overall organizational goals. In these programs managerial standard setting and the consequent appraisal is viewed as a continuous process very much a part of each manager's job.

Standards of performance of management men are best set up in terms of objectives which state what the supervisor's managerial unit is supposed to do toward attaining the objectives of the company.

When goals are set in terms of the total enterprise, a supervisor's performance is measured by what his unit contributes to the larger unit above him and what he contributes to the company through it and through teamwork with people in other departments. Management by objectives stresses and rewards teamwork and seeks to prevent empire building and conflicts between the various specialties in an organization.

In order for the supervisor to have goals to achieve, he and his boss must agree on what is expected of him and of his unit and what he will be measured by (what kind of data or records will furnish the information on the performance of his unit). Setting objectives is a good way to reach an understanding with the boss about what he expects from the subordinate's unit. Such an understanding may not be arrived at otherwise. Research reports indicate that in a number of cases there is little agreement between a subordinate and his boss on what the

---

[8] For a thorough understanding of management by objectives, see P. F. Drucker, *Managing for Results* (New York: Harper & Row, Publishers, 1964); E. C. Schleh, *Management by Results* (New York: McGraw-Hill Book Co., 1961); D. D. McConkey, *How to Manage by Results* (New York: American Management Association, 1965); G. S. Odiorne, *Management by Objectives* (New York: Pitman Publishing Corp., 1965).

subordinate's responsibilities are, which are most important, and what problems he has in carrying them out.[9] These are the matters on which a man's performance is measured; thus it is essential that there be a meeting of the minds between supervisor and boss on what the responsibilities and objectives are. The special difficulties encountered on the job enter into the evaluation of performance also; a man deserves more credit for doing a difficult task than an easy one—providing the task is necessary and the difficulties unavoidable.

The responsibilities listed in the supervisor's job description make a starting place from which to set up statements of the results he is expected to produce. These results must be matters on which records are kept so that data will be available to measure performance. As a first step in setting up standards for his own performance, the supervisor should, with his boss, make a list of the results that are expected of him and the data by which they are measured or could be measured. The sheet might start like this:

Results expected	Measured by
1. Attain high direct labor productivity.	1. Accounting records available (see the discussion below).
2. Meet quality standards.	2. Number of errors sent back for correction. Number of rejects. Number of complaints. Number of returns.
3. Keep on schedule; get work done on time.	3. Record of completion dates checked against schedules. Record of overtime.
4. Maintain good labor relations.	4. Number of grievances. Rate of turnover. Record of absences.
5. Maintain a safe operation.	5. Record of accident frequency and severity per man-hours worked. Rating on housekeeping.

After completing the listing, boss and supervisor should rate each of the items according to its importance to the company and then according to the difficulties or special problems it presents. For instance, safety may be no problem, but quality may be difficult to achieve under present circumstances. Just as questions in an exam are identified as to the amount of weight each will carry in figuring the total grade, each item on the list can be given the weight it should carry in an evaluation of the supervisor's performance.

---

[9] Norman R. F. Maier, L. Richard Hoffman, John J. Hooven, and William H. Read, *Superior-Subordinate Communication in Management* (American Management Research Study No. 52) (New York: The Association, 1961).

The next step in setting up goals is to write down what has been the performance in the past on each item, then to judge what should be the performance in the coming period of six months or a year—or whatever period is covered in a performance review. As a rule the management man in a goal-setting interview with his boss will set high goals for himself, but it is important that they be attainable; a standard that is too high may cause him to quit trying. It is important also that the data or information used for measuring performance be supplied to the supervisor in a form that is simple, usable, and measurable. Costs must be those he is responsible for and has control over, and they should be separated according to category. Such a flow of timely information is essential so that the supervisor can be alerted to substandard performance, so that he can locate the trouble spots and take action to correct them. This is *self*-control. Information that is three weeks late in arriving can be measured but it is of little use except to assess blame.

After the supervisor and his boss have worked out and agreed upon the objectives, the results expected, and the data by which they will be measured, the sheet becomes something like a charter under which the supervisor operates. In a performance review at the end of the period the boss will go over the list with him to discuss his accomplishments, the problems that he met, and what kind of help would enable him to do better. Then they will set goals for the next period. A performance appraisal such as this, which starts out with definite statements of what was expected and definite measures of achievement, provides a strong motivating force and causes a minimum of embarrassment or resentment. It reviews past performance as a preparation for the future. It discusses results and difficulties in terms of accomplishments that lie ahead.

Some companies use group meetings for setting standards. Starting at the top of the organization and working down—each boss meets with his subordinates in a group to define responsibilities and objectives, discuss results expected, and have the group set standards.[10]

Cost control

The scene of action for cost control is on the level of the first-line supervisor. He has the greatest influence on the utilization of direct labor and supplies and the greatest degree of control over scrap and

---

[10] Virgil K. Rowland, *Managerial Performance Standards* (New York: American Management Association, 1960). This is a how-to-do-it book containing transcripts of standard-setting sessions. See also William F. Treuhaft, "Executive Standards of Performance," Harwood F. Merrill and Elizabeth Marting (eds.), *Developing Executive Skills* (New York: American Management Association, 1958), pp. 56–65.

rework. Therefore it is essential that he have an understanding of the cost structure and budget system so that he can measure his own performance and take corrective action when his costs are out of line. His standard for judging whether current costs reflect satisfactory performance is the budget.

Budgets. Budgeting is a form of cost control by which the *actual* performance of a department may be measured against what that performance should be. Budgets are the estimated amounts of resources that should be sufficient to turn out a given amount of product or products during a definite period of time such as a year. Both the resources and the product may be expressed in dollars but also may be expressed in man-hours, man-dollars, or volume.

In a manufacturing department there are direct labor budgets, direct material budgets, and a variety of indirect manufacturing expense budgets such as those for indirect labor, supplies, building maintenance, machine maintenance, and utilities.

The real expenses incurred during the year are a measure of the actual performance. The difference between the actual expenses and the budgets are called *variances.* These variances measure the efficiency of the department.

In order to set up and use operating budgets effectively in a manufacturing plant it is necessary to:

1. Forecast the sales volume of the company's product for the coming year.
2. Compare this volume with the capacity of the plant.
3. Make adjustments in order to determine the probable percentage of plant utilization during the year.
4. Investigate, predetermine, integrate, and agree upon what the types and amounts of the operating expenses should be.[11]
5. Consistently check actual expenses against budget expenses.
6. Investigate the causes of variances.

Budgets are made in terms of a definite amount of plant output. A plant running at half capacity will have more than half the expenses of a plant running at full capacity, because some of the expenses are fixed. That is, building maintenance, management salaries, and so forth are the same for both situations; other expenses are variable. Direct labor and product materials vary directly with output, while other expenses like indirect labor, supplies, and machine maintenance are semi-

---

[11] These decisions must be in line with the objectives of the business, or the budget will misdirect managerial behavior. In order to stay within his budget, a manager may put off needed expenditures and let greater costs build up in some other direction.

variable—a portion of each is fixed and a portion is variable. Thus the first step in setting up the operating budgets is to make a sales forecast for the coming year. The second step is to use this tentative forecast to determine what will be the approximate percent of plant utilization. If this percentage is low, it may be necessary to allocate more money for extra sales effort to increase volume, or to take on an additional line of products, or to produce in the plant some work that is now being subcontracted. On the other hand, if the sales forecast exceeds the capacity of the plant, it may be necessary to provide for overtime or a second shift or to subcontract more work. Adjustments have to be made to balance plant utilization with forecasted sales (see Figure 9–3 illustrating the relationship of plant utilization to sales).

FIGURE 9–3
Interrelationships of Sales, Inventory, and Plant Utilization
The three should be balanced before budgets are set up.

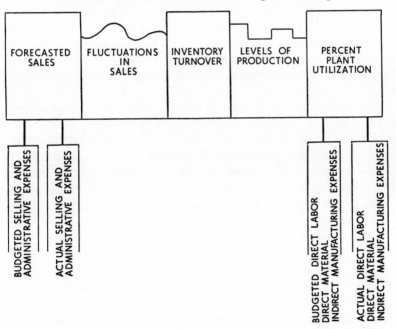

In most cases instead of setting up a single or fixed budget for a certain percentage of plant utilization, it is desirable to set up budgets for several percent levels (70 percent, 80 percent, 90 percent, and so on). These budgets are called flexible budgets. They permit adjustments between budget performance and actual performance at the different percentage levels of plant utilization that might occur during the year.

When budgets are being investigated, predetermined, and integrated, the department heads who must live within the budgets should be consulted about the amount of money available, and they should help in drawing up budgets for their departments for the coming period. If a manager has some say about his budget and expenses, he is more inclined to make an added effort to keep down the actual expenses of his department.

Actual expenses should be checked against budgeted expenses frequently during the period that the budgets are in effect. The manager should be promptly supplied with figures of actual expenses so that he can compare them with budgeted expenses and investigate the variances. When budgets are set up for several percentages of utilization of plant capacity, then the actual expenses can be compared directly with their appropriate budgets and the variance obtained directly. However, if there is a fixed budget or a *normal*[12] budget, then there is a need to make two adjustments—a capacity adjustment and a budget adjustment—in order to apportion the variance. The capacity adjustment determines which portion of the variance is due to the plant's operating at a capacity different from the expected one. This portion is not within the control of the department head. The budget adjustment determines which portion of the variance is within the control of the department head.

The adjustments are made as follows: The fixed budgets such as salaries, which are independent of fluctuations in output, are 100 percent within the control of the department head in the sense that he can keep them from being exceeded. One of his jobs is to meet these fixed expenses irrespective of output. On the other hand, with regard to variable budgets such as direct material, he is expected to control them in terms of the level at which his department is operating. For example, if his department is operating at half capacity and his variable budget is set up based on a fixed or normal capacity of 100 percent, then he is responsible for one half of the budgeted amount; that is, if he is allocated $100,000 worth of material for a period and if his department works at only half capacity during that period, he shouldn't use any more than $50,000 worth of material.

In relation to semivariable budgets, the manager can estimate what percent of them is variable and what percent is fixed. For example, if his indirect labor is 40 percent variable and 60 percent fixed, the 40 percent variable is adjustable and the 60 percent is not adjustable. If the plant is running at half capacity, then his indirect labor would

---

[12] A normal budget is one based on what should be the percentage of plant capacity for several years in the future. This type of budget is used particularly in relation to standard costs.

be 20 percent (one half of the variable 40 percent) plus 60 percent; it thus equals 80 percent of what it would be if his department were running full capacity. This new indirect labor budget which is 80 percent of his former indirect labor budget is his new adjusted budget. It is effective while his department is running at half capacity because of circumstances beyond his control.

If the department manager can't determine by inspection which proportion of a specific budget is variable, then he can solve the problem either graphically or by applying a formula.[13]

Finally, the causes of variances should be determined. If the actual expenses are above budget expenses, then steps should be taken to reduce costs (see "Cost Reduction" in Chapter 8). When actual expenses are below budgeted expenses, the budget should not be cut, but people responsible for the saving should be rewarded. Some companies cut the budget instead of giving a commendation. Budget cutting is equivalent to cutting piece rates. When production workers fear that the rate will be cut, they protect themselves by restricting production. When managers fear the budget will be cut, they may be tempted to protect themselves by uneconomical spending toward the end of the budget period.

Standard costs. Standard costs are a further refinement in cost control. The standards used should be accurately determined by time studies and other precise methods, and the standard costs should be set up in terms of *normal* conditions in a plant operating at the *normal* capacity. According to E. L. Grant:

> Where predetermined costs are based on a careful engineering analysis of the direct materials and the direct labor needed for a product, they may be described as *standard costs*. In a cost system based on standard costs, the variance balances are viewed as important tools of cost control.[14]

Standard costs are determined for direct materials, direct labor, and indirect manufacturing expenses. When actual costs are compared against these standard costs, the differences or *variances* become the basis of quick corrective action while production of the batch is still going on—thus avoiding locking the barn door after the horse is gone.

The standard costs of direct materials are divided according to price and quantity (including allowable spoilage or shrinkage). The division between price and quantity is made because the individual responsible for the efficient use of materials seldom has control over their prices.

---

[13] Both the graphic and formula solutions are shown in Eugene L. Grant's *Basic Accounting and Cost Accounting* (New York: McGraw-Hill Book Co., 1956), pp. 227–28.

[14] *Ibid.*, p. 138.

Standard costs of direct labor are often divided into time and wage rates. The reason for dividing direct labor in this manner is to uncover the use of high-priced men working on low-valued operations.

The indirect manufacturing expenses are applied as a portion of some standard cost such as standard direct labor hours or standard direct labor cost. The burden rate must be based on some normal percent of plant utilization. (*Normal* is what the output should be under good conditions over a period of several years in the future.) If a normal output were not used, then the standard cost would have to be changed for each anticipated change in level of output.

The function of standard costs can be best explained by an example:

EXAMPLE OF THE FUNCTION OF STANDARD COSTS

In the manufacture of dresses of a certain size and quality, the standard quantity of material is three yards per dress, and the standard cost of material is 50 cents per yard. If in the manufacture of a block of 100 dresses, 310 yards are actually used instead of 300 yards, and the actual cost per yard is 55 cents instead of 50 cents, the variances are as follows:

Direct Material Variance

	Actual	Standard	Variances
			− +
Quantity . . . . .310 yds.		300 yds.	10 yds.
Material cost $170.50		$150.00	$20.50

The excess of *actual* cost over standard cost is explained as follows:

      10 yds. more than standard at $0.50/yd. . . . .$ 5.00
      310 yds. at $0.05 more than standard price 15.50
            Variance (loss) $20.50

The excess of 10 yards *if it is worth investigating* might be found to be due to carelessness or lack of experience on the part of the cutter.

The excess in cost might be due to the use of a more expensive material, or the cost of material might have increased.

Direct Labor Variance

Suppose in the above example, the standard labor rate was $2 per hour, and the standard length of time to do a certain operation was one-tenth hour or six minutes per piece. For 100 pieces it is $0.1 \times 100 = 10$ hours. The actual time was nine hours, and the operator was paid at the rate of $2.10 per hour.

	Actual	Standard	Variances
			− +
Hours 9		10	1
Labor cost $18.90		$20.00	0.90

The labor saving was as follows:

      1 hour saved over standard at $2 an hour . . . .+$2.00
      9 hours at $0.10/hr. above standard rate . . . .− 0.90
            Variance (gain) $1.10

Burden Variance

In the pressing department the standard direct labor cost is $0.25 per dress. The budget for fixed expenses is $1,000 per month. The standard burden rate for indirect manufacturing expense is 0.5 or one half of the standard direct labor cost. This burden rate is based on a *normal* output of 8,000 dresses per month.

If during the month under study 4,000 dresses are produced at an actual cost of $1,800, the standard cost for the pressing department is:

```
Standard direct labor ...............................$0.25 /dress
Standard burden, $0.25 × 0.5 ......................... 0.125/dress
    (one half of the standard direct labor cost)
Standard cost for department .........................$0.375/dress
Standard cost of pressing 4,000 dresses: 4,000 × $0.375... $1,500
Actual cost (from records)........................... 1,800
    Variance ......................................$ 300
```

The variance of $300 indicates that the actual cost of pressing the dresses was $300 too much. However, when the figures are divided according to budget and capacity variances, the facts are as follows:

```
Budgeted fixed expenses ...................................$1,000
Budgeted variable expenses, $0.25/dress × 4,000 .............. 1,000
    Total budgeted expense ...............................$2,000
Standard cost, $0.375/dress × 4,000 dresses ................. 1,500
    Capacity variance ...................................$ 500
```

This capacity variance shows that $500 should have been charged against the plant's operating at a rate of 4,000 dresses instead of the normal rate of 8,000 dresses. Therefore the actual cost of $1,800 was in reality $200 below the budget of $2,000; so there was a saving of $200 instead of a loss of $300, as far as the department was concerned.

Cost control in a continuous process industry

The following quotation gives examples of cost control forms used in a continuous processing industry (Santa Clara Plant of Owens-Corning Fiberglas Corporation, which operates 24 hours a day, seven days a week). The quoted material is a portion of an article describing the development of a daily budget and stressing the control aspects of budget reporting as opposed to the purely accounting features.[15]

Reporting of budget performance is a matter that must be tailored to the organization. The budget reports discussed here are the daily and monthly report showing, in dollars, variations from allowances by cost center and

[15] John E. McDonald (Plant Auditor) and Cleon A. Johnson (Cost Control Supervisor) of the Santa Clara Plant of Owens-Corning Fiberglas Corp., "Cost Control Budgeting Which Extends to Daily Reporting," *N.A.A. Bulletin*, Section 1, November, 1957. Reproduced by permission of National Association of Accountants.

by cost account. The monthly report (Exhibit 1) is a departmental standard cost variation statement showing actual cost for the month and year to date and the budget variation for the same periods. Such a report is prepared for each cost center for distribution to all supervisory and staff people concerned with the manufacturing operation. In addition, other operating figures are included to give a comprehensive picture of the department's results in all respects other than those attributable to activity.

EXHIBIT 1

					Analysis of Net Variance			**Analysis of Budget Variance**					
									Waste	Over-				
	Department	Standard	Actual	Net	Activity	Machine	Budget	Mfg.	time	Labor	Other	Mat'ls	Craft
No.	Name	Cost	Cost	Var.	Var.	Effy.	Var.	Mat'ls	Prem.	Prem.	Labor	& Exp;	Services
211	Bonded Mat Basic												
212	Bonded Mat Fab.												

A cost variation statement summary, Exhibit 2, presents for management's use a summary of variances in which each department's variance is analyzed as to causes in activity, machine efficiency, and budget performance. Variation is further broken down into six main headings which emphasize the areas in which specific controls are effective. Basically, all variances, other than activity, are considered controllable by the supervisor. Because of the number

EXHIBIT 2

COST VARIATION STATEMENT - SANTA CLARA PLANT

Mach. Hrs.	% Activity				A MOUNT	
	Plant Std. Cost Per Average Month					
	Plant Std. Cost of Current Month's Prod.					
	Plant Std. Cost Per Scheduled Machine Hour					
	Budget Allowance Per Scheduled Machine Hour					
	Plant Actual Cost					
	Plant Std. Cost of Year to Date Prod.					

	Actual Cost		Budget Variances			
			This Month		Year to Date	
No. Description	This Month	Year to Date	Under	Over	Under	Over
LABOR:						
600 Direct Labor						
640 Direct Labor Bonus						

TOTAL COST

	Mach. Effy.	Net Variation
Current Month		
Year to Date		

of calculations required to make this report, it is not scheduled for completion and distribution until the 15th of the month. This schedule is too slow for a report designed to promote corrective action. The variation statement does, however, serve as the basis for monthly meetings of the cost control and the supervisory personnel of each department. At this meeting the cost people can amplify the figures on the statement, production people can contribute information bearing on the results achieved, and the accomplishment of the meeting is a better mutual understanding of the operation.

This daily budget report confines itself to reporting, in dollars, costs over which the supervisor can exercise direct control. Other departmental expenses not resulting directly from the supervisor's actions are not reported daily. This distinction is based on our experience that, in reporting for control purposes, it is important not to obscure controllable figures with noncontrollable figures thrown in merely to achieve the accountant's natural desire to strike a balance. A summary report, Exhibit 4, goes to the plant manager and the production superintendent. This recapitulation, supported by copies of the cost center reports, enables them to spot areas where special attention is needed without having to review a great mass of data.

EXHIBIT 3

DAILY BUDGET REPORT							
				Adjustments			
Item	Std.	Actual	Over/Under	Act.	Std.	Month/Date	Over/Under
Direct Labor							
Indirect Labor							
Other Labor							
Craft Services Labor							
Total							

The daily budget reports are distributed daily as part of the agenda of a daily production meeting of all of the production supervisors, the production superintendent, the plant manager and a representative of each of the latter's staff departments. This meeting, held at noon each weekday, considers planned operations for a day or so ahead, reviews the operating performances for the period ending at 8 A.M. the current day, and the budget for the previous day. The cost control supervisor reports the total plant budget performance and makes whatever comments he considers pertinent to the overall situation. Departmental reports distributed to the production supervisors are supported by tabulating runs and any special comments the budget analyst may wish to make. The daily reports require the greater part of the time of one person, with part-time clerical assistance.

The Ultimate Goal

Seeing the budget not as a report but as a measure of the effective utilization of men, materials, and machine—this is a final objective and can come only from continuing education. The budget people must first dispel the mysteries and uncertainties that surround their jargon and methods. If production people are to be drawn into budget preparation they must have as thorough an understanding of budget methods and objectives as the budget people can develop. The production people, on the other hand, have a responsibility to make their operations come to life for the budget people. This should

EXHIBIT 4

DAILY BUDGET RECAP SHEET   DATE_____

Department	Std.	Actual	Over/Under	Month/Date Actual	Over/Under To Date
211 - Bonded Mat Basic					
280 - Warehousing					
TOTAL					
Remarks:					

not be so difficult. The effective and efficient performance of an operation is largely the expression of the common sense and good judgment of the responsible supervisor. The function of the budget, the same as that of all other line and staff functions, is to enable the supervisor to make prompt decisions based on solid information.

Summary

A standard of work performance states the quality and quantity of work that should be performed by a normal employee working at a normal pace under normal conditions. The purpose of setting up standards and measuring performance against them is (1) to let the supervisor know if he is getting a satisfactory day's work from each man in his section, (2) to let subordinates know what is expected of them and how they are doing, (3) to enable the supervisor to plan, schedule, and distribute the department's work, and to estimate his budget needs, and (4) to enable the supervisor and his boss to delegate responsibilities and the authority to carry them out, because a delegator must have some means of judging the subordinate's performance.

The supervisor sets up standards in terms that can be easily measured and in time bundles that give representative samples of the "mix" if tasks vary in length or difficulty. Standards should be designed to encourage workers to give their best efforts to the company rather than to beat the system at the expense of the company.

Supervisors need standards by which to measure their own performance. Standards of managerial performance should be set up in terms of the objectives of the company and what the supervisor and his unit are expected to contribute to those objectives. The supervisor must be given timely information (cost data, quality records, grievance, absence, and accident records, etc.) on the performance of his unit so that he can measure it against the standards or the goals he has set for himself.

Then if the performance is substandard, he can investigate and correct it.

A budget is a statement of attainable cost performance. The differences between actual expenses and budgeted expenses are called variances and are a measure of the efficiency of the department.

CASE 1

The department preceding yours in the production line is continually sending you poor quality work, with the result that the production of your department is falling behind. You have spoken to the foreman of that department several times, but he tells you that production schedules do not permit him to finish piece parts beyond the minimum requirements.

1. Should the quality requirements be changed?
2. How can they be changed?
3. Who is responsible for the quality of the work?
4. What should you do about the situation?
5. Should people be expected to produce beyond the minimum quality requirements?

CASE 2

The operators in your department are on a wage-incentive plan. They are working hard and earning good bonuses. The mechanics of the maintenance department resent having the operators make more money than they do. As a result, the mechanics stall in repairing machines that break down, and they complain to their foreman that the men in your department are abusing the equipment.

1. Are the maintenance men justified in their attitude and behavior? Explain.
2. What should you say to the maintenance foreman?
3. What should he say to his men?
4. Should you bring the problem up to your boss? Explain.
5. How about incentives for maintenance men? Give the advantages and disadvantages.

CASE 3

You are the supervisor of a dozen employees (typists and clerks) in an office. Your boss has had limited experience in office work. He does not have many contacts with you and your group, except when he is around trying to reduce costs.

Recently one of your girls terminated for personal reasons. When you requested a replacement, your boss told you to distribute the work among the remaining girls. When you tried to protest, he told you either to try it or to show him why it couldn't be done.

Your group is a well-integrated team. They have maintained—according to your experience and observation of other groups—more than a satisfactory output. When you explained the boss's orders to them, they threatened to slow down. You know this would lead to retaliation by the boss. So you believe that the solution is to develop some sort of a report based on facts, to be presented to the boss to show him that a replacement is necessary.

1. List the steps you would follow in developing a standards of work performance program to meet the above situation.
2. List the obstacles you would have to overcome in relation to each step.
3. How would you overcome each obstacle? Illustrate by examples.

CASE 4

Jack Salerno was the supervisor of an IBM tabulating department. He had several years of experience with the equipment and in fact could operate all of it skillfully. Because of his eagerness to demonstrate to his superiors his abilities, he timed himself on all of the jobs under his jurisdiction and arrived at a productivity figure for each job. Even though he prepared a memorandum detailing all this information for his superior, he never told any of his subordinates about it.

One day he noticed that a key punch operator who had been transferred to his department recently produced considerably less work than he could. He reprimanded her, telling her that she wasn't trying and informing her that there had better be rapid improvement, indicating that his reprimand would be written up and placed in her personnel file.

She burst into tears and told him that she had never been told how much work was required of her. She further mentioned that she only had six months' experience as a key punch operator. She then said she was going to complain to Jack's superior about his treatment of her.

1. What can Jack do to salvage the situation he has created?
2. Should he allow the girl to go to his superior with her story?
3. What is wrong with Jack's approach to the setting of work standards?
4. How should he establish work standards?

CASE 5

Several of the exceptionally good mechanics in your department have to be used for meticulous work that cannot be put on a piece-rate basis. By working fast, workers of less skill often have greater take-home pay than these good mechanics. The good mechanics are resentful and say that they want to be put on the piece-rate jobs, in spite of the fact that they would have to use a great deal more physical effort.

1. To what extent are the highly skilled mechanics justified in their complaint?
2. How should the situation be remedied?
3. Should the hourly workers receive a bonus based on the productivity of the pieceworkers, even though their work is only indirectly related?
4. How might it be done?

CASE 6

You know that good housekeeping is essential to safety and good production, and you keep the general equipment in good order. However, a few of the workers who are making better than the average on the piece rate have very sloppy workplaces. You have spoken to them about this several times, but they feel that the condition of their workplaces is their business, that they are turning out more than the average, and that, if they spent time in tidying up, they would fall behind in production.

1. What is meant by "good housekeeping"?
2. What are its advantages?
3. Are the operators justified in their attitude? Explain.
4. Outline a method of promoting good housekeeping.
5. How should the above problem be handled?

CASE 7

You are the supervisor of a large group of office workers—mostly young people who are recent high school graduates. For many of them, this is their first job, and they have no idea of what constitutes a full day's work. As soon as you stop feeding them work, they stop and visit or fake working or do personal jobs.

You believe that you should set up definite standards of quantity and quality of work performance for as many jobs as you can, and measure the youngsters' performance against them; it seems to be a matter of justice both to the company and to these young people. You believe that you should get them started off right and not make them learn the hard way by being fired from the first two or three jobs they get.

1. What are some of the jobs in a large office that could be standardized without too much trouble?
2. How would you determine the quantity or the *how much* requirements for each?
3. How would you determine the quality or the *how well* requirements for each?
4. How would you go about selling standards of work performance to your employees?

5. How are you going to go about measuring the amount of output of your workers against the quantity standards?
6. How are you going to measure the quality of output of your workers against the quality standards?

CASE 8

You are the supervisor in charge of transporting materials within the plant. Your operators are all over the place, and it is difficult for you to keep track of them. The word has gotten around that your department is a spot where the work is easy.

The company is planning to purchase a number of expensive up-to-date fork trucks to take the place of the old equipment now in use. Your boss tells you the purchase will be justified if the trucks can be made to pay for themselves quickly. In other words, it will be necessary for them to be busy all the time. He tells you that this is possible if you will control your crew more closely so that they will not be wasting so much time.

1. What are some of the ways of keeping track of transportation workers to see that they are doing a satisfactory day's work?
2. Give the strong and the weak points of these methods.
3. How would you determine the quantity or the *how much* requirements for satisfactory performance for fork truck operator?
4. How would you determine the quality or the *how well* requirements for fork truck operators?
5. How would you go about selling these standards of work performance to your crew?
6. How would you check actual performance against these standards of work performance?

CASE 9

You are the supervisor in charge of a crew of electrical and mechanical maintenance men. Until recently you did not need to check up much on your men, as most of them were old-timers who took pride in keeping everything shipshape. Recently, an increase in production orders necessitated putting on a second shift of production workers, many of whom are inexperienced and do not know how to handle their machines properly. This increased the work load of your group, and you hired additional maintenance men; you got the best you could.

Your regular crew has started to complain about these new maintenance men—that they are doing sloppy work and wasting time, with the result that the old group is being overworked. You believe that you need to devise some standards of performance and a method for checking up on your crew. The old workers think this is a good idea and are willing to give you as much information as possible. They tell you that they believe that everyone should carry his own share of the load.

1. What are some of the tasks in maintenance work that are easy to standardize?
2. How would you set up the quantity or the *how much* requirements for tasks that are easy to standardize?
3. How would you set up the quality or the *how well* requirements for tasks that are easy to standardize?
4. What are some of the tasks in maintenance work that are difficult to standardize?
5. How would you go about setting up the *how much* and the *how well* for tasks that are difficult to standardize?
6. How are you going to check performance against the standards?

CASE 10

You are in charge of a drafting department and have under your jurisdiction several supervisors, checkers, and a number of draftsmen. One of the supervisors under you believes that the best way to handle his men is to keeping piling the work on, to keep them all snowed under and get all he can out of them. He believes that satisfactory performance is the maximum performance the individual can turn out.

The production of his men is high, but so is the turnover, especially among the better men. The morale is low. You believe that for the guidance of your supervisors you should set up standards of work performance for the drafting department.

1. What are the reasons that some supervisors keep their men snowed under?
2. Evaluate the argument that satisfactory performance is the maximum performance the individual is capable of turning out.
3. What determines the efficiency of a drafting department?
4. How would you set up standards of work performance for drafting work?
5. How would you go about selling these standards of work performance to the supervisors under your jurisdiction?
6. How should they go about selling them to their men?
7. How should actual performance be measured against the standards of work performance? Who should do it?

CASE 11

Mary is a very efficient machine operator with an extraordinary aptitude for the work she is doing. She can make "standard" in half the required time. Most of the girls have to put forth good effort to meet standard. Others have difficulty making it.

Instead of turning out as much work as she is capable of, she makes standard, stops her machine, goes to the restroom for a smoke or wastes her time in some other manner. Her supervisor allows her to do this. He argues that if she did extra work she would not get more pay, because the company does not have piece rates. Management is opposed to wage incentives. Mary is not supervisory material.

1. Evaluate Mary's point of view.
2. Evaluate the supervisor's point of view.
3. What are the advantages and disadvantages of having standards without wage incentives?
4. What should management do about the situation?

CASE 12

You are in charge of a department turning out a quality product. You have under you several supervisors and their men. Relations have been very cordial between you and all those under you. The men are conscientious, and the work is on an hourly basis. It would be very difficult to put the jobs on piece rates.

Recently, business has been increasing, and a backlog of work is piling up. A month ago top management asked you to increase output by 10 percent. You gave the supervisors a pep talk, and they were able to get the desired increase. Last week top management came to you and again asked for another increase of 10 percent in output. You asked for more workers, but you were told that the push is just temporary.

This morning you called together your assistants and told them the situation and asked them if they would get another increase in output of 10 percent. They refused.

1. What might be some of the reasons for their refusal?
2. To what extent are they justified?
3. Are supervisors ever justified in holding back production in order to have a cushion or factor of safety for taking care of temporary load increases?
4. Should you go directly to the men on the job in order to get the second increase in output? Justify your answer.
5. How could the situation have been avoided?
6. How should you handle the situation?
7. How can you prevent it from recurring?

CASE 13

Two years ago the head of a regional office of a government agency retired, and you were appointed to replace him. One specialized area of the agency's work has always been handled by the same man—an expert in this particular specialty—and he is now seriously ill. He had been coming to work and sitting at his desk every day even though he looked quite sick. Over the weekend he was taken to the hospital and the doctors say that his condition is serious. You doubt that he will ever be able to come back to work.

No one in the office knows anything about his work. His job just grew up around him in his 25 years in the agency. He could answer any question about how things were handled; he could remember what had gone on for years back and he kept it all in his head. You tried several times to get him to explain the work to you and he would tell you about the peculiarities of something he was working on at the moment but that was all. The girls say he wouldn't let them touch anything on his desk; he kept the drawers locked and his file cabinet locked.

Today you pried open the locks and in the drawers you found an accumulation of work awaiting handling. Some of it dates back a whole year; most of it is several months old. You also found a bottle of whiskey and his personal financial accounts including a few recently issued government bonds which you took over to his wife. She asked you where the rest of them were since he had been buying bonds on a payroll deduction plan for years and keeping them in the safe at the office rather than renting a box at the bank. You know he doesn't keep anything in the safe at the office. A check of his account book showed two dates beside each bond number—suggesting that he had cashed each bond as soon as possible after it was issued to him.

His wife then told you that he had a drinking problem and seemed unable to take care of his money. She had tried to keep close watch over him so that he would have neither the money nor the time to drink; she always stopped at the office on payday to get his check and take it to the bank.

1. When a new boss comes in, how can he find out how a well-established subordinate runs his job when that subordinate is an expert in his field and doesn't choose to put out any information?
2. How can the boss of a technical expert keep abreast of what is going on in the subordinate's job?

CASE 14

In a shop which assembles kitchen stoves on a moving assembly line, the workers are complaining that management has been speeding up the line. Management denies the accusation. The problem is to determine what *should be* the speed of the line so that the men can check the *actual* speed with a stopwatch if they wish.

A series of time studies made previously has established a standard of 52.5 minutes per man per stove. This figure is equivalent to the length of time it would take one man to build a stove if he were doing it alone. It includes all allowances for interference and personal needs. This standard was (and still is) accepted by the workers.

The work of assembling the stove is divided into 16 operations—each taking practically the same length of time—and distributed among 16 men on the assembly line. There are two 10-minute coffee breaks in the eight-hour day.

1. Determine the number of stoves that are turned out per man per eight-hour day.
2. Determine the speed of the belt in inches per minute.
3. Determine the number of minutes required for the belt to travel 7 feet (this is the distance from the leading edge of one stove to the leading edge of the next one that follows it on the line). The workers can then check for themselves to see whether a stove moves more than 7 feet in this number of minutes.
4. What are some of the ways of handling accusations of speedup?

CASE 15

Jane Blue is an old employee who has performed a variety of work in the company. She has never shown exceptional ability or incentive although her work has been generally good and her attitude cooperative. Recently, because of an increase in sales, additional people were hired and Jane was given the responsibility of training one of these new girls on an operation which Jane had performed for some years. This new girl was especially adept and within a short time she excelled Jane in the quality and quantity of her work.

Jane and another of the older employees are now cautioning the new girl against producing more than they do. Jane tells her, "It's foolish to knock yourself out when not working for piece-rate wages." The new girl reports the conversation to you, her boss.

1. What should you say to Jane?
2. What should you say to the new girl?
3. How do you take care of the situation?
4. After standards are established, if employees are holding production below the standard, what should you do?
5. If they are holding it just at standard, what should you do?

FOLLOWING UP ON THE JOB

Determining quantity standards or the "how much"

1. Are the standards attainable by the average qualified worker?
2. Is there sufficient spread between the quantity standards for day work and work on incentive?

3. Are the ranges of output too wide? Too narrow?
4. Can a more practical measure of quantity be devised than the one now in use?

Determining quality standards or the "how well"

1. Can you explain clearly and in detail the purpose of every job in your unit?
2. When you reject a job, what are the reasons? On what are these reasons based?
3. Are your quality standards higher than necessary?
4. Are your quality standards lower or higher than those of other supervisors? Why?

Introducing standards of work performance

1. Do you check each job for possible methods improvement before you determine standards?
2. Do you set up standards on a temporary basis, in order to try them out?
3. Do you discuss the standards in detail with your workers?
4. Do all your workers understand what is required for satisfactory performance in terms of quality and quantity?

Using standards of work performance

1. Do you check actual performance of your workers against the standards of work performance too often? Not often enough?
2. Do you investigate below-standard performance promptly, in order to get at the cause?
3. Do you take steps to see that outstanding performance is rewarded?
4. Do you use the standards in planning the work of your unit?

10 Fitting men and jobs

How jobs develop. Specialization and simplification. Job enlargement. Job enlargement and cost reduction. Redesigning a job. Guides for job design. The supervisor's responsibilities in placement. Matching men and jobs. The interview. The trial work period. Monotony and boredom. Misfits. Summary.

The job and the individual are basic to all organized activity. The function of organizing is presumed to be the combination of jobs and individuals in such a way as to achieve the objectives of the organization. Over the years managers have sought to make their organizations more efficient by division of labor, work simplification, and specialization. Ease of training, operational economies, and more effective utilization of men and machines have often resulted.

At the same time that these relative efficiencies were being achieved, two tragic circumstances have continually presented themselves. One is the perennial "square peg in a round hole" problem. The other is the seeming lack of meaning which characterizes work when so-called efficiency and increased specialization are the primary goals of job design.

Since the supervisor's success depends to a great extent on how well his subordinates do their jobs, it is to his advantage that jobs be properly designed and that people be well fitted to them. He must, therefore, find out what the job demands of the worker and what the worker demands of the job and then try to get the best possible fit.

Sometimes a job is so badly designed that no one fits it satisfactorily. It may have been overspecialized and oversimplified, to the extent that a monkey could do it. At the opposite extreme, the job may be a hodgepodge of unrelated activities calling for an assortment of abilities seldom found in job candidates. This chapter gives the supervisor information to guide him in designing jobs. It gives examples of what some companies are doing in enlarging rather than deskilling jobs.

To help the supervisor carry out his responsibility of matching men and jobs, this chapter offers techniques for interviewing and selecting

342

new employees, watching their progress during the probationary period, and eliminating misfits during that time.

Fitting men and jobs is a continuous managerial activity requiring a considerable expenditure of time, effort, and money. Involved in this activity are such things as recruiting, selection, placement, training, appraisal, development, job design, job analysis, and manpower planning. While many of these activities are carried out by staff specialists, supervisors are directly involved because of the human relations implications and their responsibility for effective employee performance. Any supervisor who has had to contend with a stenographer who couldn't spell, a machine operator who was all thumbs, or a salesman who couldn't sell can appreciate the need for sound selection and placement. Being responsible for performance in a group of jobs difficult to fill because of unrealistic requirements also brings home to the supervisor the desirability for sound job analysis and design.

How jobs develop

In order to discuss jobs and their design, it is necessary to distinguish between a task, a position, and a job. The following definitions were developed in the Occupational Research Program of the United States Employment Service.[1]

Task is a unit of work or human effort exerted for a specific purpose. For example, setting up a turret lathe is a task. Tending the machine is another task. Cleaning the machine is still a third task. When enough tasks accumulate to justify the employment of a worker—one person—a position has been created.

Position indicates the service of one worker who accomplishes a set of duties or several tasks. Thus a turret lathe operator's position may consist of the tasks of setting up the machine, tending and operating it, and cleaning it. Such duties comprise the individual's entire working obligation. There are as many positions in the plant as there are employees.

Job is a group of similar positions within a single establishment. Several turret lathe operators all discharging the duties of setting up, tending, and cleaning similar machines, can be said to have the same job. There may be only one turret lathe operator position in a plant or there may be many, which go to make up this job. A new job is created only when job characteristics emerge—as a result of work simplification, technological change, or mere job evolution—which are different from those that are present in any existing job.

While there has been a great amount of study of work processes and the methods of performing the separate elements of work, there

---

[1] The terms are discussed more fully in Carroll L. Shartle, *Occupational Information* (3d ed.; Englewood Cliffs, N.J.: Prentice-Hall, Inc., 1959).

has been much less attention given to the study of the design of jobs—the combining of work elements into tasks and the assembling of these tasks into jobs.

Some jobs just grow, following a traditional pattern. Jobs may be shaped to fit the requirements of the process, to fit into the setup of the organization, or to meet the existing needs of the department. Job duties evolve through changes in the volume of work. As the volume shrinks, more duties are added to jobs. As the volume expands, duties are removed from existing jobs and made up into new jobs. Jobs are designed to meet the needs of the moment, the abilities of people, and the availability of skills.

The design of many jobs is the result of taking them apart for analysis in methods improvement or work simplification programs. What was intended to simplify the work and eliminate waste was used instead to simplify the job and break it down to a few simple motions.

Specialization and simplification

The "efficiency" approach to job design assumed that men—like machines—would do their best work if each performed just a few motions. It assumed further that all planning should be removed from the performer's job and made the responsibility of someone on a higher level. Specialization limited the number of tasks in a job; simplification reduced the skill requirements. The simple machine-paced job became the accepted pattern of efficiency as exemplified in the assembly line.

Specialization is a management principle upon which mass production is based. Specialization of labor enables a worker to become extremely efficient through repetition of a task, but there is a point beyond which specialization loses its economic advantages. The more a job is subdivided, the more indirect labor is needed to plan and schedule, supervise, coordinate, and inspect the work of the performers. The more a job is subdivided, the more people there are handling it and the less becomes each person's responsibility for quality.

Simplification of work is important and necessary to improve methods, eliminate wasted effort, increase efficiency, and reduce costs. But both specialization and simplification meet a point of diminishing returns when the job uses none of the performer's human abilities, and his frustration shows up in restriction of output, irresponsibility as to quality, resistance to change, absences, grievances, transfers, and quits. These costs are more prevalent in deskilled jobs than in skilled jobs. The man on the deskilled job is expendable, "as easy to replace as a light bulb." His arm or leg might have been hired; the rest of him had to come along. But the whole man is there and just putting in his time. He becomes frustrated, tardy, absent; he fools around; he becomes a discipline problem.

A company may cut immediate costs by simplifying a job: a lower grade of labor can be used and a minimum of training can be given. But what is saved in wages and training costs in making the employee unimportant may have to be spent in efforts to counteract the effect this has upon him. After he has become apathetic, unproductive, hostile, wasteful, and destructive, then expensive campaigns are carried on to tell him how important he is and how valuable is his contribution. Off-the-job projects of athletics, sociability, and benefits may be inaugurated to improve his attitude toward the company and to substitute for the lack of satisfaction on the job.

Some years ago Peter F. Drucker analyzed traditional ideas about the assembly line and efforts to continually simplify jobs. He believes that an assembly line is not perfect engineering of human work. Rather it is imperfect engineering of machine work. His concept is stated as follows:

We know today, in other words, that wherever the one-motion one-job concept can be used effectively, we have an operation that can and should be mechanized. In such an operation the assembly-line concept may indeed be the most effective principle for human work, but human work, in such an operation, is itself an imperfection. This is work that should properly be engineered as the work of machines rather than of men.

For all other work—and that means for most of the work done today in manufacturing industry and for all the work that will be created by Automation—the principle is the organization of the job so as to integrate a number of motions or operations into a whole.

We have two principles rather than one. The one for mechanical work is Mechanization. The one for human work is Integration. Both start out with the systematic analysis of the work into its constituent motions. Both lay out the work in a logical sequence of motions. In both attention has to focus on each motion, to make it easier, faster, more effortless; and improvement of the entire output depends on improvement of the constituent motions. But the one organizes the motions *mechanically* so as to utilize the special properties of the machine, that is, its ability to do one thing fast and fault-lessly. The other one *integrates* operations so as to utilize the special properties of the human being, that is, his ability to make a whole out of many things, to judge, to plan and to change.

The technological changes under way not only make possible the realization of the correct principles but force us to apply them. They give us the means to make fully mechanic those jobs in which the human being is used as an adjunct to a machine tool. But the work that is not capable of being mechanized—above all, the work that is needed to make the new technology possible and to support it—can under Automation only be organized on the principle of integration, can, in fact, not be done at all unless so organized. Productivity will therefore increasingly depend on understanding these two principles and applying them systematically.[2]

---

[2] Peter F. Drucker, *The Practice of Management* (New York: Harper & Row, Publishers, 1954), pp. 292–93.

Job enlargement

Essentially, job enlargement is taking those tasks that have been made efficient through methods improvement and rearranging them so that there is an increase in the number and variety of tasks in a job, and so that the combination of tasks forms a job that will meet the human needs of the kind of person who will be hired to perform that job. A low-skilled man does not ask as much from his job as a high-skilled man. Still, if he is going to be a satisfactory employee giving satisfactory performance, his job must be designed in terms of human dignity.

A report on job design research in 1956 had this to say about trends in job design:

Very recently a number of organizations have begun to experiment with changing the content of jobs in the direction of specifying job content having greater complexity, containing a longer sequence of tasks, requiring greater skills, permitting rotation between tasks, and having greater responsibility for inspection, for setting up and maintaining equipment and for controlling production rates. This development, known as job enlargement, has been received with great enthusiasm by the public, press, and business community.

The results flowing from job enlargement programs that have been undertaken are not those that could have been anticipated when the bases of prediction are the classic methods of job specification through job fractionation. The results reported indicate apparent gains in productivity, quality, morale, job satisfaction, and so on. The gains may be explained—although this has not been done—by a resolution or lessening of conflict existing between the individual's motivational forces and his assigned work. Such a conflict has been observed to exist in many instances. When present, this conflict may have a deleterious effect upon productivity, costs, morale, and social organization.[3]

Job enlargement and cost reduction

The two examples of job enlargement presented here were selected because they were made for the purpose of reducing costs through improving methods. Both studies challenge some rather established beliefs about the way to organize jobs.

---

[3] Louis E. Davis (Assoc. Prof. of Industrial Engineering, University of California, Berkeley) and Ralph R. Canter (Systems Development Division, The Rand Corp.), "Job Design Research," *Journal of Industrial Engineering:* Official Publication of the American Institute of Industrial Engineers, Inc., Vol. VII, No. 6. (November–December, 1956), p. 275.

For a report on job enlargement at IBM, see Charles R. Walker and F. L. W. Richardson, *Human Relations in an Expanding Company* (New Haven, Conn.: Yale University Press, 1948).

For clerical jobs, see Robert H. Guest, "Job Enlargement—A Revision in Job Design," *Personnel Administration*, March–April, 1957, pp. 9–17.

Job enlargement at Lincoln Electric Company. Cost reductions through methods improvements have for years been a way of life at Lincoln Electric—along with guaranteed employment, piece rates that are never cut, stock ownership available to employees only, a board of directors made up of employees, and a yearly division of the profits among employees. This division is made according to their productivity and their contribution to company success, as measured in a twice-yearly merit rating.[4]

The job enlarging at Lincoln was part of a change in materials handling and manufacturing methods, and its purpose was to reduce indirect labor costs. The changes were worked out in consultation with employees and tested in the old plant; then in 1951 a new plant was built incorporating the new cost-cutting ideas. In the new factory all materials needed for manufacture are unloaded from truck or train at the dock and transported directly to the operator who will use them. They are stacked around him. Special types of handling devices and stock bins permit stacks to be 17 feet high. Each item is assigned its floor space, and inventory control is visual. Elimination of stockrooms and warehousing cuts the cost of materials handling and production control; it eliminates the perpetual inventory system, stockkeeping, and stock records.

Along the production line, related operations are grouped to form small factories. In these one-man shops an operator—or at times two or more operators—does a complete subassembly job, much like a subcontractor. For instance, one operator does a complete assembly of gas tanks of different sizes. He welds the several sections of the tank, tests it under pressure, inserts the threaded bushings, cleans the finished job, inspects it, and sends it on. Another team of two men makes the covers and guards for welders. They use a forming roll, a spot welder, an arc welder, a degreasing tank, and a paint booth.

Under Lincoln's job enlargement, punch press operators do their own setup work, their own inspecting, handle their own material, handle their own dies, and in general manage their own affairs. Workers are on piecework, have responsibility for their own work, and guarantee its quality. Costs of supervision and inspection have been cut; the number of inspectors has been reduced from over 40 to approximately 12.

---

[4] The 1961 profit bonus of this Cleveland, Ohio, company was $6.4 million, apportioned among its 1,345 employees. The costs of the product (welding equipment) were lower than in 1934 in spite of increased cost of material and wages. J. F. Lincoln challenged his company to reduce costs by 10 percent each year. Company policies reflect his convictions about the dignity of work and the limitless possibilities of people to develop their abilities if they have the incentive to do so. At Lincoln people are hired for the lowest classification jobs and given training; promotions are from within and entirely on merit. Everyone is expected to be able to do several jobs and to be willing to do whatever work is available. Everyone is expected to produce at maximum speed.

The company reports a tremendous reduction in overhead costs and an increase in production of more than 20 percent with practically no increase in personnel.[5]

Job enlargement at the Maytag Company.   Maytag, the Newton, Iowa, maker of washing machines, was able to reduce costs through job enlargement. Some of the work was taken off the progressive assembly lines and set up at individual work stations where each person performed the total subassembly rather than just a few elements of it. The individual work station permitted better material handling, better work-station layout (more compact arrangement of fixtures, tools, and materials) and a better motion pattern for the operators' longer cycle jobs.

As a result, the assembly was performed in a shorter time than when the work was divided and machine paced. The operator performed a variety of tasks and became responsible for the quality and pace of the work. Training costs evened out; while it took more time for the operator to learn the enlarged job, he stayed on it longer, so that not so many people had to be trained. Defective parts were reduced from 5 percent to less than ½ of 1 percent. Direct labor costs were reduced; grievances over work standards were reduced. Operator earnings became more stable as a result of not being dependent on other persons' efforts.[6]

The above examples of job enlargement have been successful. There is continuing evidence that this approach is effective in a variety of work. It is well to remember that jobs can be enlarged both horizontally and vertically. The Lincoln Electric example cited above is one of vertical job enlargement where the workers get involved in planning, scheduling, and inspecting as well as performing the job itself. Doing a greater variety of the operations of a job is horizontal job enlargement.

At Texas Instruments a group of 10 assemblers and their supervisor established production goals for the manufacture of complex radar equipment. The assemblers improved manufacturing processes and gradually reduced production time by more than 50 percent and exceeded labor standards based on previously approved methods by 100 percent. This approach eventually encompassed the entire group of 700 assemblers and cost reduction, less absenteeism, less tardiness, and fewer employee complaints resulted.[7]

---

[5] Information about the changes in jobs was obtained from the company. For an article about Lincoln Electric, see Blake Clark, "A Factory Full of Partners," *Reader's Digest,* June, 1962.

[6] For more details, see Irwin A. Rose, "Increasing Productivity through Job Enlargement," *Proceedings of the 15th Annual Industrial Engineering Institute* (University of California, Berkeley, February 2, 1963).

The article is also published in American Management Association, *Manufacturing and the Challenge of Change* (Manufacturing Bulletin No. 18, 1962).

[7] Earl R. Gomersall and M. Scott Myers, "Breakthrough in On-the-Job Training," *Harvard Business Review,* Vol. 44, No. 4 (July–August, 1966), p. 63.

There are some social scientists who believe that job enlargement does not in itself encourage motivation among workers. They believe that doing more than one operation is not necessarily more motivating than doing only one. Their suggestion is that the job be *enriched* by deliberate upgrading of responsibility. Job enrichment seeks to improve both task efficiency and human satisfaction by means of building into people's jobs, quite specifically, greater scope for personal achievement and its recognition, more challenging and responsible work, and more opportunity for individual advancement and growth. It is concerned only incidently with matters such as pay and working conditions, organizational structure, communications, and training, important and necessary though these may be in their own right.[8] Five studies were carried out in various British companies using job enrichment as a frame of reference. The studies demonstrated that when tasks are organized to be as authentic and motivational as possible, management receives a more accurate and a continuing feedback on individual strengths and weaknesses, ability and potential. Task support becomes a flexible instrument of management, responsive to feedback.[9]

As is the case with most concepts, there is disagreement with job enlargement or job enrichment as a motivator of more effective individual performance. The engineering modifications required for job enlargement may make the cost prohibitive and changes in the workplace may be impossible to achieve because of building design. In most instances it is assumed that all employees want to have enlarged jobs because their present specialized tasks are boring and not meaningful. This assumption may not be true in all instances and it certainly does not take individual differences into consideration. Another assumption that seems to characterize much of the discussion about job enlargement is that the employee places a great amount of value on the work he performs and he is generally dissatisfied with his job. Two researchers found that workers in an automobile plant working on assembly line operations did not demonstrate significantly different levels of job satisfaction than utility workers or supervisors in the same plant. In other words, the employees who had more routine assignments and less freedom of movement did not demonstrate any more unfavorable or favorable job attitudes than those who did.[10] Perhaps because of the ever-decreasing workweek and the concurrent increase in leisure time, work has less importance in the employee's mind and he gains satisfaction from a variety of alternative forms of fulfilling behavior such as hobbies, community or church work, and travel.

---

[8] William J. Paul, Jr., Keith B. Robertson, and Frederick Herzberg, "Job Enrichment Pays Off," *Harvard Business Review,* Vol. 47, No. 2, p. 61.

[9] *Ibid.,* p. 78.

[10] J. E. Kennedy and H. E. O'Neill, "Job Content and Workers' Opinion," *Journal of Applied Psychology,* Vol. 42 (1958), pp. 372–75.

In any event, the dominating factor in job enlargement probably evolves from our rapidly changing technology. Whenever new methods, processes, equipment and procedures are developed, the man–machine relationship changes. This requires an analysis of the present job in light of the new factors and in many instances the job has to be redesigned. When this takes place job enlargement should be considered since this is an ideal time to develop job changes which may benefit both the company and the employee. Of course there is always the possibility that present employees may not be able to handle an enlarged job even with additional training and there are usually several who refuse to try. In a tight labor market with many alternative job opportunities available, there are employees who resent any manipulation of their jobs and they would rather quit than take on additional tasks.

The employee participation implied in job enlargement means that each individual performing the job has a role in the determination of the enlarged job. Because individual differences cannot wholly be taken into consideration, the resulting job will inevitably be a compromise supposedly accepted by the group. It certainly is possible that there will be group members who are as dissatisfied with the new job as there were other group members dissatisfied with the old one. Consequently job enlargement is not the only answer to better employee performance. Perhaps more scientific selection procedures, more effective placement, better job design along with proper training, and a greater amount of employee counseling should be adjuncts to any job enlargement program.

Redesigning a job

In most companies the supervisor has a hand in the designing of jobs. He also makes or collaborates in methods improvements that result in changing the design of jobs. He works with job analysts when they are analyzing and classifying jobs into pay groups (job evaluation) for wage and salary administration. The supervisor will find that collaboration with staff groups and with his own subordinates is almost essential in changing the design of jobs, because the design must meet requirements in four areas:

1. It must fit the technical requirements of the process.
2. It must fit into the organization and be compatible with other jobs and with the informal organization of the work group.
3. The job must fit the people who are available to perform it. It must be realistic in what it demands that a person have in skills, levels of skills, energy, intelligence, responsibility, and judgment. The job should in turn provide opportunities that will encourage its performers to give their best efforts.

4. The job must accomplish its objectives at the lowest total cost. Besides direct and indirect labor the other costs that should be considered are work spoilage, poor quality, accidents, absences, turnover, grievances, work stoppages, and resistance to change.

How to analyze a job. The first step toward changing the design of a job is to list all the tasks it contains. If the workers are performing according to a job description, it will list the total tasks. However, it won't tell what proportion of the workers' time is spent on each task. It won't tell how the tasks are apportioned among the people on the job—whether each person performs all the tasks, whether people rotate from one set of tasks to another, or whether tasks are assigned to people on the job according to skills required and possessed. For instance, the newcomer may be performing only the simplest tasks on the job.

One way to collect information about what people are doing is to use the Supervisor's Log Sheet from Chapter 7. The log can be filled out by each employee to show how he spends his time. He should keep track of his daily activities for the length of time it takes to get a representative cycle, or else estimate the time spent on tasks that occur only occasionally.

Job analysis formula. Once the information is gathered, the supervisor must analyze it. He may have the help of the job analyst, and may have access to information that was collected and used for job evaluation. The purpose of analyzing the job is to find out exactly what each person on the job is doing, what skills he needs in order to perform each task, and what responsibilities he has. The job analysis formula[11] calls for a listing of:

What the worker does (the physical and mental activities).
How he does it (the machinery, tools, formulas he uses; the decisions he must make).
Why he does it (the purpose of each task and how it relates to other tasks in this or other jobs).

The skills, responsibilities, and requirements involved:

Responsibility for machinery, tools, equipment, product, materials, for the work of others; honesty, initiative.
Job knowledge amount of schooling or training and/or experience needed for proficiency on the job.

---

[11] The job analysis formula can be found in *Guide for Analyzing Jobs, Analyst's Workbook* (War Manpower Commission, Division of Occupational Analysis) (Washington, D.C.: U.S. Government Printing Office, 1944).

Or see Jay L. Otis and Richard H. Leukart, *Job Evaluation* (2d ed.; Englewood Cliffs, N.J.: Prentice-Hall, Inc., 1954), p. 218.

Mental application: amount and degree and frequency of mental and visual effort called for; amount of attention required (whether it is full or intermittent); judgments, decisions.

Dexterity and accuracy: precision, steady nerves, accuracy of measurement or calculation; coordination, reaction time, versatility.

It is necessary to identify the type of skill and level of skill required for the performance of each task, because the tasks assigned to a job should call for related skills and skills of about the same level. The employee who matched the job would then be using his highest skills most of the time.

Using the work distribution chart. The work distribution chart enters into the procedure for job enlargement when the tasks to be added to a job must be taken from other jobs. Then all of the affected jobs must be examined for the purpose of rearranging and interchanging tasks.

A work distribution chart and the instructions for using it are presented in Figures 10–1 and 10–2. The chart shows how to go about listing the tasks performed in a department and the amount of time spent weekly on each task; then how to study the way the work is distributed to people. The task lists made out by employees on log sheets are transferred to this chart because they can all be lined up together in chart form. Figure 10–2 analyzes the distribution of tasks among employees in an office, but the technique is applicable to other types of jobs.[12]

Use of the work distribution chart is a protection against overloading some employees, underloading others, and letting some responsibilities fall between the chairs.

Guides for job design

Actually there has not been enough study of job design to produce principles or systematic methods for determining what should go into a job in order that it meet the needs of the process, of the organization, and of the employee, and still fulfill its purpose at the lowest total cost.

There are social science studies of what people want from jobs; there are engineering studies of what the company wants from jobs; there are industrial psychology and human engineering studies of the capabili-

---

[12] Additional information can be had from the pamphlet *How to Analyze the Distribution of Work* (Conference Outline No. 4, Management Course for Air Force Supervisors) (Washington, D.C.: U.S. Government Printing Office). From the same office is available *Supervisor's Guide to the Work Distribution Chart*, which is part of the Government Work Simplification Program.

ties of man in the man-machine system. And there are a number of studies describing changes in job design and the results achieved. From those sources are drawn the following guides:

1. Each job should have a known purpose and be meaningful to the performer. If possible, a job should consist of a series of tasks that bring to completion some recognizable portion of a product or process.
2. Each job should have skills of about the same level. If the skills are of a variety of levels, the worker capable of performing the high-skill tasks may be bored if there are many low-skill tasks. If the skills are on the same level, the performer is using his highest talents (the ones for which the company is paying) the greater part of the time.
3. The job should be made up of related or similar skills so that the performer can become proficient in all of them. For example, the job should not demand both clerical and mechanical skills.
4. The skills that are used in the job should be available in the existing labor market.
5. The job should engender a feeling of individual responsibility. The person should have some control over what he does—some freedom to make choices. Even on rather simple jobs, most people will put more care and effort into something for which they feel responsible. When authority and responsibility are pushed down to them, people become more involved in their jobs and more concerned about the quality of their work.
6. Each job should be a member of a family of jobs; that is, the jobs should be graded according to the various related skills so that the person at the bottom of the pile can see opportunities for advancement to jobs of increasing difficulty—from Class C to Class B to Class A assembler or machine operator, for instance.
7. Jobs should be set up so that the performers can identify themselves with the work group as well as with the job and the process. Jobs should fit into the social organization so that people will help rather than hinder one another—so that high performance is an advantage rather than a threat to the group.
8. The job should be measurable in some way so that the performer can show accomplishment in terms of the quality and quantity of his output. The job should offer a challenge to the person performing it. He should, if possible, be free to vary his pace rather than be machine-paced.

Figure 10–3 is the job description of a clerk in an office of the Standard Oil Company of California. It is an example of a well-designed job.

FIGURE 10-1
How to Complete the Work Distribution Chart

WORK DISTRIBUTION CHART

FUNCTION CHARTED: ADMINISTRATIVE SECTION — DATE 5/15

OPERATION/PROCESS	M. R. Smith — Supervisor (GS-5)	G. Powers — Clerk-Typist (GS-3)	L. Grady — Clerk-Typist (GS-3)	R. Blair — Clerk-Typist (GS-3)	S. Brown — Clerk (GS-2)
1 Preparation of correspondence	Take dictation & type letters 11-30'; Prepare Corres. (Oral) 2-30'	Type teletypes 2;	Type teletypes; Take dictation & type letters; Screen 1st Corres. 50; Screen 'out' Corres. 40	Miscellaneous Typing 7-30'; Type Correspondence 3-30'; Type dittos 5-40'	
2 Reception and arrangements	Answer telephone 2-30'	Answer telephone 2-30'; Make appointments; Arrange for conferences	Answer telephone; Make appointments		
3 Recording of conference	Take dictation & prepare reports 4-40'				
4 Make reports	1½-10'	Prepare activity & history reports 5-30'; Prepare and type special reports 7-40'			
5 Maintain regulations library	39			Maintain base regulations 5-30'; Maintain AF and Command Regs. 7-20'; Research regulations 1	Maintain base regulations 9; Maintain AF and Command Regs. 11-30'; Research regulations 4-40'
6 Maintain files	4-50'	File Correspondence; File teletypes	Maintain Corres. suspense 5-40'; File Correspondence 2-30'; File teletypes	Maintain corres. 7-20'; File Correspondence 7	File teletypes 5-30'; File Correspondence 4-30'
7 Make travel arrangements	Making travel arrangements 1		File teletypes		
8 Administration and Supervision	Work planning 2½-50'; Plan and conduct meetings 4; Work review 6-20'; Assign work 7				
9 Miscellaneous Activities	Coordinate office work 2½-30'; Miscellaneous 2	Office meetings 3-30'; Miscellaneous 2	Office meetings; Miscellaneous	Office meetings; Miscellaneous	Office meetings 2; Miscellaneous 2
TOTAL (Man-hours)	200	40	40	40	40

ANALYSIS: WHAT TAKES THE MOST TIME?... IS THERE MISDIRECTED EFFORT?... ARE SKILLS USED PROPERLY?... ARE THE TASKS TOO HARD?... ARE THERE TOO MANY UNRELATED TASKS?... ARE TASKS SPREAD TOO THINLY?... IS WORK DISTRIBUTED EVENLY?

Source: Air Force Pamphlet No. 50-2-4, *How to Analyze the Distribution of Work.*

FIGURE 10–1 (*Continued*)

The Work Distribution Chart is a device for arranging *facts* about work in a clear, understandable form. It helps you to *ask* questions. It will *not* answer questions. We need certain facts which we will place on the chart. We get the facts from the task lists and operations lists.

Facts

The task lists have been prepared by each worker, stating in brief, specific, and factual terms what he does.

The operations list has been prepared by you, the supervisor, and represents operations or activities which are performed within your organization.

Having these facts, you are now ready to place the information on the Work Distribution Chart. If you properly and accurately arrange the information on the chart, you will have a clear picture of the way the work is now distributed. It will be easier to see where you can make improvements.

To prepare a Work Distribution Chart, use AF Form 1003, or a blank sheet of paper on which similar column headings have been prepared.

Procedure

1. Fill in headings.
2. Enter first, to the left, the operations you have listed as necessary for accomplishing the mission of the organization in their order of importance (in some cases there will be no significant difference between several operations). Number the operations and leave space between them.
3. Across the top of the chart enter the names, job titles, and grades of your workers. This should be done by entering the highest grade employee to the left and listing the others, from left to right, in descending order of grades of pay.
4. Review each task list and identify each task with one of the operations listed in the left hand column of the Work Distribution Chart.
5. Post the appropriate operations number on the task list beside each task.
6. Then post in the worker's column on the Work Distribution Chart each of the tasks which have been identified with Operation No. 1. For example, let us assume that the first operation listed in the left-hand column of the work distribution was that of "taking inventory." Since this entry was the first one, you will have designated it as No. 1. All tasks on the task lists which have to do with "taking inventory" will have the number "1" posted adjacent to them.
7. Then copy each of these entries on the task lists placing them on the Work Distribution Chart opposite the operation, and in the respective columns of the workers who perform them.
8. Record the number of hours (and work count, if available) for each entry.
9. Add the total number of hours spent by all employees for the listed operation across the chart and enter the total to the right of the operation. Continue this procedure until the chart has been completed.
10. Add the time entries for each worker and for each operation. The total time for all operations (totaled across) should equal the total time for all workers (totaled down).

You now have a clear, understandable picture of the distribution of work currently being performed in the organization. An analysis of the facts on the chart follows in Figure 10–2.

FIGURE 10-2
Examining the Work Distribution Chart

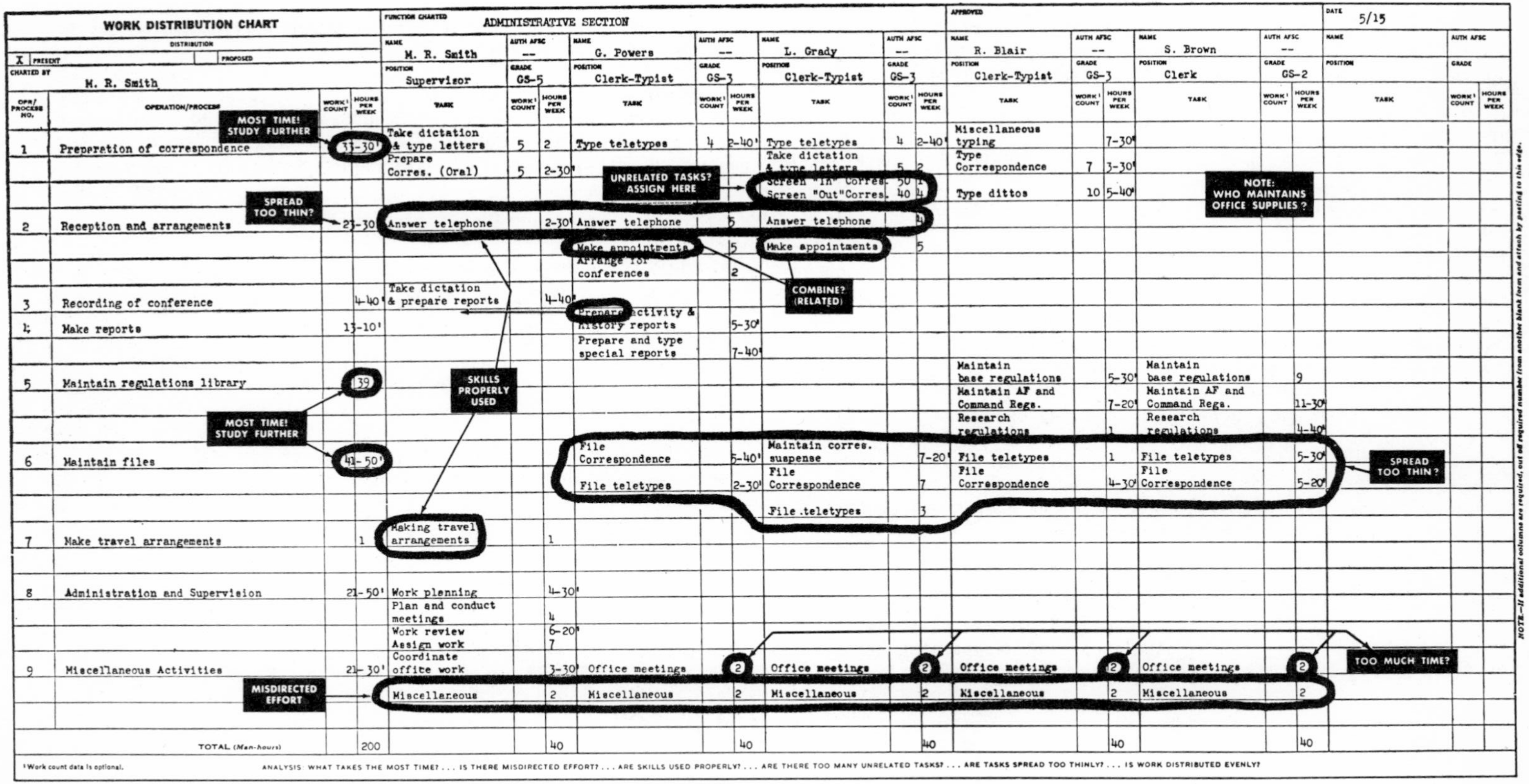

Source: Air Force Pamphlet 50-2-4, *How to Analyze the Distribution Work.*

FIGURE 10-2 (Continued)

Once the important facts about an organization are recorded on the Work Distribution Chart, it is necessary to examine the present work distribution and make improvements. Improvements are more likely if the present work distribution is systematically questioned. The following questions are suggested as a guide.

1. What operations and tasks take the most time?
   a) Other questions:
      (1) Is the most time devoted to the most important work?
      (2) Are all necessary operations and tasks included, and is the time spent on each appropriate?
   b) Hints:
      (1) Operations should be the right number and type to accomplish the mission.
      (2) Usually, operations (and tasks) which contribute most directly to the mission should take the most time.
      (3) Time totals for other operations normally should reflect the relative importance of that operation.
      (4) Operations which take the most time may require further study such as methods analysis.

2. Is there misdirected effort?
   a) Other questions:
      (1) Are all operations essential to the mission or have some been assumed which are unnecessary or done elsewhere?
      (2) Does each task contribute to the mission and to an operation?
      (3) Is too much time spent on nonessential details?
   b) Hints:
      (1) Only operations and tasks which are essential to the organization's mission should be accomplished.
      (2) Work which duplicates work done elsewhere may be misdirected effort.
      (3) Study "administrative" and "miscellaneous" operations closely for misdirected effort.

3. Are skills used properly?
   a) Other questions:
      (1) Are skilled workers doing considerably routine work or other tasks which do not use their skills?
      (2) Do workers have tasks which are above their skills for which they are not trained?
   b) Hints:
      (1) The supervisor and skilled workers should do a minimum amount of routine or other unskilled work. Willing workers may take on work below their skills.
      (2) Workers doing work far above their skills usually will do less work of poorer quality and with more accidents than workers with proper skills.
      (3) Skilled work should be concentrated in some positions and unskilled work in others where possible.

4. Are workers doing too many unrelated tasks?
   a) Other questions:
      (1) Are some workers performing tasks in every operation?
      (2) Are willing workers assigned tasks which are unrelated to their normal work?
   b) Hints:
      (1) Few people can do all types of work equally well; the assignment of unrelated tasks to workers can result in poorer work, less enthusiasm, and more fatigue.
      (2) The assignment of related tasks to a worker makes training to increase the worker's skills easier.
      (3) The willing worker should not be assigned or allowed to assume too many tasks just because of his willingness.
      (4) Tasks may be organized in related groups by type (assembling, inspecting, collecting) and then assigned to appropriate workers.

FIGURE 10-2 (Concluded)

5. Are tasks spread too thinly?

   a) Other questions:

      (1) Are many workers doing a small or unimportant task that one person could do more efficiently?

      (2) Are some tasks given to so many workers that no one is responsible for them?

   b) Hints:

      (1) If every worker is filing, answering the phone, cleaning the shop, or doing some similar task, the task may be badly performed and skills may be wasted.

      (2) One person working steadily usually can accomplish a task more effectively than many workers doing a small part of the same task.

6. Is the work distributed equitably?

   a) Other questions:

      (1) Are some workers overloaded and others underloaded or does everyone carry a "fair share" of the work?

      (2) Do the tasks of the worker look "thin" compared with others?

      (3) Does the work count information shown indicate an uneven distribution of work?

   b) Hints:

      (1) Overloading or underloading workers will get poor results and may lower morale.

      (2) Aim for a balanced work load among workers.

FIGURE 10–3
(A, B, C) Job Description of a Counter Clerk in a District Office of the Standard
Oil Company of California

```
                    JOB   DESCRIPTION

  COMMITTEE APPROVAL
                        POSITION     COUNTER CLERK
  CHAIRMAN
                        NAME
  PLACEMENT
                        DEPARTMENT  DISTRICT OFFICE    LOCATION
  DATE
                        DIVISION
```

1. NATURE AND EXTENT OF ASSIGNMENT: Describe the position accurately and concisely under the following separate subheadings: A. Basic Function: state in general terms the functions performed and the objectives. B. Scope: supply figures indicating the size or area of the assignment; omit if size is obvious. C. Functions Performed: describe the specific functions performed, indicating the percent of time.

JOB SUMMARY: Receives customer remittances and requests for service or adjustment over the counter and through the mail; follows up delinquent open and closed accounts for collection; prepares journal memos to transfer accounts; maintains Credit History Card file; assists with routine clerical work of office as time permits.

WORK PERFORMED:

1. Receives customer remittances over the counter in payment for service and merchandise. Looks up bills in accounts receivable ledgers or the merchandise register as required. Gives customer a receipt and keeps stub. Balances money received each day against stubs, searching for errors as required. Completes collector's deposit tag and gives with money to controls clerk. — 35%

2. Receives customer requests for service or adjustment over the counter. Completes Application for Service, Customer Service Order and Routine Operations Order form, as required, and files for dispatch to a Serviceman or Salesman. Completes credit reference forms as required, and mails. — 20%

3. Opens mail addressed to office. Gives other than remittances or requests for service or adjustment to Head Clerk. Balances checks received against stubs. When stubs are not enclosed, looks up amount of bills in accounts receivable ledgers or the merchandise register. Refers discrepancies back to customer. Balances amount received, completes forms, and routes checks as outlined in Duty 1 above. Completes forms for requests for service or adjustment as outlined in Duty 2 above. — 15%

4. Follows up closed accounts for collection: — 10%
   a. Files customer index cards for closed accounts per follow-up schedule, as received;
   b. Checks accounts receivable ledgers after follow-up dates for notices of payment of bill; if not paid, mails form collection letter; forwards unpaid bills to other districts and other utility companies for collection as required;
   c. If not paid by collection letter series, lists delinquent accounts and routes to General Accounting Office;
   d. If account not paid after follow-up by General Accounting Office, lists accounts for collection agency and forwards to General Accounting Office for approval; forwards approved list to agency;
   e. Destroys customer index card when paid.

5. Mails "Notice of Unpaid Bill" and "Final" notices on delinquent service accounts, and notices on delinquent merchandise accounts per established follow-up schedule, first checking accounts receivable ledgers or merchandise register to see if bill has been paid. Monthly prepares a listing of notices mailed. — 3%

CONTINUE ON ATTACHED SHEETS, WHEN NECESSARY
(Continued)

From *More Profit-Less Paper*, prepared 1953 by Joseph W. Lucas with assistance of other members of the Department on Organization. Used with permission of the Standard Oil Company of California.

FIGURE 10-3 (*Continued*)

JOB DESCRIPTION

COUNTER CLERK (Cont'd)

6. Maintains (suspense) ledger for delinquent closed accounts: 4%
    a. Sets up ledger sheets from data on closing bills and journal memos;
    b. Posts data on follow-up as outlined in Duty 4;
    c. Removes sheet from ledger as account is paid and gives to File Clerk
        and Typist for filing;
    d. If account not paid in prescribed time, prepares journal memo for
        bad debt write-off and transfers ledger stub for account to bad
        debt ledger;
    e. Periodically balances ledger per procedure.
7. Prepares journal memos to transfer accounts to closed account ledger or   3%
    to another route as required, from data on customer index cards and
    closing bills received. Routes memos for posting.
8. Maintains Credit History Card file. Sets up card for each account and   3%
    posts credit rating and changes in credit rating as notified. Recom-
    mends changes in credit ratings to Head Clerk as collections indicate
    ratings should be changed.
9. Completes form if customer requests change of mailing address or for   2%
    error in name and address, and corrects meter book sheet for account.
10. Assists with routine clerical work of office as time permits. For   5%
    example: stuffs bills in envelopes preparatory to mailing, sorts remit-
    tance stubs.

FIGURE 10–3 (*Concluded*)

COUNTER CLERK (Cont'd) **JOB DESCRIPTION**

z. **SPECIAL REQUIREMENTS:** Specify the following under separate sub-headings, where pertinent: **A. Education.** **B. Training Required:** Indicate the experience necessary to adequately perform the assignment and the name of the next lower position in which experience is required. **C. Knowledges:** list those necessary to do the assignment. **D. Other Abilities:** specify the other characteristics required for the performance of the position.

A. EDUCATION: High school graduate.

B. LEARNING PERIOD: At least six months' experience in a district office. Three months' normal training time after assignment to job.

C. KNOWLEDGES: Thorough knowledge of procedures pertaining to job as outlined in District Office Manual. Type: 45 w.p.m.

D. OTHER ABILITIES: Tact in dealing with customers; neat and pleasant appearance; completeness and accuracy when taking a customer request; appraise requests; ability to follow through on multiple step procedures.

3. **SUPERVISION AND FUNCTIONAL ASSISTANCE RECEIVED:** List the following under separate sub-headings: **A. Immediate Supervisor:** enter the position title only of the immediate supervisor to whom the employee is responsible. **B. Supervision Received:** describe the frequency and detail with which assignments are given, assistance and guidance provided, and the extent that the work of this position is reviewed, checked, and evaluated. **C. Functional Assistance:** describe the kind of functional or technical assistance available to this position, its accessibility, and its purpose.

A. IMMEDIATE SUPERVISOR: Head Clerk.

B. SUPERVISION RECEIVED: Under intermittent supervision. Work is performed according to prescribed procedures and the incumbent is expected to perform all routine in accordance therewith without reference to Head Clerk. The Head Clerk is available to answer questions on problems or work of an unusual nature.

C. FUNCTIONAL ASSISTANCE: None.

4. **RESPONSIBILITY AND AUTHORITY:** Describe the responsibility definitely fixed in this position under the following sub-headings, and specify the authority and effect of decisions and recommendations made, i.e. the latitude delegated for making independent decisions for each: **A. Men,** including number and titles of employees supervised. **B. Materials or Products. C. Operations or Functions. D. Equipment. E. Money. F. Business Relations.** Also specify the lack of responsibility or authority when none exists under any of these categories.

A. MEN: None.

B. MATERIALS OR PRODUCTS: None.

C. OPERATIONS OR FUNCTIONS: Receives customer remittances or requests for service or adjustment over the counter or through the mail; follows up delinquent open and closed accounts for collection and prepares delinquent reports.

D. EQUIPMENT: None.

E. MONEY: Accounts for money received.

F. BUSINESS RELATIONS: Daily personal and telephone contact with district personnel and the public.

5. **WORKING CONDITIONS**: General Office.

COMPILED BY_____APPROVED BY_____DATE_____

The job at the checkout stand of a market looks like a well-designed job.

Job design has been expanded to work systems design by the application of systems engineering to an organization. Gerald Nadler calls it the "IDEALS Concept," IDEALS being an acronym for *I*deal *D*esign of *E*ffective *A*nd *L*ogical *S*ystems. He lists the following seven-system characteristics as an integral part of his approach to work design:

1.	Function.	5.	Environment.
2.	Inputs.	6.	Equipment.
3.	Outputs.	7.	Human Agents.
4.	Sequence.		

His approach to work design encompasses the totality of its performance in an organization. Provision is made for design, function determination, system formulation, review, testing and installation of the system, and measuring and controlling its performance.[13]

The supervisor's responsibilities in placement

Even though the job is well designed, it will not be performed effectively by an employee who is a square peg in a round hole. People differ not only in intelligence, capacity, and skill but also in temperament, ambition, outlook on life, and ability to adjust to the technical and human demands of a particular work situation. The supervisor is in daily contact with the job factors crucial to worker success or failure. He knows better than anyone else what the jobs require of performers, and he should develop skill in judging whether applicants have what it takes to meet these requirements.

Usually applicants are recruited and screened by the personnel department and sent to the supervisor for his approval before they are hired. If the personnel department is to do a good job of selection, the supervisor must furnish detailed and accurate information about the kind of people needed. He must appraise the applicants sent to him, evaluate new employees during the trial work period, and continue adjusting people to jobs all through their employment.

The supervisor is the one who has to live with the mistakes that are made in selection. The misplaced worker—the wrong man on the job—requires more training, makes more mistakes, has more accidents. He has trouble keeping up quality and quantity of output. He gets discouraged and sick at heart. He may become physically ill from having

---

[13] For a thorough explanation of this concept, see Gerald Nadler, *Work Systems Design: The Ideals Concept* (Homewood, Ill.: Richard D. Irwin, Inc., 1967).

to face a job he can't perform properly, or having to deal with people with whom he can't get along. He may stick it out or he may avoid the unpleasantness by being absent and finally by quitting if he can find another job that meets his needs.

Estimates of the cost of turnover on simple clerical jobs are as high as $2,000; estimates on higher level jobs range up to $7,000. Costs include induction and training of the new employees, their errors, spoilage, and breakage, their low production during learning, and the lowered production of other employees whose work is affected. The company also has to pay the expenses of recruiting, interviewing, putting people on the payroll and taking them off again. Poor selection is costly whether the misfit quits or stays.

The misplaced worker who stays on the job is faced with frustration and failure. The job may take too much out of him because he lacks the native ability for it and has to put forth too much effort just to keep up. Or the job may use so little of his abilities that it holds no interest for him and he actually despises it. To gain some outlet for his emotions and energies, he may become a troublemaker.

Matching men and jobs

One supervisor's troublemaker is another supervisor's right-hand man. A job that is frustrating to one employee is challenging to another. The supervisor must study the job and all that surrounds it before he looks for the man to fill it.

What the job demands. The overall picture of what the job demands is expressed in the job specification sheet of the job description. In it will be found what education and experience the employee must bring to the job and what technical skills he must have. It will tell what physical and mental effort the employee must expend, what difficulties he must work under, and what responsibilities he must assume. The supervisor needs to know also what constitutes satisfactory performance—how much must be done and how well it must be done. This information is not usually expressed in the job description but should be in the standards of performance.

The personnel department may administer tests to measure the applicant in abilities required by the job. The supervisor may be able to get a demonstration of the applicant's proficiency in machine skills or some such sample of his work.

An employee may meet the requirements listed in the job specifications and still not work out well in the department if he doesn't fit into the work group. His presence may stir up resentment in others, and they may refuse to cooperate with him or help him in any way. The supervisor should study the group's social structure and the characteristics of the people it accepts and likes. If the personal characteristics that predominate in the group are desirable ones, they should be sought in the applicant. If the characteristics are undesirable ones, then—at the risk of dissension—they should be thinned out by the introduction of new blood.

The supervisor must also consider what opportunities exist for developing on specific jobs in his department—whether there are chances for advancement or whether the jobs are blind alleys. What types of people come and go? What types stay? What types give the most trouble? As the supervisor studies the characteristics which spell success or failure in his department, he can get a good idea of those extra things that the job demands of the new worker.

What the employee wants from the job. The question of what people want from their jobs is discussed in Chapter 11. Social scientists have asked a great number of workers what they want from their jobs and which wants are most important to them. The resulting lists are of great value in considering the wants of a group of workers, but the studies don't tell what a particular worker wants from *his* job.

Some very few people value money most highly, are self-sufficient, competitive, and not "joiners." Others would sacrifice some of the money in order to enjoy the friendliness of the work group; they want the security and comfort of congenial companionship on the job. Some housewives go to work because they want adult companionship; they have a great need for social relationships and they want a job on which they can talk. Many of them seek temporary assignments so they can have the benefits of employment along with the necessities of homemaking. Some people want a job on which they will get a minimum of bossing; they resent close supervision and want to be able to decide a few things for themselves. Others want a close relationship with the boss so that they can go to him for answers, reassurance, approval, and encouragement. Some people are content with repetitive work that lets them daydream; other people want interest, variety, challenge, and responsibility in their jobs. Some people are eager for opportunities to get ahead and are willing to make sacrifices for future gain. Others live for the moment, have lower aspirations, or have given up hope.

The particular type of work contacts required by the job may call for a certain type of personality. Is the job one in which the employee must deal with complaints, criticisms, conflicts, uncertainties, and the demands of a number of people at the same time? Is it a job in which the employee must make many demands on others—for instance, for materials, information, assistance, or just to hurry someone up? Would the applicant be able to tolerate the unpleasantness of some of these contacts or would he become flustered, angered, and upset to the point where he couldn't do his work, or would get sick, or would neglect the parts of his job that gave him too much distress? A person who has a great need to be liked, to be popular, and to be approved of may not have a thick enough skin for such a job.

In recent years there has been an increasing emphasis on the hiring and training of people from various minority groups. Since most of these individuals come from disadvantaged circumstances, they pose special problems for the supervisor. They do not have middle-class values and therefore may not place the same importance on such things as coming in on time, good grooming, socializing, hard work, and ambition as others in the work group. Some of them may be very impatient with what they perceive as the red tape of the organization and they may demand jobs for which they are not qualified. Additionally they may be difficult to discipline since they may feel attempts in this direction are discrimination. The supervisor will have to take additional time with such employees. In fact, some companies have special programs for the orientation and training of minority groups so they may be assimilated into the work force with a minimum of difficulty.

The supervisor knows what opportunities exist on the job and whether the job is monotonous or challenging. He knows his own attitude toward delegating authority. He knows whether his best workers are the docile, the independent, or the in-between. He now must find out what kind of person the particular applicant is, what he wants from the job, and whether the two sets of wants are compatible. It is seldom possible to find the perfect fit for the job; it is a matter of compromise. The supervisor must decide whether job and man are too far apart or whether the applicant has the flexibility, the variety of experience, and the possibilities for being trained up to the job. If the man is overqualified, he may be dissatisfied in a position lower than the one on which he was previously successful. He may be looking upon the job as a temporary expedient or a means of getting his foot in the door. He may be unhappy with wages and working conditions that are below those to which he has become accustomed.

The means for finding out all this information about the applicant are the application blanks, the interview, and the trial work period.

The application blank. If the supervisor receives—and in most cases he does—the applicant's application form from the personnel department, he can get some idea from it of the applicant's educational, social, and work background.

The schooling record shows what he has done in the way of education—but not what he can do or what he might have done if he had had the opportunity. A grammar school graduate may be just as intelligent as a college graduate but may have had to quit school to support himself. Certain scores on his psychological test might be a good indication of his intelligence.

Some inkling of the man's home life and social background can be obtained from his marital status, homeownership, club memberships, and other activities.

His work background will show the companies he worked for, the number and types of jobs he held, how long he stayed on them, and how their wages compared. This information may give a pretty good indication of whether he is on his way up or down and whether he is a floater.

The interview

In the employment interview the supervisor wants to find out for himself the answers to a number of questions: Can the person do the job? Does he have the ability, the skill, the knowledge, the work experience, and the education necessary? Will he do the job—that is, will he be motivated to do a good job? Is he likely to remain on the job? Is his personality suited to the job? Will he fit in with the work group? To seek these answers the interview will explore four areas: (1) work experience, (2) education and training, (3) work interests and goals, (4) background and outside interests. The application form provides the outlines of this information; the interview should fill in the rest.[14]

Most applicants in an interview are doing a selling job—putting their best foot forward. Skilled interviewers have difficulty making accurate judgments; so the supervisor must be careful not to be taken in by such things as appearance, enthusiasm, and promises. The applicant may say that he won't mind having to get up before six o'clock to drive 40 miles to the job every morning—that he'll get there on time. He may not mind it for several months, but it is too much to expect that he can keep it up.

The supervisor in his interview should try to get as accurate a picture as he can of the man's qualifications either through discussion or a work sample. Getting him to discuss his previous jobs may indicate the amount of his skill; it may also throw some light on why he left previous jobs and what the chances are of his sticking to this one.

What did he particularly like or dislike about each of his previous jobs? Of all the types of work he has done, which has he liked best? Why? Did he like work where he had responsibility? Did he prefer the closely supervised position? Did he become dissatisfied or discouraged easily? How did he do in jobs that required working with different

---

[14] The supervisor will find additional guides and techniques of selection interviewing in *Manual of Employment Interviewing* of the Employment Branch, Departmental Civilian Personnel Division, Administrative Office Navy Department (Washington D.C.: U.S. Government Printing Office, 1957).

kinds of people? Is he overcritical in the way he comments on unpleasant situations in the previous jobs? Does he show some strong dislikes that would give trouble in the job for which he is being considered? Was he bored on some jobs? How much variety does he need?

Do his education and training fit the job? Is he applying for a job that is outside his field of preparation? Are there sound reasons for the change? What are his long-range goals with respect to his work? What are his aims for the next two or three years? Do his plans fit the opportunities on the job? Will the job be a stepping-stone toward his goal?

The supervisor uses the information on the application form as the springboard to get into a discussion of the man's interests, ambitions, plans, and adjustments to past jobs. From the conversation it will be possible to tell whether this applicant is somewhat like the men who are now doing well on the job or whether he is wholly different from them.

If the applicant is not acceptable, the supervisor should terminate the interview in a friendly manner without building up any false hopes.

If, on the other hand, as the interview progresses, the supervisor feels that he would like to hire the man, this is the time to start telling him about the job—the qualifications necessary, the quality and quantity of output expected of him, the working conditions, the compensation, the type of workers with whom he will be associated. The applicant should be given a clear picture of the opportunities and drawbacks on the job; he might as well hear them now because he will find out later.

This is the time to establish a good working relationship with a new employee—to let him know that the supervisor is interested in him, wants him to be successful on the job, and is letting him know what to expect and what will be expected of him. If the supervisor oversells the job, the worker will suffer a letdown, perhaps be disgruntled, and certainly lack confidence in the boss who misled him.

The supervisor must ask himself the question: Can this job give this man what he is seeking? And he will have to answer the question himself, because the applicant is not in a position to know.

The trial work period

No matter how carefully the supervisor analyzes the application blank and appraises the applicant, there are certain things that he cannot be sure of until he has hired the man and observed him on the job. The trial work period may be for one month, three months, or even up to two years. It is to the company's advantage to have it as long as possible because the worker can be terminated at any time within the period without showing "cause." But if he is kept on past his trial work period and becomes a permanent employee, then it may be difficult to fire him. "Cause" for discharging a permanent employee might be limited to such things as insubordination, fighting, stealing, intoxication, habitual tardiness, or habitual absenteeism.

Since a probationary employee can be terminated for the reason that he is not suited to the job, it is up to the supervisor to determine definitely in the trial period whether the man can handle the job or if it is too difficult for him; whether he is a careful worker or has accidents; and whether the job is below his capacity and he will shortly be seeking opportunities for a better job—opportunities which may not exist in the department.

The supervisor also has to study the man's relations with the group: What influence is he exerting on the group? To what extent is he being accepted by the group? Is the group rejecting him so definitely that he is destined to remain an outsider?

The supervisor should study the probationary worker's behavior to determine what the indications are. Is he cooperative, dependable, and industrious? Or are there indications of stubbornness, belligerence, or laziness that would become worse once he became permanent on the job? How about his drinking habits? Do tardiness, absenteeism, and loafing indicate that he is not adjusted or is becoming dissatisfied with the job or would be an undesirable employee? Most voluntary quits take place in the first year of employment, but it isn't always the undesirables who quit.

Monotony and boredom

When a person complains that his job is monotonous, this is strong evidence that he is not fitted for the job. A job that seems monotonous to one person may not seem so to another. A young woman who was asked if her job (inspecting the same type of part all day long) was monotonous, said, "If my job looks monotonous to you, you should see my sister's job; she's a bookkeeper."

Monotony is defined as *sameness* or *lack of variety*. Boredom is defined as a *state of mind involving weariness, fatigue, disinterest, and dislike*. Boredom, then, exists in the mind of the worker: a job is boring if he finds it boring. Research studies suggest that people who suffer from boredom on the job are the young, the restless, and those who are less satisfied with things in general.

Some people, especially women, take and stay on jobs that have all the earmarks of being monotonous, but they don't complain of boredom. The social life at work may keep them interested or they may like the opportunity to daydream. They may find the job preferable to housework. They may not have a high level of aspiration, or the job may actually be somewhat of a challenge to them.

Married women are apt to look on a job as temporary rather than as a career, although this attitude may change with a higher level of education and the trend for women to spend more of their lives in the work force. Forecasts are that the majority of young women can expect to work a total of 25 years in their lives. This prospect may change their attitudes toward monotonous jobs.

A factor to be considered in monotony is that a job requires more attention from one person than from another. Anyone learning a job has to give it his full attention. People complain about jobs that require them to be alert and watchful but provide nothing to keep them alert or hold their attention. On jobs that require little attention, people may daydream about pleasant things, or brood about unpleasant things, or grumble, or fool around.

If a whole work group considers a job monotonous, there is need to create some variety in it—enlarge it or rotate the tasks or change the seating or social arrangements of the group doing the job.

Misfits

People who are subject to boredom are usually misfits on monotonous jobs. Sometimes an employee will be on a job that is far below his mental level. He may have taken it to get his foot in the door, but if the hoped-for opportunities don't develop, he becomes bored—a clock watcher who develops tricks to make the time pass faster. He wastes a lot of time and begins to interfere with others. His own dissatisfaction with the job may spread to others.

Some people are misfits because they are trying to handle a job that is beyond their mental or emotional capacity. They have to expend a great deal of nervous energy on the job; they become rattled over little things; they can't make good plans in their work.

Sometimes a person cannot fit into the group because he is far below it mentally or socially and has nothing in common with his fellow workers. Or the reverse, he may be quite a bit above the rest of the group mentally or socially and have trouble adjusting. Some such men can adjust and become the sage, the encyclopedia, the professor, for the gang, supplying facts and figures to settle the arguments brought to him for settlement.

A man's attitude toward his fellow workers may be greatly influenced by the kind of people he used to work with and the company he keeps after working hours. If a man looks upon his co-workers as the scum of the earth or a bunch of stuffed shirts, adjustment is going to be difficult.

The supervisor has the opportunity of preventing problems from arising, by eliminating the unfit during the interview and by removing the misfits that slip by and can be caught during the trial work period. He must continue to study the performance and adjustment of his people. Placement is not something that can be done once—when the man is first hired—and then be forgotten. It takes a while to find out what a person is best able to do. He should be on a job that uses his highest abilities, but people change in their interests and abilities, and jobs change in their tasks and in their methods. The job that was a challenge to a man when he was first hired may no longer hold his interest after he has mastered it. The supervisor must be alert for opportunities to move permanent employees onto jobs and into work groups for which they are better suited.

The supervisor should review the good judgments and the mistakes he made in selecting men for his permanent work group. When he is evaluating a permanent employee for the employee-evaluation record, he should recall his own reactions to the man's application blank, to the interview, and to the man's performance and behavior during the trial work period. What points sold him on the employee who turned out to be satisfactory? What did he overlook or misjudge in appraising the man who is turning out to be not so good? This knowledge he should use in the future selections of men.

Summary

The supervisor has the responsibility of fitting people to jobs and jobs to people. Some jobs may be so badly designed that no one could fit them. Oversimplified and overspecialized jobs are inefficient from a technical as well as a human standpoint. A number of companies have recognized that it is easier to make technical changes than to redesign human nature, and they are enlarging jobs instead of deskilling them.

The design of jobs must meet requirements in four areas: the human, the organizational, the technical, and the economic. The chapter provides a list of guides for designing jobs, the formula for job analysis, and a chart and instructions for analyzing the distribution of work in the department.

In fitting people to jobs, the supervisor must analyze the job and find out what it requires of the performer. The supervisor must appraise job applicants to see if they are suited to the work, to the social setup of the work group, and to the authority structure and opportunities within the organization. By means of the application form and the interview, he must judge whether an applicant has the possibilities for being successful on the job. The trial work period provides an opportunity to weed out misfits. The supervisor's responsibility for adjusting people to jobs is a continuing one because conditions change, jobs change, and people change.

CASE 1

Since it was set up several years ago, a relatively simple job (inspecting or machine operating, for example) performed by women in a group has had a high turnover. The women complain that the pay is too low. Actually, when compared to jobs of the same difficulty, the pay is in line.

In order to raise the pay and reduce the turnover, the company plans to enlarge the job by combining it with a similar job that requires more accurate work and has a higher pay scale.

Mary Morrow, the most successful operator on the simple job, was selected to try out the combined job and was trained to perform the new tasks. She has been working on the newly designed job for three months. She continues to do the tasks of the original job very well but does very poorly the new tasks—the ones requiring greater accuracy. When asked the reason, she says she does not like the new tasks because they make her nervous. If she didn't need the extra pay, she would like to go back to her old job.

1. What are some of the factors to be considered when enlarging jobs?
2. What are some of the advantages and disadvantages of combining several levels of the same type of job?
3. How should jobs be enlarged?
4. How should the above situation be handled?

CASE 2

The chief inspector, Rod Russell, has a problem of choosing between Will White and Bob Black to be his assistant. White has been with the company two years. The indications are that he has good leadership ability. He exercises good judgment and has the faculty of keeping his boss (Russell) and the operating people satisfied. He knows just about how much to give and take—an important trait at the present time because the type of inspection done requires quite a bit of judgment. Because of the nature of the product, the quality standards are not set up too well as yet, nor will they be for the next couple of years.

Bob Black, the other candidate, has been with the company for three years and has a better education than either Russell or White. He has been going to night school and taking a lot of advanced work in quality control. He has been fighting hard to introduce his ideas but Russell feels that they are premature and that the company will not be ready for them for three or maybe five years.

The company policy in promoting is to favor men who have been studying on the outside; however White seems to be better fitted for the present situation, while Black seems to be better fitted for the long-term pull.

1. Which of the two men should Russell promote, and why?
2. How should he take care of the disappointed candidate?
3. Is Bob Black overqualified for the promotion?
4. Could Russell's feelings about Black's ideas be colored by envy of Black's education?

CASE 3

A government installation is having difficulty hiring well-qualified electronics technicians. Many of the present technicians were hired during the period when skilled men were very scarce. When the more capable ones left to take higher paying jobs in private industry, the men who stayed on cornered the high-paying jobs. Thus only the low-paying jobs are left, and the pay on these is not high enough to attract well-qualified new men.

According to their job sheets, the electronics technicians are supposed to be able to do troubleshooting work, but few of the present men meet this requirement; lack of skill limits most of them to routine wiring and assembly work.

Until recently the lack of proper qualifications was not a problem because the engineers did the troubleshooting work. Lately, however, the amount of complex equipment has greatly increased and the engineers don't have time to devote to troubleshooting. The amount of equipment needing repair is piling up.

1. List the problems in this case.
2. How should each be handled?
3. What are some of the practical ways of getting relief in this situation?

CASE 4

Recently you employed a bright young high school graduate and gave him a job running a turret lathe in the shop. You believe this is a good way to break him in and acquaint him with the company. You plan to move him around from job to job so that ultimately you can use his abilities. According to tests he took in high school he has an IQ of about 130 and strong social skills. He took a number of aptitude tests in high school and passed them with high scores.

The other day he told you that he wants to become an apprentice toolmaker in your company. You asked him why. He said that according to tests he has a strong mechanical aptitude; also he took the aptitude tests for tool-and-die making (the ones administered by the state for selecting apprentices) and he passed them high. You figure that he is a test passer.

You have observed his work in the shop. As far as you can see he does not have manual dexterity. He even has difficulty grinding tools, although he knows all the reasons for the various angles. His quickness in grasping ideas and his ability to get along with people indicate that he has supervisory potentialities. You ask him why at 18 he is working and not going on to college and he tells you that he does not like to study; in fact his grades are not high enough to get him into college; he says he likes working with his hands and has high mechanical aptitude.

What should you do with him?

CASE 5

Dick Talbot had started with the company as an office boy at the age of 16. Now at age 59 he was the training director and he was in trouble.

During his career, Dick had spent time in nearly every department. While none of his service was outstanding, he was a reliable, hardworking employee. Because of his varied experience, he had been assigned to the personnel department several years ago when the company started a methods improvement program and needed a trainer. Dick was sent to school by the company to become knowledgeable in the area of methods improvement and he became very enthusiastic about the subject. Even though he had never finished high school, the company had sent him to several courses on a variety of subjects and he had done some reading on his own. He did not, however, avail himself of the company's tuition remission plan which would have allowed him to go to school at night to improve his formal education.

He conducted several classes in methods improvement and then started a program for the preparation of procedure manuals. During this period the company grew rather rapidly and the training function expanded. Having no one else available, the personnel vice president promoted Dick to the position of training director. He also hired a young man with a master's degree as Dick's assistant. As time went on, three more bright young training analysts with master's degrees were added to the staff to meet the mounting requests for training programs from the major divisions of the company.

The company was now conducting two management development programs, one for first-line supervisors and one for middle management, a college training program for college graduates hired as executive trainees, a work measurement program, an orientation program, and several skill programs. In other words, the training department was now an important function and Dick found that he was unable to cope with his increased responsibilities. He was afraid of the bright young men who worked for him but who did not respect him. He couldn't handle the dynamic executive trainees and he found his lack of formal education a definite handicap. He postponed decisions and continually withdrew from controversy. He exercised no leadership and his assistant assumed the responsibility. He longed for the days of the first methods improvement program he taught. The world was passing him by and to escape he started drinking excessively. His rate of absenteeism climbed and the personnel vice president spoke to him about the problem. Dick agreed to a complete physical as well as psychiatric help at company expense.

The personnel vice president kept Dick in his position as training director even though the department was being handled by Dick's assistant who by now was openly critical of Dick. After a period of treatment, Dick did not show any appreciable improvement and the personnel vice president wondered what to do next.

1. What course of action should be taken now by the personnel vice president?
2. What can be done with an employee whose position has outgrown his abilities and who has long service?
3. Is the personnel vice president at fault for promoting Dick in the first place?
4. Is it possible that he feels guilty about his error of judgment in Dick's case and that this is coloring his handling of the problem?
5. Should a company feel any sense of responsibility for promoting a man over his head?

CASE 6

You have three crews—six men each—employed on an assembly job. They are paid according to a group bonus system. The second and third crews are continually slowed down because production of the first crew is not ready. This crew lags because one of the members, Frank, is somewhat slower than the rest. He is a long-term employee and quite popular with the crews because of his easygoing temperament.

Any time you talk to Frank about his slowness, he replies: "Guess you're right, boss. I am a little slower than the rest; but you can't say my work isn't top quality. You can count the times I've slipped up on you in 20 years."

Frank does take pride in his work, and the crews do not object to his slowness. Ever since the group bonus system went into effect, you have felt that you should do something about Frank; but what? You know your inaction is costing money.

1. What are some of the advantages of having men on a group bonus system?
2. What are some of the disadvantages of having men on a group bonus system?
3. How much of a "right" does Frank have to his job?
4. If retaining Frank on the job is costing both the company and the other workers some—but not much—money, are you justified in keeping Frank on this job? Why or why not?
5. How would you solve the problem?

CASE 7

You are in charge of a small section consisting of a group of women, all of whom do practically the same type of work and receive the same pay. Your employees always got along well together, and supervising them was not difficult.

Recently one of the women resigned because her husband wanted her to stay home and take care of the house. As a replacement, you hired a woman who had previously held a much higher job—in fact, one quite like your own. When you employed her, you explained that her duties and pay would be the same as the other employees. You pointed out that she might not be happy in a position below the level of her previous ones; however, she was anxious to get the job and assured you that she would be quite content.

After a few weeks she began showing signs of maladjustment. She started telling the other employees what to do, and at times she even gives you instructions on how to do your job. The group resents her and her bossy attitude, and morale is suffering.

1. Should you recommend that this employee be transferred?
2. If not, should you point out her specific duties to her in order to put her back in line? How would you keep her in line?
3. Should she be recommended for a promotion in some other section, if there is an opening fitting her qualifications?
4. If she persists in her present activities, should you terminate her? Why or why not?

CASE 8

You are in charge of a large section and have two assistant supervisors under you. You have specialized these men, and each is doing a good job. One of the assistants has specialized in handling the office work;

he has had little experience on the operating end. The other assistant is a top-notch operating man but does not know the office work. You have coordinated the work of the two men.

There is a chance for you to be promoted if you can get a replacement for your job. However, it would take about six months to train either of your assistants to learn the other's job and thus be able to take your place. You do not want to hire anyone from the outside, because you have always believed in building your organization from within.

1. What are some of the advantages of specializing men?
2. What are some of the disadvantages of specializing men?
3. Give the advantages of building your organization from within.
4. Give some advantages of hiring supervisors from other companies.
5. How should you go about correcting the situation you find yourself in, in the above case?

CASE 9

Because of an increase in the work load, you plan to put on a second shift. Fortunately, you are able to make up a crew of new hires who have done night work in other companies. Since they are new, they will need some training and good supervision. You talk the situation over with your assistants, and two of them—Joe White and Bill Black—volunteer to take over this second shift.

Joe White is your most ambitious and conscientious assistant. His day crew always turns out a large volume of good work. The other volunteer, Bill Black, is easygoing and the least conscientious of your assistants. You are sorry that Bill volunteered because his crew on the day shift puts out no more work than it has to. The day crews of both men are similar and have been doing similar work. There is no difference between White's night crew and Black's night crew.

After the second shift has been under way for a while, you find out to your surprise that Bill Black's crew is doing a much better job than Joe White's crew. You ask why, and they tell you that they don't know and that they are handling their second-shift crews in the same manner as they handled their first-shift crews.

1. What are reasons why some workers prefer to work on the night shift rather than on the day shift?
2. What types of workers are better fitted for the night shift than for the day shift?
3. What kind of supervisors are able to do a better job on the night shift?
4. What are some of the advantages that the night shift has over the day shift?
5. What are some of the disadvantages?

CASE 10

Rapid expansion is making it necessary for you to hire more people. The group you will be adding to is made up of middle-aged women— mostly married—doing routine inspection work. They have little chance for advancement.

You have told the personnel department that you prefer workers of the middle-aged housewife type because they do a good job and get along well together. The personnel department informs you that this type of worker is hard to get at the present wage now that the canneries are expanding their operations in your community. The women plan to work at the canneries during the season and then stay home and collect their unemployment benefits. The type of labor available now is young girls fresh out of high school.

Several times in the past you have tried young girls on this job, and they did not work out well; they complained that the job was monotonous, that there were no chances for advancement, and that they did not like working with the older women.

1. How should you go about trying to solve the problem?
2. What technical assistance can the personnel department give you?

CASE 11

Your section consists of 15 men and 5 women doing substantially the same type of work under two new supervisors. When you were permitted to appoint these two supervisors, you chose two workers—one a man and one a woman—who had outstanding qualifications for the jobs. You put the man in charge of 10 men, and you put the woman in charge of the remaining 5 men and the 5 women.

The first few weeks under this arrangement were fine—morale and production were high. Lately you have been noticing that morale and production are off for the five men who are supervised by the woman, although the five women in her group are OK. You call two of these men to your office to find out the trouble. You gather from the way they talk that their pride is hurt because the men in the other group are making fun of them for working under the supervision of a woman.

You want to retain the woman as a supervisor, because there is no one else as well qualified. You cannot transfer the men over to the other group because it would overload the man supervisor and leave the woman supervisor with only five women to supervise—not enough to keep her busy.

1. What are the differences between the way men supervisors and women supervisors operate?

2. What is the difference between the way women respond to supervision by men, as over against supervision by women?
3. How do men react to supervision by women? Why do they react this way? Are they justified?
4. How are you going to solve the case?

CASE 12

You are the head of a production department in a large factory. Most of the jobs are repetitive machine operations on a piece rate. Most of your workers are typical factory workers—grammar or high school graduates—who live near the plant.

You are interviewing for a machine operator's job. The applicant is a Mr. Williams, formerly the manager of a local automobile agency, who had to quit his job on doctor's orders because he had had a nervous breakdown. Mr. Williams is middle aged and belongs to most of the local clubs. His application blank states that his hobby is making metal gadgets in his small basement workshop. He says that he has always liked to make things with his hands—he is happy doing manual work. His doctor thinks that a factory job would be good for him, and he believes so himself. He has an income so that the pay is not a major consideration. He just can't stand the inactivity around home; he has to get up and go to work each day.

In your plant it would be necessary for him to do repetitive work for a year before he could advance to a more interesting job. He tells you that he is sure he could get along with the group because he sold many of them cars in the past and they like him.

He looks like a man who would make a good supervisor.

1. What are his assets?
2. What are his liabilities?

CASE 13

You are in charge of a group of draftsmen, three of whom are detail draftsmen. The job description for a detail draftsman calls for a high school education or its equivalent. Of the three young men you have working on this job, one is a high school graduate, the second has had one year of college, and the third has a master's degree in foreign languages. All three were hired at the same time and at the same rate of pay.

After a few months on the job, the two men who were educated beyond the high school level showed restlessness, boredom, and dissatisfaction. The quality and quantity of their work, which at first was superior to that of the high school graduate, is now inferior.

Draftsmen are scarce, and you would like to retain these two men. You think that you could do this by changing the composition of some of the other jobs in the department and thus giving more complicated work and more pay to these two. This change would disturb the jobs of other men, and you are afraid that the plan would be unfair to them and to the high school graduate.

1. What are some of the advantages of modifying the content of jobs in order to have them fit more closely the capacities of the employees?
2. What are some of the disadvantages?
3. How should you handle the problem of people working substantially below their mental capacities?
4. How can the personnel department help you?

CASE 14

You are the supervisor of a section doing repetitive machine operations. The work is on an individual piece-rate basis. With a few exceptions, your workers are a tough crew, having limited schooling and not much job interest except to make as much money as possible on the days that they work. They make good money but spend it as fast as they make it. There is a great deal of Monday absenteeism caused by big weekends.

You would like to cut down on this absenteeism by introducing a better class of workers into your section. Several months ago you hired a young man who had just graduated from a technical high school. This is his first job, but he impressed you with his trade knowledge. You believe that his chances of getting ahead in the company are good if he is willing to take the knocks. You explained the whole situation to him during the interview.

You had Joe Smith, your oldest and best worker, break him in on the job. Smith reports to you that the youngster is having difficulty getting up to speed—always doing a better job than necessary, puttering around his machine adjusting it, instead of getting the work out slambang, as is necessary in order to make good money. Smith tells you that the young man is not adjusting well to the group. Also he says: "You're not doing the boy any good by putting him in with that gang of hoodlums."

This morning the youngster was late, and you ask him the reason. He tells you that he does not like the job. He says he is the only one in the group who understands the machines and can read blueprints, but the other fellows are making the money and they razz him.

1. Do you have any moral responsibilities to this youngster?
2. If you wish to retain him, how should you go about getting him adjusted?
3. How should you handle Monday absenteeism?

4. Should you try to change the composition of your gang? If so, how should you go about it?
5. How important are things other than getting the work out?

CASE 15

George Egan had been employed by the Link Chemical Company for three years. He was a high school graduate who came to Link with some previous business experience, but with none in the chemical industry. He was placed in the plant starting in simple jobs which he quickly learned. He evidenced a desire to learn as much as he could and this was soon noticed by Mr. Wilson, the small company's president. He encouraged Egan to acquire as many skills as possible and to familiarize himself with all jobs in the plant. Wilson then told Egan to take some technical courses at night which the company would pay for. Egan was grateful for this encouragement and he successfully completed the courses. Noting Egan's success with the technical courses, Mr. Wilson then informed him that he ought to study chemical engineering in the evening division of a nearby university. Egan did not feel that he could accomplish such a lofty goal, but when the president pressed him he felt that he would have to try since Mr. Wilson thought so much of his ability. After a year of evening study, Egan became convinced that chemical engineering was not for him. He had enjoyed the liberal arts courses and he was very interested in a course in personnel administration he had just started. Egan told Mr. Wilson of his lack of interest in chemical engineering and of his enthusiasm for liberal arts and personnel courses. While Mr. Wilson was disappointed and did not think liberal arts useful, he told Egan the company would continue to pay for his education. Because of Egan's apparent change of interests, Mr. Wilson made an appointment for him to be given a battery of tests by a local firm specializing in vocational testing. The test results indicated that Egan possessed above average intelligence and that while he could absorb engineering subjects, he could probably do much better with liberal arts and business subjects. The psychologist also pointed out that Egan did not desire to assume a leadership role, nor did he have any indicated ability, interest, or aptitude for such a role.

In the face of test results to the contrary, Mr. Wilson decided to promote Egan to the position of foreman in the plant where he would have direct responsibility for 10 employees. He told Mr. Burton, the plant manager, of his decision, mentioning that the company had a considerable investment in Egan and that it was about time they started to get a return on the investment. Mr. Burton disagreed with the decision, pointing to Egan's interests and the test results. He further mentioned that he had observed Egan's daily work carefully, and nothing in it indicated that he would be a good foreman. In addition, he stated that Egan had gained the reputation of being a fair-haired boy because of the president's close attention and that this would cause him trouble if he became a foreman. Mr. Wilson listened to Burton's arguments but he stressed his belief that Egan deserved the opportunity for increased compensation that being a foreman allowed and he expressed the opinion that test results were not always conclusive evidence of a man's ability to do a job. He told Burton to assist Egan in any way possible and ended the discussion.

Grumbling among Egan's employees started about a month after he became their boss. Burton discovered that Egan was a perfectionist and his employees could not satisfy his requirements. After two more months of smoothing ruffled waters and trying to coach Egan, Burton came to the conclusion that Egan had been given every opportunity to succeed as a foreman and had failed.

1. Was George Egan handled properly by the company president?
2. Should Egan have been promoted to recover an investment as the president put it?
3. To what extent, if any, could Egan's failure be attributed to Burton's disagreement with the president's decision?
4. Should an executive choose a so-called fair-haired boy, recognizing the awkward position in which this may place the person chosen?
5. Can the company do anything now to salvage the career of George Egan?

FOLLOWING UP ON THE JOB

Job requirements

1. Before considering a man for a job, do you always have clearly in mind what the job requires?
2. Do you have a clear picture of the type of man who would fit well into your team?
3. Are the jobs in your department designed with the thought of what people want from their jobs?

The application blank and the interview

1. What parts of the application form do you find most useful? Why?
2. Do you select items in the application form as a means of opening the discussion and putting the man at ease during the interview?
3. Do you plan in advance what you want to uncover during the interview?
4. Do you have any prejudices you have to guard against while considering an applicant?
5. Do you use the interview to get more information about items on the application blank?

6. Do you avoid overselling the job?
7. Do rejected applicants leave with a favorable impression of the department?
8. Do you talk too much during the interview?

The temporary or probationary employee

1. Is his work improving? Getting worse?
2. Is he being accepted by the group?
3. Does he learn easily?
4. Is he becoming careless?
5. Are his absences and tardiness becoming a problem?
6. Is he having accidents or near-accidents?
7. Is he beginning to loaf on the job?

Misfits

1. Are there any employees in your section working much above their mental abilities? Much below their mental abilities?
2. Are any of your workers complaining of monotony?
3. What types of workers are quitting?
4. Are you losing desirable employees? Why?
5. What types of workers are sticking to the job? Are they desirable employees?
6. Do you analyze your failures in fitting men and jobs?
7. Do you analyze your successes in fitting men and jobs?

Suggested readings

BOOKS

*For
Chapter:*

7, 8, 9   ANTHONY, ROBERT N., and HEKIMIAN, J. *Operations Cost Control.* Homewood, Ill.: Richard D. Irwin, Inc., 1967.

8, 9   BARNES, R. M. *Motion and Time Study: Design and Measurement of Work.* 6th ed. New York: John Wiley & Sons, Inc., 1968.

9   ———. *Work Sampling.* New York: John Wiley & Sons, Inc., 1956.

10   BASSETT, GLEN A. *Practical Interviewing.* New York: American Management Association, 1965.

7   BEER, STAFFORD. *Management Science.* Garden City, N.Y., Doubleday & Company, Inc., 1968.

7   BRANCH, MELVILLE C. *The Corporate Planning Process.* New York: American Management Association, 1962.

9, 10   BUFFA, ELWOOD S. *Modern Production Management.* 3d ed. New York: John Wiley & Sons, Inc., 1969.

8, 9, 10   BURGESS, LEONARD R. *Wage and Salary Administration in a Dynamic Economy.* New York: Harcourt, Brace & World, Inc., 1968.

7, 10   CHAPANIS, ALPHONSE. *Man-Machine Engineering.* Belmont, Calif.: Wadsworth Publishing Co., Inc., 1965.

7   CHURCHMAN, C. W.; ACKOFF, R. L.; and ARNOFF, E. L. *Introduction to Operations Research.* New York: John Wiley & Sons, Inc., 1957.

8   CLOSE, GUY C., JR. *Work Improvement.* New York: John Wiley & Sons, Inc., 1960.

9   DRUCKER, PETER F. *Managing for Results.* New York: Harper & Row, Publishers, 1964.

7   EWING, DAVID W. *The Practice of Planning.* New York: Harper & Row, Publishers, 1968.

10   FLEISHMAN, EDWIN A. (ed.). *Studies in Personnel and Industrial Psychology.* Rev. ed. Homewood, Ill.: The Dorsey Press, 1967.

8, 9, 10   GILMER, B. VON HALLMER. *Industrial Psychology.* 2d ed. New York: McGraw-Hill Book Co., 1961.

9   GOMBERG, WILLIAM.   *A Trade Union Analysis of Time Study.*
    2d ed. Englewood Cliffs, N.J.: Prentice-Hall, Inc., 1955.

7, 10   GOSLIN, LEWIS N.   *The Product Planning System.* Homewood,
    Ill.: Richard D. Irwin, Inc., 1967.

7   GREENE, JAMES H.   *Operations Planning Control.* Homewood,
    Ill.: Richard D. Irwin, Inc., 1967.

7, 10   HEYEL, CARL.   *Organizing Your Job in Management.* New
    York: American Management Association, 1960.

7, 10   JOHNSON, R. A.; KAST, F. E.; and ROSENZWEIG, J. E.   *The
    Theory and Management of Systems.* 2d ed. New York: Mc-
    Graw-Hill Book Co., 1967.

7   KING, DAVID I., and KING, WILLIAM S.   *Systems Analysis and
    Project Management.* New York: McGraw-Hill Book Co., 1968.

8, 9, 10   LANHAM, ELIZABETH.   *Administration of Wages and Salaries.*
    New York: Harper & Row, Publishers, 1963.

8, 10   LEHRER, ROBERT N.   *Work Simplification.* Englewood Cliffs,
    N.J.: Prentice-Hall, Inc., 1957.

7   LEVIN, RICHARD I., and KIRKPATRICK, CHARLES A.   *Planning
    and Control with PERT/CPM.* New York: McGraw-Hill Book
    Co., 1966.

7   ———.   *Quantitative Approaches to Management.* New York:
    McGraw-Hill Book Co., 1965.

10   LOPEZ, FELIX M., JR.   *Personnel Interviewing, Theory and
    Practice.* New York: McGraw-Hill Book Co., 1965.

9   McCONKEY, DALE D.   *How to Manage by Results.* Rev. ed.
    New York: American Management Association, 1968.

9   MAYNARD, H. B. (ed.).   *Industrial Engineering Handbook.* 2d
    ed. New York: McGraw-Hill Book Co., 1963.

9   ———; STEGEMERTEN, G. J.; and SCHWAB, J. L.   *Methods
    Time Measurement.* New York: McGraw-Hill Book Co., 1948.

7   MILLER, DAVID W., and STARR, MARTIN K.   *Executive Deci-
    sions and Operations Research.* 2d ed. Englewood Cliffs, N.J.:
    Prentice-Hall, Inc., 1969.

7   MORRIS, WILLIAM T.   *The Capacity Decision System.* Home-
    wood, Ill.: Richard D. Irwin, Inc., 1967.

7, 10   NADLER, GERALD.   *Work Systems Design: The Ideals Concept.*
    Homewood, Ill.: Richard D. Irwin, Inc., 1967.

9   ODIORNE, GEORGE S.   *Management by Objectives.* New York:
    Pitman Publishing Corp., 1965.

8, 9   PAYNE, BRUCE, and SWETT, D.   *Office Operations Improve-
    ment.* New York: American Management Association, 1967. ˙

8, 10   PFIFFNER, JOHN M.   *The Supervision of Personnel.* 3d ed.
    Englewood Cliffs, N.J.: Prentice-Hall, Inc., 1964.

7   St. Thomas, Charles E. *Practical Business Planning*. New York: American Management Association, 1965.

7   Schellenberger, Robert E. *Managerial Analysis*. Homewood, Ill.: Richard D. Irwin, Inc., 1969.

9   Schleh, E. C. *Management by Results*. New York: McGraw-Hill Book Co., 1961.

7   Schuchman, Abe. *Scientific Decision Making in Business*. New York: Holt, Rinehart & Winston, Inc., 1963.

7   Steiner, George A. *Top Management Planning*. New York: The Macmillan Co., 1969.

10   Strauss, George, and Sayles, Leonard R. *Personnel: The Human Problems of Management*. 2d ed. Englewood Cliffs, N.J.: Prentice-Hall, Inc., 1967.

7, 8, 9, 10   Sutermeister, Robert A. *People and Productivity*. New York: McGraw-Hill Book Co., 1963.

7, 8, 9   Timms, Howard L. *Introduction to Operations Management*. Homewood, Ill.: Richard D. Irwin, Inc., 1967.

ARTICLES

For
Chapter:

10   Bassett, Glenn A. "The Touch Job of Picking Winners," *Personnel*, September–October, 1963.

7   Cleland, David I. "Understanding Project Management," *Manage*, Vol. 19, No. 9 (1967).

10   Gomersall, Earl R., and Myers, M. Scott. "Breakthrough in On-the-Job Training," *Harvard Business Review*, Vol. 44, No. 4 July–August, 1966.

8, 9   Graves, Clare W. "Deterioration of Work Standards," *Harvard Business Review*, September–October, 1966.

8, 9, 10   Kaimann, Richard A. "Quality Control: The Man Not the Machine," *Management of Personnel Quarterly*, Winter, 1968.

7   Moore, Leo B. "Managerial Time," *Industrial Management Review*, Spring, 1968.

7   Quinn, James B. "Technological Forecasting," *Harvard Business Review*, March–April, 1967.

8, 9   Sirota, David. "Productivity Management," *Harvard Business Review*, September–October, 1966.

Part III

Developing the work team

11 Human relations

Early developments. The scientific management movement. Research in human relations. What kind of human relations? Too much human relations? Summary.

One of the many definitions of the function of management claims that it is the art of getting work accomplished through people. Even though there may be disagreement with this definition, any practicing manager knows that "people problems" usually dominate his workday and the successful solution of these problems have a considerable impact on his career.

Since the operation of any organization depends ultimately upon people, human nature should be taken into consideration in the design of jobs, the composition of work groups, the organization of work, the development of promotables, compensation, fringe benefits, and the style of leadership utilized by the supervisor.

Human beings have been trying to get along with each other since the beginning of time. The art and science of dealing with human behavior and organizations is, however, a relatively recent innovation. The study of human relations is the study of people at work. It seeks to answer questions about motivation, about things that people want from their jobs, their morale, and the ways they go about satisfying their needs. It studies differences in people, in the intensity of their wants, and in the ways they react to frustration and conflict. The study of human relations should help the supervisor develop a better understanding of the behavior of people and the effect that his own behavior has upon them.

Early developments

Everything accomplished by man has a history. His relationships with his fellow human beings in the workplace are no exception. The casual observer may look upon the American economy in wonderment or take it for granted. We use the products of its factories, do business with

389

its banks and insurance companies, avail ourselves of many offered services, and have a variety of relationships with a myriad of other organizations without giving much thought to their complexity. Rarely do we reflect on the varied knowledge, talents, and experience possessed by the individuals who are responsible for the success of these organizations. The fact that so many are successful is due in no small measure to the ability of diverse human beings to work together in organized activity toward the objectives established for the particular organization. To understand more fully the importance of effective human performance in the workplace, it is necessary to examine at least the important developments that have contributed to the present state of the art of human behavior in organizations.

The typical business at the beginning of this century was a relatively small operation utilizing few methods which are familiar today. Little attention was paid to management problems as we know them today. The factory and its growing need for machinery was preeminent in the minds of managers. One of the dominant characteristics of the era was the prevalence of the owner-manager. This individual was usually a self-made man who had personally started his own business and nursed its early growth. His thoughts were largely directed toward his machines and the processes they made possible. Men to run these machines were necessary but incidental. Though necessary, they were relatively easy to obtain, and the wages that had to be paid were the lowest possible for the maximum hours possible. There was little or no governmental regulation or interference from other outside agencies, so that the businessman was left to make his own rules. Among other things, this led to a work orientation with an emphasis on production. The newly discovered usefulness of machines and their dependability in turning out uniform products at relatively lower prices were of prime importance and interest to the manager. The resultant division of labor made it possible to hire people who had little of the artisan skill of their predecessor journeymen. The machine did the skillful operations, and the man became merely an extension of the machine.

The transfer of skill from man to machine had been developing in other countries for some time. Now it was rapidly taking hold in the United States. As in other countries, the attendant social and moral problems of this transfer were given scant attention here. The development was looked upon as an industrial one, and the social problems were not considered to be the concern of the entrepreneur. His efforts were directed toward production and profit. Because the community at large viewed industrial growth in this manner, these companies were left free to develop as they saw fit. Government generally felt that business should develop unhampered by regulation. The population was largely uneducated by today's standards, and there were little or no strong unions. Actually, economic and social pressures for growth were all on the side of any aspiring entrepreneur. The United States had a great potential waiting to be tapped by any diligent businessman. The Puritan philosophy of colonial times, which frowned on leisure and treated work and productive effort almost like a religion, created the framework for the industrial growth of this country.

The scientific management movement

It was in this climate of technological and social change taking place in the late 19th century that managers started to seek better ways to cope with the increasing complexities taking place in their enterprises. Quite naturally emphasis was placed on production efficiency but the human's contribution to this efficiency began to be recognized.

Frederick W. Taylor, frequently called "the father of scientific management," was one of the pioneers who recognized that the worker was as important to efficiency as the machine. In his early studies he found that it was the worker and not management that set the pace for production. The foreman may have given orders as to what was to be done but he didn't say how or at what speed. As a result each worker set his own pace and did the job as he saw fit, in many cases continuing poor methods that he acquired by observation of other workers. He initiated his motion studies at the Midvale Steel Company to determine the motions required for each job as well as the time required for each motion. Taylor felt that wages paid should have some relationship to the amount of work done. In this sense, Taylor is said to have rationalized production. But he saw his efforts as going beyond that goal. Believing that scientific management was not an efficiency device, a system of cost determination or just time and motion study, he felt that it involved a complete mental revolution on the part of both workers and management. Testifying before a congressional committee, he described this mental revolution as follows: "The great revolution that takes place in the mental attitude of the two parties under scientific management is that both sides take their eyes off of the division of the surplus as the all-important matter, and together turn their attention toward increasing the size of the surplus until this surplus becomes so large . . . that there is ample room for a large increase in wages for the workmen and an equally large increase in profits for the manufacturer."[1] He firmly believed that scientific management was not a collection of techniques to increase efficiency, but a philosophy of management and a way of thinking. He saw a mutuality of interests for workers and managers which would result in greater productivity and a more equitable dis-

---

[1] Frederick W. Taylor, *Scientific Management* (New York: Harper & Row, Publishers, 1947), pp. 29–30.

tribution of the economic results of this effort. Taylor's disciple, Henry Gantt, and the Gilbreths with their search for the "one best way" of doing a job also believed in the mutuality of interests of workers and managers. Lillian Gilbreth dealt with the applications of psychology to management in one of her early books and made the following claims for scientific management:

1. Physical improvement of workers (increased health, better color and general appearance).
2. Mental development (wider interest, deeper interest, increased mental capabilities).
3. Moral development (personal responsibility, responsibility for others, appreciation of standing, self-control, "squareness").
4. Contentment, brotherhood, and the "will to do." (These developments are natural consequences of item three—moral development.)[2]

It can be seen that even though the pioneers of scientific management considered increased productivity as a primary goal, they had the broader goals of society as a whole and its individual components, the worker, employer, the consumer, and business owner in mind as well. The mutuality of interests idea pervaded their thinking and they firmly believed that if scientific management was carried out properly this would result in a society with limited strife, benefiting all participants. While the pioneers were given credit for rationalizing production, they also contributed to the development of concepts of human relations.

Research in human relations

Much of the work of scientific management's pioneers took place before World War I. Many of the techniques were expanded after the war and they were refined particularly in the areas of time and motion study, wage determination, and cost analysis. Unfortunately the "mental revolution" aspects of scientific management never truly caught on in industry. In this sense the expectations the pioneers had for scientific management never were achieved. A combination of factors contributed to this failure. Many employers cut the piece rate when productivity went up thus destroying the incentive to work harder. Increasingly powerful labor unions and employees felt that increased individual productivity only meant fewer jobs. Time and motion studies frequently led to production speed up and many companies found that scientifically determined standards did not always lead to unlimited cooperation between employees and managers.

---

[2] Lillian M. Gilbreth, *The Psychology of Management* (New York: Sturgis and Walton Co., 1914), chap. 10.

Perhaps the principal reason for the failure of the "mental revolution" was the fact that the "economic man" did not exist. Financial needs are not always paramount in the mind of the worker. He might slow his pace to allow slower group members to keep up because his need for affiliation may dominate his thinking. On the other hand, he could be reluctant to be known as a "rate buster" and be derided by his fellow workers for exceeding the established rate for the job.

During the 1920's, attention turned away from the basically economic work motives emphasized by the developers of scientific management. Many writers of the period assumed that man did not like to perform work and money, therefore, would not motivate him. In many companies there were attempts to develop noneconomic fringe benefits to satisfy employee desires for recognition and security. Probably the most significant event of the 1920's was the start of the Hawthorne studies since many people believe that this was the modern beginning of the human relations movement.

The Harvard studies at Hawthorne. The most famous study of people at work was directed by Elton Mayo and a group from Harvard in the period between 1927 and 1932. The study was made at the Hawthorne (Chicago) works of the Western Electric Company and yielded a vast amount of information about workers' unfavorable attitudes toward management, about informal social organization, and about the restriction of output under an incentive plan.

The publication of the research[3] drew attention to the importance of friendly supervision, to the workers' need for association, acceptance, security, and stability in his work group, and to the disruptive effects of technological change upon his work relationships. The studies attacked the concept that the worker was an "economic man"—a person whose cooperation could be bought or whose hand could be hired and whose only concern would be to maximize his earnings. The employees interviewed at Hawthorne held down their output and earnings for reasons that involved emotion more than logic.

The Hawthorne research emphasized the group—the informal social organization—as a prime factor in motivation. Mayo theorized that man has a basic need for affiliation—a theory that has come in for questioning in later studies.

Perhaps the most significant findings were those that disrupted some of the traditional management thinking of the day and pointed the way

---

[3] F. J. Roethlisberger and W. J. Dickson, *Management and the Worker* (Cambridge, Mass.: Harvard University Press, 1939). An evaluation of the research was made 25 years later by Henry A. Lansberger, *Hawthorne Revisited* (New York School of Industrial and Labor Relations at Cornell University, 1958). The experiments are reported and evaluated in a number of books including Morris S. Viteles, *Motivation and Morale in Industry* (New York: W. W. Norton & Co., Inc., 1953).

for later study, much of which is still going on today. The formal organization structure was shown to be merely a charting of functional relationships. The organization was really a social system made up of many
small groups with their own status systems, many emotional factors,
rumors, grapevine, and a series of complex interrelationships. Mayo dis-
counted the "rabble thesis" which implied that workers in an organization were a disorganized rabble of individuals all working in their own
self-interest in as logical a manner as possible. Rather, he found that
work was a group activity and the employee placed a great deal of
importance on his relationship with the work group. The impact of
this finding is brought forth when we consider that much of present-day
human relations research centers on the work group. The findings on
morale and productivity did much to change management thinking and
resulted in greater attention to nonfinancial incentives as part of the
reward system for employees.

The Michigan studies.   The Institute for Social Research at the University of Michigan has carried on studies on work groups since about
1947.[4] These studies focus on the attitudes and behavior of first-line
supervisors and the effects these have on productivity and attitudes
of subordinates. The researchers found that in many cases the high-
producing supervisor: (1) spent more time in supervision than he did
in doing the same work as his subordinates; (2) practiced general supervision rather than close supervision, delegated authority to subordinates,
and was himself under a boss who delegated authority; (3) was employee-centered rather than production-centered; (4) supervised a group
in which people got along well together and helped one another.

An employee-centered supervisor was defined as one who established
good personal relationships with his subordinates and put the emphasis
on creating positive employee motivation. The production-centered
supervisor was one who put the pressure on for production and was
apt to supervise closely and be autocratic. Further studies revised the
concept of employee-centeredness to show that there must be concern
for production along with concern for people; just being popular isn't
enough to make a supervisor effective.

A study by Morse and Reimer at Prudential Insurance Company
in 1956 indicated that production-centered supervision could get faster
cost-cutting results. In a year's time there was a 25 percent increase
in productivity in the tightly controlled autocratically led sections and
a 20 percent increase in the groups supervised through participative
methods and general supervision. However, morale suffered in the autocratic sections; good employees began to leave the company, and the

---

[4] The Michigan studies are summarized by the Director of the Institute for
Social Research, Rensis Likert, *New Patterns of Management* (New York: McGraw-
Hill Book Co., 1961).

employees developed unfavorable attitudes toward the high producers in their group.

Rensis Likert's studies have developed a model for work groups. In his book, *New Patterns of Management*, he states it in this way:

The following description of the ideal model defines what we mean by *a highly effective group*. The definition involves reference to several different variables. Each of them can be thought of as a continuum, i.e., as a characteristic which can vary from low to high, from unfavorable to favorable. For example, a group can vary from one in which there is hostility among the members to one in which the attitudes are warm and friendly. The ideal model is at the favorable end of each variable.

The highly effective group, as we shall define it, is always conceived as being part of a larger organization. A substantial proportion of persons in a company are members of more than one work group, especially when both line and staff are considered. As a consequence, in such groups there are always linking functions to be performed and relationships to other groups to be maintained. Our highly effective group is not an isolated entity.

All the persons in a company also belong to groups and organizations outside of the company. For most persons, membership in several groups both within and outside the company is the rule rather than the exception. This means, of course, that no single group, even the highly effective work group, dominates the life of any member. Each member of the organization feels pressures from membership in several different groups and is not influenced solely by loyalty to any one group.

Since the different groups to which a person belongs are apt to have somewhat different and often inconsistent goals and values, corresponding conflicts and pressures are created within him. To minimize these conflicts and tensions, the individual seeks to influence the values and goals of each of the different groups to which he belongs and which are important to him so as to minimize the inconsistencies and conflicts in values and goals. In striving for this reconciliation, he is likely to press for the acceptance of those values most important to him.[5]

Likert then lists and describes 24 characteristics ending with the leader and his selection. Supportive relationships are given particular emphasis and the influence of the leader by virtue of his position in the organizational hierarchy is deemphasized. Likert feels that a leader who depends on his rank for maintaining group effectiveness is acting ineffectively and that he should minimize status factors between himself and the group by using a variety of ways.

Listening well and patiently.

Not being impatient with the progress being made by the group, particularly on difficult problems.

Accepting more blame than may be warranted for any failure or mistake.

---

[5] Likert, *ibid.*, p. 165.

Giving the group members ample opportunity to express their thoughts without being constrained by the leader pressing his own views.

Being careful never to impose a decision on the group.

Putting his contributions often in the form of questions or stating them speculatively.

Arranging for others to help perform leadership functions which enhance their status.[6]

Remember Likert called this an *ideal* model. Nevertheless, it would call for an unusual person to assume responsibility in the above manner and would, for that matter, call for an unusual work group. The pressures that inevitably evolve in any complex organization would make it rather difficult for the supervisor to consistently act in the manner prescribed in the above list. In some work groups, members would resent performing leadership functions, feeling it was not their responsibility. The imposition of decisions on a group is frequently out of the individual supervisor's hands. He may have a decision imposed by higher authority with no alternative but to carry it out. Obviously an entire organization would have to adhere to the ideal model and perhaps this is too much to expect from the leadership selection process, the availability of talented managers, and the vagaries of human nature.

Vroom's studies of participation.   Victor H. Vroom and Floyd C. Mann made studies in a trucking company[7] and found that employees who worked in small closely knit groups preferred employee-centered supervisors. But truck drivers and dispatchers, who worked alone or at least out of direct contact with each other, preferred authoritarian supervision.

In a further study—this time of first-, second-, and third-line supervisors at United Parcel Service—Vroom found a correlation between personality and the type of supervision preferred. The "independent" supervisors were happier and more productive under democratic supervision. But the "dependent" supervisors were indifferent to opportunities for participation in decision making.

Studies at General Electric.   Studies of supervisory styles at one of General Electric Company's turbine and generator plants classified 90 foremen as either "democratic," "authoritarian," or "mixed." A canvass of preferences of 300 subordinates showed that the majority preferred democratic supervision. But those workers who preferred authoritarian supervision had higher morale than any of the others. Perhaps this was because they were the ones getting what they wanted in supervision since democratic supervisors were in short supply in proportion to the number of employees desiring them.

---

[6] Likert, *ibid.*, p. 171.

[7] Victor H. Vroom and Floyd C. Mann, "Leader Authoritarianism and Employee Attitudes," *Personnel Psychology*, Summer, 1960.

The lowest morale in the plant was found among those men whose foremen were rated as in between the democratic and authoritarian extremes. These foremen may have been inconsistent in their behavior, permissive one time and dictatorial the next, so that their subordinates didn't know what to expect.[8]

Theory "X" and Theory "Y." No discussion of human relations would be complete without consideration of the work of Douglas McGregor. Believing that any managerial act rests on some theoretical assumption, the way in which a manager implements these theoretical assumptions is the key to the development of sound human relationships in the workplace. Human relations courses may make the manager aware of participative approaches to management and he may even answer questions on human relations quizzes in the so-called correct way but he may practice human relations on the job in quite a different manner. Essentially, McGregor was concerned with the superficiality of human relations approaches. Manager attitudes loomed large in the implementation of any human relations program in the workplace and McGregor felt that even though a manager might be aware of human relations concepts he more frequently was dominated by traditional autocratic concepts in his practice of management. He characterized this traditional view of direction and control as "Theory X" and described it as follows:

1. The average human being has an inherent dislike of work and will avoid it when he can.
2. Because of this human characteristic of dislike of work, most people must be coerced, controlled, directed, threatened with punishment to get them to put forth adequate effort toward the achievement of organizational objectives.
3. The average human being prefers to be directed, wishes to avoid responsibility, has relatively little ambition, wants security above all.

. . . Theory X is not a straw man for the purposes of demolition, but is in fact a theory which materially influences managerial strategy in a wide sector of American industry today. Moreover, the principles of organization which comprise the bulk of the literature of management *could only have been derived from assumptions such as those of Theory X.* Other beliefs about human nature would have led inevitably to quite different organizational principles. Theory X provides an explanation of some human behavior in industry.[9]

In contrast to the above approach to management, McGregor felt that many modifications in the utilization of human beings in the work-

[8] General Electric Company, *Leadership Style and Employee Morale* (Public and Employee Relations Services) (New York, 1958).

[9] Douglas McGregor, *The Human Side of Enterprise* (New York: McGraw-Hill Book Co., 1960), pp. 33–35.

place had occurred over the years. Many managements were deeply concerned with the human equation in their organizations and this was evidenced by the great number of personnel policies and procedures and fringe benefit programs developed and implemented by these organizations. Nevertheless, he believed that many of these developments had been accomplished without changes in the traditional theories of management. Changes in society caused by increased union power and social legislation gave impetus to greater emphasis on human relations. This tended to change authoritarian techniques to the "keep them happy" approach to human relations which still was quite paternalistic and certainly superficial. The work going on in the study of human behavior by social scientists gave him the backdrop for a new set of assumptions about the management of human beings. He called these "Theory Y" and they are as follows:

1. *The expenditure of physical and mental effort in work is as natural as play or rest.* The average human being does not inherently dislike work. Depending upon controllable conditions, work may be a source of satisfaction (and will be voluntarily performed) or a source of punishment (and will be avoided if possible).
2. *External control and the threat of punishment are not the only means for bringing about effort toward organizational objectives. Man will exercise self-direction and self-control in the service of objectives to which he is committed.*
3. *Commitment to objectives is a function of the rewards associated with their achievement.* The most significant of such rewards, e.g., the satisfaction of ego and self-actualization needs, can be direct products of effort directed toward organizational objectives.
4. *The average human being learns, under proper conditions, not only to accept but to seek responsibility.* Avoidance of responsibility, lack of ambition, and emphasis on security are generally consequences of experience, not inherent human characteristics.
5. *The capacity to exercise a relatively high degree of imagination, ingenuity, and creativity in the solution of organizational problems is widely, not narrowly, distributed in the population.*
6. *Under the conditions of modern industrial life, the intellectual potentialities of the average human being are only partially utilized.*[10]

McGregor then goes on to further analyze his Theory Y assumptions and contrasts them to the Theory X assumptions described earlier.

These assumptions involve sharply different implications for managerial strategy than do those of Theory X. They are dynamic rather than static: They indicate the possibility of human growth and development; they stress the necessity for selective adaptation rather than for a single absolute form

---

[10] McGregor, *ibid.*, pp. 47–48.

of control. They are not framed in terms of the least common denominator of the factory hand, but in terms of a resource which has substantial potentialities.

Above all, the assumptions of Theory Y point up the fact that the limits on human collaboration in the organizational setting are not the limits of human nature but of management's ingenuity in discovering how to realize the potential represented by its human resources. Theory X offers management an easy rationalization for ineffective organizational performance: It is due to the nature of the human resources with which we must work. Theory Y, on the other hand, places the problems squarely in the lap of management. If the employees are lazy, indifferent, unwilling to take responsibility, intransigent, uncreative, uncooperative, Theory Y implies that the causes lie in management's methods of organization and control.

The assumptions of Theory Y are not finally validated. Nevertheless, they are far more consistent with existing knowledge in the social sciences than are the assumptions of Theory X. They will undoubtedly be refined, elaborated, modified as further research accumulates, but they are unlikely to be completely contradicted.

On the surface, these assumptions may not seem particularly difficult to accept. Carrying their implications into practice, however, is not easy. They challenge a number of deeply ingrained managerial habits of thought and action.[11]

McGregor's prediction for acceptance of Theory Y have been largely borne out by later research and by actual developments in industry. Considerable emphasis has been given to attempts to change managerial attitudes. This is a recognition that managerial practices that have been long-established are difficult to modify. Theory Y assumptions have been considered controversial and still are by many present-day managers. Likewise, the attempts to change traditional managerial behavior patterns are also highly controversial. Among the most controversial is sensitivity training or "T-Groups," an approach which is supposed to help modify the participant's behavior.

Sensitivity training. This type of training started at Bethel, Maine, in the late 1940's. It was influenced by the ideas of group dynamics as developed by Kurt Lewin, a German psychologist. Called the National Training Laboratory, its work still goes on. Sensitivity training is probably the most talked about method of behavior change. Participants both strongly praise it and denounce it. For many it is a frustrating experience while others find it challenging and rewarding. Essentially it is small-group interaction under stress conditions which requires the participants to become sensitive to one another's feelings, to develop group activity, and to learn more about how their individual personalities affect other people.

---

[11] McGregor, *ibid.*, pp. 48–49.

They are encouraged to develop greater self-perception by a group leader who is largely nondirective. The group efforts are quite unstructured and this is what creates the stress and pressure among the participants. Presumably the participants begin to understand how a group interacts and to develop skills in working with others.

Initially sensitivity training emphasized the individual, attempting to induce changes in his behavior so that he could respond more effectively to human problems. More recently it has focused on both the individual and the social system of the work group. The assumption here is that if the individual is to successfully modify his behavior, he must have an environment which rewards this new behavior. In a recent book, Warren G. Bennis describes how T-Groups are presently used in organizations:

Stranger labs. Executives from organizations attend labs as "delegates" representing their organizations. The parent organization hopes to improve the organization this way by "seeding" a sufficient number of managers.

Cousin labs. Organizations set up labs for individuals with similar organizational ranks but from different functional groups, e.g., all first-line supervisors or all general foremen.

Diagonal slices. T-groups are composed of members from the same company but of different ranks and from different departments. No man is in the same group with anyone from his own work group.

Family or functional groups. These groups are identical to the intact group as indicated by the formal organization; e.g., a particular supervisor would be with his work group.[12]

It becomes obvious that one of the most controversial aspects of sensitivity training is the composition of the group to undergo the training. When people from the same company are group members some feel that their futures are inhibited by their reactions during the laboratory sessions. Other detractors of this type of training claim that people who are somewhat emotionally disturbed but functioning effectively on the job may very well suffer acute emotional consequences from exposure to a T-group. While many companies have and still are using this training, some have ceased using it and many others are reluctant to start because of its controversial nature.

The managerial grid. In an attempt to reach a compromise between scientific management and the human relations school, Blake and

---

[12] Warren G. Bennis, *Changing Organizations* (New York: McGraw-Hill Book Co., 1966), pp. 120–21. For more information on sensitivity training, see C. Argyris, *Interpersonal Competence and Organizational Effectiveness* (Homewood, Ill.: Richard D. Irwin, Inc., 1962); L. P. Bradford, J. R. Gibb, and K. D. Benne, *T-Group Theory and Laboratory Method* (New York: John Wiley & Sons, Inc., 1964); and Alfred J. Marrow, *Behind the Executive Mask* (New York: American Management Association, 1964).

Mouton have developed what they call "integrated management" (see Figure 11–1). They have shown that the most effective managers are neither "production" (scientific management) oriented nor "people" (human relations) oriented. Grid sessions are conducted which are some-

FIGURE 11–1
The Management Grid

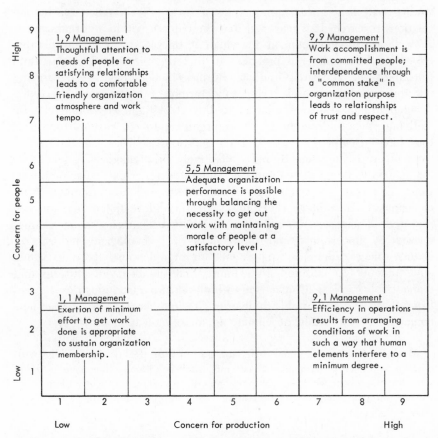

From: R. R. Blake, J. S. Mouton, L. B. Barnes, and L. E. Greiner, "Breakthrough in Organization Development," *Harvard Business Review*, Vol. 42, No. 6 (1964), p. 136. For a more thorough development of this concept, see R. R. Blake and J. S. Mouton, *The Managerial Grid* (Houston, Tex.: Gulf Publishing Co., 1964).

what similar to sensitivity training except they are more structured and directive and there is less personal criticism of the participants. The managers are induced to move toward a 9–9 type of management which shows what they call "team management" evidencing a maximum concern for people and a maximum concern for production. Best results have been achieved when both peers and superiors support the behavioral changes necessary to achieve 9–9 management. Perhaps the most desirable aspect of this approach is that it provides a useful communications device and a framework for behavioral issues. The relatively intangible ideas of organizational climate are made tangible by assigning a concrete numerical evaluation on the grid scale.

Organizational climate or environment. Recent research has stressed the organization as a social system. To a certain extent, the Hawthorne studies established this approach as a frame of reference for human relations research. It is reasoned that the climate within an organization, as well as the environment in which it operates, has a considerable effect on the managerial practices in that organization. Lawrence and Lorsch of the Harvard Graduate Business School have been carrying out this type of research trying to determine how to more effectively develop organizations in relation to their tasks and environment.[13] By studying several different types of organizations in various industries they have attempted to answer such questions as: How can the overall tasks of an organization be more effectively subdivided? What methods for achieving integration should be suggested for a particular organization? What control systems and reward systems will aid in the motivation of managers to achieve the integrated and differentiated performance required? Their research indicates that industrial environments characterized by uncertainty and rapid rates of technological and market change place different requirements on organizations than do stable environments. In addition, they found that the behavior patterns and managerial practices of managers in high-performance industries differed from those in more stable industries. Two other Harvard researchers comment on the study of climate in an organization as follows:

When students of human behavior attempt to deal systematically with environmental or situational determinants, such as climate, they soon discover some of the obstacles to developing general solutions to the problem. . . . Certain difficulties are especially common and stubborn. Particularly important among these are:

    a)   distinguishing between the objective and subjective environment;
    b)   distinguishing between the person and the situation;
    c)   determining what aspects of the environment need to be specified;
    d)   identifying the structures and dynamics of the environment.[14]

---

[13] Paul R. Lawrence and Jay W. Lorsch, *Organization and Environment* (Boston: Division of Research, Harvard University Graduate School of Business Administration, 1967).

[14] R. Tagiuri and G. H. Litwin, *Organizational Climate* (Boston: Division of Research, Graduate School of Business Administration, Harvard University, 1968), pp. 12–13.

What kind of human relations?

The Michigan studies indicate that a great many groups perform well under a supervisor who is friendly, approachable, available, and helpful—one whose supportive relationship builds the employees' sense of personal worth and importance. In getting high performance from his group, such a supervisor builds good attitudes through his own attitude—which enables him to practice good technical management without arousing hostility. Rather than putting pressure on from the top, he acts as a yeast, generating confidence, responsibility, and cooperation in working toward goals. He trusts his subordinates and gives them leeway to do their work without close supervision. His type of supervisory behavior is classified as general supervision. His type of leadership is described as democratic or participative.

The Michigan research team found much to support their premise that this was the most effective pattern of supervisory behavior. The researchers also discovered many situations in which these findings did not fit.

Other research groups[15] have sought to identify the conditions that influence the effectiveness of the supervisor's behavior. A supervisor may find democratic methods unprofitable if his own boss is autocratic, the company climate unfavorable, or the subordinates hostile. Some types of work may be unsuited to democratic human relations. Some subordinates may be overdependent and may expect and prefer autocratic behavior from the boss. Perhaps the supervisor should be selected to fit the existing human relations climate if the company has no intentions of changing it. On the other hand, the adaptable supervisor can accommodate himself to the existing situation and make gradual improvements designed to raise the level of motivation and morale.

There is evidence to demonstrate that each organization has different requirements because of environmental considerations. Because of this it is necessary to treat each organization individually and try to design a human relations approach designed to fit the situation. Recognizing the organization as a social system is of considerable importance. The formal structure may establish the formal relationships and the levels of the hierarchy but people in the organization have their own motives, abilities, likes, and dislikes and they develop many informal relationships within the formal structure. In daily contacts they form ways of working together that are different from the ways provided by the formal organization. They establish short cuts and do favors for one another. They

---

[15] For a comprehensive summary of research in human relations, see James G. March (ed.), *Handbook of Organization* (Chicago: Rand McNally & Co., 1965).

work more closely with some people than with others, and they build up loyalties toward some and antagonisms and hostilities toward others. People who give and receive help become bound together by shared work experiences and attitudes. They build detours around people they dislike and around inadequate bosses. They step up to fill weak spots in the management structure of procedures and are accorded respect for their unofficial positions.

These complex relationships that form between people and groups around the job are known as the informal social organization or, more simply, as the informal organization. Some groups are large and some are small. Some follow the lines of the organization structure, and some groups are within others or overlapping others. There are the friendship groups—tight little cliques of people who chum together off the job and on. The people in them are attracted to one another by some common ground of religion or nationality, education or culture, age or marital status. The friendship clique forms a strong bond that holds the worker to the job, and forms a tight little circle from which others can be excluded.

There are interest groups—occupational groups maneuvering for advantages and jockeying for power against other occupational groups in the total organization. The interest group puts pressure on the union and on management to get adjustment of its grievances and action on its demands.

The most essential factor when considering human relationships in organizations is the avoidance of superficiality. Any executive who believes that a short course on human relations or the reading of a few books will have a lasting effect on his behavior is deluding himself. Companies that expect miracles from human relations training programs or send to them people who should be fired, are not really coping with the deeper meaning of human relations. In an article on human relations and the nature of man, Knowles and Saxberg conclude:

> The quality of human relations in any organization, from the political state to the business enterprise, reflects first of all its members', and particularly its leaders', views of the essential character of humanity itself. It makes a great deal of difference in systems of social control whether those involved tend to view man, in general, as good or evil. If we assume that man is good, we can believe that misbehavior is a reactive response rather than a manifestation of character. This will lead to a search for causes in his experience rather than in his nature. If we are to find a cause for behavioral failure, we are more apt to look outside the offender than inside and thus consider a whole new range of variables and contributory circumstances.
>
> If, on the other hand, we assume that man himself is bad, a priori, then we are prone to assume that misbehavior is caused by something within him which we cannot alter directly. Accordingly, our attention will focus

on limiting his freedom to choose and to act through external curbs and controls. In limiting the causes of behavior, we exclude ourselves from powerful internal sources of control.

Thus the underlying human value which predominates is readily perceived in (*a*) the way social relationships are structured, (*b*) the kinds of rewards and penalties that are used, (*c*) the character of the communication process which links people together, and (*d*) the other elements of social control that characterize a relationship or an organization.[16]

Too much human relations?

There are management people who say that human relations in business and industry has been carried too far—that it is a softness toward employees which stands in the way of getting the job done, that it gets in the way of changes and improvements which might upset people. Human relations is said to let employees shuck off their responsibilities and find excuses for failure. It is accused of being a cult that would keep the inefficient on the payroll rather than support them on the tax roll.

Some complain because the practice of human relations has limited itself to being a matter of communications—getting employees to *see* things or maybe even manipulating them to make decisions. Some concede that human relations in the form of participation in decision making is necessary in the motivation of managers and of professional personnel but scarcely applicable to people in routine jobs, where it would call for a redistribution of power in an organization.

One of the most critical articles on human relations was written by Malcolm McNair for the *Harvard Business Review*.[17] He believed that far too much emphasis was being given to human relations courses in both business schools and in industry. He felt that too much preoccupation with people caused executives to lose sight of their jobs and the results they were supposed to achieve. He did not believe that human relations concepts were wrong but that they were treated too superficially and that a cynical view could be developed which could lead to the belief that the study of human relations is designed to develop skill in the manipulation of people to achieve goals.

More recently several writers have taken a critical approach to participative and democratic styles of management. Emphasis has been placed on the fact that participation does not work in all circumstances. It is entirely possible that autocratic methods may be necessary in certain situations and that some supervisors and some groups cannot function

---

[16] H. P. Knowles and B. O. Saxberg, "Human Relations and the Nature of Man," *Harvard Business Review*, Vol. 45, No. 2 (March–April, 1967), p. 178.

[17] Malcolm P. McNair, "Thinking Ahead: What Price Human Relations?" *Harvard Business Review*, Vol. 35, No. 2 (March–April, 1957), pp. 15–23.

effectively under democratic management. It is difficult to generalize about all managers and all organizations and it, therefore, may be necessary to take a highly individualized approach toward the determination of what makes for successful human relationships in a particular organization.

Any consideration of the problems of human relations must take into account the fact that a business does not exist for the purpose of providing jobs and job satisfaction. The problem of using people most effectively is one of finding ways to make them most productive in the long run. The present ways of utilizing people may be getting the most output per hour but not the most per year—or per 30 years of a man's employment. Prevailing theories and practices of management have grown up around the concept that the machine and the system must be the constant factors in production, and the man the variable one. Man has been expected to change his nature and adjust himself—and be adjusted to—the system. If he does not fit very well, he has to be influenced to be cooperative and productive.

The answer to the problem may be discovered in the kind of studies that put astronauts on the moon. In such studies, man's abilities and limitations are determined and then become the constant factor around which the machine and the system are designed. There is no question of throwing out scientific methods or abandoning a quest for utmost efficiency. The human factor is simply recognized and incorporated into the design in the way that will yield the highest efficiency. The ingenuity of these designs gives reason for belief that research and experiment will find better ways of fitting the organization of work to the human qualities of workers. The insights gained in studies of people can be put to use in the study of the organization of their work and the design of their jobs.

To the question: Is there too much human relations? the answer may be that there has been too little of it in the vital area of the relation of a man to his work.

Summary

Managers find that human relations problems occupy much of their time and the successful solution of these problems may have considerable impact on a manager's career. The development of a philosophy of human relations has to consider the contributions of scientific management and traditional approaches to supervision as well as more recently emphasized participative concepts. The Hawthorne studies contributed much to present-day thinking in the field of human relations, particularly the idea that an organization is a social system. In order to build an effective work team, the supervisor must arrange the flow of work, the

design of jobs, and the assignment of people so that the work fits the
status system of the group.

The Michigan studies indicate that many groups become very effective under a supportive supervisor who is friendly and a willing listener.
Theory X supervision using traditional methods has developed from
management theory. It gives management a rationale for the use of
autocratic concepts even though they may subscribe to human relations
concepts. Theory Y assumptions are based on social science knowledge
and could be effective in organizations if they are given a chance. Because they challenge a number of ingrained managerial habits, many
managers find it difficult to accept them.

Attempts have been made to change managerial behavior by the
use of sensitivity training and managerial grid sessions. While these
work in some instances, many companies find that such training methods
are highly controversial and are reluctant to use them. Current research
seems to be emphasizing organizational climate and environment and
is developing a highly individualistic approach to human relations in
a particular organization. Widely accepted is the idea that each organization has a particular climate and its managerial style should be
developed with that in mind.

There are many detractors particularly toward the superficiality of
the human relations approach which tries to imply that a short course
will allow for the development of skills in the manipulation of people.

CASE 1

You are in charge of a punch press section. The workers are on
piece rates and making out quite well. You are very conscientious and
want to get maximum production; you post the output of each man
twice daily, so that everyone can see where he stands. You see to it
that your workers are supplied with everything they need to keep going.
As soon as production is halted on any press, you find out the cause
and get things going again as soon as possible. You and your whole
section are businesslike.

The section next to yours, doing similar punch press work also on
a piece-rate basis, appears to be run in a leisurely and careless manner.
The foreman has no dignity and kids around with the operators. His
scrap is somewhat higher than yours, but his accident and absentee
rates are substantially lower. At the end of the day he and his workers
look fresh, while you and yours are exhausted. Finally, the production
rate of his department is better than that of yours.

You would like to run your department like his, but you are afraid
that you are not that type of person. You are reserved by nature and—try
as you may—you have difficulty being one of the boys.

1. What might be some reasons why your group is fatigued?
2. What are some of the work tensions that increase fatigue?
3. How can they be reduced?
4. What might be some of the factors promoting favorable conditions in the other section?
5. Can a "reserved" foreman develop them?
6. To what extent should a foreman be one of the boys?

CASE 2

You have working for you in your section two assistant supervisors who never could get along together, even when they were part of the rank and file. You have never been able to get at the basis of the difficulty and have decided that it is a personality clash.

Each of these assistant supervisors is setting himself and his group against the other. This is resulting in keen competition and high production, which is desirable; but, on the other hand, your section is divided into two hostile camps.

1. Should you allow this condition to continue? Why? Why not?
2. What might be some of the undesirable results if this condition grows?
3. How should you take care of personality clashes?
4. How might you correct the above situation?

CASE 3

The temperature is a problem in your department. You have young girls in their wool sweaters and suits who want the windows open. You would like them open too but if you side with the fresh-air group, you offend the other employees who are bothered by drafts and who get coughs and colds. Even when the sweater girls wear lightweight clothes, they complain that the office is stuffy and uncomfortably hot. They race to the windows every morning to get them open. Pretty soon the cold-blooded ones stomp over to bang them shut. Some hostility has developed between individuals over the opening and shutting of windows.

In the summertime there is trouble about the fans. Some of the employees claim they can't stand the heat unless the fans are running. Others get colds, stiff necks, and even more serious ailments from having the fans blow on them. Some of the women get tearful about the lack of consideration for their health.

You asked the plant engineer for help on the ventilation problem, and he says the only solution is air conditioning and that the company won't spend money for it.

1. What are some workable methods to get a compromise between the hot-blooded and cold-blooded people who have to work in the same room?
2. Should you leave this problem to the group or should you get involved in its solution?
3. Is it possible that the arguments are caused by reasons other than the temperature in the department?

CASE 4

A technician had been temporarily hired by the company to help with a special project that the electronic data processing section was developing. He was researching various programs and was given access to all of the equipment. The key punch machines and print-out machines along with other related equipment were located in a soundproof room separated from the rest of the office so that the noise level would not disturb other employees.

One day the technician was waiting for a print-out of some data and he happened to notice several speakers attached to the wall at various places just below the ceiling. He walked over to one of them, saw a volume control knob and turned it up. Music poured forth and the technician wondered why none of the speakers were turned on since the music was very pleasant. His answer came in very short order when one of the employees told him to turn off the speaker. The request was so vehement that the technician questioned the employee about his very negative reaction to the music. The employee replied, "We have to listen to the noise in here, we don't have to listen to the music."

1. How can you account for the negative reaction to the piped-in music?
2. Should the employees have been asked if they wanted music before it was installed?
3. To what extent did the isolation of these employees contribute to their attitude about the music?
4. What can management do to offset this attitude recognizing the fact that the noise level of the machines requires isolation from the rest of the office?

CASE 5

You are head of a section of workers assembling machines similar to large washing machines. As the work was previously set up, there was a heavy casting to be lifted onto a table, parts to be fitted, electrical connections to be made, some minor adjustments to be made, and finally the power was turned on and the machine run for a few minutes before it was ready for inspection. Three or four men worked as a group on the assembly of each machine. Their equipment, tools, and parts were spread around, and everything was rather unhandy. There was a fair amount of complaining about the need for lifting, some conflicts between the men as to who should do what, and a certain amount of buck-passing when the machine would not operate well while being tested. On the whole, though, they clicked and formed a good team and got the work out well. Morale was high.

You turned the whole problem over to the methods department, and they worked out a new system for you: a belt moved the main casting through the department, thus eliminating lifting; the workplaces were arranged so that tools and parts were accessible at the spot needed; the design was changed so that the tryout test was no longer made. Each worker had a specialized task to accomplish on the piece as it moved down the line. There was no need to interfere with each other, and the machine pace was not too fast.

Production increased at first, but now it is falling off. Several workers are asking for transfers. When you question them, they tell you that they don't like working on a line. You point out all the improvements, and they agree that you are correct and they see that the new way is more productive, but they say that they prefer the old way.

1. What were the relationships between the men in the old situation?
2. What are the relationships between the men in the new situation?
3. What was the relationship between the men and their jobs under the old situation?
4. What is the relationship between the men and their jobs under the new situation?
5. Why did production increase at first under the new setup?
6. Why did it fall off later?
7. What are some of the factors that have to be taken into consideration in making a change like this?
8. How should such a change have been introduced?

CASE 6

You try to distribute the work as fairly as possible according to the skills of the various workers in your department. Joe Doe, one of your better employees, is resentful whenever you assign another man an interesting or challenging job. He sulks, and the quality of his work suffers. He tells the other workers that you are playing favorites and that he is prevented from getting ahead.

1. What factors should you take into consideration when you distribute work?
2. What might be some of the causes of Joe's behavior?
3. How should you handle Joe?

CASE 7

Jim Jones has been in his present job for the past five years. He is an average worker doing an average job. During the five years he has received raises to the extent that he is now near the top of his rate range. Other workers having less seniority than he are now getting the same rate that he is, and a few of them—the more promising ones—are at the top of their rate range. Jim Jones is disgruntled because it is now a year and a half since he received a raise. His morale and his production have been on a slow decline. You don't think he should have a raise.

What are some of the ways of stimulating such an employee?

CASE 8

You receive a phone call from the wife of one of your employees, requesting you not to allow him to work overtime any more because he uses this excuse for not coming home until late at night. You have noticed that his production has been falling off lately, and there are indications of dissipation. Production is behind in your department, and your men have been working excessive hours.

1. What should you say to the man's wife?
2. How should you handle the dissipation angle?
3. What effect will your actions have on the morale of the rest of the group?
4. Should you ignore the whole situation?
5. To what extent are you your brother's keeper?

CASE 9

Ted Foster has just retired after 35 years of service with the company. During his last five years he served as a section head, supervising 15 employees including Elsie Prince. Ted's last year on the job was characterized by considerable coasting on his part and discipline in the section became very lax. Considerable freedom developed about lateness, lunch hours, coffee breaks, and quitting time.

Elsie Prince had been promoted to replace Ted Foster. She noticed the laxity of the past year but she also noticed that while several employees were abusing their privileges, the entire work group had high morale, and labor turnover was well below the company average.

Elsie is 28 years old and is career oriented. She is married with no children and she feels she has a very good future with the company. This promotion has given her further indication of her opportunities.

She feels she must establish firmer control over the employees, yet she is worried about the effect her efforts will have on the group.

1. How can Elsie enforce company rules and still maintain the same level of morale?
2. Should she seek help from her superior?
3. Should she continue the pattern of laxity established by her predecessor in view of the low labor turnover and high morale?
4. What positive things can Elsie do to offset the reestablishment of company rules?

CASE 10

Kay Miller was in charge of a secretarial pool in the executive offices of a large company. While each girl under her supervision was assigned to one or more executives, Kay was responsible for work assignment, training, performance evaluation, selection, and general supervision of the executive secretaries. Kay had few supervisory problems since assignment to the executive secretarial pool was considered a privilege and it carried considerable status in the company.

One girl, however, was getting to be a problem. Florence was an excellent secretary who performed her work flawlessly. Because of this Kay had assigned her to the company's executive vice president who was very demanding and who had a high level of expectation for all of his subordinates. He had been very pleased with the girl and he frequently complimented Kay on her wise assignment.

The executive vice president took frequent trips to visit company offices in other sections of the country. He also came in late several mornings a month because he attended meetings away from the company premises.

Kay began to notice that Florence also came in late on the days the executive vice president was at a meeting or out of town. She also took longer lunch hours when the executive vice president was absent. After several of the other girls started grumbling, Kay called Florence into a conference room and spoke to her about her lax punctuality. Florence asked if the executive vice president had complained. Kay replied that he hadn't because he didn't even know about her infractions of company rules. Florence then said that as far as she was concerned, the executive vice president was her boss and he was satisfied with her work because he frequently told her so. Kay tried to establish the fact that she was Florence's supervisor, but Florence replied that until the executive vice president complained she would not change her behavior. Kay wondered what to do next because she knew that the executive vice president was very pleased with Florence's work and she didn't have another girl as capable.

1. Can Kay effectively discipline Florence under the circumstances?
2. Should she speak to the executive vice president about Florence?
3. Why would Florence feel justified in coming in late and breaking other rules?
4. How can Kay avoid similar problems in the future?

CASE 11

You are the superintendent of a medium-sized plant and have a good hard-hitting supervisory crew that has been with you a number of years. They all know that they are necessary to the success of the business. Competition with the firms in the field is keen, and it is essential to keep driving all the time. Three months ago one of your supervisors in his late forties had a near-fatal heart attack. His doctor says he has to rest for six months and after that should do only limited work—about a half load.

Bill's illness prompted you to ask your other supervisors about their health. You learn that a number of them have the marks of modern industry—hypertension, hemorrhoids, and ulcers. They are all good men, and you don't want to lose any of them. You would like to reduce the wear and tear on your executives.

1. What are some of the causes of tension among supervisors?
2. How can each cause be removed or decreased?
3. What should you do about Bill?

CASE 12

Mary Smith was one of the best operators in your department until she became acquainted with the new setup man. Her work is of a repetitive nature and requires intermittent attention in order to avoid the formation of scrap. Lately she has taken to daydreaming, with the result that a large portion of her work is defective. You have spoken to her several times, but she tells you that she can't help it.

1. Should you try to discourage this romance?
2. Should there be a termination? A transfer? If so, who should be terminated or transferred?
3. How should you handle work requiring intermittent attention?
4. Is daydreaming on the job to be allowed? Tolerated? Encouraged, if it does not interfere with production?

CASE 13

You are office manager of a large, well-established company and have the problem of what to do with May Smith. The retirement age for women is 60. May is 51. She started work at 18 as a clerk and in her

33 years with the company has never tried to get ahead or assume responsibility. The quality of her work, never very good, has in the last few years become progressively worse. Now her health is poor, she is nervous and short tempered, and absent about one day a week.

A year ago at the suggestion of the company's physician, she started going to a psychiatrist for treatment. He persuaded her to move out of her mother's house and into a new apartment. (May had lived all her life with her widowed mother. The mother is said to be the one who kept May from marrying.) For a while the psychiatrist's advice seemed to be effective; May went out more and took greater interest in life and in her work.

Now things are bad again. May does about half a normal work load. Her work is full of mistakes that the other employees have to find and correct. She sets a bad example for the younger women who have to do a full day's hard work to keep their jobs. They resent May's poor performance.

Six months ago you asked May if she would retire voluntarily. She was outraged and said she was still a young woman. Management says to keep her as long as she wants to stay. This is probably because the psychiatrist told the company that May should keep on working.

1. What obligations does the company have toward May?
2. What obligations does May have toward the company?
3. What are advantages and disadvantages of having a definite age for retirement?
4. What are some of the problems of using *efficiency or competence* as a measure for determining retirement time?
5. How should the office manager handle the situation?

CASE 14

Recently you were appointed as the supervisor of a unit of machine operators in which you were formerly one of the rank and file. When you were selected for the job, the big boss told you that the former supervisor was being transferred because he could not get work out of the gang. He said also that the reason you were selected was because you appeared to be a natural leader, that you were close to the gang, and that you knew the tricks they were practicing in order to hold back production. He told you that he believed you could lick the problem and that he would stand behind you.

He was right about your knowing the tricks. When you were one of the gang, not only did you try to hamper the supervisor, but you were the ringleader in trying to make his life miserable. None of you had anything against him personally, but all of you considered it a game to pit your wits against his. There was a set of signals to inform the boys that the boss was coming so that everyone would appear to be working hard. As soon as he left the immediate vicinity, everyone would take it easy. Also, the operators would act dumb to get the boss to go into lengthy explanations and demonstrations while they stood around. They complained constantly and without justification about the materials and the equipment.

At lunchtime the boys would ridicule the company, tell the latest fast one they pulled on the supervisor, and plan new ways to harass him. All this seemed to be a great joke. You and the rest of the boys had a lot of fun at the expense of the supervisor and the company.

Now that you have joined the ranks of management, it's not so funny. You are determined to use your leadership position and your knowledge to win the group over to working for the company instead of against it. You know that, if this can be done, you will have a top-notch unit. The operators know their stuff, have a very good team spirit, and, if they would use their brains and efforts constructively, they could turn out much greater production and get greater satisfaction out of their jobs.

Your former buddies are rather cool to you now, but this seems to be quite natural, and you believe you can overcome it in a short time. What has you worried is that Joe Jones is taking over your old post as ringleader of the gang, and the gang is trying to give you the business just as they did to the former supervisor.

1. Was management wise in selecting you for the job? Justify your answer.
2. What advantage do you have over an outsider?
3. What disadvantages do you have? How are you going to overcome them?
4. How would you develop cooperation between yourself and the gang?
5. How would you handle Joe Jones?
6. Plan a program for changing their attitude toward the company.

CASE 15

Miss Jones, a clerk-typist, has been with the company for five years. Recently she announced her engagement and impending marriage to take place six months from now. Since the announcement, she has been doing just enough work to get by and her work has deteriorated to a point where it is barely passable. For example, the interoffice communications she types have omissions, errors, strikeovers, and dirty erasures. The quality standards for typed interoffice communications are lower than for letters sent outside the company; but even so her work falls below the standard.

The office manager does not like her performance nor the example she is setting for the newer girls. He does not want to go to the expense of making her retype her work. He has spoken to her several times, and she shows no signs of improving. She gives the impression that she is just putting in time until she gets married. He does not want to fire her.

What should he do?

FOLLOWING UP ON THE JOB

The informal organization

1. What are some of the things people attach importance to in the unit?
2. Who in the unit seem to be the leaders?
3. Who in the unit seem to be the followers?
4. Who are the insiders? Who are outsiders?
5. When changes are introduced, are they fitted to the status system?

The supervisor and human relations

1. Do you have a friendly interest in your workers?
2. Do they come to you with their problems?
3. What are some of the ambitions of your workers?
4. Are your workers getting satisfaction out of their jobs?
5. Are you able to use some of the special talents of your workers?

Fatigue and tension

1. Do your workers seem to be tense?
2. Do you supervise them too closely?
3. What factors in the unit heighten fatigue?
4. Do you try to create an atmosphere of approval?

12 Training and orientation

What is training? Induction and orientation. The new employee and the personnel department. The new employee and the supervisor. The new employee and the group. The induction procedure. The young adult's first job. On-the-job training. Choosing a trainer. Uncovering training needs. Principles of learning and techniques of training. The four-step method of job training. Summary.

Labor statistics indicate that about three fourths of the quits are people with less than six months of service with an organization. These are people who become discouraged or disillusioned before they take the time to put down any roots. A highly mobile work force and relative ease in obtaining jobs add to the problem. When the costs of such turnover are added to the costs of having a poorly trained work force, the need for effective orientation and training becomes obvious.

The training of employees has broad implications for any organization that undertakes such a task on a wide scale. A number of large companies as well as government agencies, hospitals, schools, and other organizations in our society have found that the skills available in the labor market simply do not meet their needs. Many of these organizations have recognized that employee training has to be a continuous process. Gone are the days when the new employee could be turned over to an experienced one to be given haphazard instructions in rapid sequence, observe the job for a short time, and then do it. In short, learning by trial and error has been recognized as too costly and the new employee, because of his scarcity, has to be convinced that the organization he has joined is interested enough in his future to train him properly for the job he is supposed to do.

What is training?

Training is the continuous systematic development of all employees in an organization. This means on all levels of management, supervisory and nonsupervisory positions, and in all the skills, knowledge, and atti-

417

tudes necessary for the optimum performance of these positions. Training is a never-ending task because people change and jobs change and the supervisor must keep people fitted to jobs and jobs fitted to people. This is necessary if he is to get high performance from them and they are to get satisfaction from their jobs.

A primary concern of professional management should be the development of employee interest in job assignments. An employee who is highly motivated and interested in his job will more than likely take pride in his work and be more productive. Of even greater importance are some hard facts which the managements of many organizations have had to face.

Rapidly changing technology in both factories and offices coupled with an affluent society has created shortages of skilled labor. Many young people of the type who entered the labor market as high school graduates years ago, are now going to colleges, junior colleges, and universities. In many areas of the country, the failure of educational institutions to properly prepare people for the world of work has added to the problem. The pressures of labor shortages, government, and a growing awareness of many organizations of their responsibility in our society have accelerated the entrance of various underqualified minority groups into the work force. These factors among others have caused many organizations to undertake comprehensive programs of employee training and development. Courses in good grooming, computer programming, English, arithmetic, spelling, reading, typing, shorthand, and a myriad of other skills and techniques are common in a growing number of companies and other organizations.

Management has found that there are not enough people to go around and those that are employed are given the training necessary to perform adequately on open jobs. In terms of numbers, training needs are most apparent among new employees or those just starting out on a new job. The problem is somewhat more difficult with employees already on the payroll.

Some people become unsuited to their jobs for reasons of health, accidents, aging, or change of interests. Or the jobs may change to the extent that the employee is having to struggle too hard just to keep up. People who are unsuited to their type of work may be able to perform well on some other job.

A person who has been on a job for a while may resent being told that his performance is inadequate, his methods slipshod, and that he—and nobody else—needs training. One way to get around this type of resistance to training is to have short refresher courses periodically for everybody. The instruction could combine job methods with procedures or with safety and housekeeping. Such a plan is good for the sick and not bad for the well in that a refresher course offers the supervisor a definite time and opportunity to introduce improvements in methods and techniques.

The supervisor must provide training when production schedules expand and contract, and people are shifted around as a result. Training is called for when employees get transfers, when they are upgraded, and when they are promoted. Ambitious people want to keep developing and achieving, and they are willing to put the effort into learning new jobs. Training is called for when the supervisor decides to delegate some of his routine responsibilities to his subordinates, and when he is preparing subordinates to be able to operate under general supervision. Training is called for when jobs are enlarged and when employees rotate from job to job in order to substitute for one another during absences and vacations.

Training is called for when scientific discoveries result in innovations in products, processes, and equipment. The age of automation is accelerating change at a rate that is predicted to displace a worker three times during his work life and make it necessary for him to prepare himself three times for some other kind of work. Training problems of these proportions should turn the supervisor's attention to the emotional impact of change upon people. He should develop an interest in the principles of learning and techniques of training to be used in preparing people to undertake new jobs.

Because of the growing recognition that training must be a continuous process, many companies have made considerable investments in the training function. The comprehensive programs mentioned earlier require trainers and physical facilities. Training has moved from its status as an ancillary activity to one which has become an integral part of a well-managed organization's functioning. This has caused these organizations to give careful attention to the training function and several new thoughts and ideas have been developed. Gordon Lippitt lists several trends in his recent book, *Organization Renewal.*

> A trend toward a focus on improved performances rather than on increased individual knowledge.
>
> A trend to deal with situations rather than individuals.
>
> A trend to see training as the way management gets its job done rather than as a function of a department in the organization.
>
> A trend toward building up inhouse capabilities rather than dependence on outside experts.
>
> A trend toward insistence on evaluation of the results of training rather than accepting rosy reports on faith.
>
> A trend toward designing learning that will focus on learning-how-to-learn.
>
> A trend toward training that is based on action-learning rather than on one-way communication.
>
> A trend toward training that provides reinforcement and follow-up experience for trainees rather than "graduating" them from a training program.

A trend toward dependence more on the learning to be self-motivated
by the learner rather than imposed on the learner by the trainers.

A trend for training to be goal-oriented rather than a vague assurance
that it will be "good for you."

A trend toward greater homogeneity in the persons being trained.

A trend toward emphasis on the importance of organizational climate as
an essential factor affecting change.[1]

The above list may not be all inclusive but it certainly demonstrates
that the thinking about training has become far more critical. It is now
recognized as a vital factor in sound organizational growth and development and very much a part of effective manpower planning, a topic
covered in Chapter 13.

Induction and orientation

Essentially induction and orientation programs are developed for new
employees, although, as will be discussed later, there is a need for induction of transferred and promoted employees. The need arises from the
desire of management to have a new employee learn as much as possible
about the organization in a short period of time to enhance the
employee's adjustment to his new environment. As we all know first impressions can be quite important and they are made whether or not a
management plans them. New employees will inevitably face disappointments and problems on their jobs. Some fellow employees will go out
of their way to convince the newcomer that he made a mistake in joining
the company. The induction and orientation program should help build
a reserve of positive knowledge about the organization and develop
a useful frame of reference against which to judge the varied impressions
he will receive in his early days with the company. The high incidence
of first-year labor turnover is another powerful reason for a well-planned
orientation program. Naturally, some of the turnover cannot be prevented since employees can easily find other jobs if they are disappointed
and some turnover takes place at company request because all new
hires do not succeed in their new jobs. But many employees who leave
in their first year of employment could have developed into valuable
and effective staff members if more attention was given to their orientation and initial training.

A well-planned induction and orientation program can materially assist management in the development of a uniform approach to the understanding of company policies, procedures, and rules and thereby aid
the supervisor in the handling of his subordinates.

[1] Gordon L. Lippitt, *Organization Renewal* (New York: Appleton-Century-Crofts,
Educational Division of Meredith Publishing Co., 1969), p. 210.

The new employee and the personnel department

Getting employees started off right is a two-part program: first, the personnel department introduces the employee to the company, and second, the supervisor introduces him to the work group and to the job. The personnel department's part in induction begins at the time the applicant is accepted for employment. The personnel interviewer usually gives him a booklet or employees' handbook typically containing the following information:

History of the company	Rules of conduct
Activities of the company	Safety rules
Personnel policies	Employee benefits
Employee activities	Education benefits
Career opportunities	Vacation policy
Leaves of absence	Holidays
Grievance procedure	Profit sharing

Other pertinent company policies

The personnel interviewer goes over this information with the new employee, explaining the various points and giving whatever other information will help the new man feel better acquainted with the company as a whole. More comprehensive programs are carried out by many organizations. The personnel department usually develops and implements these programs. They frequently take a half-day or one day although some companies have programs which take several days. An example of a comprehensive induction and orientation program follows. Such programs are given as frequently as is necessary so that all new hires will be exposed to the program.

Some companies include a plant tour or headquarters tour as part of the induction process. Others feel that this type of tour has little meaning for a new employee and either do not have such a tour or carry it out after the employee has been with the organization for several months. The end of the probationary period is frequently considered an appropriate time because it is felt that the new employee will know enough about the company at this time and the tour will be more interesting to him. If the tour is carried out after the employee has some experience with the company, the flow of the work is often stressed to demonstrate to the employee how the various functions take place and what part his contribution makes to the entire process.

Several organizations use films depicting the history and accomplishments of the enterprise as part of the orientation. In some companies the films are professionally made while in others they may be produced

XYZ CORPORATION
Personnel Department
New Employee Orientation Outline
Time: Five hours

Topic	Speaker
A. Welcome to company	Personnel director
1. Purpose of orientation	
2. Each employee introduces himself indicating his background and assignment	
3. Greetings	Senior manager
B. The Personnel Department	Assistant personnel director
1. Functions of personnel department	
2. Lateness and absenteeism	
3. Work schedule	
4. Time sheets or cards	
5. Payroll deductions	
6. Time off and leaves of absence	
C. Company Benefit Program	Benefits manager
1. Holidays and vacations	
2. Hospitalization insurance	
3. Major medical insurance	
4. Life insurance	
5. Disability insurance	
6. Pension plan	
7. Profit sharing	
D. Safety	Safety manager
1. Company safety record	
2. Safety equipment	
3. Importance of safety	
E. Compensation Program	Compensation manager
1. Job analysis	
2. Job descriptions and specifications	
3. Wage and salary reviews	
4. Performance evaluation	
5. Overtime	
F. Education and Training	Training director
1. Tuition remission plan	
2. Company training programs	
3. Employee eligibility	
4. Promotion from within policy	
G. Suggestion Program	Chairman, suggestion committee
1. Nature of awards	
2. Eligibility for awards	
3. Reasons for program	
H. Employee Activities and Recreation	Chairman, employee activities committee
1. Athletic teams	
2. Hobby clubs	
3. Longevity and service awards	
4. Other activity programs	
5. Charity drives	
I. Company History	Assistant personnel director

by the training department and consist of color slides depicting important aspects of the firm's activities. Visual aids enhance the program and many firms include various types of audio-visual aids to cover such topics as grooming, fringe benefits, safety and activities.

An induction program should, of course, be tailored and timed to fit the needs of the specific company. The content of the program should be evaluated periodically against the rate of turnover, the disciplinary records and accidents of new people, and any information gleaned from their exit interviews.

The personnel department's portion of the induction program may take place a day or so before the new man reports for work. From there on, induction is the responsibility of the supervisor. He must integrate the new man into the department and into the work group.

The new employee and the supervisor

The supervisor's first contact with a new man is usually in the application interview—a time when the applicant is exuding self-confidence and doing a selling job—selling his services. After he has closed the deal and is told when to report for work, he starts to worry. Quite a change comes over him while he is waiting to go on the job. He has time to think it over and ask himself a lot of questions: Was I wise to change from the old job? Will I be able to handle the new job? What kind of people will they be? What will my boss really be like? What are my chances of getting ahead of the fellows already established on the job? Or what are my chances of just getting along with them?

The more he thinks about these things, the less sure he is of himself. As a result, the morning he reports for work, instead of being a self-confident seller of his services, he is worried about what he has gotten into.

The supervisor now has the selling job to do. He is selling the company as a good place to work. He is selling the performance standards as necessary and attainable—something that the new employee is accepting as part of his contract to work. He is selling the working conditions, the rules, the requirements for quality and safety. He is selling the company's techniques for improving methods and keeping down costs. He is selling the opportunities offered in the job—or perhaps the security and congenial work associates.

He is selling himself as a supervisor—someone who will be interested in the employee's welfare and success and will provide the guidance and training to make that success possible.

A man starting on a job is interested, receptive, and eager to cooperate. He welcomes attention from the supervisor, accepts suggestions and constructive criticism. He is open to ideas and in favor of improvements because he has no involvement in maintaining existing conditions. This is the "learnable moment" and the supervisor should make the most of it to build up good attitudes toward the job, toward the level of effort that will be required, toward the behavior that will be expected, toward the quality requirements, and toward safe working habits.

Particularly the supervisor wants to build up the new man's confidence that this is a good place to work and that the training program is a well-planned means to achievement—to getting the things he wants from the job.

Orientation checklist.   An example of one company's approach toward developing cooperation between the personnel department and the new employee's supervisor is the Manufacturers Hanover Trust Company's orientation checklist. (See Figure 12–1.) It is designed to be completed by the personnel department and various people having direct and indirect relationships with the new employee. It covers a period up to the employee's first salary review and its basic purpose is to ensure that the employee is given all of the information necessary for his understanding of the various policies that have an effect on his performance on the job and his overall well being as an employee of the bank.

This company found that there was no uniformity to the amount of time spent on orientation and induction by supervisors. Some were diligent and gave as much time as necessary· while others spent no time at all, expecting the employee to pick up the information as he went along. The checklist attempts to assure that each supervisor does in fact take the time. Obviously, the quality of the effort is not assured by the checklist but since it does become part of the employee's permanent record, the bank has found that the effort is being made and fewer information requests come to the personnel department.

While such a checklist may seem to be added paper work, the need for effective information flow to the new employee is critical. Anything which enhances this flow and tends to minimize insecurities among new hires can help in lowering first-year turnover and employment costs.

The new employee and the group

Dropping a new employee into a department and letting him fend for himself is like playing a pinball game. If the ball doesn't happen to connect in the scoring area, there will be no payoff. Instead of playing a game of chance in introducing a new man into the department, the supervisor should set up provisions to keep him from losing momentum or dropping out before mastering his job and making a place for himself. During the trying days of learning his job and getting adjusted to its demands, the newcomer must somehow be made to feel wanted and

FIGURE 12–1
Orientation Checklist for New Employees

MANUFACTURERS HANOVER TRUST COMPANY

ORIENTATION CHECKLIST FOR NEW PERSONNEL

| QUESTIONS CONCERNING THIS |
| CHECK LIST SHOULD BE DIRECTED TO: |
| PERSONNEL DEPARTMENT |

NAME	PAYROLL NO:	BRANCH OR DEPT:	JOB TITLE:	DATE OF EMPL.

The majority of new employees begin their jobs with an honest, sincere desire to be successful. Each looks to the management of his department or branch for information about his job, the ultimate value of the work he performs and the regulations that apply to his work. The success or failure of a new member of the staff rests in large part upon his supervisors.

This checklist has been prepared as a minimum measure of the supervisor's responsibility for orientation and training. Reference to the Personnel Policies and Procedures manual will prove helpful in using this checklist. Please return the checklist as an attachment to the four-month review blank.

TO BE DONE		ACTION TO BE TAKEN	NOTES
BY	**WHEN**		
Personnel Department Interviewer	Date Person accepts Employment	1. Indicate starting salary and work week.	
		2. Discuss hours, employee responsibilities, salary review, opportunities, education, employee benefits, including Medical Department services. Provide benefit booklets About Manufacturers Hanover, Employee Relations Procedure. and "Conflicts of Interest".	
NAME DATE		3. Notify department of tentative starting date.	
Personnel Department Interviewer or Processor	Employment Date (First Morning)	1. Remind Supervisor of the arrival of the employee.	The employee enrolled in all benefit programs except
		2. Enroll in Benefit Programs:	

		a) Group Life
		   b) Major Medical
		   c) Blue Cross-Blue Shield
		   d) Voluntary Accident
			because _____

		3. Discuss Retirement System and Profit Sharing Plan.	☐ Check here if salary review pattern will be other than 4, 8, 12, 18 & 24 mos.
		4. Discuss:	

		a) Trial period
		   b) Regular working hours from ____ to ____
		   c) Forewarning of unusual overtime (indicate type)
			Record the salary pattern on Supervisor's History Card.

		d) Weekly salary rate, date of first pay and date of salary reviews. e) Optional deductions for charitable activities and savings plans.	Emphasize that salaries are confidential.
		5. Inform employee that he will receive within the first week of employment a booklet explaining the Employee Checking Account, an initial supply of checks and his Employee Identification (Account Number Reminder) Card.	Deductions Elected ☐ Charitable Activities ☐ U. S. Savings Bonds ☐ Savings Account
		6. Explain educational tuition refund plan.	Employee's Educational Plans (Evening Studies)
		7. Give to employee invitation to Personnel Department's Orientation Meeting.	Special Subjects _____ Higher Education _____ AIB _____ None _____
NAME DATE			Misc. _____

This space is available for additional comments which the Personnel Department interviewer believes will be of assistance to the supervisor.

FIGURE 12–1 (*Continued*)

TO BE DONE		ACTION TO BE TAKEN	NOTES
BY	WHEN		
Area Supervisor In the Metropolitan Division he is defined as the Regional V.P. or Regional Operations Officer. In other divisions or departments: Senior Officer who is responsible for the personnel function or his designee.	First Day or sometime in first week or as near thereto as is practicable.	1. Welcome to the Division/Region. 2. Explain briefly the work and organization of the Division as well as its relationship to the Bank. 3. Describe the work of the department to which employee will be assigned explaining its relationship to the division, stressing the importance of the work. 4. Encourage the new employee to request guidance at any time from his supervisor.	Inquire about schools attended. Familiarize yourself with employee's interests and ambitions. Emphasize ability of the supervisor and his role in training and counseling.
NAME	DATE		

Supervisor
Defined as:
(1) Department Head
(2) His designee responsible for operations and personnel administration in the department, or
(3) Person who will conduct salary reviews.
	First Day	1. Welcome new employee to department/branch.
		
		2. Introduce new employee to the branch/dept. officers.
		
		3. Explain:
		
		  a) Work of the department/branch.
		  b) Its purpose, organization and workflow charts.
		  c) Its relationship to the division/region.
		  d) The Job: duties, workflow chart, importance, and anticipated overtime.
		  e) Work Measurement Program.
		  f) Nature of training, the training and lesson plan, probable training period and name of trainer
		  g) Supervisory chain of command.
		
		4. Discuss the following employee responsibilities:
		
		  a) Punctuality.
		  b) Regular attendance, reporting absences to supervisor within one-half hour of starting time.
		  c) Time sheet procedure.
		  d) Coffee breaks policy, lunch periods (time schedules).
		  e) Grooming, sound finances, smoking regulations.
		  f) Leaving department.
		  g) Housekeeping-confidential nature of work-importance of accuracy-losses due to errors-waste prevention.
		  h) Form 5187-reporting change of address and status.
		  i) Location of desk-locker and/or desk key.
		  j) Introduce new employee to Sponsor and explain briefly functions of Sponsor.
			Inquire about schools attended, previous experience, family, transportation to work & ambitions. Encourage questions.
			
			Mention possibility of helping others when necessary.
			
			Give employee the operations procedure manual or its equivalent for the job.
			
			Supply new employee with your name and telephone number. During first two weeks plan to speak with new employee early and late each day to learn if he or she has any questions to be cleared up. (Be specific and thorough.)

NAME	DATE		
Sponsor Defined as: An Employee having a friendly and pleasant attitude and who is sufficiently informed in departmental functions and jobs.	First Day	1. Introduce new employee to co-workers giving a brief description of their work. 2. Show location of lockers, washroom, bulletin boards, dining facilities. 3. Discuss clothing to be worn. 4. Explain supply procedure. 5. Invite new employee to luncheon with co-workers.	Give the new employee chart of office or department layout with names of co-workers. Encourage questions, present and future. Plan to see employee twice a day for first 2 or 3 weeks.
NAME	DATE		
Trainer Defined as: The department training specialist or an experienced staff member who is regularly assigned the responsibility of training employees.	First Day (and daily for remainder of training period)	1. Explain job and training plans. 2. Commence training with the explanation of one easy task.	Use operations manual and lesson plan. Stress quality rather than quantity of work during learning period.
NAME	DATE		

FIGURE 12-1 (*Continued*)

TO BE DONE		ACTION TO BE TAKEN	NOTES
BY	WHEN		
Supervisor	Second Day	1. Discuss Salary Administration: a) Pay period (Wed. through Tues.) b) Merit salary review schedule (see Personnel interviewer's comments.) c) Authorized overtime pay policies. d) Confidential nature of salary.	Show a sample review form to the employee. Stress the factors upon which performance will be judged and who will made such judgments. Mention names of persons authorized to approve overtime work.
NAME DATE		2. Acquaint new employee with telephone etiquette; procedure for answering, limitations on personal calls.	
Supervisor	First Pay Day	Discuss Employee Checking Account a) Proper handling. b) Place and time to cash checks. c) Warning against anticipating deposits and over-drafts. d) Caution against using checks of other employees or giving own checks to others.	Encourage employee to discuss checking account with you when experiencing difficulty.
NAME DATE			
Personnel Dept. Representative	Approximately two weeks after employment.	Personnel Department Orientation a) Downtown - lounge, 40 Wall, Tel. No. 1235 b) Uptown - Room 1200, 350 Park, Tel. No. 4136	
NAME DATE			
Evening Study Representative	Second Week	Discuss: 1. Types of study qualifying under the Tuition Refund Plan and terms of the plan. 2. Employee's educational plans.	
NAME DATE			
Supervisor	Second Week	1. Discuss progress in training and get reaction to the job as well as the organization. 2. Discuss "Topics," the Suggestion System and Employee Activities.	Invite discussion of subjects which may need clarification or advice.
NAME DATE			
Charitable Activities Committeeman	Third Week	Discuss and re-solicit the employee if charitable and savings deductions were not elected at time of employment.	See Personnel Interviewer's comments on Page 1 under "optional deductions"
NAME DATE			
Dept. ESIP Representative.	Third Week	Review ESIP program and provide booklet pertaining to it.	
NAME DATE			
Supervisor	Third Week	1. Discuss progress in training and secure reaction to training, job and organization. 2. Explain Employee Relations Procedure.	Find out what the employee is thinking.
NAME DATE			
Supervisor	Fourth Week	1. Review Benefit Programs: a) Group Life Insurance b) Major Medical Insurance c) Blue Cross/Blue Shield d) Voluntary Accident Insurance e) Retirement System f) Profit Sharing Plan 2. About MHTCo. Booklet: Ascertain if employee has questions.	Stress health and welfare benefits to employee. Emphasize dollar costs to Bank as an indication of its interest. (See Page 116 - Personnel Policies and Procedures.) Include Medical Dept. services.
NAME DATE			

FIGURE 12–1 *(Concluded)*

TO BE DONE BY	WHEN	ACTION TO BE TAKEN	NOTES
Supervisor	Fifth Week	Review vacation, holiday, military leave policy and leave with pay for marriage.	Explain how and when vacations are scheduled.
NAME	DATE		
Area Supervisor	During First Three Months	Divisional/Branch Orientation — Included in one or more meetings are explanations of: a) The work of the division/branch. b) The organization. c) Terminology used in division. d) Reminder of telephone etiquette and regulations. e) Stress proper grooming. f) Miscellaneous.	Encourage questions from employee at divisional orientation.
NAME	DATE		
Supervisor	When Submitting New Employee's Four Month Review To Salary Committee	Attach this checklist to the 4 month Review along with completed answer sheets for the Programmed Instruction Course to be administered by departments and branches. (See list below)	
NAME	DATE		

CHART FOR USE OF PROGRAMED INSTRUCTION COURSES
("X" indicates programs to be administered)

HEADQUARTERS' DEPARTMENTS	Checks	Securities	Loss Prevention-Checks	HEADQUARTERS' DEPARTMENTS (con't.)	Checks	Securities	Loss Prevention-Checks
Auditing	X	X	X	Metropolitan Operations	X	X	X
Central Loan Accounting	X			Money Transfer & Wire	X		
Central Note Teller	X	X		National Control Unit	X		
Central Operations - Uptown	X	X	X	National Operations	X	X	X
Forms Control	X	X					
Central Operations - Downtown	X	X		Personal Loan Accounting	X		
Systems & Procedures	X	X	X				
Work Measurement	X	X	X	Personal Trust Division			
Check Clearance	X			P.T. Collection	X	X	
				P.T. Custody		X	
				P.T. Employee Benefit Plans		X	
Controllers	X	X		P.T. Estate Administration		X	
				P.T. Income Tax	X	X	
Corporate Trust				P.T. Investment Research		X	
Coupon Paying		X		P.T. Investment Review		X	
Stock Transfer:		X		P.T. Investments		X	
Administration		X		P.T. Order		X	
IBM & Addressograph		X		P.T. Payment	X	X	
Operations		X		P.T. Records		X	
Research		X		P.T. Security Records		X	
Stock Records		X		P.T. Trust Administration		X	
Coupon & Securities Collection		X		Real Estate & Mortgage	X	X	X
Credit	X	X	X	Secretarial	X		
Data Center	X	X	X	Securities		X	
International Division	X		X	Vaults		X	
Lock Box	X			BRANCH OFFICES			
				All Offices	X	X	X

needed. He must be protected from the embarrassment and discouragement of ignorance and isolation in front of people who all seem to know what to do and where they fit.

Even the most self-sufficient person feels lost in his first days on a new job. He might not mind isolation if he were absorbed in some project and confident of his ability to handle it. But he is insecure in his job and needs help with his work, and he is worried about how he will fit in with the people he sees around him. At lunchtime and at breaks he doesn't know what to do with himself. Everybody else seems to be comfortably established.

Most people have vivid memories of the way they felt in getting started on a new job. They can recall the strangeness and tension and tiredness. They can remember how often they felt like quitting.

The group can't be blamed for being inhospitable to the newcomer. People have their own jobs to protect and their own social relations to preserve and cultivate. Once people have achieved a kind of stability and predictability in their work lives, they find a certain joy in the routines, and they don't want to risk being crowded out.

A newcomer to a group is a threat to the stability of the group as a whole and to each member of it. The stranger may insinuate himself into the social life and edge somebody else out of position. He may break up some nice little arrangement on the job, or he may get in the way of some plans for the future. He may be overambitious. He may get somebody else's job. He may be a company man. People aren't going to give him a leg up the ladder until they know he won't kick them in the face.

It just takes time for some of these barriers to break down, but the supervisor can do a lot to prevent the original formation of much of the hostility and suspicion. If his group feels competent and confident, it doesn't have so much to fear from a newcomer. A group that is let in on the news that a new man is to be hired will feel less threatened than if one is just sprung on them without warning or explanation. The supervisor should make it a point to prepare the group for the coming of a new employee. The word should be passed along about what work he is to do and where he fits into the pattern as far as they and their plans are concerned. When the new man arrives, the supervisor should make sure that introductions are pleasant and establish some kind of bridge of interest between individuals. He should draw people into conversations with the new man to discuss job problems.

The newcomer must be started off on the right foot with the people who will be most closely associated with him on the job. Introductions should make clear the status arrangements if one is expected to give directions to the other. Introductions should also make clear whether the new man should ask for, and expect to receive, help from the other.

The newcomer should be provided with a sponsor—an employee who will eat lunch with him the first day or so and after that will look after him for a while so that he will not be standing around alone in the group.

The induction procedure

It is not only the newly hired who need inducting; anyone who is changing jobs within the company needs some kind of induction. The man who is being transferred is a stranger to the job and to the work group. He will have questions in his mind about how this job ties in with other jobs he has held and how his future is being affected by the transfer. In order to be prepared, the supervisor should get whatever information is available from the personnel department or from the man's previous supervisors.

If an inductee is a college graduate trainee, then the supervisor should find out from the personnel department what kind of program the trainee is on and what part the department is expected to play in it.

Special care must be used in inducting a supervisor into his new job, particularly if he is being moved from the rank and file into his first supervisory job. He may have received coaching for the new job, but he is now entering into a new set of relationships by moving up into a position of more authority. These relationships must be clarified and established so that there is no doubt about the man's authority, his responsibilities, and his recognition by his new associates and by his new subordinates.

If an inductee has just come to the company as a new hire, the application form will give information about his work experience, education, and previous training. This background serves as a guide to the kind of induction he needs, the kind of things he will already know, and the kind of information he should get. The employee on his first job needs many more things explained than does the experienced man. For one thing, there are so many things the beginner is uncertain about that he may be afraid to ask any questions and expose his ignorance. The following induction procedure is set up with the new man in mind and is presented in six steps:

1. Welcome the new man and learn more about him.
2. Explain the work of the section and the part he is to perform.
3. Let him know what is expected of him.
4. Show him around and introduce him to his fellow workers.
5. Turn him over to a sponsor or competent instructor.
6. Follow up on his progress.

Step 1. Welcome the new man and learn more about him. When the new man reports for his first day on the job, greet him by name and settle down for a chat with him. Appear unhurried, in order to show him that you consider this meeting important. Break the ice by mentioning something you remember from his application form or the application interview. Take this opportunity to show him that you are interested in him as a person—that his problems, his hopes, and his ambitions mean something to you. This meeting sets the tone for all your future contacts with him.

Go over some of the general points covered in the handbook. Narrow the subject to the advantages of working in this particular department. Get the man to talk about himself and his experience; then show him the relationship of his experience to the new job.

Step 2. Explain the work of the section. Start by telling the man about the job that *he* is to do. This is what is of greatest interest to him. If you start telling him about other things first, he will be wondering about his job and how it fits into all this, instead of paying close attention to what you are saying. After you have told him about what he will be doing, then show him how his job fits into the purpose of the section and how the functions of the section fit into the organization as a whole.

Tell him about the importance of his job, what opportunities there are for getting ahead, what kind of training he will get. If there are good opportunities for advancement, tell him about them; if the opportunities are limited, do not oversell them. Tell him about the people with whom he will work.

Step 3. Let him know what is expected of him. This is the time to let the man know that it is necessary for him to do a satisfactory job if he is to become a permanent employee. Start with the job description and go over it in detail so that he understands beyond question what are his duties and responsibilities. Let him know the extent of his authority. Tell him something about the person he is to report to if it is not to you. And tell him about the individuals who will report to him. Then tell him about the standards of work performance—how much and how well the job must be done for satisfactory performance.

Next, go over a company employee-evaluation sheet with him, explaining the meaning and importance of the factors on which he will be rated. Tell him the part that employee evaluation plays in getting ahead.

Then explain the rules of conduct and the customs of the department. Tell him about starting and quitting time, rest periods, lunch periods, smoking rules, and the like. Tell him how he is expected to take care of his equipment and company property. Emphasize safety. Let him know that he is expected to get to work every day and be on time. Tell him how to report if he is sick and can't get to work. Make a point of relating attendance to dependability.

The supervisor might use a checklist (see Figure 12–1) as an aid to his memory to make sure he covers each important item. And, because employees forget a lot of what they are told, it would be well to see that information about reporting sickness is written.

Be sure to tell him about payday: how and when he gets his check, how many days of work this first check will cover, and what deductions will be made.

Let him know his responsibilities for giving value for pay received, conducting himself to reflect credit upon the organization, observing rules, and meeting his fellow workers halfway. In telling the new man how he is expected to behave, the "*we* do it" approach goes over better than the "*you* do it" approach: "This is the way *we* operate." "This is what is expected of *us*."

Step 4.   Show him around.   Take the new man through the section and point out the washroom, the time clock, the first-aid station, water fountains, phones, files, storerooms, and other facilities.

If possible, let him watch employees performing jobs similar to the one he will be doing. Next, take him to his own workplace or desk and introduce him to some of the people with whom he will be closely associated. Tell him a little about each one so that he can become acquainted easily. In all the introductions, mention what the new man's duties will be and what the duties are of the person to whom he is introduced.

Step 5.   Turn him over to a sponsor.   If the new employee is to report to, or be responsible to, someone intermediate, such as a lead man or group chief, introduce the two men in a way that makes clear to both of them the superior-subordinate relationships.

If the new man is experienced in the work or in similar work, the lead man—or the supervisor if there is no lead man—should start him on the job, giving him safety instructions. The way the new man does the job should reveal his needs for training. An inexperienced man or one rusty on the job should be turned over to the trainer, who will teach him the correct way of doing the job.

Normally the supervisor is too busy to spend additional time with the new employee and turns him over to a sponsor—one of the older employees—who assumes the responsibility of looking after him and answering a lot of questions that a new employee would hesitate to ask the supervisor.

In a small company the lead man, the sponsor, the trainer may be one and the same person. In many places the supervisor is the trainer, but it is rather difficult for him to play the role of sponsor. The purpose of the sponsor is to integrate the new employee into the social system of the department as quickly and effectively as possible.

Step 6.   Follow-up.   Keep in touch with the new man. Make it a point to stop at his workplace long enough to say "Good morning" and to give him an opportunity to ask questions and get explanations. Talk to his trainer and his sponsor. Observe his performance and see if he needs more training. The time to teach the correct methods is immediately—before he has an opportunity to learn incorrect ones. Unlearning errors is a wasteful form of learning.

Set aside definite times for having longer talks with the new employee, and have them out of hearing distance of the others. Talk to him in terms of his interests, his job, his problems. Try to find out what he honestly thinks of his new job, how he is getting along, and how he feels about his fellow workers, the department, and the company. He may have some good ideas you can use. If he is doing a good job, tell him exactly what you like about his work. Don't be afraid to correct and criticize him constructively if he is on the wrong track. The majority of new employees welcome constructive criticism if it is the work and not the person that is being criticized.

These talks with the employee are time consumers, but they save time in the end. Good induction cuts down the number of first-day and first-week quits. It builds the employee's confidence that this is a good place to work. It starts him off with high morale and sustains him in his efforts to master his job. It shows him that cooperation and willingness are appreciated and will pay off. It clears up misunderstandings and irritations before they run into frustrations and uncooperative behavior.

The young adult's first job

Business needs youth, with its optimism, its enthusiasm, its daring, its willingness to try anything once, and its frequently ingenious ideas. For many of them, employment is a new world and they don't know what kind of behavior is expected of them on the job. While they are familiar with school and the teacher-student relationship which has become increasingly democratic in recent years, they may take some time in making the adjustment to the usually more autocratic boss-subordinate relationship in business and industry.

At home and in school they generally maintained close relationships with people of their own age while on many jobs their co-workers may be older and less tolerant than school friends. Breaking into the cliques existing in every work group may be difficult since the new hire has little in common with established and older employees. The workplace is usually more confining and a first job is frequently a routine assignment. At school the young person could move around more freely and each new class period meant discussion of something different. While many of them may have held part-time jobs, the workday is longer in a full-time position and tardiness is frowned upon, usually causing disciplinary action. Frequent vacations and holidays characterize the school year while few fringe benefit programs in industry include more than one or two weeks of vacation in the early years of employment. Each week at school there would be examinations or quizzes and the young person would know how he was doing. Performance measurement in business is not as frequent nor as easily understood. At the end of the semester or school year, promotion or progress to the next level took place. Promotions in business do not come with the same ordered frequency, nor are they as automatic as those in many schools. Guidance counselors, faculty advisers and teachers abound in the world of education. Usually these people take considerable interest in the young people coming to them for help. Such is usually not the case with supervisors in business whose principal concern may be meeting deadlines and coping with the pressures of management activity.

In short the work world is very different than the one from which the young adult came. In most cases the onus is placed on him for making the necessary adjustments and changes in behavior required for success in business. Not enough supervisors have the time, talent, or inclination to spend inordinate amounts of time with young employees, helping them to make the transition from school to business by smoothing out some of the rough spots. More frequently there will be complaints from these supervisors about the poor quality of the new hires and their lack of appreciation for the golden opportunity afforded them in the company.

The above difficulties have been compounded in recent years in many areas of the country by a much greater influx of young minority group members into the work force. Many of these youngsters have all of the problems of their more affluent counterparts, but they also have the added problem of coming from inadequate backgrounds, a different culture, and a different value system. Many of them have levels of aspiration beyond their education or their ability. They resent the fact that they are a minority group and inevitably some seek refuge in this fact. An orderly existence and routine work are very unusual for them. Discipline for work habits and rule infractions that a supervisor considers normal may be interpreted as discrimination by the minority group employee.

Some companies, recognizing the special problems involved in the successful induction and early job training of minority group employees have established special training programs for them which include a considerable emphasis on the behavior required for effective performance in the work environment. Very often they are assigned a "buddy" who may be a member of the same minority and who has made a successful transition on the job. In addition, companies that hire relatively large numbers of minority group members have developed special orientation programs for supervisors so that greater understanding of the special problems of these young minority group members can be enhanced. It may be quite difficult for a supervisor who has come up the hard way to understand the attention that minorities seem to be receiving. His reaction may be quite negative and he may take out his negativism on the employees. A program which tries to develop awareness of real problems and considers some of the hard facts of the labor supply and the civil rights of minorities can assist in a more successful introduction of minorities into productive job performance.[2]

On-the-job training

The most widely used method of training new employees or those promoted or transferred to new jobs is called on-the-job training. It is training at the workplace by either the supervisor or someone he has chosen as a trainer. At its worst it is a trial-and-error approach where the new employee observes the experienced performer for a short period and then is left to his own devices. At its best it can be a formal program conducted by someone versed in training techniques as well as job knowledge. Many employee complaints and some labor turnover can be traced to poor training. The pressure to get a new employee up to reasonable productivity in a short time may cause the neglect of critical steps in the learning process and not enough emphasis on safety.

When done properly, on-the-job training has many advantages for the company as well as the employee. The employee learns his job correctly and gains greater satisfaction since his performance will meet requirements and he will be usually rewarded for effective performance. He gains experience in the environment of the job thereby lessening the adjustment period. The company gets a productive worker who performs the job correctly and who may feel more favorably disposed toward the company for the effective and positive training experience he has been exposed to. DePhillips, Berliner and Cribbin list the following practices as necessary requisites for satisfactory accomplishment of on-the-job training.

1. The person selected to do the training should be a good teacher.
2. He should know the job he is to teach thoroughly.
3. He should prepare an organized training plan or have it prepared for him by the training division.
4. He should be given sufficient time to carry out the training effort and, if possible, be removed from his responsibility for work production.

---

[2] For a broader discussion of young people in business, see John S. Morgan, *Managing the Young Adults* (New York: American Management Association, 1967).

5. He should have access to information about the person he is to train, so that he is able to gauge the trainee's needs as accurately as possible.
6. He must be able to perform the job at a normal pace in the proper manner. He does not have to be an outstanding performer. In fact outstanding performers frequently lose patience if the trainee does not learn the job rapidly.
7. A timetable should be developed so that the trainer can assess the trainee's progress and report on it to both the trainee and the supervisor.
8. If the supervisor does the training, then he must be able to devote the time necessary without neglecting his other supervisory and work duties.
9. Try to assign the trainee to the work station he will ultimately be employed in, in order to maximize the advantage of working in the job environment.
10. After the trainee has developed sufficient skill to be left on his own, let him know that he can call on the trainer for further guidance.
11. The trainer should follow up on the trainee as often as is necessary to ascertain the results of the training and the amount of job knowledge retained by the trainee.[3]

Organizations of all sizes use this type of training and it is the backbone of the training effort in small companies. Where hiring frequency and job requirements make it feasible, it may be desirable to establish vestibule training for larger groups. Here the workplace is simulated and employees are usually trained by more professional methods. A vestibule school may be less expensive than the one-on-one requirement of on-the-job training. Many firms use vestibule training for entrant jobs that have a relatively large population in the company.

Whether or not he does the actual training of new employees, the supervisor needs to know training techniques. Every time he explains a process or a procedure, he is training. Every time he demonstrates a technique, he is training. Every time he explains an assignment to a subordinate, he is training. Training is the means by which he builds his work team. Training enables the new employee to perform his job properly and to meet the standards of performance. Training makes it possible for present employees to acquire more skill, to be more versatile, to be ready for promotion. Training reduces errors, accidents, spoiled work, and damage to equipment. Training reduces frictions, tensions, fears, frustrations, dissatisfactions, behavior problems, absences, and quits.

With a well-trained and flexible work group, the supervisor doesn't have to spend his day putting out fires—correcting errors, repairing damage, reprimanding the makers of mistakes—or making routine deci-

---

[3] F. A. DePhillips, W. M. Berliner, and J. J. Cribbin, *Management of Training Programs* (Homewood, Ill.: Richard D. Irwin, Inc., 1960), p. 300.

sions that his subordinates should be making. He can turn over the work to them with confidence that it will be done and done correctly.

Choosing a trainer

The supervisor as a rule knows the jobs and the men in his department better than anyone else, but he is not necessarily the best man to do the training. Because of his nature and his job, he is in a hurry to get things done. He lacks the time and the patience to do the painstaking work that teaching requires. Also, it is difficult to break down the barrier between superior and subordinate to the point where the learner can relax. In the presence of the boss, learners are often tense, afraid to make mistakes, afraid to be informal, afraid they are being judged, afraid to expose their ignorance, and afraid to ask "stupid" questions that they would feel free to ask of someone else.

In many cases it is better that someone other than the supervisor act as the instructor. In most departments there are employees who with some instruction could be made into good trainers. These are men who really know all the angles of the job, who have good attitudes, who have an interest in people, and who may have gained patience through teaching their own children. A trainer must be able to take everything calmly and to improvise when unusual situations occur.

The quality of training depends to a great extent upon the effectiveness of the trainer. The main qualifications for success in the art of training are skill, knowledge, and good attitudes, and the ability to transmit them; patience, high morale, and the ability to build confidence in the trainee.

Much of the success of teaching comes from the attitude of the trainer. He must have a strong liking for teaching. He must have a deep interest in having the learner succeed. He must have a good attitude toward the company, the department, the work, and the workers. He must be patient enough to correct the same mistakes over and over again. He must repeat instructions time and again, changing the approach and the emphasis to fit the learner. He must encourage the learner when progress is slow.

The trainer must be able to diagnose training needs and develop programs to fit them. He must be able to:

1. Tell the learner *what* he needs to do.
2. Have him learn *how* to do it.
3. Explain why it should be done in the prescribed manner.

The job of trainer is a good one on which to try out rank-and-file employees who may be potential supervisors. A rank-and-file employee doesn't get many opportunities to demonstrate managerial abilities, but when acting as a trainer he has to plan, organize, direct, coordinate, and control. A man who is successful as a trainer demonstrates that he has the ability to do these things.

Uncovering training needs

Many work difficulties have their origin in lack of training, but training is not a cure-all. When things go wrong, the supervisor should suspect other causes before he decides that training is the answer: Is selection poor? Is the wrong man on the job? Are wages low? Is equipment run-down? Are working conditions unfavorable? Is supervision lax? Are jobs poorly designed? Are attitudes bad? If the trouble cannot be charged to any of these causes, then the supervisor should suspect that a need for training is indicated by the following conditions:

Standards of work performance not being met.
Accidents.
Excessive scrap.
Frequent need for equipment repairs.
High rate of transfer and turnover.
Too many people receiving low ratings on employee-evaluation reports.
Many people using different methods to do the same job.
Excessive fatigue, fumbling, discouragement, and struggling with the job.
Bottlenecks.
Deadlines not being met.

The supervisor or the trainer should investigate the job or jobs involved in any of these conditions and observe the performance to determine what training is necessary. If close observation does not uncover the difficulty, the supervisor or his trainer should make an analysis along the following steps:

1. List the duties and responsibilities or the tasks of the job under consideration, using the job description as a guide.
2. List the standards of work performance for the job.
3. Compare actual performance against the standards.
4. Determine what parts of the job are giving the employee trouble— where is he falling down in his performance?
5. Determine what kind of training is needed to overcome the specific difficulty or difficulties.

After the training has been given, its effectiveness should be judged by whether or not it improved the conditions it was intended to correct.

Are standards of performance now being met? Are employees using better methods and getting higher ratings? Is the work going more smoothly? Has there been a reduction in accidents, damage, waste, turnover, transfers, bottlenecks?

Principles of learning and techniques of training

On-the-job training will be much more efficient if the trainer will keep in mind some principles of learning and use them when he is instructing.

Motivation to learn. Employees will not learn very much unless they are motivated to learn. Children learn because they are rewarded for doing things right and punished for doing things wrong. Research by industrial psychologists[4] indicates that rewards are much more effective than punishments in stimulating learning—that praise is superior to blame. Harsh criticism may interfere with learning, and so may fear, anxiety, tension, and emotional disturbances.

Motives for learning may be both financial and nonfiancial. A person may want higher earnings, advancement, more security, more competence, or more prestige. However, he needs immediate rewards for progress in his learning as he goes along. One such reward is his feeling of achievement in making progress. In order to get this reward he must be able to find out how he is doing—he must have some *feedback of results*. The army found that feedback was necessary in teaching marksmanship. Target shooting can't be learned unless the marksman has some way of knowing whether he has hit the target. If he missed it, he needs to know by how much and in which direction. Programmed instruction (the "teaching machine") is based upon this principle of immediate feedback. The learner studies a small segment of a subject, answers a question about it, and finds out immediately if his answer was right or wrong.

Learning by doing. Learning is accomplished through the senses. Learning a job skill is accomplished through seeing, hearing, and doing. The learner sees the demonstration of skill, he hears the instruction and explanation, and he performs the action himself. He repeats the performance until he builds up a habit pattern.

Goals and subgoals. A person learns faster if he is working toward a goal. First of all he must have a reason for wanting to learn. Then he needs a definite target—some level of accomplishment he intends to achieve. Then he should have subgoals—a definite amount of progress he expects to make that week. Goals should have been set by studying pre-

---

[4] For a deeper study of learning as a process, see Richard Bugelski, *The Psychology of Learning* (New York: Henry Holt & Co., Inc., 1956); Harold Leavitt, *Managerial Psychology* (2d ed.; Chicago: University of Chicago Press, 1964).

vious learners on the same job, charting their progress, and constructing a learning curve. If a learner can see where other people had difficulty, were slowed in their progress, and then picked up again and forged ahead, he is more confident that he can do it too.

Goals mustn't be set too high. A person has to have some successes to fortify him through periods of little progress. In learning, nothing succeeds like success, and a learner's success is his knowledge that he is making progress. On the other hand, goals shouldn't be too easy or they will be no challenge to achievement.

People who are trying to master a skill like to have their goals and subgoals set up in a timetable so they can see where they are and how they are progressing. Like the target shooters, they want definite reports of just exactly when and where they are making hits, and just how far off they are on the misses. Telling a learner he is doing fine isn't definite enough; he wants to know which part of his work is fine.

Plateaus. People sometimes hit plateaus in their learning—periods in which they seem to be making no progress. These are the times in which they get discouraged. They may quit trying, quit the job, or be absent just to escape the frustration. The trainer needs to encourage them and to assure them that trying harder will pay off. Sometimes a person thinks he has reached the limit of his learning, when actually he is on a plateau and could enter another period of improvement.

Individual differences. Not everyone learns at the same rate or achieves the same high degree of skill. Some people have to try a lot harder than others. If a learner is making nowhere near the standard rate of progress, he may lack the native ability or the motive, or the instruction may be poor.

Blocks to learning. Resistance to change is one of the blocks to learning. The causes of resistance to change are discussed in Chapter 15. Research on resistance to change has demonstrated that employees ordinarily objected so strongly to changes in their jobs that they had difficulty learning their new tasks and getting their speed up to the performance standards. But the groups that participated in designing the changes in their jobs learned their changed jobs quickly and got their speed up to the standard. Resistance to learning a changed job seems to be reduced if employees have a lot of opportunity to air their ideas about the changes.

The supervisor and the trainer should remember that an employee has no urge to learn a job that displeases him or seems to be a threat to him. A person may have difficulty relearning a job that was changed by sudden, arbitrary, or unexplained action of management. Sometimes resistance to a new method takes the form of an attempt to show that it won't work. Attitudes toward the supervisor may affect the speed with which an employee learns a changed job. Sometimes employees hold down their rate of output so they won't show up the slower members of their group.

Learning by parts. People learn in small doses; they cannot, even if they want to, attend to many details at the same time. Breaking the task into small, digestible portions expedites learning. It also creates a number of subgoals which the learner gets the satisfaction of achieving.

The four-step method of job training

Many supervisors and trainers are familiar with Job Instruction Training (JIT)—a very effective method of transmitting a well-defined, but not too complex, skill from one person who possesses it to another who does not. It is founded on the principles of good teaching and is used as the basis for the following discussion.

Before the instructor starts to instruct, he must have his whole program worked out in advance. He has to determine *which men* need instruction, *what kind, how much,* and *when* they can be fitted into his schedule. This calls for the making up of a training timetable.

After determining what training is necessary, the trainer must set up the instruction in a teachable form. This can be accomplished by using a job breakdown sheet. On the left-hand side of the sheet, he should list the *steps* and on the right-hand side of the sheet he should list the corresponding *key points*. The steps constitute the *what* is to be done, and they are set up in the sequence in which they are to be performed. Opposite each step is listed its key points—*how* it is to be done in order to perform the step successfully, and *why* it should be done in this manner. Some examples of key points are:

Do not touch leads until motor stops	in order to avoid possible shock.
Finish piece within certain limits	so that it will fit mating part.
Use a stick to push work past the saw	in order to avoid cutting hand.
Measure with micrometer	in order to get accurate reading.
Line up sheets against guidelines	so that lines will be straight.
Press down pencil or pen	to make the last carbon readable.
Boil in water 20 minutes	to sterilize.

By planning his instruction procedure in advance, the trainer will be able to move from step to step. He will foresee many of the difficulties the worker will run into and be prepared to guide the learner through them. It is also necessary to have all the equipment ready, so that there will be no delays when the actual training begins. The work place should be carefully prepared—everything clean and orderly—to set the correct example from the start and let the learner know how he is expected to keep it.

The trainer is now ready to start instructing according to the four-step method:

Step 1.   Preparation of the learner

1. Put the learner at ease—relieve the tension.
2. Explain why he is being taught.
3. Create interest—encourage questions—find out what the learner already knows about his job or other jobs.
4. Explain the why of the whole job and relate it to some job that the worker already knows.
5. Place the learner as close to the normal working position as possible.
6. Familiarize him with the equipment, materials, tools, and trade terms.

Step 2.   Presentation of the operation

1. Explain quality and quantity requirements.
2. Go through the job at the normal work pace.
3. Go through the job at a slow pace several times, explaining each *step*. Between operations, explain the difficult parts or ones in which errors are likely to be made.
4. Go through the job at a slow pace several times, explaining the *key points*.
5. Have the learner explain the *steps* as you go through the job at a slow pace.
6. Have the learner explain the *key points* as you go through the job at a slow pace.

Step 3.   Performance tryout

1. Have the learner go through the job several times, slowly, explaining to you each *step*. Correct his mistakes and if necessary you, the trainer, do some of the complicated steps for him the first few times.
2. You, the trainer run the job at the normal pace.
3. Have the learner do the job, gradually building up skill and speed.
4. As soon as he demonstrates that he can do the job, put him on his own but don't abandon him.

Step 4.   Follow-up

1. Designate to whom the learner should go for help if he needs it or if he needs to ask questions.
2. Decrease supervision gradually, checking his work from time to time against quality and quantity standards.
3. Correct faulty work patterns that begin to creep into his work, and

do it before they become habits. Show him why the learned method is superior.

4. Compliment good work; encourage him, and keep him encouraged until he is able to meet the quality and quantity standards.

The use of the term "steps" implies a strict progression from Step 1 to Step 4. In effective instruction this progression is not rigid; rather there may be a blending of the steps throughout the process. Preparing, motivating, presenting, explaining are as necessary near the end of the lesson as they are in the beginning.

Summary

The personnel department introduces the employee to the company. The supervisor introduces him to the job and to the work group. Induction by the supervisor serves to let the employee know what will be required of him if he is to be successful on the job. He is also told what there is in it for him—how the job will serve his needs. Induction and orientation are designed to assure the new man that this is a good place to work. They help build his confidence in the training program and give him encouragement while he is learning his job. Induction speeds his integration into the work group.

The induction and orientation procedure must be adapted to fit the type of job and the needs of the person; teenagers and inexperienced people need more help and attention.

Special problems and circumstances are involved in the induction and orientation of young adults. This is particularly true of minority group members. Supervisors should give extra care to the orientation of young people because of the high labor turnover among this group.

On-the-job training should probably be done by someone other than the supervisor. An employee skilled in the work might be developed into a trainer. He should have patience and a liking for teaching. He should become acquainted with the principles of learning: motivation, goals, subgoals, feedback of results, individual differences in ability and learning speed, plateaus in learning, and the importance of encouragement and confidence.

On-the-job training serves to speed up the learning of a new job and the time needed to reach performance standards. Continued training is needed to adapt to change—changes in employees and changes in jobs. Training increases employees' versatility for transfers and qualifications for promotion. It increases their skills and abilities to perform their present jobs. It reduces frustrations, frictions, errors, waste, and struggles with the job. The supervisor who has a well-trained work group can delegate responsibilities and devote his time to the important parts of his job.

The four-step method of job training (JIT) provides an effective instruction plan.

Orientation and induction

CASE 1

A few days ago you hired Harold White to replace the resigning head of the toolroom. The day White reported for work, you were out sick, and he was put to work by your assistant, Jim Jones. You had neglected to inform Jim about the new man and the job he was to fill.

As soon as you get back on the job, you ask Jim about White. He replies: "White says he is going to quit at the end of the week because he is tired of being pushed around."

You ask Jim how he started the new man on the job. He reports that since he didn't know what White was hired for, he asked him, and White said he was hired to work in the toolroom. Since Jim didn't know that the present head of the toolroom planned to resign, he couldn't see where the new man was to fit into the picture; so he kept him busy for a few hours studying the employees' handbook. Then he introduced White to the 20 people in the section; next he told him to look at the various jobs being performed and then go home. The next day Jim thought White should start earning his keep, so he gave him a job on the conveyor line. After half a day of it, White complained that he couldn't stand that type of work; so in the afternoon, Jim took White to the head of the toolroom and told him to put White to work helping his assistant. The assistant put him to work cleaning some equipment.

1. What were some of the mistakes that Jim Jones made in inducting White?
2. What would be the normal reaction of White after the first day? After the second day?
3. How are you going to correct the situation?
4. How would you have inducted White?
5. Outline the steps of a procedure for inducting a new employee.

CASE 2

The other day the personnel department informed you that one of your men had quit—Smith, an operator you had hired about a month ago. During the exit interview, he told the personnel interviewer he was quitting because in your section the regular workers were a clique, there were no opportunities for an outsider, and he had been told that he was not wanted.

You began to investigate by talking to Jack White, the old-timer whom you had selected to help Smith get acquainted with the job and with the other men. Jack informed you that he went to lunch with Smith the first day. During the meal Smith kept boasting of how he was going to be top man in the section before long because of his wonderful experience—that you had practically guaranteed him rapid advancement by stating that his past experience would be of great aid to him. Jack claimed that he tried to show Smith that this attitude wouldn't do him any good in getting along with the group. The next day Smith turned down Jack's suggestion that they go to lunch together and went instead with Bill Brown, who had recently been demoted and transferred to your section. Smith and Brown continued going to lunch together.

Then you began to check up on Smith's work. You found that he made less than normal progress during the month he was in your section. You spoke to several of the men who worked with Smith. They told you that none of the men liked him—that he criticized everything and everybody and was constantly saying that in the company where he had worked previously conditions were better and better work was turned out. One of the group said he told Smith that, if he didn't like the way things were done here, he ought to quit.

You review your actions in the hiring of Smith. You recall from the application blank and the interview that he came to work for a wage that was less than he had received on his previous job, also that he had received no raises on his last two jobs. During the interview he stated that he didn't mind getting less than his previous wage if he had the opportunity to advance—that the reason he quit his last two jobs was the lack of opportunity on them. You told him there were always opportunities in the company for a good man. During the month Smith was on the job, you spoke to him several times, and he told you that he was coming along fine.

1. What might be some of the things wrong with Smith—the man who quit?
2. Which of these might you have uncovered in the interview?
3. What mistakes might you have made in the induction?
4. How should you have inducted Smith?
5. Suppose he is right about the clique—that your group does try to discourage new men who are good workers—how are you going to clean up that situation?
6. What are you looking for in an induction follow-up?
7. How do you get this information?

CASE 3

Recently you hired Jones to work in your department. The work is such that the men have to team up in pairs. Jones has an extremely fast reaction time which enables him to work at a pace that far excels that of your best men.

Several times he has complained to you about the slowness of a partner and has asked for and received a new partner. You have been observing his performance and notice that he seems to delight in showing off by rushing and rattling the man working with him.

At first you thought that the presence of Jones would stimulate your men to greater output. However you find that spoilage has gone up and that production and morale have gone down. The men dislike Jones intensely; they think he is a show-off and speed artist. Jones thinks they are slowpokes. Before Jones came, the production was satisfactory but could have been better; now it's worse.

1. Should you try to slow Jones down? Why? Why not?
2. If you terminate Jones, what might be some of the effects on the other men?
3. What should you do?
4. What are some of the factors that you should consider when inducting into a work team a person with outstanding ability or special aptitude?

CASE 4

Recently you hired J. Gray, an experienced operator who had worked in five different companies in the preceding five years, staying about a year on each job. During the induction interview, while you were explaining the rules and what was expected of him, he did not seem to be paying much attention. Occasionally he interrupted you to say that he felt this job would be the same as his previous ones. When you showed him around, he seemed to be pretty well informed about everything. When you introduced him to some of the other workers and his lead man, his manner was somewhat abrupt.

During his first week on the job you observe him and ask other workers about his progress. You find that he works in an unsafe manner, that he smokes in forbidden areas, and that he stops work much too soon before quitting time. However, the quality and quantity of his work are excellent.

1. What are some differences between inducting an experienced man and inducting a greenhorn?
2. What are some of the things wrong with J. Gray?
3. To what extent could you have suspected these things during the induction interview?
4. How should you have inducted J. Gray?
5. How should you correct him now?

CASE 5

The personnel department has just sent you an applicant—Bill Black—for a job in your section. As you look over his application blank and talk to him, you feel quite sure that he would make a good assistant supervisor. However, you want to try him out as an operator before you inform him about what you have in mind.

Not one of your present employees is qualified for the job of assistant supervisor. A short while ago you tried out the best one of them in this position. He failed and quit the company; thus you lost a good operator.

Since Black is smarter than the rest of your men, you know that the group will suspect something. You would like to induct him in the regular way and have him get well acquainted with the workers; yet you fear that if he should be promoted in a short time, the workers would think that he was spying on them while he was an operator. That would start him off on his supervisory job with a handicap.

1. What advantages does an outsider have over the fellow promoted from within, in assuming a supervisory role?
2. What disadvantages does he have?
3. How chummy do you want Black to get with the rest of the group if you plan to make him a supervisor soon?
4. How would you handle such an induction?
5. If you were hiring him as an assistant supervisor, how would you induct him?

CASE 6

In the coil-winding department, women are employed to form small wire coils on coil-winding machines. These machines often get out of adjustment and require frequent servicing. The machines are maintained by a group of young repairmen.

The best operators of the coil-winding machines have been found to be middle-aged women. They chat while they work and don't find the job monotonous. They work very well from September to June and then most of them quit to stay home and take care of their children during the summer vacation from school. The only replacements available in June are young girls just graduated from the local high school. These girls do not work out well on the job. Their production is low and discipline is a problem. Miss Marsh, the supervisor—a spinster in her mid-fifties—seems unable to cope with them.

The young girls don't stay long. In their exit interviews (given by the personnel department to employees who are quitting or being fired) the girls say that Miss Marsh is an old maid who does not understand young girls. They say she does not keep order—that the repairmen as they go by pull the girls' hair. When the girls squeal, Miss Marsh bawls them out in front of everyone, which makes the girls indignant and some of them cry. The girls say they don't know what Miss Marsh wants until she jumps on them about something. They think what is wrong with her is that she doesn't understand young people since she never had any children. Without warning she jumps on them about not working hard enough, which is not fair because they are tired at the end of the day; besides the work is monotonous and they are entitled to some fun on the job.

A representative of the industrial relations department has spoken to Miss Marsh to get her side of the story. She says the girls are just fresh from high school and don't know how to work. They look on a job as an extension of high school. Their production is much below that of the married women because the girls don't get enough sleep at night. Miss Marsh says she can't do anything about the repairmen because they come from another department, her department can't get along without them, and besides the girls bring it on themselves by flirting with the fellows.

1. How should this situation be handled?
2. Work up an induction and orientation program that will be effective in getting young people (recent high school graduates) started on the right foot in industry.
3. Why should new, young, high school graduates be given extra consideration by their supervisors?
4. Should a supervisor take extra care with the induction and orientation of young people?

CASE 7

The company had long made it a practice to hire typists and stenographers with little or no business experience. These girls were assigned to the company's secretarial department. This department served all of the company's needs for transcription, typing, and secretarial help, With the exception of divisional executives and senior management, no one in the company had a private secretary. In addition, girls from the secretarial department were assigned to substitute for the executive secretaries during vacations and they helped when the executives needed additional assistance because of unusual work loads.

All of the girls received considerable training in the use of various typewriters and dictating machines and were encouraged to develop their stenographic skills. When a vacancy occurred in the executive secretarial staff it was the company's policy to promote the senior girl from the secretarial department. Because turnover occurred with relative frequency among the executive secretaries, the company used this promotional opportunity to considerable advantage when recruiting girls for its secretarial department. The combination of training and experience along with the opportunity to become a private secretary seemed to help the company attract applicants in a tight labor market. The policy had been working well for several years and the company's personnel director was satisfied with it.

Dave Elliot, the company's treasurer had sent a requisition to personnel for a replacement for his secretary who was leaving in a month to be with her husband who was transferred by his company. John Randolph, the personnel director, checked the list of girls in the secretarial pool and found that Betty Wright was the senior girl. He called Dave and told him he would assign Betty immediately so that she could be broken in by the time Dave's present secretary left. Dave refused to accept Betty saying that he had used her some months ago on a special job and she didn't impress him favorably. He went on to say that accuracy was extremely important in his department and Betty could not meet his requirements. The personnel director reminded him of the company policy regarding the promotion of girls from the secretarial department and told him that Betty was fully aware that she was the senior girl and was due to fill the first vacancy for a private secretary. He explained that it would be very difficult to pass over her and that this would cause a considerable loss of morale among the girls in the department who looked forward to being the senior girl because they knew the next step was promotion to a private secretary's position.

The treasurer listened to all of the reasons put forth by the personnel man but he still refused to accept Betty Wright.

1. Can any compromise be worked out so that the company policy will not be broken?
2. Is the policy a sound one?
3. How can problems of this kind be avoided in the future?
4. Is the treasurer being too inflexible in his refusal to accept Betty Wright?

CASE 8

You are the section head of a clerical customer service unit in a large insurance company's offices. The company is located in a city with a large ethnically and racially mixed population.

You have 15 employees reporting to you. Three are men and 12 are women. Three of the women are Puerto Rican, all of whom started in your department at about the same time and who have become very friendly with each other.

Your section handles customer inquiries both on the telephone and in person and in general you have been maintaining a smoothly functioning unit. Lately you have been receiving complaints from several of your staff about the three Puerto Rican girls. The complaints center around the fact that the three girls speak Spanish to each other very frequently and the other employees resent this. The complainers feel that they are being talked about and that it is unfair because they cannot understand what is being said.

You have not had any prior trouble with the three girls who are energetic, accurate, and excellent workers. There have been no customer complaints and the three girls have no difficulty at all in conversing in English although each has an accent.

1. Should you ask the three girls to speak English at all times when they are on the job?
2. Would the other employees feel the same resentment if the language spoken was some other one than Spanish?
3. Could the three girls be conversing in Spanish on a social basis because they have not felt fully welcome?
4. Could their Spanish conversations be just natural lapses into an easier method of communication with no ulterior motives?
5. Why do your other employees feel they are being talked about and what can you do about it?

CASE 9

Judy is a high school graduate hired four months ago. She is developing into one of your best workers and she is adaptable to a great variety of jobs in the department. But she is very sensitive. If things don't go just the way she wants, she pouts. If you fail to say good morning to her the first time you see her each day, she pouts. You are getting tired of this pouting.

1. What are some of the causes of pouting?
2. What treatments have you found effective in curing it?
3. Should you pay any attention at all to Judy?
4. Could Judy's sensitivity have anything to do with her effective work performance?

Training

CASE 1

Recently you were put in charge of a section of office workers. The previous supervisor was transferred because the work coming out of this particular section was of rather poor quality and quantity.

As you investigate the situation, you find out that most of the workers are young people with limited experience. They learned their jobs from one another and received no training on the job. You believe that if you can uncover their weak spots and remove these by training, the situation will be improved.

1. Set up a procedure for determining training needs.
2. What information should be on a training timetable?
3. Make up a training timetable.

CASE 2

You are in charge of shop operations. On account of the shortage of help, it will be necessary for you to train some inexperienced women to operate bench-type sensitive (hand-feed) drill presses.

1. Set down, step by step, the procedure a trainer should follow in training these women.
2. What are the key points which will spell success or failure of the above steps?
3. What is the *why* of each key point?

CASE 3

You are in charge of the milling machine section of a company producing a high-quality hand tool under its own name. Up until a month ago it also turned out the same type tool of lower quality under another brand name in order to meet price competition.

One of your men, Joe Blue, supervised the group of workers handling the milling of this lower grade tool. The objective of this group was to produce as cheaply as possible with little attention to quality. Joe and his crew worked well together in a slam-bang fashion. Their motto was "Our work may not be much good, but we turn out lots of it."

When increased demand for the high-quality product influenced the company to drop the second brand, Joe and his crew of operators were shifted over to work on the quality product. That was about a month ago. They are anxious to do a good job but are having great difficulty reducing rejects and turning out a quality product. The equipment they are working with is in good shape. You and Joe believe that it will be necessary to retrain the operators on how to do a quality job.

1. What work habits will they have to unlearn?
2. What are some of the problems the trainer will run into?
3. How should he overcome these problems?
4. What qualifications should the trainer have?
5. Set up a training procedure to take care of this situation.

CASE 4

You supervise a group of workers. You train each new worker on the job, using the four-step method. The job is simple, and most employees learn it quickly; however, you are having trouble teaching Joe

White, a new employee. Instead of listening to you and following your instruction, he tries to rush through the steps. As a result, he gets everything bungled. You have repeated the steps over and over again, but with little success. You do not wish to give Joe up as hopeless because workers are quite scarce.

1. What might be some of the reasons for Joe's behavior?
2. In terms of these reasons, how should you modify your instruction?
3. Suppose Joe is quite stupid, how should you modify your procedure?
4. Suppose Joe is naturally very awkward, how should you modify your procedure?
5. What are some of the indications that training of an individual is not succeeding and that the trainee should be shifted to some other type of work?

CASE 5

You are in charge of a large section doing office work. All your new girls come to you through the training department. They are turned over to you as being completely trained to do their jobs. However, you receive numerous complaints about the errors these new girls are making. When you approach the training supervisor with a list of recurring errors, she becomes indignant. She tells you that she is a trained teacher—that she is teaching the girls what they need to know and that she is not taking orders from you on what should be taught.

1. What are the advantages of training workers away from the job in a training department?
2. What are the disadvantages?
3. What are the advantages of training workers on the job?
4. What are the disadvantages?
5. How valid is the saying: "Forget all you learned in school and learn the way we do it on the job"?
6. How can the work of the training department and the operating departments be better coordinated?

CASE 6

You have been in charge of a shop section for the last 10 years and have been improving yourself right along by studying at night school. The young man who was just put in charge of the section next to yours is a recent graduate of a trade school.

Your boss asked you to help this young man get off to a good start—to explain company policies and procedures. You have tried, but your efforts have met with only halfhearted acceptance. You are interested in training him because the work of two sections must be closely coordinated. His lack of understanding of procedures has caused a fair amount of trouble already.

1. What parts of a supervisor's job can be learned from books?
2. What parts of a supervisor's job can be taught by fellow supervisors?
3. What parts of a supervisor's job should be taught by his superior?
4. Since there is a need for cooperation between you and the new supervisor, how are you going to handle the situation?

CASE 7

The Acme Municipal Bus Company (or substitute another type of company having this problem) has an excellent program for training its bus drivers. The course includes a very good battery of tests, visual aids, practice driving, safety training, and finally trial runs. Throughout the program, trainees receive careful instruction. As a result, the accident rate is well below the average for bus companies. The bus driver training program is known as the best in the state. Management is beginning to wonder if the program is just too good. There are rumors going around in the trade that some of the smaller out-of-town companies are telling their job applicants that they would be hired if they had completed the Acme Bus Company course. The applicants take the hint, move to the city, get employed by Acme, and take the course. Then they quit and go back to the home town and get the job. An analysis of the recent labor turnover indicates that this is what is happening. Before the training program became such a success, the labor turnover of the drivers was relatively low.

How should the situation be handled?

CASE 8

It is the policy of the company when hiring a new man to put him on probation as a temporary employee before making him permanent. The employees understand the policy. But the length of the probationary period as set by the policy is too short to really permit the evaluation of a man's performance, and it seems that nothing can be done about lengthening this period. At the end of the trial work period, each man is interviewed, his performance is evaluated, then he is either made a permanent employee or terminated.

Will West, the supervisor, has decided to terminate the temporary employee, Norm North, at the end of North's probationary period. North has been a good employee in relation to quality, dependability, cooperativeness, and such, but the amount of his production is below standard; he seems unable to turn out as many pieces as are required of, and are turned out by, the permanent employees. West has pointed this out to North on several occasions—each followed by a spurt in output, and each spurt has leveled off at a slightly higher plane. North maintains that he is a slow learner and that if he is given sufficient time he is sure he can make the grade. West knows that the trial work period is too short, but he is afraid to take a chance of getting stuck with North. It would be much more difficult to terminate North once he became a permanent employee.

1. What are the advantages and limitations of having trial work periods?
2. In what types of jobs are they useful?
3. In what types of jobs are they a handicap to management?
4. What should be done with North? Justify your answer.
5. How should you go about doing it?

CASE 9

Each supervisor has full responsibility for the training of his production employees on the job. He selects an experienced operator to do the training. All workers are on a piece rate, and the learners are guaranteed a minimum wage plus a 10 percent bonus which they will receive if the supervisor considers their progress to be satisfactory. The operator who does the training is compensated to make up for the production he loses while giving advice to the new employee.

The personnel department recommends that workers be trained in a training department where they will have the guidance of a skilled trainer. The training period will be eight weeks, during which time speed and output will be measured against a learning curve developed by observing on-the-job trainees. Whenever the learner's performance falls behind that shown on the learning curve, the 10 percent bonus will be stopped.

The production supervisors oppose this plan. They think that new employees are better off if they are put into the regular job environment at once. The supervisors claim that on-the-job training is more satisfactory and is usually completed in less than eight weeks, thus quick learners can be taken off the bonus and costs reduced.

The personnel department advocates uniformity in teaching the best work methods. It claims that supervisors are too busy to devote the time required for constant checking on learners. Consequently, inefficient learners are not weeded out soon enough, and the company loses money through low production.

1. What are some of the advantages of vestibule training?
2. What are some of the disadvantages?
3. What are some of the advantages of on-the-job training?
4. What are some of the disadvantages of having an operator do the training?

5. Is there a way to combine the advantages of the two types?
6. Is this learners' bonus plan a good one?

CASE 10

Up until now there has been no employee training in the company. The superintendent thinks that now is the time to start it and that the training should be of benefit to the person being trained and to the company. He believes that employee training should be a line function. He has asked the supervisors to discuss in their next meeting: (1) What should be taught? (2) How should it be taught? (3) Who should do the training?

1. What kind of training will be "of benefit to the person and to the company"?
2. What are some of the subjects, techniques, and skills that should be taught in terms of this objective?
3. What qualifications are necessary to teach them?
4. Who should do the training? Why?
5. How should the training needs be determined?

CASE 11

In a company manufacturing electronics equipment the training section of the personnel department handles the induction and training of new production workers, mostly women, many of them housewives. The induction or orientation program lasts for a week. Lectures and tours take two hours each day; the rest of the time is spent taking a battery of tests, receiving skill training, and doing wiring and soldering exercises. The misfits are weeded out during this week. The people who are retained are ready to produce at the shop pace when they are turned over to the shop at the beginning of the second week.

The production department contends that because operators quit without notice, a call for replacements means that they need them immediately and not a week later. They argue that a half-day's specialized training is all that is necessary—that all the rest of it is fancywork to justify the existence of the training department.

1. What are the advantages and disadvantages of induction programs?
2. What are the advantages and disadvantages of a training department?
3. What are advantages and disadvantages of training on the job?
4. How should induction be divided between the personnel and the operating departments?
5. How should training be divided?
6. Evaluate your own company's training program.
7. Evaluate your own company's induction program.
8. How can each be strengthened?

CASE 12

You are a supervisor of an office force which must deal with both top management and the operating departments. You are a great believer in an extensive training program, teaching each employee as much as you feel he is capable of handling. By so doing you have produced some highly trained men. Top management helps itself to these valuable men of yours—borrowing them and assigning them to special projects or promoting them to higher positions. This leaves you with either an insufficient number of employees to carry on the work, or the problem of training a large number of workers all the time—making it very difficult for you to plan or set up a good organization.

1. What are the advantages of continuing your present practice?
2. What are the disadvantages?
3. Should you continue to give such extensive training, or shou'd you assign each employee to one job and teach him just enough to do that job well?
4. What would be a satisfactory arrangement for taking care of the above situation?

CASE 13

Each worker in your department receives two weeks' summer vacation. The periods are staggered so as to make a full-time job for a substitute. The substitute for the last few summers has been a bright young engineer from the office who is being groomed for a managerial position. For the first week or so he works well and is interested, although he never mingles with members of your group. His interest soon wanes, and the quality and quantity of his work fall off. Your group wants to know whether his work is a sample of what it takes to get ahead with top management. At the end of each summer he returns to his office work with more knowledge of the manufacturing processes but with his stock sunk to a new low in the shop.

1. What are the causes of this situation?
2. How can the problem be solved?
3. How would you handle the young man in this situation? What would you say to him? How would you handle the group?
4. What are some of the methods that can be used to acquaint management trainees with the workings of the shop?

CASE 14

Recently you were hired as a safety supervisor and told to set up a safety department. The company feels it should have such a department because business is expanding and other companies have such departments.

It is becoming apparent to you that one of your most difficult tasks will be to indoctrinate management and the employees as to the benefits to be derived from practicing safety. Management seems reluctant to allow you to take company time to instruct the workers in safe practices. Prior to your coming, safety education was confined to posters on the bulletin board. The severity and frequency rates of accidents have been low, due to luck and the smallness of the plant. You fear that, with expansion of the plant and the hiring of new workers, things will be different.

1. How are you going to sell safety to management?
2. How are you going to sell safety to the employees?
3. What should be the content of a safety training program?
4. How should safety training be taught? By whom?

CASE 15

The industrial relations department is in charge of the program set up to train recent college graduates for supervisory positions. Part of the training consists of job rotation. Each man spends about a month in a department then moves to another department. The purpose of the rotation is to acquaint the new men with the functions of the various departments and help them find the type of work that is in line with their interests and thus find a niche in the organization. When a trainee finishes his time in each department, he writes a report outlining the functions of the department and his impressions of the department. The department head also submits a report giving his impressions of the trainee who has been working for him.

One of the trainees, Richard Rice, has had conflicts with most of the supervisors. He is supercharged with bright ideas, energy, ambition, enthusiasm, self-confidence, and tenacity. But he is tactless, abrupt, positive he is right, ruthless and outspoken in his criticism, has as his motto "survival of the fittest," and thinks that "easy does it" is a cover-up for laziness or cowardice. What he calls "speaking factually," the supervisors term as "young know-it-all shooting his mouth off." In dealing with him, the supervisors seem to figure that the best defense is a good offense. Their reports about Richard Rice, and Rice's reports about the departments, are extremely critical—much more so than reports on or by other trainees.

You, the industrial relations director, are responsible for this training program. Your subordinate, Tom Thomas, the training supervisor, has kept you informed of Rice's conflicts and has now brought in the pack of reports on Rice. You see from the reports that all he has gotten in some departments was "busywork."

1. How should the problem of Richard Rice be handled? Justify you answer.
2. Outline a plan for developing greater cooperation between supervisors and trainees in terms of the objectives of the program.

FOLLOWING UP ON THE JOB

Induction and orientation

1. Do you have a list of things to do in introducing the new employee to the job?
2. Do your new employees understand the safety regulations? The rules of conduct?
3. Do you tailor your induction procedure to fit the man being inducted? The greenhorn? The transferred employee? The experienced worker?
4. Do you take enough time to do a good job when inducting a new man?
5. Does each new employee know what is expected of him for satisfactory performance?
6. Do you put enough emphasis on fitting the new employee into the group?
7. Does each new employee know the extent of his authority and responsibility?
8. Does each new employee know exactly who is his immediate boss?
9. Do you follow up on the new employee closely enough?
10. Do you encourage him?
11. Do you let him know where he stands?
12. Do you have a high rate of quits among new employees?

Job training

1. Do you recognize the symptoms of lack of training?
2. Do you know how to uncover training needs?
3. Do you investigate the training needs of regular workers as well as those of new workers?
4. Does the person doing the training understand and follow the principles of learning when he is instructing?
5. Is the person doing the training in your section the one best qualified to be doing it?
6. Does the trainer have everything prepared in advance before he starts to train a man?
7. Does the trainer use the four-step method of job training?
8. Is safety stressed enough in training?
9. Do you follow up on the effectiveness of training?

13 Organizational development and manpower planning

Organizational growth and development. Manpower planning. Performance appraisal. Appraisal is systematic rather than haphazard. Difficulties in rating. Some common types of rating errors. Suiting the plan to the purpose. The appraisal interview as a means of improving performance on the job. Rating the probationary employee. Interview problems. Promotions and the people who want them. Advantages and disadvantages of promoting from within. Evaluating and developing supervisors. Career planning. The fast-track manager. Internal mobility. Remedial transfers. Transfers for training purposes. Transfers necessitated by changes. Transfers and seniority. Transfer policy. The environment for career development. Summary.

Most texts on management theory create the impression that the growth and development of an organization is an orderly process. Discussion centers around objectives, policies, structure, control, direction, planning, staffing, and several other management functions. Once goals are identified, a suitable formal structure is designed and the enterprise is off and running.

That this rather simplistic approach to organizational development rarely, if ever takes place, is both one of the most perplexing problems and significant challenges presented to managers. To understand the impact of those problems and challenges and the various factors involved in them is a necessary part of the manager's responsibility.

The purpose of this chapter is to show the manager what organizational development and manpower planning mean to him from career as well as managerial viewpoints.

Organizational growth and development

Managers make several decisions over a period of time which have a variety of consequences for their organizations. Increased demand for the products or services a firm offers may require decisions to hire more people. More people could require more space and, therefore, a decision to enlarge a plant or an office may be required. Pressure on a manager to increase production could cause him to ask for more help. A positive response from his superiors would enlarge his span of control causing him to decide to promote someone to be his assistant. Thus a new supervisory position is created changing the nature of the formal organization structure and the established reporting relationships. An opportunity to acquire a company in a related field results in a decision which may take the firm into a different set of circumstances and problems than those with which its managers are familiar. Increased size usually means greater complexity and this could result in more levels of management as well as requirements for additional supervisors and other employees.

While the growth of some organizations may appear to be "Topsy-like," in actuality it is usually not spontaneous. It is the result of management decisions made by individuals who try to move the organization toward its goals as they perceive them. This does not imply that some of the decisions are not haphazard. In fact the decisions that may have the most effect on an organization are frequently made without full consideration of their total impact. What results in some cases is an organization resembling a patchwork quilt that becomes very difficult to manage.

It is relatively easy for an individual manager to plan for his own area of responsibility. Understanding the relationship of his plans to the rest of the organization is a more difficult task. It is precisely this difficulty that causes many of the problems in dynamic organizations.

Growth and development are frequently thought of as synonymous. That they are not is pointed out by Herbert Hicks in his book, *The Management of Organizations*. He states:

> . . . we will consider organizational growth to be any increase in the size of the organization or any movement toward a given objective. Organizational development, on the other hand, will be considered as the formation of new combinations of resources or the formulation of new attainable and visionary objectives. Development is the broader of the two concepts; it occurs through innovation and it provides the framework within which growth can occur. Growth, being narrower, occurs within a given stage of development. Reaching or attaining the maximum output with a given stage of development is a process of attaining maximum growth. Growth asks: How does the organization get more out of what it now has? Development asks: How can the organization achieve something different?[1]

Longevity is not necessarily characteristic of an organization. The number of business failures of both large and small companies each

---

[1] Herbert G. Hicks, *The Management of Organizations* (New York: McGraw-Hill Book Co., 1967), p. 82.

year attests to this. Likewise the large number of mergers and acquisitions of recent years also indicates that a particular organization can disappear as a separate entity by being taken over. To a very great extent, the length of time that an organization exists has a direct relationship to the effectiveness of its managers. Their ability to handle growth and development while establishing and achieving objectives and encouraging efficient operation has a good bit to do with organizational longevity.

In Chapter 11 mention was made of recent research indicating that organizational climate had a definite effect on the requirements of that organization. The philosophy of its management in relation to present situations and future considerations is also a dominant factor. The effective utilization of resources, especially human resources, contribute much to organization longevity. Assuring a constant and adequate supply of capable managers and other employees is vital to sound organization development. This means the creation of a development environment which will demonstrate that senior management is serious about growth and development and that it will encourage employees on all levels to take advantage of the internal climate to optimize their individual careers.

In the early 1950's, Peter Drucker in discussing the development of managers described his thinking and it is still very timely.

The prosperity if not the survival of any business depends on the performance of its managers of tomorrow. This is particularly true today when basic business decisions require for their fruition an increasingly long time-span. Since no one can foresee the future, management cannot make rational and responsible decisions unless it selects, develops and tests the men who will have to follow them through—the managers of tomorrow.

. . . Manager development cannot be just "promotion planning," confined to "promotable people" and aimed at finding "back-up men" for top-management vacancies. The very term "back-up man" implies that the job of a manager as well as the organization structure of a company will remain unchanged so that one simply has to find people to step into the shoes of today's executives. Yet, if one thing is certain, it is that both job requirements and organization structure will change in the future as they have always done in the past. What is needed is the development of managers equal to the tasks of tomorrow, not the tasks of yesterday.

. . . The concept of the back-up man for top-management jobs also overlooks the fact that the most important decisions regarding tomorrow's management are made long before a man is promoted to a senior position. Tomorrow's senior positions will be filled by men who today occupy junior positions. By the time we have to find a man to take over the managership of a big plant or sales organization, our choice will already be limited to three or four people. It is in appointing people to positions as general foreman or department superintendent, as district sales manager, as auditor, etc., that we make the decisions that are crucial. And in making these decisions the typical back-up planning helps us little, if at all.[2]

These rather prophetic remarks form a suitable frame of reference for what we today call organization development. In addition to managers, staffing of the entire organization, the climate created, and the seriousness of management's purpose are the totality of organization development. This includes several factors. Among these are:

1. Effective recruitment, selection, training, and placement of new employees.
2. The creation of a climate that will encourage self-development and upward mobility.
3. An effective compensation and reward program.
4. Performance appraisal carried on systematically and as objectively as possible.
5. An effective program of internal mobility including promotion and transfer of employees that is mutually acceptable.
6. Early identification of promotables.
7. Supervisor and management development programs both on-the-job and structured programs, which recognize the inevitability of organizational change.
8. Career planning for employees in which they, as well as their superiors and the personnel department have a role.

Manpower planning

The above list certainly will not appear as anything particularly new to the reader. Many organizations have been carrying out such practices in one form or another for several years. The point is that in many instances there is no attempt at any coordination of all of the factors. By carrying them out in a fragmented and haphazard manner, the organization cannot reap the total benefit of their efforts.

In recent years the combination of rapid technological change and a growing shortage of capable people to fill open jobs of all kinds has caused forward-looking organizations to develop comprehensive manpower planning programs. Such coordinated and systematic effort is therefore new for most of these organizations. Accurately anticipating manpower needs is both complex and obscure. Making a rather definite commitment to an employee about his career may be difficult for a management that has preferred to carry on discussions about an employee's promotability without including him in the discussion.

---

[2] Peter F. Drucker, *The Practice of Management* (New York: Harper & Row, Publishers, 1954), pp. 182–84.

Two factors which are basic have encouraged the development of sound and comprehensive manpower planning. In the first, promotion from within policies have become very common among all types of organizations in our society. A variety of reasons have caused such wide acceptance of this policy. Probably most critical is the ever-increasing costs of recruiting and training an effective work force in a rapidly changing and relatively prosperous economy. Retention of employees becomes critical when the labor market does not have a plentiful supply of potentially capable employees and supervisors.

Secondly, and closely related to the first factor is the wide choice of job opportunities available to the capable, and frequently the not so capable, individual. The full employment policies followed by the federal government has had a considerable impact on the type of unemployment existing in our economy. Frank H. Cassell of the Inland Steel Company quoted the following statistics in a speech published by the Industrial Relations Center of the University of Minnesota.

A full employment policy, however, has varying degrees of impact upon employment, depending on the level of skill, knowledge, and experience needed, and the availability of those qualities in the work force by geographical area.

For example at a 4.1% overall employment rate unemployment for people with varying skills are as follows:

Managers and officials..0.9
Professional, technical and kindred workers.........................1.5
Craftsmen, foremen and kindred workers............................2.2
Clerical and kindred workers......................................3.7
Service workers, ex. private workers...............................5.1
Operatives and kindred workers...................................5.4
Laborers (non-farm)...8.1[3]

When geographical differences and specific occupations along with age of employables is taken into consideration the problems confronting an organization's personnel department become more apparent. It is easy to see why effective manpower planning is an absolute necessity.

When a person is already employed, it is quite natural for him to look to his own company for career opportunities. This is certainly true if he is satisfied with his present job. Part of his job satisfaction should come from his knowledge of the quality of his performance as indicated to him by his supervisor.

Performance appraisal

Most organizations have some formal or informal way of evaluating employees—for judging their performance, behavior, abilities, and poten-

---

[3] Frank H. Cassell, *Corporate Manpower Planning* (Industrial Relations Center, University of Minnesota, Special Release 6, February, 1968), p. 3.

tialities. Formal evaluating is done by filling out an appraisal form. The second step is usually an interview with the appraised employee and a discussion with him of the evaluation. In most cases the immediate supervisor does the evaluating—or is one of the evaluators—and he handles the interview.

The program may be called employee evaluation, merit rating, employee rating, efficiency rating, service rating, performance review, performance appraisal, progress report, personnel review, employee appraisal, or some such name. It may be tied to pay raises or it may be separate from salary adjustment. It may be part of a program of identifying promotable people, or it may concentrate on improving effectiveness of performance on the present job. It may be a perfunctory "handing out of report cards" or it may be a constructive session reviewing performance for the purpose of planning for future performance. It may be an embarrassing or hostile session probing into personality flaws, or it may be a means of increasing the effectiveness of performance. Of course, some people do not want to hear about their performance particularly if the report is negative and too critical. Such an appraisal may destroy an employee's self-image and his attitudes about his ability. Nevertheless, feedback on employee performance is vital to an effective supervisor-employee relationship and the majority of employees find it to be a useful and frequently rewarding experience.

Evaluating and developing employees is a continuation of the supervisor-subordinate relationship begun in induction and carried on in training. Evaluation is a means by which the supervisor lets the employee know how he is doing. It is part of the feedback of results and can be used to stimulate the employee's continued learning and continued improvement on his job. It is a way to direct his efforts into channels that will enable him to become more valuable to the company.

Evaluation is of particular importance to the new man. It gives him an opportunity to find out whether he and his boss agree on what is expected of him and how well he is doing it. It gives him guidance to help him prepare for his future with the company. If he wants to advance, he is concerned about the opportunities and what he should be doing to prepare himself for them. If he is not doing well, he is entitled to a warning and to counseling on what's wrong and what he can do about correcting it. If he isn't suited to the work, he should find out before he invests too much of his life in it.

On some jobs the employee can measure the quality and quantity of his own performance against the standards of work performance and know where he stands on production. But there are other factors that enter into his job performance and his value to the company. Does he get along well with others in the performance of his work? Is he steady, interested, and willing? Is his job knowledge adequate or does he need constant help? Does he comply with instructions, rules, and regulations? Does he work safely and influence others to work safely? Is he self-starting or does he have to be prodded? Does he go ahead with his work without close supervision or does he fool around? Is he punctual and regular in attendance? Can he be relied on to carry through a job properly? Does he use his initiative, contribute good ideas, and cooperate in improving methods? Is he flexible and adaptable in adjusting to changed conditions? Does he have knowledge of related jobs he could handle in emergencies? Is he willing to learn new duties? Does he have potential for promotion? Is he immediately promotable?

Appraisal is systematic rather than haphazard

The supervisor makes informal evaluations of his employees in his everyday decisions about them. He is making judgments about them when he assigns special jobs to them, when he gives them training, when he asks for raises and promotions for them. He is making judgments when he recommends them for transfer, demotion, or dismissal. Some of the decisions may be impulsive ones made to fit the needs of the moment. A planned system of employee evaluation should make the decisions more deliberate, factual, and fair, because it will be based on systematic comparison of person against person and person against standard.

Having to write an evaluation periodically forces the supervisor to be more analytical about his people and their performance. When he has to back up some of his opinions he may realize that they were unfounded and unfair. Since he has to have evidence for his evaluation, he has to measure the amount of work his people are doing and the quality of it. He has to compare it to the standards of work performance to see if people are measuring up to requirements and if they are improving or slipping. He must study attendance records to see which employees are getting to work on time every day and which ones are taking a lot of time off.

If an employee's work and behavior record are so unsatisfactory that he should be discharged, or if his work is so poor that he should be demoted, the evidence collected and recorded on the rating form is support for the action. It is difficult to discharge or demote an employee who has been getting good ratings on his job; so the supervisor must collect objective evidence over the whole rating period and be as factual as possible in his evaluations.

Evaluation of people involves subjective judgment as well as performance records and it is subject to error. But if supervisors are given training, they can improve their rating abilities. The act of gathering, studying, and comparing information on all the employees improves the quality of decisions concerning each one of them and reduces the danger of being unfair.

Difficulties in rating

In this chapter forms for rating hourly employees and for rating supervisors are reproduced (Figures 13–1 and 13–3). The form for hourly employees lists factors of quality, quantity, dependability, job knowledge, and adaptability. The managerial forms list a greater number of factors.

Ratings on these factors may be used to compare performances on a companywide basis rather than just within a department. It is important therefore that supervisors be trained to rate on a uniform basis. If some rate tight and others loose, an injustice will be done to the employees who are being appraised for promotion, training, discharge, merit increases, salary changes, or bonus payments. Some of the criticism of employee evaluation stems from the lack of uniformity among raters.

Forced choice. In order to get away from supervisors' leniency or bias in rating, some companies use forms that don't list factors or degrees (such as unsatisfactory, fair, good, excellent, outstanding—or their numerical or alphabetical equivalents). Instead, a "forced choice" form is used, presenting groups of statements describing behavior. In each group of statements the supervisor is required to check the one most applicable to the person being rated. On some forms he must also check the statement that least resembles the person being rated.[4] The grading of the statements and the totaling of the scores is done by the personnel department. The supervisor can only guess how the statements will be scored and whether he is giving an employee a good or a poor rating.

Defining factors. Where forced choice is not used, raters must have a common understanding of the definition of the factors they are rating. *Dependability,* for example, could mean a number of things: Does it mean that the employee shows up for work every day and gets there on time and in condition to work? Does it mean that he can be trusted to carry the money to the bank? Does it mean that he can be relied upon to get his work done properly? This third meaning is the one given in the Lockheed rating form (Figure 13–1). If it were not defined, then under *dependability* one supervisor would be rating attendance, another would be rating honesty, and the third would be rating work performance.

Defining the degrees. When the rating form lists factors and degrees of factors, there is a problem of getting agreement between the raters as to what is meant by the various degrees. The degrees (such as excellent, superior, average, fair, or poor) constitute the measuring stick,

---

[4] For more about rating methods, see M. J. Dooher and V. Marquis (eds.), *Rating Employee and Supervisory Performance* (New York: American Management Association, 1950).

FIGURE 13–1
Form for Rating Hourly Employees

LOCKHEED AIRCRAFT CORPORATION - MISSILE SYSTEMS DIVISION

EMPLOYEE PERIODIC HOURLY REVIEW

DEPT.	PLANT	S	NAME	M/ /W	OCCUPATION	SENIORITY DATE MO. DAY YEAR	EMPLOYEE NO.

EFFECTIVE DATE OF THIS REVIEW	PRESENT RATE	WAS EFFECTIVE MO. DAY YEAR	SENT TO DEPT. MO. DAY YEAR	THIS REPORT MUST REACH INDUSTRIAL RELATIONS BEFORE	MO. DAY YEAR

Describe specific work employee has been performing during this review period

State approximate length of time on this type of work in your department.

THIS FORM WILL ACT AS A CHANGE-OF-STATUS IF A MERIT INCREASE IS RECOMMENDED AT THIS TIME.

NOTICE PREPARED BY	DATE	KARDEX POSTED	(IF NO CHANGE, ENTER "SAME") NEW PAY RATE→	CHANGE CODE	GRADE	DIFFERENCE
				1		

APPROVALS   LAST RATE CHANGE

IMMEDIATE SUPERVISION	PERSONNEL REPRESENTATIVE
DEPARTMENT HEAD	EXECUTIVE

The following factors are to be rated. The order in which these factors are listed in no way reflects their respective value.

DEPENDABILITY
Your Confidence in Employee's Ability to Accept Responsibility

Refuses to or not able to carry much responsibility; needs constant follow-up.	Usually follows instructions; needs some follow-up	Willing and able to accept responsibility; requires little follow-up.	Outstanding ability to follow through on all assignments with no detail supervision.

QUANTITY
Output - Speed

Exceptionally fast; unusual output.	Does more work than expected; is fast; exceeds requirements	Output meets acceptable standards; is satisfactory	Output below normal requirements; definitely slow.

ADAPTABILITY
Versatility; Adjustment to Job or Changed Conditions; Ease with which New Duties are Learned.

Meets changed conditions with little effort; has outstanding ability to pick up new jobs.	Learns well with minimum amount of instruction; adjusts himself well in a short time.	Learns fairly well but needs detailed instruction for each new job.	Is slow to learn; has trouble adjusting himself to changed conditions; needs constant instruction.

JOB KNOWLEDGE
Technical Knowledge of Job and Related Work.

Has limited knowledge of his job; knows nothing of related work.	Knows his job fairly well; has little knowledge of related work.	Seldom needs help; has good knowledge of his job and related work; is well-informed.	Has excellent knowledge of his job and related work; is very well-informed.

QUALITY
Accuracy in Work; Freedom from Errors

Makes practically no mistakes; highest accuracy.	Makes very few errors; is accurate; does high grade work.	Makes some errors but does passable work.	Makes mistakes frequently.

COMMENTS:

RATED BY

Used in Lockheed Aircraft Corporation—Missile Systems Divisions (reproduced with their permission).

and it is essential that all raters use the same stick. What is "excellent" to one rater should not be "superior" to another, and what is "fair" to one rater should not be "poor" to another. The rating system must set up some kind of bench mark for what is average, and some kind of guide for judging the degrees above and below it.

Forced distribution. This method is similar to what students call "grading on the curve." The supervisor is supposed to rank subordinates in categories such as superior, above average, satisfactory, and inadequate. Typically, the top 20 percent would be rated superior, the next 30 percent as above average, the next 30 percent as satisfactory, and the bottom 20 percent as inadequate. This system is designed to minimize overlenient ratings by supervisors. It assumes that all work groups have a distribution of performance quality which can be neatly "curved" and this is the principal objection to this approach by supervisors who use it.

Fairness in rating. In judging people against a bench mark, the fairest way to do it is to take one factor at a time and rank all of the people on that one factor (rather than take one person at a time and rank him on all of the factors). In rating people on job knowledge, for instance, it is not too difficult to identify the highest and the lowest people in the group. It is the in-between people who are difficult to place. They can be compared one to another and then ranked in order of best to worst on that one factor.

The supervisor must base his rating on evidence that is as objective as possible and that is gathered over the whole rating period. He should not rely on impressions or base his judgments on a few outstanding successes or failures. Daily observations over the entire rating period help to put any "off-day" difficulties or unusual performances into their true perspective. Incidents that are going into the record to be used against employees must be discussed with them at the time of their occurrence so that they have an opportunity to explain what happened.

In order to protect against prejudice and errors in judgment, some companies have more than one person work on the rating of an employee. A number of people who are acquainted with him and his work may act as a committee in making an appraisal. Or a personnel representative may act as a counselor to assist the supervisor in making out his ratings. Or the rater's boss may go over the ratings to judge their accuracy. The employees may be able to appeal the ratings if they consider them unfair.

Some common types of rating errors

Some supervisors have a tendency to rate their groups too high. They don't want to cause hard feelings, and they think that low ratings reflect on their own abilities as trainers and leaders. Some groups will be out of the ordinary in one direction or the other, but the supervisor should be able to produce evidence to prove it.

Some supervisors who have not gathered evidence about all of the factors they must rate will rate the ones they are in doubt about as "average," which is an injustice. This error is called the "central tendency." Other supervisors make a worse mistake in handling factors on which they have too little evidence. They rate the unknowns the same as some other factor they do know about. That error is called the "halo effect." For example, a supervisor has evidence that an employee's quality and quantity are poor but doesn't know the man well enough to know his attitude. He just assumes that the attitude must be poor also and he rates it that way.

Supervisors must not let their ratings be influenced by conscious or unconscious prejudice against a race, nationality, or religion or by partiality to friends, relatives, and lodge brothers. When a supervisor is rating his employees, he must guard against softness—a tendency to be good to everybody; spinelessness—an unwillingness to take the risk of unfavorable decisions; hurry—failure to take the time to do a good job; and harshness—a tendency to underrate everybody.

Suiting the plan to the purpose

There are a number of types of evaluation plans and a number of purposes which they are designed to serve. *Merit rating* plans are designed to stimulate people to high performance in order to get pay increases and upgrading. Merit rating is based on the belief that people who perform better on the job should be paid more, and it provides a system for judging their performance and rewarding it. Rewards of pay increases follow a pattern upward on a range set by job evaluation. On the same job a person of outstanding ability might be paid quite a bit more than a person who was just adequate. The factors on the rating sheet get a numerical rating, and the score determines whether the employee gets an increase that period. In unionized companies, seniority may be more of a factor in advancement than merit, and the prevailing sentiment may favor raises for everybody rather than just for the high performers.

Measuring potential for advancement. Some types of employee evaluation plans are heavily slanted toward management development. The rating forms emphasize personality, appearance, enthusiasm, mentality, sociability, and other traits considered desirable for a higher job. The assortment of traits may be designed to identify people who are outstanding in the qualities necessary for particular jobs. A person's score on the appraisal may be compared to the scores of employees in all parts of the company in order to determine which ones should be groomed for promotion.

When employee evaluation is used primarily for appraising potential for advancement, then raises, promotions, and preparation for higher jobs become the central theme. But the future just doesn't hold quick promotions for everybody. Overemphasis on promotion frustrates and demoralizes the employees who are passed over time after time. For this reason some companies have two types of evaluation: the one (just discussed) for appraising potential for advancement, and the other (discussed below) for evaluating current job performance.

The appraisal interview as a means of improving performance on the job

Accurate information about employee performance on their present jobs is a very necessary aspect for effective manpower planning. Not only can the appraisal interview aid in helping the employee toward better performance on his present job but it also may give some idea of his transferability to other work of a similar nature. In other words, this kind of information increases the options of both the employer and his supervisor.

If the employee evaluation is to result in improved performance on the job, the appraisal interview should be centered on performance and not on innate abilities or personality traits. In order to discuss performance, the supervisor should have evidence of the quality and quantity of work and whether it meets the standards. In telling the subordinate what parts of his work are satisfactory and what parts unsatisfactory, the supervisor should talk in terms of results rather than faults. He should try to get the subordinate to fill in the information about the circumstances that led to the results. The subordinate should be encouraged to discuss his own performance and anything in the situation which made it hard for him to do his job. If his job difficulties are matters of personality, he should be asked to evaluate and discuss them in terms of job performance and suggest what he could do about them. Employees seem to be able to accept correction that relates to their performance and behavior but not to their personalities. A subordinate may criticize himself on his own lacks and weaknesses, but if the supervisor has to do the criticizing he had better confine it to observed behavior rather than to the flaws in the personality that caused the behavior.

If a subordinate has weaknesses that can't be changed or if he is working right up to the limit of his capacity, there is nothing to be gained by deflating his ego.

The subordinate who is doing a passable but uninspired job and could do much better should be asked to appraise his own performance

FIGURE 13–2
Suggestions for Appraisal Interviews

To help their supervisors handle merit-rating interviews, the Industrial Relations Division of Bell & Howell Co., Chicago, gives each supervisor a folded card outlining the purposes of the interview and giving suggestions and a check list for conducting it.

REMEMBER TO . . . . Select a good time and place to talk. Begin discussion on mutually familiar ground. Be relaxed, natural and a good listener. Can you lead into your points indirectly? Keep the discussion out of irrelevant or emotional areas. In a direct approach, let the man "save face." Make the man sure your primary interest is in him. Don't "talk down" to him. Make him want to come back.	 PRINCIPLES OF GOOD MERIT RATING INTERVIEWING Industrial Relations Division Bell & Howell Co.

CHECK LIST FOR INTERVIEW	PURPOSES OF COUNSELING INTERVIEW FOLLOWING MERIT RATING

OUTSTANDING ABILITIES OR QUALIFICATIONS
 	
AREAS REQUIRING IMPROVEMENT
 	
SPECIFIC TRAINING RECOMMENDATIONS
 	
ANALYZE DISCUSSION RESULTS:
 	
  What does he hope to achieve
  within the Company?
 	
  What is he doing to improve
  himself?
 	
  What immediate plans for improve-
  ment did you agree upon?
	A. Getting the employee to do a better job through making clear your standards of performance. You, too, have peculiar traits. Here is a chance for the employee to learn your preferences in quality, quantity and methods of work and to understand your reasons for these standards.
	B. Giving the employee a clear picture of how he is doing with emphasis upon strengths as well as weaknesses. Much trouble can result in business and industry from employees whose self rating is sharply at variance with their supervisor's evaluation.
	C. Discussing plans for improvement, and projects to better use employee's abilities.
	D. Building strong, personal relationships between supervisor and employee in which both are willing to talk frankly about the job, how it is being done, what improvement is possible, and how it can be obtained. Improving person-to-person understanding so that closer, stronger relationships exist.

Reproduced by permission of the Industrial Relations Division of Bell & Howell Co., Chicago.

and abilities. He should be pressed to work out a plan for improving his performance and to set up a schedule for it. People seem to need definite plans with deadlines built into them so that they can get started and keep going until they achieve the goals they set. The supervisor should follow up at specified times to see if the employee is improving.

Interviewing the unsatisfactory performer. If an employee's performance is unacceptable, the supervisor should find out—before the interview—whether to talk in terms of transfer, demotion, or discharge. The appraisal sheet should show cause to support the action. The appraisal interview should give warning of what the employee is to expect.

If the employee is capable of satisfactory work but is not trying, he should be told what is unsatisfactory about his performance and what he must do to correct it. There should be a date set by which he should show the required amount of improvement. The plan and the timetable should be put in writing as evidence that the employee was given a warning and an offer of help. Then if he does not improve, the supervisor will be in a position to take action.

If a man is making an effort but is failing on the job—and training can't solve the problem—the supervisor must find out if it is possible to transfer or demote him to a job for which he is better fitted. Often separation from the company is really a kindness to the person. Too often supervisors procrastinate and allow the unsuited employee to struggle on year after year while the problem becomes worse rather than better. The supervisor would do well to consult the personnel department before interviewing the employee who can't make the grade.

Rating the probationary employee

Many of the problems of the unfit employee could be avoided through a more careful rating of him during his probationary period. This is the time to study his ability, performance, and behavior, and to decide whether he should be permitted to become permanent. The decision has long-range significance, since dismissal will never again be this easy and the employee may stay on in the company for 30 years. Many an unsatisfactory, disgruntled employee is the result of the supervisor's failure to take decisive action.

The trial work period is the most reliable test for determining whether the new man is going to become a desirable employee. It is superior to any of the techniques of selection developed thus far. If the trial period is long enough, the new employee will show his true colors during it. If he is undependable, has a tendency toward tardiness, absenteeism, drunkenness, troublemaking, or other undesirable behavior, some symptoms will show up. If he fails to make satisfactory progress toward proficiency in the work, he is probably not suited to it and never will become a good producer. If it is doubtful whether he has the minimum qualifications necessary to become a successful employee, he should be terminated.

On the other hand, when a trial employee has the qualifications, and his evaluation sheet shows that he has reached the standards of performance for the tasks he is performing, the supervisor should make sure to tell him so. At the end of the trial work period, he should call the man in, congratulate him for making the grade, show him his rating, and praise him for the progress he has made. Then the supervisor should spend the greater portion of the interview working out a program for the employee's future development.

Some companies provide for a follow-up evaluation three months later. Frequent evaluations of new employees provide an opportunity to counsel them, guide them, help them become more effective on their present jobs, and show them that it is worth their while to be ambitious and cooperative.

Interview problems

The supervisor has to use the type of interview that suits his own personality, the personality of the subordinate, and the circumstances and problems involved.

One of the problems that turns up in an appraisal interview is that the subordinate objects strongly to the evaluation put on his performance; he simply doesn't see it that way. Some supervisors meet this one by narrowing the area of disagreement. They ask the subordinate to fill out a sheet the way he believes it should be. Then they find the points on which the two sheets do agree. They ask the subordinate to tell them why he rates the remaining factors as high as he does. If the explanation isn't convincing, they go back and review the points of agreement. Then they return to a discussion of the disputed items and try to get agreement on some of them. If the subordinate won't change his stand, they ask him to take a few days to think it over.

When a subordinate is not getting an expected raise or promotion, and he loses his temper, he should be allowed to blow off steam. If he accuses the supervisor of unfairness, he should be encouraged to talk himself out. If he brings up old gripes that are still bothering him, this is a good time to let him get them off his chest. Whatever the subordinate's reaction, the supervisor should avoid getting dragged into an argument. Arguing with an angry man doesn't lead to a plan for future development.

It is not the supervisor's purpose to tell the employee how to run his life, but to help him see realistically the qualities of his performance, his problems, abilities, skills, strong and weak points, and the areas for possible development and self-improvement. The employee has to look at himself realistically and see where he stands before he is ready to think about self-improvement.

When the supervisor starts to discuss an employee's work performance, the employee is naturally apprehensive and defensive. The more he is on the defensive, the less advice he will take. If lack of effort is the reason for inadequate performance, the supervisor should make it clear that he is not implying a lack of ability.

Evaluations of ability and personality may strike at the employee's ego. To imply that a person has a serious lack is to risk wounding him to the point of barring any further communication with him. When it is necessary to call attention to weaknesses, the supervisor should try to get the employee to do it for him. Much of the hostility in an appraisal interview comes from the employee's feeling that his personal worth is being attacked.[5] If the supervisor will keep this in mind, he will talk about performance rather than about traits. When he is talking about strong points and weak points he will do it from the standpoint of their application to the performance of a particular job and as they look from the evidence at hand. He will put the emphasis on the *job* and its objectives and responsibilities, and on the problems encountered in carrying out the job. He will talk about what the subordinate does and not what the subordinate is. He will talk about the problems the subordinate runs into but not about the problems of his personality.[6]

Generally most employees will react favorably to constructive criticism. If it is presented in a positive manner, the employee can be made to recognize that his own welfare will benefit from a positive reaction. On the other hand, an employee who does not have the talent or desire to do the job well may react negatively and try to blame environmental

---

[5] For suggestions on handling the appraisal interview, see Earl G. Planty and C. E. Efferson, "Counseling Employees after Merit Rating and Evaluation," M. Joseph Dooher and Vivienne Marquis (eds.), *Effective Communication on the Job* (New York: American Management Association, 1956), chap. 18.

Robert Hoppock, "The Salesmanship Theory in Appraisal Counseling," *Journal of the American Society of Training Directors,* April, 1961, pp. 51–52. (He thinks the salesmanship approach is the wrong one to get employees to change their behavior.)

Spencer J. Hayden, "Getting Better Results from Post-Appraisal Interviews," *Personnel,* Vol. XXXI, No. 6 (May, 1955), p. 542.

Kenneth E. Richards, "A New Concept of Performance Appraisal," *Journal of Business,* Vol. XXXII, No. 3 (July, 1959), pp. 229–43.

For Douglas McGregor's proposal to substitute goal-setting interviews for performance appraisals, see "An Uneasy Look at Performance Appraisal," *Harvard Business Review,* Vol. XXXV, No. 3 (May, 1957), p. 90.

[6] For excellent suggestions on an interview of this type, see Mortimer R. Feinberg, "Is the Performance Review a Threat or a Promise?" in Elizabeth Marting, Robert E. Finley, and Ann Ward (eds.), *Effective Communication on the Job* (rev. ed.; New York: American Management Association, Inc., 1963), pp. 233–42; and Robert Hoppock, "Seventeen Principles of Appraisal Interviews," *ibid.,* pp. 242–45.

conditions such as the workplace, fellow employees, tools, and even the supervisor.

Promotions and the people who want them

Not everyone in the organization is eager to become the big boss. Some want to stay put; some want to advance part way; some want to get to the top. Many employees don't want the risks that go with advancement and with the assumption of authority and responsibility. They may be top-notch performers right where they are, and that is where they feel comfortable. They will take their advancement in the form of wage increases and service pins.

The man who is capable of becoming a supervisor has more belief in his own competence and his ability to control circumstances and shape results. He has more of what is called "tolerance for ambiguity." He is willing to take some risks and he gets a certain enjoyment out of carrying responsibility and exercising authority. He is willing to trade some of his comfort for accomplishment. He will keep pushing until he finds himself at a level at which he likes to operate. He may stop at the first, second, or some higher level of management where he has fulfilled his ambition or is near his capacity. At his proper level such a man usually has a good team, has everything under control, is stable, and can always be depended upon. He handles his group with skill and has his men working efficiently. He and they are happy working together. Such a man is valuable right where he is; he should get recognition for the good job he is doing. He should be made to feel secure in that job and not be pushed to advance to a higher one. He is a carry-the-load man who has found the spot at which he is happiest and can operate the best.

Some other man may have his sights set on the top job. He takes a special joy in the competition and excitement of fighting his way up. His idea of achieving is steady advancement, and he is discontent if he has to stay in one spot too long.

The successful organization needs a good mixture of the three types of people. The system of rewards should be designed so that each one can work toward his own level of satisfaction. For the people who want to get ahead there should be definite paths of promotion and guidance in preparing for them.

Advantages and disadvantages of promoting from within

Promotion stimulates a man to greater effort, enables him to develop to his capacity, and keeps him from leaving the company to seek opportunities elsewhere. A policy of promotion from within builds high morale because employees can see that extra effort is rewarded.

When a man moves up the line, he brings with him knowledge and experience gained in the jobs he handled in the company on his way up. He knows the way the company operates, the way its people operate, the policies and problems of the organization, and what has and has not worked in the past. His closeness to the organization is a mixed blessing, though; he is not a new broom or new blood; he is not bringing in the fresh viewpoint or the new ideas that come with an executive recruited from another company. Disadvantages of inbreeding can be overcome to some extent by getting new ideas from outside sources— evening-school courses, books in the management field, trade publica-tions, professional meetings, and business clubs.

Promotions must be made with great care because mistakes are hard to rectify. Whenever a man is promoted, someone else may be disappointed or jealous. If the wrong man is chosen for the job, there are charges of favoritism. If the man chosen does not have the ability to fill the job, the efficiency of every man under his command is impaired. If he has to be replaced, there is the problem of what to do with him; it may be impossible to put him back on his old job. If he leaves the company, then a man is lost who was at least good enough to be considered for promotion.

Evaluating and developing supervisors

The supervisor is evaluated on his performance in his present job and he is evaluated on his potential for advancing into higher management jobs. His strongest personal characteristics and the area in which he excels are important indications of the direction in which his development should be planned. His training for higher jobs should build on his strong points and shore up his weak points.

The executive appraisal form, Figure 13–3, is an example of a trait-measuring form used for evaluating a supervisor's potential. Bell & Howell Company reports using the form successfully for many years.

If a company does not have a printed form for appraising potential, it may use the performance appraisal form and supplement it with personal information. When upper management is appraising the promotability of its supervisors it asks questions like these:

1. What are his outstanding abilities? What are his weaknesses?
2. What is his age? What is the state of his health?
3. What are his ambitions? What progress has he been making? How near is he to the top of his capacity?

FIGURE 13–3
Form for Appraising Supervisors

Routing: 1. Supervisor Making Appraisal
          2. W. L. Johnson, Dept. 881 (For Scoring)
          3. Supervisor for Interview
          4. W. L. Johnson, Dept. 881 (For File)

BELL & HOWELL COMPANY

EXECUTIVE APPRAISAL

1. Purpose
    To measure, objectively as possible, the caliber of executive personnel.
    The results of this appraisal will be considered when (a) reviewing
    salary status (b) making organization changes.

2. Plan
    To have each executive employee appraised by his immediate superior at least
    once a year. Executive Appraisal forms will be prepared and distributed by
    the Industrial Relations Division.

3. Instructions for Appraisal
    a) Consider, and mark only one element at a time.
    b) Review the employee on the position he holds now.
    c) Do not allow personal feelings to govern the appraisal. Be completely
       fair.
    d) Do not be entirely influenced by recent unusual cases pertaining to
       any element to be considered. Each executive employee should be
       judged on the basis of his normal performance.
    e) Check the square that most aptly applies. However, if you feel the
       executive's performance is in between the descriptions indicated,
       please check the square provided for this purpose.
    f) Two levels of supervision must approve each appraisal whenever practical.
    g) Summary will be completed by Dept. 881.
    h) Per cent effectiveness is secured by dividing total rating, by number of
       factors rated - multiplied by 5.

APPRAISAL FOR

Name_____Dept._____Position_____

Appraised By_____Date_____Date Interviewed_____

	Total Possible Points	Actual Appraisal Score	Per Cent Effective	SUMMARY
				1. Outstanding_____
Supervisor's Appraisal	_____	_____	_____	2. Excellent_____
				3. Good _____
Exec. Self-Appraisal	_____	_____	_____	4. Fair
				5. Unsatisfactory__

COMMENTS:_____

_____

_____

Form #35111 Rev. (9-29-54)

Source: Bell & Howell Company (reproduced with their permission).

FIGURE 13–3 (*Continued*)

A. WHAT HE KNOWS

   1. Knowledge of Job--Refers to: familiarity with the various procedures of the work.

( )   ( )   ( )   ( )   ( )   ( )   ( )   ( )   ( )

Exceptional mastery of all phases of his work.	Thorough knowledge of practically all phases of his work.	Adequate knowledge of particular job.	Insufficient knowledge of particular job.	Inadequate comprehension of requirements of job.

   2. Experience--Refers to: skill and practical wisdom gained by personal knowledge.

( )   ( )   ( )   ( )   ( )   ( )   ( )   ( )   ( )

Broad background and training for particular job.	A comprehensive background.	An adequate background.	Has some background but requires direction.	Inexperienced or unsatisfactory progress.

   3. General Company Information--Refers to: knowledge of major and minor Company policies.

( )   ( )   ( )   ( )   ( )   ( )   ( )   ( )   ( )

Thorough understanding and appreciation of all Company policies.	Knowledge of practically all Company policies.	Acceptable knowledge of Company policies.	Limited knowledge of Company policies.	Does not have enough information to be efficient.

B. WHAT HE IS

   1. Health--Refers to: soundness of body and mind, and freedom from physical disease or disability.

( )   ( )   ( )   ( )   ( )   ( )   ( )   ( )   ( )

Robust, energetic	Sufficiently healthy and energetic to handle the job.	Sufficiently healthy to handle job but not overly energetic.	Frail, affected by pressure.	Sickly, Affects his work.

   2. Enthusiasm--Refers to: a positive, ardent and eager response.

( )   ( )   ( )   ( )   ( )   ( )   ( )   ( )   ( )

Believes wholeheartedly in the Company and expresses both orally and in his attitude that belief.	Works enthusiastically, not too expressive.	Matter-of-fact attitude.	Definitely passive or indifferent.	Negative in attitude

   3. Personality--Refers to: the external mannerisms consciously or unconsciously adopted in meeting situations.

( )   ( )   ( )   ( )   ( )   ( )   ( )   ( )   ( )

Radiant, confident, poised courteous.	Pleasant, forceful.	Likeable	Ill at ease, not too forceful.	Negative colorless person.

FIGURE 13–3 (*Continued*)

4. Appearance--Refers to: the outward impressions made by a person.

( ) ( ) ( ) ( ) ( ) ( ) ( ) ( ) ( )

Superior style, grooming, taste and a sense of the fitness of things.	Well dressed and neat.	Neat, but not particularly striking.	Intermittently careless.	Slovenly and untidy.

5. Character--Refers to: the integrity of an individual.

( ) ( ) ( ) ( ) ( ) ( ) ( ) ( ) ( )

Has the courage of his convictions and unquestioned habits.	Morally sound. Tolerant.	An average human being possessing average personal weaknesses.	A person whose behavior harms no one but himself.	A person who is a bad influence on the behavior of the group.

6. Mentality--Refers to: the quality of mind, mental power and creative intellectual ability of a person.

( ) ( ) ( ) ( ) ( ) ( ) ( ) ( ) ( )

Superior ability to think clearly and arrive at sound conclusions.	Worthwhile ideas of his own, and ability to make useful decisions	Well informed on certain subjects useful in his daily work.	Little ability to comprehend, interpret or grasp new ideas.	Unable to reason logically.

7. Sociability--Refers to: sense of mutual relationship, companionship and friendliness with others.

( ) ( ) ( ) ( ) ( ) ( ) ( ) ( ) ( )

A genuine interest in people and extremely well liked by others.	A friendly, pleasant person, happy in a group.	Willing to be a part of a group but makes little contribution.	Poorly adjusted to the group.	Unwilling to be a part of any group activities.

C. WHAT HE DOES

1. Ability to get things done--Refers to: the ability to perform, execute and achieve an assigned task.

( ) ( ) ( ) ( ) ( ) ( ) ( ) ( ) ( )

Completes assignments in the shortest possible time.	Completes assignments in unusually short time.	Completes assignments in a reasonable time.	Slow in completing assignments, or does not complete them.	Takes a long time to accomplish little.

2. Cooperative--Refers to: an appreciation of collective action for mutual profit or common benefit.

( ) ( ) ( ) ( ) ( ) ( ) ( ) ( ) ( )

Greatest possible cooperativeness.	Very cooperative.	Cooperative.	Difficult to handle	Obstructive

FIGURE 13-3 (*Continued*)

3. Acceptance of responsibility--Refers to: a willingness to assume duties.

(_)   (_)   (_)   (_)   (_)   (_)   (_)   (_)   (_)

Greatest possible sense of responsibility.	Very Willing	Accepts but does not seek responsibility.		Does assigned tasks reluctantly.		Irresponsible	

4. Judgement--Refers to: the ability to grasp a situation and draw correct conclusions.

(_)   (_)   (_)   (_)   (_)   (_)   (_)   (_)   (_)

Superior ability to think intelligently and use sound judgement.	Excellent Judgement.	Good common sense.		Poor judgement		Neglects and misinterprets the facts.	

5. Initiative--Refers to: the desire and ability to introduce a new course of action.

(_)   (_)   (_)   (_)   (_)   (_)   (_)   (_)   (_)

Seeks and sets for himself additional tasks, highly ingenious.	Very resourceful.	Progressive		Rarely suggests		Needs detailed instruction.	

6. Expression--Refers to: the ability to articulate and orally express one's thoughts and feelings.

(_)   (_)   (_)   (_)   (_)   (_)   (_)   (_)   (_)

Unusually articulate in expressing thoughts and feelings; master of good speech techniques.	Speaks well.	Nothing about his speech that is distinctive or distasteful.		Careless speech habits and mild physical defects.		Inarticulate and physical defects.	

7. Rate of work--Refers to: the time taken to finish a specific assignment.

(_)   (_)   (_)   (_)   (_)   (_)   (_)   (_)   (_)

Greatest possible rapidity.	Very rapid.	Good speed.		Slow		Hopelessly slow	

8. Accuracy--Refers to: a high percentage of freedom from mistakes.

(_)   (_)   (_)   (_)   (_)   (_)   (_)   (_)   (_)

Highest possible accuracy	Very careful.	Careful, no more than reasonable time required for revision.		Careless, time required for revision greatly excessive.		Practically worthless work.	

9. Budget Accomplishment.

(_)   (_)   (_)   (_)   (_)   (_)   (_)   (_)   (_)

Performs within budget even under severe circumstances.	Performance almost within budget. Deviation.	Performs within budget more than two-thirds of the time and seldom are deviations substantial.		Misses budget frequently and deviations are substantial.		Almost always misses budget and deviations are often substantial.	

FIGURE 13-3 (*Concluded*)

10. Condition of Department.

  (▭)   (▭)   (▭)   (▭)   (▭)   (▭)   (▭)   (▭)   (▭)

| Extremely orderly. | Very orderly. | No particular disorder. | | Disorderliness in department | Department very disorderly. | | |

D. **MANAGERIAL QUALITIES**

1. **Handling People**--Refers to: the ability to appreciate, understand, and direct individual differences.

  (▭)   (▭)   (▭)   (▭)   (▭)   (▭)   (▭)   (▭)   (▭)

| Extremely successful in helping and training his men to progress and attain their ambitions. | Capable leader. | Fails to develop and obtain maximum results from men. | | Fails to command confidence. | Antagonizes his subordinates. | | |

2. **Developing Assistants**--Refers to: the ability to delegate responsibilities to the right individual.

  (▭)   (▭)   (▭)   (▭)   (▭)   (▭)   (▭)   (▭)   (▭)

| Superior ability in selecting suitable men and training them to assume specific responsibilities. | Very capable in recognizing and training subordinates. | Good in selection, but little attention is given to training. | Allows subordinates to shift for themselves. | Hinders the natural development of his men. | | | |

3. **Delegating Work**--Refers to: the assignment of specific responsibilities.

  (▭)   (▭)   (▭)   (▭)   (▭)   (▭)   (▭)   (▭)   (▭)

| Superior ability in recognizing individual's capacities, when he assigns tasks. | Capable supervisor. | Fails to recognize individual's capacities. | Fails to see work to be done. | Does all the work himself. | | | |

4. **Planning and Organizing**--Refers to: success in organizing, by delegating authority and planning.

  (▭)   (▭)   (▭)   (▭)   (▭)   (▭)   (▭)   (▭)   (▭)

| Highest possible effectiveness. | Effective under difficult situations. | Effective under normal circumstances. | | Lacks planning ability. | Inefficient. | | |

5. **Vision**--Refers: to the power to see and image.

  (▭)   (▭)   (▭)   (▭)   (▭)   (▭)   (▭)   (▭)   (▭)

| Superior ability to think creatively foresee and imagine. | Very capable in anticipating the future. | Ability to plan in advance. | | Overly realistic. | Devoid of imagination. | | |

6. **Selling Company Policies**--Refers to: Company loyalty and an eagerness to tell others.

  (▭)   (▭)   (▭)   (▭)   (▭)   (▭)   (▭)   (▭)   (▭)

| An extremely loyal employee eager to express to outsiders his enthusiasm. | A very loyal employee. | Passive in his attitude toward Company policies. | | Critical of all Company policies. | Disloyal and traitorous. | | |

4. What kind of a person is he?
5. How good is his judgment? His planning? His organizing? His initiative?
6. What is the cost picture in his department? Is production satisfactory? Is he meeting his budgets?
7. What is the state of morale in his unit or department? How about labor turnover, absenteeism, tardiness, discipline problems, accidents, grievances, and complaints?
8. What type of supervisory techniques does he use?
9. Is he able to train subordinates, delegate authority to them, and accomplish results through them?
10. What specific results has he achieved during the year?
11. Does he work harmoniously with other supervisors?
12. Is he competent technically? How well does he keep up with developments in his field?
13. What are the reactions of those who hear him talk? Of those who read his reports?
14. Are his work habits good or bad?
15. Does he dress appropriately?
16. What types of extra assignments could he take over? What types of committee work could he do? What types of jobs could he be promoted to—if any?
17. How can his long-term growth be developed and maintained?

Career planning

The answers to questions such as those above frequently constitute one of the first steps in career planning for an individual. When the supervisor's boss rates him high on performance and the forecast for his promotability is favorable, then higher management becomes interested in his development. Some companies set up *appraisal panels* to watch over the development of managerial talent. A panel would consist of three or four higher managers who would (1) evaluate present and potential abilities of the management man, and (2) plan his future development for advancement in management. The findings of the panel are reviewed by top management. This review permits top management to become acquainted with the sources of executive replenishment over the next 5 or 10 years. The appraisal panel, meeting as a committee, inaugurates and maintains a program of planned future development for each supervisor by means of coaching, committee work, job rotation, special assignments, and, often, more formal education.

From an organization's viewpoint, career planning must take place for individuals both as individuals and as an assurance that there will be a pool of capable persons available for promotions as the need arises. In fact, there is some current thinking that indicates that opportunities should be created for high-talent employees so they can be given responsibility as soon as possible.

An organization must conduct a constant search for managerial talent and lay plans for systematically developing it for orderly progress up the ladder. If a company is to be able to promote from within, it must plan its manpower needs, discover suitable candidates, provide training for them, and constantly evaluate the progress that people are making toward preparing themselves for higher responsibilities. A large corporation may keep track of its talent pool by using the computer to store up-to-date information on the skills, experience, and job desires of its managerial, scientific, and technical personnel.

Manpower replacement chart. The personnel inventory maintained on the organization's computer is often supplemented by manpower replacement charts. (See Figure 13–4.) These charts enable management appraisal committees and the personnel department to know at a glance the status of employees in a given department. For instance, in the example given it is readily apparent that the department head will retire in two years when he reaches age 65. It is also apparent that the assistant department head will probably not be his replacement because of the quality of his present performance and his promotability rating. Further it can be seen that the supervisors of sections C and E have outstanding ratings in both categories. If these ratings continue for the next two years then one solution could be to promote one of them to department head and move the other one to another higher opening in the company. Of course there are other possibilities, but the point is that such a chart prepared and reviewed annually is a very useful managerial tool.

Benefits to individuals. When a company carries out systematic manpower planning using a personnel inventory and replacement charts which are updated annually, they also make forecasts five or six years in advance each time the inventory and charts are updated. Retirement illness, and other reasons create openings. Expansion and organization changes are also anticipated. Naturally when one promotion takes place it sets off a chain reaction if the company follows a promotion from within policy. Such an approach to manpower planning tends to minimize the chance that a talented individual would be missed when considering candidates for promotion. It also makes it difficult for a manager to hoard capable individuals.

Probably the most important benefit of this approach is the career opportunities it makes apparent to individuals in the company. The personnel department, the employee's supervisor, and the management appraisal committee can meet with the employee and design suitable career tracks or paths for him. He can express his interests and desires also. By taking the usual mystery out of promotion decisions, the company can help assure that talented individuals will not seek opportunities elsewhere.

FIGURE 13–4
Manpower Replacement Chart

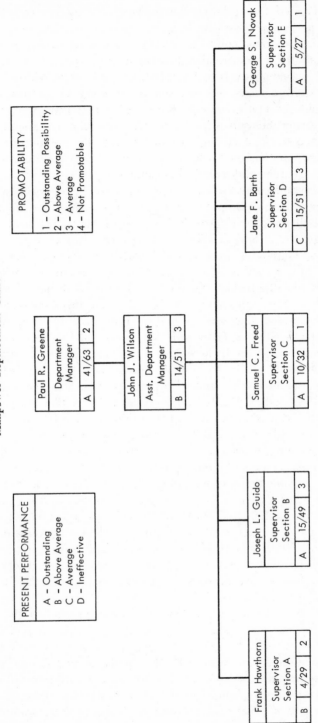

PRESENT PERFORMANCE

A – Outstanding
B – Above Average
C – Average
D – Ineffective

PROMOTABILITY

1 – Outstanding Possibility
2 – Above Average
3 – Average
4 – Not Promotable

Paul R. Greene		
Department Manager		
A	41/63	2

John J. Wilson		
Asst. Department Manager		
B	14/51	3

Frank Hawthorn		
Supervisor Section A		
B	4/29	2

Joseph L. Guido		
Supervisor Section B		
A	15/49	3

Samuel C. Freed		
Supervisor Section C		
A	10/32	1

Jane F. Barth		
Supervisor Section D		
C	15/51	3

George S. Novak		
Supervisor Section E		
A	5/27	1

This is a simplified version of a replacement chart. Normally an entire organization's formal structure would be included. The qualitative measures are self-explanatory and would be derived from the results of performance appraisals. The first number in the center of each box is the employee's tenure with the organization. The second number is his age at the time the chart is prepared. Such charts are usually prepared annually after the performance appraisal takes place.

Staff assistance in supervisory development. While the development of supervisors is primarily a line responsibility, sound manpower planning helps create an atmosphere of cooperation between line managers and the personnel department. Since line managers may tend to be somewhat parochial in their approach to staffing and promotions, the personnel department can assist them in developing a companywide viewpoint. Over a period of time it can be demonstrated that even though a particular department may lose a talented individual to another part of the company, they will also receive talented people from other departments. It also enables reinforcement of the idea that one of the manager's prime responsibilities is to develop promotables. Among other ways that the personnel department can assist line departments in the development of supervisors for the entire organization are:

1. In the selection of candidates—it can bring to his attention people from other sections and departments and even those within his own department that he may have missed. It can furnish the results of tests administered to applicants. Working together, the line and personnel departments can uncover hidden talents, and the line superior can escape charges of favoritism.
2. The personnel department can design and conduct supervisory training courses and orientation courses whereby actual and potential supervisors are trained in seeing the relationships between production, marketing, engineering, personnel, and other departments— trained to consider the broader picture in their thinking and their decision making.
3. The personnel department can handle job rotation whereby candidates for higher positions spend time working in various departments, particularly switching from line to staff jobs so that they can work more cooperatively later on when they are promoted.
4. The personnel department can suggest education and other self-improvement programs for people being groomed for supervisory positions.

Taking the time and effort to train supervisors pays off to both the line department and the personnel department because it cuts down on the work of handling grievances, turnover, and absenteeism, and on the positive side it builds up morale and production.

The fast-track manager

In recent years, another approach to career planning has been receiving attention in the business periodicals and in some texts. Earlier in this chapter it was pointed out that many people in a company do not desire the responsibilities that accompany promotions to higher levels of management. Some reach a level at which they feel comfortable and they desire no further advancement. On the other hand, many organizations have found that there are people who have both the desire and the capability to reach senior management positions. It is estimated that approximately 10 to 15 percent of an organization's managerial manpower are in this category.

Obviously the identification and careful nurturing of these managers is a critical necessity. The business pages of any large city newspaper carry daily news of managers who change their jobs. Executive search firms are constantly looking for high-talent managers to serve the needs of their clients. Some companies find out about their talented people the hard way. Losing a bright, young manager to another firm can be a sobering experience to a company that already has a shortage of such people.

There seems to be a high degree of mobility among managers of this type.[7] They are highly competent, young, ambitious middle managers who are strongly motivated by responsibility and challenge. To keep them, many companies have placed them on a "fast track" of increasingly greater responsibility. When a manager of this type is identified, usually by a combination of testing, performance, and recommendations by superiors, he is rapidly promoted often with significant increases in salary. In some organizations, the "sink or swim" approach is used by giving the manager a position which may be too difficult for him. Naturally it is hoped that he will succeed and in many instances companies have found that the person chosen does succeed. In fact notions about long years of seasoning in a variety of so-called understudy jobs have been dispelled. In several companies the "fast track" has come about out of necessity. There simply are not enough managers to fill open positions and they are not readily available in the open market.

When a manager is placed on a fast track, he is carefully watched by his superiors and his career plan is given considerable attention. Jobs are chosen for him which will continually broaden his knowledge and responsibility. Rotational assignments are quite common. So are geographical moves if the company has several locations. Companies who follow the "fast-track" approach are openly developing a cadre of young managers who will succeed to top-management positions relatively early in their careers.

Internal mobility

The tight labor market prevalent in recent years has caused many organizations to look to its internal labor market for more effective place-

---

[7] For a more thorough analysis, see E. E. Jennings, *The Mobile Manager* (Ann Arbor, Mich.: Bureau of Industrial Relations, University of Michigan, 1967).

ment of employees. Rather than waiting for emergencies, management has encouraged and developed systems enabling transfers of employees with greater ease and efficiency. Companies have found that most transfers take place within a department or division. While this is desirable, they also want to encourage transfers on an interdepartmental basis. In this manner there can be more effective utilization of the present work force and possible lower labor turnover. This is usually true where an employee is unhappy with his present position and is able to find a new one in the company rather than by quitting and seeking employment elsewhere.

A transfer serves to move an employee to another job in the same company. The move may be made to rotate jobs for training purposes, to accommodate organizational changes, to satisfy a disgruntled employee or his supervisor, or to protect an employee from a layoff. While most transfers are lateral in nature to jobs usually paying the same amount, there are some transfers which result in demotion of the employee.

Even though moving people around in a company can be costly and in some cases complicated, it is usually beneficial to both the company and the employee. The costs involved in recruiting new employees are generally greater than those incurred by transfers. Most important of all is the effective use of the internal labor market and the greater flexibility this gives the management of the company.

Remedial transfers

There are many reasons why a person may need to be transferred out of his present job. Initial placement may have been poor, or the job may have changed to the extent that the person is no longer suited to it. He may have changed in physical condition or in knowledge, skill, interests, or attitude. He may have run into problems of social adjustment to the work group or to the supervisor.

If the supervisor made a mistake in fitting a man to a job, it may be possible to correct it by moving him to another job in the department and training him for it. If the right job doesn't exist within the department—or if the problem is one of relationships between people—the supervisor should ask help from the personnel department in getting the man placed in another department.

Fitting men and jobs must be a continuing activity if the company is to make maximum use of the abilities of its people, and if the people are to get maximum satisfaction from their work.

Health and safety. Physical disabilities can incapacitate a person for his present job. He may be partially disabled by an accident, by poor health, or by age. His job may make too heavy physical demands upon him or be too hazardous for him. He may be a hazard to other people if he is having accidents or near accidents. His physical or emotional state may make him fear that he is going to be injured on the job. His sight, hearing, or coordination may be impaired. His condition may make him unable to learn new skills called for by changes in his job.

Sometimes the job can be redesigned to accommodate the physical disabilities, but more often the employee is given a transfer or demotion to some job he can handle.

Change of interest or skill.   Sometimes a man's interests may be along a different line than the job he is doing. He may be going to school at night preparing himself for a type of work entirely different from the job he is on. The field in which he is studying may require several years of preparation, during which time he is being upgraded and receiving raises on his regular job. Then when he wants to change over to the type of work he has been preparing for, he finds that he has to start at the bottom at a low salary. Rather than make the financial sacrifice, he may remain on his present job, discontented and discouraged. The supervisor can prevent misfits of this kind by keeping in close touch with his men, and keeping informed of their ambitions and their outside training. Before it is too late for them to make the change, he can arrange transfers into jobs related to their fields of training.

Sometimes a man will take any job in order to get his foot in the door. If he proves his worth, he should be helped to get into the type of work for which he is best suited. Occasionally a person will have special skills for which there was no demand when he was hired. When the opportunity does arise, the supervisor should shift him into the job in which he can use his highest skill.

Personality problems.   Often, transferring employees to another department is a means of solving human relations problems. In any group of people working together, there are bound to be personality clashes. If they are minor, people learn to adjust to one another, but occasionally there arises a situation in which two people cannot get along with each other, no matter how they try; then their work suffers, and they should be separated. Such a separation is especially desirable when there is conflict between a superior and his subordinate. No superior should be expected to keep under his jurisdiction a subordinate who is a constant irritation to him or whose actions are continually hindering him. The supervisor should first look upon the man as a challenge to his skill as a leader and try to win him over. If he cannot do this, then he should have the man transferred. The subordinate who is a headache to one supervisor and a misfit in one group may turn out to be a star performer somewhere else.

The failing employee. Occasionally an employee who is a failure in one department and should be fired can be saved to the organization by a transfer to another department. Under such circumstances, the supervisor should tell the personnel department the whole story about the man and ask to have him placed elsewhere in the organization. Such an employee should be told the truth about his transfer—that he is being given a chance to make good and that this is his opportunity to prove that he has been misjudged. Sometimes such people change; but, if they do not improve after one or two such transfers, serious consideration should be given to terminating them.

Whenever a person is transferred, he should be told the reason. He should have the opportunity of protesting a transfer. Knowing the *why* of a transfer, no matter what it is, is better than not knowing. A person transferred without knowing the cause suffers quite a shock to his feeling of security. A person transferred to a new department should receive an induction that will enable him to adjust easily and achieve satisfactory performance rapidly. The new group should be given preparation to receive him.

Requests for transfer. Employees often initiate the requests for transfers, either requesting them of their supervisor or bypassing him and going directly to the personnel department. When the supervisor is by-passed on such requests, he should ask himself whether he has been showing his employees that he has their interests at heart—if he has been holding onto men when he should have been taking the initiative in helping them transfer to jobs better suited to them. When a number of people request transfer out of a department, the supervisor should suspect something wrong in the department and take action to correct it.

Transfers for training purposes

The employee whose abilities slate him for advancement into management might be moved from one job to another within a department for two reasons: (1) to gain a wider job knowledge and (2) to be gotten out of a blind alley and placed in a position from which promotion is a logical and likely step.

Some transfers within a department are made to increase the flexibility of the work group. If employees learn how to handle several jobs, they can substitute for one another during absences and vacations. They are able to handle emergencies and to shift to other work in case of machine breakdown, shortage of materials, or rush jobs. Short-run transfers of this type can be taken in stride by employees who feel competent to do the work to which they are transferred. Such transfers are facilitated if job descriptions are not too narrow and if induction and training emphasize broad duties for the job.

People who have some flexibility have less to fear from changes in technology, method, or procedure, although most people resist being shunted around from job to job. The amount of transferring done for training purposes will depend upon the union contract, the needs of the company, and the costs of training. The supervisor who understands the social arrangements in his work group can do much to smooth the way for short-run transfers that are in the company interest. He may be able to show the employee that in times of rapid technological change an employee is in a more favorable position if he knows how to perform several jobs.

Transfers necessitated by changes

Employees may be routed out of their jobs by changes in the volume of work or by changes in technology, product, equipment, procedure, or method. The company has an investment in these employees and in most cases it wants to protect the investment by transferring them to other jobs and retraining them. If employees are laid off frequently, the best of them will find other jobs that are more stable. The others when they are called back become wary of implementing changes and they find ways to make their work stretch over longer periods.

A company that has a good reputation for taking care of its people will have less turmoil in introducing new methods and improvements. Introduction of a computer may require that employees be transferred several times while the changeover is being made. Each transfer calls for training, induction to a new work group, and preparation of that group to receive the new members. The supervisor who understands the emotional problems involved in learning changed jobs can help people adjust to transfers to new work groups and to new duties.

Transfers and seniority

The supervisor must know and abide by the provisions of the union contract and the company policy covering transfers and seniority. He must know whether employees can be required to do work outside the job duties defined in the job description. Contract provisions may permit the senior employee to transfer to a more desirable job if he can perform the duties.

If seniority is on a companywide basis, the bumping in times of layoff may bring people from all parts of the company into a department, with the resulting problems of training them and integrating them into a team. If seniority is on a job basis or a departmental basis (rather than on a companywide basis) an employee may be unwilling to transfer out of the department or out of the job on which he has seniority. Even though a job in another department might suit him better or offer better chances for advancement, it involves a risk. In case of a cutback in the new department, he would be the low man, vulnerable to bumping and maybe out of a job. If seniority is on a companywide basis, a work group may strongly resist receiving a transferred employee who has high seniority and would displace someone in the group in case of a cutback.

These problems involving security and fairness complicate the handling of transfers, and the supervisor must be sure he understands the particular arrangements in his company. Even if there is no union, these matters will very likely be regulated by company policy and procedure.

Transfer policy

An organization obviously must have transfer policies which protect it against possible abuse of the transfer privileges. Attempt should be made to prevent transfers from becoming a method of unloading problem employees from one department on to another. Policies should discourage supervisors from trying to pirate workers and should deter employees from seeking easier jobs in other departments. If reasonable equity is maintained between employee requests, supervisory requests, and company needs, then transfer policies can aid the company in establishing optimum use of its internal labor market. This should be the overriding force in the handling of transfers.

The environment for career development

There is no doubt that the policies a company has concerning organizational development and manpower planning play a considerable part in creating an atmosphere of encouragement for employees who are willing to assume responsibility and who have the capabilities for advancement. Nothing is so frustrating as working for a boss who stifles initiative and discourages individual growth. In the chapter on human relations, sensitivity training and management grid programs were mentioned as possible vehicles for changing managers' attitudes toward their jobs and their subordinates. In the final analysis, it is each individual supervisor that really creates the growth climate for his capable subordinates. His daily relationships with subordinates can really aid young, ambitious employees to grow or they can stifle these employees if the supervisor is negative.

Not every company can offer rapid promotion and some supervisors may spend several years under the same boss. The influence the boss has on his subordinates in such situations can be very important in the development of their abilities.

In capsule form, here are some suggestions for providing an environment that will foster supervisory development.

1. Delegate authority and responsibility. There is no use in just telling a subordinate supervisor that he needs to assume more responsibility: put it on his shoulders.
2. Expect a lot from your subordinate supervisors. Most assistants can do and are willing to do more than they are now doing. Make each supervisor's job a challenge to him.
3. Make accomplishment the basis of security and advancement.
4. View mistakes by subordinates as a necessity for their growth. Convert these mistakes into opportunities to learn.
5. Recognize that success breeds success.
6. Develop a spirit of mutual concern, trust, and confidence between you and your subordinates.
7. Reduce the social distance between you and your assistants.
8. Provide your subordinates with experience so that they can grow.
9. Have a development program in process for each of your subordinates. Have it tailored to fit his needs.

Of course, the basic factor in career development is the individual himself. He must want to get ahead and must also want to willingly perform the work necessary to achieve his goals. Most companies want to promote from within. Superiors look for talent in their subordinates. They often give special assignments to test the attitudes and ability of those people seeking promotions. When a vacancy occurs they are certainly going to consider the person who has demonstrated some evidence of self-development by keeping up with the managerial and technical developments in his field and who continues to improve his performance on his present job while fully cooperating in the acceptance of special assignments and greater responsibility.

Summary

Organizational development is rarely spontaneous. It comes about as a result of managerial decisions which result in change. Even though some of these decisions may be haphazard, they have an impact on the company and its managers. If an organization is going to continue to achieve its objectives over the long term it must develop an effective manpower planning program to assure an adequate supply of capable managers for the future.

Most companies have promotion from within policies developed largely because of tight labor markets and high-recruitment and training costs. To effectively carry out its manpower planning, an organization should systematically appraise the performance of its employees. Performance appraisal permits a company to try to improve present job performance and to identify promotables. There are several methods available and the one that suits the company's purpose should be chosen.

Not everyone wants to be promoted to higher level jobs for a variety of reasons. Those that do, however, providing they are capable, should be given every opportunity to grow in the organization. Once a promotable employee has been identified, the company should develop a career plan for him. He, his supervisor, and other interested managerial personnel should be involved in the development of the career plan. Job assignments, education, increased responsibility and other special assignments should be carefully planned to optimize the growth of the employee.

Companies should plan for replacement of managerial personnel years in advance of need. Career plans and replacement charts will assist in this effort. These are particularly desirable for they tend to minimize labor turnover among capable candidates for higher management positions. Some of these capable individuals may be young and highly mobile and have given evidence of potential for top-management responsibility. In such cases some companies have developed "fast-track" career paths where promotions and salary increases come rather rapidly and responsibility increases as fast as the employee can absorb it.

The internal labor market is more effectively utilized by having an enlightened transfer policy. Transfers should be made with the employee's welfare as well as the company's in mind. While transfers may be costly, they generally are less costly than recruiting and training new employees.

Each company should try to create an environment which encourages career development for its employees. But in the final analysis, it is the individual who must want to grow and he can demonstrate this to his superiors by undertaking a program of self-development.

CASE 1

You recently rated the employees in your group according to the company's employee-evaluation plan. You find that John Brown, one of your young workers, turns out more than a satisfactory quantity and quality of work, but that is about all you can say for him. You have noticed that he has as little as possible to do with other workers—seems to consider himself better than they are. He shows no initiative on the job—never goes ahead with anything on his own—and takes as much time off as he can get away with. You know that he is taking some kind of college courses at night.

You call in Brown and start going over his evaluation with him. You tell him that the quality and quantity of his work are high but that his value as an employee is lowered by his tardiness and absentee record and by his attitude toward his fellow workers. During the interview, he tells you that he is studying management courses at night and that in three years he will graduate; then he is going to quit and get a good job somewhere.

You know that the company is always looking for good men and that there are many opportunities within it for advancement.

1. What might be some of the reasons for Brown's attitude toward his fellow workers?
2. What might be some of the reasons for his lack of initiative?
3. What might be some of his reasons for his taking time off?
4. How would you straighten him out in relation to each of the above?
5. How would you go about getting Brown to change his attitude?

CASE 2

You have just finished rating John Jones, and the quality and quantity of his work for this period are far below that shown on his previous ratings. When his work fell off suddenly several months ago, you asked him the reason, and you have talked to him about it several times since then. The only information you could get from him was that he was having trouble at home and that, as soon as it cleared up, he would be his old self again.

Now, when you discuss his rating with him and show him his previous ratings, he tells you that his wife left him several months ago and that he has been taking care of the three children. He says that as soon as school reopens in the fall, he will not be worrying about having the children running loose all day, and he will be able to concentrate on his job.

1. Should you accept this as an excuse? Justify your answer.
2. If other workers notice that you are tolerating Jones's low production, should you tell them the reason why?
3. What are Jones's obligations to the company?
4. What are the company's obligations to Jones?
5. What should you say to Jones?

CASE 3

You have been reviewing the employee evaluations you made of Joe Doe over the last five years, and you find that they are better than average. In the present rating, he is poor in all categories. You have observed that something is wrong with him, but you have no idea what it could be.

Now when you start to talk to him about the ratings, he tells you that he is washed up as far as the company is concerned. You ask him why, and he tells you that six months ago Harry White was promoted instead of him to be one of your assistants. He states that he thought that he was being groomed for the job and that he is sorely disappointed.

This comes as quite a surprise to you, because you never thought of him as having enough ability to do supervisory work. It is true that he did minor jobs for you, but they were of the office-boy type.

Even though his past ratings were better than good, there is no indication that he could handle a crew of men. Most of the men in the group are older and more experienced than he is.

1. How does Joe Doe see the facts?
2. How do you see the facts?
3. How are you going to change Doe's attitude?

CASE 4

You have heard numerous reports that Jack Black has been running the company down and telling the group that the place is a sweatshop. He is always going around with a chip on his shoulder. Whenever you have asked him about this attitude, he has retorted with such remarks as "My production is up," or "The company is getting its money's worth out of me."

You now show him his evaluation sheet, on which you have rated him low in attitude and cooperativeness. He says that this is OK with him and then starts to tell you that management is not entitled to anything but quality and quantity of output, and all the rest of it is a lot of bunk; its only purpose is to get the workers to bow down and salve management's ego. He asks you to prove otherwise. He says that a fellow might have a good attitude, be cooperative and dependable, and show initiative, but if his production is not up, he gets fired.

1. Is the company entitled to anything in addition to production from its employees? Why? Or why not?
2. What arguments would you use to prove to Black that he is wrong?
3. What would be the results of a spreading of Black's attitude?
4. How would you go about changing his attitude?
5. What would you do if you were unsuccessful in changing his attitude?

CASE 5

A year ago you were brought into a fairly large staff department as its supervisor. The men within your group are aggressive. They get action on their recommendations by selling, cajoling, or going up the line to a place where they can convince a big boss who will turn their recommendations into direct orders. All the men are intelligent, gifted with good judgment, analytical ability, and common sense. Most are young college graduates and strong on theory.

J. Jones is one of your problem subordinates. Shortly you will have to make out an annual appraisal sheet on him, discuss it with him, and get him started on a self-improvement program. From reports, inquiries, and your own observations, you have gathered the following information about him:

a)   He is gifted with a great deal of intelligence.
b)   He is a tireless worker on projects which appeal to him, but very laggard when he has to handle details or uninteresting work.
c)   He fails to recognize authority.
d)   He has few, if any, friends in the organization.
e)   He possesses an extremely high opinion of his own ability and worth.
f)   He is ambitious to the point of fixation.
g)   He has an attitude of animosity toward the supervisors of other departments.
h)   He is irascible, argumentative, and far from receptive to constructive criticism.
i)   Frequently he comes up with a brilliant idea which he easily sells to the big boss who shoves it down everyone's throat. Most of these ideas turn out to be worthwhile.

Your immediate superior, A. Smith, had your job before he was promoted and you were brought in. He had Jones as an immediate subordinate and apparently still has a high regard for him. Further, he currently confides in Jones regularly and spends much time in private conversation with him. Smith has gone on record praising Jones's worth to the company. However he did not recommend that Jones be promoted to the job which you now hold.

1.   Evaluate each of Jones's liabilities and assets as a staff man.
2.   Would you evaluate each differently if he were a line supervisor? Why? Why not?
3.   Outline how you would discuss the evaluation with him. Be specific.
4.   Set up a self-improvement program and a career plan for Jones.
5.   How are you going to get him to adopt it?

CASE 6

The company hires recent college graduates who are potential managerial material and then it has a problem keeping them interested in their jobs until the young men are sufficiently prepared to take over supervisory work and until supervisory openings occur. The average college graduate needs a year or two of experience before he can successfully run a section. Usually he has to spend an additional year or two waiting for a supervisory job to open up. Sometimes unusual circumstances shorten or lengthen this waiting period.

These young men are anxious to get ahead and they do a good job as long as it is a challenge to them. However, after the glamour wears off they get bored and their work suffers to the extent that some of them—in justice to other people—are no longer promotable.

1. Develop a training program that will keep these young people interested until the vacancies occur.
2. To what extent is the company responsible for their boredom?
3. How could more effective manpower planning help this situation?
4. Are the young men expecting too much from their jobs?

CASE 7

Each year the company recruited 50 to 75 college graduates for its management training program. This program lasted 18 months and the successful trainee usually was placed in a lower level managerial responsibility at the completion of his exposure to the training. The program was highly competitive and even though selection was careful, approximately 25 percent of the participants were released by the company before they completed the program.

It was decided to expand the company's promotion from within policy and allow present company employees to apply for the management training program along with those people recruited from the outside. While a bachelor's degree was necessary for the outside applicant, the company decided to waive that requirement for present staff provided they had at least five years' experience within the company and had availed themselves of the company's tuition remission program and were presently enrolled in an evening bachelor's degree program at one of the colleges in the area. In addition, they would be required to take the same personality, aptitude, intelligence and skill tests that outside candidates took. They would also be subjected to the same multiple and depth interviewing process that the outside applicant was given.

Lou Swanson met all of the requirements, having worked for the company six years since his high school graduation. After a variety of clerical jobs he had been promoted to a group leader's job. After receiving the promotion, he enrolled at an evening college and was presently one third of the way through the bachelor's degree program. His job as a group leader was not really a management position since he had no real responsibility other than as a pacesetter in one of the large, clerical departments.

Lou decided to apply for the management training program and made an appointment to see the personnel director. He impressed the personnel man with his enthusiasm, apparent ambition, and interest in the company. Everything was going along very well until Lou stated that he could see no reason to take any of the tests that the department used in the screening process. He felt he had already proven himself in the company and the tests were not necessary. He also felt they were an invasion of his privacy. Because of Lou's adamant refusal to take the test battery, his application for the management training program was denied.

1. Was the personnel director correct in refusing Lou Swanson's application?
2. Should an employee who has a successful record in a company be subjected to testing for a job whose requirements are different than the one in which he is presently engaged?
3. Should Lou have applied for the training program feeling the way he did about the testing requirement?
4. Based on the information available, do you think Lou would have been a good risk for the training program?

CASE 8

You have under your jurisdiction several supervisors. It is part of their job to discuss periodically with their workers the employee-evaluation sheet. Most of these supervisors dislike this task. They put it off until the last minute and then get it over with as fast as possible.

1. What are some of the reasons for this attitude?
2. What are some of the advantages of discussing ratings with employees?
3. What are some of the important things for the supervisor to consider during such discussions?

CASE 9

Tom Merrill started with the company when he was discharged from the service at the end of World War II. He had been a combat pilot and had risen to the rank of captain. The company, a major petroleum firm, placed Tom in its aviation marketing division to take advantage of the knowledge he had acquired in the service. Tom was successful and he progressed through various positions receiving raises and promotions as time went on. Tom was sent to several company training programs to develop his managerial ability and he was given continually increased responsibility. After several years in the aviation division, Tom was given a variety of rotational assignments in other divisions to broaden his knowledge of company operations. Clearly Tom was a young man with a great future. During this period, the company prided itself on its promotion from within policy placing great emphasis on experience in company operations. Little emphasis was placed on education and several executives had not gone to college. There were many success stories in the company of men who had started in minor jobs and had risen to high managerial posts. Tom, who had not gone to college, apparently was emulating this type of company success story. After serving in a variety of posts, Tom was assigned to the sales staff of the marine division. He continued his pattern of success, receiving merit increases and promotions until he was placed in charge of marine sales reporting directly to the divisional vice president. Tom had participated in more company-sponsored executive development programs and these along with his experience had apparently developed him into a very capable, articulate administrator.

During the period of Tom's service in the marine division, the company effected a change in policy. While they still basically adhered to a promotion from within policy, more emphasis was placed on education. College graduates were hired for executive training, thus bypassing the time-honored office boy to president approach of the past. Master's degree holders were recruited for several understudy positions and, in fact, Tom had a few working for him.

Tom's boss, the divisional vice president, was pleased with Tom's performance and frequently told him so. Each year it was his responsibility to conduct a formal performance evaluation of those managers reporting to him. Part of the evaluation program provided for the ranking of peer group managers in the order of their worth to the company. This ranking reflected the opinion of the evaluator as well as his superior. For four years Tom was told that he received a high ranking each year and his raises reflected the esteem in which he was held. Tom questioned his superior about promotional opportunities and each time he was told not to worry and be patient. Tom did not press the issue since he was reasonably satisfied with his progress and he was flattered by the high ratings he received. He began to reflect on his career, however, and wondered when he would be promoted. He had been with the company almost 25 years and was now 45 years old. He felt he could assume major management responsibility and his ratings seemed to prove this to him. He also believed that a promotion must come in the near future or he would be bypassed by younger men in the company. He felt he was still marketable as an executive for another company but that if he waited much longer, he would be too old. After considerable thought in this vein, he decided to have a heart-to-heart talk with his superior.

He opened the discussion by questioning his boss on the meaning and value of the peer-ranking aspect of the performance evaluation program. His boss told him it had considerable importance in determining a man's promotability and the size of his annual increase. Tom then pressed for more specific information regarding his evaluation. While reluctant to do so, his superior then told him that he had been ranked number one for the past four years by both the executive vice president and himself. His boss went on to say that the size of increase Tom had received reflected this thinking and that he was now being paid a salary over the top of the range for his position. Tom then asked the logical question, "Why have I not been promoted?" His boss then replied, "It's because of your lack of formal education." "The company has decided that only college graduates will be considered for promotion to senior management positions," he added.

1. Do you feel the company is justified in the position they have taken with regard to the promotability of Tom Merrill?
2. Should Tom's superior have told him about his rating and the decision about his promotability? Should he have been told sooner?
3. What should Tom do now?
4. Does a company's management have any responsibility to communicate how a policy change may affect an employee's career?
5. To what extent did Tom contribute to his predicament by not getting a degree by going to evening college during his career with the company?
6. Is the company placing too much emphasis on the value of a college education and by so doing, discriminating against employees like Tom Merrill?
7. Is there a possibility that there may be another reason for not promoting Tom and his superior may have used his lack of education as a convenient excuse? If so, to what extent should a superior be frank with a subordinate when discussing his career?
8. Can the company justify paying Tom a salary higher than the top of the range for his position and still not promote him?

CASE 10

You are a department head, have been with the company for 25 years, and have under you two assistant supervisors—John Black and Bill White. Black has been with the company 20 years, and White has been with the company 6 years. Black has always been dependable, cooperative, and loyal, but he lacks initiative and he is slowing down on account of his age. White is a younger man, has initiative, is dependable, and grasps problems quickly.

Several months ago the company installed an employee-evaluation plan in which employee ratings are based on loyalty, initiative, ability to work under pressure, cooperation, dependability, and quality and quantity of work. These ratings are now the basis for raises, promotions, demotions, and layoffs.

You rated both men carefully, with the result that White—the younger man—got a better rating than Black. Then you discussed each man's rating with him. Black was satisfied with his rating.

A short while ago, business fell off, and a reduction in force was put into effect. A number of people were laid off, while others were demoted. Under the employee-evaluation plan, it was necessary for you to reduce Black from the status of a supervisor to that of a rank-and-file worker. Everyone in the department, including White, feels that an injustice has been done.

1. What might be some of the reasons for this feeling?
2. Should the employee evaluation be used as the sole basis of raises? Demotions? Layoffs?
3. Should other factors be taken into consideration in relation to raises? Demotions? Layoffs? If so, what should they be?
4. How can the employee-evaluation or merit-rating system now used in the company be made more effective?

CASE 11

For a long period, the company was behind in its orders, and the labor market was tight. Since workers were hard to get, you and the other supervisors had a tendency to overrate your employees on the evaluation sheets; and, in discussing the ratings with them, you emphasized their good points in order to keep them happy. As a result, practically every employee is rated "superior."

Now business is falling off, and it is necessary for a number of employees to be demoted or laid off. Top management tells all the supervisors to use their employee-evaluation sheets as the basis for such actions and to discuss these ratings with the employees when they are being demoted or laid off.

1. How should the supervisors handle the situation?
2. What should they say to the workers?
3. What are some of the cautions to be considered in evaluating employees?

CASE 12

A valuable and long-time employee, Sam Smith, does an excellent job in your department, especially on detailed and highly skilled work. His one drawback is that he talks endlessly. Every job subject that is brought up will start Sam off on a long-winded recital of its history and related incidents and a string of anecdotes that he manages to tie to it. People avoid opening conversations with him because they don't want to get him started talking and then be unable to shut him off. You and several supervisors before you have tried to caution him against being so long-winded but it had no effect on him. Every subject that he discusses he goes into in such fine detail that he bores everyone who comes in contact with him. To turn this liability into an asset you made him one of your trainers and he has become quite successful at it.

There is to be a supervisory opening soon in his section and you know that Sam feels he is in line for it. He has intimated as much to you by pointing out that he has been doing training work which he considers a chore, and doing it successfully because it has been the normal stepping-stone to promotion in the department. Your associates tell you that they wouldn't relish having Sam Smith as an associate; he is too boring and he would waste too much of their time. You feel that you will have to bypass Sam but you certainly don't want to discourage or lose him.

How would you handle the situation?

CASE 13

The following display advertisement appeared in the newspaper of a suburban town located about 40 miles from the central city. It covered about one quarter of a standard size newspaper page, had enough white space and a large size type face, so that it could be easily seen by even a casual reader of the particular issue of the paper. It represents a somewhat novel approach to management development.

ARE YOU A RECENTLY RETIRED TOP CALIBER VICE PRESIDENT—FINANCE AND ADMINISTRATION?

We are an exciting, active consumer goods company, located in _____, with annual sales over $50,000,000 and an excellent growth record that needs you for not more than three years to give seasoning and training in broad gauge responsibilities to a brilliant 28 year oldster who will then take over. If you're looking for the enjoyment of being active and seeing a potential vice president "bloom and develop," please write in confidence to Box XYZ, _____ News.

1. Comment on the desirability of this approach for the development of a young executive.
2. What can the company do to help ensure the success of such an approach?
3. What disadvantages may be encountered by the company?
4. As an executive taking this job offer, what would you expect the company to do to effectively utilize your abilities?

CASE 14

Joe Smith has been in your inspection department for the last five years, during which time he has been doing good work and getting periodic raises so that he is earning a good wage. About four years ago he developed an interest in radio, and he has an amateur radio station at home. On the few occasions when he tried to transfer into the radio experimental department, the supervisor always turned him aside with some excuse or other. About six months ago a new supervisor was put in charge of the radio experimental department. He offered Joe a job but told him that the pay his skill could command in this or any other company would be about half his present pay rate.

Joe tells you that he is disgusted, that he tolerated his present type of work in the hope of getting into radio work eventually, and that now he finds he can't make the financial sacrifice. His work is suffering.

1. How would you go about solving this problem?
2. What should you say to Joe?
3. How could this situation have been avoided?
4. If Joe's work does not improve, should he be terminated?

CASE 15

The toolroom has three employees, and you are to select a supervisor for it. One possibility is a young toolroom worker who has made a very good record in the short time he has been with the company. He is capable, intelligent, a good worker, and a born leader.

The other possibility is a man who has been working in the toolroom for a number of years and who could handle the job, but he is a slow learner and lacks leadership ability. There is no seniority clause in your labor contract.

1. How important is leadership in the toolroom?
2. Which man are you going to promote? Why?
3. What are you going to say to the man who is not promoted?
4. What weight should be given to seniority?
5. What weight should be given to merit?

CASE 16

Recently the personnel department asked you to accept Joe Brown as a transfer into your section, in order to give Joe one last chance to make good. He has a wife and three children and has been with the company a little more than a year, working on a punch press. He claims that the noise of the presses tires him out and that he is afraid of getting hurt. His output has never been satisfactory.

You know about Joe. He has the nickname of "Lazy Joe." Most of the workers wonder why he wasn't fired long ago. You are willing to give him a last chance on account of his wife and children. Your section does light machine work.

1. Should the personnel department ask you to take Joe? Justify your answer.
2. What should you say to Joe when he is transferred to your section?
3. How would you induct Joe?
4. What would you say to the other workers? Justify your answer.
5. To what extent should "lemons" be transferred?
6. If a man has been transferred as a misfit three or four times, what are his chances of making good?

CASE 17

Bill Jones, the supervisor in charge of another section, habitually comes over to your section to chat with your men. It seems that his section does not require his presence all the time; so he spends many afternoons in your section, being one of the boys. Your men are beginning to think that you are too strict with them; several of them have already asked to be transferred to Jones's section.

1. What are some of the methods you might use to discourage Jones?
2. If you are not successful, should you consult your boss?
3. What are some of the ways to discourage pirating?
4. What are some of the advantages and disadvantages of familiarity between supervisors and workers?
5. Where should the line be drawn?

CASE 18

It is the policy of the company to rotate first-level supervisors periodically, so that they will have the opportunity to get acquainted with the various activities of the organization. However, the full value of this plan is not realized because a great deal of time is spent getting people adjusted after each move.

1. What are the advantages of rotating first-level supervisors?
2. What are the disadvantages of rotating first-level supervisors?
3. What are the adjustments that have to be made?
4. How can each of these adjustments be made easier for the first-level supervisors?

CASE 19

A superintendent of an operating division resigns, creating a vacancy that must be filled with the least possible delay. Top management knows about a good man who could fill the job; he is now doing similar work in another company.

The supervisors in the division believe that the position should be filled by promotion from within. Such a promotion would necessitate moving two other men, so that actually three men would be promoted along the line. The supervisors contend that hiring an outsider would have a serious effect on morale and cause greater disturbance than promoting three men within the division.

1. What are the advantages of promoting from within?
2. What are the disadvantages?
3. What are the advantages of recruiting management men from other companies?
4. What are the disadvantages?
5. What should top management do in this case? Justify your answer.

CASE 20

Jeff Roberts has worked for the company for 18 months—all of it as a test technician on the production test line of one of the company's products. He is fast and accurate and takes pride in the quality and quantity of his work. He has been testing this particular instrument longer than anyone else on the line. The company has a policy of moving its production test line personnel around in its various test lines but didn't move him because the product he tests is a rather complicated device and it takes two or three weeks to train a person to test it. Several other technicians have been moved from the line after they requested a transfer to another instrument.

Several new employees have been added to the test line recently, and the number of instruments required for shipment has decreased. The test line therefore is overstaffed. Twice during the past month Jeffrey has been approached by management about transferring to another test line. Both times he said he would rather stay where he is. The section manager feels that a transfer would benefit both the employee and the company, but is not really necessary since two other technicians on the test line have requested a transfer to other product lines.

Jeffrey is about 38 years old, unmarried, and has some income from investments. His salary is comparable to other technicians at the same experience level.

1. Should employees be required to move around to get wider experience?
2. If an employee doesn't want to move around, does that make him of less value to the company?

CASE 21

One of the employees in the accounting department is a young unmarried woman, a university graduate, who began work eight years ago when the company was just getting started. She is extremely competent, highly intelligent, and very well liked by her associates, but she has not been promoted even though the company has expanded rapidly and there have been openings she could fill. The promotions have been given to men; the only reason she hasn't been advanced is that she is a woman.

During the last two years her tardiness has become a matter of concern. She is from 15 minutes to an hour late to work every day. Predicting the time of her arrival has become something of a game in the office. She continues to do a superior job, doing what would take others twice as long to accomplish. Her boss can't get a promotion for her; he has tried.

1. Should a woman be promoted into a job where she would be supervising male accountants?
2. What substitutes for promotion might there be?
3. What should be done about her tardiness?

CASE 22

Mr. Smith, aged 60, has been with the company for the last 15 years as a first-level supervisor. Lately his age has been handicapping him; he is absent frequently, and his memory is failing. During his absences the assistant takes over; in fact, the assistant does most of the work even when Smith is on the job.

Because of periodic raises over a number of years, Smith is receiving good pay. There is quite a spread between his salary and that of his assistant. This annoys the assistant, who says that he does the work but Smith gets the pay.

Smith has been a faithful employee. He is well acquainted with the personnel and the policies of the organization. He will not be eligible for retirement until five years from now.

1. Should Smith be demoted and his assistant put in his place? Justify your answer.
2. Should the situation be allowed to continue? What might be some of the consequences?
3. What should you do with Smith?
4. What should be done with the older supervisory employee who is no longer able to do his job efficiently?
5. What should be done with the older rank-and-file worker who is no longer able to do his job efficiently?

CASE 23

John Green, a middle-aged man, has been a first-level supervisor under your jurisdiction for the last five years. He and his crew do an excellent job. He is by far the best man under you. You would like to make him your understudy so that he could take over your job if you should be promoted.

You tell him of your plans. He replies that, if it would not make much difference to you, he would prefer to remain on his present job for the rest of his life. You ask him why. He says that for the last several years work has been a pleasure to him—he has everything under control, he knows his men, they know and respect him, he is getting good pay, the company knows that he is doing a good job, his house and his car are all paid for; so why should he get ulcers?

1. What are the advantages of having men like Green at various levels in the organization?
2. What are the disadvantages?
3. Is Green justified in his attitude? Explain.
4. Should you encourage Green to try to advance in the organization? Why? Why not?
5. Do you think that Green would be offended if you promoted some less-successful supervisor to be your understudy?
6. Are you justified in accepting a second-best man to be your assistant?

CASE 24

Tom Jones has been with his company for over 45 years. For the past 15 years he has been supervising a small section in one of the departments located at the company's headquarters. His job requires a great amount of detail work and over the years Tom has developed his own methods and systems to assure that everything that leaves his desk is without mistakes. Some of his methods are duplications and could be simplified, but Tom is completely satisfied with his own procedures. Tom is scheduled to retire within two years under the company's mandatory retirement program and he has been frequently absent in the past year due to illness.

Because Tom's work involves a great deal of detail and because of his frequent absences, Bob Stevens who is over 20 years younger than Tom was assigned to Tom's section to learn the job and to take over in Tom's absence.

They have been working together for three months and Bob is already quite familiar with the procedures and methods established by Tom. He feels, however, that some of the duplications of effort can be eliminated and the job simplified. Tom, however, insists that everything should be done the same way he has done it for the past 15 years. These arguments have caused a good deal of friction between the two. Of particular annoyance to Bob is Tom's practice of answering any question with an explanation of the entire procedure along with case histories and several repetitions. He will not listen to reason, insisting on completing the entire explanation each time.

Tom has been asked by his superior to give special assignments to Bob and to let him employ his own methods as long as the end result is the same. He promises to do this, but before long he will again insist that Bob should follow his established procedures. Bob has indicated that if this keeps going on, he will ask for a transfer because he cannot work under such conditions for two years. On the other hand, Tom's knowledge of the job is valuable and he is needed to fully train Bob. Bob is the only person who is qualified to be trained for Tom's job, and the department does not want to lose him.

1. Can the two men be convinced to work together more effectively? How?
2. Is it a good idea to place Bob in an understudy position two years in advance of Tom's retirement?
3. Why do you think Tom is reacting to the training of Bob in the manner described in the case?
4. Is Tom the only one at fault as the case implies?
5. Assume that Tom continues his present behavior pattern. How would you then handle the situation?

CASE 25

Ed Davis had been assistant department head of the accounting department for eight years. During this period he assumed he was doing a good job since he had heard nothing to the contrary. He had been receiving periodic salary increases and his boss seemed satisfied with the way things were going. Ed was 42 years of age and he was looking forward to taking over as department head in one year when his superior was to retire.

The financial vice president had decided, however, to promote Ken Forest, a 28-year-old supervisor of the accounts payable section. Ken had been a supervisor for three years and he reported to Ed Davis. During this period Ken had considerably impressed the vice president as a knowledgeable and effective manager. He felt that Ed Davis did not have the ability to be department head, but that he was a competent number two man. None of the vice president's thinking had been communicated to either individual. Neither had it been told to the department head slated for retirement.

Ken had been attending a management development program conducted for the company by an outside consultant. He had impressed the consultant and when he asked for advice, the consultant listened with interest. It seems that Ken Forest had analyzed his situation and felt that his opportunities in the company were limited. He mentioned that Ed Davis would probably be department head and since he was 42 this meant 23 years of waiting for Ken. Ken did not want to wait until he was 51 to become head of the accounting department. The consultant told him that even though it appeared somewhat dark, many things could happen in a large company and that Ken should not be discouraged. Ken replied that he probably would seek other employment so that he could advance more rapidly.

The consultant thought about Ken's dilemma and his indicated potential. He felt that the personnel director should be aware of Ken's thinking because he felt the company should not lose a person of Ken's caliber if it could be avoided. When the consultant spoke to the personnel director about Ken he was told of the financial vice president's plans for Ken. The consultant then asked why Ken had not been told and the answer was that management was not yet prepared to make a firm commitment.

1. Was the financial vice president handling his manpower planning properly?
2. How can a company keep a bright, young executive satisfied without clearly delineating his future for him?
3. Is it wise to allow the assistant department head to assume that he will be promoted when his superior retires?
4. Can the company do anything to resolve the problem they are facing?
5. Will they be able to keep both Ed Davis and Ken Forest?

FOLLOWING UP ON THE JOB

Evaluating employees

1. Do you and the other supervisors agree about the meanings of "initiative," "cooperativeness," "dependability," and such other characteristics on which you rate employees?
2. Do you and the other supervisors agree about the meanings of the degrees with which you measure—such terms as "poor," "fair," "good," "superior," and "excellent"?
3. Do you gather information about every employee, with reference to all the factors, throughout the whole period covered by the rating?
4. Do you allow unusual incidents to have undue influence on your ratings?
5. Do you rate your group as a whole too high? Too low?
6. Do you allow a worker's rating on one factor to influence you when you are rating him on other factors?
7. Do you rate as "average" those factors you do not have much evidence about?
8. Do you always take one factor at a time and rate all your employees, one against the other, in relation to it?
9. Do you allow prejudices to influence you when you are rating your workers?

Using employee evaluations

1. Do you base your recommendations for raises, promotions, layoffs, etc., upon your ratings?

2. Do you use extra care in rating temporary employees to determine whether or not they should be made permanent?
3. Do you terminate undesirable temporary employees? Or do you hope that they will improve after they have become permanent?
4. Do you make it a point to develop those employees whose ratings indicate that they have good possibilities?
5. Do you provide additional training for those employees found to be in need of it?
6. Do you work out with your employees a timetable for their self-improvement programs?

Interviewing employees

1. When discussing an appraisal, do you give the employee a chance to talk?
2. Do you try to get him to criticize his own performance?
3. Do you criticize performance rather than personality?

Promotions

1. Do you try to develop your men so that they will be eligible for promotion?
2. Do you ever try to hold back a good man because you do not want to lose him?
3. When you are planning to fill a supervisory position under you, do you make a careful study of that position?
4. When considering the promotion of a man from a rank-and-file job to a supervisory position, what abilities do you look for?
5. How do you discover each of these abilities in the candidate?
6. Do you have a well-worked-out procedure for training understudies?
7. Do you cooperate with the personnel department in any manpower planning that they carry out?
8. Do you resent a man being promoted over you even though he may be more capable?
9. Would you recommend a subordinate for promotion who was very capable but whom you did not like personally?
10. Would you suggest that a subordinate seek a position elsewhere if you believed his promotion was blocked in your company?

Transfers

1. Do your employees have any special skills that they are not using but which are needed elsewhere in the company?
2. Do you keep yourself informed about the night school courses some of your employees are taking?

3. Are there some serious personality clashes in your section that should be cleared up by transfers?
4. Do you ever have people transferred without giving them the reason?
5. Do you ever attempt to pirate workers from other sections?
6. Do you correct initial placement mistakes by having workers transferred to more suitable work?
7. Do you use transfers as a means of avoiding responsibilities?
8. Do you always work within company policies in relation to transfers?
9. Are there a great number of requests for transfers out of your section?

Suggested readings

BOOKS

For
Chapter:

11, 12   AMERICAN MANAGEMENT ASSOCIATION. *Leadership on the Job*. Rev. ed. New York: The Association, 1966.

11   ARENSBERG, CONRAD M.; BARKIN, SOLOMON; CHALMERS, W. ELLISON; WILENSKY, HAROLD L.; WORTHY, JAMES C.; and DENNIS, BARBARA D. *Research in Industrial Human Relations: A Critical Appraisal*. Industrial Relations Research Association, Publication No. 17. New York: Harper & Row, Publishers, 1957. (Gives both union and social science angles on the research studies.)

11   ARGYRIS, CHRIS. *Understanding Organizational Behavior*. Homewood, Ill.: The Dorsey Press, 1960.

12   BASS, BERNARD M., and BASS, VAUGHAN. *Training in Industry: The Management of Learning*. Belmont, Calif.: Wadsworth Publishing Co., Inc., 1966.

11   BASSETT, GLEN A. *Management Styles in Transition*. New York: American Management Association, 1966.

11   BENNIS, WARREN G. *Changing Organizations*. New York: McGraw-Hill Book Co., 1966.

11   BLAKE, R. R., and MOUTON, J. S. *The Managerial Grid*. Houston, Tex.: Gulf Publishing Co., 1964.

12   BUGELSKI, RICHARD. *The Psychology of Learning*. New York: Henry Holt & Co., Inc., 1956.

11   DALTON, MELVILLE. *Men Who Manage*. New York: John Wiley & Sons, Inc., 1959.

11, 13   DAVIS, KEITH. *Human Relations at Work*. 3d ed. New York: McGraw-Hill Book Co., 1967.

12   DePHILLIPS, FRANK A.; BERLINER, WILLIAM M.; and CRIBBIN, JAMES J. *Management of Training Programs*. Homewood, Ill.: Richard D. Irwin, Inc., 1960.

13   DRUCKER, PETER F. *The Practice of Management*. New York: Harper & Row, Publishers, 1954.

11, 12, 13   FLEISHMAN, EDWIN A. (ed.). *Studies in Personnel and Industrial Psychology*. Rev. ed. Homewood, Ill.: The Dorsey Press, Inc., 1967.

11 GELLERMAN, SAUL W. *Motivation and Productivity.* New York: American Management Association, 1963. (A review and appraisal of 40 years of motivational research. Studies included are Harvard, Michigan, Pittsburgh, Whyte, Argyris, McGregor, McClelland, Schacter.)

11 HERZBERG, FREDERICK; MAUSNER, BERNARD; PETERSON, RICHARD O.; and CAPWELL, DORA F. *Job Attitudes: Review of Research and Opinion.* Pittsburgh, Pa.: Psychological Service of Pittsburgh, 1957. (Summarizes research studies.)

11 ———; MAUSNER, B.; and SNYDERMAN, B. B. *The Motivation to Work.* New York: John Wiley & Sons, Inc., 1959. (Study of engineers and accountants, and the relationship of job satisfaction to motivation.)

11, 13 JENNINGS, EUGENE E. *The Mobile Manager.* Ann Arbor, Mich.: Bureau of Industrial Relations, University of Michigan, 1967.

13 KELLOG, MARION S. *What to Do about Performance Appraisal.* New York: American Management Association, 1965.

11 LAWRENCE, PAUL R., and SEILER, JOHN A. *Organizational Behavior and Administration: Cases, Concepts, and Research Findings.* Rev. ed. Homewood, Ill.: Richard D. Irwin, Inc., 1965.

11, 13 ———, and LORSCH, JAY W. *Organization and Environment.* Boston: Division of Research Harvard University Graduate School of Business Administration, 1967.

12 LEAVITT, HAROLD. *Managerial Psychology.* Rev. ed. Chicago: University of Chicago Press, 1964.

11, 12 LIKERT, RENSIS. *New Patterns in Management.* New York: McGraw-Hill Book Co., 1961. (Summarizes social research at University of Michigan Institute for Social Research.)

11, 13 ———. *The Human Organization.* New York: McGraw-Hill Book Co., 1967.

11, 12, 13 LIPPIT, GORDON L. *Organizational Renewal.* New York: Appleton-Century-Crofts, Educational Division of Meredith Publishing Co., 1969.

13 LIVINGSTON, ROBERT T., and WAITE, WILLIAM W. (eds.). *The Manager's Job.* New York: Columbia University Press, 1960.

12 LYNTON, ROLF P., and PAREEK, UDAI. *Training for Development.* Homewood, Ill.: Richard D. Irwin, Inc., 1967.

13 MAIER, NORMAN R. F. *The Appraisal Interview.* New York: John Wiley & Sons, Inc., 1958.

12 McGEHEE, WILLIAM, and THAYER, PAUL W. *Training in Business and Industry.* New York: John Wiley & Sons, Inc., 1961.

11 McGREGOR, DOUGLAS. *The Human Side of Enterprise.* New York: McGraw-Hill Book Co., 1960.

11, 12, 13   ———. *The Professional Manager.* New York: McGraw-Hill Book Co., 1967.

13   MERRILL, HARWOOD F., and MARTING, ELIZABETH (eds.). *Developing Executive Skills.* New York: American Management Association, 1958.

11, 12, 13   MINER, JOHN B. *Personnel Psychology.* New York: The Macmillan Co., 1969.

12   MORGAN, JOHN S. *Managing the Young Adults.* New York: American Management Association, 1967.

11   MORSE, NANCY C. *Satisfactions in White Collar Jobs.* Ann Arbor, Mich.: Survey Research Center, University of Michigan, 1953.

11   PFIFFNER, JOHN M. *The Supervision of Personnel.* 3d ed. Englewood Cliffs, N.J.: Prentice-Hall, Inc., 1964.

11, 13   PIGORS, PAUL, and MYERS, CHARLES A. *Personnel Administration.* 6th ed. New York: McGraw-Hill Book Co., 1969.

11   ROETHLISBERGER, F. J., and DICKSON, W. J. *Management and the Worker.* Cambridge, Mass.: Harvard University Press, 1939.

11   ROY, ROBERT H. *The Administrative Process.* Baltimore: The Johns Hopkins Press, 1958. (Contains a study of informal organization and authority relationships in an X-ray department.)

11, 12, 13   SALTONSTALL, ROBERT. *Human Relations in Administration.* New York: McGraw-Hill Book Co., 1959.

11   SAYLES, LEONARD R. *Behavior of Industrial Work Groups.* New York: John Wiley & Sons, Inc., 1958. (Study of groups classified as conservative, strategic, erratic, and apathetic.)

11   ———. *Managerial Behavior.* New York: McGraw-Hill Book Co., 1964.

12   STOKES, PAUL M. *Total Job Training.* New York: American Management Association, 1966.

11, 13   STRAUSS, GEORGE, and SAYLES, LEONARD R. *Personnel:* The *Human Problems of Management.* 2d ed. Englewood Cliffs, N.J.: Prentice-Hall, Inc., 1967.

11, 13   TAGIURI, RENATO, and LITWIN, GEORGE H. (eds.). *Organizational Climate.* Boston: Division of Research, Harvard University Graduate School of Business Administration, 1968.

11, 13   TANNENBAUM, ARNOLD S. *Social Psychology of the Work Organization.* Belmont, Calif.: Wadsworth Publishing Co., Inc., 1966.

11   TAYLOR, FREDERICK W. *Scientific Management.* New York: Harper & Row, Publishers, 1947.

11, 12   VAN DERSAL, WILLIAM R. *The Successful Supervisor in Government and Business.* New York: Harper & Row, Publishers, 1962.

13 VETTER, ERIC W. *Manpower Planning for High Talent Personnel.* Ann Arbor, Mich.: Bureau of Industrial Relations, University of Michigan, 1967.

11 WHYTE, WILLIAM FOOTE (ed.). *Money and Motivation: An Analysis of Incentives in Industry.* New York: Harper & Row, Publishers, 1955.

13 ZALEZNIK, A. *Foreman Training in a Growing Enterprise.* Boston: Harvard University Press, 1951.

11 ———; CHRISTENSEN, C. R.; and ROETHLISBERGER, F. J. *The Motivation, Productivity, and Satisfaction of Workers: A Prediction Study.* Boston: Graduate School of Business Administration, Harvard University, 1958.

ARTICLES

For Chapter:

11 ARGYRIS, CHRIS. "T-Groups for Organization Effectiveness," *Harvard Business Review,* March–April, 1964.

13 BASSETT, GLENN A. "The Tough Job of Picking Winners," *Personnel,* September–October, 1963, pp. 8–17.

12 CHRISTIAN, ROGER W. "Guides to Programmed Learning," *Harvard Business Review,* November–December, 1962, pp. 36 ff.

11 DROTNING, JOHN. "Sensitivity Training Doesn't Work Magic," *Management of Personnel Quarterly,* Summer, 1968.

12 ———. "Programmed Learning," *Factory Management and Maintenance,* March, 1962, pp. 108–116.

13 FERGUSON, LAWRENCE L. "Better Management of Managers' Careers," *Harvard Business Review,* March–April, 1966.

13 FIEDLER, FRED, E. "Engineer the Job to Fit the Manager." *Harvard Business Review,* September–October, 1965.

13 GEISLER, EDWIN B. "Manpower Planning: An Emerging Staff Function," Bulletin 101, *American Management Association,* 1967.

11 GLUECK, WILLIAM F. "Reflections on a T-Group Experience," *Personnel Journal,* July, 1968.

11 KATZ, ROBERT L. "Human Relations Skills Can Be Sharpened," *Harvard Business Review,* July–August, 1956.

13 KELLY, PHILIP R. "Reappraisal of Appraisals," *Harvard Business Review,* Vol. XXXVI, No. 3 (May–June, 1958), pp. 59–68.

11 KNOWLES, H. P., and SAXBERG, B. O. "Human Relations and the Nature of Man," *Harvard Business Review,* Vol. 45, No. 2 (March–April, 1967).

11 LEAVITT, HAROLD J. "Unhuman Organizations," *Harvard Business Review,* July–August, 1962.

13   MacGuffie, John V.   "Computer Programs for People," *Personnel Journal,* April, 1969.

11, 13   McNair, Malcolm P.   "Thinking Ahead: What Price Human Relations," *Harvard Business Review,* Vol. 35, No. 2 (March–April, 1957), pp. 15–21.

13   Maier, N. R. F.   "Three Types of Appraisal Interview," *Personnel,* Vol. XXXIV, No. 5 (March–April, 1958), pp. 27–40. This article and the one by Kelly (above) is reprinted in Pigors, Myers, and Malm. *Readings in Personnel Administration,* Part 4-C. 2d ed. New York: McGraw-Hill Book Co., 1959.

13   Meyer, Herbert H.; Kay, E.; and French, J. R. P., Jr.   "Split Roles in Performance Appraisal," *Harvard Business Review,* January–February, 1965.

13   Murray, Thomas J.   "The Rise of the Fast Track Executive," *Dun's Review,* January, 1968.

11   Odiorne, George S.   "The Trouble with Sensitivity Training," *Training Directors Journal,* October, 1963.

13   Richards, Kenneth E.   "A New Concept of Performance Appraisal," *The Journal of Business,* Vol. XXXII, No. 3 (July, 1959), pp. 229–43.

11, 13   Schoen, Donald R.   "Human Relations: Boon or Bogle?" *Harvard Business Review,* November–December, 1957, pp. 41–47.

11   Schoonmaker, Alan N.   "Individualism in Management," *California Management Review,* Winter, 1968.

11, 13   Whyte, William F.   "Human Relations Theory—A Progress Report," *Harvard Business Review,* September–October, 1956, pp. 125–32.

Part IV

Maintaining the work team

14 Supervisory leadership

To paraphrase the well-known television commercial, *"leadership is the secret ingredient."* The quality and type of leadership will very often mean the difference between successful and inadequate performance by a work group. A quite common occurrence in business is a change in supervision which results in much higher quality performance of employees in the same environment using the same resources. "The crux of leadership is the acceptance of responsibility—the idea or fantasy that one can make a difference in the course of events. This sense of personal involvement in life is not simply a passive experience. It is an impelling urge to make a difference and use oneself in effecting outcomes."[1]

This chapter considers the supervisor's job of leadership as one of carrying out company objectives with and through people and making the best possible use of the company's most valuable asset—its people. Since people tend to follow a leader who can help them get what they want, the supervisor's leadership is based on demonstrating to subordinates that they will get some of the things they want if they provide the organization with what it wants—and that they will fare better by following his leadership than by working against it.

The supervisor wants his leadership of employees to achieve:

1. Willing, sustained, and high-level job performance.
2. Readiness to accept change.
3. Acceptance of responsibility.

---

[1] Abraham Zaleznik, *Human Dilemmas of Leadership* (New York: Harper & Row, Publishers, 1966), p. 1.

4. Involvement of people so they will use their brains, abilities, initiative, and ideas.
5. Improvement in problem solving, in cooperation, and morale.
6. Development of people to be self-starting and self-controlling.
7. Reduction of turnover, absences, grievances, tardiness and waste.

The talents, skills, and interests of subordinates—be they scientists, clerks, salespeople, production workers—and their attitudes and expectations may determine the kind of leadership that will be appropriate. Other factors that influence the supervisor's leadership and the freedom with which he can exercise it are: the kind of organization he is in, the kind of boss he has, the conditions surrounding the job and the labor market, the kind of fellow supervisors he has, and the kind of person he is himself.

This chapter will consider the ways in which these factors limit a supervisor, how he can best operate within these limitations, and how he can overcome some of them through increasing his own effectiveness.

Attitudes and motivation

Subordinates can be lazy, indifferent, and uncooperative. They can deliberately waste materials, neglect their duties, and cheat the company. Or they can be enthusiastic, self-starting, and responsible, as personally involved in their jobs as if they owned the company. Motivating forces lie in the person himself—his character, how he feels about the job, what he wants from it, and what he thinks he can get from it in return for his efforts. The leader who would convert these motivating forces into high performance must understand the subordinate's wants and abilities and help him find satisfaction for them through working for the success of the enterprise.

Money alone does not motivate a man to do his best even though the size of his paycheck is important in shaping his attitude toward his job. People differ in their feelings of what is important to them in a job, and as a man changes in age, health, mobility, and outlook, he changes also in what he wants from the job. But more or less a person needs the assurance that the job is secure, that he is adequate to it, that his future on it is up to him and not at the mercy of favoritism or whim. He would like a sense of belonging and acceptance by his associates, and approval and recognition by the boss, some assurance that what he is doing is worthwhile. These wants are discussed in Chapter 16.

A new man on a job gauges his security, adequacy, acceptance, and future prospects by the boss's behavior toward him. Almost all the things a man wants from the job depend in some way upon the boss's attitude. If the supervisor is not interested in people, his attitude is going to show through his actions. If he is not genuinely concerned about the welfare and development of subordinates, his attempts to "show interest in people" will be labeled as phony. His attitude toward subordinates is a mirror in which they see what they are going to get from the job. It shapes their attitudes toward the job and plays a big part in determining whether they will just go along doing what they are told or whether they will put their brains and initiative to work. If the supervisor feels that people are lazy, obstinate, and irresponsible, his treatment of them will tend to make them act that way.

Leadership

Leadership has been a popular discussion topic for centuries. Even today it ranks high in the research efforts of behavioral scientists. Some of the broad area of study may aid in understanding the elusive nature of this very important ingredient of organizational performance. Many individuals pattern their efforts after those of successful leaders by studying their actions. Studies of leadership patterns have resulted in the many "how to" books and articles written on the subject.

The trait or personality characteristic approach. Leaders are observed for their personality characteristics. Lists of many qualities result. Such characteristics as integrity, perception, sense of humor, tact, honesty, drive, enthusiasm, and initiative among others are usually found. Of course, the writer's bias may be reflected in the list, leaving the reader to decide which list is best and how many qualities are necessary for successful leadership. These studies have shown that all leaders do not possess the same characteristics and vastly different personalities are successful as leaders. Nevertheless, they are useful because they do indicate that personality factors are important in leadership and that people can be effective leaders despite considerable individual differences.

We have all known of situations that have required leadership in an unusual degree. Studies of these situations have given rise to the following approach.

The situation or circumstance approach. A situation arises which requires leadership and a leader emerges from the group. Group behavior is studied to determine the nature of its behavior and what occurs to produce leadership. The informal leadership theories are based on this approach. Many groups have informal leaders even though there is a formal leader designated by higher management. Usually a combination of situational and environmental factors contribute to the emergence of the informal leader. In fact, there is a management development technique which attempts to create leadership opportunities in various situations so that group members can exercise leadership and develop themselves for greater responsibility. Research in this area has demonstrated that job differences and environmental factors require different types of leadership.

In the final analysis, the success of any leader depends upon the acceptance or rejection of that leadership by those followers under his jurisdiction. Studies in this area are described as:

The follower approach. In any group situation the reaction of followers reflects on the effectiveness of the leader. Additionally, the personality of the follower determines the kind of leader for whom he will perform effectively. The type of work performed, as well as the age, sex, status, and background of the followers have a definite relationship to the effectiveness of the leader. Results of studies in this area indicate that any leader has to pay close attention to the individual differences that exist among those he supervises. He must treat each person as a unique individual in order to maximize his performance on the job.

The following approach to the study of leadership is often called the opposite of the trait approach.

The leadership structure approach. This approach is based on the idea that there is no such thing as a "one-man show" in the leadership of a group and that each individual in the group has some influence over the behavior of the group. Such an approach hopefully results in cohesiveness of group behavior. While there is no doubt that multiple influences affect any group, someone has to assume responsibility, make decisions, set examples, and communicate with the group. Of course it is possible that more than one person in a group may perform these functions, but a group usually looks to one individual for its direction.

All of the studies agree that leadership is a complex subject and that no single approach can give all the answers. One idea, however, becomes apparent; leadership is a continuing process for any supervisor. We all know that a particular managerial position includes certain leadership prerogatives and that the amount of influence and power an individual possesses affects his ability to lead. Command, which is the power granted by the formal organization structure, continues with the job, regardless of the incumbent. There is no doubt that knowledge and skills, along with personal characteristics, contribute to the effectiveness of the leader. A supervisor should remember that, most importantly, leadership means continuing to learn from experience and understanding that each individual reacts differently to a given set of circumstances.

Styles of leadership

For most people, leadership is highly personal. The way it is carried out is usually a summary of past experience and personal convictions.

A particular approach to a problem is tried and if it works, the individual will use that approach whenever a similar situation arises. These situational and environmental approaches combined with the individual's inherited characteristics and his collected learning experiences contribute to his leadership style. Generally environmental factors play the dominant role in the development of a leadership style. Education, work experience, people an individual admires, and the nature of his behavior loom large in the development of the manner in which he leads others. The type of leadership that an individual exercises is frequently the kind which he has most admired and respected in his own life experience.

An individual's leadership style will influence acceptance of his leadership by the members of his staff. Among the ways a leader exercises influence are:

Personality characteristics. We have all used the terms "strong personality" or "weak personality" to describe people. At times the supervisor must use the force of his personality to lead. His ability to influence staff members may be based on his attitude about the work, the example he sets, his own work habits, and the amount of enthusiasm he displays. All of these things have a direct bearing on subordinates' reactions to the supervisor.

Rank or position in the organization. The expression, "pulling rank" is well known in superior-subordinate relationships. There may be times when work pressure demands immediate acceptance of orders rather than discussion and on these occasions the supervisor may depend upon his position to gain acceptance of the orders.

Knowledge and experience. Subordinates frequently respect a supervisor because he knows more about the work than they do. This knowledge along with his past experience and his overall education can have a powerful effect on subordinates. The supervisor can use his knowledge and experience in a positive way by effectively training and developing subordinates and by setting a fine example for them to follow.

Another theoretical approach to leadership style that has been popular over the years is that there are three basic power styles adopted by persons in leadership positions. This theory supports the idea that the way a manager uses power determines his style of leadership. The popularity of this approach is probably based on the notion that we can easily categorize leaders as using one of the three styles most often discussed.

Autocratic leadership. Persons in this category are usually characterized as "hard-boiled autocrats" or "benevolent autocrats." In both cases the leader centers decision making in himself and he completely dominates the work situation for his employees by paternalistically structuring everything they do. He assumes full responsibility and demands unquestioning acceptance of his orders. There is no encouragement of individual initiative among subordinates. In fact such initiative would be considered a threat by the authoritarian supervisor. There is little or no free flow of communication and the subordinates are insecure in their relationships with the supervisor. He maintains control and exercises power by keeping them insecure and fearful.

While both types of autocrat are very similar in their style, the "hardboiled" autocrat's leadership is more negative in nature. His employees are more resentful and turnover is likely to be higher. On the other hand, the "benevolent" autocrat is often popular with his work group. He makes himself the dispenser of all rewards and takes credit for all the good things that happen to his work group. Many people respond quite positively to this style of leadership. This is probably due to their having grown up in a culture of benevolent autocracy with this style of leadership exercised by parents, teachers, clergymen, boy scout leaders, military superiors, and other leaders to whom they were exposed. Another reason given for the relatively wide acceptance of benevolent autocracy[2] is that most people prefer to work in a strongly structured climate, knowing what is expected of them and not having to make any decisions about their work. They expect the boss to be a strong person and prefer not to assume any responsibility themselves.

Nevertheless, frustration, conflict, and poor morale tend to develop more readily when the boss is an autocrat. When his leadership is negative it tends to destroy any attempt at self-development and very few promotables evolve from such a work group. People do not try to give their best because they are not really encouraged to do so. One of the prime ways the autocrat exercises power is by keeping aspirations low.

Democratic leadership. In contrast to the autocratic supervisor, the supervisor who practices a democratic style of leadership rarely makes unilateral decisions. He tries to develop his subordinates by having them participate in decisions which affect their work. This approach is often called consultative management. Attempts are made to develop group problem solving by keeping all group members informed about all of the factors that may have an effect on their jobs and the work unit's relationships with the rest of the organization. Initiative and self-development are encouraged and ideas and suggestions for improvement frequently result. Promotables are far more likely to come from this type of work group than from the groups supervised by autocratic supervisors. There are some people, however, that do not respond to this kind of

---

[2] For an interesting discussion of this style, see R. N. McMurray, "The Case for Benevolent Autocracy," *Harvard Business Review,* January–February, 1958, pp. 82–90.

leadership. They may even interpret supervisory attempts at group problem solving and consultative management as signs of managerial weakness. They believe that the manager is paid to assume responsibility and they are paid to do the work and they want no part of activities they believe are the province of the manager.

Free-rein or laissez-faire leadership. In this style the supervisor really does not exercise any leadership at all. He tends to avoid power and the responsibilities of management. He may be an authority symbol because of his position and he usually does serve as a contact between his work group and the rest of the organization, but that is about as far as his leadership goes. Employees in this kind of situation set their own goals and hopefully provide their own impetus for their achievement. What can happen in such a work group is a chaotic approach to the job. There is little or no attempt at coordination and people frequently work at cross-purposes. Obviously this is not a desirable leadership style but it does occur when a person who is an outstanding work performer is promoted to a supervisory position he really does not want. He merely continues to perform his job as he has done it before without any regard for the managerial implications of his new position.

Other approaches to leadership style were mentioned in Chapter 11 in the discussion of human relations. They were the Theory X (authoritarian) and Theory Y (democratic-consultative) of Douglas McGregor and the managerial grid which established managerial styles based on position on a grid designed to measure style.

One outstanding fact becomes apparent in the study of leadership. There is no one best method which, once learned, will solve all leadership problems. The very nature of leadership is based on a fluid superior-subordinate relationship. To be effective, supervisors must recognize this fluidity and the fact that it exists on all levels of an organization. Most satisfactory performers of the art of leadership use the various approaches as they are called for by the confronting situation. If autocracy is called for they will use it. In a situation that indicates a democratic approach this will be the approach and so on. Of course the style a person develops more than likely polarizes around one of the approaches because of his personality and experience.

In any event, leadership is always judged by what others do rather than by what the leader does; therefore, it can be concluded that a successful leader is one who influences others to respond in the direction intended. Simply stated, the possession of certain personality characteristics, a position of authority and the desire to influence others are not enough. A person can be called a leader only when he obtains a positive reaction to his direction more often than not and the group accepts him as its leader.

How to choose a leadership pattern

The leader who involves his subordinates in decision making and the leader who makes all the decisions himself represent the two extremes of leadership behavior (loose *versus* tight control, democratic *versus* autocratic, permissive *versus* strong or directive). In between is a whole range of leadership behavior as measured by the amount of authority exercised by the leader himself and the amount of freedom he gives to his subordinates to make decisions. The following classification of leadership behavior and the discussion of it is based on a study by Tannenbaum and Schmidt.[3]

1. The manager who exercises tight control makes all the decisions himself, announces them, and expects them to be accepted and obeyed on the power of his authority.
2. Next in line is the manager who makes all the decisions but tries to "sell" the decisions by showing the employees that they have something to gain by going along with them.
3. The manager makes the decisions but gives his subordinates an opportunity to discuss them, to ask questions about them, and to get an explanation of his thinking and his intentions.
4. The manager makes a tentative decision which he presents to his subordinates and asks for their reactions to it. He might change the decision if there are serious objections to it.
5. The manager defines the problem, presents it to the group, asks for suggestions as to what would be good decisions. Then he selects the decision that seems best to him.
6. The manager defines the problem, sets the limits within which the decision must be made, and asks the group to make the decision. (He is responsible and accountable to his superior even though the group and not he makes the decision.)
7. The manager lets the group define the problem and make the decision within the prescribed limits. This type of decision making might be done by scientists in a research organization.

It is important that the manager be honest in letting the group know how much authority he is keeping for himself and how much he is giving to the subordinates. If the boss intends to make the decision himself, he should not try to fool the subordinates into thinking it was

---

[3] Robert Tannenbaum and Warren H. Schmidt, "How to Choose a Leadership Pattern," *Harvard Business Review*, Vol. 36, No. 2 (March–April, 1958), pp. 95–101. Reprinted in Edwin A. Fleishman (ed.), *Studies in Personnel and Industrial Psychology* (Homewood, Ill.: The Dorsey Press, 1961), pp. 376–87.

their idea in the first place. Using participation as a technique to manipulate employees is a shortsighted policy that is apt to backfire.

From Tannenbaum and Schmidt comes the following list of forces or factors (in the manager, in the situation, and in the subordinate) which play a part in determining what types of leadership are practical and desirable.

Forces in the Manager:
His attitude toward sharing the decision making.
His confidence in his subordinates' ability.
His own leadership inclinations.
His feelings of security in an uncertain situation (his "tolerance for ambiguity").

Forces in the Situation:
The type of organization.
   The way the manager is expected to behave.
   The size and geographical distribution of the work unit.
   The need for keeping plans confidential.
The effectiveness of the group in working together.
The difficulty of the problem itself.
The pressure of time.

Forces in the Subordinate: Each subordinate has a set of expectations about how the boss should act in relation to him. . . Generally speaking, the manager can permit his subordinates greater freedom if the following essential conditions exist:

1. If the subordinates have relatively high needs for independence. (As we all know, people differ greatly in the amount of direction that they desire.)
2. If the subordinates have a readiness to assume responsibility for decision making. (Some see additional responsibility as a tribute to their ability; others see it as "passing the buck.")
3. If they have a relatively high tolerance for ambiguity. (Some employees prefer to have clear-cut directives given to them; others prefer a wider area of freedom.)
4. If they are interested in the problem and feel that it is important.
5. If they understand and identify with the goals of the organization.
6. If they have the necessary knowledge and experience to deal with the problem.
7. If they have learned to expect to share in decision making. (Persons who have come to expect strong leadership and are then suddenly confronted with the request to share more fully in decision making are often upset by this new experience. On the other hand, persons who have enjoyed a considerable amount of freedom resent the boss who begins to make all the decisions himself.)

The manager will probably tend to make fuller use of his own authority if the above conditions do *not* exist; at times there may be no realistic alternative to running a "one-man show."

The restrictive effect of many of the forces will, of course, be greatly modified by the general feeling of confidence which subordinates have in the boss. Where they have learned to respect and trust him, he is free to vary his behavior.

. . . Thus the successful manager of men can be primarily characterized neither as a strong leader nor a permissive one. Rather, he is one who maintains a high batting average in accurately assessing the forces that determine what his most appropriate behavior at any given time should be and in actually being able to behave accordingly. Being both insightful and flexible, he is less likely to see the problems of leadership as a dilemma.[4]

Effective leadership within the limitations

Employee-centered behavior, general rather than close supervision, willingness to delegate authority to subordinates and to let them share in decision making—all these things have their roots in the supervisor's attitude toward his subordinates. This attitude is a belief in their value, their capacity to grow, their ability and willingness to handle responsibility and to do a good job.

Sometimes the supervisor's attitude has to be based on faith because he is the one who must make the first move even though subordinates seem to be suspicious and resentful. He has to establish a climate of approval before people will be willing to take the risk of assuming responsibility. He has to train the subordinates, help them, encourage them, forgive their mistakes, and make them less dependent on him. Giving employees any amount of freedom to regulate themselves and to participate in decision making is not something that can be done overnight. Rather it calls for a period of careful preparation, particularly if subordinates are accustomed to and expect tight control.

The effectiveness of the supervisor's leadership rests mainly on recognizing and understanding the various factors that limit him and adjusting his operations to cope with them. Some of the limiting factors he can change and improve. Others are beyond his control, but rather than be hamstrung by them, he should accept them as challenges to build up his effectiveness in whatever directions are open to him.

Personality factors. The supervisor's own personality plays a big part in determining what type of leadership role fits him most comfortably. Perhaps he doesn't have a warm and outgoing nature that enables him to establish friendly and informal relationships with his subordinates. He may not be interested in their home lives, but some of his subordinates will be just as glad that he isn't. He does not have to be a backslapper in order to be employee-centered. Employee-

---

[4] *Ibid.*

centeredness is essentially a sincere concern for the welfare of subordinates and a willingness to listen to them, help them, and stand up for them. If he is scrupulously fair in his dealings, his subordinates will respect him and have confidence that they will get a fair break from him.

Some of the supervisor's own personal limitations he can't do much about, so he should take a realistic attitude toward them, quit worrying about them, and build on his strong points. For one thing he can increase his own energy and enthusiasm for the job by a deliberate campaign of good mental hygiene. A mentally healthy person neither underestimates nor overestimates his own abilities. He accepts his short-comings, is comfortable about himself and his relationships with others. If he has been dissipating his energies in needless conflicts and prolonged hostilities he may find it helpful to analyze his own attitudes. If he can see what it is within himself that makes him hostile to some people or oversensitive to criticism, he can be more understanding of the behavior of others. If he can remember that a whole lifetime of experiences and ingrained beliefs go into shaping a man's personality and the way he will react to a situation, the behavior of others and his own behavior will be less upsetting. Bitterness and chagrin over disappointments, mistakes, and criticisms sap a supervisor's energy and make it difficult for him to get along with people. Maybe he can write them off as sunk costs or look at them from an angle of "win a few, lose a few—and some are rained out."

Supervisory skills. The supervisor's job is not an easy one but no matter how frustrating the situation is, he can improve it by learning how to get his work under better control. His job calls for more technical skill than a higher management job does. In order to make good decisions about the work and to lead people to successful performance of it, he should make sure that he has adequate knowledge and technical competence in its methods, processes, procedures, and techniques. He should make it a point to study trade journals and texts to keep up to date on his specialty. The confidence that is the mark of a good leader comes from knowing the job.

In order to guide and direct subordinates to successful performance of their jobs, the supervisor must run his section or department in a way that makes it *possible* for people to do their jobs right. He must have the technical competence and planning ability to keep the work running smoothly, the materials on hand, the equipment in repair, the workplace in order, and the day's work planned carefully in advance. Employees object to needless waste. Few things are as demoralizing to subordinates as a boss who putters around in the morning and pushes in the afternoon, who can't plan far enough ahead to keep people supplied with work but lets them stand around wasting time.

In order to avoid going from one crisis to another, he should develop skill in planning and organizing the work, and avail himself of all the staff assistance at his disposal. He can keep on top of the job by planning the distribution of his own time and setting up procedures for handling recurring problems. He should teach his subordinates how to apply the rule of the exception, so that only the matters that can't be covered by routines have to be brought to his attention. He should make his section more efficient by improving methods. He should practice using problem-solving techniques in order to be able to make sound decisions. A leader who is confident because he is competent can command the respect of his work group and of the other people who are dependent upon his performance.

The boss as a limiting factor

Some bosses want to make all the decisions and are simply unable—as well as unwilling—to turn over any authority to subordinates. By their very nature they want tight control over everything for which they are responsible. They want to give strict and definite orders and to be obeyed in every detail. Some subordinates, even those in supervisory positions, are happy with this type of leadership. They like to have what they are to do spelled out for them exactly so that they in turn can give detailed orders to their subordinates. They don't want to use their own judgment or make decisions, and they don't want their subordinates doing it either. They don't want to take any risks or be blamed if things don't turn out well; they have to be covered at all times. They like to follow clear-cut rigid orders, to obey and be obeyed. When boss and subordinate are both of this type, they work very well together. They understand each other and get satisfaction out of operating in this manner.

But the supervisory subordinates who want to be free to use their ideas and abilities on the job just want to be told the goals and allowed to choose their own way of reaching them. Actually they want a minimum of bossing and they are willing to take the risks involved in making their own decisions. They are the ones who operate well under general supervision. Luckily there are bosses who have this philosophy of management. These bosses just naturally tend to exercise loose control. They give their subordinates as much freedom as possible to choose their own leadership pattern, to work out their own problems and use their own judgment. They set up goals and let their subordinates choose the means to attain them. In a relationship such as this, an ambitious and capable subordinate has an opportunity to learn by his own mistakes and prepare himself for a position of greater responsibility.

It is the exceptional boss (or subordinate) who is an extreme example of either tight control or free rein. Most people could be classified as somewhere in between. The way most bosses operate depends on circumstances—the kind of training they have had, the nature of the work that is being done, the kind of boss *they* have, and the kind of people they are supervising. Most superiors believe in the principle that authority and responsibility should be delegated as far down the line as possible, but many of them have trouble in carrying this out. The boss may hold back authority and responsibility for a number of reasons. For instance:

1. He may simply like to exercise a great deal of authority.
2. There may be certain types of jobs that he enjoys doing himself.
3. He may not have a system of controls worked out to enable him to keep track of delegated jobs to be sure they are being performed properly.
4. The amount he can delegate may be restricted by established job descriptions.
5. He may feel that the subordinates are not capable of carrying out certain responsibilities.
6. He may have no policies for the subordinates to use as guides in making decisions.
7. He may be unable to communicate his ideas to the subordinates.
8. His subordinates may be unwilling to accept responsibility.
9. He may be unable to train subordinates or unwilling to take the time to do it.

The supervisor who is frustrated by a boss who won't give him enough authority can do a number of things to improve the situation. First of all he should make a real attempt to find out if he is handling his present responsibilities in the way the boss wants them handled. The performance review may present an opportunity to come to a better understanding with the boss about the amount of authority the boss is willing to give him, the problems he meets in doing his job, and the projects he would like to undertake. Communicating skill will help him present his ideas in terms of the boss's viewpoint and get a better hearing for them. If the boss is against an idea for improving employee motivation, maybe it is because he tried it and it didn't work or because his own boss is against it. A subordinate who wants to sell his boss a plan of action must have it well thought out, intelligently organized, carefully worded, and presented from the boss's angle.

If the boss insists on maintaining tight controls, maybe it is because he lacks confidence in the subordinate's ability to handle the job. The way to earn the boss's confidence is to build a high degree of efficiency in the work group so that the boss can depend on the work's being out on time and done in the way he wants it.

In order to avoid conflicts with the boss, the subordinate should study the boss's personality, the way he operates, the kind of decisions he makes, his strong and weak points, and his sore points. A subordinate should realize that the boss faces problems and difficulties on the job, carries the responsibility for the department, and is accountable for everything that happens in it. Being mindful of the boss's welfare includes keeping him informed of the things he needs to know and will have to answer for, being loyal to him, and never short-circuiting him.

If the boss doesn't believe in turning over any authority and responsibility to rank-and-file employees, there is no point in doing it. Employees who take on extra responsibilities expect rewards, recognition, and promotion for their extra efforts but they won't get anything unless the boss approves. While the supervisor may feel that the boss is cramping his style, he should remember that flexibility and followership are a part of leadership and that new ideas have to be introduced a little at a time. If he can't operate on the amount of authority he gets from his boss, he should quit. As long as he keeps the job, he is obligated to carry out the boss's orders.

The setup of the organization as a limiting factor

The setup of the organization may limit a supervisor either by directly defining and curtailing his authority or by putting pressures on him to conform to the accepted pattern of behavior. If the company is a large one, the need for uniform action leaves little room for making a special case out of every problem and settling it on its merits. The supervisor must learn to operate within the framework of the organization, and he can do this more effectively if he will learn the history and the why of the policies, procedures, and rules that he must observe.

In the small plant or branch, personal leadership is the general rule, and personalities have a much greater impact on the organization. Everyone knows everyone. The personality of the head man strongly influences the operations of everyone down the line. Quick decisions can be made; mistakes show up rapidly. Policies, procedures, and rules are often not set forth clearly. Problems are handled according to their individual merits, and decisions are often arbitrary. Authority and responsibility tend to gravitate toward those who grasp most vigorously. In the small concern, the leader must have a keen understanding of personalities and the relationships between people.

The reputation of the company, its policies on salary, and the steadiness or seasonality of employment all combine to influence the style of leadership. People may be hired and laid off in great waves as production schedules change or contracts are completed or canceled. The leader under such circumstances can scarcely do anything about developing his people on a long-term basis. He must do the best he can with people who are more concerned about prolonging their jobs than about giving their best to the company. If the organization is in a constant state of crisis or crash programming, leaders are inclined to exercise a high degree of authority. They don't take time to consult with subordinates on decisions, but these periods of organizational upset are the very ones in which subordinates need to discuss managerial plans, air their fears, objections, and resentments, and ask questions about things which are bothering them.

The line-staff relationships within the organization may reduce a first-level supervisor's authority and influence. He may be smothered by staff experts giving him information and advice, performing services for his department, checking up on his performance, and insisting that he adhere to prescribed policies, procedures, or methods. The effective supervisor learns as much as possible about the various staff specialties and the services they can provide for him, and he avails himself of everything he can use. His attitude toward staff experts promotes employee acceptance of staff innovations.

Fellow supervisors as a limiting factor

Fellow supervisors influence the supervisor in the exercise of his leadership. The departments preceding his and following his in the work flow can either hamper or help him. Cliques, jealousies, and unbridled competition can interfere with his operations. The old gang may resent the eager beaver, the Johnny-come-lately, or the wonder boy. But no matter what a man has to put up with in the way of fellow supervisors, he can feel sure that his own actions can improve the situation.

Competence, dependability, and good work are essential to building a good relationship, because fellow supervisors resent being hampered by a weak sister who can't get his work done properly or on time. The supervisor can show his concern for their success and welfare by doing his own job properly, not passing the buck to them, and not building his prestige at their expense. He should make good use of every occasion on which fellow supervisors get together. By comparing notes he can clear up misunderstandings and conflicts over who is responsible for what and he can find out if any of his actions are putting the other fellow on the spot.

Tact and good humor will go a long way toward gaining goodwill. It may take time, but meeting fellow supervisors halfway and cooperating with them more than competing against them will help the supervisor become an influential member of the supervisory team.

The union as a limiting factor

The existence and the status of the union in the plant will have an influence upon the exercise of leadership by the supervisor. The shop steward may usurp or be permitted to usurp some of the supervisor's authority. Union members may look to the steward instead of to the supervisor for leadership. The steward's operations may make it difficult to build up a spirit of teamwork. Contract provisions must be followed in rewarding and punishing employees. Promotions, discharges, transfers, and layoffs must be handled according to contract. Enforcement of rules and standards may be appealed through the grievance procedure and have to be defended before an arbitrator. Mistakes become more serious in that they set a precedent (past practice) that may give away management rights. The need for prudence and uniformity of action may cause decision making to be transferred from the supervisor to the labor relations department.

In order to operate effectively under a union contract, the supervisor must understand and abide by contract provisions. He should study the types of grievances that go through the grievance machinery and the settlements that come out of it. He should study the decisions and opinions of arbitrators. He should forestall the occurrence of grievances by observing the provisions of the contract. He must guard against even the appearance of discrimination or arbitrary action. His handling of grievances must be correct as well as perceptive. His handling of discipline must measure up to the requirements of just cause and due process.

Since the union limits the supervisor's authority, he must develop compensating skills in dealing with people. By avoiding threats, displays of anger, head-on collisions of wills, and mistakes in handling personnel matters, he can minimize the chances of having his decisions reversed or of having to back down. By knowing more about people and the needs and wants they seek to satisfy, he can build positive motivation. By knowing the shop steward's rights and obligations, the supervisor can build better relations all around.

The work group as a limiting factor

The supervisor must adapt his pattern of leadership to the employees he is supervising. His work group may be young girls on a routine clerical job with relatively low pay and little chance of advancement. Here it is important to help the girls find satisfaction in their association with the group. It may be possible to design the job so that there is a feeling of group responsibility for getting out the work and seeing that each one carries her fair share of it. It may be possible to let the girls divide up the work themselves or rotate. It may be possible to stimulate interest by setting up competition with another group.

The leader's job here is to teach, train, guide, and encourage young people who have little experience in settling down to a full day's work and are not considering it as a career. His role is one of friendliness and firmness, showing what he expects and demands in good work habits, responsible behavior, and emotional maturity.

A work group may be made up of relatively uneducated and unskilled production workers performing simple repetitive tasks paced by a conveyor. The nature of the work may limit the contacts between people. A foreman on an assembly line may not be able to do anything about redesigning the jobs, but he can teach his men how to handle several different jobs so they can at least get some variety by rotating. He can take some of the pressures off them by being friendly and understanding, by listening to them, and explaining why the job has to be done just that way. He can be there to help them when they get into trouble. If they feel pushed, he can let them alone until they call him.

The supervisor may be confronted by a group of workers who are restricting production and sabotaging changes and improvements. Coming into such a situation he should set about building up trust and confidence in his leadership. He can show people by his actions that he has their interests at heart. He can stand up for them, treat them with absolute fairness, help them with job problems, clear up points of friction, remove unnecessary unpleasantness, and respect the customs that are important to them. He should study the informal organization to see if it is possible to work through its leaders.

A supervisor wants to motivate people by making it possible for them to get satisfaction from working for the aims of the organization. Since people have needs for security and satisfactory personal relationships, he tries to provide satisfaction for them on the job. His relationships with subordinates will be shaped by his own personality and by their expectations of the way a good boss should behave. Some employees are much more dependent than others and want close, personal, and sympathetic attention. Others want independence in varying degrees. All of them want the security of knowing that the boss will listen to them, that he is fair, that he will stand up for them, that he will help them to get ahead, and that he will give them a break when they need it. The supervisor gains his subordinates' confidence and goodwill by doing things voluntarily for them, sticking his neck out for them, giving breaks and doing favors of the type that meet group approval. He must avoid doing anything that smacks of favoritism or discrimination.

The job as a motivating factor

Some jobs are so badly designed that no one can fit them or get satisfaction from their performance. In order to lead people to high performance it may be necessary to redesign these jobs. Factors that must be considered in the design of a job are discussed in Chapter 10.

Fitting people to jobs. If people are to perform well, they must be fitted to their jobs. Placement is a supervisory skill calling for technical knowledge to analyze the tasks that make up a job and determine the amount of skill, knowledge, judgment, and exertion demanded of the performer. In order to choose a man who can do the job and will do it and get satisfaction from it, the supervisor must know the man and his abilities, ambitions, and limitations. How much variety is needed to hold his interest? How much responsibility does he seek? How much judgment is he able to exercise? Some people are stimulated by challenging jobs and should have responsibility thrust upon them. Others become upset and discouraged by anything unusual. The person who has to struggle to keep up in one job may distinguish himself in another. Placement is a continuing activity because jobs change and people change.

Putting meaning into jobs. A leader is expected to create job enthusiasm—to show employees the significance of what they are doing and to make them want to do it better. On many jobs people just don't know the meaning of what they are doing unless they are told. They don't know what uses will be made of the hole they are digging or the figures they are handling. They don't know what failures or losses will result if their work is not done properly. Dramatic improvements in quality and in job interest have resulted from showing employees what happens to the product or process if their work is defective. ("Nobody told me it made any *real* difference which way those things were put. I just thought some fusspot had decided that's the way he wanted it.")

Building meaning and interest into the job begins at the time a new man is inducted into the department. It should be stressed in the training he gets and in the emphasis on quality standards. It should be a continuing thing because people need to be reminded and have fresh examples brought to their attention.

One person may come to see meaning in his job in terms of the total enterprise; he is contributing to an important work. Another may see the purpose of his job in terms of service to the customer. Still another may see his job in terms of his work group; he is carrying his share and not throwing a burden on his work associates. Each man sees his job from his own viewpoint—which isn't the same as the supervisor's. This divergence of viewpoint is a reason for emphasizing the need for a leader to know his followers. He has to know what they respond to in order to be able to influence them to want to do the job right. Is it pride in workmanship? Ambition to get ahead? Fear of failure?

The supervisor can add meaning to the job by the way he matches assignments to the performer, by the way he explains the purpose of the work, by the amount of confidence he shows in the subordinate's ability and judgment, by the way he gives suggestions and criticisms, and by the way he evaluates the performance and gives recognition for good work.

Building meaning into the job is a powerful motivator in that it enables the performer to see that what he is doing is important and enlists his interest in doing it better. Pride in workmanship and a sense of accomplishment generate enthusiasm for the job and give people the courage to tackle a heavy work load.

Maintaining high standards on the job. Supervisory leadership is not a matter of being popular and keeping people happy no matter what they do or don't do. The leader who lets people get by with poor performance and undesirable behavior is then annoyed and dissatisfied with his subordinates but his disapproval does nothing to improve their performance; actually it tends to make it worse. People are insecure and resentful when the boss disapproves of them. Lax discipline leads to misunderstandings, antagonisms, and blowups when rule-breaking or poor performance gets out of hand. Conscientious employees are uneasy under a leadership that lets people get by with sloppy work and disregard for rules. They don't like to carry the load while others fool around, and they are afraid they will be hurt in the crackdown when it comes.

People have respect for, and confidence in, a leader who insists on high standards. He lets them know what is expected of them and how they are doing. He gives them constructive criticism and makes it possible for them to accomplish something worthwhile. By insisting on high performance and the kind of behavior that merits his approval, the supervisor is *able* to approve of his subordinates and give them recognition for the good work they do.

It takes backbone and forthrightness as well as diplomacy and tact to tell people that their performance is inadequate or their behavior unacceptable. Leadership requires courage to face up to the difficult problem of talking to people about their shortcomings. It is much easier to put it off and hope for the best. Sometimes people who are not doing well on a job actually feel relieved when the supervisor brings the problem out into the open and sets up with them a plan of action for improving the situation. Sometimes, however, an employee is a goldbricker and doesn't respond to leading and has to be pushed. For him, orders must be given as commands.

Fortunately most employees are not allergic to work. When management sets up a climate favorable for it, they accept responsibility and direct their own efforts toward objectives which they understand and support. Many employees can practice a high degree of *self*-control and do their best work under a leadership pattern of management by objectives. (See Chapter 9.) Such a leadership gives people high goals to shoot for, and sets up definite measures by which to review performance. It sets agreed-upon quantitative standards and provides the information by which a person can measure his own performance. If conditions permit a supervisor to use this type of leadership, he does not have to breathe down the necks of his subordinates to get work out of them. He can give them the freedom that fits their self-respect and stimulates them to excel.

The newly promoted supervisor

In any dynamic organization people are promoted to supervisory positions frequently. Such people are usually inexperienced in supervision and they can face difficulty on their new jobs. When a man is promoted through the ranks to a supervisory job, he brings with him his job knowledge and technical skills and a pretty good idea of the way the work of the section is handled. It is up to him now to learn management principles, practices, techniques, and skills, and to make the best use of the professional assistance available to him. Through association with the work group, he knows what is behind its attitudes, opinions, habits, and behavior. He knows how the group interprets management's actions, and what influences inside and outside of the group cause it to give or hold back cooperation with the supervisor.

A man promoted from the ranks shares some of these attitudes, and his problem now is to make a shift of viewpoint so that he can look at job problems from the point of view of management as well as from that of his men, and so that he can get the cooperation of his men by helping them derive satisfaction from their jobs.

The college-trained supervisor

The young man just out of college hasn't much experience in understanding the behavior of people at work, nor has he had much opportunity to practice team effort. His schoolwork emphasized and rewarded individual effort and he has been actively competing for grades; he expects to keep right on competing on the job. He is in the habit of, and frame of mind for, learning, and he is in a hurry to get ahead.

He needs a boss who gives him goals to compete against and who sets the stage for cooperation with fellow supervisors. The new supervisor needs to be introduced to his work group in a way that establishes his authority and shows that he has management backing. He should be presented to his fellow supervisors in a way that sets him up in his own job without being a threat to theirs and in a way that will set a pattern for cooperative relationships. Every new man introduced into an organization is a threat to somebody's security or a block in somebody's way toward promotion. If the other supervisors are uncertain where they stand with the boss or fearful of losing their jobs, they may try to undermine the new man as a means of protecting themselves.

Cooperation versus competition. A new supervisor should learn how to cooperate with his fellow supervisors before he thinks about competing with them for advancement. A new man operating as a lone wolf has a hard time getting a good start in a highly specialized organization where there is a great deal of interdependence between sections. His most immediate need is to be accepted by his teammates so that he can get the help and information he needs to get established. Young people who are going to get ahead in companies look around and study the way the management operates. They compare the abilities, tactics, and accomplishments of their fellow supervisors and line up, and keep up, with the ones who are going places in the company rather than with the ones who are marginal.

The company should find ways to stimulate, protect, and guide lively and healthy competition without turning teammates against one another. Competition in management can be destructive when it results in undermining the other fellow, putting obstacles in his path, and grabbing part of his job. One way to direct competition along productive and constructive lines is to set high goals for management men. Then they are working to beat a goal rather than block a teammate. Then they can help one another.

Getting started on a supervisory job. The coming of a new supervisor may bring on behavior problems in a work group. Employees are apprehensive of changes he may make. Many of them feel that in hiring a supervisor from college, the company has betrayed them and shut them off from opportunities to advance through the ranks. Some are resentful because they wanted or expected to be chosen for the job themselves. A disappointed candidate has had a blow to his pride, and if he is going to be a satisfactory employee from this point on, he must be shown that the selection was made on some basis other than favoritism. He needs to know why he was passed over and what his chances are for the future. He must be helped to gain a realistic attitude about his opportunities and about the value of improving his performance on his present job. Too often the fellow who also ran (or at least thought he was in the running) loses interest in his work or refuses to cooperate with the new boss and thereby disqualifies himself for future chances at promotion. The job of explaining should be done by the previous supervisor or by the supervisor's boss.

While some of the work group will hold back on cooperation until they feel safer about the new boss, others will fall in line because they hope this is their chance to get a new break.

The new supervisor will in most cases have the backing of upper management. Management selected him and feels a certain responsibility for its choice and a desire to prove it a wise choice. It will be slow to reverse itself and admit making a mistake. Each new supervisor should have received preliminary training as an understudy so that he can be prepared for the job he is to take on. Here are some suggestions for starting on a new supervisory job in a way to get teamwork:

1. Make sure you know the extent of your authority and responsibility. Try to find out the basis on which the boss is going to judge your performance. Which of your duties does he consider most important?
2. Find out why things are as they are and don't make unnecessary changes; just changing a seating arrangement can disturb a relationship that means a great deal to people. If things *have* to be changed, sometimes the new broom can do it better than the man who has become personally involved in the situation.
3. Try to find out how the previous supervisor operated. Find out from him or from other supervisors about the people in the work group: Who are the old-timers and who are the come-latelys? Who are the leaders and who are the outsiders? What are the symbols of prestige? What are the social arrangements for getting the work done?
4. Demonstrate by your actions that you are trustworthy and considerate. Respect the dignity of people. Remember that people want the satisfaction that comes from doing a good job and that they respect a boss who does a good job. It is more important in the long run to be respected than to be liked.
5. Go out of your way to cooperate with other supervisors. Ask their advice. Remember that you will be working with them and needing their help.
6. Be loyal to the boss or no one will trust you.

Coaching the new supervisor

The new supervisor's on-the-job training from his boss is both coaching and counseling. Counseling was discussed in the previous chapter as part of the employee evaluation and development program. A boss counsels subordinate supervisors by telling them how they are doing and how they can do better. A person just starting in management is receptive to criticism of his performance. The more achievement-minded he is, the more he wants to be told precisely what is wrong and what is right about the way he is working. If there are things about his behavior, speech, dress, or attitude that stand in the way of his getting ahead, this is the time to tell him about them.

Coaching, on the other hand, relates to the daily how-to-do-it part of the job of supervising. The following coaching suggestions are presented for the boss who is training a subordinate for a supervisory position. (They are for the subordinate too, so that he can recognize that he is being coached and can make the best use of it.)

1. Start him on some of your more routine activities.
2. As soon as possible, give him complete authority and responsibility for some phase of the work—give him some task he can call his own.
3. Show him how you analyze and solve some of your management problems.
4. Show him how to plan his work.
5. Let him know the *present* extent of his authority and responsibility.
6. Let him know what *will be* the full extent of his authority and responsibility.
7. Increase his authority and responsibility gradually.
8. Keep others informed of his authority and responsibility.
9. Correct his mistakes as they occur and show him how you would handle the situation.
10. Keep him advised of your problems.
11. Get him acquainted with your associates and your boss.
12. Teach him to come to you with decisions instead of for decisions.
13. Protect him from short-circuiting.
14. Back him up.

And, depending upon circumstances, you might give him informal training by means of:

1. Special projects in which he designs a procedure or improves a method (often in cooperation with a staff man) thereby increasing his ability to solve problems.
2. Work rotation, whereby he works on various types of jobs in the department in order to become more familiar with them and, later on, better able to supervise them.
3. Training assignments whereby he develops and conducts on-the-job training and thus improves his human relations techniques.

4. Committee work, in which he attends or substitutes for you on inter-department committees.
5. Participation in technical or professional societies, with attendance at local meetings so as to keep abreast of the field.
6. Acting as an "assistant to"—being in the same office with you, taking over details of your job, listening in, and learning how you operate.
7. "Sending him upstairs" to the boss's office to represent you. This is good practice for the man and it also gives your boss the opportunity of becoming acquainted with him.

Successful leadership on the job—an application

Leadership should be judged from the results it accomplishes in performance and in building an effective work group. As a practical example of leadership judged by results, Figure 14–1 gives a report on a supervisory leader's performance as viewed by his boss, his fellow supervisors, his subordinates, and by himself. Their judgments are recorded on the chart and from them can be extracted six essential elements of the leader's job. These elements have been discussed from various angles throughout the chapter but not under these particular headings.

FIGURE 14–1

The Performance of a Successful Leader Named Jones as It Looks to His Boss, to His Fellow Supervisors, to His Subordinates, and to Himself

His Boss Says That Jones:	Fellow Supervisors Say That Jones:	Subordinates Say That Jones:	Jones Says:
Keeps production up	Does top-notch work	Explains jobs well	My boss consults me
Keeps costs down	Does it on time	Sees all angles of jobs	He likes my ideas
Makes good decisions	Has good ideas	Has things thought out	He gives me freedom
Has good ideas	Cooperates	Gives a square deal	He gives me more more authority and responsibility
Has initiative	Delivers what he promises	Is not taken in	
Is dependable, loyal, and well liked	Speaks well of us, of company, of boss	Has job under control	My department runs smoothly
Takes responsibility	Handles problems well	Has gang under control	There is a minimum of conflict
Has few grievances	Handles men well	Plays no favorites	My men work well
Has few accidents	Has loyalty of his subordinates	Protects his men	My men are loyal
Has low turnover	Does not pass buck	Helps men get ahead	My men don't ask for transfers out
Turns out good work	Can be trusted	Lets them know where they stand with him	
Carries out orders		Praises good work	
Doesn't short-circuit		Reprimands properly	

These four reports can be summarized into six essential things a leader does:
1. He makes good decisions.
2. He motivates people to work with him.
3. He has control of the situation.
4. He assumes responsibility.
5. He gives everyone a square deal.
6. He inspires confidence.

The six essential elements of effective supervisory leadership are reviewed here briefly.

A leader makes good decisions. He has technical knowledge of the job. He knows company policy. He knows and understands his subordinates and is able to predict their reactions. He has a problem-solving technique for gathering, sorting, and evaluating information, for working out solutions and selecting the most practical solution.

A leader motivates people to work with him. He finds out what type of leadership gets the best results with his subordinates and what will stimulate each person to give his best efforts. He provides opportunities for people to satisfy their wants through giving high performance. Where it is possible and appropriate he builds the will to work by giving subordinates responsibilities and freedom to use their own judgment in attaining definite goals. He knows when to make people toe the mark. He realizes that there are people who do not respond to leading and who have to be pushed.

A leader has control of the situation. He has the technical competence and planning ability to make it possible for his subordinates to do a good job. He has high standards of performance and insists that his subordinates live up to them. He is emotionally mature and able to deal with other people's behavior problems perceptively and correctly. He knows company policy and union contract so that he avoids mistakes that set unwanted precedents and cause grievances. He maintains good discipline.

A leader assumes responsibility. Because the supervisor is ambitious he seeks opportunities to widen his experience and prepare himself for advancement. Because he wants to get additional authority from his boss, he makes sure that he is handling his present responsibilities properly.

A leader gives everyone a square deal. He is honest and does not make promises he can't keep. He doesn't exploit the willing workers but sees that they are rewarded for their extra efforts. He doesn't let people lie down on the job. He avoids favoritism and arbitrary action. He cooperates with his associates and does not put them on the spot or build his prestige at their expense. He is loyal to his boss, keeps him informed, does not short-circuit him or try to get his job.

A leader inspires confidence. He is competent on the job and concerned for the welfare of his subordinates, his fellow supervisors, and his boss. He helps subordinates achieve security, sees that they get their rights, and helps them to get ahead. His fellow supervisors can depend on him to do his work properly and on time. His boss can depend on him to carry out orders and to accomplish the technical and human objectives of the department.

Summary

This chapter's discussion of supervisory leadership covered various approaches to the study of leadership and leadership style because of their importance in developing an understanding of the entire subject of supervisory leadership. Emphasis was given to the idea that there is no one general purpose type of leadership which will suit all situations or all individuals. In reality, supervisors usually develop a style based on their personalities, knowledge, experience, and the style which they have responded to over the years. While inherited characteristics play a role in an individual's leadership style, environmental factors are more important.

The effective leader recognizes that different approaches are required for each situation and each individual. He will, however, tend to adopt a style which suits him and practice it most of the time. The supervisor does have restrictions on his freedom to make decisions and these restrictions may limit the type of style he can use. The amount of decision making that can be turned over to subordinates and the kind of leadership that will be appropriate and effective depend on the setup of the organization, the presence or absence of a union, the abilities, attitudes, and expectations of subordinates, the work they are doing, the supervisor's own personality and ability, the operations of fellow supervisors—all these things plus his boss's attitude toward delegation of authority. The supervisor through increasing his own effectiveness can overcome some of these factors that limit him. He can learn to operate within the ones he can't change.

Employees are motivated in greater or less degree to satisfy their wants for status, recognition, approval, and accomplishment, as well as their basic needs for security. The leader must know his people as individuals and understand their wants and abilities in order to fit them to jobs that enlist their interests and to stimulate them to high performance. Some employees are stimulated by general supervision. Almost all employees will respond well to participation in some of its many forms and degrees.

In order to get people to follow his leadership, the supervisor must show them by his attitude and behavior that he values them as people, that he can be trusted, and that he is able and willing to help them get some of the things they want from the job. Effective supervisory leadership calls for character and courage as well as managerial, technical, and human relations skills and good practices. In order to establish and maintain his leadership, a supervisor must—among other things—make good decisions, motivate people to work with him, have control of the situation, assume responsibility, give everyone a square deal, and inspire confidence.

CASE 1

About six months ago you promoted Jim Jones, an excellent worker, to be first-level supervisor over the group he had been working with. You gave him the same type of training that you gave the other supervisors, but he is failing on the job. Production in his section is low; tardiness and absenteeism are high. His main difficulty is that he cannot discipline his men. He does not seem to be able to reprimand; he is apologetic and softhearted. The men call him "Caspar Milquetoast" behind his back.

Jones is well liked by the other supervisors. Recently he purchased a house in the neighborhood where several of them live.

You are afraid that, if you demote him, his pride will be hurt and he will quit. You do not want to lose a good man.

1. What might have been some indications that Jones would turn out to be a poor supervisor?
2. How can you make a man into an effective supervisor?
3. What arguments can you give Jones so that he will accept a demotion and not leave the company?
4. Give the advantages and disadvantages of making a man the supervisor over a crew that he has worked with.

CASE 2

You have recently been appointed supervisor. One day as you walk through the department, you receive a Bronx cheer from one of the workers in a far corner of the room. You know who it is. All the workers stop their jobs to see what you are going to do about it.

1. Should you ignore it?
2. Should you return it?
3. Should you reprimand the guilty party immediately in front of the other workers? Justify your answer.
4. What steps should you take to prevent the recurrence of the offense?

CASE 3

You have under your jurisdiction a roving inspector named Joe Smith. He is a member of a minority group. You have rated him below par in everything because you were not able to get enough evidence to rate him differently.

You call him in to go over his rating with him. You show it to him and tell him that this is the way you see him. He immediately goes on the defensive, saying that the rating is unfair and that he is getting a raw deal and is going to protest to top management. He states that, on his job, production can't be measured closely; as far as initiative, cooperation, and attitude are concerned, he can't get very far in any of these because he is a member of a minority race and everyone in the department is against him.

There is some truth to his accusations, but the situation is not nearly as bad as he paints it.

How are you going to handle this one?

CASE 4

Harold Connors had been an informal leader in his department for several years. The other men came to him with their gripes and problems and the discussions which took place usually were fruitful. The department head was an autocratic boss and did not encourage upward communication among the employees.

Among the topics Harold discussed with the group in several conversations was leadership style. Quite naturally, autocratic supervision was much criticized and the men constantly pointed out the virtues of democratic or participative management to each other. In fact, there was general agreement among the group that participative management was the best approach for a supervisor to follow.

In general, the group was self-motivated and most took considerable pride in their work which was analytical and technical. They were all engineers and they were quite interested in the maintenance of their professional competence. The fact that they could not effectively communicate with their superior rankled them but their animosity was partially offset by the frequent discussions during which Harold Connors acted as informal leader.

The department head retired and Harold Connors was offered the post. He welcomed the opportunity to get credit for what he had been doing informally for several years. The rest of the work group was very pleased with the choice and they pledged their support and cooperation. Harold assumed his position and proceeded to implement his democratic approach to the leadership of the department. He continued the same type of discussion he had with the group before and he willingly shared his responsibility with his subordinates. Group goals were discussed freely and then assignments were made by voluntary acceptance by various individuals. While the previous department head had done all recruiting, Harold shared this effort and any group member was able to make recommendations. This same kind of participation characterized the setting of departmental priorities and goals as well as the utilization of manpower and other resources.

After six months, Harold began to notice that group participation was not working. The theory discussed favorably many times with the group was not successful in practice. He found that he had to use autocratic measures to meet departmental deadlines. Some group members who had accepted responsibility for the accomplishment of a particular goal were not achieving the goal. The discussions that were formerly friendly now became gripe sessions. Individual members sought Harold out to curry favor for their own pet projects and requested special treatment without considering its impact on the group. Harold learned from several of his employees that the formerly popular group meetings were now considered a waste of time and while some were necessary, they should be infrequent. Harold was quite disillusioned but he vowed to himself to continue to try participative management.

1. Why did the efforts to achieve a participative work group apparently fail?
2. Could they have succeeded if an outside manager had been placed in charge of the group?
3. Was Harold hoping for too much in his desire to continue the same kind of relationship he had with the group when he was its informal leader? Why?
4. Should Harold continue to try to develop a participative atmosphere or should he revert to more traditional autocratic methods?

CASE 5

Six months ago Bob Boyle was promoted from first-level supervisor to the job of second-level supervisor in charge of six sections. Ray Rich was brought in from a smaller branch of the company to take Boyle's old job of first-level supervisor; Boyle is now his boss.

While Boyle was a first-level supervisor he was a hard-hitting disciplinarian always pushing for more production. Some of the first-level supervisors call him a slave driver, others call him a snoopervisor. But in all fairness to him, he was a square shooter and his section turned out more production than any other section. When Ray Rich came to take over Boyle's former job, Boyle said to him in front of the group of first-level supervisors: "The job is all yours. Run the section any way you want. However, I want a reasonable amount of production from your section." This treatment seemed suited to Ray's personality. He is relaxed and so are his men. He does not push them and they produce at a steady pace. Morale is higher in his section than in any other, and production is steady. In the other sections morale seems to be going down but production is going up.

The honeymoon period between Boyle and Rich seems to be coming to an end rapidly. Boyle has let it be known that he thinks Rich is a poor leader—a Caspar Milquetoast. Rich, on the other hand, is telling the other supervisors that Boyle is a slave driver and that they should not let him push them around.

How can the situation be saved?

CASE 6

For the last 10 years, Mrs. Schmidt has been the supervisor of a group of women. Her group maintains satisfactory production but she gets it by playing favorites. To get along with Mrs. Schmidt, a woman employee has to win her favor by flattery, then do exactly what she is told and in the manner she is told to do it. If Mrs. Schmidt takes a liking to her, she is accepted and her work made easier. The women Mrs. Schmidt doesn't like get the dirty and difficult jobs. There is a feeling among the women that "if Mrs. Schmidt doesn't take you as one of her pets, you'd better get a transfer out of her department or quit."

The information about this situation came to you (her supervisor) from the head of the personnel department. He is worrying because the labor turnover in Mrs. Schmidt's group is getting out of hand.

You have spoken to her about the situation. She admits that this is the way she operates even though it is against company policy. She states that women have to be handled in this manner; otherwise they will walk over a woman supervisor.

1. What are some of the drawbacks to practicing favoritism?
2. How is the supervision of women different from the supervision of men?
3. List, step by step, a program for training Mrs. Schmidt in how to supervise women.

CASE 7

Five years ago the company opened a small branch plant in a distant city. J. White, one of the first hires of the branch, showed supervisory ability and was soon put in charge of a rapidly expanding department. He was very successful. The production and morale were high in his group.

Since the branch plant had limited chances for advancement and the home plant had greater opportunities, White was moved to the home plant and placed in a supervisory position in a department similar to the one he had been handling so successfully. However, in a large well-established plant things are run differently than in a small branch plant. Six months have passed and White is trying hard but he hasn't gotten his new job under control.

1. List and give the reasons for differences between running a department in a large well-established plant and in a small branch plant.
2. Can a man be a success in one and a failure in the other? Why? Why not?
3. How should White have been inducted into and trained for his new job?

CASE 8

The central stenographic pool is your responsibility. One of the stenographers, Laurie, is an unusually attractive and competent young married woman. When Purchasing for Research asked that she be permitted to concentrate on their work you agreed. The other girls were glad to be rid of it because the work is technical and difficult.

Now there is an office scandal—the romance between Laurie and the head of purchasing. He has a wife and four small children. Everybody seems to know about it but no one has taken any action. The engineers who are in and out of the purchasing office all day complain that "all this passion in purchasing is embarrassing." They are suggesting that you take care of the situation by firing Laurie since she is not as essential to the business as the purchaser.

1. Whose problem is this?
2. Should you do anything about Laurie? If so, what?
3. Should the purchasing manager's superior take action?
4. Is this something that should be handled by the personnel department?

CASE 9

Don Doyle is an assistant supervisor. Shortly he will come up for his periodic employee evaluation. As his supervisor, J. Jones, sees him, Doyle maintains his so-called leadership by pampering his men—taking their part whether they are right or wrong. His attitude toward the company is poor and so is that of his men. Their morale is low and their production is average. Doyle is not management-minded. A month ago one of his employees put in a grievance because he did not receive sick-leave pay for a day he took off. There were strong indications that he attended a baseball game on the afternoon of that day. Doyle, instead of taking management's viewpoint, backed the man's grievance up to the hilt. There are other instances of similar behavior.

When Jones, the supervisor, talked to Doyle about management-mindedness, Doyle replied: "I'll always go to bat for my men to get them raises, better working conditions, and to protect their rights to sick pay. If the company policies are unfair, I'll let you know and my men know exactly where I stand." During the previous periodic interview, the supervisor (Jones) recommended to Doyle that he take a supervisory training course given in the evenings at a local college. Doyle took the course and received a very high grade, but the course didn't change his behavior in the least. The supervisor wants to develop Doyle and get him ready for promotion.

How should the supervisor, J. Jones, handle this problem when he is discussing Doyle's employee evaluation with him?

CASE 10

You are a supervisor of a section and have been summoned to a conference with your boss. He informs you that you are to assume control of a neighboring section, where schedules are lagging. The supervisor you are to replace is well liked by his men. The boss tells you that you can either terminate the other supervisor or demote him to the position of assistant supervisor.

1.   What are some of the problems you are going to run into?
2.   Would you terminate or demote the other supervisor? Why?
3.   How would you go about winning the confidence and cooperation of the men who will be under you?
4.   How would you go about determining the cause for the lag in schedules?

CASE 11

One of your assistants, Joe Blue, was graduated from a small midwestern college several years ago. In his school days he was a leader in campus activities, president of his fraternity, manager of the track team, etc. He has a superabundance of enthusiasm, initiative, and aggressiveness. These qualities, while necessary for leadership, seem to be overdeveloped in his case. You recently put him into a minor supervisory position with the hope of developing him into an executive.

His group turns out a satisfactory amount of work. He is well liked by his subordinates because he has a lot of bounce and he helps them with the details of their jobs. However, he does not get along well with the other supervisors of equal rank. He competes actively against them, grasping any of their authority and responsibility that comes his way. Occasionally he makes decisions that should be reserved for you. In fact, you have been informed that he is telling his subordinates how he would run the whole section if he were in your position.

He seems to have no interest in life other than getting ahead rapidly. He is unmarried and lives alone in a room. He spends practically all his waking hours on the job—the first one to get to the office and the last one to leave. Thus he gets quite a bit of extra work done. The other supervisors do not care for this behavior either.

1. How do the other supervisors see the facts?
2. How does Joe Blue see the facts?
3. How do his subordinates see the facts?
4. How do you see the facts?
5. What are some of the leadership qualities Joe lacks?
6. How can you develop Joe without destroying the good qualities he now has?

CASE 12

Ray Foster had been with the company for 35 years. He has worked in your department as a senior clerk for as long as you have been there. You have found him to be a loyal, efficient employee. Although he has limited ability, he has done his job well and his attendance and punctuality record has been excellent.

He comes to you with a personal problem. His wife has become chronically ill and the woman who cares for her during the day must go home before Ray gets home from work. Ray has asked to leave a half-hour early each day so that his wife will not be alone. He cannot come in early in the morning because the practical nurse does not get there early enough, having her own family to care for. Ray mentions the difficulty in securing such help and the fact that he is lucky to have a dependable woman to care for his wife during the day. Ray even offers to take a cut in pay if you will grant his request.

You listen to his problem with considerable sympathy. His long, loyal service to the company weigh considerably in your decision. Even though there is no company policy to cover such a situation, you decide to allow him to leave early each day. You turn down his offer to accept a pay reduction. Ray is very grateful and you feel very good about your decision.

Two weeks go by and three employees come to you to ask for similar privileges. All have been with the company less than five years, and they are average performers. None of their reasons are as compelling as Ray's in your judgment.

1. Should you grant the requests of the three employees?
2. Should you have granted Ray's request in the first place?
3. How can you explain special treatment for a long-service employee to other employees in the department?
4. Should a company have special privilege policies for long-service employees?

5. Should you go to higher management with your problem and suggest a company policy to cover such problems?

CASE 13

You are an assistant supervisor. Your immediate boss, J. Jones, has been with the company 30 years—15 of them as supervisor. Few situations arise which he has not experienced previously. When he gives you orders he spells them out, telling you exactly how he wants them carried out. He leaves no leeway for initiative or mistakes. If a job is not done in just the manner he prescribed, he is quick to tell you about it. His philosophy is, "I know how things should be done. You do as you are told and don't ask questions."

You don't particularly care for this type of supervision. You prefer to give your subordinates as much freedom as possible in choosing methods as long as the desired results are obtained. You have good production and high morale in your group.

Your boss often criticizes you for your manner of supervising. He says you are wasting time by giving people freedom to choose methods and thus make mistakes—that when you have had more experience you will be a better manager. He says, "Management plans and the workers perform. If we expect them to think or plan, then they should be the managers."

1. What are the strong and weak points of your boss's method?
2. What are the strong and weak points of your method?
3. In what kind of an organization is his method better?
4. In what kind of an organization is your method better?
5. Could you both operate more effectively if you were using the same method? Explain.

CASE 14

John Benson had been head of the department for about eight years. Over this period the department had high labor turnover and a considerable current of discontent among its 25 employees. Because John was an autocratic supervisor and he seemed to have the support of the division manager, the people in the department did little outward complaining about his leadership.

Nevertheless it was common knowledge in other departments in the division that the majority of the people in John's department were very dissatisfied to say the least. These people were career employees performing technical work and they received personal feelings of accomplishment from their work. Few compliments were forthcoming from their boss and while they resented this, their personal pride and possible fear of retribution kept them from saying anything to John. One of the things they resented most was John's frequent practice of taking credit for ideas and efforts of subordinates so that he could enhance his own reputation with his superior, the division manager.

One of his subordinates, Will Michaels, had become the informal leader of the department although he did not seek the role. Other employees sought him out for advice and guidance and he became the focal point of the gripe sessions which had become more frequent as time passed. These gripe sessions were quasi-social occasions such as lunch, and they usually ended with Will telling his fellow employees to openly complain about their grievances to both John and his superior. Will had done this several times and while he gained no positive results, he at least had the satisfaction of having a clearly stated position. This may have been one of the reasons why the other employees turned to him for advice. In any event, Will evidenced no fear of his boss and he was generally recognized as a superior employee by his peers.

The division manager retired and was replaced by a member of one of the departments in the division. He had not had prior administrative experience in the company, although he had managerial responsibility at prior places of employment. Because he was familiar with the problems in John Benson's area of responsibility he recognized it as a trouble spot and after some consultation with the assistant division manager he decided to replace John Benson as department head. John was quite surprised since he assumed that he could continue under the new division manager as well as he had under the one who had recently retired. When the new division manager demoted John, he said he could stay with the company as a technician in the department he had previously managed. This was done because of John's long tenure with the company and the fact that he was only eight years from retirement. John accepted the demotion with considerable dejection and malice since he felt he had no choice under the circumstances.

Will Michaels was called in by the new division manager and asked to assume the department head position. He was informed of his former superior's demotion and the fact that John would now be working for him. The division manager told Will that he was chosen because it was believed that he could weld the department into a cohesive operating unit of the division. Will accepted the responsibility with what could be called confident apprehension.

1. In making the transition from informal leader to formal leader, can Will maintain the same relationship with his fellow employees?
2. What problems do you feel he will have with his former superior in the changed relationship which now exists?
3. Did the new division manager handle the situation properly?
4. Should Will have accepted the position as department head?

5. What kinds of problems does an informal leader face when he becomes the formal leader?
6. Is it wise for management to promote a generally recognized informal leader to a managerial responsibility?

CASE 15

You are the head of an inspection department. Recently a new product was added to the line. The inspection requirements on this new product cannot, for the present, be expressed very definitely. This necessitates the exercise of quite a bit of judgment on the part of the inspectors, who have to be located in the production department.

To avoid disturbing your present group of inspectors, you hired experienced inspectors from the outside to handle this job. You put Bill White, one of your best assistants, in charge of them. He had been getting along very well in charge of a group of old-timers doing routine inspection.

This morning you dropped into Bill's office to see how he is making out on his new job. You found him arguing with someone on the phone. When he finished, he slammed down the receiver and said to you: "Not one of these damn inspectors uses his head."

He tells you that he is swamped with work and is being run ragged by his men. They are always phoning him either to come and check on borderline cases or to get them out of disputes they are having with the production people.

1. What might be some of the reasons why Bill White, a previously successful supervisor, is now having difficulties?
2. What parts of the situation can't he control?
3. What parts of the situation can he control?
4. Outline a program for him to follow in order to get the situation under control.

CASE 16

J. R. was recently brought in from the outside and made general manager of a major operating unit of a large company. The president is convinced that he is doing an outstanding job. Formerly J. R. had been the manager of a small family-owned concern that was very successful in a highly competitive industry.

He is very impersonal and holds himself aloof. It is difficult to find out what he thinks about anything or anybody. When his subordinates ask questions, he has a trick of making them look foolish. When he sets up a policy, he formulates it in advance and then calls in his assistants and attempts to convince them that such a policy should be adopted as their joint decision. He does not encourage any suggestions or discussion. Several of his assistants have resigned because they could not understand him or agree with his policies. These men have been replaced by yes men who had worked with J. R. in the other company.

When presented with operating problems, he makes snap judgments which might have worked in the small concern, but they are disturbing the setup of this organization. When objections are brought up by his subordinates, he intimates that if they can't get results, he will hire men who can.

You are one of J. R.'s assistants. You have been with the company for a long time and don't want to lose your job.

1. What might be some of the reasons for J. R.'s behavior?
2. How might his experience with the small company be influencing his behavior? Explain.
3. Contrast leadership in a small and in a large organization.
4. What might be some of the unfortunate results if J. R. continues to operate in this manner?
5. What should you do in this situation? Why?

CASE 17

Allen Adams recently took a job as a shop foreman in a young, growing, medium-sized company manufacturing a variety of items on a jobbing basis. Previously he had worked for 20 years as a shop foreman in a well-run automobile manufacturing plant. His predecessor in the jobbing shop (Bill Barnes) was made the general foreman and is now Adams' boss. In Adams' opinion, Barnes is a poor disciplinarian and does practically no work. According to Adams, Barnes dumps his responsibility and authority onto the shoulders of his shop foremen. His shop foremen now have to figure out how the jobs are to be done and they often have to call their men together in order to dope out methods, instead of going to Barnes for information. This seems foolish to Adams. According to him, a real boss should know what he wants done and how he wants it done and then tell his subordinates how to do it. Thus his people are not going around leaderless and wasting time by using trial-and-error methods.

On the other hand, Barnes thinks that Adams' 20 years experience in automobile manufacturing is of little value in a jobbing shop. According to Barnes, Adams lacks initiative—wants policies to cover all his decisions and wants procedures and directions spelled out in detail so that nothing can go wrong. Then all Adams will have to do is be a go-between or an expediter of top management's detailed orders. But it is impossible for the general foreman to spell out everything in a jobbing shop because policies and procedures have to be continually adjusted to fit situations as they develop. Barnes thinks that if he had to spell out everything the way Adams wants, he would not need any supervisors.

1. What are the differences between being a successful foreman in a large manufacturing company and in a medium-sized jobbing shop?
2. Evaluate Allen's arguments: (*a*) in general, (*b*) in relation to a large automobile manufacturing company, (*c*) in relation to a jobbing shop.
3. Evaluate Barnes's arguments: (*a*) in general, (*b*) in relation to a large automobile manufacturing company, (*c*) in relation to a jobbing shop.
4. Where should each compromise in order to get better cooperation between them?

FOLLOWING UP ON THE JOB

1. Do you make good decisions?
2. Do you motivate people effectively?
3. Do you always have control over the situation?
4. Do you assume all your responsibilities?
5. Do you give everyone a square deal?
6. Do you earn the confidence that you want others to have in you?
7. Are you trying to increase your span of control?
8. Are you showing by your work that you are willing to assume greater responsibilities?
9. Are you operating in harmony with the setup of the organization?
10. Are you the captain of your work team?
11. Are you an influential member of the supervisory team?
12. Do your workers come to you for guidance and advice?
13. Are your workers volunteering their best efforts?
14. Do any of your subordinates short-circuit you?
15. Does your boss short-circuit you?
16. Are you loyal to your workers? To your fellow supervisors? To the boss? To the company?

15 Managing employee problems and change

Policies and the supervisor. Disciplinary policy. Rules. Penalties. The effects of the union contract on rule enforcement. Due process and procedure. Incompetence and negligence. Gripes and grievances. The grievance machinery. Foreman and shop steward. Grievance handling by foremen. The handling of gripes. The emotional content of gripes. Absenteeism and tardiness. Effects of tardiness and absenteeism. Finding and treating the causes. Problems with alcoholics. Techniques for reducing absences and tardiness. Counseling the absentee. Penalties for absences. Preventing disciplinary problems. Talking with offenders. Discharge. Managing change. Resistance to change. Summary.

Each workday the supervisor is faced with a variety of tasks. Among those which occupy most of his time are problems generated by the employees reporting to him and the changes caused by technology, new knowledge, organizational development, and our society in general. In some instances, there is little he can do about either employee problems or change because they are beyond his area of responsibility and control. On the other hand, he is reinforced in the handling of many employee problems by company policies, standards, procedures, rules, tradition, social mores, union contracts, and the employees themselves. In the management of change he should recognize that change is a constant. It permeates his life. In fact, the human being has adapted to change since the dawn of history. The present problem confronting the supervisor, however, is the rapid acceleration of change that has occurred in recent years and that gives every promise of continuing at an increased rate in the immediate future. Even though the supervisor is principally concerned with work change, this does not diminish the impact of change because every alteration to the work environment is a work change.

If the tempo of change has increased, so has its nature. In his most recent book, Peter Drucker visualizes us as entering into an age of discontinuity and he believes his book to be an "early warning system." He mentions major discontinuities as existing in four areas:

1.   Genuinely new technologies are upon us. They are almost certain to create new major industries and brand-new major businesses and to render obsolete at the same time existing major industries and big businesses. . . . The coming decades in technology are more likely to resemble the closing decades of the last century, in which a major industry based on new technology surfaced every few years, than they will resemble the technological and industrial continuity of the past fifty years.

2.   We face major changes in the world's economy. In economic policies and theories, we still act as if we lived in an "international" economy, in which separate nations are the units, dealing with one another primarily through international trade and fundamentally as different from one another in their economy as they are different in language or laws or cultural tradition. But imperceptibly there has emerged a world economy in which common information generates the same economic appetites, aspirations, and demands—cutting across national boundaries and languages and largely disregarding political ideologies as well. The world has become, in other words, *one market,* one global shopping center. . . . It is not yet a viable economy. . . . Either we learn how to restore the capacity for development that the nineteenth century possessed in such ample measure—under conditions for development that are quite different—or the twentieth century will make true, as Mao and Castro expect, the prophecy of class war, the sidetracking of which was the proudest achievement of the generation before World War I. Only the war now would be between races rather than classes.

3.   The political matrix of social and economic life is changing fast. Today's society and polity are pluralistic. Every single social task of importance today is entrusted to a large institution organized for perpetuity and run by managers. Where the assumptions that govern what we expect and see are still those of the individualistic society of eighteenth-century liberal theory, the reality that governs our behavior is that of organized, indeed overorganized, power concentrations.

Yet we are also approaching a turning point in this trend. Everywhere there is rapid disenchantment with the biggest and fastest-growing of these institutions, modern government, as well as cynicism regarding its ability to perform. We are becoming equally critical of the other organized institutions; revolt is occurring simultaneously in the Catholic Church and the big university. The young everywhere are indeed, rejecting *all* institutions with equal hostility. . . .

4.   But the most important of the changes is the last one. Knowledge, during the last few decades, has become the central capital, the cost center, and the crucial resource of the economy. This changes labor forces and work, teaching and learning, and the meaning of knowledge and its politics. But it also raises the problem of the responsibilities of the new men of power, the men of knowledge.[1]

---

[1] Peter F. Drucker, *The Age of Discontinuity* (New York: Harper & Row, Publishers, 1969). pp. ix–xi.

Drucker has a reputation for controversy and we may not agree with his prophecies but his observations are based on realities which already exist. The years ahead may not produce the results Drucker predicts but there is no doubt that basic changes will take place in many areas that will affect the organizations in our society and the chain reaction will certainly cause supervisors to cope with problems undreamed of today.

The purpose of this chapter is to help the supervisor understand employee problems and change and their effect on his own work efforts. The constructive handling of discipline is emphasized. Absenteeism and tardiness are singled out for special attention because they are daily headaches and costly ones at that. The nature of grievances and gripes is also discussed along with ways of handling them to the satisfaction of management and employees.

Change is considered as a constant but resistance to change and other effects of change on the work situation are also mentioned. The supervisor usually bears the brunt of change implementation and he must learn to cope with it if he is to be an effective manager.

Policies and the supervisor

Handling discipline calls for close cooperation between line management and the personnel or industrial relations department. The supervisor may be required to consult with the industrial relations department to make sure that a penalty is consistent with penalties elsewhere in the company, that it would hold up if challenged, and that it would not set an unwanted precedent.

In most companies the first-level supervisor does not have the authority to discharge employees from the company or to hand out long suspensions. Even though he does not have such final authority, he does have the obligation to initiate the action and to recommend the penalty. What is more important than the amount of his authority is his knowledge of the policy under which he must operate. He needs to know what kind of action upper management expects and will support, so that his decisions won't be reversed.

Disciplinary policy

Good management seeks to make the most effective use of employees; so the aim of a disciplinary policy should be to prevent misbehavior and to catch backsliding before it becomes serious. A good disciplinary policy is designed to warn, correct, and reform offenders rather than just give them what is coming to them. Such a policy of *corrective* or *progressive* discipline provides for:

1. Rules that are reasonable, necessary, definite, known, and understood.
2. Enforcement that is certain, reasonable, uniform, consistent, and fair.
3. Penalties that are appropriate and corrective. Immediate discharge for gross offenses only. For other rule-breaking, lighter penalties for the first offense and harsher penalties for repetitions, then discharge when other methods of correction fail. There should be flexibility in the penalty schedule to take into account the degree of guilt, the contributing causes on the job or at home, the employee's length of service and his record.
4. A procedure specifying the steps of the discipline process from the time of the rule violation to the closing of the record. The procedure should be designed to achieve line and staff cooperation in handling discipline. It should protect the rights of the employee, provide for informing him of the charges against him, give him an opportunity to explain and to defend himself before a penalty is assessed, and provide a channel through which he can appeal a penalty he considers to be unjust.
5. Provision for furnishing the supervisor with the information, training, and help he needs to handle discipline problems and maintain his leadership. He must know the extent of his authority and what kind of decisions will be supported by upper management.

Rules

The purpose of company rules is to tell people how they should act as members of a specific group. Without the rules they would have no way of knowing what time they were expected to be at their desks or workplaces, what time they could leave, whether they must get permission to leave their own area, and when and where they could smoke. Rules tell employees that they can't use company time for their own personal phone calls, visitors, and mail, for reading magazines, chatting, overstaying coffee breaks and rest periods, loafing, taking long lunch hours, and leaving early. Punching the time clock for a fellow employee looks like a friendly act rather than a serious offense. A person could scarcely be discharged for it unless it was established as a rule and specifically brought to his attention. Ignorance of the law is a perfectly good excuse within a business organization. There, as in the army, is "always somebody who didn't get the word."

Rules must be clear and definite in order to avoid being misinterpreted. They should be direct and specific so that people can't get around them. And in order to be effective they must be known and enforced. They should be published in employee handbooks, in memos, letters to employees, and on bulletin boards in work areas and restrooms. They should be explained to new employees in the induction procedure and reviewed periodically. Some companies require the supervisor to review the rules with his subordinates every six months.

Normally people are willing to abide by rules of conduct if these rules make sense to them, if practically everyone is obeying the rules, and if the few who do violate them are penalized. On the other hand, rules set up arbitrarily and without explanation are looked upon as encroachments on personal liberty rather than protection of the general good. People are slow to figure out the *why* of rules. They will grumble about a no-smoking rule with never a thought of the fire hazards it protects them against. They complain about the inconvenience of using safety equipment. Safety rule enforcement entails constant reminders, campaigns, slogans, displays, gimmicks, cautions, warnings, and penalties. Safety is emphasized in induction and training. Some employees still don't become safety-conscious until they have served a turn on the safety committee and had the responsibility of enforcing the rules and investigating accidents and hazards.

If there is general violation of a rule, there may be something wrong with the rule itself or the way it is presented or explained. Even though the supervisor does not have the power to change the rules, he does have the job of enforcing them, and he should make strong recommendations for revisions of rules that do not work well. Too many rules or rules that seem petty, arbitrary, or unreasonable defeat their own purpose. Giving highly motivated people as much freedom as possible and treating them as responsible adults pays off in cooperation, team spirit, and high morale.

Having few rules and depending on the spirit rather than the letter of the law works better in small groups than in large, however, and may run into penalty reversals in a unionized company. An arbitrator may ask for evidence that the rule really existed and that the employees were aware of it—particularly if the prohibited act is something that is permitted in other companies.

Penalties

This discussion of penalties and the discussion on rule enforcement that follows it take into account that a union contract places definite restrictions on the type of penalty that can be assessed. Extremely serious offenses—immorality or sabotage, for example—usually call for immediate dismissal—no need for a warning, no need for a notice, and no obligation to try to reform the offender. Offenses that are less serious call for some milder penalty aimed at correction. Corrective (progressive) discipline calls for lighter penalties for the first offense and harsher penalties for repetition. After a certain number of offenses—regardless of whether they are identical—the company resorts to discharge. The schedule of penalties under a union contract is essentially as follows:

1. Oral warning of which no record is made in the employee's folder.
2. Oral warning with a record of it put into the employee's folder. This warning notice is proof that the employee was advised of management's intention to discipline him for repetition or continuation of his behavior. Such a record is needed to justify a discharge for repetition of the offense or a discharge for a series of offenses. It is needed to justify a discharge for repeated failure to meet production standards.
3. Written reprimand. This form may carry one or more signatures— that of the immediate supervisor, the department head, superintendent, or labor relations officer.
4. Suspension (disciplinary layoff) for a definite period of time, which might be for a few hours, a day, a number of days, or months. During a suspension an employee does not report for work and does not get paid. Some companies don't use suspension as a penalty because they find it creates too many operating difficulties. While the suspended employee is gone, his work has to be done by someone else, which creates a hardship for the other employees. Or else a replacement must be brought in temporarily and trained to do the work. A company that does not suspend employees would add one or more warnings to the sequence of penalties leading up to discharge.

   Some people use the word "layoff" only for reduction in force. They feel that the use of the word "layoff" in connection with discipline may give the idea that disciplinary layoff is a way to get rid of undesirables without having to go through the discharge procedure and without having to answer for violating seniority rights. A disciplinary layoff is a penalty whose length is in proportion to the seriousness of the offense it punishes. The exception to this definition is the practice of sending a man home while his offense is being investigated. Such a suspension enables the supervisor to handle offenses that require immediate action but may warrant a penalty more serious than he has the authority to assess.
5. Discharge—the capital punishment of industry. A discharge cuts off the rights and benefits an employee had in his job. He may even be unable to collect his unemployment benefits if the law of his state provides that no benefits will be paid to a person found to be discharged through his own fault.

There are several other types of penalties used in some organizations. Demotion or downgrading to a lower paying job is a rather special type of penalty that in unionized companies is usually restricted to cases of unsatisfactory performance caused by incompetence. Withholding of benefits is another penalty whose use is usually restricted by the union contract. Benefits that might be withheld are merit increases, promotions, overtime work, holiday pay, or vacation pay. At one time the trend was to incorporate into the contract a schedule of all possible offenses with the exact penalty that would be assessed for the first offense, the second, and third, and the fourth and fifth if there were that many before discharge. In recent years the "price list" approach to penalties has fallen to disfavor and most contracts have a broad "just cause" provision which is less rigid than the price list and allows for the exercise of more judgment.

The effects of the union contract on rule enforcement

The fundamental provision of a union contract is for the security of a worker in his job. Most contracts provide that he can be disciplined and discharged for "just cause" and this puts the burden on management to prove that the cause *is* just. If the union feels that a penalty is unjust, it can carry an appeal up the steps of the grievance machinery to successively higher levels of management and finally to arbitration. An arbitrator is a disinterested third party who hears management's argument and the union's argument and then passes judgment on which one is right.[2]

The rulings of arbitrators and the reasons they give for them[3] form a body of opinion defining "just cause" and shaping answers to such questions as what constitutes proper grounds for discipline, proper procedures for handling it, and proper penalties.

Arbitrators reverse or reduce a substantial number of penalties appealed to them.[4] The reasons they give for doing so are worth studying

---

[2] Arbitration's purpose, procedures, and techniques, the disputes it handles, and the significance of the decisions it hands down are analyzed by Frank and Edna Elkouri in *How Arbitration Works* (rev. ed.; Washington, D.C.: Bureau of National Affairs, Inc., 1960), chaps. 13, 14, 15.

[3] A number of decisions are published (serially since 1946) by the Bureau of National Affairs, Inc. in *Labor Arbitration Reports*. Also by Prentice-Hall in *American Labor Arbitration Awards*. Published awards on discipline disputes outnumber published awards on any other type of grievance. Statistics drawn from these awards do not take into account awards that were not published or grievances that were compromised without going to arbitration.

[4] Another arbitrator would not necessarily make the same decision on a like offense in another company. The circumstances would be different and the contract would be different. Examples that conform to trends do give a basis for predicting what to expect, however. The examples used in this chapter are in line with trends

because they show up weaknesses in supervisors' enforcement of rules and they point out areas in which the supervisor should improve in knowledge, attitude, and skill. Some of these mistakes in handling discipline are:

Inconsistency or discrimination.
Condonation of offenses.
Failure to warn offenders.
Inadequacy of evidence.
Failure to follow specified disciplinary procedures.

These weak spots are discussed in the next few pages. They should serve to alert the supervisor in a unionized company to study the provisions of the bargaining contract he is working under and to look for arbitrators' decisions that have been made in his company and in his industry.

The supervisor of nonunionized employees should examine his own disciplinary actions to see if they conform to the requirements of just cause.

Consistency of discipline. If two employees commit the same offense and one of them is left unpunished while the other is singled out for harsh treatment, the discipline is inconsistent. It is also discriminatory. If a rule-breaking is overlooked in rush times and punished by a 10-day suspension in slack times, the discipline is inconsistent. Fairness requires that everyone committing the same offense be treated substantially alike. Yet absolute consistency is impossible and actually undesirable because the circumstances surrounding an offense add to or lessen the guilt. (Did the employee falsify one production record so as not to show up his slower fellow workers, or has he been making out false reports and cheating the company for 20 years?)

Identical penalties are not called for in a case where two employees violate the same safety rule and one employee has an unblemished record and the other has a record of warnings and discipline for previous violations.

---

reported in texts that classify, count, and analyze the published decisions. Some of these texts are:

Elkouri, *op. cit.*

Orme W. Phelps, *Discipline and Discharge in the Unionized Firm* (Berkeley and Los Angeles: University of California Press, 1959). This interesting study is based on statistical analysis of penalties for incompetence, unreliability, troublemaking, endangering safety, dishonesty, disloyalty, insubordination; immoral, illegal, or subversive acts; and improper behavior of union representatives.

J. Fred Holly, *The Arbitration of Discharge Cases: A Case Study in Critical Issues in Labor Arbitration* (Washington, D.C.: Bureau of National Affairs, 1957). This is a study of 1,055 arbitration awards on discharge cases covering a period from 1942 to 1956.

There are a number of extenuating circumstances that warrant reducing a penalty, for instance: (1) The employee's length of service and good record. (2) The degree of his guilt (Did he do it through lack of care and thought rather than deliberately and maliciously?). (3) The amount of provocation by fellow employees or by the supervisor (Who started the fight and why? What led up to the insubordinate action?). (4) The contributing negligence of supervisors or fellow employees (Did he get any instruction, direction, or help?). (5) Past practice in the company that would bear upon the case (What has the employee been led to expect?). Arbitrators consider these circumstances in deciding whether a penalty is just, and a supervisor should consider them also.

Condoning offenses. Laxness in enforcing discipline is poor practice. It builds up outright disregard for rules among the less conscientious and causes uneasiness and resentment among the more law-abiding who don't want to risk being hurt in a crackdown. If the supervisor tolerates rule-breaking and takes no disciplinary action against misconduct, then cracks down suddenly and makes an example of someone, the work group becomes distrustful and resentful. The disciplined employee becomes a martyr. He may file a grievance that he was discriminated against, that the behavior was common practice, that it had been condoned for a long time, that he was not warned to stop, that he had not received a reprimand, that he had been led to think that he would not be punished. Arbitrators reverse discharges and reduce other penalties when the evidence shows that the supervisor has been letting people get by with the violation.[5]

When violations have been condoned for some time and the company wants to tighten up on the enforcement of a rule, the best thing to do is to dust off the rule, post it with a notice that beginning such and such a time it will be enforced. Then call everybody's attention to it, warn the offenders, and carry out the warnings. Giving people warnings and then failing to carry them out is condoning the offense. An arbitrator reversed a discharge when the company, after warning the employee he would be fired next time he was absent, permitted several "next" times to go by before taking action.[6]

---

[5] See BNA's *Labor Arbitration Reports* 3 LA 557 Alan Wood Steel Co. case. The employee damaged a crane he was moving. He had moved the crane many times before even though there was a rule against it. The arbitrator held that the company's failure to enforce the rule had established a practice which the workers might believe was proper. If the company intended to start enforcing the rule, it should have given definite warning. This employee had not been given a warning or a reprimand. The five-day layoff was reversed.

8 LA 177 Allis Chalmers Co. The arbitrator said that the company cannot condone a violation of a plant rule for a long time and then impose discipline when loss or inconvenience results from a violation.

[6] *Ibid.* LA 678 Michigan Steel Castings Co.

Warning. Immediate dismissal is the penalty for acts that are flagrantly immoral or illegal. Some companies dismiss instantly for stealing, fighting, gambling, drunkenness, destroying company property, gross insubordination, falsification of records, sleeping on the job, punching the time card of another employee. But less serious violations of plant rules are not punished by dismissal on the first offense; instead the offender gets a warning or a suspension. Then he gets a heavier penalty if he repeats the offense.

Records of warnings must be made and put into the employee's personnel folder to be used as evidence in future actions. Some companies set a limit on the number of warning notices, reprimands, and suspensions an employee can accumulate. If he exceeds the number permitted he is discharged. Under such a system it is essential that the offender be kept informed of his score and his nearness to discharge. When he has only one more to go, he must get a warning that the next violation will result in discharge.

Warnings are an essential part of discipline for poor production or poor performance. Such a requirement is in line with the supervisor's duty to let employees know what the standards are, how they are measuring up to them, what improvements they must make, and how quickly they must make them. An employee warned of poor performance must be given an adequate period of time in which to correct his performance. If a continuation of his poor work is going to lead to dismissal, he must be warned of the fact. As an illustration of this point, here is a case selected from cases submitted by supervisors in management training conferences.

The union contract provided for discharge for good cause, also for a system of warning tickets (records of warnings given to employees). An instrument repairman was discharged for poor, inefficient, sloppy work. The instrument foreman had warned the man and had made out a ticket but did not state on the ticket that this was a final warning or that a repeat would mean discharge.

The arbitrator ruled that the man, although warned of his poor work, was not warned of discharge, so ordered him reinstated but with pay to start at time of reinstatement. When the man returned to work, the foreman warned him and made a record so stating that he (the foreman) would check the repairman very closely and that at the first evidence of poor work he would be terminated. The man stayed only a day and a half and then quit.

Adequacy of evidence. In discharge and discipline cases that go to arbitration, arbitrators demand proof of the employee's guilt in order to establish that proper grounds exist for punishment. Evidence must be substantial and believable—not gossip or hearsay—and it must be directly related to the offense.

Evidence of misconduct cannot be secret data stored away in a little black book and brought out as a surprise. Old offenses, if they are to be offered as evidence, must be acts that were brought to the employee's attention at the time they were committed or discovered. The supervisor is not permitted to build up a case by hoarding violations without calling them to the offender's attention. Arbitrators have ruled that if an offense is to be punished it must be investigated and acted upon soon after it is discovered. Furthermore the employee must be given an opportunity at that time to explain, contest, or defend himself against any charges that will be put into the record to be used against him.

These rules of evidence show the need for taking action on serious violations and making a record showing the circumstances and the penalty.

Due process and procedure

Just as the U.S. citizen looks to the Constitution for guarantee that he will not be deprived of his rights except by due process of law, so does the employee look for protection from being deprived of his job. The due process specified by the union contract takes in three points that have already been discussed: proper grounds for discipline, appropriate penalties, and fair play in enforcement. The fourth point is correct procedure.

Union-designed procedures governing discipline and discharge provide for publicity, formality, and time limits to give an employee an opportunity to defend himself. To the supervisor the procedures are cumbersome and restrictive but it is important that he abide by them. If there is good cause to separate an employee from the company, it should be done promptly and correctly. A slipup, such as failing to give an employee proper notice or depriving him of his right to talk to the steward, can result in having him restored to his job.

Some of the procedures covering discharge are: (1) giving adequate notice to the offender and to the union; (2) making a full statement of the charges on which the discipline is based; (3) providing time for the offending employee to consult with his steward; (4) providing for the accused to be represented by the steward at a hearing or other disciplinary action; (5) permitting the steward or other union officials to investigate the charges; (6) observing the time limits covering the steps for appealing the discharge through the grievance machinery.

The grievance procedure provides that if the employee is found to have been unjustly discharged, he will be reinstated with full back pay and seniority. If the penalty being appealed is a suspension, the arbitrator may rule that the length of it should be reduced. In that case the employee gets back part of the earnings he lost between the time of the sentencing and the time of reinstatement.

Incompetence and negligence

The supervisor's disciplinary problems include the job performance of his subordinates as well as their behavior. Unsatisfactory job performance may be due to incompetence or to negligence, and, because one calls for different treatment than the other, a distinction should be made between them.

Incompetence. Incompetence is defined in various ways: (1) being substantially deficient in the work, (2) being incapable of performing the work safely, (3) being unable to turn out work in proper quality or quantity, (4) being unable to keep up with the standard of performance of others on the job. A man may be incompetent because he never had the required ability. Or his performance may have been satisfactory at one time but deteriorated because of illness, aging, or lack of motivation. The job itself may have been changed and made more difficult. Production standards may have been raised. The employee may have been promoted to, or transferred to, a job that he was unable to handle.

While management has the right to discharge the inefficient employee, it must be prepared to support that action with proof both of the inefficiency[7] and of the supervisory efforts that were made to correct it. If an employee grieves that his discharge for incompetence was unjust and the grievance reaches arbitration, the arbitrator wants to find out if this employee is being singled out for harsher treatment than others, if he has been given sufficient training, instruction, help, and supervision, and what his merit ratings were. It is hard to prove a charge of incompetence if a worker has had good merit ratings right along. And it may be hard to explain how an employee was permitted to finish his trial work period and become permanent if he was so poorly fitted to the job. One of the reasons arbitrators give for reversing penalties on incompetence is that the supervision was faulty.

An employee who is incompetent on one job may be able to perform another one satisfactorily. The company is expected to make an honest effort to place a long-service employee in a job he can do if such a

---

[7] See Sumner H. Slichter, James J. Healy, and E. Robert Livernash, *The Impact of Collective Bargaining on Management* (Washington, D.C.: The Brookings Institution, 1960), chaps. 17, 18, 21, 27, 29. The authors report on some current practices in enforcing standards of work performance under collective bargaining. Also they give an excellent report on company practices with regard to rules, penalties, procedures, and arbitration. Their information came from a survey of a number of companies.

job exists—and if his inefficiency is not a result of laziness. Demotion, transfer, and retraining are the means the supervisor is expected to use before resorting to discharge for incompetence. However, if the worker is chronically inefficient, lazy, or indifferent, he should be discharged and the records should show unmistakable evidence of his lacks and the supervisor's efforts to remedy them.

Negligence. Negligence (as distinguished from incompetence) indicates that the employee is able to do the job but is careless, thoughtless, or doesn't follow instructions. He botches up the job and causes loss of materials, customers, or money. He doesn't pay attention to what he is doing, has accidents, damages machinery, or wrecks vehicles. He neglects to lock up valuables. He lights a match at the gas tank.

An employee's failure to use reasonable care may cause heavy property damage and may endanger life as well. The incidents may be so costly, dangerous, and frequent that he cannot be trusted on the job. (Deliberate and malicious destruction of company property is counted as sabotage rather than negligence and—if it can be proved—is punished by discharge.) Negligence is considered to be more a matter of attitude than of ability, and the standard penalties are warning, suspension, and discharge. Demoting an employee to punish him for his carelessness is considered an improper penalty unless specifically provided for in the contract. There are exceptions, however, and the dividing line between negligence and incompetence becomes very thin at times. There are cases in which repeated accidents indicate that an employee is unable to perform a job safely. In such cases arbitrators may rule that demotion or transfer to less hazardous work is the proper treatment.

Gripes and grievances

The term *grievance* has come to mean an employee's formal complaint about his job—usually a written complaint—presented to management. A company's contract with the union may narrow the definition by specifying that the complaint must concern matters covered in the contract. Then a grievance is considered to be a dispute between the employee and the company concerning the violation or interpretation of the terms of the contract. This definition is important in that it labels certain complaints as illegitimate and not subject to arbitration.

Complaints that don't fit the definition of a grievance may be labeled as *gripes.* These definitions obviously are management definitions. From the standpoint of the employee, he has a grievance if he feels that he has suffered an injustice. And he has a gripe if something is annoying or irritating him.

The supervisor has to deal with every type of complaint—real or imagined, oral or written, covered by a contract or not covered by a contract. He also has to deal with dissatisfactions that haven't been put into words but are having a bad effect on performance or morale. In any job there are irritations, annoyances, vexations, disappointments, conflicts of interest, and real or imagined injustices that give rise to gripes and grievances. An accumulation of these dissatisfactions creates a contagious kind of unrest that interferes with performance of the job.

An employee may be griped by the people he works with, by the way the boss orders him around, by last-minute requests to work overtime. He may be griped by discomforts and inconveniences—warm water in the drinking fountain and restrictions on his use of the telephone.

A sense of injury from a long-standing gripe has a way of transforming itself into a complaint that fits the company's definition of a grievance. This substitution of one complaint for another complicates the handling of grievances. The supervisor has to dig beneath the surface explanation to find the real basis of the trouble.

Typical grievances are claims by an employee that his job was improperly classified, his wages improperly figured, his seniority violated in a layoff, transfer, or promotion, that he was disciplined unjustly or too severely, discriminated against for union activities, that the foreman discriminates against him, gives him the dirty jobs, or doesn't give him his share of overtime.

The grievance machinery

One of the benefits of a union to its members is its grievance machinery. Through it, members have the right and the opportunity to appeal managerial actions that seem unjust. Since some of these appeals are against actions of the immediate supervisor, the grievance machinery offers a channel that can be used without fear of reprisal. Almost all union agreements outline the steps to be followed in adjusting grievances. The short and simple procedure of a retail store is illustrated in Figure 15–1.

Some companies require that complaints be given an oral hearing before they are entered as grievances. The aggrieved employee can go alone or he can ask the steward to accompany him in presenting the complaint orally to the foreman. (The steward is legally entitled to be present.) If the foreman's handling of the complaint does not satisfy the employee, he may then turn it over to the union for handling in the grievance machinery. Figure 15–2 shows the path followed by a grievance in a manufacturing company's procedure.

Following is a rather general description of what takes place in the steps of a five-step grievance procedure.

Step 1. Employee and steward fill out and sign the formal grievance papers and take them to the foreman, who must write his answer on

FIGURE 15–1
Grievance Procedure of a Retail Store and Retail Clerks'
Union

The employee takes up his grievance with his immediate supervisor. Then, if not satisfied with the handling of it, he appeals for a hearing before the Adjustment Board. If the Board cannot reach an agreement, an arbitrator is added to it to decide the dispute.

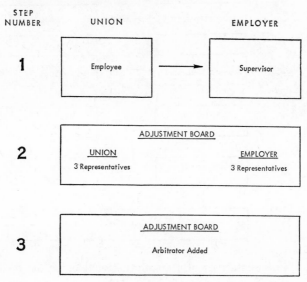

the grievance. There may be a time limit for this step and for each of the steps in the procedure. The foreman usually has a few days in which to study the problem, consult others about its implications, and give his answer. If he denies the grievance, the union decides whether to drop the issue or appeal it to the next step.

Step 2. The union representative at Step 2 may be the chief plant steward, the union business agent, the chairman of the union grievance committee of the plant, or several members of the grievance committee. He (or the committee) presents the written grievance to management. The management man here may be department head, superintendent, general superintendent, or plant manager. He investigates the charge, confers with the foreman, consults with others in both line and staff departments, and discusses the matter with the union representative. If no agreement is reached, the union can appeal the grievance to Step 3.

Step 3. Here the plant's union grievance committee, with the possible assistance of a representative of the international union, meets with someone in the top level of plant management to negotiate the issue. If it isn't settled here it can be carried to Step 4.

FIGURE 15–2
A Grievance Procedure Having Four Steps of Negotiation
Plus One of Arbitration

At Step 3 the Plant Personnel Director enters into direct
negotiating alongside the Plant Manager.

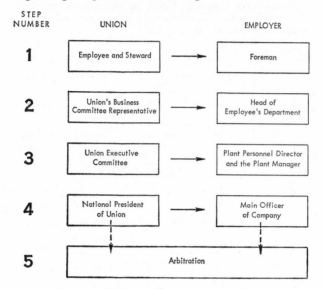

Step 4. Representatives of the international office of the union (or regional or district representatives) meet with the general officer of the company (the president or vice president). If the dispute is still unsettled, it goes to an arbitrator.

Step 5. Arbitration. Arbitration is used to avoid strikes and walkouts over disputes during the life of a union contract. The arbitrator is a disinterested third party selected and paid by company and union. He may be appointed on a permanent basis to hear all the grievances that arise in the company or he may be selected[8] on an *ad hoc* basis— that is, chosen to deal with a particular dispute. The arbitrator studies the case, questions witnesses, and makes a decision based upon his interpretation of the contract provisions. The decision is binding. The decisions and opinions coming from arbitration and the settlements reached in negotiation should be reported to supervisors to give them guidance. Some supervisors complain that the first they hear of a settlement is when the employee tells them what he got.

There are any number of variations to the negotiating procedure just described. The head of industrial relations or of personnel may take an active part as a negotiator in one or more of the steps. In

---

[8] Arbitrators may be selected from a list prepared by the American Arbitration Association, or a list from the Federal Mediation and Conciliation Service, or from a state agency.

those companies where the negotiating is done by line management, industrial relations or personnel acts in a staff capacity, interpreting policy and contract, showing how previous grievances were handled, and maintaining consistency of action throughout the company.

Not every grievance enters the procedure at the first step. Grievances over discharge, suspension, or layoff may skip the first two steps and go at once to a high level. Short cuts are used for several reasons: (1) to speed up the process in cases where feelings run high, where sympathy spreads to a great number of employees, and where resentment and pressure may show up in slowdowns or wildcat strikes; (2) to get quick settlement of cases that may call for retroactive pay; or (3) to enter the procedure at the point where authority exists to establish new policy or precedent. Grievances which can be settled on the lower steps are those coming under established policy or precedent.

Foreman and shop steward

The foremen are the ones who live with the union contract all day long in dealings with employees and their elected representatives, the union stewards. The type of relationship that the foreman has with the steward probably reflects the relationships at the top between company and union.

The steward's position is a unique one. On one hand, he is an employee of the company, doing a regular job under the supervision of the foreman; on the other, he is an elected officer in the union, with freedom and rights that other employees don't have. In his official capacity he is protected by contract provisions and labor laws. He has an obligation to his constituents to hear and investigate their grievances and argue them vigorously with the foreman. The vigor he may use in his official capacity is beyond that permitted to him as a regular employee. He has the job of policing the contract and seeing that its provisions are lived up to. He can question the foreman's decisions and advise employees of their rights under the contract.

Contract and plant practice govern the amount of time and the conditions under which he may be away from his workplace to handle union matters. The contract also regulates the type of union business he can handle on company time. It is customary for the company to pay him for the time that he spends handling grievances.

Understanding the steward's position calls for understanding a little of the internal politics of the union.[9] Political rivalries within the union

---

[9] For a study of personalities of union officials and the influence of internal union political pressures on the union's handling of plant grievances, see Leonard R. Sayles and George Strauss, *The Local Union: Its Place in the Industrial Plant* (New York: Harper & Bros., 1953).

may influence the attitude of its leaders toward supporting and settling grievances. Grievance rates may rise around the time for electing local officials. Certain types of grievances may be pushed just before contract negotiating time. Under some circumstances grievances may be cooked up to embarrass the company. A union must decide whose cause to support when a grievance by one group of members asks for something at the expense of another group. An adjustment of seniority, for instance, or a promotion is always made at the expense of another employee.

A good working relationship between foreman and steward can facilitate the settlement of grievances at the first level. The foreman should take the initiative in establishing courteous and businesslike relationships with the steward. The foreman can be agreeable rather than grudging in regard to the time the steward is entitled to spend on his union duties. The foreman can make it a point to introduce each new employee to the steward. He can set a pattern of courtesy in the way he keeps the steward informed of production schedule changes, overtime expected, layoffs proposed, and disciplinary actions pending. The steward can't be expected to cooperate in meting out punishments to his constituents but he can reinforce warnings to members whose misbehavior is endangering their jobs.

Grievance handling by foremen

Grievance handling at the foreman's level is both rewarding and dangerous to the company. The dangers lie in the chance of poor decisions made without adequate understanding of the total situation. The foreman may lack information about the union contract and the company's policies. He may be unfamiliar with the workings of the union. A foreman's handling of a grievance may set an expensive and unworkable precedent. What looks like a good decision in his department can spell trouble elsewhere. For instance, on a grievance involving truck driver and helper, a foreman wrote: "Only truck drivers will operate vehicles." Unfortunately this was a tender issue elsewhere in the company where electricians and others outside the driver classification worked with equipment that had to be moved occasionally. The company had hoped these employees would continue to move their own equipment rather than stand by and have a driver do it for them.

Handling grievances wisely calls for consultation with someone who is acquainted with the total situation and will give guidance without

---

See also Slichter, Healy, and Livernash, *op. cit.*, chaps. 22–28. Of particular interest are the reports on union pressure tactics; the internal operations of the union and their effect on the grievance rate and on the level at which settlements are made; management policies and their effects on grievance settlement; arbitration procedures; the effects of grievance handling on production standards in high-cost plants.

dominating the decision. Ordinarily the industrial relations or personnel department should be expected to do this and to act as a clearinghouse of information on matters relating to grievance handling.

If foremen are to get all the information they need to make good decisions, the company must provide opportunities for them to study and discuss the provisions of the contract and the implications of the decisions that arbitrators hand down. Training for grievance handling has a plus value in that it helps the foremen avoid making the kind of mistakes that give rise to grievances. Understanding the seniority provisions of the contract helps prevent mistakes in arranging transfers, promotions, and layoffs. Knowing arbitration decisions on disciplinary grievances makes for better practices of rule enforcement. One company reported[10] that its foremen became better contract administrators through a program of participation in the new contract negotiations. The foremen suggested contract changes, were briefed on each day's progress in negotiations, and then analyzed and discussed each article in the new contract.

The alternative to giving foremen the training they need is to have grievances handled at a higher level—a practice that has a number of drawbacks. For one thing, a grievance when it is passed up the line changes in character. It may become a "cause" to be fought over, aligning the company against its employees and creating tensions and disturbances. The foreman understands the shop problems better than higher levels of management can know them. He is in a position to work out better settlements at his level. He knows the employee and sees the grievance in the setting that gave rise to it. If he and the employee can handle it there before it can be made into an issue, they can be solving a problem rather than preparing for a contest. And while they are solving the problem they can often bring about needed adjustments in their ways of working together.

A decision that comes down from on high does nothing to improve the understanding between a man and his boss. The bypassed foreman loses the status and authority he needs to maintain his group's high performance and good behavior.

The handling of gripes

The discussion of grievances concentrated on a shop environment in order to show the operation of union grievance machinery. The handling of gripes is informal, and supervisors everywhere must handle them as they come or have them build up to the point of interfering with the job.

---

[10] See "Foremen Can Aid Bargaining at Four Stages," *Factory Management and Maintenance,* April, 1962, pp. 108–09.

A gripe is something more than just being unsatisfied with the job. Few people are completely satisfied with their jobs, and few people consider work as a joy and a blessing, although they would be lost without it. To most people work is a necessary chore that requires sacrifice either to a small or to a great degree. Beefing about the job may be the employee's way of letting off steam about a situation that he realizes cannot be corrected. Or beefing may indicate that he has a gripe.

Gripes may be real or imaginary. They may have their origins in something that is actually wrong in the work situation or in something that the employee only thinks is wrong in it. Having someone bang the window shut every time he opens it for a breath of fresh air may be one of the most irritating things in a man's life. The hot-blooded and the cold-blooded people may have a running feud about temperature, drafts, windows, and fans. The discomfort involved can assume the proportions of a persecution.

Minor unsatisfactory conditions cause undue annoyance to an employee whose actual gripe is something else. A poorly lighted work area may send a typist into a frenzy of errors and complaints when actually she is burning up because her good typewriter was taken away without explanation and given to another girl.

Gripes may manifest themselves by some sort of change in the behavior of the aggrieved employee: the happy-go-lucky one becomes sullen; the center of the crowd keeps more to himself; the enthusiastic worker becomes a daydreamer; the safe worker becomes careless; the good housekeeper becomes sloppy; the good attender starts taking time off. Sometimes there will be a flare-up and the employee will refuse to follow orders. Occasionally someone will "boil over" and "tell the boss off."

When a group of employees has a gripe, it may show itself in quarreling, gossiping, faultfinding or stalling on the job, mistakes and waste, a drop in quality and quantity of work done, or an increase in absences.

The supervisor can't afford to ignore gripes and leave their handling to upper management or to the personnel department. And he certainly shouldn't leave them undiscussed and unsettled to be turned into grievances to be handled by the union.

The open door.   Even if upper management has an open-door policy welcoming employees to carry their job problems up to the big boss, most problems won't be taken care of that way because most employees avoid the big boss. The few who go to him with complaints have a personal ax to grind or are seeking attention, or their complaints have already reached a serious stage.

The big boss can't get a true picture of a situation without investigating and calling people in to get their sides of the story. Often he lacks the time; so he makes a quick decision which creates more disturbance than it settles as it goes down the line. The supervisor who passes gripes up the line instead of settling them in his section may be making more trouble for himself than he is avoiding.

The supervisor and gripes. The supervisor may try to avoid handling gripes by passing them over to the counselor or some other member of the personnel department. Counselors have a definite and useful function to perform, but there should be a distinction made between their activities and those reserved for the supervisor. The supervisor who avoids handling gripes often finds that he has a lot of explaining to do. Also he finds himself on the defensive. The gripe develops into a case of subordinate *versus* supervisor. When this situation exists, it is very difficult to build a team in which the supervisor is working *with* the employees.

When the supervisor doesn't take care of gripes, the union may turn them into grievances. When this happens regularly in the company, upper management may be partly to blame. If upper management ignores the recommendations of supervisors but acts promptly when the union presents the same request in the form of a grievance, the employees soon realize that the way to quick action is through the union. Then the supervisor begins to question the value of handling gripes.

The immediate supervisor is the logical man to handle gripes. He is close to the scene, in a position to detect a gripe in its early stages. He probably had some of the same gripes when he was a member of the rank and file. He knows, or should know, his employees and what is important to them. He knows what to look for in the way of causes. Supervisors have seen the same problems recurring from time to time and have either had to solve them or live with them. The way supervisors analyze and solve the case studies in this book is evidence that many of their solutions are better than those of the experts.

Some of the gripes of employees are against the supervisor; so the employees should have an avenue of appeal. However, the experienced supervisor, skilled in interviewing, can solve many of these problems. In some cases he is just the substitute cause. The employee may be blaming his difficulties on the supervisor rather than on his own inadequacies. The employee may build up resentment until the supervisor becomes the personification of all his troubles. In such cases the skilled supervisor can clear the air by letting the aggrieved employee blow off steam and can—better than any third party—show that he has no grudge against the subordinate.

The emotional content of gripes

Gripes have a high emotional content. An employee's job becomes almost a part of his personality; anything that threatens the job is an attack upon him. The man whose job importance has been reduced gets headaches or stomach pains and can't say a civil word to anybody. An employee feels personally wronged and cheated if someone else gets special advantages. The girls at the store are boiling because the boss's two favorites can saunter in any time they please and can wander away from their work. The girls with the gripe are snappish to the customers.

Gripes reflect the emotional upheavals at home—the disappointment and tears over plans frustrated by schedule changes; the indignation and resentment about job conditions that trigger the employee's allergy or aggravate his ulcer. The man who is kept beyond his turn on the night shift becomes a nervous wreck; he can't sleep, can't eat; his family can't adjust to the hours; he quarrels with his wife; he has accidents on the job.

The fact that something gripes a person shows that it has hit a tender spot and he is stirred up about it emotionally. He can't think about it calmly and he can't do his job well while he is in this state of mind. The employee with a gripe has a lowered boiling point; any little annoyance can set him off.

The supervisor has to watch his own emotional involvement in a gripe case. The aggrieved employee may be one who is hard to get along with. He may always be having difficulties. He may be oversensitive, suspicious, and not well adjusted. His manner of making the complaint may be offensive. His complaint may be a sharp criticism of the way the supervisor is doing his job. The supervisor's own reaction to a combination like this may prevent him from investigating the situation carefully and from understanding why the employee is behaving as he is. It isn't easy to be calm and listen quietly while a wrought-up subordinate presents charges that could be embarrassing. The supervisor has to learn how to overcome his own annoyance and listen. Just giving full attention to the aggrieved employee has a mollifying effect, and somewhere in the complaint there is a clue to what is causing the trouble.

In the first chapter of this text is a discussion of attitudes and how they affect judgment. With it there is a chart illustrating the personality factors that affect a person's interpretation of a situation. The legend under the chart applies equally to the griever and his boss:

Each person's perception of a situation is distorted by his values: his expectations, loyalties, prejudices, likes, dislikes, attitudes, ideals, and objectives. These factors may prevent him from seeing the real situation and understanding why others are behaving as they are.

Absenteeism and tardiness

Absenteeism and tardiness are considered together because they cause the same kind of problems for the supervisor and because penalty systems treat them as related offenses. If an employee is several minutes or hours late in getting on the job, he is tardy. If the time stretches out beyond a half day, he is considered absent. In measuring absences, some companies don't count as an absence the time lost by employees who are away from their jobs because of sickness, injury from accidents, death in the family, or a legitimate excuse of that type. Other companies count as an absence *any* failure of an employee to report on the job on a day he is scheduled to work.[11]

Effects of tardiness and absenteeism

Absences and lateness upset the supervisor's planning. Jobs have to be shifted; the relationship of each job to others has to be revamped. Employees have to be put on work they are not familiar with. They have to be given additional instructions and directions. Their work has to be inspected more frequently. An employee who is unfamiliar with the work makes more mistakes, turns out less work, and reduces the efficiency of others. If a number of employees are absent, their work may have to be done by scheduling overtime.

Other costs that may be charged against absences are salaries paid to the absentees, benefit payments, salaries of replacements, and salaries of people who must check up on absentees, interview them, and keep records. Overhead costs of the plant go on even though equipment stands idle and the work is not done while people are absent. Estimates of the cost of absenteeism range from 4 percent of the payroll up to 40 percent.

The absences of professional people are costly. One study[12] reported that the total direct and indirect cost of a one-day absence of an engineer amounted to $273.10. This included eight hours of overtime to catch up on his work.

---

[11] Absence statistics and costs, therefore, don't compare very readily from one company to another. The following formula is one of many in use for figuring the percentage rate of absence.

$$\text{Absence rate} = \frac{\text{No. of man-days lost through absence during month}}{\text{Average no. of employees} \times \text{no. of working days}} \times 100$$

Count all man-days lost except vacations and unpaid leaves of absence. To compute the average number of employees, add the total work force figures for each pay period within the month being measured and divide by the number of pay periods. An absence rate of 2 percent is considered excellent.

[12] Made at Stevens Institute of Technology and reported by Frederick J. Gaudet, *Solving Problems of Employee Absence* (American Management Association Research Study 57) (New York: American Management Association, Inc., 1963). This thorough study of absences doesn't claim to solve the problems but it does describe them and report what a number of companies are doing about them. It also gives a survey and evaluation of research studies of absences and absentees. It presents 41 formulas for measuring the absence rate.

In some companies the tardiness of professional people becomes a problem. Some of these people like to work irregular hours—start an hour or so late in the morning and work until midnight. Even though they as individuals may be making great contributions to the company, some of their value is lost because their activities are not coordinated with the activities of other people in the organization. The work of dozens of people might be held up pending information to be obtained from the professional who has not shown up for work as yet. Sometimes resentment is built up against him: "Who does he think he is anyway?" and "If he can come in late, why can't I?" Some companies have found it necessary to insist that everybody in the organization *with no exceptions* start the work day at the regular time.

Finding and treating the causes

In order to study the attendance problems in his own department, the supervisor should be supplied with company figures on absences and their costs. Rates and costs should be broken down by departments so that he can see how his unit compares to others. He should get regular reports showing who in his group was absent or tardy, how many times, how many days in a row, what days they were, what excuse was given.

A certain amount of tardiness and absence is to be expected for causes of illness, accidents, family emergencies, deaths, and funerals. Sudden increases in the rates might indicate excessive overtime, job-caused fatigue, gripes, or unsettled grievances. Low morale may manifest itself in absences as well as in turnover. People may be disturbed to the point of taking time off to go job hunting. When a job becomes too disagreeable, employees may develop such headaches or stomach-aches that they feel justified in staying home.

Employees' personal troubles. One school of thought lays the blame for excessive absences on the personality of the high-absence employee; he is typed as *absence-prone*. In a good many instances, a small number of employees account for a majority of the absences. These employees usually don't get along well with people, don't like their supervisors, have trouble at home, or are generally dissatisfied with their jobs.

Some studies show a correlation between the employee's attendance and his opinion of the supervisor. In a University of Michigan study, the high attenders felt free to discuss their personal and job problems with the supervisor.[13] In a study by Noland the poor attenders thought

---

[13] Floyd Mann and Howard Baumgartel, *Absences and Employee Attitudes in an Electric Power Company* (Ann Arbor, Mich.: Survey Research Center, 1952). This study was made in the Detroit Edison Company. The findings were supported in studies made in insurance, railroading, and manufacturing groups also. The high attenders also had better feelings toward their fellow employees.

their foreman was difficult to get along with, unfair, and never showed appreciation of good work.[14]

Keith Davis comments on the relationship of organization size and employee absenteeism. "Increasing size of operations introduces what might be called a *behemoth syndrome,* by which increasing size develops a series of interrelated symptoms and problems. For example, larger size is associated with lower employee satisfactions, which tends to increase absenteeism."[15] Employees can feel overwhelmed in a large organization, believing that they are insignificant and unimportant. Such feelings of insecurity can cause them to feel sorry for themselves, develop imaginary illnesses and take days off to get even.

Women tend to have higher absence rates than men. This is particularly true of younger women who are not career-oriented and look upon their jobs as way stations on the route to marriage. Young married women may take time off for medical care and not want to tell the company about it so they may manufacture excuses for their absences. This is particularly true when the company does not allow pregnant women to work. They may also take days off when their husbands are home and call in sick even though they are not. As a rule older women and women executives in general tend to have low absence rates.

With the increasing amount of underprivileged minorities employed in industry, there is an increase in absenteeism and tardiness. Habits of punctuality, responsibility, the desire to advance are learned through a lifetime of training, work opportunities, family pressure, and through encouragement and reward on the job. The person who grows up surrounded by these attitudes will have his behavior shaped by them. Unfortunately, large numbers of minority group employees have not been exposed to this type of environment. Many of them have living conditions that are not conducive to getting up and being on the job everyday. They may sleep four or more in a bed, lack medical care, have such bad home conditions that they stay out all night and their friends may not be concerned about being in shape for work. Supervisors may have special problems in trying to discipline these people because the same techniques that have worked for other employees may not work for them. A good deal more attention and patience may be necessary before the supervisor is able to convince members of minority groups that his values and those of the company should also be theirs.

---

[14] William E. Noland, "Foreman and Absenteeism," *Personnel Journal,* June, 1945, pp. 73–77. In this study of 500 workers in New York, the good attenders were satisfied with the treatment they got from the foreman.

[15] Keith Davis, *Human Relations at Work, The Dynamics of Organizational Behavior* (3d ed.; New York: McGraw-Hill Book Co., 1967), p. 192.

Studies of people who are frequently absent serve to emphasize the effect that attitudes have on attendance. In looking for causes of absences the supervisor should keep in mind that an absence seems to be the result of a number of factors working together to influence an employee to take time off.

Talking with employees about their absences will often bring to light personality clashes, fears of being hurt on the job, suspicions of discrimination, feelings of not getting a square deal, and a host of other causes of low morale—including problems at home. All of these complaints must be listened to. Talking with offenders and helping them find ways to solve their problems is discussed later in this chapter.

Social relations on the job affect attendance. A tightly knit group with high loyalty seems to have fewer absences than a group that is beset by conflicts. A person who is absent excessively may be separating himself from the group for some reason; or the group may be rejecting him. The supervisor needs to know his people and understand where and how they fit into the group. Then he will be in a better position to avoid setting up conflicts within the group.

Job factors.   Causes and remedies for absenteeism are not all in the field of human relations. The design of jobs, the way a man fits his job, and the adequacy of his training influence his attendance. The opportunity to make decisions and to feel useful and necessary keeps people from taking time off. Absences tend to be high where the skill level of the job is low. If certain jobs have high absences, the supervisor should consider redesigning them to make them more interesting, challenging, responsible, or agreeable. This might be accomplished through job enlargement, job rotation, partnership work, or even just an improvement in the seating arrangement.

The supervisor's ability to plan affects attendance. If employees stand around waiting for work, they get the idea that they won't be missed.

Accidents causing injuries on the job result in absences and may indicate the need for a better management of safety. Other causes of absence are poorly maintained equipment,[16] poor light, fumes, noise, and inadequate ventilation. People try to escape from unpleasant situations, job irritations, and frustrations. Women are more easily annoyed than men by discomfort and poor housekeeping. If it is drafty or uncomfortable at work or if there is no clean place to lie down and rest during the breaks, women may decide in favor of staying home when they have a slight ailment.

---

[16] George S. Odiorne, "Some Effects of Poor Equipment Maintenance on Morale," *Personnel Psychology,* Summer, 1955, pp. 195–200. This was a study of the behavior of the operators of well-maintained machines and poorly maintained machines. The 10 men on the poor machines had more absences, tardiness, grievances, arguments, and quits.

Problems with alcoholics

The heavy drinker who is actually an alcoholic is usually an attendance problem. He is a problem in other ways too—putting off work because he is too foggy to handle it, delaying decisions, being evasive, elusive, and undependable, and being hard to get along with until he has had a drink. It is difficult to confront a subordinate with specific instances of this type of behavior, but an attendance record is something concrete on which to base a discussion of performance and of drinking.

The Federal Labor Department estimates that alcoholics lose about 28 man-days per year. A few studies of alcoholics' attendance indicate that their days off may be scattered through the week and not just concentrated on Mondays and Fridays. These same studies indicate that tardiness does not seem to be a problem typical of the alcoholic employee, but that he may disappear and leave before the day is over.

The supervisor should realize that alcoholism is an illness and not a moral problem, and that it does not improve by itself. In fact it is apt to get worse; so he is not doing the employee a kindness by protecting him and covering up for him. There is nothing to be gained by getting angry with an alcoholic for his failures to handle his work. There is no point in lecturing him about the dangers to his health or suggesting that he drink beer or save his drinking for weekends. He would if he could.

There is a distinction that must be made between the heavy drinker who doesn't let his drinking interfere with his job, and the alcoholic who seems to let nothing interfere with his drinking. Since very few people will admit to being alcoholic, the supervisor should seek some expert help in identifying the alcoholic employee. It is important to find out if the company has any policy or program for treating alcoholics. Some companies have recognized that the alcoholic is worth treating and that the company is repaid many times over for its part in restoring him to health and to a useful life. Companies with alcoholism programs report that over half the employees who have *sought* treatment have been helped. In fact, some companies boast that many of their restored alcoholics have moved up to higher jobs.

The supervisor's difficulty is to get the alcoholic to seek treatment, because treatment cannot be forced upon him. The alcoholic himself must take the action, and he probably won't do it unless he is made to realize that he has to do it in order to keep his job. He seems to be unable to recognize that he has a problem on which he must take action.

If the company has no program for taking care of alcoholic employees, the supervisor would be doing a great kindness if he made a contact with Alcoholics Anonymous to have someone take the employee to a meeting. He could go with the employee himself, since meetings are attended by nonalcoholics—wives, husbands, friends, doctors, and sociologists, as well as bosses. The professional person may be there because he is an alcoholic himself or because he is concerned about someone else who is one.

Techniques for reducing absences and tardiness

The following techniques are suggested for companywide use:

1. To remedy transportation or parking problems causing tardiness: Shift the starting time a few minutes in one direction or the other. Stagger the times at which various departments start work. Enlarge the parking lot. Assign the parking spaces. Get public transportation companies to shift their schedules.
2. Increase the number of time clocks or shift their location.
3. Make it inconvenient to be tardy: A few minutes after starting time, pick up the unpunched time cards and replace them with colored cards directing the employee to write his excuse on the card and take it to his supervisor for OK (or to the timekeeper or personnel office). The employee returning from an absence is required to do the same thing.
4. Send a nurse to the home of the absentee. If he is really sick, she can help him get proper treatment. If he isn't, he is not apt to risk it or to malinger. The nurse's services are particularly effective in cutting down on sick leave abuse that accompanies a generous policy of paying for time lost.
5. Require a doctor's certificate for an illness absence longer than two days. Most employees would rather come back to work than make a visit to the doctor and pay for it.
6. Give recognition to the perfect attender—a letter of commendation or gift at the end of each year of perfect attendance. A special award with some ceremony for each five years of perfect attendance.
7. Pay employees for days of sick leave they don't use during the year. Or add these days to their next vacation. Or add them to their retirement benefits.
8. Pay a bonus for good attendance. To be effective a bonus period should be short and should provide for a fresh start soon after a fall from grace. The bonus has drawbacks. Some companies complain that it brings employees to work when they are too sick to work. It makes them angry if they get hurt on the job or are sent home sick.
9. Post the departmental attendance records.

10. Mail to the employee's home a monthly statement of his attendance record with the request that he check it over to see if the reasons listed for his absence are the correct ones.
11. Have labor-management committees deal with absentees.
12. Turn the chronic absentee over to the union officials for counseling and warning of the nearness of discharge.

Suggestions for the supervisor in handling tardiness. The supervisor's own attitude toward tardiness will shape the employee's attitude toward it and will determine the amount of effort the employee will make to be on time. If the supervisor just gets in under the wire, is late, or doesn't take any action when people come in late, the conscientious, well-organized employee comes to feel that nobody appreciates his effort—and it is an effort—to be on the job on time every day.

The employee who would be late to his own wedding goes on thinking that punctuality just isn't very important. It takes a great deal of effort on his part to regulate his life so that he can be punctual. And it takes a certain amount of constant pressure to keep him reminded of the need to sustain that effort. Young people need to be helped to value time and to build good work habits. People under 20 have the worst attendance records.

Counseling the absentee

Almost any company plan for reducing absences will work for a while, not because of the method used but because the employees become fully aware that the company is deeply concerned about their absences. But gimmicks for improving attendance don't take the place of direct personal contact between supervisor and employee. When an employee returns to work after an absence, the supervisor must talk to him about the reasons for his absence. Points to be put across are that the company is extremely concerned about absences, that the employee was missed and needed, and that the lack of his services caused difficulties for others.

If the employee's absences are chronic, the supervisor should go on from this·point to try to find out the reasons. This is an opportunity to clear up misunderstandings and to show an interest in the employee's welfare.

The employee should be shown his attendance record and asked to set up a plan of correction. In many cases, employees simply don't realize how bad their records are. They don't understand the purpose of the company's policy for sick leave benefits. They have no idea of the cost of absences or of all the trouble caused by poor attendance. Some employees, when they get the total picture, will see that their poor attendance is a violation of fair play.

The employee should be shown that his absences are hurting his chances of getting ahead in the company. The important assignments are given to people who can be depended upon to show up for work. The chronic absentee will be passed over in promotions. Unreliability will show up in his merit rating and prevent his getting a merit increase. He should be warned of the penalties awaiting a continuation of his behavior.

Penalties for absences

Penalties for absenteeism and tardiness vary in stiffness from one type of business to another. In a continuous process industry they are heavy. The process (molten glass or steel, for instance) can't be shut off without great loss, and every job has to be covered around the clock. The nature of the work likewise influences the time limits within which the absentee must call in to say that he is not coming to work, to give the reason, and get an OK on it. He may be required to call in before the shift starts or within an hour or two after. It is part of the induction procedure to tell the employee whom to call, when to call, and what happens if he doesn't call.

In tight labor markets employers sometimes find it difficult to control absenteeism and tardiness. Even though such poor practices may be costly, the companies find that recruiting new hires may be very difficult and they may tolerate more absences and lateness than they would if replacements were easily obtained. Large white-collar employers in big cities who employ mainly young female clerical help tend to have more problems with lateness and absence. Attempts to control it by passing over employees for merit increases may work but more often than not the employee will quit and seek employment elsewhere. In some critical skill areas such as typing, stenography, key punch, computer programming, and proof machine operation, there is a strong likelihood that employers will overstaff to diminish the effect of absenteeism on the work pace.

Another reality that employers have had to face is the deterioration of public transportation in big cities and the increased traffic on highways feeding into these cities. Tardiness is often caused by poor transportation and it is very difficult to convince an employee to get up an hour earlier to get to work on time particularly when large numbers of employees are late and the poor transportation gets considerable news coverage.

Preventing disciplinary problems

It is clear that there is both a legalistic approach and a human relations approach to the handling of employee problems. While a union contract or narrow interpretations of rules in a nonunion organization may reinforce the supervisor in many problem situations, it is not the only answer. Building a case is not as important as building a man's will to work and his willingness to live up to the rules and standards. Studying penalties and the problems attached to assessing them serves to emphasize the need for preventing violations. Preventing future problems begins with analyzing the present ones to see what caused them.

Studies indicate that the majority of discharges are not for inability to do the work but are rather for some undesirable personal trait in the employee—dishonesty, laziness, carelessness, unreliability, or lack of initiative. The best way to avoid problems with such people is to avoid hiring them. If they slip through the selection procedure, it may be possible to catch them in the probationary period. Most companies have such a period of from 30 to 90 days (or even up to two years) during which the new employee is on trial and can be dismissed for any reason except for his union activity. This is the time to find out if he is willing to put out the effort to produce in a satisfactory fashion, if he has good work habits, if he gets to work every day and on time, if he has a good attitude toward the job, and if he gets along well with the other employees. This is the time to get acquainted with him and find out if the job suits his abilities, interests, ambitions, and plans.

If an employee's work habits, motivation, and behavior are good during the trial period and change some time later, why do they change? Why does he start doing poor work, being careless, taking time off, coming in late, fooling around? Why does he get irritable, quarrelsome, or insubordinate? It is up to the supervisor to find out and do something about the situation. The employee's problem may be a personal one— illness, finances, difficulties at home. He may get some relief by talking about it, and the supervisor should help him by listening. The supervisor must find out the company's policy for going along with employees whose off-the-job difficulties are interfering with their work. The company's medical department, personnel department, or credit union may be able to help.

If home problems aren't to blame, the job itself may be the problem. The duties may have changed and the employee needs more training. The organization of the work may bring him into conflicts he can't handle. The design of his job may be such that he doesn't know what he is responsible for and what is expected of him. He may see no possibility of achieving anything on it. He may find it monotonous. The distribution of assignments may seem unfair. Failure to get a promotion may have discouraged him or made him resentful.

Correcting the situation may call for reorganizing the work to remove points of conflict, changing work partners, redesigning jobs, training people to handle a greater variety of tasks, arranging for transfers. Job enlargement may give employees more of what they want out of a job. Job rotation may relieve monotony in some types of work. People differ in the amount of frustration they can tolerate. If the job yields no satisfaction to the worker, his behavior will reflect it in one way or another. One person may stay away from the job and be sick; another may become quarrelsome, another may become apathetic—just do what is required of him.

Behavior problems may be caused by the supervisor's attitude. Employees have rather intense feelings about what they are asked to do on a job and the manner in which they are asked to do it. Locking horns over assignments or failing to carry them out properly may be a result of resentment against a supervisor whose manner of giving orders is abrupt, tactless, threatening, or belittling. Employees' unreasonable behavior may have its roots in lack of job security. Preventing problems of this type calls for a better understanding of what employees want from their jobs and from their supervisors.

Talking with offenders

When an employee's behavior or performance is unsatisfactory, it is up to the supervisor to talk to him about it. The interview might be simply a friendly inquiry about a slump in performance or a minor infraction of rules. Or an interview might be for giving a reprimand or a penalty. The supervisor must know his people and suit his technique to the person. A mild reminder or reproof may make more of an impression on one person than a suspension would on another.

Some principles of reprimanding.   The cardinal principle of any reprimanding is that it be done in private. A reprimand is intensely personal; it is a blow to an employee's self-esteem to be told that he is not measuring up. If a person is bawled out in public, he seems to need to strike back in some way to maintain his self-respect.

A second principle of reprimanding is to do it immediately after the offense. If tempers are too hot at the moment, there should be just enough time to cool off. The supervisor may need the time to calm down so he won't make any angry blasts or threats. The reason for handling a rule-breaking promptly is to establish a cause-and-effect relationship between offense and penalty. If there is a delay, the rule breaker thinks maybe he won't be punished and he thinks up excuses to justify his behavior. Then, when he finally gets a penalty, he blames the supervisor for having a grudge against him. Punishment should flow directly from the employee's own action, just as a burn comes from touching a hot stove. There is no need to be apologetic about assessing a deserved penalty or to say, "I hate to do this to you but it's a rule and I can't get around it." Shifting the blame from the offender to the company indicates that the offense wasn't really serious enough to warrant the penalty.

The supervisor should plan and carry through a reprimand so that the offender has no doubts about:

1. What was unsatisfactory about his behavior or performance. What he did that was wrong.
2. Why it was wrong. What rule it violated. What damage it caused. What bad effects it had.
3. What punishment (if any) is being meted out for this offense and why the penalty is a just one.
4. What will happen if he does it again.
5. How he is going to avoid recurrence of the offense. Or how he is going to improve his performance.

Criticizing performance. It is important not to discourage an employee or dwell on how poorly he has done and what future mistakes he might make. The supervisor should be sure that when he criticizes, he is referring only to the particular behavior that is under discussion. He is not belittling the person. He is not dragging up old mistakes and implying that the offender does everything wrong. An employee needs to know that the supervisor has confidence in his ability and intentions to do a good job.

If an employee has mishandled an assignment because he made a mistake in judgment, it may be better to let him criticize his own performance and suggest the improvement needed. If he was doing what he thought was right, a severe reprimand may cause him to refuse to accept responsibility or use his initiative in the future.

If the shortcoming is poor quality work, carelessness, low production, or lack of effort, the supervisor should try to get the employee to analyze his job difficulties. It may be that the employee does not understand the purpose of his job, the reasons for the quality requirements, and the cost and trouble caused by errors. The positive side of the requirements should be emphasized so that the employee can see that he was at fault; otherwise he will consider the reprimand undeserved.

Getting results. The purpose of the disciplinary interview is to get an improvement in behavior or performance. In order to get an employee to make up his mind that he is going to do better, the supervisor must appeal to the man's self-interest. The employee must see the advantage to himself in changing, and he must accept the responsibility for making the change. People can change their attitudes and habits for the better if they see the need to do it and if there is sufficient incentive to make it worth their while. When an employee leaves a disciplinary interview it should be with a plan to do better because it is to his advantage to do so.

Discharge

Discharge is the capital punishment of the industrial world. An employee who is discharged loses the income he and his family depend on, loses the benefits he has accumulated through seniority—his protection from layoff, his pension, the pay increases he has gotten through merit increases and promotions, the longer vacations, and the choice of shifts. He loses his company-paid insurance and other fringe benefits.

Because of its seriousness, discharge should be a last resort, and it should be a matter of justice, not a spur-of-the-moment consequence of anger, personality clash, or misunderstanding. Personalities, differences in viewpoint, and honest differences of opinion figure largely in discipline cases. Therefore a proposed discharge should be investigated and approved by authority higher than the immediate supervisor. Because of the possibilities of injustice there should be provision for appeal. Employees under collective bargaining have a channel of appeal through the grievance machinery. Employees in civil service have an appeal board or commission. People in private business or industry who are not union members may or may not have a formal appeal channel. In the small company they may appeal at the open door of the owner or top manager. In larger companies the personnel department may act as an appeal channel. The employee gets a chance to state his case if the personnel department gives every person leaving the company an exit interview before he gets his final check.

Some companies have a policy that a supervisor can discharge a man from the department but not from the company. The personnel department then makes the decision as to whether the man should be separated from the company or given an opportunity to transfer to a job in another department.

In some cases an employee is given an opportunity to resign rather than have the discharge on his record. (The supervisor can mark the record that he would not want the man to work for him again.) In a unionized company a man who quits under such circumstances may be reinstated. His quit can be processed through the grievance machinery as a discharge if there is evidence that the employee's rights were violated or that he didn't intend to quit. In matters of work assignments and transfers, for example, if the employee is given only the alternatives of taking it or leaving it—accepting the assignment or quitting—an arbitrator may call such a quit an unjust discharge.

Whoever is responsible for the behavior of a discharged employee during his final hours in the plant must see that he is escorted off the property and that he has no opportunity to give vent to his resentment by damaging anything before he leaves.

Managing change

Before one can do anything about an activity that has an effect on the managerial process, he must develop an understanding of that activity. Understanding change is no exception. Perhaps one way of approaching this understanding is to recognize that change has both an external and an internal dimension as it relates to a particular organization. Changes can occur in society at large which may have little effect on an individual organization. There are many companies and other organizations in the country that continue to use time-honored methods and procedures in face of advancing technology. Of course this approach may lead to difficulties. Witness the problems of many stock brokerage firms with their back-office or clerical operations. Nevertheless, some companies seem insulated from the changes occurring in society. As mentioned in Chapter 13, they may be those which are less growth and development minded and in relatively stable industries.

On the other hand, many organizations are directly affected by change in the society. In New York City, changes in the ethnic and racial population, educational changes, social and political pressures, and a tight labor market have caused many employers to hire large numbers of so-called minority group members for clerical work. For some of these employers this has meant a considerable increase in training cost not only for the new employees but for supervisors who have responsibility for these new employees. Among the nonbusiness organizations who are going through similar experiences are the colleges and universities who are now actively recruiting minority groups and who have experienced a variety of problems which they were not prepared for.

The quotation from Peter Drucker's new book earlier in this chapter indicate several factors which are present realities and which he believes will have a direct bearing on the future of this society. There are several other present realities which give every indication of having a future effect on organizations in this country. The ever-increasing level of education of our population with more young people going on to college and the great increase in adult education will certainly have wide impact on such things as the quality of the labor supply, the level of aspiration of individuals, demand for various products and other marketing implications, and a host of other possibilities.

The change in our population mix as far as its age is concerned is another factor having a direct bearing on the way organizations operate. In 1960, more than half of our population was over 33 years of age. In 1970, more than half will be under 25 years old. In one decade, we have seen a change from people who have had their formative years during the depression dominating our society to a majority who have

been born after World War II. Any business organization that employs
large numbers of young people and that has many supervisors that are
in their forties and fifties are already experiencing the impact of the
generation gap in the number and type of problems and the ways they
are handled.

Anyone marveling at the magnificent effort which placed our astronauts on the moon should recognize the complex organizations required for the accomplishment of this feat. Organizations are getting
more complex and it is entirely possible that private corporations will
be unable to meet all of the needs of the society. We may see more
private-public corporations such as Comsat developed to fill needs with
which private industry may be reluctant or unable to cope. In fact
it has been recently suggested that the problem-ridden U.S. Post office
be developed in this manner.

The internal view.   The point of the above discussion is to demonstrate that there is a societal frame of reference for each organization
in our society. Some may be more directly and more rapidly affected
by general changes in the society than others but each will have to
reckon with the external developments which take place if they are
to continue their existence.

In a sense, given the above societal frame of reference, most of the
chapters in this book deal with aspects of internal change. Planning,
work measurement, methods improvement, organization development,
manpower planning, and training, among others all imply change and
what the supervisor can do to cope with it. In other words, individual
supervisors are both agents of change and implementers of change. An
individual supervisor may not be aware of certain broad changes in
the society but he must train 10 minority group members assigned to
his department. He may also have to learn how to deal with a larger
influx of college graduates even though he is only a high school graduate.
Advancing technology may mean nothing more to a supervisor than
a changed method or procedure which he has to introduce to the work
force and help them understand it and overcome their resistance to
the changes it implies. The changes that have most meaning for him
are those that affect his job and the jobs for which he is responsible.
Of particular significance will be those changes which diminish or increase his importance in the organization.

One such possibility may result from the current emphasis on organizational change based on changes in the entire approach to supervision.
Organizational climate, sensitivity training, Theory Y assumptions and
other nonauthoritarian approaches mentioned in this book may have
a very direct bearing on the nature of the organization itself. It is possible that the formal organization structure with its traditional bureau-

cratic processes may be supplanted by more democratic approaches to supervision.

Warren Bennis, a well-known behavioral scientist, has put it this way:

It seems to me that we have seen over the past decade a fundamental change in the basic philosophy which underlies managerial behavior, reflected most of all in the following three areas:

1. A new concept of *man*, based on increased knowledge of his complex and shifting needs, which replaces the oversimplified, innocent push-button idea of man.

2. A new concept of *power*, based on collaboration and reason, which replaces a model of power based on coercion and fear.

3. A new concept of *organizational values*, based on humanistic-democratic ideals, which replaces the depersonalized mechanistic value system of bureaucracy.[17]

Jay Forrester of the Massachusetts Institute of Technology proposes a new corporate design which will include the 11 following characteristics:

1. Elimination of the superior-subordinate relationship.
2. Individual profit centers.
3. Objective determination of compensation.
4. Policy making separated from decision making.
5. Restructuring through electronic data processing.
6. Freedom of access to information.
7. Elimination of internal monopolies.
8. Balancing reward and risk.
9. Mobility of the individual.
10. Enhanced rights of the individual.
11. Education within the corporation.[18]

The proposals made by Bennis and Forrester may seem radical but anyone with a sense of perspective and a recognition of what has happened in the last 30 years in our organizations would have to say that they have at least a chance of being adopted in the future. In any event, there is no doubt that behavioral scientists, operations research people, and others will continue to offer ideas and concepts which, if implemented, will mean drastic change for supervisors.

[17] Warren G. Bennis, "The Idea of Change," in William G. Scott, *Organization Concepts and Analysis* (Belmont, Calif.: Dickenson Publishing Co., Inc., 1969), p. 148.
[18] Jay W. Forrester, "A New Corporate Design," in Paul Pigors, Charles A. Myers, and F. T. Main, *Management of Human Resources* (New York: McGraw-Hill Book Co., 1969), pp. 229–43.

Resistance to change

The success of an enterprise depends upon making changes that will enable it to keep up or ahead in its field. Companies race to be the first on the market with a new product. They buy new equipment that will do the job faster and better. They devise new systems to handle the increase in paper work. They reorganize part or all of the company to meet problems of growth and change. They introduce new procedures, methods, techniques, work rules, and standards. They rearrange desks and equipment to fit changes in the work flow.

All of these changes must be introduced and accepted at the work level if they are to be put into successful operation. But some changes provoke hostility, restriction of output, grievances, sabotage, refusal to cooperate, errors, tears, work stoppages, absences, and quits. New equipment designed to increase output may instead result in a drop in production.

The engineer says of the reaction to the newly installed incentive wage system: "You'd think that people would jump at the chance to make just as much money as they're willing to work for. But no. The morning the rate goes into effect, there're more women in the nurse's office than at the machines."

It's up to the supervisor to introduce and get compliance with changes that are originated by others and to make improvements and changes on his own. He is the one who must somehow adapt changes to fit the needs of his people and help people adapt to fit the demands of the change.

Motives for resisting change. Not every change is resisted. People ask for changes that they feel will be an improvement. Some people actively seek new experiences—promotions, more interesting work, more responsibility.

Whatever people do, they are seeking the things they feel will be to their advantage. And conversely, they oppose things (and that includes changes) that they feel will be to their disadvantage. "Advantage" in this sense is psychological since it is the person's private notion of what constitutes his own self-interest. His idea of what is to his advantage is based upon what he thinks it is possible for him to accomplish and what he thinks is desirable. And this may be something quite different from what management expects it to be. The theory of "economic man" was based on the idea that everyone is motivated to make the maximum amount of money. And some people are, but probably not too many. People restrict their output—and thereby their earnings—when they feel that it is to their own self-interest to do so.

Actually, everyone has a great many motives, and no two people have quite the same assortment. Each person therefore has his own particular concerns over what a proposed change in his job is going to mean to him. Furthermore, his attitude is affected by the attitude of the group. People on the job fit themselves into social groups to get a feeling of belonging in an environment of uncertainties. These groups, known as "informal organizations," are described in Chapter 11. The group takes on a character of its own and dictates the behavior of its members. It puts pressure on members to resist changes that might upset group stability. If the group is hostile to the company, then members look upon change as just another management trick to get something more out of them.

Fear and insecurity are at the roots of much of the hostility toward changes originated by management. People fear the loss of the job itself or the loss of some of their psychological advantages—status, for instance. The prospect of unemployment is a frightening one that makes people take strange measures—restriction of output, for example—to protect their jobs. When a person behaves badly on a job he is trying to protect, he seems to be cutting off his nose to spite his face. Changes in technology carry a threat that the job will be abolished or changed so that a person's particular skills will no longer be needed.

If major changes are introduced in a time of business expansion, a company may be able to guarantee that employees will be reassigned or retrained rather than cut off the payroll. But job security encompasses more than money. People come to feel that they *own* their particular jobs and the status attached to them. This is all to the good under stable conditions; it is the basis of their taking responsibility for getting out the work, for taking pride in the company, for using their initiative, and for cooperating with others. But pride and personal involvement in the job make an employee vulnerable to the threat of loss of power or prestige. People who have influence in the present setup may be afraid of losing it in a change, and they have a real stake in proving that the change can't possibly work. Some people feel that a change in their job implies a criticism of the way they were performing it; they too are eager to prove that the new arrangement is no better.

Status problems of change. Status anxiety exists on all levels of the organization, and people are angered, frustrated, and humiliated by changes that curtail their authority. The introduction of a computer may spread resentment throughout a company when the change of system deprives people of authority to use their own discretion in handling accounts.

A person's job and his status in the work group become part of the image he has of himself—what kind of person he is and how valuable he is. Revising it downward is painful, and the prospect of being "told" by some newcomer is galling. An older employee suffers in a change because he sees himself in danger of losing the advantage he won by getting there first. In an office this advantage might be his knowledge of the company's paper work-handling procedures. If these are changed, he will lose his status as an expert. Furthermore, he may be shifted to a job in which he may not be so adequate. A skilled craftsman suffers much the same kind of severe blow to his ego if he must move to a less-skilled job.

Changes in relationships between people on the job are loaded with conflicts. A group at work has its status system: some jobs have higher status—are "higher class"—than others. People within the system develop ways of working together, adjusting to the system, and helping each other. If a change of duties reverses the relationship and has the low-status person giving orders to the high-status person, the two people may be unable to work together. Such problems can be avoided if the supervisor protects the status system when he introduces changes into his department.

Preparing people for changes. Sometimes a person's only objection to a change is that it was sprung as a surprise, or—as he feels—pulled over on him or shoved down his throat. Independent, energetic, provident people want to feel that they have some control over their destinies, and they want some say about their jobs. What's more, they feel that they are in a better position than anyone else to know the things that need changing. They resent the implication that they are workhorses but not bright enough or important enough to be consulted. If they are left out of the planning, the company is the loser.

Changes should be discussed in advance with the people who will be affected by them. Their questions should be solicited, their fears, problems, and objections drawn out and discussed. Companies installing computers have found it necessary to develop long-range plans for giving employees detailed information about the changeover—just what each one's job would be at each stage of the change and what it would be when the installation was completed. One company admitted an oversight: it forgot to prepare employees in unaffected departments that would be receiving employees transferred from clerical jobs taken over by the computer. The people in these uninformed departments were the ones who had trouble adjusting.

Any kind of change to a person's job makes it necessary for him to break old habits and learn new ways of doing things and new ways of looking at things. If he can't adjust, he becomes a problem to the supervisor. It is essential that an employee find something in a change that is to his advantage, and the designers of change must learn how to design jobs that satisfy human needs along with the technical needs. As a rule, the benefits that management is seeking can be attained in a number of ways, and the way that is most acceptable to employees is the one most likely to succeed. Sounding out employee ideas and attitudes and taking them into account in the plans for change calls for good two-way communication in which the supervisor must be willing to lend a sympathetic ear.

Some research studies indicate that group participation in the planning of changes can take care of many of the problems. In group discussions, employees can let management know their objections—and can do it without being labeled as malcontents or troublemakers. A certain amount of beefing to management seems to relieve employees of pent-up resentment and helps them to settle down and adjust.

Summary

A considerable part of the supervisor's time is involved in the handling of employee problems and the management and implementation of change. To be an effective manager and achieve organizational goals he must carry out the disciplinary policies of the company. By so doing he helps assure overall compliance with rules and procedures. Even though the discipline policies are reasonable and fair there will be some employees who break rules and because of this penalties must be imposed. Rule enforcement and the imposition of penalties for infractions should be uniformly applied. Favoritism will only cause trouble, but the wise supervisor will recognize that each case must be handled individually.

Union contracts usually restrict the supervisor's flexibility in the handling of discipline so he should fully understand it and the grievance procedure also included in most union contracts.

While grievances are often considered formally and grievance procedure applied, employees have many informal problems which could be called gripes. In any event the supervisor must deal with all employee problems and complaints and rule infractions.

Among the most common problems the supervisor must deal with are absenteeism and tardiness. These are very costly to the company and in many cases the supervisor will find that a relatively few employees account for the majority of absenteeism and tardiness. There are many things which may cause absence such as trouble at home, job dissatisfaction, poor transportation, and inadequate supervision. Special problems in this area may be encountered in large cities with tight labor markets and a greater incidence of minority group employees.

The union contract and narrow rule interpretation by the supervisor may lead to a legalistic approach to discipline. The supervisor should also be concerned with the human relations aspects of handling employee problems. It is generally better to develop understanding and effective work habits than to become a strict disciplinarian. Discharge of an employee is usually the last resort as a problem solver in discipline cases. It should be carefully considered because of its impact on the employee as well as the rest of the work group.

The management of change should be approached by the supervisor as both an external and internal phenomenon. There are many changes occurring in the society at large that will have varying effects on the internal functioning of the organization. The supervisor should make an effort to understand the external changes and how they may affect his job. Internally he must act as both a change agent and an implementer of change. Among his most difficult tasks is the handling of resistance to change. Most humans prefer the comfort of status quo and the supervisor must encourage acceptance of changes if he is to aid in the achievement of organizational goals.

CASE 1

Mary Kay has been employed by the company for seven years. She started as a clerk-typist after graduating from high school. Over the years she has compiled an excellent performance record and has received several promotions and pay increases. Her most recent promotion which took place one month ago was to the position of chief clerk. She now has the responsibility for 10 employees and they all think very highly of her as a supervisor.

For the past six months Mary has been arriving at work late very frequently. Usually it is 15 or 20 minutes but at times she arrives as much as an hour late. Because she is so well regarded by superiors and subordinates alike, her superior spoke to her after the lateness developed into a constant pattern. He found that personal problems involving her mother, sister, and brother-in-law were troubling her. She lived with these people and they relied on her for guidance and assistance.

Her boss suggested that she move, and she moved in with an aunt. For a short time this helped but then the family sought her out once again and got the aunt involved as well. She does not want to live by herself since she has strong family ties. She recognizes that her job responsibiliy is very important and she seems to be career-oriented, yet she is reluctant to remain aloof from her family.

1. Should Mary Kay have been given her last promotion in view of her lateness record?
2. Can a company tolerate an employee who is excellent in every respect, except in lateness?
3. Should Mary be placed on probation with an ultimatum to improve her lateness record or be fired?

4. To what extent should her superior become involved in Mary's personal affairs to help her solve her problems?
5. Can Mary continue to be an effective supervisor under the circumstances?

CASE 2

There are three fork-lift truck operators in the warehouse. Two of them are young fellows who have both been warned twice (the second warnings in writing) about carelessness in operating the trucks. Last week one of them (Jack) made a fast turn and spilled a shipment. The dropped cartons had to be opened and inspected and a number of damaged items sent back for repair.

The foreman said it was inexcusable carelessness and gave him a three-day layoff. He warned the truck operators that any damage with trucks would be punished by layoff from here on.

Today Ray Harrison, the third truck operator, smacked into a door frame overhead and spilled the entire load he was carrying. He had simply failed to lower the truck. He is a valued employee and never had an accident before or any disciplinary record in all his years on the job. He is a friend and neighbor of the foreman and they ride to work together. Everybody is watching to see what the foreman is going to do about it.

1. If a foreman makes a threat that is contrary to policy or to the union contract, does he have to carry it out?
2. What should he do?

CASE 3

You have a salesgirl in the store who is a real problem; she just doesn't use her head. She has been making the same stupid mistakes for three years but you don't fire her because she sells at least a third more than anyone else. She studies the sales blurbs on new merchandise and learns how to operate all the gadgets. She can fill in anywhere. She works hard and doesn't fool around.

The customers love her. She acts sincere and friendly and interested in what they need, but then she forgets to put part of their purchase into the bag. You have a drawerful of guarantees and cords for electric shavers, earphones for radios, batteries and parts for toys, instruction sheets—all things that she forgot to put into the packages. On gift merchandise people don't always come back for the missing parts.

She wants to be a schoolteacher. She is 23 and away from home, supporting herself on this full-time job while she goes to college part-time. You can't figure out what is wrong with her. She is intelligent; she is serious; she is not silly. She doesn't look tired or hung over. She is really a very nice girl and everybody likes her. But she does the stupidest things. She forgets to order stock or else she makes out the order for a gross instead of a dozen or puts the wrong stock number on it. She puts things back in the wrong boxes. She forgets to lock the display cases. She gets her money mixed up. She gets very upset if you say anything to her about her mistakes.

1. What is the distinction between incompetence and negligence?
2. What can be done about this girl's faults?

CASE 4

A recent rule published by the company states that if an employee is caught smoking in the shop he will be punished by disciplinary action. The type of penalty is left up to the supervisor. Top management says that the rule is necessary because there were two rather serious fires in the plant within the year.

Many of your workers—experienced mechanics—disregard the rule by sneaking off to hidden corners for a smoke. These men would be hard to replace if they should quit or be fired. You think that upper management will crack down one of these days, and you want to be in the clear.

1. Evaluate the above smoking rule.
2. What are the advantages of leaving the penalty up to the supervisor?
3. What are the disadvantages of leaving the penalty up to the supervisor?
4. If a crackdown comes, who is in the middle? Why?
5. Would you establish a rule of three days off without pay for the first offense, seven days for the second offense, and an indefinite layoff for the third offense?
6. What kinds of penalties should you set up?
7. To what extent can your men help you to establish penalties?

CASE 5

The production in your group has been steadily decreasing, and you strongly suspect that the men have deliberately organized a slowdown. You question several of your good workers, and they admit that they are being pressured into holding back production, but they refuse to incriminate any of their fellow workers by naming the ringleaders of the slowdown. When you ask the cause of the slowdown, they tell you that the cost of living is increasing and that they need to make more money by working more overtime.

You believe that right now there is no justification for more overtime. In addition, you feel that, if you submit to this type of pressure, you will lose control over your group. The work of your group is of such a nature that individual output is difficult to measure.

1. What are the possible solutions to this problem?
2. What are some of the possible consequences of the above solution?
3. How can the situation be prevented from recurring?
4. What leadership characteristics do you need to develop? Explain.

CASE 6

The written rule of your company states that employees caught gambling are subject to immediate dismissal. However, various degrees of violation have been going on for years. There are baseball pools; some employees play poker or blackjack during the lunch period; some of the men are playing the horses and the numbers; there is even betting on production output.

You and the other supervisors know about these practices but do nothing about them because they do not seem to be detrimental. In fact, some of them build up the team spirit. However, you supervisors have been careful to avoid getting involved, because of the policy prohibiting gambling.

This morning your boss called you into his office to tell you that he received a phone call from the wife of one of your workers, complaining that her husband did not bring home any pay last week because he lost it all gambling in the plant, and she threatened to inform the police.

You ask him for the name of the employee, and he says that he will tell you later, after you have cleaned up the situation. He tells you that the company's written rule is your authority. You don't know how well he is acquainted with the situation; so you ask him how far you should go. He tells you all the way—all gambling must be stopped because he hears that it is getting into the hands of professionals in other plants. You ask him about clamping down on other departments, and he states that you are trying to pass the buck to him. He tells you to remember that it was the wife of one of your workers who called up.

1. What are your responsibilities in the above situation?
2. What are the responsibilities of the other supervisors in the situation?
3. What are the responsibilities of your boss in the situation?
4. How could it have been prevented from getting out of control?
5. How are you going to handle the situation?
6. Write up a realistic rule covering gambling.

CASE 7

The general foreman in the shop of a utility company has under him four foremen, each bossing a street work gang that installs and maintains the company's lines. He received a call from the company nurse asking if he would transfer a street mechanic from one of these crews to another. She said the mechanic had become a nervous wreck on his job, was sick to his stomach every morning before work, and had lost 25 pounds. The general foreman promised to give the man every possible break and said to send him over.

When the mechanic came in, the general foreman recognized him as the workman he had reprimanded severely the day before out on a street job. The mechanic now told him this story: His foreman was usually drunk on the job and insisted that the men drink with him. The gang loafed around in the mornings and then rushed through the work in the afternoons, doing it the quickest way and not according to company instructions. This is why the mechanic deserved the reprimand when the general foreman appeared suddenly at the job and found him doing it wrong. The mechanic said that his foreman and the gang didn't like him because he was afraid to drink on the job. Now he was afraid of what would happen to him if they found out he squealed.

1. What actions should the general foreman take?
2. Is there any way to detect drinking on a job performed away from the plant?
3. How can a general foreman check up on road gangs when they are spread over a wide area?
4. How active a part should the company nurse take in the affairs of employees who are having trouble with their foreman?

CASE 8

A large financial institution in a major metropolitan city had been experiencing considerable difficulty recruiting a sufficient supply of clerical employees for entrant jobs. The labor market for clerical help was extremely tight and in fact all employers in this city were experiencing similar difficulty.

The company inserted an advertisement in a large Sunday newspaper to recruit the needed clerical help. The advertisement requested people over 20 years of age to apply for the openings. The salary offered for inexperienced persons was $90 per week while experienced applicants were offered higher, but no specified salaries.

In one of the departments which utilized the same type of clerk the advertisement had specified, there was a young lady performing the job who had been with the company about one year at the time of the advertisement. She had started in the same position for $75 weekly and had just received her anniversary increase which brought her salary to $85.

She complained about the inequity involved and her supervisor requested a special increase for her which would bring her salary into line with that being offered to new employees. The supervisor mentioned further that she was a capable performer. His request was turned down by his superior who mentioned that she would have to wait for her next salary review which was six months away.

The clerk, when informed of the increase denial, told her boss that she would be better off if she resigned and then applied for the same job as an experienced worker.

1. If you were the supervisor how would you explain the salary inequity to this clerk?
2. Should the company advertise for clerks and mention salary?
3. How can a company cope with the need to pay for new employees and still keep present employees satisfied?
4. Should salary differentials be maintained in a rising labor market and if so, how should it be done?

CASE 9

You, a department head, have been insisting that your subordinates put a stop to the whistle jumping. It is really getting out of hand. Employees wanting to avoid the traffic jam in the parking lot line up at the time clock to wait for the quitting bell.

Today one of your new first-line supervisors saw three of his men standing at the clock at two minutes before five. He took their time cards from them and punched the cards out. The company rule about punching another's card is that the offense can be punished by dismissal.

1. How should this action of his be handled?
2. What are some ways to discourage whistle jumping?
3. What would be the wording of a good whistle-jumping rule?

CASE 10

Dave Carter, the manager of a branch office of a large commercial bank, was telling one of his fellow branch managers about a problem he recently had in his branch.

Dave said, "Approximately six months ago, my branch was involved in a misappropriation of funds. The persons involved were two tellers. One was a young girl functioning as a savings teller and the other a young man who was a paying and receiving teller. Both had been with the branch over a year and we considered them efficient employees. Customer complaints led to the discovery that both tellers were not returning cash overages to depositors, yet they would balance their accounts at the end of the day. On three separate occasions deposits with cash overages were planted on the two tellers and the money was not returned to the bank's auditing staff members who were playing the role of customers to check on the two tellers.

For about a month before the misappropriations occurred the two tellers were seen arriving and leaving the branch together and it became apparent that a romance had developed. I want to know at what stage of a romance do you step in and arrange for a transfer of one of the parties to prevent any undesirable conditions to arise?"

1. As Dave's fellow manager what would you tell him?
2. Was Dave correct in assuming that the romantic attachment was the sole cause of the misappropriation of funds?
3. Should a company try to discourage such romantic attachments and how can they do it?
4. Would a transfer of one of the employees in the above situation have removed the temptation to keep cash overages?

CASE 11

You are the head of a large department and you have several supervisors reporting to you. Recently you were confronted with a knotty problem. It seems that one of the supervisors had gotten into a loud and disagreeable argument with an employee. You called the supervisor to your office to hear his story.

The supervisor admitted losing his temper and shouting at the employee, but he believed it was justified. He had been observing the employee over the one year the man had been with the company. During this period the employee had been frequently late and his absentee rate was above average. In addition, the supervisor went on to say that the employee was a socializer on the job, frequently leaving his work to talk to other employees, and to use the telephone for personal calls. The supervisor then said that the proverbial last straw caused his outburst. The employee had come in late and after about an hour of work he made a telephone call which the supervisor had timed as lasting 14 minutes. The supervisor then started his tirade. The employee denied being on the telephone that long and the supervisor called him a liar and that started the vituperative exchange which ended when you called the supervisor to your office.

After listening to the supervisor, you asked him if he had disciplined the employee before since apparently he had a poor record. You also asked if the employee had been placed on probation or had been warned. The supervisor looked at you sheepishly, and seemed reluctant to answer. You pressed him for an answer and he finally blurted out that he was afraid to discipline the employee because he was a Negro. He stated that the impression he had from you and higher management was that

Negro employees should be given special treatment so that they would feel welcome and not discriminated against. He felt the company wanted to impress the public with its forward-looking employment practices and that they didn't want any trouble with the Negro community. As a result, he was lax in discipline and he had kept a hands-off approach with all Negro employees until his outburst. He said he couldn't stand it anymore and the 14-minute telephone call caused him to lose his temper.

1. What would you now tell the supervisor?
2. Should minority group employees be given any special attention by management?
3. Could the company have done anything to offset the misunderstanding that the supervisor apparently had about the treatment of Negro employees?
4. To what extent did the lack of discipline encourage the Negro employee to accept his behavior as satisfactory?
5. What can a company do to help supervisors handle minority group employees in view of the tensions which exist in our society among various racial and ethnic groups?

CASE 12

The function of one of the sections under your jurisdiction is to receive and determine the disposition of expensive used equipment that is sent to the company in trade-ins on more modern equipment. The shipments may consist of whole units or only subassemblies. The men in the section have to be able to identify the items and determine whether they should be repaired or junked.

Jack Black has been in charge of this section since its beginning, three years ago. He knows his business and is an excellent supervisor. He trains his men well, and they respect his knowledge and leadership. There is evidence that he may be an alcoholic, but, since he runs his section so well, you have pretended not to notice this failing.

One day recently he was intoxicated on the job. You called him in and notified him of the company policy that intoxication on the job is grounds for dismissal. He said that he could do the job in spite of his drinking and claimed that, because of his heavy work load and responsibilities, he needed to drink to relax. You told him again about the policy, sent him home, and told him to report for work the next day. You said also that this incident would be ignored.

Black did not report for work again for almost a week, and when he did come back, he said that he had been ill.

During his absence, you kept a close check on his section. In going over the work with his assistant and the men in his section, you realized that Black was the backbone of the group. This section was not functioning well without him, even though the assistant was good. The assistant volunteered the information that Jack Black was the best supervisor in the plant, even when he was drunk.

Upon Black's return, you reprimanded him, reminded him of his responsibilities and of how much depended upon him. You told him how much his work was appreciated by top management.

Everything went smoothly for two weeks; then Black did not show up for work, nor did he report his absence by phone, as is required. You sent an investigator to his home, but he was not there. His wife said that he had left for work at the regular time, although he had been drunk the night before. She appeared to be a very fine, intelligent woman. The investigator talked to her about Black's ability and about his drinking. She said she was afraid his case was hopeless and that she was disgusted with his habitual drinking.

She said that on his previous job his work was so outstanding that the boss called for him every morning in order to be sure he would be on the job and gave him a weekly bonus for behaving himself. Finally, though, the boss had to fire him because of the time lost through drunkenness.

You don't want to fire Black. He is a valuable man, and you want to save him.

1. What are some of the ways of handling this type of problem?
2. How effective are they?

CASE 13

The company employs a number of female employees to perform the intricate wiring and soldering tasks necessary in the assembly of complex control panels. It was found that women could generally perform this type of work better than men. Beverly was one of the first women hired by the company and she came with considerable work experience in similar jobs at other companies in the area. According to the production manager she proved to be an excellent worker, performing her assigned tasks with speed and efficiency. He felt she set an excellent work example for the other female workers who were hired to perform the same kind of work. Difficulty started when the general manager noticed that Beverly wore particularly tight, form-fitting slacks. He mentioned this to the production manager since he believed this type of apparel was not proper and would cause distraction among the male employees. The production manager replied that he hadn't noticed any distraction taking place, but that he would speak to Beverly about her apparel. When he did, she became quite adamant stating that she felt she could wear anything she desired unless the company furnished a uniform. She also mentioned that she could get a similar position in a variety of other plants in the vicinity and that none of her previous employers found any fault with her clothing. The production manager let the matter drop because she was an excellent worker and she would be difficult to replace in the tight labor market which existed. He did wonder, however, what he was going to tell the general manager.

1. Does a company have any right to specify what an employee will wear on the job?
2. Should the general manager have gotten involved in this matter?
3. Did the production manager handle the problem effectively?
4. What can he tell the general manager in view of the result of his conversation with the girl and his own opinions?
5. What would you do if confronted with Beverly's reaction?

CASE 14

The fire chief has reported one of your men, Jim Smith, for violation of the no-smoking regulation. Your boss passes the report on to you and recommends a three-day suspension—which is the penalty for violating this regulation.

This is the first time Smith has broken any of the rules. Upon investigating, you find that he was caught with a lighted cigaret just outside of the smoking zone. You bring this information to the attention of your boss. Because his wife recently made him give up smoking, he wants an example made of Smith and wants all employees lectured on the hazards of fire. When you inform Smith of the action taken, he points out to you the following violations going on at that moment:

1. Joe Jenkins,   working without gloves.
2. Plug Jones,   spitting on the floor.
3. Speedy Malone,   running downstairs.
4. Forklift Jackson, excessive speed.

Also 10 other men violating regulations, all habitual offenders. He asks how it could be fair to suspend him.

1. How can you justify your action to Smith?
2. What should you do about the other violations?
3. What is wrong with your boss's attitude?
4. How should you go about building respect for rules after there has been continuous and widespread violation of them?

CASE 15

J. Jones has been a first-level supervisor for the last 20 years. He is on a salary, does not have to punch the time clock as do his assistants and the rank and file. Jones has fallen into the habit of coming in 10 or 15 minutes late each day. This is a bad example to the other supervisors (who all get there on time); also it annoys his assistants and the rank and file who claim Jones thinks he is a big shot.

You, the assistant superintendent, have spoken to Jones several times about the poor example he is setting. He states that his assistants see that everyone in the section starts to work on time—that most of the other sections don't get started until 10 or 15 minutes later. He further argues that he puts in overtime whenever necessary, and without receiving extra compensation.

His coming in late is not sufficient reason to demote him because he has been with the company so many years. He is not interested in further advancement.

1. Evaluate Jones's arguments.
2. Should tardiness among supervisors who put in an hour or so overtime each day be tolerated? Why? Why not?
3. How should Jones be handled?

CASE 16

One of the employees is a bright, willing, conscientious, well-educated young woman. She works hard, gets along very well with people, and would possibly make a good supervisor, but she just can't seem to get to work on time. She runs all the way from the bus stop and either just makes it or just misses it by a couple of minutes. She doesn't overstay her coffee breaks or lunch periods and she is willing to stay after hours to finish up work or handle rush jobs.

In the appraisal interview she told the supervisor that she has never been able to be punctual or get things done on time. She can't estimate how much time things take or what time it is. She is always being surprised and shocked by how late it has gotten. In order to improve she makes lists of things she has to do and checks them off. She checks and rechecks the setting of her alarm clock and the position of the "on" button. She keeps a little kitchen timer in the bathroom so she won't spend too much time getting dressed in the morning. But still things go wrong. Something breaks or she can't find her keys or the office manual she took home to study. Mornings are just one emergency after another. If she absolutely has to be somewhere at a certain time, the worry of it keeps her from concentrating on what she is doing. If the company makes a big issue out of promptness, the worry about being late keeps waking her up during the night.

1. Is punctuality a part of personality?
2. Is judgment of time something that people have or don't have, like dexterity, perfect pitch, or artistic ability?
3. Would a system of rewards for promptness get her to work on time?

4. Would a system of penalties for tardiness get her to work on time?
5. Can the supervisor do anything to get her to work on time?
6. Should she be considered for a supervisory job?

CASE 17

You are in charge of production in a company making a mass-produced product. Orders are increasing, and labor in the community is scarce.

Yesterday one of your production-line foremen came to you about Joe Brown, an employee on the line. Joe is in his early twenties and is a satisfactory worker. Recently, however, his tardiness has skyrocketed: he reports for work from 5 to 50 minutes late. As a result, the line is slowed down and output suffers.

Joe's excuse is that he has moved to the next town. He depends on public transportation, and the buses do not run on a dependable schedule. The foreman feels that Joe could get to work on time if he tried hard enough, and he quotes statistics to show that tardiness is highest in young men. On this theory, he has given Joe several reprimands. Lately, Joe has been absent several times without any plausible excuse, which serves to strengthen the foreman's suspicions.

1. Do you feel that Joe's tardiness is avoidable or unavoidable?
2. Assuming it to be unavoidable, what measures should you take to protect your production output?
3. What steps might be taken to correct Joe's tardiness and absenteeism?
4. What should your interests be in this matter?

CASE 18

You are a supervisor of a section and have two stenographers assigned to you. One of your stenographers is 10 to 15 minutes late each morning and usually takes from 10 to 15 minutes longer than the allotted time for lunch. You call this to her attention, and she tells you that the practice is common in the rest of the department and she doesn't know why she should do differently. Your investigation confirms her statement.

1. Is she justified in her attitude?
2. How should you go about correcting her?
3. What arguments against tardiness can you give your fellow supervisors?
4. If you cannot get action from your fellow supervisors, should you see your chief? What should you say to him?

CASE 19

One of your best machine operators returned from an excused absence and—according to the new rule—had to retrieve his time card from the personnel department before he could report to his own department.

His report of what happened was this: The young girl in the personnel department paid no attention to him but continued a personal chat on the telephone. After 10 minutes of waiting for his card, he told her to shut off the yak and get to work so that he could get to work. The girl's version was that he shouted at her in an insulting manner and swore at her.

You, the supervisor, were called to the scene where he and the girl were glaring at one another and her boss was standing by. You tried to smooth things over by asking the operator to apologize. He said it was no more his fault than hers; he would trade apologies with her. She refused.

Having reached an impasse there, you told him to go home and think it over and he could come back to work when he got ready to apologize. He walked out. Now a week has gone by and you have heard nothing from him and you need him. Your boss tells you that you handled the situation improperly and that the man is going to be discharged for being absent without leave. The company is tightening up on enforcement of penalties for unexcused absences and is now in the process of getting rid of a number of undesirables who took a week off to go hunting even though the company had announced, as usual, that no hunting absences would be excused. There will probably be grievances carried to arbitration, and the company is not going to risk any inconsistency.

1. Were you within your rights in insisting that the man apologize as a condition of returning to work?
2. How should you have handled the whole incident?
3. If he files a grievance and is restored to his job, what attitude should you take about the incident?

CASE 20

You are in charge of a department which employs both men and women. The jobs that the women can do are limited by the state labor code, whereas the men have to do any job that is assigned to them. There is a strong feeling of resentment among the men, with the result that they are slowing down and refusing to help the women. The department output is falling off. You are not responsible for employing the women, but you are informed by top management that it is necessary to retain them.

1. Should there be "equal pay for equal work"?
2. Would you appeal to the men on a chivalry basis?
3. How would you handle the situation?
4. Would you turn the matter over to your chief?
5. Would you talk to the women? What would you say to them?

CASE 21

You are the head of a production department. One of your foremen is getting another job. He says he has to get out of this one because he is getting an ulcer from dealing with the union steward. You would like to be rid of the steward but there are not sufficient grounds to discharge him. He is a highly competent worker and he is careful to stay within the law. But he files three times as many grievances as any other steward. He challenges every small thing the foreman does. He keeps people stirred up all the time. He has been steward for two years.

You are considering the idea of promoting him to the job of foreman and then firing him because he would be out from under the protection of the bargaining unit. Your contract with the union has no provision for protecting the seniority of a man promoted out of the ranks; so he wouldn't be able to bump back into his old job.

1. What might be some of the consequences of this plan?
2. Would some other course of action take care of the problem?

CASE 22

You are the supervisor in charge of the procurement section of a local company. You supervise 10 buyers. Each buyer has a stenographer who takes dictation, types letters, types purchase orders, and so forth. You have good teamwork among all members of your section, and morale is high.

Recently the company inaugurated a coffee break and hired a woman to make and distribute the coffee twice daily to the office personnel. The woman is Mrs. Adams, a widow, a very nice-looking gentlewoman in her early sixties. She puts in an eight-hour day. Today Carolyn, who has been with your group for quite some time and is one of the better stenographers, came to your office quite upset and angry. She told you that she heard that the coffee woman gets a higher hourly rate than she does and it isn't fair; anyone can make coffee and wash the cups, but education and experience are necessary for a stenographer. You check with personnel and you find that Mrs. Adams is getting more pay than Carolyn; you also hear that Mrs. Adams is a long-time friend of the boss's family.

1. What should you tell Carolyn, the stenographer?
2. What is the procedure for handling this situation?
3. What are some possible solutions?
4. How could the situation have been prevented?
5. Show how a job evaluation program could have prevented the situation from arising.

CASE 23

An employee, Sally Smith, is a widow and works to support herself and her 12-year-old son John. During the year she has been absent from work four times for periods of from two to five days each because John was home sick from school. He gets severe colds. She can't find anybody to come into her home on short notice to take care of him when he becomes ill. Now John has the flu, and Sally has been absent for more than a week taking care of him. Yesterday her boss, Bill Black, told one of her co-workers, Lilly Lee, in confidence that Sally is absent too much and he is going to get rid of her. Lilly promptly relayed the message to Sally, asking her not to repeat it because if Black heard it back, then Lilly would be in trouble. Black has the reputation among his subordinates of having a knack for working employees out of a job if they displease him. He uses various tricks—hounding them by close supervision, giving them menial work or sometimes no work, or overloading them with work until they quit or get a transfer out of his department.

Sally feels that she is on Black's list and does not know which way to turn. If she reports to personnel what Black said to Lilly, then Lilly will get into trouble. If she goes over Black's head and reports the situation to his boss, Mr. White, the results won't be any better. On other occasions when employees went to Mr. White, he called in Mr. Black but it only delayed the execution temporarily. Sally likes her job and needs it.

What should Sally do? Justify your answer.

CASE 24

A packing plant (or cannery) that is semiseasonal employs about 25 women and 85 men most of the year. At the peak of the season there may be three times that many union-member employees. For 25 years this plant was supervised by the same superintendent, foreman, and forelady. They operated with very tight reins and showed a great deal of favoritism to certain plant employees. When the union organized the plant 15 years ago these three bosses were very definite in showing the employees that they did not like the union and would not cooperate with it in solving plant personnel problems. The superintendent would take the word of his foreman and forelady as Gospel and he made all his decisions in his office on the basis of their say-so; the union was "always wrong." The forelady (Lola Locurto) became tyrannical. So many grievances arose that the personnel director from the main office of the company used to have to meet regularly with the union president to try to settle them.

When the superintendent was close to retirement age, top management decided to break up this regime. The foreman was transferred to another plant and a rank-and-file worker promoted to be foreman. A new man, Bob Brown, was brought in as assistant to the superintendent, and 18 months later was promoted to be superintendent when the old man retired. The two new men got along very well together and with the union steward, with the result that grievances of the male employees dropped to a minimum.

The old-line forelady was very valuable to the new superintendent because she knew the operations and was capable in organizing her crews of women workers. She cooperated with the new superintendent and he tried to help her overcome her faults. She has improved but at times still shows favoritism; she still has her cliques around her. She sometimes forgets herself and shouts at the women and is not very diplomatic. The union stewardess has never liked her and continues to make grievances out of little things. The new superintendent makes it a practice to have the forelady come in whenever the union stewardess has asked to see him. Although she has asked for private meetings, he has refused—telling her that the women will have to learn to cooperate, that they both have their faults, that the forelady is very competent and that he is helping her improve her relations with the women. He always assures the stewardess that he knows there are two sides to every story and that he always investigates both sides before he makes a decision. The union stewardess continues to run to the superintendent with complaints against the forelady.

The superintendent has never considered moving or transferring the forelady, because when he was the assistant the female union employees let him know that they did not like the forelady and were out to get her. The superintendent feels that if he were to transfer or discharge the forelady he would be losing a very helpful employee and that the union would consider it "their victory."

1. What should top management have done when the union first entered the plant?
2. What should the new superintendent have done when he first took over?
3. Should the new superintendent have discharged the forelady or had her transferred to another plant?
4. What can the superintendent do now to improve relations between the forelady and the stewardess?
5. How can the superintendent help the forelady to overcome some of her old habits?
6. How can relations between supervisors and union stewards be improved? List and explain.

CASE 25

You are the department head of a large department and you have six supervisors reporting to you. Recently one of them retired and you replaced him with a young, ambitious girl who had been with the firm for five years. She had evidenced leadership ability and she had a good understanding of the work of her unit as well as the department as a whole. Things have been going well and you have been congratulating yourself on your wise choice for promotion. You had instructed her to introduce the new methods and procedures developed by the systems and procedures group and it seemed as if they were working out smoothly.

Just as you were completing your self-satisfied analysis of the situation, the new supervisor walked into your office with a problem. She had introduced the new work methods and procedures carefully explaining and demonstrating them and had met with success with all of her employees, except one. This girl had been with the company almost as long as the new supervisor. When the supervisor asked her why she wasn't going along with the new methods, she replied that her methods were as good and that she got the work out and that was all that mattered.

The supervisor felt her authority was being undermined by the uncooperative employee and she wanted to fire her. Before she took action, she came to you for advice.

1. Would you allow the supervisor to fire the uncooperative employee? Why? Why not?
2. Should the supervisor have done anything before she came for advice?
3. What kind of advice can you give her?
4. What can be done about such an uncooperative employee?

CASE 26

Recently you were advanced to the position of supervisor. You wondered at the time why Jim Jones, a fellow worker, did not get the job instead of you. Jones's work was the best in the section. He is in his early sixties, and, before coming with the company five years ago, he had run his own shop until he was forced out of business by a dishonest partner. When he had his own shop, he supervised twice the number of men you now supervise.

Since you became supervisor, his work is falling off, and he is bitter about being passed over. You ask your boss why Jones didn't get the job, and he says the only reason was Jones's advanced age.

1. Is it your responsibility or your boss's responsibility to tell Jones why he was not promoted?
2. What are the advantages and disadvantages of having a man in his sixties as a supervisor?
3. How are you going to gain Jim Jones's cooperation?

CASE 27

The foreman in a manufacturing company saw two of his men scuffling near their machines just before they resumed work after lunch. They were evidently just having fun, but it was dangerous and against the rules, and this was their second offense. The penalty for the first offense is a warning, and for the second offense a three-day layoff. Since the foreman did not have the authority to give a three-day suspension, he bawled them both out, pointed out the hazards of horseplay around machinery, and told them they could expect to be suspended for it, since they had been warned before.

It was a busy afternoon and he didn't get a chance to talk to his boss about it until almost quitting time. The boss said to suspend them both for three days and signed the forms. Before the foreman had time to notify the two offenders, the shift ended and they left for home.

In the morning though, he was waiting for them with the suspension slips and told them that they were both laid off for three days beginning at once. They asked for four hours reporting pay since they had made the trip expecting to work. They insisted that the union agreement guarantees four hours reporting pay if they report to work and the company hasn't notified them in advance that they won't be working.

1. Do they have a legitimate claim?
2. Do they get paid if it is their own fault that they are not going to be working?
3. What should the foreman do about it now?

CASE 28

You are the manager of a branch of a large commercial bank. Your assistant manager is a 53-year-old woman who has been with the bank 30 years, all of them in this branch. She is familiar with every job, having done each one in her rise to assistant manager. Over the years her performance has been excellent.

In the last few years changes in the operating patterns of the branch have been necessitated by ethnic, racial, and economic changes in the neighborhood in which the branch is located. Because of these changes you now feel that this woman is no longer appropriately assigned. There have been several recent touchy situations where you have had to take over customer interviews that had been started by the assistant manager. These developed mainly because of lack of understanding between the assistant manager and the customers. She has considerable difficulty communicating with customers and seems to treat them in a patronizing disdainful manner. This is not the case, however, with those old customers whom she knows very well and with whom she has been doing business for years.

You have mixed feelings about the situation as it has developed. In one sense, you would prefer not to lose her because she is an excellent worker, knows many customers personally, and has served in the branch for her entire career. On the other hand, she cannot get along with the newer customers and these are increasing in number, while those she can get along with are decreasing.

You have made no formal transfer request for her, but in several informal conversations with your superior you have gotten the impression that he would prefer to maintain the status quo. The assistant manager has told you that she too has informally sounded out your superior about a transfer to no avail.

1. Should you make a formal request for transfer for this employee?
2. If you do, what reasons will you give?
3. Why do you think your superior has not acted on your informal discussions with him?
4. If this employee cannot adjust to the new customers in your branch, can she adjust to a different branch after having been in yours for 30 years?
5. If the employee stays at your branch, what can you do about her apparent inability to relate to the newer customers?

CASE 29

Recently a worker, Joe Blue, submitted a written grievance stating that he is being discriminated against because of his race. He states that Jim Smith (one of your assistants) prevented him from advancing to a supervisory position; he names several men less qualified technically who were promoted over him; he mentions that one other member of his race in the group was also passed over; and he lists dates on which he claims Smith told him to his face that he did not like him.

You call Smith into your office and show him the grievance. He tells you that Blue is very active in leading minority group movements and can twist anything into a race issue. Smith admits that he dislikes Blue and cannot disguise it. He says that Blue is superior technically to the rest of the group but has no leadership ability except aggressiveness in relation to the race issue. Smith justifies his position by saying that he gets along well with the other member of the minority race—a slow and contented individual.

You do not want to have any discrimination issue in your organization, nor do you want to shift either Blue or Smith out of their present positions.

1. Evaluate the case as presented by Blue in the grievance.
2. Evaluate the case as presented by Smith, the assistant.
3. How are you going to investigate the case in order to get a clearer picture?
4. What kind of written answer are you going to give?
5. What is the procedure for handling a written grievance?

CASE 30

Jack Carlson came back from a meeting with the budget committee and proudly announced to his secretary that he was able to obtain for her one of the new electric typewriters the company was buying. It took much haggling but the fact that Ginny's typewriter was over 20 years old clinched Jack's argument.

Ginny Morton had been with the company somewhat longer than her typewriter and she had worked for Jack Carlson for the past 10 years. They had an easy-going relationship so Jack was quite taken aback by Ginny's frosty behavior after his announcement. "It was no easy job getting you that new electric," he said. "Don't you like my typing?" she replied. "But its got nothing to do with your typing—of course, you're an excellent typist," Jack said. "In fact the new typewriter will make your job easier and you'll be able to make more carbons." "I happen to prefer my typewriter to any of those new machines—they only break down frequently," Ginny said. Jack was amazed at Ginny's reaction particularly since he was proud of the effort and argument which had enabled him to obtain the new typewriter for his secretary. He ended the discussion by telling Ginny that the electric typewriter was coming and she might as well get used to it.

1. Indicate the reasons for Ginny's reaction to the new electric typewriter.
2. Did Jack handle the situation properly?
3. What can be done to create understanding when new equipment is introduced?

FOLLOWING UP ON THE JOB

Discipline

1. Do all your workers understand the rules of conduct?
2. Do you refresh their memories often enough?
3. Do your workers accept the rules of conduct voluntarily or out of fear of penalties?

4. Do you have enough facts and a tentative plan of action before you reprimand?
5. Do you seek additional facts during the disciplinary interview?
6. Do you always give the employee a chance to tell his side of the story?
7. Do you always show the employee how to correct his behavior?
8. Do you always fit the penalty to both the violation and the violator?
9. Do you always follow up to see if the penalty had constructive results?
10. When your disciplining backfires, do you try to find out why?
11. Do you ever discharge a worker while you are angry?

Discipline under a union contract

1. Do you know the provisions of the contract?
2. Do you know how arbitrators have decided disputes over penalties?
3. Do you know the company's policy on discipline?
4. Are you consistent in enforcing rules?
5. Do you crack down suddenly on offenses previously condoned?
6. Do you make complete records of warnings?
7. When it is necessary to discipline or discharge, do you have evidence that is admissible, and do you follow the proper procedures?

Tardiness and absenteeism

1. Do you pay enough attention to tardiness and absenteeism?
2. Do your employees realize the full cost of tardiness and absenteeism?
3. Do you analyze tardiness and absenteeism records?
4. Do you use tardiness and absenteeism investigations as a means of uncovering undesirable conditions in your section?
5. When tardiness and absenteeism have their origin in home problems, do you try to help?
6. Do you try to make your section a pleasant place in which to work?
7. Do you set a good example by being prompt and on the job every day?

Grievances

1. Do you abide by the contract in distributing overtime, handling layoffs, transfers, promotions?
2. Do you study the settlements negotiated in the grievance machinery?
3. Do you study the decisions made by arbitrators?
4. Do you consider the effects of your grievance handling on other areas in the company?
5. Do you avoid provoking grievances?

Uncovering gripes
1. Do you recognize the signs of a gripe?
2. Do you investigate tardiness and absenteeism with the idea of uncovering gripes?
3. When quantity and quality of output are off, do you look for gripes?
4. Do your subordinates avoid expressing their gripes to you?
5. Do your subordinates present their gripes to you in a friendly manner? In a belligerent manner?
6. When you are investigating gripes, are your other employees willing to give you good information?
7. Do your subordinates feel that you give them a square deal?
8. Do you ignore gripes in the hope that they will disappear?
9. Do you avoid settling gripes by passing them on to your boss? To the personnel department?
10. Do you try to solve gripes and thus prevent them from becoming written grievances?

Handling gripes
1. Do you gather information from as many sources as possible?
2. Do you formulate solutions in terms of policies and principles?
3. Do you follow up the effectiveness of the solution?
4. Is the manner in which you settle gripes bringing management and the worker closer together?

Handling resistance to change
1. Do you try to understand the reasons why people resist changes?
2. Do you analyze changes to find out what fears and status anxieties they would arouse?
3. Do you introduce changes in a way that gains acceptance of them and speeds relearning of the changed job?

16 Motivation and morale

Individual needs. Motivation problems. Personal problems of employees. Tensions on the job. What people want from their jobs. Motivation and morale. Determinants of morale. Morale and productivity. Today's employee. The job as a factor in promoting high morale. Teammates as a factor in promoting high morale. The supervisor as a factor in promoting high morale. The company as a factor in promoting high morale. Communication as a factor in promoting high morale. Summary.

There have been several statements in this book which relate to this chapter. Probably the most important is the discussion on teamwork in management in Chapter 6. The creation of an effective group working toward organizational objectives is, after all, a very basic function of the manager. Any experienced manager knows that this is most likely his principal responsibility and most difficult task.

Recognition of the uniqueness of individuals inevitably leads to the conclusion that there will be some goal conflict between those of the individual and those of the organization. It logically follows that those individuals whose personal goals are most related to those of the organization he works for have a greater chance for success. Going a step further, he is more highly motivated by his work and the environment in which he performs it. His morale is usually high and his attitudes about the organization are overwhelmingly positive.

This chapter concerns itself with motivation and morale as they relate to individual and organizational well-being.

Individual needs

There is no doubt that we are a technological society. Much attention is given to the production miracles performed by the factories in this country. The space program leading to the moon landing is a case in point. Preventive maintenance on equipment is carried far more effectively in our factories than it is on the human beings who work in them. As individuals we tend to take better care of our automobiles and tele-

620

vision sets than we do of ourselves. Only recently have we begun to turn our attention to some of the human problems caused by technology, such as air and water pollution, noise, urban blight, and improper utilization of resources.

When a machine does not perform efficiently we look for the cause and fix it. Similar malfunctioning in human beings is more difficult to isolate and repair. Because of this there is a tendency to either minimize or turn away from human problems. In some cases, there are attempts to seek simple solutions to the human problems. Perhaps the simplest solution for the handling of problem employees is to fire them. The effective supervisor, however, seeks greater understanding of his fellow employees.

Finding out what makes humans "tick" has occupied people for many years. Probably the most significant findings to come out of Mayo's Hawthorne experiments is that human beings are unpredictable and they do not always do what is expected of them. The attention given to the Hawthorne studies down to the present day is our indication of how little is known about human behavior. In fact many writers believe that the human relations movement started with Mayo's work in the late 1920's.

Psychologists have attempted to define human needs in a variety of ways. To understand motivation and employee attitude, it is desirable to be acquainted with the major theories relating to human needs.

The hierarchy of human needs. Psychologist A. H. Maslow has developed a theory based on the assumption that people exert effort to satisfy their needs and that once these needs are satisfied, they no longer are motivated toward further effort. The key, of course, is related to timing. When do people decide that their needs are satisfied? Maslow suggests that there is a hierarchy of human needs and that once a lower level of need is satisfied, the individual can only be motivated by a desire to satisfy the next level of need in the hierarchy. Maslow describes his need hierarchy as follows:[1]

1. *Physiological needs.* Essentially these are concerned with the needs necessary for survival such as food, clothing, and shelter. For most people in our society, these needs are relatively well satisfied. The high level of employment with its obvious implications of reasonable material well-being tend to minimize the motivating effect of need fulfillment on this level.
2. *The safety needs.* When physiological needs are reasonably gratified, the individual wants to protect this attainment. He then becomes concerned with such things as pension plans, job security,

---

[1] A. H. Maslow, *Motivation and Personality* (New York: Harper & Row, Publishers, 1954), material paraphrased from chap. 5, pp. 80–106.

personal safety, workmen's compensation, and other related things which would minimize future deprivation and economic-social security. In this sense, safety needs are related to physiological needs with the emphasis on future fulfillment of survival needs.

3. *Belonging and social activity needs.* Once the first two levels of needs are fairly well satisfied, man turns his attention to the need for friendship, association, love, and social activity. He joins clubs, athletic teams, other social groups, and his affiliation with a desirable work group within a larger acceptable organization becomes more critical to him. Off the job this level of need is fulfilled by marriage, family relations, and neighborhood social activity. Maslow calls this level of need one of the higher needs. The first two levels are finite and once fulfilled have little impact on the motivation of effort. The higher level needs tend to be infinite and can continue as motivators since their level of fulfillment is hard to define in concrete terms.

4. *Esteem and status needs.* People want to have a stable, firmly based, high evaluation of themselves. They must feel that they are worthy and that they are doing worthy things. There is a desire for prestige and good reputation, for achievement and competence. Since the first three levels of needs are usually partly satisfied in our society, this need becomes very important as a motivator for the individual. In the workplace he wants recognition, approval, and appreciation for his efforts. This relates not only to the type of work he performs, but his relationships with his superiors and his fellow employees. Satisfaction of this need leads to feelings of self-confidence, personal worth, capability, adequacy, usefulness in the world, self-respect, and a sense of purpose. The most stable self-esteem is based on deserved respect from others.

5. *Self-actualization, self-fulfillment, and self-realization needs.* The needs on this level are the capstone to all of the other levels of needs. The needs on this level are related to the realization of the individual's potential. To fulfill this need he seeks work that is challenging and difficult. He wants opportunities for self-development and self-expression. The desire for creativity and freedom to express this creativity are very important on this level of the need hierarchy. Inner satisfaction is the goal sought by the person as a motivator on this level. Essentially fulfillment on this level means becoming everything that one is capable of becoming.

Some conclusions become apparent from an analysis of Maslow's need hierarchy. Needs have a priority for the individual and once needs on one level are at least partially satisfied, he seeks fulfillment on the next level. The two lower levels of needs are more or less universal but their satisfaction may have different intensities with each person. One person may need more food than another. Shelter needs may be satisfied with a tent or a substantial private home. One could argue that the expensive home does more than satisfy shelter needs and could be classified as filling status or self-esteem needs. This is probably true of other low-level needs as well.

The lower level needs are largely fulfilled by economic efforts. The individual works for enough money to exchange for the food, clothing, and shelter he believes necessary. As he becomes motivated by higher level needs, social effort and behavior become entwined with economic effort. Managers who believe that people are solely motivated by money still believe in the "economic man" concept which is based on the notion that all of man's desires can be met with economic motivators. This idea only applies to the first two levels in Maslow's hierarchy. Managers who fail to recognize this will more than likely have difficulty with some of their employees. The implications of the higher levels in the need hierarchy are important to the supervisor since he can contribute significantly to the satisfaction of needs on these levels. While the listing of needs may seem to be an oversimplification of the complex behavior of human beings, there is little doubt that considerable satisfaction is derived from recognition, status, and the opportunity to develop one's capabilities to the fullest extent possible. The work environment including supervisory input which allows the employee to achieve fulfillment of higher level needs is usually the most satisfying to that employee.

Supportive-participative management style as a motivator. Using Maslow's basic idea of a need hierarchy and assuming that lower level needs are satisfied to a great extent, then the higher level needs loom as most important. Argyris and Likert[2] are two well-known believers of this idea. Essentially, they feel that the nature of the managerial and organizational environment contribute significantly to the satisfaction of higher level needs. In particular, their assumptions are built on relationships of the individual to the organization and to its management. Where the employee is part of a group which can participate in such managerial functions as goal setting and decision making, the chances for self-realization become much greater. The work takes on more meaning for the employee and he has a greater feeling of belonging and identification with the work group and the organization as a whole. By being able to participate in decisions which affect his life, he can exercise creativity, have it recognized, and gain self-actualization. Organizations which do not practice this style of management, therefore, create an environment which minimizes the chance for self-actualization.

---

[2] For a thorough treatment, see Chris Argyris, *Integrating the Individual and the Organization* (New York: John Wiley & Sons, Inc. 1964); and Rensis Likert, *The Human Organization* (New York: McGraw-Hill Book Co., 1967).

The motivation-hygiene theory. Frederick Herzberg and his colleagues[3] conducted studies of 200 or so engineers and accountants to determine what factors made them feel exceptionally happy and exceptionally unhappy about their jobs. Out of this study evolved the motivation-hygiene theory which, put simply, indicates that there is a duality about the person's feelings about his job. Further, these feelings were not expressed as opposites of each other. In other words, lack of job dissatisfaction did not mean job satisfaction. Conversely, the opposite of job satisfaction was not job dissatisfaction, but rather no job satisfaction. Two essential findings came out of the studies. Factors which produced job satisfaction were separate and distinct from the factors which led to the job dissatisfaction. Employees named different types of conditions for positive and negative feelings. For example, if opportunity for advancement was given as a cause of positive feelings, the lack of such opportunity was rarely given as a cause for negative feelings about the job. Instead some other reason was given such as poor administration or inadequate company policies.

Herzberg's original studies included the following 16 factors.

1. Achievement.	10. Interpersonal relations—
2. Recognition.	superior.
3. Work itself.	11. Interpersonal relations—peers.
4. Responsibility.	12. Supervision—technical.
5. Advancement.	13. Company policy and
6. Salary.	administration.
7. Possibility of growth.	14. Working conditions.
8. Interpersonal relations—	15. Personal life.
subordinate.	16. Job security.
9. Status.	

It should be noted that six of these are motivational factors. They are factors 1, 2, 3, 4, 5, and 7 on the preceding list. All of the rest are maintenance factors. Motivational factors relate directly to the job and the employee's performance and are therefore job-centered. The rest are related to environment. Herzberg found that the job-centered factors were more significant motivators than the maintenance factors. Interestingly enough is the fact that most fringe benefit programs are based on maintenance factors. The traditional approach to motivation includes environmental aspects rather than the job-centered ones. This is partly based on the idea that management can better implement environmental

---

[3] For a complete description of the studies and philosophy behind them, see F. Herzberg, B. Mausner, and B. B. Snyderman, *The Motivation to Work* (2d ed.; New York: John Wiley & Sons, Inc., 1959); and F. Herzberg, *Work and the Nature of Man* (Cleveland, Ohio: The World Publishing Co., 1966).

factors than they can job-centered factors. The motivational factors require changes in leadership style on the part of supervisors, particularly if they are following autocratic-paternalistic methods. This naturally is more difficult to accomplish and that is the principal reason for managerial emphasis on maintenance factors for motivation of employees.

Keith Davis compares Maslow's theories to those of Herzberg as follows:

Maslow centers on human needs of the psychological person at work or anywhere else. Herzberg focuses on that same person in terms of how job conditions affect his basic needs. What the Herzberg motivation-maintenance model seems to say in general is that managerial and professional (and to some extent white-collar) workers have reached a stage of socioeconomic progress in modern society such that the two higher-order need levels are now primarily the motivating ones. The three lower-order need levels are now minimally achieved so that they are no longer strong, driving forces to an employee. Rather, they are merely necessary for his *maintenance* at his current level of progress.[4]

Motivation problems

Many of management's problems with motivation of employees are based on their trying to induce the employee to be more productive by offering him rewards to be enjoyed off the job, rather than on it. Relatively few companies try to make actual job performance a rewarding experience. On the "pay for pain" basis high salaries enable the employee to have a hobby into which he can pour the creative energies and enthusiasm not called for on his job. The routine job offers very few of these intangible rewards. An employee comes home from his job and goes to work on some project of his own that he enjoys and on which he does the planning and makes the decisions. If some of this enthusiasm could be harnessed to the job there could be a considerable increase in productivity and job satisfaction.

 There are some situations in which an employee is blocked or frustrated in all his attempts to get satisfaction from his job. Frustration of needs may lead employees to aggression expressed in hostility, conflict, grievances, spoilage, slowdowns, destruction of property, insubordination, or similar undesirable behavior. Or a frustrated person, instead of striking back in hostility, may simply withdraw in spirit from the job. He may refuse to use his initiative or participate in the work situation beyond just performing what is required of him. He may become indolent, passive, unwilling to accept responsibility, and unreasonable in his demands for wages and other economic benefits.

---

[4] Keith Davis, *Human Relations at Work, The Dynamics of Organizational Behavior* (3d ed.; New York: McGraw-Hill Book Co., 1967), p. 36.

The money motive. The money motive is not a simple one to diagnose. A few people are "economic men" and all their lives the money motive is uppermost. For them, money seems to serve as a substitute for love or emotional security.

In other people the money motive is something that changes with the changing of their circumstances. Young people starting out with high hopes and expectations have strong money motives because they need so many things. After they have achieved the standard of living to which they aspire, money may take on a more symbolic meaning. It may be thought of less for its purchasing power and more as a measure of personal worth. The money motive may drop in importance but it can rise in a hurry if someone else gets a raise.

At the low end of the financial and social scale, among people who live from hand to mouth, money and savings don't represent security. Security lies in the steady job. Money is something to be enjoyed at the moment because not enough of it could be accumulated to make any real improvement. A person has to see some solid possibility of bettering his situation before he is ready to respond to the incentive of money.[5]

Individual differences. Any discussion of people's motives and wants should emphasize that each person is unique. He is different from all others in his wants. He is different in his heritage of size and strength, in his dexterity and muscular coordination, in the quality of his sight and of his hearing. Each is different from others in intellectual abilities and emotional makeup. To compound the differences, each person is further changed by his life with his parents and the influence of his friends. He is changed by all his experiences, his education and training. All the things in a man's life—plus the situation at the moment—enter into shaping his thinking about what he wants out of life, how he will go about getting it, and how much effort he will put into it.

People differ in their work aptitudes and abilities, in the work habits they have learned, in the pace they can maintain, in their susceptibility to boredom. They differ in their emotional stability, in the strength of their needs for security, for autonomy, and for affiliation. They differ in the strength of their motives for achievement.[6]

But people change. Physical changes add to or take away from their strength and energy. New experiences affect their way of looking at things. The footloose young fellow becomes the family breadwinner

---

[5] For studies of the money motive, see William F. Whyte *et al.*, *Money and Motivation* (New York: Harper & Row, Publishers, 1955), chap. 14.

[6] For research on the achievement motive, see David C. McClelland, J. S. Atkinson, R. A. Clark, and E. L. Lowell, *The Achievement Motive* (New York: Appleton-Century-Crofts, Inc., 1953).

David C. McClelland, *The Achieving Society* (Princeton, N.J.: D. Van Nostrand Co., Inc., 1961).

looking for opportunities and needing more money. The man who started his job with such enthusiasm becomes bored with it as his interests change, or dissatisfied with it if his friends distinguish themselves in other fields. The girl who looked on her job as a fill-in until marriage starts considering it as a career when her friends get married and she is still single.

Considering the differences between people and the changes within a person during his lifetime, it becomes obvious that there is no simple formula for solving all the human problems at work. The supervisor finds that he can't treat all people alike because the treatment will bring a favorable response from some and an unfavorable response from others. He must take individual differences into account in fitting people to jobs, in making assignments, in praising, rewarding, criticizing, and disciplining.

When supervisors in a conference discuss individual differences and the treatment of people as individuals, some supervisor will usually say that the way to treat people is to follow the Golden Rule: *Do unto others as you would have them do unto you.* Some other supervisor usually answers, "How do you know the other fellow wants to be treated the way you want to be treated? If I treated the girls in my department that way, they'd cry."

Personal problems of employees

Every supervisor knows there are problem employees—irresponsibles, troublemakers, crybabies, alcoholics. Some people never mature emotionally; they find and make problems. They have difficulty adjusting to life and to the demands of the job. Other people have temporary upsets in their emotional lives. They find some combinations of difficulties and frustrations just too much to handle at one time.

The alcoholic employee is a problem calling for expert help. He may be shy, withdrawn, and supersensitive. Problem drinkers may be overambitious perfectionists who are seeking escape from less-than-perfect conditions at home or on the job. Some companies have medical programs for restoring them to health, and they report that in the majority of cases they are successful: the restored employee advances to higher jobs and repays the company in gratitude and high performance. The alcoholic employee and others with severe emotional problems need professional help and should be put in contact with a person or an agency able to help them. Problems with the alcoholic employee are discussed in Chapter 15.

When an employee's personal problems are affecting his behavior and interfering with his performance, it is up to the supervisor to do something about it. He may find that the employee's mental distress is caused by poor placement, insecurity, fear of getting hurt, gripes, grievances, resentments, and frustrations. Sometimes he can help an employee over a low spot by changing his job assignments, injecting some new interest into the job, or moving him into a more congenial group. He may be able to let the employee know just how far the company is willing to go along with substandard performance resulting from off-the-job problems. Bringing the matter out into the open may give the troubled person some relief. Sometimes when the supervisor hears the problem, he can suggest avenues of assistance—for instance, if the employee is over his head in debt and doesn't know where to turn.

Sometimes the employee can be helped to arrive at a more accurate evaluation of his difficulties. The supervisor should not, however, take upon himself the responsibility of *solving* subordinates' problems. He can point out solutions, but the person who has to live with the solution should make the choice.

Tensions on the job

At the end of the day some employees are all worn out, have stiff necks and other symptoms of nervous tension, and have to stop at a bar for a drink to relax before going home. Some people are much more susceptible than others to strain and nervous fatigue. The tension they feel can come from improper light, intense vibration, or noise. It can come from having to keep alert and watchful on an operation not sufficiently interesting to hold their full attention. It can come from boredom—the kind of weariness that results from disinterest and dislike of a job that offers no challenge. The job may be poorly designed or the person may be emotionally unsuited to repetitive work.

There are other causes of fatigue and strain on the job: the snooping supervisor, the feeling of not knowing how to do a thing, the fear of making a mistake, the fear of being bawled out, the fear that "something will happen." These feelings of insecurity and inadequacy cause continuous strain that drains the energies during the workday.

Tension is caused by the supervisor's behavior when he is impatient and irritable, when he's behind schedule, when somebody is putting pressure on him and he is taking it out on his subordinates. The supervisor needs to be sensitive to his own behavior because his employees have a tendency to be oversensitive to it. If he is grumpy, belligerent, nervous, or upset, the reason may be that he was out too late, had an argument at home, or damaged the car on the way to work. But his subordinates relate his behavior to the job and to his feelings about them. His behavior sets the mood of the section and either adds to or lightens the stresses of the job.

A supervisor who has himself and the job under control and can be calm, friendly, and understanding can do much to alleviate tension. He is the key person in promoting the mental health of his subordinates. In the way he conducts himself and deals with others, he sets up a work climate that is harmonious or one that is full of stress. By seeing that things go well, he can provide an environment in which subordinates can make effective use of their energies and can get some pleasure from the day's work.

What people want from their jobs

Surveys have been made of the wants of people on jobs, out of jobs, applying for jobs, and quitting jobs. Some surveys were made by asking people to think of the things they desired from their jobs and to list them in the order of their importance. Other surveys used this information to compile "ready-made" lists of wants which the employees or the job applicants were asked to rank in importance to them. The following list was taken from several surveys.[7] People said they wanted:

Security	Fair wages
Work that is meaningful	Freedom from arbitrary action
Opportunity for advancement	A voice in matters affecting them
Recognition	Congenial associates
Competent leadership	Satisfactory working conditions.

The most important thing to be remembered in studying a list of wants is that it does not represent a profile of the wants of any one person. It is simply a combination of many lists. A person would not list his wants in the same order this year as he did five years ago. Quite possibly the things he lists as most important to him are the things that he lacks or is dissatisfied with at the moment. A satisfied want seems to drop in importance until something threatens the satisfaction. The fact that wages and working conditions are so far down the list could mean that people were fairly well satisfied with them at the time—that they were not burning issues. The fact that security, meaningful (or interesting) work, and opportunity for advancement were 1, 2, 3 on the list may indicate that they were the things lacking in many jobs.

Figure 16–1 shows a different type of survey. It was designed to find out whether bosses know what their subordinates want. The results

[7] For an analysis and compilation of a great number of surveys, see Frederick Herzberg, Bernard Mausner, Richard O. Peterson, and Dora F. Capwell, *Job Attitudes: Review of Research and Opinion.* (Pittsburgh: Psychological Service of Pittsburgh, 1957). Herzberg's compilation found that security, intrinsic aspects of the job, and opportunity for advancement were in the 1, 2, 3 positions; wages were sixth.

FIGURE 16–1

What Subordinates Say They Want in a Job Compared to What Their Superiors Expect Them to Want

The survey that produced these figures was made in a household appliance company in the midwestern United States. The following question was asked of 2,499 workers and their 196 foremen and 45 general foreman:

"Different people want different things out of a job. What are the things you yourself feel are *most important* in a job?" The three top wants of each person were tabulated. The percentage of workers who gave high rank to steady work and steady wages was 61, the percentage of foremen 62, the percentage of general foremen 52—as shown on the top line.

The foremen and general foremen were asked another question: "What are the things you think most of the people you supervise feel are *most important* in a job?" And 61 percent of the foremen estimated that their subordinates would rank high wages of major importance; yet only 28 percent actually did so. All along the line the bosses overestimated the importance their subordinates attach to financial factors and underestimated the importance to them of nonfinancial factors.

Percent Who Give a Rank of 1, 2, or 3 to:	*Men*	*Foremen's Perception of Men*	*Foremen*	*General Foremen's Perception of Foremen*	*General Foremen*
Steady work and steady wages	61%	70%	62%	86%	52%
High wages................	28	61	17	58	11
Pensions and other old age security benefits............	13	17	12	29	15
Not having to work too hard.	13	30	4	25	2
Getting along well with the people I work with........	36	17	39	22	43
Getting along well with my supervisor...............	28	14	28	15	24
Good chance to turn out good quality work.............	16	11	18	13	27
Good chance to do interesting work...................	22	12	38	14	43
Good chances for promotion..	25	23	42	24	47
Good physical working conditions...................	21	19	18	4	11
Total..............	*	*	*	*	*
No. of cases.........	2,499	196	196	45	45

From Robert L. Kahn, "Human Relations on the Shop Floor," in E. M. Hugh-Jones (ed.), *Human Relations and Modern Management* (Amsterdam: North-Holland Publishing Co., 1958), p. 49. The study was made by the Survey Research Center of the University of Michigan and used with their permission.

are interesting from the standpoint that the bosses overestimated the importance their subordinates attach to financial wants and underestimated the importance to them of nonfinancial wants.

Studying a list of wants should serve the purpose of alerting a supervisor to the variety of things people may want, the varying degrees in which they want them, and the fact that some wants may be in conflict with others. The person who wants to advance and still keep his congenial associates is going to have to choose between these two wants. People will trade off wants. Some people will take distasteful jobs for the high earnings. Other people will turn down a high-pay job because it doesn't offer enough security, or the work isn't interesting, or they don't want to put a barrier between themselves and their friends. The supervisor has much more influence in the satisfaction of some wants than of others. His area of motivation may be in the "trade-off"—helping people to get a little more of one thing to compensate for their having to get along with less of another.

Security. A breadwinner's need for security is most often expressed in terms of steady work and steady wages. The lack of job security plays havoc with people. The resultant worry interferes with learning a job and performing it. People who are insecure on the job will try to protect themselves in peculiar ways: they will resist changes, play it safe, pass the buck for responsibilities, refuse to take initiative, restrict production, and manufacture and pass along rumors.

Insecurity brought on by automation or threats of automation is reflected in featherbedding, conflicts over work standards, and demands for a shorter workweek.

The security that the supervisor can provide is the assurance that as long as the employee keeps on doing his job well, his position is safe except for circumstances outside the supervisor's control. An employee needs to feel that continuing tenure on the job is the normal situation. Except for the few individuals who respond only to threats, the supervisor should not use fear as a motivator. The "heads will roll" and "one mistake and you're out" relationship is not the way to develop initiative and responsibility in subordinates. People need security and approval in their relationship with the boss before they can develop their abilities and give their best performance.

The supervisor can build his subordinates' sense of security by letting them know what is expected of them and how they are doing, by training them, making them more valuable, by consulting with them, keeping them informed, and being willing to listen to their problems. When changes are impending, he must recognize that people become severely upset by real or fancied threats to their job, or to their prestige or to their feelings of adequacy. They suffer from headaches, sick stomachs, sleeplessness, "nerves," and any number of occupational ailments. They need a sympathetic listener who can give them information, reassurance, and encouragement.

Work that is meaningful. A job that is absorbing and challenging to one person may be a frustration to another. The professional man wants a job on which he can make a significant contribution to knowledge or to his own success and that of his company. The skilled worker

wants a job that uses his highest skill. People want a feeling of achievement from their work. The achievement motive may be the one that
is most effective in sustaining high performance. People keep on achieving long after they have provided for their financial wants.

Achievement-motivated people want jobs that produce some identifiable results. Many industrial jobs have been overspecialized and oversimplified to the point that they use none of the performer's human abilities. It may be possible to redesign such jobs, to combine tasks into
jobs better suited to people's physical and mental abilities and psychological needs. See Chapter 10's discussion of job enlargement and Chapter 14's discussion of the job as a motivating factor.

Many jobs have no meaning to the performer because no one took
the time or trouble to explain to him the purpose of what he is doing.
He doesn't know the ultimate use of the part he is working on, the
reasons for the methods, or the difficulties that will be caused by defective work.

Wherever possible, the supervisor should find ways of making work
more meaningful so that the performer can get some kind of satisfaction
over mastery of the job. Designing jobs, fitting people to jobs, training
people for jobs, and explaining the purpose of jobs, are ways in which
the supervisor can help subordinates find meaning in their work.

Opportunity to advance.   Whether or not people take advantage of
the opportunity to advance, they like to feel that it is there. Lack of
opportunity and dissatisfaction with pay are the two reasons most frequently given for changing jobs. They may not be the true reasons,
but they look good on the next application blank. People don't want
to burn their bridges behind them or label themselves as troublemakers
or misfits; they need references for the next job.

Ambitious upward-striving people certainly need to see an opportunity to advance. They are willing to prepare themselves for higher
level jobs and to make present sacrifices for future gains.[8] They desire
the money or the status or the challenge or the achievement that comes
with advancement. Advancement is one of the incentives that drives
them to put out extra effort, and they expect to get the advancement
as recognition and reward for their efforts. Advancement when it is
received is a spur to still higher effort. If the advancement does not
come, employees may lose interest in the job, reduce their efforts, become
embittered, or look elsewhere for a job. Professional employees are
highly motivated to advance. They seek status not only in the company
but also in the professional society and in their group of professional
friends.

---

[8] For a study of the ambitions of clerical workers and the limited opportunities
for advancement, see Nancy Morse, *Satisfactions with White Collar Jobs* (Ann
Arbor, Mich.: Institute for Social Research, University of Michigan, 1953).

On the other hand, many employees who have reached the top of their salary classification continue to give devoted service. Many people reach a spot on the advancement ladder and wish to stay there because they have attained the height of their ambitions or because they have the job under control and feel comfortable at that level.

Some people just are not interested in advancement. A man with alimony trouble or one with no dependents may not be interested in putting more into his job. Young girls looking forward to marriage may not be concerned about advancement. A married woman might prefer shorter hours to an advancement. Some people are not willing to put out the effort and make the personal sacrifices entailed in advancement; other enjoyments in life are more important to them. Some people are comfortable with their friends on the job and would be uncomfortable with the people on a higher level. (The socially mobile person may be one who doesn't make deep attachments and can shuck off old teammates and adjust himself readily to new ones.) Some people find a job they like and just want to stay on it.

Some people have to face up to the fact that there are no opportunities for them to advance on their jobs. One map-making concern employing many detail draftsmen had no upper positions for them. The company met the problem by making the plant a beauty spot in a good locality and by maintaining the best of working conditions and relationships. When draftsmen wanting advancement complained to the chief draftsman that they were dissatisfied on a dead-end job, he told them that if they wanted to leave he would help them get jobs elsewhere. If they wanted to stay, they should accept the limitations of the job and find enjoyment in the recreations available in the community or in becoming leaders in community activities.

In a unionized job, seniority with its privileges and security may become a substitute for promotion. Through seniority a person may be able to transfer to a job that is easier, cleaner, or "higher class" even though it may not involve higher pay. A work group may push for advancement in the form of improvements or concessions that represent evidence of getting ahead of another group.

A person who is stymied in his ambitions to advance may transfer them to his children, make sacrifices to put his children through college, and take glory in their achievement. He has the satisfaction of knowing that his son with the engineering degree may not have to take any guff.

Getting ahead may be a matter of being able to buy a big car, a cabin, a boat, and having the time to enjoy them.

People at the bottom of the heap who never had much hope of getting ahead and haven't accumulated any money or improved their situation at all may become embittered by failure and futility. They may find their outlet in getting ahead of the company and outwitting the supervisor.

The supervisor, when he hires people, must match their ambitions to the opportunities in the department and in the company. If there are opportunities, he should help his people develop for them. He should remember that people change in their interests and goals. An employee studying in one field and working in another may find himself stuck in the wrong job if no one steers him in the right direction. He may be unable to afford the financial sacrifice of quitting his job and starting at the bottom in the field of his choice. Some employees who have not considered promotion as a possibility become interested in preparing for openings if the supervisor takes an interest in guiding them.

Recognition   The desire for recognition, for praise, appreciation, importance, prestige, and esteem is a powerful drive in some people. The desire for distinction in the group or in the community can inspire a man to undertake responsibility for a project and to put tremendous effort into making it a success. The desire for prestige—when accompanied by the ability and energy to achieve it—can motivate a person to high performance.

Even if a person does not have a high drive for achievement, he still desires recognition and appreciation as an individual. He is the center of his own world and very important in it. He needs recognition to bolster his belief in his own worth. His dignity is affronted when he is addressed as "Hey you" or is considered as only a number on an IBM card. If he cannot get attention in the form of approval, he may get it by being negative or aggressive. When workers feel ignored, they may call attention to themselves by complaining, showing off, displaying aggression against the company, and occasionally by having accidents.

The supervisor should try to help his people achieve something worthwhile and then see that they get the credit for it. Glad-handing isn't enough. He should help them get recognition outside the department also—in the company newspaper, social committees, safety committees, in athletics and similar activities. The supervisor's special problem in giving recognition is to do it in a way that does not arouse the jealousy or ill will of the group. One person should not get all the credit for something accomplished by group effort. Credit given to one member must somehow be made to reflect credit on everybody.

Competent leadership.   An employee has a stake in his job; he has tied his future to it. He has to rely on the leadership of the company to maintain a productive and profitable business that will survive and be able to provide steady work and good wages. The company leadership sets up the environment, the policies, the leadership climate, and the spirit of the organization within which the employee and his immediate supervisor must operate. The company's policies and controls shape the attitudes and actions of its supervisors.

An employee's emotional state on the job is influenced to a great extent by his supervisor' attitudes and ability. An employee wants a boss who has the job under control and is able to plan and schedule the work so that deadlines can be met without frenzy. A man wants a boss who doesn't blow up under pressure or take it out on his subordinates—a boss who is willing and able to spare them from unecessary anxieties, frictions, pressures, and frustrations. He wants a boss who is not too fearful for his own security and can tolerate a few mistakes.

A man wants a boss who will help him to get what he wants out of the job. It may be achievement, recognition, appreciation, security, advancement, friendliness, help—all these things are desired to some degree. The boss must be able to appraise the intensity of the desire, the employee's ability, the opportunities open to him, and to help him achieve some kind of satisfaction from his job.

Fair wages. The burning issue with wages is *fairness.* Is the pay in line with the status of the job? Is it as much as other groups are getting for work of this class and difficulty? Is it as much as other people are getting for like amount of effort and achievement? Is it more than people are getting for lower class jobs? There are traditional relationships between jobs in status and pay, and any disturbance of the accepted arrangement will arouse bitter resentment in the person or group that feels itself to be injured.

The supervisor should be close enough to his subordinates to know their attitudes about the pay they are getting. He should get the information he needs to handle rumors about the good wages that are being paid "for practically no work" in other departments and in other companies. If raises are based on the employee-evaluation system, he should see that his subordinates get their share. He should know the company's job evaluation plan and should explain it to his men.

If wages in the department are in line and the employees are complaining about them or quitting for jobs elsewhere, the supervisor should suspect that there is something else wrong with the job. If people are getting very little satisfaction from their work, money becomes more important to them as a means of buying off-the-job satisfactions. If the job is unpleasant, they want more money for putting up with it. If they feel pushed around, they'll push back with a money demand. Money is something concrete to complain about when personal satisfactions are lacking on the job.

Freedom from arbitrary action. Freedom from arbitrary action means that there is no favoritism, no discrimination, no prejudice, no preferential treatment for the lodge brothers; it means there are no black sheep, no insiders or outsiders.

If an employee feels himself to be a victim of discrimination, he is in a frame of mind to put an unfavorable interpretation on every management action and communication. After he mulls over his grievance for a while, it may become almost an obsession. His resentment may erupt suddenly in undesirable behavior or unreasonable demands. The grievance procedure provides an outlet to drain off some of the ill will of an employee who feels he has been the victim of an injustice.

Because some employees seem to find injustices where they don't exist—or at least were not intended—the supervisor must avoid even the appearance of favoritism. Employee evaluation, transfers, raises, promotions—when within the control of the supervisor—should be based on merit and on accomplishment. They must not be made on hunches, prejudices, or because the employee is a likable fellow. Whenever a promotion or a transfer is made, the reason should be explained, not only to the person being moved, but also to those who thought they were in the running.

A voice in matters affecting him.   Not everyone has strong needs for autonomy or for having a say about how things should be done on the job. Some employees are more comfortable doing what they are told and they don't want to get involved in anything that would increase their own risk on the job. Because of their personalities, their upbringing, and their work experiences, they prefer the tight ship nononsense kind of supervision. They are willing to let the boss make the decisions, make the mistakes, and hold the responsibility.

At the other extreme are the scientific and professional employees. They want to select their own projects, go about them in their own way, and be freed from organizational regulations and controls.

In between the two extremes are the great numbers of employees who know they must trade some of their freedom for employment but who still want some say about things that concern them and their jobs. They are unable to accept the idea that a job is nothing more than doing what they are told. Much of what looks like unreasonableness or stubbornness on the part of such employees is their reaction to feeling pushed around—having to take it or leave it. They want to feel that they are offering their cooperation freely. They don't want anyone telling them what to do if they already know. On the other hand, they become upset if they don't know what they should be doing, and can't get the help they want from the supervisor. Their jobs put them in a position of dependence, yet they feel that independence is essential to their self-respect.

The supervisor can reduce the frustrations of the independent employee by minimizing the need for orders and by giving information and soliciting suggestions on job problems. The employee who has participated in planning changes that affect his job is less apt to feel that they are being shoved down his throat. An effective supervisor will give him the freedom he wants to use his own initiative.

Congenial associates. People in an office or a shop form a community. Since they have to be together on the job for so much of their lives, they don't want to be griped by one another all the time. They want to be with people like themselves—people with whom they can share their plans, jokes, and ideas. They want teammates who will pitch in with them when the going is rough, who will lend a helping hand, a sympathetic ear, or a pat on the shoulder. When people who must work together are able to get along well, there are fewer frictions on the job; people catch and correct mistakes for one another; they look out for one another's safety. People who are accepted into the group are happier on the job and less apt to be absent or quit. Being a member of a congenial group may make up for some of the lack of interest or challenge in a repetitive job.

There are a few people who want to work by themselves, to mind their own business, and to be let alone. Sometimes they are let alone, but at other times they may be made the butt of jokes or horseplay. Often these loners do a better-than-average job and the supervisor might wish he had more like them if he could just put them on jobs where they would not have to work with others.

A person may be a troublemaker on the job because his personality doesn't fit the group or because his job keeps him in hot water with everybody. Relationships in the work group depend to a great extent on the way the work is organized, on the location of workplaces, and on the demands that people must make on one another in carrying out their duties. If these demand relationships do not correspond to the status relationships—the pecking order—then frictions and personal conflicts will develop. If a youngster is making demands upon an old-timer, the two may not be able to work together. Congenial working relationships depend upon good organization of work flow, careful selection of employees, and keeping assignments in line with the social structure of the group.

Satisfactory working conditions. An employee's satisfaction with his working conditions depends to a great extent upon his background, education, and expectations. And it depends a whole lot on what kind of conditions other people in the company are having to put up with.

Women seem to place more importance upon working conditions than men do. Women complain about lighting, heating, and drafts, about the condition of the rest rooms, lack of mirrors, lack of a clean and comfortable place to rest or to smoke. They are unhappy about furniture that snags their stockings and equipment that breaks their fingernails.

If a man is satisfied with the status of his job, he seems able to put up with necessary discomforts—provided his department is no worse off than any other. The postman is proud of getting the mail through in spite of the weather. People may be proud of a rugged job and their ability to handle it. There is a certain satisfaction in job mastery, but it doesn't extend to putting up with unnecessary inconveniences and hazards. Certain types of minor annoyances and discomforts make people think that the company doesn't care what happens to them. Things like fountains and fans unrepaired or hot water and soap cut out to save expenses can become gripes of major proportions. Unfairness or lack of consideration in scheduling hours of work can distress an employee to the point of looking for another job.

The supervisor can show his concern for his group by making his own department clean, orderly, and safe. He can see that things are kept in repair and can go to bat for his subordinates to correct conditions that gripe them.

Motivation and morale

Morale is the spirit of an organization. It is the state of mind of employees—individually and as a group. It is the way they think and feel about the work itself, the working conditions, the supervisor, fellow workers, the company and its management, the fairness of the pay, and the prospects of a steady job.

Morale is a measure of the satisfaction employees are getting in their attempts to satisfy their needs. It is a measure of their confidence in the job as something in which they can invest their most precious asset—their futures. It is an indicator of the degree to which they are getting what they want from the job. Or, more importantly, it is a measure of their confidence that in the future they will get what they want from the job.

If the above description of morale on the job is analyzed, it can be seen that there is some relationship between morale and motivation. The factors which, if satisfied, motivate employees also lead to the development of higher morale among these employees. High motivation does not always mean high morale but it is reasonable to assume that employees who are highly motivated will tend to have high morale more often than not. Problems arise in discussions of morale and motivation because of the lack of concrete understanding of the term "morale." William G. Scott describes three approaches to the problem of morale definition:

1. *The "classical" approach* stems from the "needs psychology" school. Personal determinants of morale are emphasized in this approach. Needs are visualized as emanating from the ultimate problem of human survival. Thus, satisfaction of basic needs is seen as a primary morale factor.

2. *The psychological approach* stresses the hierarchial and dynamic nature of needs. When basic needs are satisfied, then higher motives, such as accomplishment, recognition, and participation, emerge to dominate an individual's behavior. High morale from this point of view results from a continual satisfaction of the so-called "higher" motives.

3. *The social approach* to morale is a product of the work of Elton Mayo and the Hawthorne researchers. Morale is considered as a social phenomenon caused by the strong desire of man to be associated with his fellow man. Thus morale is determined by the social situation at work.[9]

Determinants of morale

Morale must be considered as both an individual and a group attitude. On an individual basis, morale has frequent ups and downs. An individual's morale goes up as he sees prospects of getting ahead on his job; it goes down when the prospects grow dim. It goes up when he gets an opportunity to show what he can do and gets recognition for doing it. It goes down when the plums go to someone else and his own role and opportunities are curtailed. It goes up when he achieves status and prestige; it goes down when a technological development or organizational change pulls the rug from under him. It goes up when things are going well in his personal life; it goes down when the situation fails to measure up to his expectations.

Morale on a group basis is less volatile. In a company that has maintained good relations with its employees over a long period of time, there is a backlog of goodwill that supports group morale through some minor grievances and temporary dislocations. Morale has a kind of momentum that prevents it from reversing itself promptly with each company action. If it is on a steady upward trend, it can absorb some minor jolts. As long as the unfavorable conditions don't last too long, the flare-ups they cause are just temporary disturbances. When employees have confidence in the company's good intentions, morale sinks rather slowly under stress and can regain its losses if management doesn't delay too long in taking remedial action.

It is only when pressures have gone on for considerable time that employees lose their optimism and suffer a collapse of morale. Then there may be a rash of absences. Or the low morale may show up in a less spectacular way in apathy, malingering, sloppy work, waste of materials, destruction of property, disregard for the rules, hostility, and unwillingness to carry out orders or to cooperate.

Once the employees have lost faith in the company and their morale is down, even trivial events or rumors can send it plunging lower. What-

---

[9] William G. Scott, *Organization Theory, A Behavioral Analysis for Management* (Homewood, Ill.: Richard D. Irwin, Inc., 1967), pp. 293–94.

ever the company does is suspect. Even significant concessions made by management get at best a grudging acceptance. Employees whose experience has taught them not to trust the company are slow to change their attitudes; so the company's job of rebuilding morale is a slow and discouraging one. The alternative to rebuilding morale is to operate on a police state basis.

Some companies make morale surveys in order to measure the state of morale and prevent a collapse. The surveys yield some enlightening statistics on employee dissatisfactions—information that would not otherwise find its way to upper management to influence policy making. Just providing the survey as a channel through which employees can complain serves to improve morale. Some employees won't complain otherwise because they don't want to be labeled as troublemakers. But they need a channel through which to express their grievances. The channel can be the opinion survey or a formal grievance procedure or a boss who will listen to gripes, recognize their bearing on motivation and morale, and take action.

Just having a voice in matters affecting their own working lives is a powerful sustainer of employee morale. Upward influence—the ability to affect managerial actions—builds confidence and optimism in employees and raises the level of both motivation and morale.

There are many other factors that affect employee morale, and the supervisor doesn't control them all. He is, however, the company representative who has closest and most personal influence on the morale of his subordinates. The knowledge, attitudes, and skills he needs for the job of managing work and worker have been the subject of this text.

Morale and productivity

The relationship between morale and productivity is a complex one. Company measurements of the two factors have shown them existing in the following combinations:

Morale	High	High	Low	Low
Productivity	High	Low	High	Low

One reason that high morale doesn't always result in high productivity is that just being *willing* to work isn't enough to assure high output. High productivity involves a combination of ability, training, work habits, technical advances, organizational arrangements, performance goals, motives, and rewards. In the illustration above where morale was high and productivity was low, the company may have been keeping everybody contented but neglecting its technical job of planning, improving methods, setting standards of work performance, and reducing costs. It may have had good human relations but it also needed good discipline, placement, training, evaluation and development of individual employees, and it needed to get the work group to accept high performance goals.

In the example of high production with low morale, the workers may have been on machine-paced jobs that were specialized and simplified to the point that they called for no judgment or responsibility. Morale tends to be low on jobs with rigid systems and controls, where there is minimum delegation of authority and responsibility, and where there is constant emphasis on increasing production through technical means rather than through getting people to want to be more productive.

Today's employee

The blue-collar job that was machine paced is now being automated, and there are very few white-collar jobs that could be classified as unskilled. The new jobs being created in an age of automation are jobs calling for judgment, analysis, and creativity. They are the types of job in which productivity is affected by worker attitude. They are jobs calling for specialized technical training—training which must be kept up to date by continued study and schooling on the employee's own time.

A company whose technical advantage depends upon talents that are both scarce and perishable has no choice but to maintain a high level of morale and motivation. The company's talent supply depends upon its employees' willingness to study and to stay on the job. The company's ability to attract top quality talent is dependent upon the reputation it has as an employer of talent.

The old and the young. Another factor to be considered in connection with employee morale is the age composition of today's work force. The low birthrate of depression years accounts for the relative scarcity of people in their thirties and the high proportion of older employees and very young ones.

Older employees whose skills are being replaced by machines present a morale problem that gets in the way of the smooth introduction of technological change. To understand the emotional basis of this problem, the supervisor needs to study the status problems resulting from introducing change. In order to be able to retrain older people for changed jobs, he should study the motivational factors that influence the learning process.

The young people in the work force present a morale problem of a different type. They have had more schooling than the majority of the oldsters. In 1940 the proportion of workers with high school education or better was 39.1 percent. By 1968 it had increased to 62.1 percent. The person of higher education expects more from his job. He expects it to have interest and variety, to use his abilities, and to let him make decisions.

The college-educated employee has usually had several job offers and has been led to expect opportunities for exercising initiative and leadership, earning recognition, and making rapid advancement. He does not expect close supervision or tight controls. On the other hand, he is generally not a rebel against the organization. He is eager to get ahead in it and achieve recognition, advancement, and status. He is apt to be critical of the company's policies and working arrangements because he is concerned about the way the business is managed and the opportunities it offers him. He may think that the management of the company is preventing him from doing as good a job as he is capable of doing. There is a 50 percent chance that he will be dissatisfied with his first job and quit it before the year is over if it doesn't offer enough dignity, stimulation, and opportunity for personal growth.

The supervisor who understands the expectations which today's employee brings to the job can help him adjust to the reality that promotions in business don't come every year as they did in school. While waiting for promotions, the ambitious young person has to be provided with opportunities to develop his abilities on the job, to make accomplishments, and to get recognition. He needs assurance that the company has plans for using his abilities and that the future holds opportunities for him in the company. It is up to the supervisor to provide the upward contacts through which young people are absorbed into the life of an organization.

The essence of building morale and the will to work is to make it possible for employees to achieve personal satisfaction through working for the success of the enterprise. The basis on which to build high morale is compatibility of goals and mutuality of interests. The employee must be enabled to see that he can achieve some of his goals while working for the goals of the organization.

The job as a factor in promoting high morale

A man's adjustment to the job that he is doing is an important factor contributing to the state of his morale. If the job is too far below his abilities he will be dissatisfied with it. If it is too far above his abilities he will be faced with failure and discouragement. The best performance and most satisfaction result when a man is doing a job that is somewhat of a challenge to him and he has the training and ability to meet that challenge. Knowing how he is doing on the job is a morale builder, so there should be some means by which he can measure his progress.

In order to have high morale a man must believe in the importance of his job and have a feeling of personal significance in performing it. The proper design of a job becomes more important with the rise in educational level of employees. Individual differences in education, ability, skill, background, age, and level of aspiration account for some of the differences in what people expect in intrinsic satisfaction from the performance of their work. The low-skilled man doesn't expect or get as much job satisfaction as the man of higher skill.[10]

The supervisor must get the best possible fit between what the person demands of the job and what the job demands of the person. A man's adjustment to the job can be helped by improving the design of the job, training him up to the job, by explaining the why of the job, by letting him know what is expected of him and how he is doing.

Working conditions have an effect on morale in that they indicate the degree of the company's concern for the employee's safety and well-being. People seem to be able to tolerate and even feel heroic about unavoidable hazards and difficulties of the job, but they are griped by inconveniences and discomforts that the company *could* remedy but doesn't. Some of these job conditions that lower morale are poor lighting, heating, and ventilation, badly maintained equipment, and unsafe conditions. Correcting such conditions will remove the dissatisfaction they cause, but mere contentment with conditions surrounding the job is not a motivator to high performance.[11] See the discussion of Herzberg's theory of motivation earlier in this chapter.

Teammates as a factor in promoting high morale

An employee wants to belong to a group that has likes and dislikes somewhat resembling his own. He depends upon his teammates for the satisfaction of some of his needs for belonging and approval. He

---

[10] For a review of research studies on attitudes of people toward their jobs, see Herzberg, Mausner, Peterson, and Capwell, *op. cit.* Studying collected research reports on a particular topic permits comparison and evaluation of the findings. For instance, there is some disagreement about the relationship of age to morale. Some research findings indicate that morale takes a sharp drop in early years and is slow to build up again. However there was no correlation between age and morale in the study by Philip Ash, "The SRA Employee Inventory: A Statistical Analysis," *Personnel Psychology,* Autumn, 1954.

[11] For a further discussion of the theory of the relationship between motivation and morale, see Herzberg, Mausner, and Snyderman, *op. cit.* They suggest that the unfavorable conditions surrounding the job are the *dissatisfiers.* The job *satisfiers* are an entirely different set of factors and are associated with performing the job and being rewarded, promoted, and given more responsibility. They suggest that the satisfiers motivate people to high performance.

wants to feel secure in his own special place on the team and to feel that he and his job are important to the team effort. He wants to feel that the team depends upon him.

Company morale is sometimes described as team spirit. One of management's jobs is to build teamwork or cooperation throughout the organization. Without it, people in the company go their separate ways and spend their energies building up and defending their own territory rather than working for company goals.

It is part of the supervisor's job to build the team spirit among his employees so that they will work together cooperatively and productively. Conflicts, antagonisms, and hostilities make teamwork impossible. Criticizing, belittling, and excessive kidding will break down the cohesiveness of the group and waste its energies in defensiveness and buck-passing. The supervisor wants his people to be friendly, sociable, and willing to help one another. He wants their job relationships to be such that they will get satisfaction out of working together.

When selecting new employees, the supervisor should choose people who will get along reasonably well together. He should use care in mixing people of certain nationalities, regions, and personalities. He should keep in mind that people of dissimilar ages and social backgrounds may break the work group into factions and refuse to cooperate.

It is the "no-belongs"—the people who don't fit with the others and are not accepted by the group—who quit. Because first impressions form attitudes, newcomers must be inducted carefully. Their duties and place in the group must be arranged in a way that promotes their acceptance and integration into the activity. A feeling of personal identification with the group and with the job is one of the factors contributing to high morale. If the work itself offers little satisfaction, then friendly relationships with fellow workers become even more important to the morale of the worker.

While there is no doubt that a compatible work group is a desirable goal, the supervisor may find it increasingly difficult to achieve that goal by controlling the selection process for his work group. Social pressures, fair employment practices legislation, and the nature of the labor market all limit his flexibility in this regard. The generation gap, ethnic, racial, and religious differences may all pose difficulties for the supervisor. Yet it must be his responsibility to try to weld the varying differences among his subordinates into reasonable performance toward the achievement of group goals in the context of organizational goals. Supervision is a difficult assignment and the responsibilities are becoming more complex with each passing day. Creating a team spirit among people with varying backgrounds and aspirations is one of the most difficult challenges facing the supervisor. The extent to which he accepts this challenge and successfully copes with it has a good bit to do with the nature of morale in his work group.

The supervisor as a factor in promoting high morale

An employee is dependent upon his supervisor for some of the satisfactions he wants from the job—security, recognition, fair dealing, satisfactory working conditions, competent leadership, and a voice in matters affecting him. The supervisor builds the morale of his subordinates by the extent to which he is able and willing to take care of their needs. While financial security, raises, and promotions depend upon company action, it is the supervisor who makes it possible for people to qualify for them. He is the one who makes it possible for people to do a good job. He is the one who recommends that they be rewarded for it.

The supervisor builds the security of his people in a number of ways. He lets them know what is expected of them and how they are doing. He trains them so that they will be more valuable and successful. He is fair, consistent, and friendly in his dealings with them. He is willing to listen to them and encourage them. He is understanding about mistakes. He approves of his people and he is able to do this because he insists upon high standards of performance and behavior.

The supervisor contributes to morale by being a competent leader, able to plan and schedule the work and keep everybody working effectively. He sees to it that the working conditions are as good as possible—the equipment in repair, the materials on hand, the place in order.

He lets people know the reasons for things, gives them a chance to take part in working out changes that affect them. He listens to complaints and takes care of gripes; he is fair and consistent in his discipline. He asks people's opinions, shows respect for their ideas, and sees that they get credit for their suggestions. He entrusts employees with responsibility, shows appreciation for extra effort, gives praise and recognition for achievement, and helps people prepare for advancement.

The company as a factor in promoting high morale

How much the first-level supervisor is free to do in satisfying the wants of his subordinates and building high morale in his team depends to a great extent upon what his boss expects of him and what the company makes it possible for him to do. He has an opportunity to build high morale in his group if he is not being hounded for production and forced to breathe down the necks of his subordinates to get out more work; if he can spend more time in leading instead of pushing his men; if he has the time to train and develop them; if he has the time to encourage them; if he has the chance to correct them constructively; and if he has the time to show an interest in them.

As for the supervisor himself, he must feel secure. He must feel that upper management is behind him. He must know where he stands in the company, and he must feel that his recommendations carry some weight. He must be a definite part of the management team.

For high morale to exist in an organization, there must not be a conflict between the employees' goals and the company's goals. Employees must feel that the goals of the organization are compatible with their interests and attainable more completely and effectively by team action than by the performance of individual stars. Each person must feel that he is making a worthwhile contribution to the team and that his team depends upon him.

The company's system of pay is of vital importance in the morale of employees. High pay won't of itself assure high performance or high morale, but a system of pay that seems fair and is tied to merit and output is an essential ingredient. Fringe benefits are morale builders in providing assurance of sickness pay, hospitalization, pensions, and death benefits to the family.

The organization structure of the company influences morale by providing for good working relationships between people and between departments. The procedures for handling the work, and the policies governing the delegation of authority, effect the design of jobs and the satisfaction to be derived from performing them.

The company's ability to forecast, plan, and make decisions determines the stability of employment. The company's way of improving methods, making changes, setting goals, and measuring performance is a determinant of morale. The policies for dealing with people set the tone of morale.

Communication as a factor in promoting high morale

Employees want information that will assure them that the company has a worthwhile purpose—something in which they can believe. They want to know that the company is doing a good job; they want to feel pride in its reputation. They get satisfaction from being on a winning team.

In order to have high morale, employees need to have confidence in the company, in the ability, integrity, and intentions of its leaders, and in the prospects that it can and will give them steady employment and a good break. They want to trust the management that controls their futures. But the effects of managerial decisions can be so devastating to employees that they read meanings into even the most insignificant occurrences. Every act of management is open to misinterpretation, and employees need constant reassurance and explanations. Supervisors can answer questions and give information only to the extent that upper management provides the information. Employees are hungry for information about anything that relates to their jobs.

They want to know about the company—its background and present organization.

They want to know what its products are—how they're made and where they go.

They want to know what the company's policies are—especially new policies—as they affect themselves and their fellow workers.

They want to know the reasons for changes in methods, and to have information about new products—and they want this information in advance.

They want to know what is expected of them and how they're measuring up.

They want to know how their jobs fit into the scheme of things, and what their chances for advancement are.

They want to know what the outlook is for the business, and what the prospects are for steady work.

They want to know about the company's income, and about its profits and losses.

Should circumstances make layoffs necessary, they want to know as far in advance as possible, the reasons and how they as individuals are affected.[12]

The foregoing quotation came from the National Association of Manufacturers. In the same article are the following reasons why the employer should provide the information.

The efficient operation of your plant depends, first of all, on the respect of the employee for the capacity and performance of management.

Employees who know where they fit in the company, why their work is important, and the ultimate uses of the products, *have better work attitudes.*

Greater satisfaction of the individual employee with his job and his employer stems from a thorough knowledge of what's going on in the company.

Work interruptions are often caused by misunderstandings. A good communications program can *minimize the possibility of such misunderstandings.*

A good two-way information program *gives management a better understanding of what employees want* and what they're thinking.

Failure of the company to tell its story *leaves the way open for misinformation* and demoralizing rumors.

The kind of economic system we have in America depends on the wishes of its citizens. Only when the employees understand what the individual enterprise system is doing for them and feel they have a part in it, can we expect them to believe in and support it. . . .[13]

---

[12] *Employee Communications for Better Understanding* (New York: National Association of Manufacturers, July, 1951), pp. 8, 9–11.
[13] *Ibid.*

Summary

The motivation of employees and the development of high morale
in the work group is perhaps the supervisor's most difficult task. The
fact that relatively little is known about human behavior significantly
contributes to this difficulty. Several theories about human behavior
have been developed over the years which add to our understanding
of humans but by no means furnish complete answers. Among these
theories are Maslow's hierarchy of needs, the supportive-participative
management style advocated by Argyris and Likert, and Herzberg's motivation-hygiene theory. An understanding of these theories among others
will help the supervisor to create a more effective climate for job performance but it becomes obvious that he cannot control all of the variables which contribute to human behavior on the job.

Most of the fringe benefit programs in industry are maintenance programs designed to offer rewards which the employee can utilize off
the job. Not too many organizations have turned their attention to what
may be the most fruitful source of motivation and high morale—the
work itself. The supervisor should recognize the limitations of money
as a motivator. There are few "economic men" who are solely motivated
by economic rewards. Individual differences, job tensions, personal problems, and group relations all contribute to how the human feels about
his job. People want a variety of things from their jobs and it is difficult
to neatly categorize the wants of a particular individual. Among the
things they want are: security, meaningful work, advancement opportunity, recognition, competent leadership, equitable compensation, congenial associates, participation in decision making, freedom from arbitrary action, and satisfactory working conditions.

A relationship has been established between motivation and morale
even though morale is difficult to define. Essentially morale should be
considered as both an individual and a group attitude. There are many
things that contribute to individual and group morale. These are: the
job itself, the level of group productivity, fellow workers, the supervisor,
the organization, individual pride, age, background, education, and the
effectiveness of communication.

The successful development and maintenance of high morale among
a work group with varying backgrounds and aspirations and differing
reasons for working is a most challenging assignment for the supervisor.

CASE 1

You are the supervisor of the assembly department of a company
manufacturing electronics equipment. You have 50 women doing assem-

bly work, most of which is routine. About eight months ago the company received an order for some special and rather complicated equipment. You selected three of your best girls to handle the assembly work on this order. You explained to them that the job would be tough and that they would have to work apart from the rest of the girls. The job turned out to be a nightmare; the engineers hardly waited for the solder to cool before they changed their minds. Work had to be done over, time and again. The big bosses were always dropping in to observe the progress of the work. The girls worked under continuous pressure until the job was completed, about two months ago. They appeared happy and took no time off.

When the girls returned to their old jobs, they were the center of attention, telling their experiences. Now things have settled down into the old routine. However, the three girls seem to be listless in doing the simple assembly work. You had to seat them far enough apart to put an end to their continuous chatting about things that happened on the special job.

A while back, the three girls started coming in to work late together. You reprimanded them. Now they are beginning to take days off together.

1. Why did the girls appear to be happy when working under the strain of the special job?
2. Why are they not adjusting to the old routine?
3. What steps might you have been able to take to help them make the adjustment?
4. How are you going to handle the absentee problem?

CASE 2

You are in charge of a department of 35 men, and there is another department doing similar work and employing the same number of men. The other supervisor often does favors for his men, such as letting them off early, especially before holidays, and giving them more free time during working hours. As a result, your men want the same breaks; they grumble and feel that you are taking advantage of them. The other department is now turning out more work than yours because of this upset.

1. Should you follow the example set by the other supervisor?
2. Should you talk to the other supervisor? If so, what would you say to him?
3. How should you correct this situation?
4. Should you see your superior?
5. Who should handle the situation?
6. Discuss the setting-up of a policy to take care of the situation.

CASE 3

Mary Lou Stern was assigned to the department as an accounting clerk trainee. After a training period of one month, she was performing her work satisfactorily and getting along quite well with the other employees. With experience, she became very efficient in her job and because she frequently finished her assigned work early, she helped out her fellow workers in both her own section as well as others in the department. Mary Lou was becoming the ideal clerk, conscientious, efficient and cooperative.

Although maintaining her high-performance standards, Mary Lou developed the practice of using the telephone for frequent personal calls. During the monthly staff meeting, correct telephone usage was discussed as part of the agenda. At the end of the meeting the department head called Mary Lou to his office and told her that she was using the telephone excessively. She replied that she would stop the abuse. Things went quite well for two weeks and then the personal calls began again. The other employees started to complain, for they felt that Mary Lou was getting away with something they were not permitted to do.

The department head once again spoke to her, but this time he was rather strong in his manner and particularly emphatic about the need for obeying company rules regarding personal calls.

Mary Lou's personal calls ceased and she continued to perform her own work satisfactorily but she now stretched her work so it would last all day. She was no longer available to help other employees. There was a noticeable change in her demeanor as well. While she had been cheerful and friendly in the past, she was now just civil and she only spoke when spoken to.

1. Could the department head have disciplined Mary Lou and still retain her goodwill?
2. How much of the other employee's complaints may have been jealousy of Mary Lou's skills as a clerk?
3. Can the supervisor do anything to help Mary Lou return to her former level of cooperative effectiveness?
4. Should an employee who is doing an outstanding job be disciplined for breaking rules which do not affect work performance?

CASE 4

You are an assistant in a department where a great many forms and reports must be made out to be signed and forwarded by your chief. He always sends these forms and reports back to you with trifling corrections—often no more than one or two words—necessitating a complete redoing of the work. Your subordinates resent these corrections of their work and the need to do it over. They seem overcome with frustration and futility on the job. They snap at one another and take more days off than the average of other departments.

1. What should you tell your subordinates?
2. Should you talk the matter over with the chief? What would you say to him?
3. To what extent is a man in complete charge of his responsibilities?
4. To what extent should a superior show his authority?
5. How would you handle this situation?

CASE 5

You are the supervisor of a section in a large data processing department. Forty IBM proof machine operators report to you. The operators are scheduled on a staggered basis on your shift. Some start at 7:30 A.M., others at 8:00 A.M. and still others at 8:30 A.M.

Usually the operators use the same machine each day. However, this procedure is not always possible because the machine may be inoperable mechanically or the night shift operator (12 midnight–8:00 A.M.) may still be using the machine.

The operators who are displaced from their regular machines and are required to use another machine frequently complain rather strenuously to you about this inconvenience.

1. Why would an employee complain about being displaced from his regular machine?
2. Should an operator have a regular machine since all the proof machines are the same?
3. What can you do about the complaints?

CASE 6

You are the office manager of a small company. Your office force is made up of two middle-aged women—Mazie and Annie—and one young one, Joan (just out of high school) who was hired as switchboard operator when Susie retired a year ago. Mazie has been the payroll clerk for 10 years; Annie, the general stenographer for 15 years. When Susie was there relative harmony prevailed and the three women carried on a routine developed over a period of years.

When Susie retired, Joan was hired by the head of the company "as young blood to freshen up the office a bit." Soon both older women were "picking on" her. After six months of it, Mazie changed sides and joined Joan in quarreling with Annie. A few weeks ago Joan and Annie teamed up against Mazie. They all do their work satisfactorily but the atmosphere in the office, instead of being "freshened up," is icy and uncomfortable.

1. What might be some of the causes?
2. What might be some remedies?
3. Should an older woman have been hired instead of Joan? Why? Why not?
4. Should Joan, who is doing satisfactory work, be fired in the interests of peace and quiet? Justify your answer.

CASE 7

Harry Barnes was called to the president's office one afternoon. Naturally he greeted this summons with some nervousness. Harry was a very capable employee and had been with the company for several years. The company was a large international firm with offices in several countries. Overseas experience was considered to be very necessary for promotion to senior management positions in the company and all of the young, ambitious men employed by the firm coveted such assignments.

When Harry entered the president's office, he was greeted very cordially and told that he was being considered for the post of assistant manager of the company's London office. The president then asked Harry if he was interested in the position. Harry's reply was enthusiastically affirmative. The president told Harry to discuss it with his wife before accepting the offer. Harry replied that he and his wife had considered the possibility of an overseas assignment because of the nature of the company's business and that they both looked forward to the opportunity it presented. The president then confirmed the offer and told Harry to make the necessary arrangements to go to London in about one month. He said the company would offer assistance in finding a home, school for Harry's son, and other necessary arrangements. Harry was elated and when he left the president's office he called his wife to tell her the good news. He also told several fellow employees and received their congratulations. That evening Harry and his wife started their planning for the impending move. They decided to rent their house since these assignments usually lasted three years and they wanted to return to their present home. A real estate broker was called and the home was placed on the rental market. Harry's wife proceeded with other arrangements including securing a mover and his son told all of his friends at school of the exciting adventure which he anticipated. Harry made arrangements with other members of his family to look after his affairs in this country and informed all his relatives and friends of his good fortune. All in all, this was quite an event in the Barnes family.

Two weeks went by and everything was progressing smoothly. Packing was under way and excitement in the Barnes family was at a fever pitch. Harry was training his successor and he had discussed several things with his new superior in London by telephone. A family had been found to rent the Barnes home and they planned to move in soon after Harry and his family left for England.

Approximately one week before he was due to leave for London, Harry was called to the president's office again. He anticipated further instructions and last minute details regarding his promotion. Instead, the president told Harry the promotion was being withdrawn. He went on to say that the company's board of directors of which he was a member had decided to use foreign nationals in as many overseas managerial positions as possible. He said they felt this course of action was a desirable one in view of the changing conditions in most of the countries in which the company carried on business. Because of this change in policy, the company had decided to promote a British national for the assistant manager's post in London, which had been offered to and accepted by Harry Barnes. Harry was shocked by the president's withdrawal of the promotion. He tried to counter the president's reasoning and went on to delineate his preparation for the overseas assignment including the embarrassment and inconvenience the change of plans would cause him and his family. The president sympathized with Harry but said the decision was final and ended the discussion.

1. What responsibility, if any, does the company have to Harry and his family for the inconvenience and embarrassment that has been caused by the policy change?
2. Should the company have gone through with Harry's promotion regardless of the policy change?
3. What should Harry do in view of what has happened to him?
4. What can the company do to regain Harry's enthusiasm, confidence, and loyalty?
5. Can such events be prevented by the management of a company? How?
6. To what extent does good corporate citizenship require that Harry accept the president's reasoning at face value?

CASE 8

In your bookkeeping department there are two unmarried women about 30 years of age who are in active competition with each other—taking accounting courses at night, pirating work, and undermining each other, evidently with an eye to promotion to the one job that will be open above them when an older bookkeeper reaches retirement age in three years. Either young woman could qualify for the promotion.

Both girls have known for 10 years that there was only one job to advance to, but it never made any difference to them until just recently. Before that they were good friends, helped one another, and got a great deal of pleasure from the social life of the office. Several of the men in the office were married recently, and now the only single men are very young clerks.

1. What might be some of the reasons for this change of attitude toward each other?
2. Should the situation be allowed to continue? What might be some of the results?
3. What should you do?
4. Is the situation any of your business?

CASE 9

You are a section supervisor. At the last monthly meeting of section supervisors, the boss said he would like to try out full-scale participation by the supervisors in handling the problem of whistle jumping. He said he was just handing the problem over to them. They should confer on it, work out a group solution, and put the solution into effect without coming to him for a decision.

The section supervisors held a conference on whistle jumping and agreed that the problem was serious, that each supervisor was responsible for curbing it in his own section, that uniformity in enforcement was necessary, that the penalty for the first offense within a specific period should be an oral reprimand, and that the penalty for the second offense should be a written reprimand.

You explained to your men the conclusions of the supervisors' conference. You have given several oral reprimands and they seem to be effective. Your men ask you to go slow about issuing written reprimands because whistle jumping is not decreasing in some of the other sections and the offenders are not being penalized. Your men state further that the men in some of the other sections have not been informed of the penalties, thus it would be unfair of you to stick too close to the line. You observe that whistle jumping is being controlled in only about one third of the sections.

You believe that uniformity in enforcement of rules is necessary and that participation by supervisors is one of the ways to achieve this.

1. What are some of the advantages and disadvantages of the boss's plan?
2. On what kinds of problems is it effective? Why?
3. On what kinds of problems is it not effective?
4. Can the whistle-jumping problem be solved this way? Why? Why not?
5. Assuming that it can, what more should have been done at the previous meeting?

CASE 10

Top management recently decided that everyone in the organization who was responsible for money or stock should take a polygraph (lie detector) test. A sheet was received asking each manager's consent to submit to a test this first time and again at any time the company might request. The tests were conducted by a member of the security force from company headquarters. Now everyone tested is doing a slow burn. The resentment is reflected in the following comments on the test and the questions asked in it. Analyze them and make suggestions for preventing losses from dishonesty.

1. The character who administered the test must have been thrown off a police force for graft. What use might he make of the information he had obtained? What use did the company plan to make of this intimate information?
2. The company had no right to ask whether a person intended to make a career of his job or whether he had feelers out for other jobs.
3. The company had no right to ask one person for information damaging to another.
4. The company had no right to ask how a person felt toward his immediate boss.
5. The company must be crooked; otherwise it wouldn't go in for this sort of thing.
6. Do they expect me to stick my neck out now to save them from loss?

CASE 11

You graduated from college a year ago and were taken into a company to be trained for a supervisory position. You are a hard worker and anxious to move up in the ranks of management. After the first six months of the company's junior executive training course, your work is recognized, and you are given a supervisory job as part of your executive training.

Three assistants are under you, and it is necessary for you to work very closely with them. These assistants are much older than you and have been with the company for a number of years. From the very start you run into difficulties with your oldest assistant, John Brown. He is lazy, and he always changes your orders in carrying out his assigned tasks. When you speak to him about work in front of the other employees, he always has the comeback that he knows what is to be done and that in years past it was always done differently. To avoid his back talk, you give most of his work to the other assistants or do it yourself.

After a while you get tired of Brown's behavior. You do some discreet inquiring to find out if he was always that way, and you learn that years ago he was in the private employ of the owners of the concern and he is still well liked by them. The other supervisors have always stayed clear of him.

Your boss lets you know that he will have nothing to do with the situation. If you go over his head and complain, it will not look good for you, because Brown has been working in the plant for 10 years with never a complaint against him. You feel that this is a test of your supervisory ability, and you want to do something about it.

1. How might Brown be viewing the situation?
2. How might your boss be viewing the situation?
3. How do you view the situation?
4. What might be some of the mistakes you are making?
5. How should you go about disciplining Brown?
6. What must have been wrong with the way the previous supervisor handled Brown?

CASE 12

Your boss has several sections under his control. You and the other supervisors of these sections are called into his office quite often for conferences and instructions. The boss is the type of man who pounds his desk and shouts when giving instructions; also he is sarcastic. You don't like being shouted at, and neither do the other supervisors. Many of the men working under you and under the other supervisors have felt the bite of his tongue; as a result, morale is very low and all resent the boss's attitude. The efficiency of all his sections is low, and there are many requests for transfers out of the department.

1. Should you, being senior supervisor, talk this situation over with your boss? If so, what should you say to him?
2. What are some ways of handling this type of boss?
3. Would it be advisable for you, or for all the other supervisors, to go to someone higher in authority than your boss?
4. How could the personnel department help in this situation?

CASE 13

Paul Nathan was president of his own company, a medium-sized concern enjoying moderate success in a very competitive industry. Quite naturally Paul was very enthusiastic about the firm's prospects and he kept telling all of his employees how successful they would be if they stayed on his team.

Mr. Nathan was generally the first to arrive each morning, usually at 7:00 A.M. By the time the rest of the group arrived at 9 o'clock, he had frequently dictated several letters and memoranda and his secretary was expected to transcribe these immediately. He frequently reminded her and other employees that he had done a day's work before they arrived. He also stayed late each day, frequently starting a meeting with some of the executives at 4:00 P.M. or 4:30 P.M. and these meetings usually lasted well past the normal quitting time. Because of his great interest in the company, Paul Nathan made it a practice to work on Saturdays even though that day was not a part of the normal work week. His efforts on that day also produced a large amount of memoranda and he frequently asked his secretary to come in on Saturday to transcribe his output from the dictating machine. The willingness to come in on Saturdays or the lack of it on the part of the company's executives was used by Paul Nathan as a rather significant standard to measure their degree of enthusiasm for their jobs and the welfare of the company. Because his own work habits included the devotion of so much time to the business, he felt that all senior executives should follow the same pattern. Of the 10 executives concerned, 3 did not mind following Nathan's lead. The others grudgingly came in one or two Saturdays a month and they resented the time spent. Their particular criticism centered on the general lack of accomplishment and the fact that much time was spent merely satisfying Paul Nathan's ego. None of the executives had any stock in the company, although they were involved in profit sharing on gross revenues in addition to their salaries.

Quite naturally, those executives who came in every Saturday received an inordinate amount of praise from Nathan and the others were keenly aware of the need to demonstrate enthusiasm and dedication. Nevertheless they felt it was unfair to be measured by the amount of time expended on the job rather than by what was accomplished. They believed it necessary to spend time away from the firm and that their families deserved a portion of this time. Paul Nathan was aware of the feelings of most of his executives and he claimed that no one was pressured to work on Saturdays or any evening of the week for that matter.

1. Is Paul Nathan realistic in his desire for executive performance?
2. Can the chief executive and owner of a company expect the same amount of dedication and enthusiasm that he has?
3. What can the president of this company do to change the attitude of his immediate subordinates?
4. What can the executive do to change Paul Nathan's approach to performance evaluation?

CASE 14

The job of secretary to a senior officer of the company had long been considered an honor. It was traditional to promote one of the secretaries to major department heads when such a position opened. Usually the person chosen had long tenure with the company and had demonstrated ability as an effective private secretary.

Such a person was Louise Miller. She had been with the company for 27 years and she was presently serving as the secretary to the chief engineer. When the production vice president's secretary retired everyone including Louise believed that she would be promoted to fill the vacancy.

A week after the vacancy occurred, it became apparent to Louise that she was not being offered the promotion. She went to see the personnel manager and was told that he was recruiting a girl for the job from outside the company. He felt that the girl should be a college graduate and be able to pass the battery of psychological, intelligence, and aptitude tests the company had recently started to use as part of its selection and placement procedure.

Louise Miller was quite discouraged when she left the personnel manager's office. She felt slighted and was rather bitter about the fact that her years of successful secretarial experience did not seem to qualify her for the opening. She went to her boss, the chief engineer, to ask for advice. He felt she was an excellent secretary who was eminently qualified for the promotion. He believed that her knowledge of company policy and procedures, her loyalty and her strong motivation should result in a promotion for her.

1. What should Louise Miller's boss do to help her?
2. Is the personnel manager correct in his efforts at outside recruitment to fill the open secretarial position?
3. Should Louise Miller's long and successful experience be considered a valid substitute for her lack of qualifications established by the personnel manager?
4. How should long service, experienced employees be handled when they believe they are qualified for an opening and new standards indicate they are not?
5. Should Louise be given the opportunity to take the test battery?
6. Is Louise Miller justified in her feelings of bitterness and discouragement?

CASE 15

You were appointed to a job in a government agency to replace the retiring manager of a large group of women clerical workers. One thing you intend to change is the reform-school routine that starts the day. The women clerks (all in the 40 to 65 age bracket) mill around in the lobby until a warning bell rings at five minutes to eight. Then they walk silently into the department, each to her own place, and sit down. At one minute to eight a tap on the bell brings them to attention; they pull their chairs up into working position, take the covers off their office machines, and are ready. The eight o'clock bell rings and they plunge into their work.

The assistant manager, who has been there a long time, suggests that before making any changes, you conduct a poll and ask the women if they want to change this routine. You go along with him and hand out ballots for an unsigned vote on how they like this way of beginning the day. Seventy percent of the women write that they think it is a wonderful system and they wouldn't want it changed.

Can you explain it?

CASE 16

You are the personnel director of a large company. While there was no written policy regarding coffee breaks, they were a long-established tradition and all employees availed themselves of the privilege each morning and afternoon of the workday. In fact, company management had allowed a vending machine company to place their machines in several locations throughout the building in which the company was located. As a result, employees took coffee breaks, usually 10 minutes long at any time of the day they desired.

In general, this approach did not cause too much difficulty in work accomplishment, but in one department, in the opinion of its supervisor, the work suffered. There was socializing around desks while the coffee was consumed and telephones went unanswered and work came to a halt. In some instances, the employees in that department took breaks longer than 10 minutes and this too upset work patterns.

Because of this the supervisor issued a memorandum to all employees under his jurisdiction. In it he reaffirmed the tradition of the coffee break, but he restricted it to 10:15 to 10:25 in the morning and 3:15 to 3:25 in the afternoon. He also requested all employees to be back at their desks at the end of each break.

When the memo was received, many of the employees reacted negatively. Indignation ran high and two employees were designated as spokesmen to come to you with their grievance without first going to their supervisor.

1. What reaction would you have to the two-man committee?
2. Was the supervisor justified in trying to establish orderly breaks in his department?
3. Could he have handled it in other ways?
4. Are the employees justified in their indignation and what, if anything, can you do to minimize it?

CASE 17

You are the supervisor of a large office section. Several of the units in the section are under the jurisdiction of assistant supervisors, and each contains a half-dozen or so typists. A separate unit for tabulating figures is run by Sam Smith who has one typist to assist him. Smith is middle-aged, married, and all business.

This morning Smith asked you to replace Betty, the typist he has had for the last six weeks. (She took the place of the previous girl, who left to be married.) Smith tells you that Betty is making deliberate mistakes and not correcting her errors because she wants to be transferred back to her former job in one of the other units. Smith says that from the beginning Betty was never very good at typing columns of figures and has been getting progressively worse. He states that he has explained the importance of her work to her and pointed out her errors to her. He believes that she needs glasses. When he suggested that she should get her eyes examined, she said that she had no intention of getting glasses and looking like an old maid. Frequently in the presence of Smith she complains over the phone to the girls in her former unit that she is cooped up, that her work gives her a headache, and that she wishes she were back in her old unit where there were good-looking fellows who were single, there was lots of fun, and the living was easy.

You ask Smith what he thinks the trouble is. He replies that Betty— like most of the girls in the section—is a dumb, sweet, pretty kid who is more interested in landing a husband than in doing a fair day's work. There is no reason for you to doubt Smith.

Betty's former unit is the source of supply of typists for Smith's unit. Practically all the girls are young graduates of the local high school. While Betty was in that unit her work was satisfactory. You do not want to terminate her. As a last resort you could send her to Personnel for assignment elsewhere.

1. What are your problems in this situation?
2. How should you handle each?
3. Should you discipline Betty? What would be effective?
4. What might be some of the consequences of sending her back to her old job?
5. What are some of the principles one should have in mind when considering transferring employees?

CASE 18

You are in charge of a section normally employing 30 men. The product is seasonal; so once a year it is necessary to double the number of employees for two or three months in order to get the product out. There is no way of avoiding it.

Through the rest of the year you have your organization running smoothly: morale is high, and scrap is low. On several occasions you and your section have been commended for efficiency. However, with the hiring of the seasonal help each year, efficiency and morale go down on account of the crowded conditions and the confusion caused by the new men.

The new help generally falls into two categories: those who give a minimum amount of production because they realize that their employment is only temporary and those who work very hard in the hope of being retained when the rush is over.

1. How can morale and production be improved during the rush season?
2. How can you build morale and production among the new men whose output is low?
3. Should the supervisor encourage seasonal workers to give good output, by hinting that there is a good chance that the best workers will be made permanent—even though he has no basis to support such a promise?
4. Can you have high production and low morale?
5. Can you have high morale and low production?
6. Upon what foundation is a combination of high production and high morale based?

CASE 19

You are the superintendent of the small but rapidly growing Acme Manufacturing Company. In general, everything is coming along well except in the central inspection department. You think the problems there could also arise elsewhere; so you want to get the situation under control.

From the beginning of the company eight years ago one of the stated policies has been: *No time clocks. Management depends upon everyone to deliver a satisfactory day's work for a satisfactory day's pay. If an employee is tardy he is expected to make up the lost time by putting in extra time or effort.*

The policy was not written but generally understood. There are no abuses except in J. Smith's inspection department where tardiness, slow starting, and visiting are taken as a matter of course. Smith, like most of the other supervisors, started as a rank-and-file worker. Any supervisory training that he may have, he has gotten on his own. Smith has told you of his concern over the way his people abuse the coffee break and that he was trying out schemes for solving the problem. These coffee breaks are twice a day for a period of 10 minutes each. In Smith's department the people line up long before the coffee wagon is due and wait for it. After they get their share of free coffee and doughnuts, they start bull sessions or wander off into other departments. Later, individually or in groups, they drift back to their work stations. The 10-minute break has become in many cases a half-hour break.

Performance in the inspection department—never too good—got so bad three months ago that Smith felt he should do something about the coffee break. He told his assistant, J. Jones, to signal the end of the 10-minute break by clanging a hammer on a piece of sheet steel and shouting "Time's up. Time's up." At first this was considered to be quite a gag and good for a laugh, and it had some good effect. However, when the supervisors and employees in the rest of the plant saw what was going on, they began to kid the members of the inspection department by banging on pieces of metal and shouting "Time's up." This caused the inspectors to feel that they were the objects of ridicule; so they openly expressed antagonism against the supervisor and his assistant. Resentfulness and dissatisfaction were expressed in gripes and grievances concerning trivial conditions that had long been overlooked or tolerated. Housekeeping became more slovenly. Performance went down and errors went up.

In your investigation you find that the inspection department has lost sight of the policy regarding tardiness; some of the newer employees never heard of it. You learn that the assistant supervisor was hired in spite of the company policy against hiring relatives (he is a relative of a member of top management) and that he was promoted to his present job after he had been with the company only a few weeks. You learn that all this was done over the objections of Smith, the inspection department supervisor. Smith had been holding open the position of assistant supervisor as bait to encourage some of his men.

You find that there are no standards of performance in the inspection department. Departmental planning is poor. Jobs are either rush jobs or to be dawdled over.

1. List the violations of good management practices in this case.
2. Show how each should be corrected.
3. Set up a training program for supervisors. What should be included? Why should it be included? How should the various subjects be taught?

CASE 20

The big boss of a medium-sized manufacturing company has been reading articles (similar to those quoted in this chapter) about keeping employees informed about the company. He thinks it is a good idea. Up until now practically no such information has ever reached the rank and file. The boss has called in the head of the industrial relations department and told him to find out what other companies are doing about keeping employees informed, then to come up with a program for his company.

1. Outline the steps to be taken in investigating, evaluating, designing, inaugurating, and maintaining a program of keeping employees informed about the company.
2. Gather (if practical) information from books, periodicals, and companies to illustrate each of the above five steps.
3. What are some ways of measuring the effectiveness of such programs?

FOLLOWING UP ON THE JOB

Morale changes within the department

Has there been an increase or decrease in:

Gripes and grievances	Tardiness	Accidents
Quality of output	Absenteeism	Quits
Quantity of output	Transfers out	Scrap

The employee and his job

1. Are jobs well designed?
2. Is each worker fitted to his job?
3. Do some need additional training?
4. Does each one know what is expected of him?
5. What is the condition of the equipment?
6. How are working conditions?

The employee and the team

1. Are cliques forming?
2. Is anyone being made the goat?
3. Is there buck-passing?
4. Is there a friendly give-and-take?
5. Is there quarreling?
6. Are group members cooperating?

The employee and you

1. Do you let each subordinate know how he is getting along?
2. Do you point out ways to improve?
3. Do you take a friendly interest in his problems?
4. Do you give credit when due?
5. Do you tell him in advance about changes that will affect him?
6. Do you give him encouragement?
7. Do you give him opportunity to participate in decisions?

The employee and the company

1. Do you squelch rumors with facts?
2. Do you sell the company to your men?
3. Do you point out the advantages of working for this company?
4. Do you keep your superiors informed on employee thoughts about the company?
5. To what extent do you create a motivational climate in your area of responsibility?
6. How does the company, its policies, working conditions, and the nature of the work contribute to the fulfillment of employee needs?

Suggested readings

BOOKS

For Chapter:

14   ARENSBERG, CONRAD M.; BARKIN, SOLOMON; CHALMERS, W. ELLISON; WILENSKY, HAROLD L.; WORTHY, JAMES C.; and DENNIS, BARBARA D. *Research in Industrial Human Relations: A Critical Appraisal.* Publication No. 17 of Industrial Relations Research Association. New York: Harper & Row, Publishers, 1957.

14, 15, 16   ARGYRIS, CHRIS. *Integrating the Individual and the Organization.* New York: John Wiley & Sons, Inc., 1964.

14, 16   BASSETT, GLENN A. *Management Styles in Transition.* New York: American Management Association, 1966.

16   BIRCH, D., and VEROFF, J. *Motivation: A Study of Action.* Belmont. Calif.: Brooks/Cole Publishing Co., 1966.

15   BUREAU OF NATIONAL AFFAIRS, INC. *Labor Arbitration Reports.* Washington, D.C.: BNA, Inc. (Selected arbitration cases published serially since 1946.)

14, 15,16   CUMMINGS, L. L., and SCOTT, W. E. *Readings in Organizational Behavior and Human Performance.* Homewood, Ill.: Richard D. Irwin, Inc., 1969.

14, 15, 16   DAVIS, KEITH. *Human Relations at Work, The Dynamics of Organizational Behavior.* 3d ed. New York: McGraw-Hill Book Co., 1967.

14, 16   DRUCKER, PETER F. *The Practice of Management.* New York: Harper & Row, Publishers, 1954.

14, 16   DUBIN, R.; HOMANS, G. C.; MANN, F. C.; and MILLER, D. C. *Leadership and Productivity.* San Francisco, Calif.: Chandler Publishing Co., 1965.

14, 15, 16   FLEISHMAN, EDWIN A. (ed.). *Studies in Personnel and Industrial Psychology.* Rev. ed. Homewood, Ill.: The Dorsey Press, 1967.

15, 16   FITTS, P. M., and POSNER, M. I. *Human Performance.* Belmont, Calif.: Brooks/Cole Publishing Co., 1967.

15   GAUDET, FREDERICK J. *Solving Problems of Employee Absence.* Research Study No. 57. New York: American Management Association, 1963.

16 GELLERMAN, SAUL W. *Motivation and Productivity.* New York: American Management Association, 1963.

15 GUEST, ROBERT H. *Organizational Change: The Effect of Successful Leadership.* Homewood, Ill.: Richard D. Irwin, Inc., 1962.

14, 15, 16 HAMPTON, DAVID R. *Behavioral Concepts in Management.* Belmont, Calif.: Dickenson Publishing Co., Inc., 1968.

16 HERZBERG, FREDERICK. *Work and the Nature of Man.* Cleveland, Ohio: The World Publishing Co., 1966.

16 ———; MAUSNER, BERNARD; and SNYDERMAN, BARBARA. *The Motivation to Work.* 2d ed., New York: John Wiley & Sons, Inc., 1959.

14, 16 LIKERT, RENSIS. *The Human Organization.* New York: McGraw-Hill Book Co., 1967.

14, 16 McGREGOR. DOUGLAS. *The Human Side of Enterprise.* New York: McGraw-Hill Book Co., 1960.

14 ———. *The Professional Manager.* New York: McGraw-Hill Book Co., 1967.

14, 15, 16 MAIER, NORMAN R. F. *Problem-Solving Discussions and Conferences: Leadership Methods and Skills.* New York: McGraw-Hill Book Co., 1963.

14, 16 MARROW, A.; BOWERS, D. G.; and SEASHORE, S. E. *Management by Participation.* New York: Harper & Row, Publishers, 1967.

16 MASLOW, A. H. *Eupsychian Management.* Homewood, Ill.: Richard D. Irwin, Inc., 1965.

16 ———. *Motivation and Personality.* New York: Harper & Row, Publishers, 1954.

14, 15, 16 MORSE, NANCY C. *Satisfactions in White Collar Jobs.* Ann Arbor, Mich.: Survey Research Center, University of Michigan, 1953.

14 NILES, HENRY E.; NILES, MARY CUSHING; and STEPHENS, JAMES C. *The Office Supervisor: His Relations to Persons and to Work.* New York: John Wiley & Sons, Inc., 1959.

15, 16 O'CONNELL, J. J. *Managing Organizational Innovation.* Homewood, Ill.: Richard D. Irwin, Inc., 1968.

14, 15, 16 PFIFFNER, J. M., and FELS, M. *The Supervision of Personnel.* 3d. ed. Englewood Cliffs, N.J.: Prentice-Hall, Inc., 1964.

16 ———, and SHERWOOD, FRANK P. *Administrative Organization.* Englewood Cliffs, N.J.: Prentice-Hall, Inc., 1960, chaps. 22 and 23.

15 PHELPS, ORME. *Discipline and Discharge in the Unionized Firm.* Berkeley and Los Angeles: University of California Press, 1959.

16   ROETHLISBERGER, F. J. *Management and Morale*. Cambridge, Mass.: Harvard University Press, 1941.

14, 16   ROY, ROBERT H. *The Administrative Process*. Baltimore: The Johns Hopkins Press, 1958.

15   SAYLES, LEONARD R. *Behavior of Industrial Work Groups*. New York: John Wiley & Sons, Inc., 1958.

14, 16   ———. *Managerial Behavior*. New York: McGraw-Hill Book Co., 1964.

14, 15, 16   SCOTT, WILLIAM G. *Organization Theory. A Behavioral Analysis for Management*. Homewood, Ill.: Richard D. Irwin, Inc., 1967.

15   ———. *The Management of Conflict*. Homewood, Ill.: Richard D. Irwin, Inc., 1965.

15   SLICHTER, SUMNER; HEALY, JAMES J.: and LIVERNASH, E. ROBERT. *The Impact of Collective Bargaining on Management*. Washington, D.C.: The Brookings Institution, 1960.

14, 15, 16   STAFF OF SUPERVISORY MANAGEMENT (eds.). *Leadership on the Job*. New York: American Management Association, 1957.

15   STAGNER, ROSS, and ROSEN, HJALMER. *Psychology of Union-Management Relations*. Belmont, Calif.: Wadsworth Publishing Co., Inc., 1965.

15   STESSEN, LAWRENCE. *Employee Discipline*. Washington, D.C. Bureau of National Affairs, Inc., 1960.

15, 16   TANNENBAUM, ARNOLD S. *Social Psychology of the Work Organization*. Belmont, Calif.: Wadsworth Publishing Co., Inc., 1966.

14, 15, 16   THAYER, LEE. *Communication and Communication Systems in Organization, Management and Interpersonal Relations*. Homewood, Ill.: Richard D. Irwin, Inc., 1968.

15   TRICE, HARRISON. *The Problem Drinker on the Job*. Bulletin No. 40. Ithaca, N.Y.: New York State School of Industrial and Labor Relations,

14, 16   VROOM, VICTOR H. *Some Personality Determinants of the Effects of Participation*. Englewood Cliffs, N.J.: Prentice-Hall, Inc., 1960.

16   ———. *Work and Motivation*. New York: John Wiley & Sons, Inc., 1964.

14, 15, 16   WHYTE, WILLIAM F. *Organizational Behavior: Theory and Application*. Homewood, Ill.: Richard D. Irwin, Inc., 1969.

ARTICLES

For Chapter:

15   "Act of Handling Grievances: When Is a Gripe Not a Grievance?" *Supervisory Management*, April, 1959.

15 "Alcoholic Executive," *Fortune*, Vol. LXI, No. 1 (January, 1960), pp. 99 ff.

15 BAUMGARTEL, H. E., and SOBEL, R. "Organizational Factors in Absenteeism," *Personnel Psychology*, Vol. XII (Autumn, 1959).

14 BESCO, ROBERT O., and LAUSCHE, C. H. "Foreman Leadership as Perceived by Superiors and Subordinates," *Personnel Psychology*, Winter, 1959.

15 CALEO, ROBERT L. "Cracking down on Absenteeism," *Administrative Management*, June, 1963.

16 DAUW, D. C. "Creativity and Vocational Needs of Clerical Personnel," *Personnel Journal*, December, 1968.

16 HERZBERG, FREDERICK. "One More Time: How Do You Motivate Employees?" *Harvard Business Review*, January–February, 1968.

14, 16 HOPPER, KENNETH. "The Growing Use of College Graduates as Foremen," *Management of Personnel Quarterly*, Summer, 1967.

15 "Identifying the Problem Drinker on the Job," *Personnel*, Vol. 33, No. 6 (May, 1957), pp. 527–33.

15 KELLEY, JAMES W. "Case of the Alcoholic Absentee," *Harvard Business Review*, May–June, 1969.

14, 16 KOPROWSKI, E. J. "Toward Innovative Leadership," *Business Horizons*, Winter, 1967.

14 KURILOFF, A. H. "Management by Integration and Self-Control," in *Proceedings Fifteenth Annual Industrial Engineering Institute*, University of California, Berkeley and Los Angeles (February, 1963). (A report on a company organized and managed according to Douglas McGregor's Theory Y. The company (Non-Linear Systems, Inc. of Del Mar, California) is the subject of the following article.)

14 ———. "An Experiment in Management—Putting Theory Y to the Test," *Personnel* (November–December, 1963), pp. 8–17.

14, 16 LIVINGSTON, J. S. "Pygmalion in Management," *Harvard Business Review*, July–August, 1969.

16 MASTERSON, THOMAS R., and MARA, THOMAS G. "Motivating the Underperformer," Bulletin No. 130, *American Management Association*, 1969.

15 MORGAN, F. M. "Toward Better Control of Absenteeism," *Personnel Journal*, April, 1969.

15 MOSER. GEORGE V. "Rules and Discipline," *Management Record* Vol. XXIII, No. 5 (May, 1961), pp. 21–23.

16 MYERS, M. SCOTT. "Who Are Your Motivated Workers?" *Harvard Business Review*, January–February, 1964.

16 PORTER, LYMAN W., and LAWLER, EDWARD E. III. "What Job Attitudes Tell about Motivation," *Harvard Business Review*, January–February, 1968.

15 ROSSMAN, H. D. "You Can't Fire Us—We Just Quit," *Personnel Journal*, April, 1968.

16 STERNBACH, RICHARD A.; GUSTAFSON, LAWRENCE A.; and COLLIER, RONALD L. "Don't Trust the Lie Detector," *Harvard Business Review*, Vol. XL., No. 6 (November–December, 1962), pp. 127–134.

14 TANNENBAUM, ROBERT, and SCHMIDT, WARREN H. "How to Choose a Leadership Pattern," *Harvard Business Review*, Vol. 36, No. 2 (March–April, 1958), pp. 95–101.

16 TINGEY, SHERMAN. "Six Requirements for a Successful Company Publication," *Personnel Journal* (November, 1967).

15 "What to Say to an Alcoholic," *Management Review*, Vol. LIII, No. 1 (January, 1964), pp. 34–39.

15 WOLLENBERGER, JOSEPH B. "Acceptable Work Rules and Penalties: A Company Guide," *Personnel*, Vol. XL, No. 4 (July–August, 1963), pp. 23–29. (A labor relations lawyer suggests the wording for 26 rules and the penalties for violations.)

Part V

Professional personnel

Part V

17 The management of professional personnel

Definition of professionals. The meaning of professionalism. What professionals want from the job. The professional as a supervisor. The job of managing research. Training for research management. Paths of advancement. Project management. Professional development. Leadership skills for professionals. Utilizing professional talent. The growing use of professionals. Summary.

Technical excellence is one of this country's major resources. To keep ahead in a competitive and increasingly complex world, many companies are initiating and expanding such activities as research and development, project management, operations research and other mathematical techniques, and pure and applied research in a variety of fields. For these activities they employ engineers, scientists, and other technical personnel. These people prepare plans, design new products, discover new applications for old products, develop new processes, and perform a host of other tasks which require their professional expertise. Professional employees are being employed by all types of organizations and are one of the fastest growing groups in industry, government, and organizations in our society. The effective utilization of professional employees is a matter of concern to both the employer and the employee. The dichotomy that exists between managers and professional personnel can be easily seen in this quote concerning James Webb, the first administrator of the National Aeronautics and Space Agency. Webb was neither a scientist nor an engineer, his background being political and managerial. "At first, scientists were suspicious of him and somewhat condescending, considering him "only a bureaucrat."[1]

This chapter discusses some of the problems that complicate the management of professional talent—problems that stand in the way of achieving maximum output for the company and maximum satisfaction for the individual.

[1] John N. Wilford, We Reach the Moon (New York: Bantam Books, 1969), p. 56.

Definition of professionals

In an industrial society traditionally divided into managers and operatives, the professional occupies a unique position. The National Labor Relations Act distinguishes him from the rank and file by defining him as one engaged in work (1) predominantly intellectual and varied as contrasted to routine mental, manual, mechanical, or physical; (2) involving the consistent exercise of discretion and judgment—the results of which cannot be standardized in relation to a given period of time. The work must also require knowledge of an advanced type in a field of science or learning customarily acquired by a prolonged course of study. This course of study is distinguished from a general academic education, from an apprenticeship, or from training in the performance of routine mental, manual, or physical processes. The law goes on to describe the professional as an employee who has completed courses of study in an area of advanced knowledge and who performs related work under the supervision of a professional person.

These qualifications of a professional set him apart from the rank-and-file employee but do not make him a member of management. He is a manager only if his position in the organization structure is a managerial position—that is, if he is responsible for the results of some unit of the organization, or accountable for the action of other people whose work he plans, organizes, directs, coordinates, and controls.

The essential difference between the professional employee and the manager is that the line or operations manager gets things done through others and is responsible for the actions of others. The professional employee engaged in the technical work of his profession is a staff man responsible for his own contribution of ideas, for making these ideas usable, and for helping other people to make use of them.

The meaning of professionalism

The code of ethics of the medical profession is instilled into the medical student as a part of his education. A code of ethics is a set of standards which is a protection to the profession—a guard against unworthy behavior by its members. Standards are to assure that the doctor will have the knowledge and skill he needs, that his judgment can be relied on, and that he can be trusted to do what should be done.

The scientists and the engineer in their college training are indoctrinated with the codes of their professions. The profession establishes standards of training and performance. It sets up criteria by which it judges the competence of its members and the integrity of their work. It establishes the expectation that a professional has the competence to know what should be done and how it should be done and that he will do it that way. The professional code establishes that the scientist is responsible to the scientific community and that it will be the judge of his actions.

Professionalism in science and in engineering—just as in medicine—has as its primary function the protection of standards and the preservation of integrity.

The scientist and engineer who go on to get Ph.D. degrees as a preparation for research work may become deeply committed to their professions. They absorb more of the methodology and the idea of the colleague type of control—a social system in which a professional's behavior and performance are regulated by the judgments of his equals. The traditional superior-subordinate relationship of industry doesn't fit into this pattern.

In the years of study for a doctorate, graduate students get a prolonged exposure to the academic world. There, scholarly people have status without going into administrative work. The scholar can have power and influence through being sought out as an authority in a particular field and having his colleagues recognize the significance of his contributions to it. To an extent related to the length of exposure, these influences of the academic environment are absorbed into the values and attitudes of the professional.

When the professional takes an industrial job he doesn't think of himself as just another employee. He thinks that his judgment should be respected. He objects to getting detailed directions about how he is to do his work. And he objects even more strongly to having anyone look over his shoulder to see if he *is* doing it. He may be more concerned about professional standards than about business results.[2] He may find that his professional standards are in conflict with the company's need for something practicable and profitable rather than the best that could be done if time and money were unlimited. He wants to do a piece of work that will merit the acclaim of his scientific colleagues, and when he does such work, he wants to publish it. He wants to attend the meetings of his scientific society in order to talk about his achieve-

---

[2] The science-oriented person is sometimes described as one who just happens to be doing his work in a particular organization but hasn't let it affect his goals or standards. The institutional-oriented professional is one who is working for company goals.

A study done by Barnes in two engineering-technician groups doing design work on electronic equipment illustrates a type of organizational relationship in which the professional has high attachment to the values of his profession without withdrawing from the values of the organization. See Louis B. Barnes, *Organizational Systems and Engineering Groups: A Comparative Study of Two Technical Groups in Industry* (Boston: Harvard University Press, 1960).

ments, to find out what others are doing, and to get new ideas to use in his work.

In place of these rewards that he wants—and as incentives to future performance—the company may offer him more money or an administrative job or a status spot in the parking lot. Since organizations use rewards as a means of influencing behavior, they need to find out what things—in addition to money—will motivate people to give the organization what it wants. Since the organization needs what the professional has to offer, management would be well advised to find out what kind of treatment will yield the highest output to the company and highest satisfaction to the professional.

The picture of the professional[3] presented fits some of the scientists and engineers in industry and may explain the basis for demands that seem unreasonable to management but entirely logical to the professional. The picture of the science-oriented professional doesn't fit all scientists and engineers and it doesn't take into account individual differences in personality and motivation. In fact, scientists and engineers shouldn't be lumped together and considered as a type, even though the engineer's education has become quite scientific.

Social studies of professional personality.   Personality factors of scientists and engineers have been the subject of a number of studies attempting to determine the human factors involved in creativity and success in creative work. Two studies of small selected groups of outstanding scientists present a picture of the creative person as someone basically different from other people—highly independent, totally dedicated to his work, and lacking in social interests.[4] Other studies made on an unselected basis[5] found scientists and engineers in industry to

---

[3] To go much deeper into the study of professionalism and the adjustments involved in adapting it to organizations, see William Kornhauser, *Scientists in Industry* (Berkeley and Los Angeles: University of California Press, 1962). Also Robert Teivot Livingston and Stanley H. Milberg (eds.), *Human Relations in Industrial Research Management* (New York: Columbia University Press, 1957).

[4] Ann Roe's psychological study of 22 outstanding physical scientists fits this pattern. "A Psychological Study of Physical Scientists," *Genetic Psychology Monographs*, May, 1951, pp. 121–39.

Also Francis Bello's study of 100 outstanding scientists, "The Young Scientists," *Fortune,* June, 1954, pp. 142 ff.

[5] A survey that Booz, Allen, & Hamilton made of 3,500 scientists and engineers contradicts the opinion that they are "different." It found that the scientists and engineers wanted to know what management required of them and preferred working under relatively close administrative controls. For more about this survey, see James L. Wyatt, "Are Creative People Different?" *Management Review,* Vol. XLVIII, No. 7 (July, 1959), pp. 20 ff.

This same survey is discussed by C. Wilson Randle, "Problems of R&D Management," *Harvard Business Review,* Vol. XXXVII, No. 1 (January–February, 1959), pp. 129 ff.

Interviews with 277 engineers and scientists and their superiors were the basis

be very much like other highly educated and ambitious people. One study found them willing to work under relatively close controls. Another study found a number of them interested in moving out of technical work and into higher paying jobs in management and sales. It is these differences in personality, ability, and interest that make it possible to find scientists and engineers who fit the various types of work to be done and who have the combination of technical competence and managerial ability needed for managing scientific and engineering work.

What professionals want from the job

While there are wide individual differences between professionals, a number of attitude surveys found some striking similarities between them in the complaints they made about their jobs and the things they said were important to them in their work.[6]

They complained of salary inequities—that people were not paid according to their contributions and that the only way to get raises was to job hop. They complained that their talents were poorly utilized on their jobs—that much of the work they were doing was below their skill level. They complained of lack of freedom to follow up interesting research leads and said that they were being forced to overspecialize.

A number of scientists and engineers in aircraft, oil, utilities, and electrical companies formed unions. Their demands were much the same as the complaints expressed in the surveys. They wanted training and planned advancement, merit reviews, and salaries based on ability and output. They wanted to be recognized and treated as professionals. And they wanted the company to pay professional dues and tuition costs,

---

for a study by Lee E. Danielson. His subjects, although intensely interested in their work, were also interested in the cash and recognition; many of them expected to move out of technical fields and into higher paying ones such as management or sales. (*Characteristics of Engineers and Scientists Significant for Their Motivation and Utilization.* [Report No. 11] [Ann Arbor, Mich.: Bureau of Industrial Relations, University of Michigan, 1960].)

[6] The University of Chicago's "Employment Inventory" surveyed the attitudes of 587 professional employees—engineers, chemists, and physicists. See David G. Moore and Richard Renck, "The Professional Employee in Industry," *Journal of Business,* Vol. XXVIII (January, 1955), pp. 58–66.

Opinion Research Corporation of Princeton, N.J., questioned 622 professionals, half of whom were in scientific work. ("The Conflict between the Scientific Mind and the Management Mind," *The Public Opinion Index for Industry,* Vol. 17, No. 9 [Princeton, N.J.: Opinion Research Corp., 1959].)

The U.S. Government quizzed 20,000 scientists in order to compare attitudes of those in government with those in private industry. The attitudes in this survey were not as critical as the ones in the two surveys above. (*Summary of Report of Attitudes of Scientists and Engineers in Government and Industry* [Washington, D.C.: Government Printing office, 1957].)

to finance attendance at professional meetings and to give leaves of absence for educational purposes.[7]

Some attitude surveys inquired about the satisfactions of professional work as well as the dissatisfactions.[8] The scientists and engineers gave high ranking to such satisfactions as seeing their ideas put to use; seeing a project through from beginning to end; doing work that is new, varied, creative, and challenging; getting recognition for achievement; having opportunities for training and for keeping up with developments in the field.

Turnover figures indicate that satisfactions actually realized on many jobs were not sufficient to hold the professionals to them in the face of a high market demand for their talents. College placement estimates are that half the graduates change jobs within the first year out of college and that three fourths of them have changed by the end of the fifth year. The cost of this turnover is high—recruiting expense, training expense, and the fact that an inexperienced man can contribute very little in his first year or so on a professional job.

Since the surveys were made, many companies have improved their salary structures and advancement policies and are offering training and opportunities for more education.[9]

The professional as a supervisor

Most scientists, engineers, and other professionals come to their jobs with a value system that is different from that which is considered typical by managers. They tend to emphasize loyalty to their disciplines and to their ability to practice these disciplines. Such loyalty has been imbued by the university world since many of their professors have similar loyalties. Generally they are not prepared for the goal orientation of the business world and many of them seek careers in nonbusiness organizations because of this. Some find that their technical knowledge will only carry them so far in industry and that the higher rewards come

---

[7] For a study of contract demands and provisions, see "Unionization among American Engineers," *Studies in Personnel Policy* No. 155 (New York: National Industrial Conference Board, 1956).

Unionization didn't fit very well with professionalism, and by 1960 the number of dues-paying members had dwindled. See "Engineering Union Fights for Life," *Fortune,* Vol. LXI, No. 5 (May, 1960), pp. 248 ff.

[8] "Career Satisfactions of Professional Engineers in Industry," *Public Opinion Index for Industry* (in cooperation with the National Society of Professional Engineers) (Washington, D.C., 1957).

John W. Riegel, *Intangible Rewards for Engineers and Scientists* (Ann Arbor, Mich.: Bureau of Industrial Relations, University of Michigan, 1958).

Danielson, *op. cit.*

[9] In the American Management Association reports in the reading list, various companies report on what they are doing in the management of their professional employees.

from administrative or sales work. Even though many professionals move to administrative work, they may be frustrated and feel that they have deserted their disciplines for material reward rather than professional gratification. Many would prefer to be rewarded for technical excellence and do not desire the managerial responsibility. If he redirects his goals toward managerial ones, he still may feel that his promotion to a first-level supervisory position was a reward for technical ability rather than management potential. In fact, he may have given little thought to the managerial implications of the supervisory job.

When he starts his supervisory job he finds that he must disentangle himself from the work of his subordinates. While this is desirable from a management point of view, the scientist-supervisor finds this a difficult transition. He must realize that his responsibilities now include several things about which he knows little. Communications skills, understanding the role of his group in the context of the total organization, his role as its manager, motivation of employees, salary administration, and other administrative considerations. Additionally, he may find that members of his staff resent him because they may feel he has sold out for the financial rewards of a managerial position.

Because of these pressures the relationship between the new scientist-supervisor and his superior are very important. Unfortunately, in many cases his superior has not successfully made the transition from technical specialist to manager either. He may still treat the first-level supervisor as a technician rather than as a member of management. Under such circumstances it is very difficult for the first-level supervisor to understand the role of manager and he frequently accepts the technical role since he more fully understands it. Relations with his subordinates require him to maintain effective understanding of the state of knowledge in his technical specialty while his redirected managerial goals require developing knowledge and understanding of entirely new subject areas. Obviously if he is to be a successful manager he has to sell his group to higher management. Under these pressures he may abandon the supervisory role and revert to the technical areas from which he receives satisfaction. It is therefore necessary for middle managers to be supportive and developmental when handling first-level supervisors who are professionals. The middle manager must create a climate which allows the supervisor to meet his managerial goals and still maintain effective relationships with the professionals on his staff. While this approach may sound no different from that which is desirable for any first-level supervisor, it is particularly significant in the managerial development of a scientist because his initial ambitions probably are not toward management goals. He has to be convinced that making the transition is worthwhile from a career viewpoint. His nonprofessional counterpart already has this idea as part of his value system.

The job of managing research

Companies have found that the man most outstanding for his scientific or technical abilities may have no ability in management. To make up for his lacks in his managerial job, they back him up with a good administrator—a business manager—and hope that the combination will cover the job. If the scientist is pursuing knowledge for its own sake, and the administrator has no scientific background, the resulting two-headed leadership may have its heads faced in opposite directions. The one will be looking toward technical excellence and freedom from organizational restraints, and the other will be looking toward business results. The professional people in the department may feel that their careers are suspended between a financial manager who can't evaluate the quality of their work, and a technically brilliant boss whom they describe as the worst manager they ever saw, and who describes himself as "simply not interested in their silly personal problems."

Surveys of a number of research departments[10] indicate that companies want the research director to be a good administrator even if he isn't a brilliant researcher. They want him to be oriented toward the business and to be able to operate as a member of top management in integrating the work of the research department into company planning and company objectives. He should be able to work with finance, marketing, and production in evaluating the profit possibilities of proposals for new products and new technologies. He should be able to measure progress on projects and judge if they should be continued or abandoned. The job of directing the company's research is a managerial one, calling for managerial ability as well as technical competence.

The administrative responsibilities of a research department are, as a rule, separated from the technical responsibilities and concentrated under an administrator who is responsible to the director. The administrator and his staff take care of contracts, budgets, personnel matters, and stenographic, clerical, and other services. The administrative group provides its services throughout the research organization in order to relieve scientists and engineers of nonprofessional work.

Training for research management

Managerial jobs below the research director also call for technical competence plus skill in dealing with people and in managing work. The scarcity of this combination of talents has led to the establishing

---

[10] One such survey reporting on organization structures and managerial responsibilities is by George W. Howard, *Common Sense in Research and Development Management* (New York: Vantage Press, 1955).

of management training programs for professionals. Some companies offer the training to nonmanagers and give as the reasons: (1) to discover professionals who have a talent and a liking for management, (2) to prepare people for supervisory positions, (3) to make the professional aware of the company's administrative and business problems, (4) to improve man-boss relationships and teamwork throughout the organization.

For managers and administrators in research, a number of companies and universities are offering courses in management, industrial relations, human relations, finance, marketing, economics, and other subjects designed to:

1. Develop competence in managing and an understanding of the social and economic factors that enter into decision making.
2. Enlarge the professional's area of interest to include aspects of management outside his own department and get him to think and act in the interest of the business as a whole.
3. Develop skills in human relations and leadership.

Still another type of training being offered is the cram session to update the technical knowledge of the present manager in research or engineering. In order to keep abreast of the work of his younger and more highly specialized subordinates, he takes intensive short courses in science, engineering, and mathematics.[11]

Paths of advancement

Going into management to get ahead was the logical and expected career path for the scientist and engineer of an earlier day. His practical training prepared him to rotate from staff to line jobs and gain wide experience with the company's technical and managerial problems. Many of today's engineers are prepared for a different type of job—a career in the scientific and technical work of research, development, and design. Their college courses gave them scientific backgrounds for going on to graduate work and getting advanced degrees.

The demand for engineers in research-oriented industries has influenced engineering colleges to concentrate on the theoretical aspects of engineering rather than the applied aspects. Engineering now includes an area of knowledge that used to be considered purely scientific. The new courses are more general, more abstract, and more related to analysis than to application. They have crowded out shop courses and other practice courses that used to be part of the engineer's training.

---

[11] For a description of a six-week course designed by U.C.L.A. and adapted by General Electric to offer to its men in high-level engineering management, see George A. W. Boehm, "Bringing Engineers up to Date," *Fortune*, Vol. LXVII, No. 5 (May, 1963), pp. 120 ff.

Furthermore, jobs in research call for continued study of scientific courses. The more scientific and theoretical a man's work and his course of study, the more he is apt to regard managerial duties as a waste of scientific time and talent. But if going into management is the only way to get ahead in the company, he may take that route and become an unhappy and ineffective manager.

Some companies are attempting to handle this problem by setting up separate paths of advancement so that the creative and talented researcher can stay out of management and still get recognition through promotions and pay increases. As a reward for his research achievements, he is given greater autonomy and status, a title, and a management salary. And he keeps on doing research work. He may direct special projects. In a team system of organization he may represent his field of science or branch of engineering as an expert, working on complex problems that involve several fields of learning and call for cooperative effort.

Project management

In most advanced technology organizations an organizational unit has been created which is called a project. This unit is concerned with achieving a highly specific goal such as the development of a new product. Time, budget, and performance specifications are carefully worked out and the project group is expected to achieve them. The colleague relationship which many professionals find desirable is the hallmark of project management. The project unit is made up of a high proportion of those professionals necessary to complete the project. While they may come from different disciplines, they are engaged in the professional work for which they were trained and which is so important in their value system. To a certain extent the authority relationships are professional-technical rather than managerial. The project manager has clear instructions for completion of the project and he therefore must utilize his staff of professionals in ways which will achieve the project goals. Scientists and engineers are treated as professionals and they can readily see their contribution to the project as it moves toward completion. The manager can assume that his group will perform as professionals and he directs his attention to budget, time, and performance considerations. While some professionals may not look with favor on time, cost, and related deadlines, the manager at least can reinforce his position by calling on the professional values of his subordinates to help meet deadlines.

It is essential that corporate planning in organizations utilizing project management take project completion into consideration. Once the team is established it must be utilized. Completion of a project should be rewarded by the assignment of another project. Effective functioning of teams of this kind require that they be kept occupied with meaningful effort.

Professional development

The engineer must recognize that his college training provided the fundamentals and that he must continue to build upon them throughout his career. A number of companies provide or finance the training for developing the abilities needed in the particular work of the establishment. Some companies repay part or all of the tuition for graduate study. Some companies finance attendance at a certain number of professional society meetings. They have several reasons for doing so: (1) Professionals feel very strongly about it. (2) Some studies of research organizations indicate that the professional does a higher quality of work if he is motivated by the desire to merit approval from his scientific society. (3) The company stands to gain from the knowledge that is exchanged at professional meetings. New approaches to problems and new techniques are discussed at such meetings before the information appears in print.

No matter how generous the company is in its provisions for training, professional development is essentially self-development. It can't be forced on a person if he doesn't see the need for it or if he doesn't see opportunities for profiting from it.

In order to encourage people to develop their talents and at the same time make sure that the company will avail itself of them, some of the larger companies maintain central talent agencies (actually internal employment agencies) for their professional and managerial personnel. Active records are kept of employees' abilities, experience, education, and career desires. Then when opportunities arise anywhere in the company, a search of the talent file is made for qualified candidates to be considered for the positions.

Leadership skills for professionals

The professional who wants to develop his abilities for stimulating and guiding the mental output of others will profit from analyzing the case studies and the complaints and wants reported in this chapter. A professional who is a manager may feel that he knows what other professionals want. But the viewpoint and career wants of the manager are somewhat different from those of the nonmanager. One manager who was asked to list gripes and grievances of professional subordinates said he didn't know of any; he guessed the people who weren't satisfied just moved on to some other company.

Professional treatment.   People who are not members of the science
and engineering professions grow weary of the tune of incessant demands for professional treatment. They wonder why the engineer and
scientist can't be satisfied with the treatment that others get in a business
organization. Since professionalism is the basis on which engineers and
scientists expect "different" treatment, it (professionalism) is central to
the problem of trying to adjust organizations to professionals and professionals to organizations. This adjusting and accommodating is one of
the skills of leadership. The manager of professionals needs to create
a working environment in which professionals, while serving their own
career goals, are yielding maximum output to the company.

The crux of the matter is that the training that made a man capable
of carrying on sustained mental effort under his own power was based
on creating an image of himself as a person who didn't need to be
watched or prodded. The image a professional has of the type of person
he is or wants to be does not fit into an organizational setup in which
bosses tell subordinates what to do, how to do it, when to do it, where
to do it, and—perhaps—why to do it. That is, the professional's image
of himself doesn't fit into the lower end of such a superior-subordinate
relationship. If it fits into the upper end of it, he is in trouble also.

The type of leadership behavior that will be appropriate and effective
in dealing with professionals depends upon the environment, the type
of work being done, and the performer's age, experience, ability, personality, and degree of dedication to his career. Although a business
can't be operated as if it were a college, a model for supervising mental
and creative work can be drawn from the academic environment. The
relationship between a professor and a mature graduate student producing a thesis is one in which the performer has the responsibility for
managing his own work. The professor's function is to set high standards
and demand high performance, to teach and to explain requirements,
to guide work without dominating it or doing it himself. Furthermore,
the relationship is one in which there is freedom to admit ignorance
and ask questions.

Creating the climate for professional teamwork.   A leadership skill
essential to the professional is the ability to create the type of personal
and group relationships in which creativity is fostered and in which
professionals will produce ideas and help other people to use them.
One of the deterrents to contributing ideas to a common pool is the
professional's very normal desire to get proper credit for his brainchil-
dren. If the leader of a group appropriates ideas and fails to give credit
to the originators, the flow may be slowed to a trickle.

Similarly, the leader of a group puts a damper on creative effort
if he is dictatorial and overcritical.

Cooperative effort in creative work is essential when each specialist knows only a branch of a subject. Getting people to work together is an art that is practiced in conference leadership of case studies. If the leader can move out of the limelight and act as a catalyst, the group members will exchange information.

The commodity of the technical specialist is ideas, and the production and communication of them is the business of the research department. Informality and freedom to move about seem to be factors in the circulation of ideas. Studies made of professional groups lend support to the theory that creativity and productivity are stimulated by interaction of people who have a variety of backgrounds.[12] If people are divided into small rigid permanent groups, there is always the danger that the leader of the group may take over the contacts and shut off the members from free interaction with people outside the group.

Making challenging assignments. The desire for challenging, varied, and creative assignments is associated with the desire for professional recognition and development. A person's status on the job is proclaimed by the kind of assignments he gets. Stimulation from the challenge of important work and responsibility is important in mental and creative work, which by its nature calls for a high degree of self-motivation.

An assignment can be stimulating because it fits into a man's plans for broadening or deepening his knowledge, or because it points toward opportunities for the future. It can be stimulating because it offers variety that gets a man out of a rut and awakens new interests, or because it enable him to achieve, advance, or get recognition. A professional has good reason to fear that if his assignments don't keep him abreast of developments, his knowledge will become obsolete and his professional future will be endangered.

It is not always possible to give assignments that are stimulating. Every job has its routine aspects, and the work of an organization has to be done by the people who are available to do it. But a leader can do more about suiting assignments to individual interests if he knows the abilities, career plans, and educational projects of individuals. He can make assignments more challenging by the way he presents them and explains their purpose.

Guiding the new man. The supervisor plays an important part in the career development of young engineers and scientists in training. The new man needs to be assured that someone has a continuing interest

---

[12] University of Michigan studies in the National Institutes of Health describe these interactions and relate them to productivity. See Donald C. Pelz *et al., Interpersonal Factors in Research, Part II: Leadership and Group Factors in Scientists' Performance and Motivation* (Ann Arbor, Mich.: University of Michigan, 1957).

A Columbia University study of 1,436 industrial research laboratories reports on ways companies use team research and on the communications patterns involved. (David B. Hertz and Albert H. Rubenstein, *Team Research* [New York: Eastern Technical Publications, 1953].)

in his progress and problems. He needs to be assured that there is a definite plan to use his abilities, increase his value, and promote his career. His interest in each training assignment will be in direct proportion to the relation he can see between it and his goals on the job. He needs to be shown how it fits in the pattern and what he can get out of it that will help him get ahead.

If a junior is assigned to assist a senior engineer or scientist, the training must be evaluated periodically to be sure it is what the new man needs and that he is not just being used to fill in for a technician.

Reviewing performance. Performance evaluation and the appraisal interview were discussed in Chapter 13, and the Bell & Howell Company's forms used for examples. Their form for engineer appraisal is included in this chapter. (See Figure 17–1.)

The young professional employee looks upon performance review as a right and he complains if he doesn't get it. He wants feedback on his work—both to get recognition for good work and to find out what the company expects of him. He wants to know what use was made of his work and why some of his proposals were not accepted.

The performance review provides an opportunity to discuss training needs for the present job and to show the professional how he can accomplish his career goals through preparing himself for the demands of the job ahead.

Utilizing professional talent

A professional is more apt to be well utilized as a consultant than as an employee. As a consultant his price per hour dictates that he be assigned to important problems and that the company make good use of his time. Management should give serious consideration to using consultants on problems calling for talents not regularly needed in the company. The consultant's status as an expert called in on a particular problem puts him in a position where he must complete the assignment and teach others how to use his work.

If he were kept on the payroll as an employee, he would be trying to carve out some kind of a secure job for himself. He might be promoting projects that would use his talents but wouldn't fit the company's needs. Or he might be doing work that could be handled by someone of less talent.

Utilizing professional talent calls for observing the principle of staff economy: making talent go a long way. Not every job requires the brilliant thinker with broad scientific background and top academic attainments. Some jobs can be performed as well—or better—by the careful, methodical practical man. When problems call for a combination

FIGURE 17–1

Form for Appraising Engineers

ROUTING:

1. Supervisor Making Appraisal
2. W. L. Johnson - Dept. 7781 (For Scoring)
3. Supervisor For Interview
4. W. L. Johnson - Dept. 7781 (For File)

BELL & HOWELL COMPANY

ENGINEERING APPRAISAL FORM

1. PURPOSE

> To measure, objectively as possible, the individual performance of engineering personnel. The results of this appraisal will be considered for (a) individual development, (b) reviewing salary status, (c) promotional purposes.

2. PLAN

> To have each engineering employee appraised by his immediate superior at least once a year. Engineering appraisal forms will be prepared and distributed by the Industrial Relations Division.

3. INSTRUCTIONS FOR APPRAISAL

> a) Consider and mark only one element at a time.
>
> b) Review the employee on the basis of the position he holds now.
>
> c) Do not allow personal feelings to govern the appraisal. Be completely objective.
>
> d) Do not be entirely influenced by recent unusual cases pertaining to any factor to be considered. Each engineer should be judged on the basis of his normal performance.
>
> e) Place a small check for each factor under the heading that most aptly applies. Join each succeeding check mark with a straight line to indicate the employee's profile.
>
> f) Two levels of supervision must approve each appraisal whenever practical.
>
> g) Appraisal will be scored and averaged by Dept. 7781.

FORMAL TRAINING RECEIVED SINCE LAST APPRAISAL:_____

_____

ADDITIONAL COMMENTS:_____

_____

Used in Bell & Howell Company (reproduced with their permission).

FIGURE 17-1 (Continued)

BELL & HOWELL COMPANY
ENGINEER APPRAISAL FORM

NAME _____ CLOCK NO. _____ POSITION _____ DATE _____

APPRAISED BY _____ DATE INTERVIEWED _____

	UNSATISFACTORY	FAIR (Somewhat below average)	GOOD	EXCELLENT (Somewhat above average)	OUTSTANDING (Well above average)
	1 2 3	4 5 6	7 8	9 10 11	12 13 14 5

1. **INITIATIVE**
   Enterprise; drive; capacity for independent action; degree to which he assumes responsibility when orders are lacking; degree to which he follows through on a job despite obstacles.

2. **COOPERATIVENESS**
   The trait of working wholeheartedly both with and for others in an open-minded objective fashion; possession of the qualities of tact, courtesy, friendliness and tolerance.

3. **EXPRESSION**
   Facility in expressing ideas both orally and in writing. This implies the ability to communicate ideas in a logical, coherent fashion and the ability to summarize.

4. **QUANTITY OF WORK**
   Amount of useful output in the light of the opportunities afforded by the job. The output may be written or otherwise.

5. **QUALITY OF WORK**
   The general excellence of all kinds of output, including written material, with consideration given to the difficulty of the job. Accuracy, thoroughness and dependability of output should be considered, but not quantity. In the case of supervisors, this trait includes skill in directing and guiding others.

6. **CREATIVENESS**
   Originality, including imagination and inventiveness.

7. **ENGINEERING OR TECHNICAL JUDGEMENT**
   Skill in analyzing situations and arriving at sound conclusions from available facts even though the available data may be incomplete or seemingly contradictory.

8. **VERSATILITY & ADAPTABILITY**
   Willing and capable of doing successfully several lines of work, as need arises.

9. **GENERAL COMPANY INFORMATION**
   The degree of understanding of procedures of major and minor company policies and conformance to them. (See Inst. 3 B)

10. **BUDGET AND/OR SCHEDULES**
    Ability to perform within budget limitations and/or according to schedules and commitments.

11. **PROFESSIONAL INTEGRITY**
    Degree of willingness to face facts and follow course of action indicated.

of knowledge and talents not possessed by any one person in the group, a team should be formed.

Organizing and planning of work should be such that each person is using his highest abilities most of the time. Theoretical people shouldn't be spending their time building apparatus, running tests, and making routine calculations. Sometimes professional people are reluctant to turn over work to others and don't make good use of the technical assistance available to them. Sometimes they spend their time running errands, copying lists, and taking care of administrative detail, when they should be turning these tasks over to administrative and clerical people.

Organizational arrangements to foster innovation. In the final analysis, talent isn't being utilized fully unless the intellectual output is carried through to profitable innovation. Staff people are hired to supply new ideas, but organizations by their nature resist innovations. Managers of line departments are occupied with the pressing problems involved in accomplishing the present job, and new ideas mean changes and upsets that interfere with getting out the day's work. Managers are necessarily concerned about making a good showing where it counts for them, and managerial performance is usually measured on a short-term rather than a long-term basis.

Seeing new products and technologies through from inception to completion calls for special organization structures, policies, and procedures. It calls for some kind of coordinating authority to cut across jurisdictional lines between research and manufacture. Companies have devised various procedures for planning and controlling the progress of technical projects.[13] Some organizations use job rotation to place in strategic spots people who are acquainted with the work of the research department and receptive to its services.

The growing use of professionals

Industry, government, hospitals, universities, and other complex organizations in our society have discovered an ever-increasing need for professionally educated individuals of all kinds. The development of sophisticated mathematical techniques for forecasting and decision making and quantitatively based control systems has brought mathematicians, economists, and statisticians to positions of increasing importance. Computer technology requires people trained in the new field of computer science. Graduate and undergraduate business schools as well

---

[13] For descriptions of some of these organizational forms and procedures, see James Brian Quinn and James A. Mueller, "Transferring Research Results to Operations," *Harvard Business Review*, Vol. XLI, No. 1 (January–February, 1963), pp. 49–66.

as engineering schools have developed major courses of study in this area. Increasing emphasis on effective utilization of human resources is resulting in the recruitment of behavioral scientists by large organizations. Included here are psychologists, sociologists, anthropologists, and Ph.D's from graduate business schools who are trained in the application of behavioral theory to organizations.

Operations research, described in Chapter 7, introduced the notion of a team of varied scientists working on problems and this concept is constantly being enlarged in all types of organizations. It is therefore becoming necessary for management to develop a fuller understanding of the ways in which professionals are motivated and to create the kind of climate which allows them to grow and develop. Working at the frontiers of knowledge often requires management of a higher order than that which is concerned with day-to-day routine.

Summary

The problems of professionals in industrial organizations are illustrated in this discussion of the management of scientists and engineers in research, development, and design. An understanding of professionalism and professionals' abilities and career wants is needed in order to set up a working environment conducive to getting high output from their talents while yielding satisfaction to the individuals.

Ideally a director of research should be able to guide company planning in terms of the profit possibilities of innovations. He should be able to coordinate the work of research with the work of other parts of the organization—particularly with marketing, finance, and production. He should be able to plan, organize, direct, coordinate, and control the work of the research department. In the levels of management below the director, scientists and engineers also need to combine managerial ability with technical competence.

Following are some ways that companies meet this problem and other problems of professionals in the organization:

1. Concentrate administrative work, clerical work, and support functions under an administrator or administrative assistant to the research director. Have professionals turnover nonprofessional work to administrative assistants and clerks.
2. Establish dual ladders of advancement so that the professional doesn't have to go into management to get ahead. Give training in management to scientists and engineers who want to manage and have managerial potential. Also give them technical training—broad rather than detailed—to familiarize them with the work of their more highly specialized subordinates. Establish a promotion ladder on which talented and creative people can advance through

doing theoretical and technical work. Give them status and rewards equal to those of managers, but have them do professional rather than managerial work.

3. Provide training to recruits from college, so that they will be able to do their jobs; their education may have tended more toward analysis than toward application. Provide training to keep people abreast of their specialties and to develop their abilities.

4. In hiring, follow the principle of staff economy and make a little talent go a long way.

5. Hire talent to fit the work to be performed, and take into account that recent engineering training tends toward science rather than toward shop courses.

6. Engage consultants for talents not regularly needed in the company.

7. Develop a leadership pattern of the participative type—resembling that of college professor to mature graduate student. Leadership must stimulate creative effort and foster the teamwork necessary to bring diverse talents to bear on the solution of problems.

8. Use operations research as a means of bringing together various types of scientific talent and focusing them on organizational problems. O.R. offers a route through which the professional and his work can be integrated into the organization.

9. Develop an organization structure which allows for creativity and the full utilization of professional talent. One such approach is project management.

10. Allow for the constant development of professionals who are constantly worried about obsolescence of their education. Create a climate of free inquiry and skeptical curiosity to encourage professionals to optimize their abilities.

11. Recognize the need for differing styles of management and leadership to encourage professionals in the pursuit of careers with the organizations.

CASE 1

A young engineer was assigned to the position of acting first-level supervisor over 15 engineers, with the understanding all around that if he performed well he would be given the job permanently.

Within the group of 15 there are 5 engineers (mechanical and aeronautical) who are specialized in airframe design. All five are considerably older than the new supervisor, have been with the company a long time, and have close friends in higher management. As a group they have always performed their jobs well and with very little supervision or help. Their previous supervisor gave them a great deal of freedom in making job decisions. Now they are demanding frequent field trips, claiming them necessary to proper performance of the job.

The acting supervisor feels strongly that these trips are not necessary—at least not to the extent that the five are claiming. But his training is in electronics and he isn't sufficiently familiar technically with the airframe field to be able to judge which of the requests are legitimate and which are unreasonable. He is afraid to consult his boss about it and reveal his lack of knowledge.

What should he do?

CASE 2

The manager of the engineering department is complaining that the job of managing the department demands all of his time. He would like to be able to get away from his desk and do some design work of his own. As he expressed his dissatisfaction to an associate: "I have to waste all this time on petty details involving people and I'm simply not interested in their silly personal problems."

1. Recommend organizational changes that might reduce this dissatisfaction.
2. What avenues of promotion for engineers and scientists would you recommend?
3. What major qualifications should an engineering manager bring to his job?
4. Is technical competence any indication of ability to get work done through others?

CASE 3

The engineers of a large company complain that their tasks are not challenging. Portions of every job to be done require a great deal of initiative, knowhow, and technical ability, but the greatest part of the project is routine and requires little of the above qualities.

1. What makes an assignment challenging?
2. Is it realistic to expect all the tasks to be challenging ones?
3. What tasks in addition to the creative assignments are necessary to achieve completion of an engineering development project?
4. What modifications to the organization might merit serious consideration in this case?

CASE 4

The nontechnical people assigned to the research division complain that they are looked down upon by the research engineers and administrative staff (also engineers). The engineers insist that this attitude isn't allowed to affect personal relationships.

Purchasing is handled for (and at) the research division by a purchasing department headed by a local purchasing agent. He reports to the head of the purchasing division at another location. Purchasing department personnel are not employees of the research division. The purchasing department runs into problems in placing for bid the complex technical materials required. It must in most cases rely on the specifications of the engineering staff, who feel that engineers should have the prerogative regarding source, quantity, and price.

The engineers do not question stockroom items unless there is a short part; then they inform the research director that his activities are being interrupted by a stock shortage. He storms into the purchasing agent's office to complain that valuable engineering time is being lost because a two-cent part is not available. It is company policy to control these items on a minimum-maximum basis using six-month usage to set the maximum. In items of low use the entire stock is often withdrawn on a single requisition.

Another difficulty arises out of the research engineers' dislike for paperwork. They bring materials into the plant from vendors without getting a purchase order; they buy materials from petty cash; they "borrow" items brought into the plant in the briefcases of vendors. The purchasing agent learns of these purchases when he receives the bill from the supplier. Engineers often promise an order to a vendor before the purchasing agent receives the requisition. Sometimes there are thousands of dollars' worth of materials being assembled on vendor premises without covering paperwork.

The engineers take pride in this freedom and flexibility in their operations. Engineering department heads and the director of research share this feeling.

1. List the technical problems involved in this case.
2. What controls might be established to minimize them?
3. Will such controls reduce the personal problems?

CASE 5

A young company doing research and development work brought in a new general manager. In investigating costs he discovered that there was a 30 percent turnover rate. The men who had been leaving the organization were highly educated and trained engineers and scientists. There were no exit interviews nor records of complaints. The company had no formal policies applying to its professional personnel.

1. What are some of the reasons for high turnover of professional personnel?
2. Estimate the cost of replacing these people. Are costs incurred in addition to recruiting costs? Where would such additional costs be reflected? Would accountants be alert to such costs?
3. What policies would you recommend to the general manager?

CASE 6

A project leader in charge of a small engineering group has guided his project through the initial phases of design and he hopes to have all the hardware assembled in a few weeks. During the design phase of the project his supervisor gave him complete responsibility and authority to handle any matters concerning the project. But now as the hardware stage is beginning, the supervisor has jumped in and is duplicating his subordinate's efforts in the procurement of parts and the supervision of technicians responsible for the fabrication of the engineering prototype.

1. What should the project leader do about it?
2. Why would such a situation arise?
3. How can the situation be improved?

CASE 7

The company has expanded rapidly and its middle- and upper management positions are held by engineers who were part of the original organization. You, the sales manager, are new. You report to one of these engineers who is now vice president in charge of sales.

When a customer's order involves any change in specifications, you are not authorized to make a decision on your own but must get confirmation from the heads of engineering and production. These two engineers are always tied up in their own technical problems and show little concern for problems originating in the sales department. They seem to have no appreciation of the urgency of sales decisions. You have talked to your boss about this, but without results. You wonder if you should carry this problem to the president of the company.

1. Recommend a course of action for the sales manager.
2. What orientation to their management jobs should engineers receive?
3. Should accountants and salesmen receive any special orientation when promoted to management positions?

CASE 8

Bob Edwards joined the company when he graduated from engineering school. Stan Nelson, the department head, soon found Bob to be one of the best workers he had ever had in the department. Not only was he very willing and cooperative, but he soon was very popular with the other employees.

Things went along very well for several months and then Stan began to notice a certain amount of tension among the employees. None of them wanted to talk about it and Stan became worried. Over the next two weeks, he carefully observed his staff and the reason for the tension became apparent. Bob Edwards who had been popular was now treated with icy politeness. It appeared that his fellow employees now resented him. Stan called one of the older engineers to his office and questioned him in depth about the situation. Prudent probing led the employee to admit the general resentment against Bob. The employee mentioned that while the feelings toward Bob were foolish, they nevertheless were real. "Bob never makes mistakes, he's the best engineer we have and he has many excellent ideas," the employee said. "He gets more work done than any of us and then he tries to help others," he went on to say. "Bob has just become too effective in too short a period of time and the other employees feel he is making them look bad," he explained.

Stan now knew the reason for the tension, but he decided to do nothing about it, since he felt it would work itself out as time passed. Unfortunately, time did nothing but worsen the situation. Resentment increased because the employees felt that Bob was too efficient for his own good. The icy politeness changed to open bitterness. Stan definitely felt that Bob did nothing to provoke this reaction. He was just a highly intelligent and skilled engineer who was doing his job in the best way he knew. In fact, he went out of his way to be pleasant and seemed to be confused with the negative reaction he received. He simply could not understand that the others did not appreciate his high performance standards.

Stan was faced with a perplexing dilemma. He had an excellent employee who was doing an outstanding job, yet the rest of the department was deteriorating. Clearly, something had to be done.

1. What can Stan do to alleviate the problem which confronts him?
2. Should Bob be transferred to another department?
3. Is there any way Bob's ability can be effectively utilized by Stan without causing resentment among the other employees in the department?
4. How does a very effective employee get along in a peer group that is not as bright and capable as he is?
5. Why do you feel the employees resent Bob rather than be proud to have such a capable fellow employee?

CASE 9

You are the head of an engineering department. One of your sections consists of a small group doing experimental work. This group is made up of a half-dozen men and a supervisor, John Roe, who is technically brilliant but has a nasty temper. The work requires a great deal of judgment, and there are arguments and spirited disputes among the members.

This morning Roe caustically told one of his subordinates, Jim White, to quit stalling on the job and hurry up. White told Roe to go to hell. Roe, on the spur of the moment, fired him.

White came and told you about it, saying that a man can't do experimental work with anyone snapping at his heels. You then call in Roe and ask, in the presence of White, the reason for the firing. Roe says the reason is gross insubordination. When you start to smooth over the situation, Roe stops you by saying that if he is going to be boss, he has to have control over his men. He then says: "Either he goes or I go." You don't want to lose either man.

1. What mistakes did you make in this situation?
2. What should you have done?
3. What can you do about it now?
4. How should you handle White?
5. How should you handle Roe?

CASE 10

The manager of a group of project engineers considers his subordinates to be the best in their fields. Through their efforts the company has been able to achieve and maintain a reputation for producing the most technically advanced and reliable equipment of its type. Company management imposes few restraints upon the engineering department but does insist that time schedules be met.

At or before the halfway point on each project, management requires that a reanalysis be made with respect to time and money and that the reevaluated time schedule be met. The engineers are careful about money expenditures for materials. But as the scheduled date for completion draws near, they insist that the network is just not good enough and that another month or two (and maybe a little more money) will yield superior results.

1. Why do engineers misjudge time and money requirements? What factors are they likely to miss?
2. What can the engineers do to minimize the possibility of missing estimated completion dates and funds requirements?
3. What are some of the reasons for shortening the time between research and sale of a product?
4. What factors enter into a decision to shorten the development time and rush a product onto the market?

CASE 11

One of the chemists in the laboratory is so outstanding that the industrial customers bypass the salesmen to deal with him directly. Customers phone him about their problems and the products he is developing and adapting for their use. He spends his time visiting their plants, talking and writing to them, and getting involved in production problems on their orders.

His activities are cutting into the authority of other departments who now have to consult with him before they can carry on their ordinary business with his customers. While he is giving these particular customers excellent service in tailoring products to fit their needs, he is no longer giving the company the scientific services it wants from him: the investigation of new fields and the development of new products.

1. How should objectives be set for people in research and development?
2. In a company that tailors products to fit the needs of industrial customers, how can the contacts between scientists and customers be controlled?

CASE 12

Ralph Jameson is a project engineer who directs the work of a sizeable group of engineers. He considers them to be well qualified and endowed with initiative and imagination. They are also ambitious and would like the opportunity to advance in rank and supervise a few other engineers. Judging from the way they supervise the draftsmen and technicians who are assigned to them from time to time, he feels that they possess managerial potential. There are no supervisory positions for them on their present project.

On several occasions when the company obtained new contracts for extensive, challenging projects, Jameson suggested that some of his best men be promoted to supervisory positions on them. In each case management rejected the recommendations and staffed the new projects with men recruited from outside the company. The reason given was that the present employees were being utilized fully and to the best benefit of the company.

Jameson is at a loss to explain to his men why jobs that would be advancements and challenging opportunities for them have been filled from outside the company. He is afraid that they will leave the company.

1. Why would management staff new projects completely with new men recruited outside the company and overlook—at least apparently—its own experienced personnel?
2. What qualifications should an engineering supervisor possess?
3. What channels of advancement could be provided for engineers and scientists?
4. What satisfactions do engineering and scientific personnel seek?
5. What communications do you recommend between management and professional people in this case?

CASE 13

A young company of about 100 employees has been unusually success-ful, mostly because of new products coming from its research and devel-opment effort. The R&D staff consists of 10 chemists, 2 of whom are group leaders. The laboratory runs smoothly. Working conditions, salary, morale, and fringe benefits are above average.

The bench chemists are under 30 years of age and have been with the company between three and five years. The two group leaders are 38 years old; they both joined the company shortly after it was organized 10 years ago. The research director, the president, and the sales manager are all under 45 years of age and are stockholders.

Bench chemists begin to think of promotion to group leader or equiva-lent after about five years of experience, but in this small company there is no place to go. Because of this lack of promotional opportunities, the company loses its creative chemists after it has had them about five years.

1. How can professional people be induced to remain on the job when salary is not the prime issue?
2. Can positions be created to provide promotion for them?
3. Should chemists be hired who are less ambitious and aggressive?
4. Can present jobs be redesigned to yield more satisfaction?
5. What costs should be considered in replacing chemists every five years?
6. How realistic are expectations of advancement for everyone?

CASE 14

Recently as a part of a program to reduce overhead, management succeeded in tightening work schedules and discipline in the "ordinary" engineering departments of the company. But some extraordinary mea-sures are going to be required to bring into line the scientists, engineers, and administrative staff in the applied research departments. These highly qualified people (many of them Ph.D.'s) consider it "unprofes-sional" to have to work under conditions that require them to get to work or back from lunch within a five-minute leeway.

This attitude poses a problem: If management lays down the law, it may result in some of the professionals leaving the company. If man-agement backs down, it will be setting up a double standard of conduct, possibly damaging to morale in the much larger group of engineers who are forced to obey the rules.

1. Does creative technical output occur only during certain periods of the day?
2. How closely is creative technical output related to job satisfaction?

3. Should there be a dual standard of behavioral expectations?
4. Can professionals be made to adhere to everyday rules?
5. Is management short-sighted in trying to reduce costs in this manner?

CASE 15

J. Smith joined the company after graduation from college several years ago. While in school he received very high grades but did not engage in any extracurricular activities. On the job he has shown marked technical ability.

The engineering department is small and the opportunities in it are limited. Most of the promising young engineers move out into supervisory positions in other parts of the organization. The others, seeing little chance to get ahead in the engineering department, quit after a while.

You, the assistant superintendent, had been planning to move Smith out of engineering to a supervisory job. His immediate supervisor and others in frequent contact with him present this report of his attitudes: (1) All technical problems are simple and any fool can solve them. (2) Management work does not require brains but only common sense. (3) Engineers go into management work because they can't make a success of straight engineering work. Smith is critical of management in general to the extent of being nearly antimanagement. He dresses like the rank and file instead of like the other young engineers. The people he works with tolerate him but are not friendly to him. You and his immediate supervisor are interested in helping young people adjust to the working world.

How would you handle each of Smith's difficulties?

FOLLOWING UP ON THE JOB

Managing the professional employee

1. Should there be a dual standard of rule application; one for regular employees and one for professional employees?
2. Why do professional employees frequently make poor managers?
3. Should a special career track be designed to reward professional employees for their technical excellence?
4. How does the professional employee's loyalty to his discipline conflict with organizational loyalty?
5. What can be done to resolve the conflict between the scientist's and engineer's desire for perfection and the compromises which are often characteristic of problem solving in organizational life?
6. What can an organization do to encourage professional employees to continue their development?

7. Are the positions offered to professional employees frequently over-sold by the recruiter in his efforts to secure talent?

8. To what extent are the talents, education, and knowledge of professional employees underutilized in many organizations?

9. Can an organization justify special salary considerations for professional employees?

10. Should professional employees be supervised by one of their own or by a nonprofessional person who is an effective administrator?

Suggested readings

BOOKS

For
Chapter:

17   AMERICAN MANAGEMENT ASSOCIATION (New York) Reports:
Achieving Full Value from R&D Dollars, No. 69 (1962).
Management of Scientific Talent, No. 76 (1963).
Optimum Use of Engineering Talent, No. 58 (1961).
The Human Element in Modern Business, No. 1 (1957).

17   BARNES, LOUIS B. *Organizational Systems and Engineering Groups: A Comparative Study of Two Technical Groups in Industry.* Boston: Graduate School of Business Administration, Harvard University, 1960.

17   BLOOD, JEROME W. (ed.). *The Management of Scientific Talent.* New York: American Management Association, 1963.

17   DANIELSON, LEE E. *Characteristics of Engineers and Scientists Significant for Their Motivation and Utilization.* Report No. 11, Ann Arbor, Mich.: Bureau of Industrial Relations, University of Michigan. 1960.

17   DRUCKER, PETER F. *The Practice of Management.* New York: Harper & Row, Publishers, 1954.

17   GELLERMAN, SAUL W. *Motivation and Productivity.* New York: American Management Association, 1963.

17   HINRICHS, JOHN R. *Creativity in Industrial Scientific Research: A Critical Survey of Current Opinion, Theory, and Knowledge.* New York: American Management Association, 1961. (This is a 39-page bulletin.)

17   HOWARD, GEORGE W. *Common Sense in Research and Development Management.* New York: Vantage Press, 1955.

17   HOWER, R. M., and ORTH, C. D., III. *Managers and Scientists—Some Human Problems in Industrial Research Organizations.* Boston: Division of Research, Graduate School of Business Administration, Harvard University, 1963.

17   KORNHAUSER, WILLIAM. *Scientists in Industry.* Berkeley and Los Angeles: University of California Press, 1962.

17   LIVINGSTON, ROBERT TEVIOT, and MILBERG, STANLEY H. (eds.). *Human Relations in Industrial Research Management.* New York: Columbia University Press, 1957.

17   MARCSON, SIMON. *The Scientist in American Industry.* New York: Harper & Row, Publishers, 1960.

17   PELZ, DONALD C.   *Motivation of the Engineering and Research Specialist.* General Management Series No. 186. New York: American Management Association, 1957.

17   RAUDSEPP, EUGENE.   *Managing Creative Scientists and Engineers.* New York: The Macmillan Co., 1963.

17   RIEGEL, JOHN W.   *Administration of Salaries for Engineers and Scientists and Intangible Rewards for Engineers and Scientists.* Ann Arbor, Mich.: Bureau of Industrial Relations, University of Michigan, 1958.

17   RONKEN, HARRIET O., and LAWRENCE, PAUL R.   *Administering Change: A Case Study of Human Relations in a Factory.* Boston: Harvard University Press, 1952.

17   SAYLES, LEONARD R.   *Individualism and Big Business.* New York: McGraw-Hill Book Co., 1963.

17   WOLFE, D.   *America's Resources of Specialized Talent.* New York: Harper & Row, Publishers, 1954.

ARTICLES

For
Chapter:

17   BOEHM, GEORGE A. W.   "Bringing Engineers up to Date," *Fortune*, Vol. LXVII, No. 5 (May, 1963), pp. 120 ff.

17   ———.   "Research Management: The New Executive Job," *Fortune*, Vol. LVI, No. 4 (October, 1957), pp. 222 ff.

17   COLLIER, DONALD W.   "Solving the Research Department's Interface Problems," *Management Review*, September, 1969.

17   COOK, LESLIE G.   "How to Make R & D More Productive," *Harvard Business Review*, July–August, 1966.

17   DRUCKER, PETER F.   "Management and the Professional Employee," *Harvard Business Review*, May–June, 1952.

17   GADDIS, PAUL O.   "The Project Manager," *Harvard Business Review*, May–June, 1959.

17   HARTMAN, R. M.   "Selection, Appraisal, and Training of Your Engineering Department," *Journal of the American Society of Training Directors*, October, 1958.

17   HOWELL, ROBERT A.   "Multiproject Control," *Harvard Business Review*, March–April, 1968.

17   KAPLAN, NORMAN.   "The Role of the Research Administrator," *Administrative Science*, June, 1959, pp. 41 ff.

17   MENDELL, JAY S.   "The Case of the Straying Scientist," *Harvard Business Review*, July–August, 1969.

17   MOORE, DAVID G., and RENCK, RICHARD.   "The Professional Employee in Industry," *Journal of Business*, Vol. XXVIII, (January, 1955), pp. 58–66.

17   ORTH, CHARLES D., III.   "The Optimum Climate for Industrial Research," *Harvard Business Review*, Vol. XXXVII, No. 2 (March–April, 1959), pp. 58 ff.

17   PHELPS, ERNEST D.   "Help Your Engineers to Get Ahead," *Harvard Business Review*, January–February, 1962.

17   QUINN, JAMES BRIAN, and MUELLER, JAMES A.   "Transferring Research Results to Operations," *Harvard Business Review*, Vol. XLI, No. 1 (January–February, 1963), pp. 49–66.

SHAPERO, ALBERT.   "Managing Technical and Intellectual Resources," *Business Horizons*, April, 1969.

Index

Index

This book has been set in 10 and 9 point Caledonia, leaded 2 points. Part and chapter numbers are in 24 point Univers Bold No. 65. Part titles are in 14 point Univers Bold No. 65. Chapter titles are in 18 point Univers Bold No. 65. The size of the type page is 27 by 45½ picas.